III. As you APPLY THE KNOWLEDGE

Feature	Description	Benefit
Sample Documents	Sample letters, discussion memos, communication strategy memos, and press releases are included at key points throughout the book.	These samp̲ ͜ ͜͜ ͜esswork in document p̲ ͜.͜. ͜pecific illustrations include formats, framing, and content for each of these important documents.
Chapter Cases	At the end of each chapter, at least two (and in some chapters, three) case studies are included. These are authentic, detailed descriptions of issues and problems faced by real business managers and executives.	Each case study asks you to define the business problem, analyze critical issues, identify key stakeholders, and propose options for action for the managers involved.
Writing Exercises	In response to the case studies in each chapter, students are asked to produce strategy memos and professional North American business letters.	You will learn how to design business documents that work. In each instance, memos and letters are drafted in response to authentic issues, events, and challenges facing business managers.
Discussion Questions	Each case study contains between 6 and 12 questions designed to stimulate thought about the issues in the case and to prompt an engaging, spirited classroom discussion.	This is an opportunity to share what you know, to try out your ideas in response to the issues in the case. Classroom discussion, though, is more than simply expressing opinion. It's an opportunity to be held accountable by your peers for the ideas you offer.

IV. What you will DISCOVER

Special Features	Description	Benefit
New Case Studies	New case studies including authentic business challenges faced by Google Domino's Pizza, L'Oreal, Taco Bell Corporation, and Face book. These are fresh cases with current issues from corporations students will recognize.	While many of the cases in this book remain from previous editions, these new cases offer you an opportunity to think about current problems as the twenty-first century approaches its second decade.
Revised Content in Most Chapters	Content in most chapters, particularly those dealing with Technology, the Internet and online behavior, and Intercultural Communication has been updated, revised, and made current.	Enduring principles remain, just as they were expressed in earlier editions of this text, but new, current and highly recognizable information has been used to update most chapters.

Business Communication

Business Communication Today, 11/e
Bovée & Thill
0132539551

Excellence in Business Communication, 10/e
Thill & Bovée
0132719045

Business Communication Essentials, 5/e
Bovée & Thill
0132539713

Keys to Business Communication, 1/e
Carter
0136103332

Business Communication, 1/e
Shwom & Snyder
0136078079

Writing and Speaking at Work: A Practical Guide for Business Communication, 5/e
Bailey
0136088554

International/Intercultural Communication

Intercultural Business Communication, 5/e
Chaney & Martin
0132127903

Managerial Communication

Management Communication, 4/e
O'Rourke
0136079768

Prentice Hall "Guide To" Series in Business Communication

Guide to PowerPoint Version 2010
Munter & Paradi
0132568888

Guide to Presentations, 3/e
Munter & Russell
0137075081

Guide to PowerPoint, Version 2003
Munter & Paradi
0131452401

Guide to Managerial Communication, 9/e
Munter
0132147718

Guide to Business Etiquette, 2e
Cook & Cook
0137075049

Guide to Interpersonal Communication
Baney
0130352179

Guide to Managerial Persuasion and Influence
Thomas
0131405683

Guide to Media Relations
Schenkler & Herrling
0131405675

Guide to Electronic Communication
DeTienne
0130933481

Guide to Meetings
Munter & Netzley
0130338567

Guide for Internationals: Culture, Communication, and ESL
Reynolds & Valentine
0131705245

Guide to Report Writing
Netzley & Snow
0130417718

Management Communication

A Case-Analysis Approach

FIFTH EDITION

Management Communication

A CASE-ANALYSIS APPROACH

James S. O'Rourke, IV

Teaching Professor of Management
Arthur F. and Mary J. O'Neil Director
The Eugene D. Fanning Center for Business Communication
Mendoza College of Business
University of Notre Dame

Prentice Hall

Boston Columbus Indianapolis New York San Francisco Upper Saddle River
Amsterdam Cape Town Dubai London Madrid Milan Munich Paris Montreal Toronto
Delhi Mexico Sao Paulo Sydney Hong Kong Seoul Singapore Taipei Tokyo

Library of Congress Cataloging-in-Publication Data

O'Rourke, James S
  Management communication : a case-analysis approach / James S. O'Rourke. -- 5th ed.
    p. cm.
  Includes bibliographical references and index.
  ISBN-13: 978-0-13-267140-8 (alk. paper)
  ISBN-10: 0-13-267140-9 (alk. paper)
  1. Communication in management. 2. Communication in management--Case studies. I. Title.
  HD30.3.O766 2013
  658.4'5--dc23

                            2011033216

Editorial Director: Sally Yagan
Acquisitions Editor: James Heine
Editorial Project Manager: Karin Williams
Editorial Assistant: Ashlee Bradbury
Director of Marketing: Maggie Moylan
Senior Marketing Manager: Nikki Jones
Marketing Assistant: Ian Gold
Senior Managing Editor: Judy Leale
Production Project Manager: Debbie Ryan
Art Director: Jayne Conte
Cover Designer: Suzanne Behnke
Composition: Integra Software Services, Pvt.Ltd.
Printer/Binder: Courier/Westford
Cover Printer: Lehigh-Phoenix Color/Hagerstown
Text Font: Times New Roman, Arial

Credits and acknowledgments borrowed from other sources and reproduced, with permission, in this textbook appear on the appropriate page within text.

10 9 8 7 6 5 4 3 2
ISBN 10: 0-13-267140-9
ISBN 13: 978-0-13-267140-8

To: Pam, Colleen, Molly, and Kathleen. And to Jay, Cianan, and Ty. Your inspiration, patience, and support have been indispensable. Thank you for making this possible.

To my colleagues: Sandra, Sondra, and Liddy. You are among many who have encouraged me, corrected me, kept me honest, and held me accountable for my ideas. And to Andrea and Judy: Teaching and writing are so much easier with your help.

And, of course, to my friends in MCA and the Arthur Page Society: Thank you for the support, counsel, and good ideas. My life is richer for having shared your company.

CONTENTS

NEW TO THE FIFTH EDITION

Six brand-new, current-issue case studies:

Case 1-3: Domino's "Special" Delivery: Going Viral through Social Media.

Case 3-3: The Tiger Woods Foundation: When Values and Behavior Collide.

Case 3-4: Google's New Strategy in China: Principled Philosophy or Business Savvy?

Case 5-2: Carnival Cruise Lines: Fire Aboard a Stranded Cruise Ship

Case 5-3: AntennaGate: Apple's Loss of Signal (A).

Case 7-2: Johnson & Johnson's Strategy with Motrin: The Growing Pains of Social Media.

New writing assignments for several case studies, including:

Case 6-3: Kraft Foods, Inc.: The Cost of Advertising on Children's Waistlines.

Case 7-3: Facebook Beacon (A): Cool Feature or an Invasion of Privacy?

Case 11-1: Hayward Healthcare Systems, Inc.

Case 11-3: Hershey Foods: It's Time to Kiss and Make Up.

Case 13-1: L'Oreal USA: Do Looks Really Matter in the Cosmetic Industry?

Case 13-2: Taco Bell: How Do We Know it's Safe to Eat?

Approximately 10% of new anecdotes and examples, including extensive new examples in the Managing Conflict chapter.

A new section on social media and its uses, as well as updated content on the Internet and online behavior.

Newly updated chapter on Technology and its applications in business.

Up-to-date census data in the chapter on Intercultural Communication.

PREFACE

Many years ago, as an Air Force officer assigned to a flight test group in the American Southwest, I had the opportunity to speak with an older (and obviously wiser) man who had been in the flying business for many years. Our conversation focused on what it would take for a young officer to succeed—to become a leader, a recognized influence among talented, trained, and well-educated peers. His words were prophetic: "I can think of no skill more essential to the survival of a young officer," he said, "than effective self-expression." That was it. Not physical courage or well-honed flying skills. Not advanced degrees or specialized training, but "effective self-expression."

In the years since that conversation, I have personally been witness to what young managers call "career moments." Those moments in time are when a carefully crafted proposal, a thorough report, or a deft response to criticism saved a career. I've seen young men and women offered a job as a result of an especially skillful speech introduction. I've seen others sputter and stall when they couldn't answer a direct question—one that fell well within their area of expertise—during a briefing. I've watched in horror as others simply talked their way into disfavor, trouble, or oblivion.

Communication is, without question, the central skill any manager can possess. It is the link between ideas and action. It is the process that generates profit. It is the emotional glue that binds humans together in relationships, personal and professional. It is, as the poet William Blake put it, "the chariot of genius." To be without the ability to communicate is to be isolated from others in an organization, an industry, or a society. To be skilled at it is to be at the heart of what makes enterprise, private and public, function successfully.

The fundamental premise on which this book is based is simple: Communication is a skill that can be learned, taught, and improved. You have the potential to be better at communicating with other people than you now are. It won't be easy, but this book can certainly help. The fact that you've gotten this far is evidence that you're determined to succeed, and what follows is a systematic yet readable review of those things you'll need to pay closer attention to in order to experience success as a manager.

WHAT THIS BOOK IS ABOUT

This book will focus on the processes involved in management communication and concentrate on ways in which business students and entry-level managers can become more effective by becoming more knowledgeable and skilled as communicators.

The second premise on which this book is based is also simple: Writing, speaking, listening, and other communication behaviors are the end-products of a process that begins with critical thinking. It is this process that managers are called on to employ every day in the workplace to earn a living. The basic task of a manager, day in and day out, is to solve managerial problems. The basic tools at a manager's disposal are mostly rhetorical.

Management Communication supports learning objectives that are strategic in nature, evolving as the workplace changes to meet the demands of a global economy that is changing at a ferocious pace. What you will find in these pages assumes certain basic competencies in communication, but encourages growth and development as you encounter the responsibilities and opportunities of mid-level and higher management, whether in your own business or in large and complex, publicly traded organizations.

WHAT'S DIFFERENT ABOUT THIS BOOK

This book is aimed directly at the way most professors of management communication teach, yet in a number of important ways is different from other books in this field.

First, the process is entirely strategic. We begin with the somewhat nontraditional view that all communication processes in successful businesses in this century will be fully integrated. What happens in one part of the business affects all others. What is said to one audience has outcomes that influence others. Without an integrated, strategic perspective, managers in the twenty-first century economy will find themselves working at cross-purposes, often to the detriment of their businesses.

Second, the approach offered in *Management Communication* integrates ethics and the process of ethical decision making into each aspect of the discipline. Many instructors feel either helpless or at least slightly uncomfortable teaching ethics in a business classroom. Yet, day after day, business managers find themselves confronted with ethical dilemmas and decisions that have moral consequences for their employees, customers, shareholders, and other important stakeholders.

This text doesn't moralize or preach. Instead, it offers a relatively simple framework for ethical decision making that students and faculty alike will find easy to grasp. Throughout the book, especially in case studies and role-playing exercises, you will learn to ask questions that focus on the issues that matter most to your classmates and colleagues. The answers won't come easily, but the process of confronting the issues will make you a better manager.

Third, this text includes separate chapters on Technology (Chapter 7) and Listening and Feedback (Chapter 8), as well as Nonverbal Communication (Chapter 9), Intercultural Communication (Chapter 10), and Managing Conflict (Chapter 11). These are topics that are often either ignored or shortchanged in other texts. These kinds of interpersonal communication skills are clearly central to relationship building and the personal influence all managers tell us they find indispensable to their careers. And, you'll find a newly revised chapter devoted to Persuasion (Chapter 6), which explores the science that underlies the process of influence.

Finally, *Management Communication* examines the often tenuous but unavoidable relationship that business organizations and their managers have with the news media. A step-by-step approach is presented to help you develop strategies and manage relationships, in both good news and bad news situations. Surviving a close encounter with a reporter while telling your company's story—fairly, accurately, and completely—may mean the difference between a career that advances and one that does not.

THE ADDED VALUE OF A CASE STUDY APPROACH

The fifth edition of this book contains nearly three dozen original, classroom-tested case studies that will challenge you to discuss and apply the principles outlined in the chapters. Two of the chapters (8 and 13) include role-playing exercises. Appendix A, "Analyzing a Case Study," will introduce you to the reasons business students find such value in cases and will show you how to get the most from the cases included in this book. A rich, interesting case study is always an opportunity to show what you know about business and communication, to learn from your professors and classmates, and to examine the intricate processes at work when humans go into business together. Reading and analyzing a case are always useful, but the more profound insights inevitably come from listening carefully as others discuss and defend their views. Appendix B, "Writing a Case Study," will provide enough information for you and a small group of classmates to begin researching and writing an original business case on your own.

THE REST IS UP TO YOU

What you take from this book and how you use it to become shrewder and more adept at the skills a manager needs most is really up to you. Simply reading the principles, looking through the examples, or talking about the case studies with your friends and classmates won't be enough. You'll need to look for ways to apply what you have learned, to put into practice the precepts articulated by successful executives and discussed at length in this book. The joy of developing and using those skills, however, comes in the relationships you will develop and the success you will experience throughout your business career and beyond. They aren't simply essential skills for learning how to earn a living; they're strategies for learning how to live.

—James S. O'Rourke, IV

Chapter *1*

Management Communication in Transition

This book will argue that management communication is the central skill in the global workplace of the twenty-first century. An understanding of language and its inherent powers, combined with the skill to speak, write, listen, and form interpersonal relationships, will determine whether you will succeed as a manager.

At the midpoint of the twentieth century, management philosopher Peter Drucker wrote, "Managers have to learn to know language, to understand what words are and what they mean. Perhaps most important, they have to acquire respect for language as [our] most precious gift and heritage. The manager must understand the meaning of the old definition of rhetoric as 'the art which draws men's hearts to the love of true knowledge.' "[1]

Later in the twentieth century, Harvard Business School professors Robert Eccles and Nitin Nohria reframed Drucker's view to offer a perspective of management that few others have seen. "To see management in its proper light," they write, "managers need first to take language seriously."[2] In particular, they argue, a coherent view of management must focus on three issues: the use of rhetoric to achieve a manager's goals, the shaping of a managerial identity, and taking action to achieve the goals of the organizations that employ us. Above all, they say, "the essence of what management is all about [is] the effective use of language *to get things done.*"[3]

The job of becoming a competent, effective manager thus becomes one of understanding language and action. It also involves finding ways to shape how others see and think of you in your role as a manager. A number of noted researchers have examined the important relationship between communication and action within large and complex organizations and conclude that the two are inseparable. Without the right words, used in the right way, it is unlikely that the right actions will ever occur. "Words do matter," write Eccles and Nohria, "they matter very much. Without words we have no way of expressing strategic concepts, structural forms, or designs for performance measurement systems." Language, they conclude, "is too important to managers to be taken for granted or, even worse, abused."[4]

So, if language is a manager's key to effective action, the next question is obvious: How good are you at using your language? Your ability to take action—to hire people, to restructure an organization, to launch a new product line—depends entirely on how effectively you use rhetoric, both as a speaker and as a listener. Your effectiveness as a speaker and writer will determine how well you are able to get others to do what you want. And your effectiveness as a listener will determine how well you understand others and can do things for them.

This book will examine the role language plays in the life of a manager and the central position occupied by rhetoric in the life of business organizations. In particular, though, this book will help you examine your own skills, abilities, and competencies as you use language, attempt to influence others, and respond to the requirements of your superiors and the organization in which you work. If you think that landing your first really big job is mostly about the grades on your transcript, think again. Communication skills are most often cited as the primary personal attribute employers seek in college graduates, followed by a strong work ethic, teamwork skills, initiative, relating well to others, problem-solving skills, and analytic abilities.[5]

Management Communication is about the movement of information and the skills that facilitate it—speaking, writing, listening, and processes of critical thinking—but it's more than just skill, really. It's also about understanding who you are, who others think you are, and the contributions you as an individual can make to the success of your business. It's about confidence— the knowledge that you can speak and write well, that you can listen with great skill as others speak, and that you can both seek out and provide the feedback essential to your survival as a manager and a leader.

This chapter will first look at the nature of managerial work, examining the roles managers play and the characteristics of the jobs they hold. We'll also look at what varies in a manager's position, what is different from one manager's job to another. And we'll look at the management skills you will need to succeed in the years ahead. At the heart of this chapter, though, is the notion that communication, in many ways, is the work of managers, day in and day out. This book goes on to examine the roles of writing and speaking in your life as a manager, as well as other specific applications and challenges you will face as you grow and advance on the job.

WHAT DO MANAGERS DO ALL DAY?

If you were to consult a number of management textbooks for advice on the nature of managerial work, many—if not most—would say that managers spend their time engaged in planning, organizing, staffing, directing, coordinating, reporting, and controlling. These activities, as Jane Hannaway found in her study of managers at work, "do not, in fact, describe what managers do."[6] At best they seem to describe vague objectives that managers are continually trying to accomplish. The real world, however, is far from being that simple. The world in which most managers work is a "messy and hectic stream of ongoing activity."[7]

Managers are in constant action. Virtually every study of managers in action has found that they "switch frequently from task to task, changing their focus of attention to respond to issues as they arise, and engaging in a large volume of tasks of short duration."[8] Professor Harvey Mintzberg of McGill University observed CEOs on the job to get some idea of what they do and how they spend their time. He found, for instance, that they averaged 36 written and 16 verbal contacts per day, almost every one of them dealing with a distinct or different issue. Most of these activities were brief, lasting less than nine minutes.[9]

Harvard Business School professor John Kotter studied a number of successful general managers over a five-year period and found that they spend most of their time with others, including subordinates, their bosses, and numerous people from outside the organization. Kotter's study found that the average manager spent just 25 percent of his or her time working alone, and that time was spent largely at home, on airplanes, or commuting. Few of them spend less than 70 percent of their time with others, and some spend up to 90 percent of their working time this way.[10]

Kotter also found that the breadth of topics in their discussions with others was extremely wide, with unimportant issues taking time alongside important business matters. His study revealed that managers rarely make "big decisions" during these conversations and rarely give orders in a traditional sense. They often react to others' initiatives and spend substantial amounts of time in unplanned activities that aren't on their calendars. He found that managers will spend most of their time with others in short, disjointed conversations. "Discussions of a single question or issue rarely last more than ten minutes," he notes. "It is not at all unusual for a general manager to cover ten unrelated topics in a five-minute conversation."[11] More recently, managers studied by Lee Sproull showed similar patterns. During the course of a day, they engaged in 58 different activities with an average duration of just nine minutes.[12]

Interruptions also appear to be a natural part of the job. Rosemary Stewart found that the managers she studied could work uninterrupted for half an hour only nine times during the four weeks she studied them.[13] Managers, in fact, spend very little time by themselves. Contrary to the image offered by management textbooks, they are rarely alone drawing up plans or worrying about important decisions. Instead, they spend most of their time interacting with others—both inside and outside the organization. If you include casual interactions in hallways, phone conversations, one-on-one meetings, and larger group meetings, managers spend about two-thirds of their time with other people.[14] As Mintzberg has pointed out, "Unlike other workers, the manager does not leave the telephone or the meeting to get back to work. Rather, these contacts *are* his work."[15]

The interactive nature of management means that most management work is conversational.[16] When managers are in action, they are talking and listening. Studies on the nature of managerial work indicate that managers spend about two-thirds to three-quarters of their time in verbal activity.[17] These verbal conversations, according to Eccles and Nohria, are the means by which managers gather information, stay on top of things, identify problems, negotiate shared meanings, develop plans, put things in motion, give orders, assert authority, develop relationships, and spread gossip. In short, they are what the manager's daily practice is all about. "Through other forms of talk, such as speeches and presentations," they write, "managers establish definitions and meanings for their own actions and give others a sense of what the organization is about, where it is at, and what it is up to."[18]

THE ROLES MANAGERS PLAY

In Professor Mintzberg's seminal study of managers and their jobs, he found the majority of them clustered around three core management roles.

INTERPERSONAL ROLES Managers are required to interact with a substantial number of people in the course of a workweek. They host receptions; take clients and customers to dinner; meet with business prospects and partners; conduct hiring and performance interviews; and form alliances, friendships, and personal relationships with many others. Numerous studies have shown that such relationships are the richest source of information for managers because of their immediate and personal nature.[19]

Three of a manager's roles arise directly from formal authority and involve basic interpersonal relationships. First is the figurehead role. As the head of an organizational unit, every manager must perform some ceremonial duties. In Mintzberg's study, chief executives spent 12 percent of their contact time on ceremonial duties; 17 percent of their incoming mail dealt with acknowledgments and requests related to their status. One example is a company president who requested free merchandise for a handicapped schoolchild.[20]

Managers are also responsible for the work of the people in their unit, and their actions in this regard are directly related to their role as a leader. The influence of managers is most clearly seen, according to Mintzberg, in the leader role. Formal authority vests them with great potential power. Leadership determines, in large part, how much power they will realize.[21]

Does the leader's role matter? Ask the employees of Chrysler Corporation (now DaimlerChrysler). When Lee Iacocca took over the company in the 1980s, the once-great auto manufacturer was in bankruptcy, teetering on the verge of extinction. He formed new relationships with the United Auto Workers, reorganized the senior management of the company, and—perhaps, most importantly—convinced the U.S. federal government to guarantee a series of bank loans that would make the company solvent again. The loan guarantees, the union response, and the reaction of the marketplace were due in large measure to Iacocca's leadership style and personal charisma. More recent examples include the return of Starbucks founder Howard Schultz to re-energize and steer his company, and Amazon CEO Jeff Bezos and his ability to innovate during a downturn in the economy.[22]

Popular management literature has had little to say about the liaison role until recently. This role, in which managers establish and maintain contacts outside the vertical chain of command, becomes especially important in view of the finding of virtually every study of managerial work that managers spend as much time with peers and other people outside of their units as they do with their own subordinates. Surprisingly, they spend little time with their own superiors. In Rosemary Stewart's study, 160 British middle and top managers spent 47 percent of their time with peers, 41 percent of their time with people inside their unit, and only 12 percent of their time with superiors.[23] Robert H. Guest's study of U.S. manufacturing supervisors revealed similar findings.[24]

INFORMATIONAL ROLES Managers are required to gather, collate, analyze, store, and disseminate many kinds of information. In doing so, they become information resource centers, often storing huge amounts of information in their own heads, moving quickly from the role of gatherer to the role of disseminator in minutes. Although many business organizations install large, expensive information technology systems to perform many of those functions, nothing can match the speed and intuitive power of a well-trained manager's brain for information processing. Not surprisingly, most managers prefer it that way.[25]

As monitors, managers are constantly scanning the environment for information, talking with liaison contacts and subordinates, and receiving unsolicited information, much of it as a result of their network of personal contacts. A good portion of this information arrives in oral form, often as gossip, hearsay, and speculation.[26]

In the disseminator role, managers pass privileged information directly to subordinates, who might otherwise have no access to it. Managers must not only decide who should receive such information, but how much of it, how often, and in what form. Increasingly, managers are being asked to decide whether subordinates, peers, customers, business partners, and others should have direct access to information 24 hours a day without having to contact the manager directly.

In the spokesperson role, managers send information to people outside of their organizations: An executive makes a speech to lobby for an organizational cause, or a supervisor suggests a product modification to a supplier. Increasingly, managers are also being asked to deal with representatives of the news media, providing both factual and opinion-based responses that will be printed, broadcast, or posted to vast unseen audiences, often directly or with little editing. The risks in such circumstances are enormous, but so too are the potential rewards in terms of brand recognition, public image, and organizational visibility.

DECISIONAL ROLES Ultimately, managers are charged with the responsibility of making decisions on behalf of both the organization and the stakeholders with an interest in it. Such decisions are often made under circumstances of high ambiguity and with inadequate information. Often, the other two managerial roles—interpersonal and informational—will assist a manager in making difficult decisions in which outcomes are not clear and interests are often conflicting.

In the role of entrepreneur, managers seek to improve their businesses, adapt to changing market conditions, and react to opportunities as they present themselves. Managers who take a longer-term view of their responsibilities are among the first to realize that they will need to reinvent themselves, their product and service lines, their marketing strategies, and their ways of doing business as older methods become obsolete and competitors gain advantage.

While the entrepreneur role describes managers who initiate change, the disturbance or crisis handler role depicts managers who must involuntarily react to conditions. Crises can arise because bad managers let circumstances deteriorate or spin out of control, but just as often good managers find themselves in the midst of a crisis that they could not have anticipated but must react to just the same.

The third decisional role of resource allocator involves managers making decisions about who gets what, how much, when, and why. Resources, including funding, equipment, human labor, office or production space, and even the boss's time are all limited, and demand inevitably outstrips supply. Managers must make sensible decisions about such matters while still retaining, motivating, and developing the best of their employees.

The final decisional role is that of negotiator. Managers spend considerable amounts of time in negotiations: over budget allocations, labor and collective bargaining agreements, and other formal dispute resolutions. In the course of a week, managers will often make dozens of decisions that are the result of brief but important negotiations between and among employees, customers and clients, suppliers, and others with whom managers must deal.[27]

MAJOR CHARACTERISTICS OF THE MANAGER'S JOB

TIME IS FRAGMENTED Managers have acknowledged from antiquity that they never seem to have enough time to get all those things done that need to be done. In the early years of the twenty-first century, however, a new phenomenon arose: Demand for time from those in leadership roles increased, while the number of hours in a day remained constant. Increased work hours was one reaction to such demand, but managers quickly discovered that the day had just 24 hours and that working more of them produced diminishing marginal returns. According to one researcher, "Managers are overburdened with obligations yet cannot easily delegate their tasks. As a result, they are driven to overwork and forced to do many tasks superficially. Brevity, fragmentation, and verbal communication characterize their work."[28]

VALUES COMPETE AND THE VARIOUS ROLES ARE IN TENSION Managers clearly cannot satisfy everyone. Employees want more time to do their jobs; customers want products and services delivered quickly and at high-quality levels. Supervisors want more money to spend on equipment, training, and product development; shareholders want returns on investment maximized. A manager caught in the middle cannot deliver to each of these people what each most wants; decisions are often based on the urgency of the need and the proximity of the problem.

THE JOB IS OVERLOADED In recent years, many North American and global businesses were reorganized to make them more efficient, nimble, and competitive. For the most part, this reorganization meant decentralizing many processes along with the wholesale elimination of middle management layers. Many managers who survived such downsizing found that their number of direct reports had doubled. Classical management theory suggests that seven is the maximum number of direct reports a manager can reasonably handle. Today, high-speed information technology and remarkably efficient telecommunication systems mean that many managers have as many as 20 or 30 people reporting to them directly.

EFFICIENCY IS A CORE SKILL With less time than they need, with time fragmented into increasingly smaller units during the workday, with the workplace following many managers out the door and even on vacation, and with many more responsibilities loaded onto managers in downsized, flatter organizations, efficiency has become the core management skill of the twenty-first century.

WHAT VARIES IN A MANAGER'S JOB? THE EMPHASIS

THE ENTREPRENEUR ROLE IS GAINING IMPORTANCE Managers must increasingly be aware of threats and opportunities in their environment. Threats include technological breakthroughs on the part of competitors, obsolescence in a manager's organization, and dramatically shortened product cycles. Opportunities might include product or service niches that are underserved, out-of-cycle hiring opportunities, mergers, purchases, or upgrades in equipment, space, or other assets. Managers who are carefully attuned to the marketplace and competitive environment will look for opportunities to gain an advantage.

SO IS THE LEADER ROLE Managers must be more sophisticated as strategists and mentors. A manager's job involves much more than simple caretaking in a division of a large organization. Unless you are able to attract, train, motivate, retain, and promote good people, your organization cannot possibly hope to gain advantage over the competition. Thus, as leaders, managers must constantly act as mentors to those in the organization with promise and potential. When you lose a highly capable worker, all else in your world will come to a halt until you can replace that worker. Even if you should find someone ideally suited and superbly qualified for a vacant position, you must still train, motivate, and inspire that new recruit, and you must live with the knowledge that productivity levels will be lower for a while than they were with your previous employee.

MANAGERS MUST CREATE A LOCAL VISION AS THEY HELP PEOPLE GROW The company's Web site, annual report and those slick-paper brochures your sales force hands to customers may articulate the vision, values, and beliefs of the company. But what do those concepts really mean to workers at your location? What does a competitive global strategy mean to your staff at 8:00 A.M. on Monday? Somehow, you must create a local version of that strategy, explaining in practical and understandable terms what your organization or unit is all about and how the work of your employees fits into the larger picture.

MANAGEMENT SKILLS REQUIRED FOR THE TWENTY-FIRST CENTURY

The twenty-first century workplace requires three types of skills, each of which will be useful at different points in your career.

TECHNICAL SKILLS These are most valuable at the entry level, but less valuable at more senior levels. Organizations hire people for their technical expertise: Can you assess the market value of a commercial office building? Can you calculate a set of net present values? Are you experienced in the use of C++ or SAP/R3 software? These skill sets, however, constantly change and can become quickly outdated. What gets you in the door of a large organization won't necessarily get you promoted.

RELATING SKILLS These are valuable across the managerial career span and are more likely to help you progress and be promoted to higher levels of responsibility. These skills, which help you to form relationships, are at the heart of what management communication is about: reading, writing, speaking, listening, and thinking about how you can help others and how they can help you as the demands of your job shift and increase at the same time.

CONCEPTUAL SKILLS These skills are least valuable at the entry level, but more valuable at senior levels in the organization. They permit you to look past the details of today's work assignment and see the bigger picture. Successful managers who hope to become executives in the highest levels of a business must begin, at a relatively early age, to develop the ability to see beyond the horizon and ask long-term questions. If you haven't formed the relationships that will help you get promoted, however, you may not be around long enough to have an opportunity to use your conceptual skills.

TALK *IS* THE WORK

Managers across industries, according to Deirdre Borden, spend about 75 percent of their time in verbal interaction.[29] Those daily interactions include the following:

ONE-ON-ONE CONVERSATIONS Increasingly, managers find that information is passed orally, often face-to-face in offices, hallways, conference rooms, cafeterias, rest rooms, athletic facilities, parking lots, and literally dozens of other venues. An enormous amount of information is exchanged, validated, confirmed, and passed back and forth under highly informal circumstances.

TELEPHONE CONVERSATIONS Managers spend an astounding amount of time on the telephone these days. Curiously, the amount of time per telephone call is decreasing, but the number of calls per day is increasing. With the nearly universal availability of cellular, satellite, and online telephone service, very few people are out of reach of the office for very long. The decision to switch off your cellular telephone, in fact, is now considered a decision in favor of work-life balance.

VIDEO TELECONFERENCING Bridging time zones as well as cultures, videoconferencing facilities make direct conversations with employees, colleagues, customers, and business partners across the nation or around the world a simple matter. Carrier Corporation, the air-conditioning manufacturer, is now typical of firms using desktop videoconferencing to conduct everything from staff meetings to technical training. Engineers at Carrier's Farmington, Connecticut, headquarters can hook up with service managers in branch offices thousands of miles away to explain new product developments, demonstrate repair techniques, and update field staff on matters that would, just recently, have required extensive travel or expensive, broadcast-quality television programming. Their exchanges are informal, conversational, and not much different than they would be if both people were in the same room.[30]

PRESENTATIONS TO SMALL GROUPS Managers frequently find themselves making presentations, formal and informal, to groups of three-to-eight people for many different reasons: They pass along information given to them by executives; they review the status of projects in process; they explain changes in everything from working schedules to organizational goals. Such presentations are sometimes supported by PowerPoint slides or printed outlines, but they are oral in nature and retain much of the conversational character of one-to-one conversations.

PUBLIC SPEAKING TO LARGER AUDIENCES Most managers are unable to escape the periodic requirement to speak to larger audiences of several dozen or, perhaps, several hundred people. Such presentations are usually more formal in structure and are frequently supported by PowerPoint or Corel software that can deliver data from text files, graphics, and photos, and even motion clips from streaming video. Despite the more formal atmosphere and sophisticated audio–visual support systems, such presentations still involve one manager talking to others, framing, shaping, and passing information to an audience.

THE MAJOR CHANNELS OF MANAGEMENT COMMUNICATION ARE TALKING AND LISTENING

A series of scientific studies, beginning with Rankin in 1926,[31] and later with Nichols and Stevens (1957)[32] and Wolvin and Coakley (1982),[33] serve to confirm what each of us knows intuitively: Most managers spend the largest portion of their day talking and listening. E. K. Werner's thesis at the University of Maryland, in fact, found that North American adults spend more than 78 percent of their communication time either talking or listening to others who are talking.[34]

According to Werner and others who study the communication habits of postmodern business organizations, managers are involved in more than just speeches and presentations from the dais or teleconference podium. They spend their days in meetings, on the telephone, conducting interviews, giving tours, supervising informal visits to their facilities, and at a wide variety of social events.

Each of these activities may look to some managers like an obligation imposed by the job. Shrewd managers see them as opportunities to hear what others are thinking, to gather information informally from the grapevine, to listen in on office gossip, to pass along viewpoints that haven't yet made their way to the more formal channels of communication, or to catch up with a colleague or friend in a more relaxed setting. No matter what the intention of each manager who engages in these activities, the information they produce and the insight that follows from them can be put to work the same day to achieve organizational and personal objectives. "To understand why effective managers behave as they do," writes Prof. John Kotter, "it is essential first to recognize two fundamental challenges and dilemmas found in most of their jobs." Managers must first figure out what to do, despite an enormous amount of potentially relevant information (along with much that is not), and then they must get things done "through a large and diverse group of people despite having little direct control over most of them."[35]

THE ROLE OF WRITING

Writing plays an important role in the life of any organization. In some organizations, it becomes more important than in others. At Procter & Gamble, for example, brand managers cannot raise a work-related issue in a team meeting unless the ideas are first circulated in writing. For P&G managers, this approach means explaining their ideas in explicit detail in a standard one-to-three-page memo, complete with background, financial discussion, implementation details, and justification for the ideas proposed.

Other organizations are more oral in their traditions—3M Canada comes to mind as a "spoken" organization—but the fact remains: The most important projects, decisions, and ideas end up in writing. Writing also provides analysis, justification, documentation, and analytic discipline, particularly as managers approach important decisions that will affect the profitability and strategic direction of the company.

WRITING IS A CAREER SIFTER If you demonstrate your inability to put ideas on paper in a clear, unambiguous fashion, you're not likely to last. Stories of bad writers who've been shown the door early in their careers are legion. Your principal objective, at least during the first few years of your own career, is to keep your name out of such stories. Remember, those who are most likely to notice the quality and skill in your written documents are the very people most likely to matter to your future.

MANAGERS DO MOST OF THEIR OWN WRITING AND EDITING The days when managers could lean back and thoughtfully dictate a letter or memo to a skilled secretarial assistant are mostly gone. Some senior executives know how efficient dictation can be, especially with a top-notch administrative assistant taking shorthand, but how many managers have that advantage today? Very few, mostly because buying a computer and printer is substantially cheaper than hiring another employee. Managers at all levels of most organizations draft, review, edit, and dispatch their own correspondence, reports, and proposals.

DOCUMENTS TAKE ON LIVES OF THEIR OWN Once it's gone from your desk, it isn't yours anymore. When you sign a letter and put it in the mail, it's no longer your letter—it's the property of the person or organization you sent it to. As a result, the recipient is free to do as he or she sees fit with your writing, including using it against you. If your ideas are ill-considered or not well expressed, others in the organization who are not especially sympathetic to your views may head for the copy machine with your work in hand. The advice for you is simple: Don't mail your first draft, and don't ever sign your name to a document you're not proud of.

COMMUNICATION IS INVENTION

Without question, communication is a process of invention. Managers literally create meaning through communication. A company, for example, is not in default until a team of auditors sits down to examine the books and review the matter. Only after extended discussion do the accountants come to the conclusion that the company is, in fact, in default. It is their discussion that creates the outcome. Until that point, default was simply one of many possibilities.

The fact is managers create meaning through communication. It is largely through discussion and verbal exchange—often heated and passionate—that managers decide who they wish to be: market leaders, takeover artists, innovators, or defenders of the economy. It is only through communication that meaning is created for shareholders, for employees, for customers, and others. Those long, detailed, and intense discussions determine how much the company will declare in dividends this year, whether the company is willing to risk a strike or labor action, and how soon to roll out the new product line customers are asking for. Additionally, it is important to note that managers usually figure things out by talking about them as much as they talk about the things they have already figured out. Talk serves as a wonderful palliative: justifying, dissecting, reassuring, and analyzing the events that confront managers each day.

INFORMATION IS SOCIALLY CONSTRUCTED

If we are to understand just how important human discourse is in the life of a business, several points seem especially important.

INFORMATION IS CREATED, SHARED, AND INTERPRETED BY PEOPLE Meaning is a truly human phenomenon. An issue is only important if people think it is. Facts are facts only if we can agree upon their definition. Perceptions and assumptions are as important as truth itself in a discussion about what a manager should do next.[36]

INFORMATION NEVER SPEAKS FOR ITSELF It is not uncommon for a manager to rise to address a group of his colleagues and say, "Ladies and gentlemen, the numbers speak for themselves." Frankly, the numbers never speak for themselves. They almost always require some sort of interpretation, some sort of explanation or context. Don't assume that others see the facts in the same way you do and never assume that what you see is the truth. Others may see the same set of facts or evidence but may not reach the same conclusions. Few things in life are self-explanatory.

CONTEXT ALWAYS DRIVES MEANING The backdrop to a message is always of paramount importance to the listener, viewer, or reader in reaching a reasonable, rational conclusion about what she sees and hears. What's in the news these days as we take up this particular subject? What moment in history do we occupy? What related or relevant information is under consideration as this new message arrives? We cannot possibly derive meaning from one message without considering everything else that surrounds it.

A MESSENGER ALWAYS ACCOMPANIES A MESSAGE It is difficult to separate a message from its messenger. We often want to react more to the source of the information than we do to the information itself. That's natural and entirely normal. People speak for a reason, and we often judge their reasons for speaking before analyzing what they have to say. Keep in mind that, in every organization, message recipients will judge the value, power, purpose, intent, and outcomes of the messages they receive by the source of those messages as much as by the content and intent of the messages themselves. If the messages you send as a manager are to have the impact you hope they will, they must come from a source the receiver knows, respects, and understands.

YOUR GREATEST CHALLENGE

Every manager knows communication is vital, but every manager also seems to "know" that he or she is great at it. Your greatest challenge is to admit to flaws in your skill set and work tirelessly to improve them. First, you must admit to the flaws.

T. J. Larkin and Sandar Larkin, in a book entitled *Communicating Change: Winning Employee Support for New Business Goals*, write: "Deep down, managers believe they are communicating effectively. In ten years of management consulting, we have never had a manager say to us that he or she was a poor communicator. They admit to the occasional screw-up, but overall, everyone, without exception, believes he or she is basically a good communicator."[37]

YOUR TASK AS A PROFESSIONAL

As a professional manager, your first task is to recognize and understand your strengths and weaknesses as a communicator. Until you identify those communication tasks at which you are most and least skilled, you'll have little opportunity for improvement and advancement.

Foremost among your goals should be to improve existing skills. Improve your ability to do what you do best. Be alert to opportunities, however, to develop new skills. Add to your inventory of abilities to keep yourself employable and promotable.

Two other suggestions come to mind for improving your professional standing as a manager. First, acquire a knowledge base that will work for the years ahead. That means speaking with and listening to other professionals in your company, your industry, and your community. Be alert to trends that could affect your products and services, as well as your own future.

It also means reading. You should read at least one national newspaper each day, including the *Wall Street Journal*, the *New York Times*, or the *Financial Times*, as well as a local newspaper. Your reading should include weekly news magazines, such as *Bloomberg BusinessWeek,* and the *Economist.* Subscribe to monthly magazines such as *Forbes* and *Fortune.* And you should read at least one new hardcover title a month. A dozen books each year is the bare minimum on which you should depend for new ideas, insights, and managerial guidance.

Your final challenge is to develop the confidence you will need to succeed as a manager, particularly under conditions of uncertainty, change, and challenge.

For Further Reading

Axley, S. R. *Communication at Work: Management and the Communication-Intensive Organization.* Westport, CT: Quorum Books, 1996.

Christensen, L. T., Morsing, M., and Cheney, G. *Corporate Communications: Convention, Complexity, and Critique.* Thousand Oaks, CA: Sage Publications, Inc., 2008.

Clutterbuck, D. and Hirst, S. *Talking Business: Making Communication Work.* Burlington, MA: Butterworth-Heinemann, 2002.

Drucker, P. F. *Management Challenges for the 21st Century.* New York: HarperBusiness, 1999.

Ferguson, N. *The Ascent of Money: A Financial History of the World.* New York: The Penguin Press, 2008.

Hamel, G. and Breen, B. *The Future of Management.* Boston, MA: Harvard Business School Press, 2007.

Krisco, K. H. *Leadership and the Art of Conversation.* Schoolcraft, MI: Prima Publishing, 1997.

Mintzberg, H. *Managing.* San Francisco, CA: Berrett-Koehler Publishers, Inc., 2009.

Van Riel, C. B. M. and Fombrun, C. J. *Essentials of Corporate Communication.* New York: Routledge, 2008.

Wishard, W. V. D. *Between Two Ages: The 21st Century and the Crisis of Meaning.* Washington, DC: Xlibris Corporation, 2000.

Endnotes

1. Drucker, P. F. *The Practice of Management.* New York: Harper &amp, Row, 1954.
2. Eccles, R. G. and N. Nohria. *Beyond the Hype: Rediscovering the Essence of Management.* Boston, MA: The Harvard Business School Press, 1992, p. 205.
3. Ibid., p. 211.
4. Ibid., p. 209.
5. *Job Outlook 2008.* National Association of Colleges and Employers, Chart A.
6. Hannaway, J. *Managers Managing: The Workings of an Administrative System.* New York: Oxford University Press, 1989, p. 39.
7. Eccles and Nohria. *Beyond the Hype*, p. 47.

8. Hannaway. *Managers Managing*, p. 37. See also J. P. Kotter. *The General Managers.* New York: The Free Press, 1982.

9. Mintzberg, H. *The Nature of Managerial Work.* New York: Harper &amp, Row, 1973, p. 31. See also: Mintzberg, H. *Managing.* San Francisco, CA: Berrett-Koehler Publishers, Inc., 2009.

10. Reprinted by permission of *Harvard Business Review* from Kotter, J. P. "What Effective General Managers Really Do," *Harvard Business Review,* March–April 1999, pp. 145–159. Copyright © 1999 by the Harvard Business School Publishing Corporation; all rights reserved.

11. Kotter. "What Effective General Managers Really Do," p. 148.

12. Sproull, L. S. "The Nature of Managerial Attention," in L. S. Sproull (ed.), *Advances in Information Processing in Organizations.* Greenwich, CT: JAI Press, 1984, p. 15.

13. Stewart, R. *Managers and Their Jobs.* London: Macmillan, 1967.

14. Eccles and Nohria. *Beyond the Hype*, p. 47.

15. Mintzberg. *The Nature of Managerial Work*, p. 44 (emphasis mine).

16. Pondy, L. R. "Leadership Is a Language Game," in M. W. McCall, Jr. and M. M. Lombardo (eds.), *Leadership: Where Else Can We Go?* Durham, NC: Duke University Press, 1978, pp. 87–99.

17. Mintzberg. *The Nature of Managerial Work*, p. 38.

18. Eccles and Nohria. *Beyond the Hype*, pp. 47–48.

19. Reprinted by permission of *Harvard Business Review* from Mintzberg, H. "The Manager's Job: Folklore and Fact." *Harvard Business Review*, March–April 1990, pp. 166–167. Copyright © 1990 by the Harvard Business School Publishing Corporation. All rights reserved.

20. Mintzberg. "The Manager's Job," p. 167.

21. Ibid., p. 168.

22. McGregor, J. "Bezos: How Frugality Drives Innovation," *BusinessWeek*, April 28, 2008, pp. 64–66.

23. Stewart, R. *Managers and Their Jobs.* London: Macmillan, 1967.

24. Guest, R. H. "Of Time and the Foreman," *Personnel*, May 1956, p. 478.

25. Mintzberg. "The Manager's Job," pp. 166–167.

26. Ibid., pp. 168, 170.

27. Ibid., pp. 167–171.

28. Ibid., p. 167.

29. Borden, D. The Business of Talk: Organizations in Action. New York: Blackwell, 1995.

30. Ziegler, B. "Video Conference Calls Change Business," *Wall Street Journal*, October 13, 1994, pp. B1, B12. Reprinted by permission of *Wall Street Journal*, Copyright © 1994 Dow Jones & Company, Inc. All rights reserved worldwide.

31. Rankin, P. T. "The Measurement of the Ability to Understand Spoken Language" (unpublished Ph.D. dissertation, University of Michigan, 1926). *Dissertation Abstracts* 12, No. 6 (1952), pp. 847–848.

32. Nichols, R. G. and L. Stevens. *Are You Listening?* New York: McGraw-Hill, 1957.

33. Wolvin, A. D. and C. G. Coakley. *Listening.* Dubuque, IA: Wm. C. Brown and Co., 1982.

34. Werner, E. K. "A Study of Communication Time" (M.S. thesis, University of Maryland, College Park, 1975), p. 26.

35. Kotter. "What Effective General Managers Really Do," pp. 145–159.

36. Searle, J. R. *The Construction of Social Reality.* New York: The Free Press, 1995. See also Berger, P. L. and T. Luckmann. *The Social Construction of Reality.* New York: Doubleday, 1967.

37. Larkin, T. J. and S. Larkin. Communicating Change: Winning Employee Support for New Business Goals. New York: McGraw-Hill, 1994.

CASE STUDY 1-1

Odwalla, Inc. (A)

Stephen Williamson's worst nightmares were about to come true. As chief executive officer of Odwalla, Incorporated, he was at the helm of a company worth nearly $400 million whose products in the premium juice market were widely regarded by customers and competitors alike for quality and freshness. The company's reputation was solid throughout the Pacific Northwest, but the press release on his desk was filled with nothing but bad news.

Williamson had just met with his corporate communication director, reviewed the crisis communication plan, and was now applying the last few corrections to a press release before faxing it to PR Newswire. The date was October 30, 1996, and less than an hour ago, the Seattle–King County Department of Public Health and the Washington State Department of Health had reported an outbreak of E. coli (0157-H7) infections that were "epidemiologically" associated with drinking Odwalla apple juices and mixes. More specifically, the public health physicians had uncovered a direct link between people who had the infection and those who had consumed Odwalla's product. Some 66 people had become sick from drinking Odwalla juices in recent weeks.

E. coli Bacteria

Escherichia coli is a species of microscopic bacteria named for the German biologist who discovered it during the early 1900s. Virtually all large animals, including humans, benignly host some form of the bacterium in their large intestinal tracts. But a particularly virulent form of the organism, known specifically as 0157-H7, can sicken and kill those whose immune systems may be compromised.

E. coli 0157-H7 can grow quickly in uncooked food products, including meat, cheeses, fruit, dairy products, and juices. The bacteria may be completely destroyed, however, by heat or radiation. If meats are cooked to a temperature of 160 degrees Fahrenheit, or if juices and other potable liquids are pasteurized, the danger posed by such organisms is dramatically reduced or eliminated completely. For example, consumers can assume "frozen concentrate" juices are free from bacteria because their preparation requires heating to 170 degrees.

Odwalla's juice products, however, were not pasteurized. E. coli and other harmful bacteria were kept at bay with a multistep production process that selected only the finest fresh fruit, washed each piece twice, and then refrigerated the squeezings to slow the growth of microorganisms. Deliveries were made to retailers each day in refrigerated trucks, and products were displayed and sold from special Odwalla coolers. The process was repeated each business day, with the previous day's unsold products gathered up by Odwalla's drivers and returned to the plant for disposal. Thus, the product customers bought from Odwalla retailers each day was guaranteed to be fresh-squeezed that very day—a feature that loyal customers willingly paid premium prices to obtain.

The question remained: How could the lethal strain of E. coli bacteria get into Odwalla juice? How could the careful, meticulous production process have failed? Over the past 16 years, Williamson and the company's founder, Greg Steltenpohl, and the Odwalla team had worked hard to establish a stellar reputation for the company and their premium, trendy products. Yet, all of their hard work was at this moment on the line. The future of their growing company would depend on how Williamson and his senior team reacted to events over the next few hours. Gathering the papers on his desk, he took a deep breath and began dialing fax numbers.

Odwalla, Incorporated

Greg Steltenpohl, his wife Bonnie Bassett, and a friend named Gerry Percy founded Odwalla in September of 1980. A backyard shed served as the manufacturing facility for three longtime friends, who used a $200 hand-juicer (purchased with borrowed funds) and one box of oranges to make freshly squeezed orange juice. They distributed the juice to local restaurants in a Volkswagen microbus, earning just enough profits from their first day of business to purchase two more boxes of oranges for the next day's run. Thus, began this fruit juice empire.

Over the years, the Santa Cruz–based company had grown to become the leading Western United States supplier of freshly squeezed fruit juices. Currently, it markets more than 20 flavors of juice, smoothies, and vitamin-packed drinks. "If it's not fresh squeezed, then it's not part of Odwalla . . ." said Steltenpohl. In 1993, Odwalla went public and sales skyrocketed from $9 million in 1991 to $59 million in 1996. Odwalla had experienced approximately 40 percent annual sales growth during those five years.

Steltenpohl, Bassett, and Percy's entrepreneurial inspiration was a suggestion drawn from a paperback tradebook entitled *100 Businesses You Can Start for Under $100.* Based on their concerns about social trends and environmental issues, the founders decided to create a company with a social conscience. The name Odwalla came from a musical piece by The Art Ensemble of Chicago, in which the hero Odwalla guides his followers from the gray haze. Similarly, during a hazy gray time in the processed foods business, this company could guide their customers, friends, and neighbors by providing fresh citrus alternatives.

The vision of Odwalla encompasses the idea of "nourishing the whole body." The foundation of the company had been maintained through Odwalla's dedication to providing superior fresh fruit juices, preserving the product. The environment, and fostering community relationships. This people-centered approach is focused both internally on employees and shareholders as well as externally on customers and the broader community.

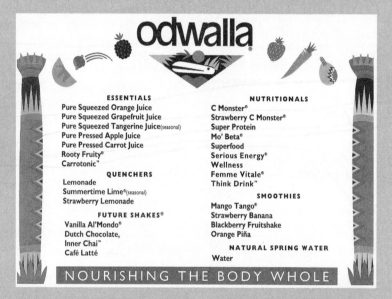

A Diverse Product Line

The diverse product offerings of fruit juices, smoothies, all natural meal replacements, quenchers, and geothermal natural spring water comprise what Odwalla terms *Nourishing Beverages.* The core competencies of the organization involve the use of minimal production processes to deliver superior taste and nutritional value as compared with concentrate and artificially flavored substitutes. This is accomplished through strict quality production systems, selective agreements with suppliers and vendors, and the continued adaptation to changing consumer tastes and preferences. Moreover, the nutritional value and flavor qualities are complemented by artful packaging.

The product line is distributed throughout California, Oregon, Colorado, Washington, New Mexico, Texas, and Nevada. Despite this large seven-state territory, a company goal remains to deliver "day of juicing quality." Such stringent standards preserve both the nutritional and flavor integrity. Thus, the shelf life of the fruit and vegetable products is limited to between eight and seventeen days after retail purchase.

The fruity flavors, outrageous names, and all-natural ingredients have allowed the company to achieve tremendous success based on the health benefits derived from consumption of the product. Their products have attracted a loyal customer base of health-conscious adults seeking nutritious vitamin supplements but also are extremely popular among young children. Parents, aware of the nutritional goodness of Odwalla juices, see them as a healthy alternative to other commercially prepared fruit drinks.

Odwalla's "All Natural" Production Process

Odwalla has strategically differentiated itself based on the "all-natural" composite of their products. The company uses strictly pure fruit extracts in the creation of their juices, smoothies, and vitamin supplements. However, the "all-natural" base of Odwalla's products holds implications for virtually every aspect of the procurement and production processes. For example, the majority of their fruit is grown in the state of Washington. The seasonal nature of the fruit industry, however, necessitates a switch at some point in the season to less expensive California fruit.

As part of their purchasing agreement, Odwalla mandates that all of the fruit they purchase be handpicked. This reduces the number of bruised and rotten pieces received in the shipments. Aside from the actual procurement of basic ingredients, the company also maintains both a production and quality control division. The production division is responsible for overseeing the creation of the product. This division not only employs people to run the presses, mix the ingredients, and bottle the juices but also employs "sorters" whose main function is to determine which pieces of fruit are acceptable for production. The company uses a quality control division to monitor all processes and uphold strict safety guidelines.

Though 98 percent of the nation's fruit juice went through a pasteurization process, Odwalla's products were unpasteurized. Steltenpohl feared that the use of a pasteurization process and other cleaning agents would kill important nutrients and detract from the taste of the final product. "Absolute freshness," he observed, "is a key component of Odwalla's product offering."

Production versus Quality

In mid-1995, juice makers in Florida were hit by an outbreak of salmonella in orange juice served at Walt Disney World. This outbreak sickened more than 60 children and adults. Consequently, the state of Florida drafted strict rules that required larger juice companies to take additional measures to ensure the safety of their production processes. As a California-based company, Odwalla was under no obligation to adhere to these standards, and very few juice companies outside of Florida actually did.

In early 1996, Odwalla hired two managers from the Florida juice industry. One of them, Dave Stevenson, who oversaw quality assurance, suggested that Odwalla add a chlorine-based rinse for precautionary measures. However, the other executive, Chip Beetle, feared chlorine would leave an aftertaste and was simply not necessary. Williamson agreed and Odwalla continued with their previous procurement, production, and distribution processes. By the summer of 1996, business was booming. In fact, sales were so strong that Odwalla was struggling to keep up with the demand for their product. Some former company officials say that production demands became more important than safety concerns.

Will an Apple a Day Keep the Doctor Away?

Throughout the 1990s, as consumers became more health conscious and supportive of environmentally sensitive causes, Odwalla's sales exploded. In addition to being passionate about Odwalla juice products, Odwalla's extremely loyal customers identified with the company's wholesome mission and social values. During the three years preceding the crisis, Odwalla expanded rapidly and achieved 40 percent annual earnings growth.

As Steve Williamson returned to his office, he picked up the phone and dialed the director of corporate communication's extension. When she answered, he simply said, "I sent the press release. What do we do now?"

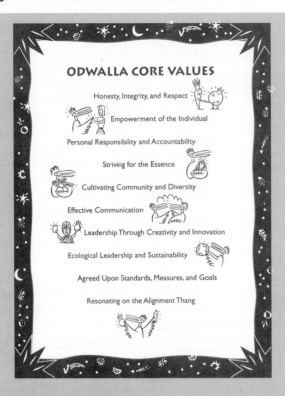

DISCUSSION QUESTIONS

1. What are the key communication issues for Odwalla?
2. How can the communication strategy focus on retaining consumer confidence?
3. Does Odwalla appear to have an effective crisis management system in place?
4. How should a company such as Odwalla go about developing guidelines before a crisis occurs?
5. Does a company such as Odwalla have a responsibility to change its production processes?
6. If the things Odwalla is saying about itself (in its advertising and its core values) are really true, what should they do? What's their next move?

WRITING ASSIGNMENT

Please respond in writing to the issues presented in this case by preparing two documents: a communication strategy memo and a professional business letter.

In preparing these documents, you may assume one of two roles: you may identify yourself as an Odwalla manager who has been asked to provide advice to Stephen Williamson regarding the issues he and the company are facing. Or, you may identify yourself as an external management consultant who has been asked by the company to provide advice to Williamson.

Either way, you must prepare a strategy memo addressed to Stephen Williamson, President and Chief Operating Officer of the company, that summarizes the details of the case, rank orders critical issues, discusses their implications (what they mean and why they matter), offers specific recommendations for action (assigning ownership and suspense dates for each), and shows how to communicate the solution to all who are affected by the recommendations.

You must also prepare a professional business letter for Williamson's signature. That document may be addressed to Odwalla retailers or Odwalla retail customers. If you have questions about either of these documents, please consult your instructor.

This case was prepared from personal interviews and public sources by Research Assistants Suzanne Halverson, Kristan L. Rake, and Jay Gallagher under the direction of James S. O'Rourke, Concurrent Professor of Management, as the basis for class discussion rather than to illustrate either effective or ineffective handling of an administrative situation.

CASE STUDY 1-2

Great West Casualty v. Estate of G. Witherspoon (A)

A. C. Zucaro, Chairman and CEO of Old Republic International Corporation, arrived at work on January 15, 1999, and picked up that morning's edition of *The Wall Street Journal,* as usual. As he worked deliberately through his first cup of coffee, his well-honed business instincts told him this would be a good day: Interest rates were down, the market was up, and the many subsidiaries of Old Republic were performing well. For the moment, Mr. Zucaro was a happy man.

As he moved to section two of the *Journal,* his optimism sank. There, on the front page of the Marketplace section, was an article discussing a lawsuit involving a subsidiary of Old Republic, Great West Casualty Company. Nothing new for a company with $2 billion in revenues and nine operating subsidiaries. But Zucaro knew from the headline that this Friday morning would be less pleasant than most: "An Old Woman Crossed the Road, and Litigiousness Sank to New Low."

The Events of July 1, 1998

On her way to work at 4:30 A.M. on July 1, 1998, 81-year-old Gertrude Witherspoon blew out a tire and careened into a roadside ditch. With her automobile disabled, Mrs. Witherspoon left her car and began walking along U.S. Route 71 near Adrian, Missouri. Still dazed from the accident, she attempted to cross the highway to reach help. At just that moment, two semitrailers traveling almost side by side spotted the small figure in the road as they passed under a bridge. Traveling nearly 70 miles per hour, the truckers were unable to avoid hitting her. According to the police report, the driver of the rig slammed on his brakes and skidded more than 100 feet. Mrs. Witherspoon was pronounced dead at the scene.

Friends and relatives were stunned and saddened, particularly at Dave's Wagon Wheel Restaurant, where Mrs. Witherspoon worked 50 hours a week as a waitress. No one took the news harder than Joyce Lang, Mrs. Witherspoon's only daughter. "The family was crushed," she said, "and I was determined to find out more about what happened that morning."

A Relative Contacts the Insurance Company

In the days and weeks following the accident, Ms. Lang sought more information about the accident. She received only indifferent statements from the Missouri Highway Patrol and the truck owner, Rex Williams, of Vernon County Grain & Supply. Frustrated in her attempts to learn more about her mother's death, Ms. Lang telephoned a claims adjuster at Great West Casualty Company to ask a few questions.

The adjuster at Great West Casualty explained that the police report and witnesses' statements showed no fault on the part of the truck driver[s]. "Is that all you can tell me?" she asked.

"The case is closed," the adjuster responded.
"Well," said Ms. Lang, "I can open it."

Believing the family was preparing legal action against Great West Casualty Company, the claims representative moved to file suit on behalf of his company against Mrs. Witherspoon's estate. "It was never my intention to sue the company," Ms. Lang said later. "I did contact an attorney, but it was only to find out what our rights were. We filed no claims or lawsuits."

About five months later—just a few days before Christmas—on December 18, 1998, Joyce Lang received notice of a legal claim filed against the Witherspoon estate for damages to the truck that struck her mother. Specifically, the claim sought $2,886 "on account of property damage caused to a vehicle due to the negligent actions of Gertie Witherspoon on July 1, 1998."

The local news media first reported this incident on September 4, 1998, when Barbara Shelly, a reporter for the *Kansas City Star* and an acquaintance of Ms. Lang, wrote a brief article elaborating on the life of Mrs. Witherspoon. By coincidence, Ms. Shelly happened to be speaking with Ms. Lang on the day the claims notice arrived. "Seeing my mother's name in print like she was a criminal," said Ms. Lang, "I was devastated."

Ms. Lang received the notice because she was serving as executor of her mother's estate. "I'm not paying them for killing my mom," she said. "I'll sit in jail first."

Amazed by the insurance company's actions, Ms. Shelly wrote a second article discussing the accident and the insurance company's response. Details in the second article appeared in the January 8, 1999, edition of the *Kansas City Star*. The story was then picked up by *The Wall Street Journal* and reported on January 15, 1999 (Attachment 1). It was at that moment that A. C. Zucaro sensed trouble. Covering the claim filed by Rex Williams was a fairly small matter. The more immediate problem for him would be the company's response to the storm of media criticism.

Old Republic International Corporation

In January 1999, Old Republic International Corporation was a financially strong and efficient insurance enterprise with substantial interests in each segment of the insurance and reinsurance industry. Old Republic International was primarily a commercial line underwriter, serving many of America's leading industrial and financial services companies as valued customers. For the year ended 1997, the company's net income was $298 million on revenues of $1.962 billion.

Old Republic International had grown steadily as a specialty insurance business since 1923. The company was regarded as independent and innovative, which was reflected in its growth. Most Wall Street insurance analysts thought the company's performance reflected an entrepreneurial spirit, sound forward planning, and an effective corporate structure that promoted and encouraged the assumption of prudent business risks. At the time, Old Republic International had nine subsidiaries across four general business lines, including General Insurance Group, Mortgage Guaranty Group, Title Insurance Group, and Life Insurance Group.

Old Republic International's corporate communication department consists of one individual who handled investor relations. All other forms of communication were outsourced to a large public relations firm in Chicago, Illinois, that reported directly to the company's president. The work performed by the public relations firm was financially oriented and included such tasks as preparing annual reports and earnings announcements.

Great West Casualty Company

Great West Casualty Company was an independent subsidiary of Old Republic. Founded in 1956, the company served the special needs of the trucking industry. By 1999, it served 29 states and had regional offices in Boise, Idaho (Western Region); Bloomington, Indiana (Eastern Region); Arlington, Texas (Southern Region); and Knoxville, Tennessee (Southeastern Region). The corporate headquarters in South Sioux City, Nebraska, served the central and northern regions. Great West Casualty employed more than 600 professionals companywide. Their policies included automobile liability, cargo coverage, general liability, inland marine floaters, physical damage, property coverage, umbrellas, and workers' compensation.

The Great West Casualty communication department also had just one employee, Ms. Leslie Bartholomew. As corporate information director, she handled all communications for the firm. Aside from an operational manual provided by Old Republic International, consisting mostly of general guidelines for handling corporate communication, Great West Casualty made virtually all communication decisions independently.

For Zucaro and his senior team at Old Republic International, the questions were direct and fairly simple: What should they do, how soon should they do it, and how should their actions be communicated? Would they need professional help from a public relations firm? And, more to the point, what did this series of events say to the company about its corporate communication strategy?

WRITING ASSIGNMENT

Please respond in writing to the issues presented in this case by preparing two documents: a communication strategy memo and a professional business letter.

In preparing these documents, you may assume one of two roles: you may identify yourself as a corporate officer who has been asked to provide advice to Mr. A. C. Zucaro regarding the issues he and the company are facing. Or, you may identify yourself as an external management consultant who has been asked by the company to provide advice to Mr. Zucaro.

Either way, you must prepare a strategy memo addressed to A. C. Zucaro, Chairman and CEO of Old Republic International, that summarizes the details of the case, rank orders critical issues, discusses their implications (what they mean and why they matter), offers specific recommendations for action (assigning ownership and suspense dates for each), and shows how to communicate the solution to all who are affected by the recommendations.

You must also prepare a professional business letter for the signature of a corporate officer whom you think is appropriate. That document should be addressed to Ms. Joyce Lang. If you have questions about either of these documents, please consult your instructor.

This case was prepared by Research Assistants Eric Gebbie, John Nemeth, and Jeffrey White under the direction of James S. O'Rourke, Concurrent Professor of Management, as the basis for class discussion rather than to illustrate either effective or ineffective handling of an administrative situation. Information was gathered from corporate as well as public sources.

CASE STUDY 1-3

Domino's "Special" Delivery: Going Viral Through Social Media

"We all have our secret ingredients . . . and in about five minutes they will be sent out on delivery where somebody will be eating these. Yes, eating 'em. And little did they know that cheese was in his nose and that there was some lethal gas that ended up on their salami. Now, that's how we roll at Domino's!"[1]

Mondays are never anyone's favorite day to be at work. But, for Tim McIntyre, VP of Corporate Communications at Domino's Pizza, Monday, April 13, 2009, might rank as the worst Monday he had experienced in his 25 years with the company.[2] While wrapping up his workday at the corporate office in Ann Arbor, Michigan, McIntyre received an e-mail alerting him that videos featuring company employees contaminating food in an unidentified store had been posted on the online video sharing site, YouTube. What had been a quiet day following Easter weekend suddenly turned into the first day of a full-fledged communications and marketing nightmare.

The Nightmare Begins

At 4:30 p.m. on April 13, McIntyre received an e-mail from the webmaster of www.GoodAsYou.org, a GLBT advocacy blog site, alerting him of the existence of a number of damaging videos the group had discovered posted on YouTube.[3] (The GLBT site showed interest in the videos because the words "gay" could be heard several times in the narration.)

After just one viewing, McIntyre knew that the five amateur videos could seriously damage the Domino's brand, not to mention putting the company at legal risk. He said, "You know what, this is a bad one— they're in uniform, they're in the store. We need to do something about it."[4] Each video, recorded by a current female Domino's Pizza employee featured a male employee performing various acts of food contamination. To make things worse, the director and actor are in full Domino's uniforms, are at work during normal store hours, and imply in the narrative that the contaminated food will soon be delivered to unsuspecting customers. It wouldn't be until much later that night that McIntyre and team would discover the identity and location of the people responsible for the videos.

Thankfully for Domino's, Good As You felt obligated to quickly notify corporate headquarters as soon as the videos were found; however, to protect the public, the bloggers also posted the video links on their own site.[5] (Refer to Appendix A for McIntyre's response and correspondence with Good As You.) McIntyre said that this initial notification came about fifteen minutes prior to his corporate social media team discovering the existence of the videos online.[6] Within that same hour, another popular consumer affairs blog site, www.consumerist.com, also posted the videos on their site. Within 24 hours, McIntyre would learn that the most popular video had received 250,000 YouTube views.[7] And that was just the beginning—the videos were going viral before McIntyre's eyes.

McIntyre scanned through the past experiences of his long tenure with Domino's to recall a situation in which he had dealt with something similar—crimes, accusations, and brand problems—something to use as a reference point on how to proceed. When nothing similar came to mind, he realized that no plans, protocols or off-the-shelf solutions in a communications handbook could help remedy the situation before him.[8] It was up to him to pull his team together to face this unprecedented threat. But what should his first step be? And what kind of irreparable damage might Domino's suffer if he chose the wrong course of action?

The Vulgar Videos

McIntyre credits two savvy readers at The Consumerist who used clues in the videos and innovative geo-mapping and investigative tools to identity the location of the videos' creators by 11:00 p.m. on Monday, just six-and-a-half hours after the videos originally surfaced.[9] The two culprits in their early 30s, Kristi Hammond and Michael Setzer, turned out to be full-time employees at a Domino's Pizza franchise location in Conover, North Carolina.

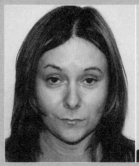 

Kristi Hammond
Director/Narrator

Michael Setzer
Actor

Hammond's "opus piece" is a two minute, twenty-six second video named, "Dominos Pizzas Special Ingredients" (sic) in which the two employees joke about being lazy workers and mention that their manager is in the back reading a newspaper, as usual. The video shows Setzer in vivid detail passing gas on salami and stuffing cheese for sandwiches up his nose, all while Hammond laughs and jokes in the background about this being business as usual at Domino's. The camera then pans to the overhead order screen, which Hammond says displays the name of the customer who will receive the delivery.

The other videos, called "Sneeze Sticks," "Poopie Dishes," and "Dominos Pizza Buger," contain Setzer sneezing on cheesy bread, wiping his behind with a sponge and then cleaning pizza pans, and stuffing a pepper up his nose while making oven-baked sandwiches. The following are a sample of quotes transcribed from one of the videos:

Kristi: "Hello, this is Kristy back again. And here at Domino's I like to be lazy . . . . You see Michael over there hard at work—yeah, not really. Did y'all see that? He just blew a booger on those sandwiches! Do you remember the time when you sneezed? [laughter] Do it again, do it again!"

Video 1: "Dominos Pizzas Special Ingredients"

Video 2: "Sneeze Sticks"

Michael: "This is Michael's special Italian sandwich."

Kristi: "And on the sandwich it goes. Now, Michael, I think that these sandwiches are going to be full of protein. . . ."

Domino's Pizza Background

Started in 1960 by Tom Monaghan as a single store, Domino's Pizza quickly grew through a network of company-owned and franchise-owned stores. With more than 5,000 stores in the United States and 3,700 stores in international markets, the chain is now recognized as the world leader in pizza delivery, based on reported consumer spending.[10] Domino's employs 125,000 team members in the U.S. and more than 60 countries around the world.[11] These employees crafted and delivered well over 400 million pizzas worldwide in 2008.[12]

Domino's Pizza is a publicly traded company on the NYSE under the symbol DPZ. In 2008, the company had global revenues of $1.4 billion. Sales were split with 55% in the U.S. and 45% international. Between 2004 and 2008, Domino's experienced growth primarily from international expansion, with just 39 new stores opening in the U.S. and 977 stores opening internationally.[13]

Franchisees. While the network of Domino's stores consists of company- and franchise-owned stores, the latter remain the primary driver behind the company's growth. Over 90% of U.S. and 100% of international stores are franchise-owned. Franchise owners are required to operate their stores in compliance with written policies, standards, and specifications drafted by Domino's corporate headquarters, but there are numerous of matters in which franchise owners have autonomy, including setting menu prices and hiring employees. The corporate headquarters provides franchisees with training materials, comprehensive operation manuals, and franchise development classes, but it is up to the franchisee to ensure operations and employees meet the standards of the Domino's brand.[14]

Corporate Communications Team. Tim McIntyre began his tenure at Domino's Pizza immediately after graduating from college. Twenty-five years later, as vice president of corporate communications, he now reports to the executive vice president of corporate communications, who reports to the company's CEO.[15] McIntyre's long, successful tenure at Domino's contributes to what he refers to as high levels of trust and "full support from the management team" on critical issues.[16]

McIntyre's internal team handles all of the company's public relations, but partners with two external agencies for advertising and new media strategy work.[17] A new team focused specifically on social media formed at Domino's about one month prior to the outbreak of the YouTube videos. This team had been planning to launch the company's presence online through several social media outlets just one week later—before Hammond beat them to it.

The Competitive Pizza Industry

Domino's Pizza operates in the highly competitive food service industry in the Quick Service Restaurant (QSR) sector. The QSR pizza category is large and fragmented and, at $33.9 billion a year, is the second largest category in the $230.0 billion U.S. QSR sector. Competition within the QSR sector is particularly intense with regard to product quality, price, service, convenience and concept. Within the U.S. there are approximately 69,000 pizzerias serving about 3 billion pizzas annually, but the main pizza delivery and carry-out competitors are Domino's, Pizza Hut and Papa John's. Together these three comprise 47% of pizza delivery in the U.S. Internationally, Pizza Hut is the principal competitor to Domino's.[18]

In general, individual customers in the QSR sector do not comprise a large portion of sales. Instead, businesses rely on volume and repeat purchase. For Domino's Pizza, no customer accounts for more than 10% of sales.[19] If customers perceive a problem in product quality, price, service or convenience, the implications to future business success could be serious. For this reason, there is nothing more important or sacred to Domino's than the trust of its customers.[20]

Social Media Players

Due to the growth of social media web sites on the Internet, individuals now have the ability to instantly share messages, images, and videos with a global audience. Once a posting is made, it can also be copied by other users and uploaded to other sites, thus compounding the impact of the posting. In this case, three sites were immediately involved. www.YouTube.com had the original posting by Hammond and Setzer, and two prominent blog sites, www.GoodAsYou.org and www.consumerist.com, copied the posting and put it on their own web sites within hours.

In today's technologically advanced world, the Internet instantly connects people all over the globe. In the United States alone, estimates of broadband Internet connection show that 84 million of the 119 million U.S. households, or 71%, had broadband connection to the Internet by 2010.[21] With the simple click of a mouse, Internet users can quickly access unprecedented amounts of information. Much of that information is posted by companies, news outlets, or other organizations, but increasingly, information is being posted and shared by common users on social networking websites.[22]

Some of the most popular social networking and content sharing websites in the U.S. are Facebook, MySpace, Twitter, and YouTube.[23] Facebook boasts a network of more than 350 million active users with an average of 50% logged on every day,[24] MySpace has more than 100 million active users,[25] and Twitter had the largest yearly growth of members at 1,382% when it hit 7 million members in February 2009.[26] YouTube started in 2005 and is now the most widely viewed video service in the U.S. ahead of Fox Interactive Media, CBS Corporation, Yahoo! sites, and others.[27] By January of 2009, YouTube claimed more than 100 million unique U.S. visitors.[28] YouTube's users, according to the website, watch "hundreds of millions of videos a day" on YouTube, and every minute, an additional 20 hours of video is uploaded to YouTube by users.[29]

The uploaded content by users on many social networking sites does not go through a formal review or approval processes by the website, so the users have great authority to post information they deem as appropriate. Once a posting is made, the content can easily be copied by other users and uploaded to other sites. This compounding effect of information being shared across websites is difficult to control and contain, so information can quickly spread and reach other users. "Viral" is a term commonly used to describe Internet content that is quickly popularized through sharing by users.[30]

In this situation with Domino's Pizza, the videos posted by Hammond and Setzer went viral. YouTube had the original posting that was uploaded by Hammond and Setzer, but within hours, two prominent blog sites—GoodAsYou.org and consumerist.com—copied the posting and put it on their own websites.[31] Once this occurred, Hammond and Setzer, as well as Domino's, lost the ability to control where the videos were posted and who was able to view them. This trend of everyday users posting and sharing information, and the impact of information going viral, is summarized well by Tim McIntyre in a response to consumerist.com about the Domino's video pranks. McIntyre said, "The 'challenge' that comes with the freedom of the Internet is that any idiot with a camera and an Internet link can do stuff like this—and ruin the reputation of a brand that's nearly 50 years old, and the reputations of 125,000 hard-working men and women across the nation and in 60 countries around the world."[32] A single Internet user, according to McIntyre, can have an immediate impact felt globally.

Putting Out the Fire

Tim McIntyre knows that the most valuable asset of Domino's is the unfailing trust of its customers. Because of the nature of the industry it is in—home food delivery—Domino's customers literally invite the company and its delivery drivers into their homes at the same time they hand over home addresses, credit card information, phone numbers, and names as they place an order. It was this trust that McIntyre was afraid would be forever damaged if this issue were not contained quickly and quietly.[33]

Instinct was telling McIntyre that the videos were most likely a hoax—a stupid prank pulled by two bored workers—but he didn't know for sure. But, whether the videos were pranks or not, Domino's customers would soon decide for themselves if he didn't come up with a plan.

When talking about that first day, McIntyre said, "My first reaction when I saw it was anger. I was angry because I love this place, I love this brand, I love the franchisees that I work with. And I took it personally. . . we [the immediate response team] channeled anger into action."[34] Needless to say, Monday's events were not a practice fire-drill for McIntyre and his team; the following weeks were going to need a lot of that action to contain this rapidly spreading media fire.

DISCUSSION QUESTIONS

1. What appears to be the business problem facing Domino's in this case?
2. Who are the key stakeholders?
3. What should Tim McIntyre and the communications team do first?
4. What should Domino's do about the employees who made the video?
5. What should Domino's do about the store where the video was made?
6. What steps should Domino's take to resolve this crisis?
7. How should Domino's respond at the local, national, and/or global level?
8. Which media should Domino's use to communicate its message?
9. How can Domino's ensure a similar crisis does not occur in the future?
10. How should Domino's work with franchisees?

WRITING ASSIGNMENT

Please respond in writing to the issues presented in this case by preparing two documents: a communication strategy memo and a professional business letter.

In preparing these documents, you may assume one of two roles: you may identify yourself as a senior communications manager for Domino's Pizza who has been asked to provide advice to Mr. McIntyre regarding the issues he and the company are facing. Or, you may identify yourself as an external management consultant who has been asked by the company to provide advice to Mr. McIntyre.

Either way, you must prepare a strategy memo addressed to Mr. Tim McIntyre, Vice President for Corporate Communications at Domino's, that sum-marizes the details of the case, rank-orders critical issues, discusses their implications (what they mean and why they matter), offers specific recommend-ations for action (assigning ownership and suspense dates for each), and shows how to communicate the solution to all who are affected by the recom-mendations.

You must also prepare a professional business letter for Mr. Patrick Doyle, President and Chief Operating Officer, to sign. That document may be addressed to any of Domino's key stakeholders, including customers, franchisees, investors, or others. If you have questions about either of these documents, please consult your instructor.

Appendix A

**UPDATE: From Domino's corporate:

> Thank you for bringing these to our attention. I don't have the words to say how repulsed I am by this - other than to say that these two individuals do not represent that 125,000 people in 60 countries who work hard every day to make good food and provide great customer service. I've turned this over to our security department. We will find them. There are far too many clues that will allow us to determine their location quite easily.
>
>
> Regards,
>
>
> Tim McIntyre
>
>
> Vice President, Communications
>
>
> Domino's Pizza, LLC

***

This case was prepared by Research Assistants Adam Peeples and Christina Vaughn under the direction of James S. O'Rourke, Concurrent Professor of Management, as the basis for class discussion rather than to illustrate either effective or ineffective handling of an administrative situation. Information was gathered from corporate as well as public sources.

References

1. Direct quote from Kristi Hammond, narrator of Domino's prank video.
2. Personal interview with Tim McIntyre, September 25, 2009.
3. Ibid.
4. Jacques, Amy. *The Strategist,* "Domino's Delivers During Crisis," Summer 2009, page 7.
5. http://www.goodasyou.org/good_as_you/2009/04/video-let-the-dominoes-appall.html.
6. Personal interview with Tim McIntyre, September 25, 2009.
7. Ibid.
8. Ibid.
9. Jacques, Amy. *The Strategist,* "Domino's Delivers During Crisis," Summer 2009, page 8.
10. Domino's Pizza Corporate Website, About Us section: www.dominosbiz.com. Accessed 10/5/2009.
11. Domino's Investor Relations. http://phx.corporate-ir.net/phoenix.zhtml?c=135383 &p=irol-homeProfile&t=&id=&. Accessed 10/5/2009.
12. 2008 Domino's Pizza Annual Report.
13. Ibid.
14. Ibid.
15. Personal interview with Tim McIntyre, September 25, 2009.
16. Ibid.
17. Ibid.
18. Ibid.
19. Ibid.
20. Ibid.
21. Mintel report, "Social Networking and Connectivity in the Digital Age - US - January 2008." Section called, "Demographics and Trends." http://academic.mintel.com.proxy.library.nd.edu/sinatra/oxygen_academic/search_results/show&/display/id=294369.
22. Ibid.
23. Ibid.

24. "Press Room: Statistics." Facebook.com. Dec 2009. http://www.facebook.com/press/info.php?statistics.

25. "Fact Sheet." MySpace.com. Dec 2009. http://www.myspace.com/pressroom?url=/fact+sheet/.

26. Carlson, Nicholas. "Twitter Traffic Grows 1,382% In a Year." BusinessInsider.com. 19 Mar 2009. Dec 2009. http://www. Business-insider.com/twitter-traffic-grows-1382-in-a-year-2009-3.

27. Research by comScore. Posted by emarketer.com in the article, "YouTube Hits 100 Million." 18 Mar 2009. Dec 2009. http://www.emarketer.com/Article.aspx?R=1006981.

28. Ibid.

29. "YouTube Fact Sheet." YouTube.com. Dec 2009. http://www.youtube.com/t/fact_sheet.

30. "Viral Internet Marketing: Why Viral Content is Great." Articlesbase.com. 22 Oct 2009. Dec 2009. http://www.articlesbase.com/internet-marketing-articles/viral-internet-marketing-why-viral-content-is-great-1369574.html.

31. Personal interview with Tim McIntyre, September 25, 2009.

32. Letter to Jonathon Drake by Tim McIntyre on 14 Apr 2009. Posted by Chris Walters. "Consumerist Sleuths Track Down Offending Domino's Store." Consumerist.com. 14 Apr 2009. Dec 2009. http://consumerist.com/2009/04/consumerist-sleuths-track-down-offending-dominos-store.html#comments-content.

33. Ibid.

34. Jacques, Amy. *The Strategist,* "Domino's Delivers During Crisis," Summer 2009, page 7.

Chapter *2*

Communication and Strategy

In Chapter 1, we looked at the role communication plays in the life of a manager—we examined why managers communicate. In this chapter, we look much more closely at how managers communicate—we examine the process itself. Elsewhere in this book we will examine the products of that process: writing, speaking, listening, conflict management, and group interaction.

DEFINING COMMUNICATION

First, though, a definition may be helpful. If you read enough books on this subject, you'll find more definitions than you can understand or remember. Here's one that is both easy to understand and easy to remember: Communication is the transfer of meaning.[1]

> "I sent you an e-mail," your manager asserts. "Didn't you get it?" You got 40 e-mails that day. What did his say?
>
> "We put out a memo on that subject just last month," a junior VP claims. "Why aren't the employees complying?" They get dozens of pieces of paper in their in-boxes each day. Are you surprised no one read it? For those of you who remember the memo, did you understand it? For those who think they understood what the vice president meant, what was your reaction? Wasn't that just a backgrounder? An update of some sort, meant to provide you with information about the development and implementation of some policy that won't really affect you? For those who received, read, understood, and remembered the memo: What was your incentive for complying with the vice president's request? How does this affect you and, more importantly, what's your motivation for getting involved?
>
> "That memo is crucial to the future of this company," your boss thunders. "It's about the vision our senior team wants to see throughout the entire organization." Gee, all that in one memo, and you just glanced through it and tossed it aside. Maybe it's still around somewhere. When you get a few minutes, you really should read it. For now, though, there's a lot more on your plate that seems much more urgent, and "vision memos" will have to wait.

Sounds familiar? It's all too familiar in many organizations because people, particularly managers, confuse the act of communicating with the process of communication. They honestly believe that a message sent is a message received. And a message received would certainly be understood and complied with, right? For them, communication is mostly, if not entirely, about sending messages.

For managers who truly understand the process, however, communication is about much more than sending messages. It's about the transfer of meaning.

When I understand a subject the way you understand it—with all of the intricacies, complexities, context, and detail—then you have communicated with me. If I am aware of not only what you know about a subject but also how you feel about it, then you have communicated with me. When I comprehend just how important a subject is to you and why you think it's important to take action now, you have communicated with me. All of this may be possible in a memo to the staff, but it's certainly not easy. Because communication is a complex, ongoing process that involves the whole substance of ourselves, it would be an unusual memo that could capture all of that. The transfer of meaning may take more than just a phone call or an e-mail message.

ELEMENTS OF COMMUNICATION

To successfully transfer meaning, you must understand that every message you receive comes from a sender who encodes the details of its content and selects a medium through which to transmit what she knows or feels. That message may be impeded by noise, primarily because of the cultural context against which it will be delivered as well as the field of experience of the receiver. The effect of the message will also depend on the frame of mind or attitudinal set you bring to the situation, along with the system of ethics that governs communication in your organization, your industry, and your society.

If all of this looks complex, congratulations, you now have a firm grasp on the obvious: Human communication is intricate, delicate, difficult, and, above all, complex. The remarkable fact is, however, we do it every day, and, more often than not, we achieve some degree of success. Orders get placed, deliveries are made, customers are satisfied, people do what you ask of them, and the business you work for runs—more or less—the way it's supposed to.

The real question here isn't whether you can communicate. You showed that you can do that when you filled out a business school admissions application. The real question is whether you can get better at it. Can you impress your clients enough to keep them? Can you encourage a reluctant employee to give the best he's got? Can you convince the boss that you are the one to take on those new responsibilities? We each have basic skills. What we need is a set of higher-level competencies that will serve the world-class organizations we will work for in the years ahead.

PRINCIPLES OF COMMUNICATION

Communication is a process that involves several basic principles. They are things we know to be true about human communication across time and cultures, across organizations and professions, and across nations and economies. Above all, we know that communication is:

DYNAMIC Human communication is constantly undergoing change. One message builds on another; one experience adds to another.

CONTINUOUS Communication never stops. Even when you hang up the telephone, you're communicating the message that you have nothing more to say. Silence, in fact, can be among the more powerful forms of communication. Simply said: You cannot *not* communicate.

CIRCULAR Communication is rarely ever entirely one-way. We each take in information from the outside world, determine what it means, and respond. The cycle we refer to as feedback is nothing more than receivers becoming senders, and vice versa. When we stop speaking to listen, we join the feedback loop.

UNREPEATABLE Heraclitus, a Greek philosopher-mathematician, once wrote that "No man can step in the same river twice." What he meant was that if you attempt to repeat an experience, the experience will be different—circumstances change and so will you. So it is with communication. Even if we say something again in precisely the same way, our listeners have heard it before. The same message delivered to two different listeners amounts to two different messages. That's also true of the same message delivered twice to the same listeners. Once we have heard or seen a message, we have some notion of what to expect. Thus, it's not the same experience as when we heard it or saw it for the first time.

IRREVERSIBLE Some processes are reversible—we can freeze water into ice and then thaw it back into water again—but not communication. We may wish we could unsay something, but we can't. All we can do is explain, apologize, and say more—but we can't ever get it back.

COMPLEX Communication is complex, not only because of the various elements and principles at work in the process, but also because it involves human beings. Each of us is different in a number of important and meaningful ways, which means that each of us will assign slightly different meaning to words, react in slightly different ways because of our background, education, and experience, and behave in slightly different ways around other people. Nothing is simple or entirely straightforward about the ways in which people communicate.[2]

LEVELS OF COMMUNICATION

Human communication also occurs at various levels. The complexities of the process, particularly audience analysis and message construction, increase as the level of communication elevates.

INTRAPERSONAL When we communicate within ourselves, sending messages to various parts of our bodies, thinking things over, or working silently on a problem, we are communicating intrapersonally.

INTERPERSONAL When we communicate between or among ourselves, sending messages from one person to another—verbally and nonverbally—we are communicating interpersonally.

ORGANIZATIONAL When we communicate with one another in the context of an organization, sending and receiving messages through various layers of authority, using various message systems, discussing various topics of interest to the group we belong to or the company we work for, we are communicating organizationally.

MASS OR PUBLIC Occasionally, when we send messages from just one person or source to many people simultaneously, as in a newspaper advertisement, television commercial, or Twitter message, we are communicating publicly.[3]

BARRIERS TO COMMUNICATION

If we each understand the principles of communication and the levels at which it can take place, and if we each use and understand the same language, why don't we succeed more often than we do? What's holding back the transfer of meaning? Broadly speaking, two barriers keep us from communicating successfully.

PHYSIOLOGICAL BARRIERS Because all the information we receive about the world must come through one or more of our five senses (sight, sound, touch, smell, and taste), we depend on those senses to report accurately on what's going on around us. It is possible, though, for our senses to be impaired or for the source of the message to provide inadequate information (insufficient light to read a message, an announcement not loud enough to be audible, and so on). In sending messages to others, we must be sensitive to the fact that they may not see, hear, touch, smell, or taste in the same way we do.

PSYCHOLOGICAL BARRIERS Communication is much more than simply sending and receiving messages. It's about understanding them, as well. Remember, communication is the transfer of meaning, and if I don't know what you mean—even though I may see and hear you well enough— no communication has taken place. Everything from the culture in which we live to the norms or standards of the groups we belong to can influence how we perceive and react to the messages, events, and experiences of everyday life. Even individual mind-sets, including prejudice and stereotypes, can affect what we understand and how we react to others. We examine each of these barriers in greater detail in Chapter 4, "Speaking."

COMMUNICATING STRATEGICALLY

To communicate strategically means several things. First, it means that your plans for communication, your proposed messages, the medium (or media) you select, the code you employ, the context and experience you bring to situations, and the ethics you adopt will all have a direct effect on the outcome. Remember the elements of communication we discussed earlier? Those are the keys to successful strategic communication.

You should know, however, that those are all just tools; they are means to an end. You should first ask what end you hope to reach. What are your communication goals? If you are communicating strategically, those goals will be aligned with and will directly support the goals of the organization you work for. And, at each level of your organization, the ways in which you communicate will be consistent and aimed at the same objectives.

To develop a communication strategy that will help you and your organization achieve the goals you have set for yourselves, you first must ask yourself a few questions related to the elements of communication we've discussed:

SENDER Who should communicate this message? Will your signature compel people to action? Should you ask your manager or vice president to sign this letter? Should someone closer to the intended audience send the message?

RECEIVER Who is the intended audience for this message? What do you know about them? More important, what do they know about you and your subject? What feelings do they have about it and you? What's their previous experience with this subject and this sender? What's their likely reaction?

MESSAGE What should your message contain? How should your message say what you intend for your audience to know? Should your message contain the bare minimum to evoke a reaction, or should you provide greater detail? Should the message focus on just one topic or should you include many issues for them to consider?

MEDIUM What's the best way to send this message? Is one medium quicker than another? Will one medium offer your audience better opportunities for feedback? Will one medium carry more detail than another? Does one medium carry a greater sense of urgency than another? Will one medium cost more than another?

CODE Encoding your message simply means selecting the right words and images. Style and tone matter as you approach readers and listeners with new information. Will they understand the words you plan to use? Will they understand the concepts you offer them? For your audience, decoding is a more complex matter of assigning meaning to the words and images you have selected. Will they mean the same thing to your receiver as they mean to you? Do these words and images have multiple meanings for you and your audience?

FEEDBACK What's the reaction of your audience? How will you know if you've communicated successfully? What measure will you use to determine whether they understand this subject the same way you understand it? Will the audience response be delayed? Will it be filtered through another source? How much feedback will you need before you decide to communicate again?

NOISE How many other senders and messages are out there? Whose message traffic are you competing with? Will others try to deflect, distort, or disable your communication attempts? How can you get the attention of your intended audience with all that they have to read, see, hear, and think about each day?

EFFECT To achieve the goals you've set for yourself and your organization, you must know how to motivate others. You must show them how the information or ideas you have offered are useful and worth acting upon.

SUCCESSFUL STRATEGIC COMMUNICATION

Getting people to listen to what you say, read what you write, or look at what you show them isn't easy. More often than not, people up and down the line have other interests that seem more immediate and other concerns to focus on. How, then, do you persuade them that paying attention to your message and cooperating with you is in their best interest?

Successful strategic communication usually involves the following six steps:

LINK YOUR MESSAGE TO THE STRATEGY AND GOALS OF THE ORGANIZATION What are the strategic objectives of your business? Chances are good that your organization has published a document outlining its vision, values, and beliefs. Of course, the corporate annual report to shareholders is a good place to look for business strategy. If you can't find what you're looking for, call corporate communication and explain what you want and why you want it.

Every division within a business should have a set of simple, easy-to-understand business objectives (e.g., "Increase cash flow by 10% during this fiscal year," or "Increase market share by 15% within the next three years"). All of your communication—no matter what the audience, no matter what the medium, no matter what the purpose for communicating—should be consistent with and directly supportive of those business objectives. If your writing and speaking don't fit that description, either you don't understand the company's objectives or you don't agree with them. If that is the case, you should make an effort to learn and understand them or look for work elsewhere.

ATTRACT THE ATTENTION OF YOUR INTENDED AUDIENCE Appeal to basic needs or to the fundamentals of physiology to attract the attention of your intended audience. Basic needs would include the bottom rungs of Abraham Maslow's Hierarchy of Human Needs. This hierarchy explains the frequent focus on issues related to survival, food, water, sex appeal, and other needs.[4] The fundamentals of physiology are simply activities designed to appeal to the sight, hearing, taste, touch, or smell capacities of the audience. Loud noises, bright lights, and similar devices can attract attention; the more important issue is whether you can hold that attention once the audience knows who you are and what you want.

EXPLAIN YOUR POSITION IN TERMS THEY WILL UNDERSTAND AND ACCEPT If your audience is willing to spend time and effort attending to your message but cannot understand what you intend, you'll raise nothing other than their frustration level. As you will see in Chapter 5, using language they are likely to understand and accept will make comprehension and compliance that much easier. This implies knowing your audience: knowing who they are, how much they know about this subject, how they feel about it, and their level of sophistication.

MOTIVATE YOUR AUDIENCE TO ACCEPT AND ACT ON YOUR MESSAGE Several motivational appeals are available for you to reach and move your audience. First, consider an appeal to authority. If you are either in a position of organizational authority or an acknowledged expert on the matter, you may legitimately ask your audience to respond to those forms of authority. It is the equivalent, to some, of hearing ". . . because I'm you're mother," but it works more often than not. And, in some instances, you may have neither the time nor the patience to explain in detail why the audience should comply. Successful appeals to authority usually involve a follow-up stage in which the authority figure provides justification for the request.

Second, you might consider social conformity to move your audience, which is equivalent to the "celebrity endorsement" or "millions of satisfied customers can't be wrong" approach. The vast majority of people don't like to be out of step with other members of the society in which they live; they appreciate and value conformity and what it does for society. An endorsement to your intended audience from a person they respect (it doesn't matter if *you* respect him or her) may prove helpful. If not, you can always resort to opinion polls ("Four out of five dentists who chew gum recommend our product").

Finally, you might use rationality and consistency theory to motivate your audience. Just as the majority of people wish to conform to what others think is proper, so too do they want rational, consistent behavior in their lives. If they see what you are advocating as irrational or inconsistent with their existing beliefs, they won't buy it. You must show them that it is consistent with what they already believe and—for those who admire logic—entirely rational.[5]

INOCULATE THEM AGAINST CONTRARY MESSAGES AND POSITIONS Persuasion theorists have shown that beliefs persist in the face of contrary evidence if the holder of those beliefs has been inoculated against counter-persuasion at some point. Several means exist to make those actions you advocate resistant to the appeals of your competitors. First, you can ask for a tangible commitment from your audience. If that commitment is public, or at least known to other members of the target audience, so much the better. Everything from signing a pledge card to wearing a campaign button will bolster the beliefs of your audience.[6] A Los Angeles restaurateur dramatically cut the number of reservation "no-shows" by asking diners a simple question as they called for reservations: "Do you promise to call us if your dinner plans change?" The act of saying "yes" on the telephone committed them to a course of behavior that benefited the restaurant substantially.[7]

MANAGE AUDIENCE EXPECTATIONS People are disappointed in the service or the products you deliver only if their expectations exceed the quality of what they receive. The same is true of communication. Always deliver what you promise, never less. Always meet or exceed your audience's expectations. Manage those expectations by cueing your audience about what to expect from your communications with them. If you deliver what you say you will, your audience will reward you with its attention and consideration for your message.

WHY COMMUNICATING AS A MANAGER IS DIFFERENT

Communication is a fundamental skill central to the human experience. We each know how to do it; we've done it since birth and receive additional practice each day. So, why is it so difficult to communicate on the job? What does the workplace do to change the nature of communication? Several factors in business life alter the way we look at communication. These factors influence the way we write and speak with others, right down to word selection and format. They influence our willingness to listen or to devote time to the concerns of others. And they influence the way we think about our daily problems, responsibilities, and challenges.

LEVELS OF RESPONSIBILITY AND ACCOUNTABILITY The higher your level of responsibility in an organization, the more you have to think about. If you spend the majority of your day focused on just one or a few fairly well-defined issues, your communication will tend to be much more keenly focused. If you have many problems, many challenges to address during the day, your communication style will be more fragmented and broadly focused. As you read in Chapter 1, time management and communication efficiency become core skills.

Additionally, as you become more accountable, you tend to keep better records. If you know you'll be asked about particular issues, it's to your advantage to update and maintain what you know about those subjects. A phone call from your boss, posing questions you can't answer, is always a difficult experience.

ORGANIZATIONAL CULTURE Some organizations have a very written culture. Procter & Gamble, for example, requires that every issue be written in memo form and circulated to team members before it can be raised as an agenda issue in a team meeting. Other organizations, such as 3M Canada, are more "oral" in nature, offering employees an opportunity to talk things through before writing anything down. Many companies rely on a particular culture to move day-to-day information through the organization, and to succeed in such a business, you must adapt to the existing culture rather than try to change it or ask it to adapt to you.

ORGANIZATIONAL DYNAMICS Organizations, like the humans who populate and animate them, are in constant flux. Businesses change with the conditions of the marketplace and the lives of the managers who run them. Your communication will have to adapt to the conditions in which you find yourself.

That does not mean signing your name to a document that is false or passing along information that you know isn't true, even if the organization presses you for time or will not give you access to information you really need to do your job. It does mean adapting your style to the standards and norms of the industry. It may mean greater concision or more detail than you might personally prefer. It may mean shorter turnaround times on requests than you think are reasonable. Or it may mean sharing or withholding information from those you work with each day. Each organization has its own style that is conditionally and temporally affected by a range of issues from market share to target-status in a takeover.

PERSONALITY PREFERENCES Finally, it's important to acknowledge that each of us has his or her own preference for gathering, organizing, and disseminating information. Each of us also has a style for making decisions. You'll have to accommodate those you work with and work for in order to succeed in business.

If the boss wants plenty of detail and plenty of time to think it over before making a decision, accommodate that. Provide an executive summary, but give her the detail in tabular or annex form if that's what she wants. Meet or beat submission deadlines. And provide the information in the form your reader or listener most wants. If your client likes e-mail, learn to live with brief, typewritten messages and attached text files. If your client likes personal briefings, schedule the time it will take to go over the information in detail. It is counterintuitive, but if you put the information-gathering and decision-making needs of others—particularly your boss and your clients—ahead of your own preferences, you'll get what you want faster and with much less pain.

CRISIS COMMUNICATION

Crisis can come in many shapes and forms. Some crises unfold slowly over many months or years. Others arrive quickly or explosively, without notice.

The Coca-Cola Company's mishandling of a product contamination crisis in Europe during the summer of 1999 is a case in point. A bad batch of CO_2 found its way into Coca-Cola products bottled in Belgium and onto grocery store shelves in the cities of Bornem, Lochristi, and Kortrijk. When reports of school children feeling nauseous and seeking hospital treatment after consuming Coca-Cola products hit the local press, company executives dismissed the incidents as overblown and "hardly a health hazard."[8]

CEO Doug Ivester, in fact, was in Paris at the time of the incident, yet chose to fly back to Atlanta rather than address it directly. He not only misread local sentiment regarding the company's obligations but failed to grasp the larger cultural implications of the crisis. Belgian Prime Minister Jean-Luc Dahaene had been forced out of office because of a scandal involving contamination of the food supply, and others seized the opportunity to take cheap shots at the American soft drink giant. Sweden's *Svenska Dagbladet* proclaimed, "200 Poisoned by Coca-Cola," and Italy's *La Stampa* declared, "Alarm across Europe for Coca-Cola Products."[9]

Following a recall of the company's products that cost $103 million over a six-week period and resulted in a drop of more than 20 points in Coca-Cola's share price, the brand did recover. It took just less than a year for consumers in Europe to resume their pre-crisis consumption patterns and for the company's stock value to return to the $75 per share level. The damage to the company's reputation cost Doug Ivester his job, however, as key investors lost confidence in his ability to protect the brand.

Other crises are years in the making. On the morning of February 5, 1995, Jim Adamson arrived at the corporate offices of Flagstar Companies in Spartanburg, South Carolina. As the firm's newly appointed CEO, his task was to reshape the future of a troubled company. His predecessor, Jerry Richardson, had struggled to keep the company alive with $2.3 billion in debt from a series of restructuring attempts. Despite those efforts, the company lost money for five consecutive years from 1985 to 1990.[10]

More ominously, Adamson had to confront the issue of racial discrimination. Flagstar was the parent company of Denny's Restaurants, a chain of restaurants that had become a symbol for racism in the United States. He also had serious questions about the company's business model as a holding firm for quick-service and convenience-dining restaurants. With few assets and no experienced management team at his disposal, Adamson was brought to Flagstar from his position as CEO at Burger King by Henry Kravis, the New York junk-bond buyout king from Kohlberg Kravis & Roberts. His instructions were clear: Turn this company around. Make money or make way for someone who can.[11]

Each of these events represents a crisis and a potential threat to the reputation, financial health, and survival of the companies involved. And while each executive responded in a different way to the threats, each was faced with a moment of decision. "What am I facing, and what shall I do?"

CRISIS DEFINED Let's draw a line between business problems and a genuine crisis. "Problems," according to author Lawrence Barton, "are commonplace in business. What differentiates crisis from the routine or even extraordinary management dilemma is this: a crisis is a major, unpredictable event that has potentially negative results. The event and its aftermath may significantly damage an organization and its employees, products, services, financial condition, and reputation."[12] Ordinary business problems can be addressed in a limited time frame without arousing public attention and draining the resources of an organization. By contrast, a crisis is more expensive and often takes considerable time to understand and react to. And, of course, a crisis is far more threatening.

TYPES OF CRISES Some professionals draw further distinctions within crisis management, observing that some crises are *internal* in nature. Think of the accounting scandal and misappropriations for which Tyco CEO Dennis Kozlowski was convicted. The problems were almost entirely internal, as were those created by William Aramony at United Way. By contrast, other crises are *external* or *oppositional* in nature. When People for the Ethical Treatment of Animals attacked Procter & Gamble and its Iams Dog Food division in March of 2003, alleging mistreatment of animals in a research facility, the crisis involved one organization opposing another.

PREPARING FOR A CRISIS When it comes to crisis communication, British physician Thomas Fuller got it right in 1732, when he wrote, "A man surprised is half beaten."[13] Clearly, it pays to be prepared.

"Preparedness planning is definitely *not* a waste of time," says J. Adaire Putnam, Director of Corporate Communications at the Kellogg Company in Battle Creek, Michigan. "Because, when a crisis strikes, it usually strikes without warning, only giving you time to react and respond to whatever it triggers. Your foresight in getting ready for a crisis," she says, "will get you 80 percent of the way at a time when—in the chaos a crisis unleashes—all you can afford is the time to go the additional 20 percent."[14]

How an organization reacts to an incident or emergency can be a defining moment that can salvage or destroy a reputation. And it is often impossible to know when an emergency will occur. Arthur Andersen's accountants, Firestone Tire's executives, the makers of Tylenol, and Wendy's restaurant officials certainly didn't anticipate a calamity happening to them. But managers with responsibility for safeguarding the reputation of a product, a brand, or an organization can certainly prepare for communicating in a crisis.

Here are five rules that Adaire Putnam thinks all managers should consider as they approach crisis communication:

1. **Develop a detailed crisis management action plan that includes detailed research.** "Assess all potential issue-and-crisis vulnerabilities and plan accordingly," she says. With a system in place, you'll be less likely to waste valuable time trying to decide how to communicate. When cable-TV operator Cox Communications prepared for contract negotiations with broadcasters several years ago to carry their programs, the company asked Putnam and her former employer, public relations firm Ketchum, to help manage the issue because if the programming agreement were to fail, it would result in a "dark channel." Careful research helped the company define their message points, audiences, and best position on the issue. When a crisis struck on New Year's Day and Fox Television precluded Cox subscribers from watching college bowl games and the NFL playoffs, the crisis communications plan went into effect. Cox and their partners at Ketchum continuously reviewed media treatment and customer correspondence to determine the effectiveness of their strategy and message points.[15]

2. **Set specific objectives and principles.** The Cox Communications crisis-preparedness plan established three objectives: to motivate broadcasters to provide retransmission consent, to minimize customer defections to satellite, and to minimize the damage to the company's public image. Those objectives each proved to be measurable and achievable.

3. **Establish a crisis-control team and an outline of responsibilities and authority for taking action when a crisis develops.** Decide who will comprise your crisis team, creating that team around the expertise you will need and the personalities involved. Assign at least one hands-on person, says Putnam, as the crisis-communications team leader and then choose a backup.

    Additionally, you must select your primary and secondary spokespeople. Line up the outside experts and help you will need, possibly including outside legal counsel, an environmental cleanup expert, and mental health workers for trauma victims, among others. Develop a communications contact tree with everyone's phone numbers on it, including cell phones, and make sure they're updated regularly.

    Contact a local hotel or motel and inform the proprietor that a day may arise when you will need all the rooms and you'll pay what he or she wants. Establish a "war room" or conference facility where the entire team can work. Make sure there are enough phone lines there and that those in the room will have cell phone service.

    Also, establish a separate press room away from the "war room" so that the media won't know who is there and demand access to other potential spokespeople.[16]

4. **Speak with one voice.** Create a communications plan that ensures all of your stakeholders—employees, customers, suppliers, community, regulatory officials, and others—receive the same clear, valid information. Consider making your Web site or even a special crisis Web site *the* place to get crisis-related information.

    Your Web site can prove invaluable for responding to a crisis, explaining the company's position, or rallying public support behind an issue. In September 2004, when the pharmaceutical firm Merck & Company made the decision to pull its important pain-killing drug Vioxx from the market, company vice president Joan Wainwright realized she would have to reach millions of concerned patients, physicians, pharmacists, and others. More than 100 million prescriptions had been written for the drug. Within 60 hours of the initial announcement, she and her communications team launched a Web site at www.vioxx.com and established a toll-free telephone number to answer questions and address concerns.[17]

During October and November 2004, Merck's public affairs efforts generated more than 4 billion media impressions on the topic. The company's Vioxx Web site traffic grew from about 4,000 daily visits on September 29 to 234,000 on October 1. By early December, the vioxx.com Web site had attracted more than 2 million visitors, and the company's merck.com Web site had experienced an additional 1 million visitors. The team's toll-free telephone number received more than 120,000 calls in the first six days following the announcement. Additionally, the company reported issuing more than a half-million refunds for Vioxx prescriptions worldwide. Without the Web presence and a competently staffed call center, Merck would simply not have been able to address the enormous public concern that arose literally overnight.[18]

5. **Train for a crisis.** Develop scenarios in advance and work out responses on a case-by-case basis. Anticipating what information you will need can help to ensure that you have it when a crisis occurs. Establish what-ifs, contingencies you can employ if needed and experts you can tap to work side-by-side with you. Consider holding a mock crisis, a simulation, to test your procedures and better prepare your team and its resources.

Prepare background materials that will be needed, including press release templates, fact sheets, biographies, and position statements that can be formatted for easy revision and updated during an actual crisis.

In May 2005, FedEx gathered its main communications forces for such a crisis simulation. It was a global exercise involving more than 75 participants from FedEx's four operating companies in offices around the United States, Europe, Asia, Canada, and Latin America. FedEx and their partners at Ketchum developed a scenario involving a terrorist attack on the FedEx system, infecting employees around the globe with a chemical warfare agent. FedEx communicators faced the threat of serious damage to the company's reputation and the possible shutdown of the entire system.

Armed with 93 scripts that advanced the storyline, facilitators in seven cities role-played a variety of FedEx personnel, media outlets, and customer contacts to make the situation as real as possible for the players. After the exercise, facilitators addressed gaps that the simulation exposed and incorporated the best practices that emerged into all FedEx communicators' crisis processes. The company also made a commitment to testing its crisis preparedness annually.

"Preparation really is the key," says Adaire Putnam. "Simply expect the unexpected. The better prepared you are for the worst to happen, the more quickly and effectively you can respond. The best way to manage communications during a crisis truly is to plan for it in advance."[19]

For Further Reading

Argenti, P. "Crisis Communications," in *Corporate Communication*, 5th ed. New York: Irwin McGraw-Hill, 2009, pp. 257–283.

Coombs, T. *Ongoing Crisis Communication: Planning, Managing, and Responding*, 2nd ed. Thousand Oaks, CA: Sage Publications, Inc., 2007.

Goodman, M. B. and Hirsch, P. B. *Corporate Communication: Strategic Adaptation for Global Practice.* New York: Peter Lang Publishing, Inc., 2010.

Hatch, M. J. and Schultz, M. *Taking Brand Initiative: How Companies Can Align Strategy,* *Culture, and Identity Through Corporate Branding.* San Francisco, CA: Jossey-Bass, 2008.

Mitroff, I. I., Pearson, C. M., and Harrington, L. K. *The Essential Guide to Managing Corporate Crises.* New York: Oxford University Press, 1996.

O'Hair, D., Friedrich, G. W., and Shaver, L. D. *Strategic Communication in Business and the Professions*, 7th ed. Boston, MA: Allyn & Bacon, 2010.

Quirke, B. *Communicating Corporate Change: A Practical Guide to Communication and Corporate Strategy.* London: McGraw-Hill, 1996.

Endnotes

1. Fabun, D. *Communication: The Human Experience.* New York: William Morrow, 1968.

2. See DeVito, J. A. *The Interpersonal Communication Book*, 10th ed. New York: HarperCollins Publishers, 2003, pp. 23–36. See also Watzlawick, P., J. H. Beavin, and J. D. Jackson. *Pragmatics of Human Communication: A Study of Interactional Patterns, Pathologies, and Paradoxes.* New York: Norton, 1967.

3. DeVito, J. A. *Human Communication: The Basic Course*, 9th ed. New York: HarperCollins Publishers, 2002, p. 5.

4. Maslow, A. "A Theory of Human Motivation," *Psychological Review* 50 (1943): 370–396.

5. Bem, D. J. *Beliefs, Attitudes, and Human Affairs.* Belmont, CA: Brooks/Cole Publishing Company, 1970, pp. 24–38.

6. Cialdini, R. B. *Influence: The Psychology of Persuasion.* New York: Quill Books, 1993.

7. Grimes, W. "In War Against No-Shows, Restaurants Get Tougher," *New York Times*, October 15, 1997, pp. B1–B6. Copyright 1997 © by the New York Times Company. Reprinted with permission.

8. Smith, H. and A. Feighan. *Coca-Cola and the European Contamination Crisis (A), (B).* Notre Dame, IN: Eugene D. Fanning Center, Mendoza College of Business, 2000.

9. Ibid.

10. Adamson, J., R. NcNatt, and R. B. McNatt. *The Denny's Story: How a Company in Crisis Resurrected Its Good Name.* New York: John Wiley & Sons, 2000.

11. Abes, M. J., W. B. Chism, and T. F. Sheeran. *Denny's Restaurants: Creating a Diverse Corporate Culture (A), (B).* Notre Dame, IN: Eugene D. Fanning Center, Mendoza College of Business, 2000.

12. Barton, L. *Crisis in Organizations: Managing and Communicating in the Heat of Chaos.* Cincinnati, OH: South-Western Publishing Company, 1993, p. 2.

13. Fuller, T. www.inspirational-quotes.org/competition-quotes.html. Accessed November 7, 2005.

14. Putnam, J. A. In a personal interview with the author, August 1, 2005, Chicago, IL.

15. Ibid.

16. Ibid.

17. Wainwright, J. Vice President for public affairs, Merck & Company, in a teleconference interview from her offices at Merck corporate headquarters, Whitehouse Station, NJ, December 9, 2004.

18. Ibid.

19. Putnam. In a personal interview with the author.

CASE STUDY 2-1

Starbucks Coffee Company: Can Customers Breastfeed in a Coffee Shop?

Audrey Lincoff sat back in her office chair, looking at the numerous newspaper articles that covered her desk. As the spokeswoman for Starbucks, she knew she played a major role in Starbucks' response to the current dilemma. The question was all over the news and the office: How would Starbucks handle the pressure from a new activist group, breastfeeding mothers? Led by a powerful woman and skilled negotiator, the disgruntled breastfeeders had gathered at a Maryland Starbucks to stage a "nurse-in." Ms. Lincoff worried about the media attention and had to make a decision: cater to the group's demands or ignore them in hopes that they would either fade away or choose another target.

History of Starbucks Coffee Company

Starbucks began as a coffee importing and roasting company in 1971. The Seattle-based corporation was named after the first mate in Herman Melville's classic novel, *Moby Dick*. The name reflected the quirky nature of the company's founders, Gerald Baldwin, Gordon Bowker, and Zev Siegl, who had become friends during their college days at the University of Seattle.[1]

The Starbucks Coffee, Tea, and Spice Company sold roasted coffee beans to restaurants and to the public from its store in the Pike Place Market next to Puget Sound. Starbucks had grown to four stores by 1982, the year their Hammerplast sales rep decided to pay them a visit. Howard Schultz was selling a lot of coffee percolators to the little company in Seattle; he flew out from New York City to see why. He fell in love with the company and pushed the founders to create the job of Director of Retail Sales for him.

The next year, Schultz spent his vacation in Milan. He experienced Italian café culture and realized America had nothing like it. More importantly, he decided America was ready for such a "third place," a location outside of the home and the office for people to gather. However, his employers did not share his vision. Schultz left to follow his dream, starting the Il Giornale chain of cafés in the Seattle area in 1985.

Two years later, Starbucks' owners decided they were ready to leave the coffee business. Schultz put together a group of investors, including Bill Gates, Sr., and bought the company. He rebranded the Il Giornale stores as Starbucks and didn't look back. It took him five years to prepare the company for a public offering, but by 2004, SBUX was number 8 on *Fortune* magazine's list of "America's Most Admired Companies."

Since 1987, the company has expanded at an astonishing rate. Schultz's hunch was right; America was ready for the third place provided by Starbucks. In 1987, Starbucks opened its first store outside of the State of Washington. Over the next eight years, the company spread throughout North America before opening its first overseas location in Japan. The company continues to open new stores at an impressive rate: 1,500 new stores have been planned for 2006. Starbucks has also grown through licensing relationships and by offering bottled drinks and bags of coffee for sale in grocery stores. Retail sales for 2003 were \$3.45 million.[2]

Corporate Culture

Starbucks' unique culture was what led Howard Schultz to leave his successful appliance sales career and move his family from one coast of the country to the other. As it has grown, the leadership has been careful to maintain and grow the company's culture. As Schultz has said, "Building Starbucks has been very much about building the company my father never got a chance to work for."[3]

All Starbucks' employees who work more than 20 hours per week are eligible for benefits. The company also works with the farmers who grow the coffee beans to improve their lives, as coffee growing regions tend to be very poor and the cost of coffee has been depressed because of oversupply.[4] Starbucks' baristas tend to be proud of both the company they work for and the training they receive. Upper management is more diverse than most large companies in the United States.[5] All of this has built the company's reputation for being progressive, even liberal, for a large corporation.

Training

Barista training involves 20 hours of online and in-store on-the-job training. Many of the stores have wireless Internet routers. While the Wi-Fi connection is a great draw for customers, it also complements the company's training program. After entry-level training, advanced programs are also available online, including the recently introduced "black apron" training for baristas to achieve *Coffee Master* status.[6]

The management training program involves another ten weeks.[7] Starbucks knows that an important part of developing superior managers is making sure the right people go through the training program. Training for store development managers is conducted at headquarters in Seattle after the managers have worked for at least three months in a store.[8]

Customers

While employees clearly come first in the Starbucks culture, the customer is a close second. Starbucks' fourth guiding principle is to "Develop enthusiastically satisfied customers all the time." "We recognized early on that the equity of the Starbucks brand was going to be the retail experience that the customers had in our stores," says Schultz.[9]

As an industry analyst recently noted, "The two things that make them great are real estate and making sure no one has a bad experience in their stores." Schultz says this is because "our customers see themselves inside our company, inside our brand—because they're part of the Starbucks experience."[10]

The Breastfeeding Protest: Got Milk?

On August 8, 2004, a new item was added to a Maryland Starbucks menu, but for a much younger crowd. About 100 people, including babies, the babies' mothers and fathers, grandmothers and friends, filed into a Silver Spring, Maryland Starbucks coffee shop to stage a "nurse-in." Holding signs, feeding babies, and passing out fliers on the benefits of breastfeeding, the mothers were focused.

The idea of the "nurse-in" began a month earlier, after a Starbucks employee received several complaints and asked Lorig Charkoudian to relocate to the bathroom or cover up as she breastfed her 15-month-old daughter in the Maryland coffee shop. Inspired by the incident, Lorig gathered about 30 mothers to breastfeed at the store and protest actions that they felt belittled the importance of breastfeeding, which they saw as a natural, healthy process. Lorig argued that covering is uncomfortable for the baby and that "When women breast-feed, you see less breast than you do in the average Coors Light ad."[11]

By 2005, Starbucks did not have an official policy regarding breastfeeding in its coffee shops. In Lorig's case, the law was on her side. In Maryland, an act passed in 2003 prohibits stopping mothers from breastfeeding in public. Starbucks spokeswoman, Audrey Lincoff, responded by stating that "Starbucks complies with all applicable state and local laws regarding breastfeeding" and that Starbucks would "instruct our Maryland store partners to inform any concerned customer that by Maryland law, mothers have their right to breastfeed in public and to suggest to the customer that they either avert their eyes or move to a different location within the store."[12]

Unfortunately for Starbucks, Lorig was not satisfied with this effort. She wanted Starbucks to allow breastfeeding in all of its 5,882 U.S. shops. To support her efforts, Lorig started a Web site, www.nurseatstarbucks.com, to allow mothers to send letters to Starbucks chief executive, Orin C. Smith.[13] "It's all about public acceptance of breastfeeding," said Lorig.[14] Supporting mothers seemed to agree with the decision to use Starbucks for their demonstrations. One participating "nurse-in" mother responded by saying, "If you look at the clientele during business hours, you'll find a lot of young mothers with children who come to congregate and talk. If they want to continue to attract this clientele, they need to change their policies."[15] On the other hand, a regular, loyal customer inside the shop at the time of the demonstration responded by stating that Lorig's decision was an "overreaction" and that in a place where he is eating or drinking, a "nurse-in" was the last thing he wanted to see.[16]

The Leader of the Pack

Lorig Charkoudian is no stranger to public confrontation and conflict. From the death penalty to elephant rights, she has been involved in a number of causes and movements. Recently voted one of "Maryland's Top 100 Women," Charkoudian has a history of public confrontation and public demonstrations.

From 1995 to 2005, Charkoudian served as the founder and executive director of the Community Mediation Program (CMP) in Baltimore. The CMP was established initially to help Baltimore residents resolve conflicts nonviolently but developed into a much larger program spanning the State of Maryland. She is also employed as an adjunct professor in the University of Baltimore's Negotiation and Conflict Management Program. Charkoudian is the recipient of numerous local awards in the Baltimore area, including the Unsung Hero Award (1999), the Brick Award (1997), and the Human Rights Community Builder (1997).[17] Thus, it would appear the breastfeeding conflict at Starbucks is not the product of amateur activists; it is led by an experienced professional who knows how to lead and convince others to follow.

Past Problems

The breastfeeding issue is not the first to involve conflict and controversy in a Starbucks store. In 1995, Starbucks' Corporate Customer Relations Manager, Betsy Reese, became aware of several problems associated with an espresso machine purchased by a customer named Jeremy Dorosin. In just six weeks, the problem had escalated to a point unforeseen by any Starbucks executive.

In April of 1995, Mr. Dorosin purchased an espresso machine from a California Starbucks, which left him unsatisfied because of defects. Upon returning the machine for repair, Dorosin received a "loaner" from the company. Apparently pleased with the performance of the machine he'd been loaned, Dorosin purchased another as a wedding gift for a friend. Unfortunately, his friend found the gift to be in unacceptable condition—dirty, wet, and not functioning properly—as if it had been previously used. Embarrassed, Dorosin returned the wedding gift to the Starbucks store and complained to the manager. After several interactions with the manager, the corporate service supervisor, and the district manager, no resolution could be reached. Even when Starbucks offered apologies and gifts, Dorosin responded with "too little, too late." In response, he chose to take the disagreement public and confront the company in the media.[18]

Jeremy Dorosin ran an advertisement in [the] *Wall Street Journal* on May 5, 1995, describing what had happened to him and asking if other people had similar or comparable bad experiences with Starbucks. In response, he received thousands of calls from angry customers, competitors, and employees. Although Starbucks' and Dorosin's stories differ concerning exactly when the company offered to apologize, one thing is crystal clear: the short timeline between problem and escalation. Between the first advertisement on May 5, 1995, until mid-June of that year, Dorosin received nonstop attention in four *Wall Street Journal* articles, three radio shows, three television program appearances, and one *New York Times* article.[19] He even launched a Web site entitled, www.starbucked.com. Dorosin's name serves today as a reminder to Starbucks of how small problems can escalate out of control.

Breastfeeding Legislation

On May 22, 2003, Maryland Governor Robert L. Ehrlich, Jr., signed legislation regarding breastfeeding in public. The State of Maryland Code, Title XX, Subtitle XIII states that:

- A mother may breast-feed her child in any public or private location in which the mother and child are authorized to be.
- A person may not restrict or limit the right of a mother to breast-feed her child.[20]

This law gives a mother the right to breastfeed her child virtually anywhere in the State of Maryland but does not clarify whether or not an individual has the right to request that a mother cover her nipple during breastfeeding.

Maryland was not the first to enact legislation specifically governing breastfeeding in public places. In fact, close examination of other state laws regarding breastfeeding reveals the complexity of the situation. By 2005, 16 U.S. states had no legislation exempting breastfeeding from indecent exposure laws. This leaves mothers who breastfeed in public at risk of violating a criminal statute.

Some states, such as Missouri, give mothers the right to breastfeed in public, but with as much discretion as possible. Georgia laws previously incorporated similar language, until 2002 when it was removed. Conversely, nine states have legislation stating, "a mother may breast feed her baby in any location, public or private, where the mother is otherwise authorized to be, irrespective of whether or not the nipple of the mother's breast is covered during or incidental to the breast feeding." New Jersey and Connecticut state laws impose a fine and even potential imprisonment for persons discriminating against breastfeeding mothers. State law[s] in Hawaii and Illinois give breastfeeding mothers the right to bring proceedings against any person engaging in a discriminatory practice. Connecticut, Hawaii, and Louisiana refer to the restriction of the right of a mother to breastfeed her child as a discriminatory practice.[21]

Not only do numerous state laws address public breastfeeding, but many states have enacted legislation regarding breastfeeding in the workplace, deferral of jury duty, and the exemption of sales and use tax on breastfeeding related items. Coincidently, Maryland was the first state to exempt breastfeeding supplies from sales tax. Considering that thirty-four states have some form of legislation regarding public breastfeeding, it was becoming obvious to Starbucks management that breastfeeding mothers had become a powerful special interest group.

Breastfeeding Everywhere

Starbucks is not the only organization attempting to assess the impact that a breastfeeding policy (or lack thereof) might have on company performance. McDonald's experienced a similar incident as women across the country protested at local fast-food restaurants in support of Jamie Lovett. Ms. Lovett was asked to stop nursing her 9-month-old at a McDonald's in Birmingham, Alabama, on June 27, 2004. The McDonald's manager referred questions to marketing representative, Stacy Cox, who could not be reached for comment.[22]

Burger King also experienced a similar incident at a franchise in Salt Lake City. Burger King implemented a policy that allows breastfeeding in its restaurants the night before a scheduled protest. A spokesman for Burger King responded to the incident by saying, "We want to be a family-friendly place." The new policy requires Burger King employees to ask complaining customers to move to a different area of the restaurant. While Burger King's public apology and policy implementation satisfied the Utah woman, the same cannot be said for all breastfeeding advocates. Some women assert that a policy allowing breast-feeding is not enough. Advocates want restaurants claiming to be "family friendly" to provide a special room where mothers can breastfeed their children.[23]

The array of responses from breastfeeding advocates makes it clear that satisfying all of their needs will be very difficult for any company. Any organization that succumbs to the demands of one breastfeeding mother will open itself up to even more demands. Organizations must decide how far is too far and address this issue before it becomes a major crisis.

Going Forward

Ms. Lincoff swept the clippings into a folder to take to the communications strategy meeting. She wondered what shape the final plan would take. Even a small incident could damage the brand if it were mishandled. As she headed down the hall, she thought about the conflicting goals of the stakeholders and possible ways to satisfy them. With growth and success in the marketplace come challenges and opportunities of many sorts; breastfeeding mothers and their babies appeared to be next.

DISCUSSION QUESTIONS

1. Should Ms. Charkoudian's group's demands be taken seriously, or are they just another case of ridiculous requests which can be safely ignored by the company?
2. Is there a reasonable way for Starbucks to satisfy all customer segments?
3. Assuming Starbucks adopts an official policy, how can it effectively communicate the policy throughout the company?

4. When state laws that affect store operations change, how can Starbucks communicate the new laws to stores in that state to ensure that all stores are in compliance?

WRITING ASSIGNMENT

Please respond in writing to the issues presented in this case by preparing two documents: a communication strategy memo and a professional business letter.

In preparing these documents, you may assume one of two roles: you may identify yourself as an external communication consultant who has been asked to provide Ms. Lincoff with advice, or you may identify yourself as a communication manager within Starbucks Corporation. Either way, you must prepare a strategy memo addressed to Ms. Audrey Lincoff, Vice President for Corporate Communication.

You must also prepare a professional business letter for Howard Schultz's signature. That document should be directed to Starbucks customers and should explain the company's policy and the reasons why the company has adopted that policy. If you have questions about either of these documents, please consult your instructor.

Your strategy memo should provide analysis of the business problem, the relevant background details, critical issues, audience factors, options for action, and your specific recommendations. Think broadly and pro-vide comprehensive advice for Ms. Lincoff regarding the issue of customers breastfeeding in Starbucks stores.

References

1. Serwer, A. "Hot Starbucks to Go," *Fortune*, January 26, 2004, p. 60.
2. Starbucks corporate Web site: www.starbucks.com. Retrieved December 23, 2004.
3. O'Connell, P. "A Full-Bodied Talk with Mr. Starbucks," *BusinessWeek*, October 15, 2004. Retrieved from yahoo.businessweek.com
4. Stopper, W. "Establishing and Maintaining the Trust of Your Employees," *Human Resource Planning*. June 21, 2004.
5. Fellner, K. "The Starbucks Paradox," *ColorLines*, Spring 2004. Available from www.arc.org
6. Wolff, L. "Coffee Chains Perk Up Training, Store Design," *Gourmet News*, May 1, 2004.
7. Coeyman, M. "Loving the Daily Grind," *Restaurant Business*, October 10, 1996, 82.
8. H. D. "Boot Camp Brewhaha," *Training*, July 17, 2004.
9. Dann, Schultz, Somberg, and Levitan. "How to . . . Find a Hit as Big as Starbucks," *Business 2.0*, May 2004, 66.
10. Smith, S. "Experiencing the Brand—Branding the Experience," February 2001. Available from www.personaglobal.com
11. Helderman, R. "Maryland Moms Say No to Coverup at Starbucks," *Washington Post*, August 9, 2004. Available from www.washingtonpost.com/ac2/wp-dyn/A50610.
12. "Mothers Stage 'Nurse-in' at Starbucks Store," *MSNBC*, August 10, 2004. Available from www.msnbc.msn.com/id/5662809.
13. Ibid.
14. Charkoudian, L. Resume. *Maryland Daily Record*, October 26, 2004. Available from www.mddailyrecord.com/top100w/01charkoudian.html.
15. Helderman, R. *Washington Post*, August 9, 2004.
16. Ibid.
17. Charkoudian, L. *Maryland Daily Record*, October 26, 2004.
18. Rosenthal, D., T. Barr, and T. Boyd. "Dorosin v. Starbucks," *Case Research Journal* (1998). Retrieved October 2, 2004 from www.starbucked.com
19. Ibid.
20. "Maryland Code 20-81, S.B. 223, Chap. 369," Maryland General Assembly Home Page. May 22, 2003 Available from mlis.state.md.us/2003rs/chapters/Ch_369_SB0223T.rtf
21. Vance, M. "A Current Summary of Breastfeeding Legislation in the U.S.," *La Leche League International*. September 21, 2004. Available from lalecheleague.org/Law/summary.html
22. Daley, J. "Local Breastfeeding Advocate to Join Nationwide Protest," *The Marion Star*, August 7, 2004. Available from www.marionstar.com/news/stories/20040807/localnews
23. "Breastfeeding OK at Burger King," Online posting. *A Sassy Lawyer in Phillipine Suburbia*. November 25, 2003. Available from journal.houseonahill.net

This case was prepared by Research Assistants Jenny E. Bailey, Shannon J. Rainer, and Cameron A. McHale under the direction of James S. O'Rourke, Concurrent Professor of Management, as the basis for class discussion rather than to illustrate either effective or ineffective handling of an administrative situation. Information was gathered from corporate as well as public sources.

CASE STUDY 2-2

Taco Bell Corporation: Public Perception and Brand Protection

Our concern, of course, is whether or not this product, which is registered for animal feed, is somehow illegally finding its way into food that people eat.[1]

Late in the afternoon of Friday, September 15, 2000, Laurie Gannon, Public Relations Director at Taco Bell Corporation, received a phone call from the company's government Relations team. Gannon typically receives periodic phone calls from this department, bringing her abreast of Taco Bell's involvement with governmental agencies. When she picked up the phone, Laurie figured it was another update; however, things quickly took a turn for the worse. She was informed that a special interest group in Washington DC would hold a press conference early the next week to discuss Taco Bell–labeled taco shells sold by Kraft Foods, Inc.

Inquiring further, Laurie learned that the product in question—Taco Bell taco shells sold in grocery stores—might contain a corn ingredient unapproved for human consumption. Although the report specifically targeted taco shells distributed and sold by Kraft, the media and subsequent consumer reaction could potentially prove damaging to the Taco Bell brand.

Details were sketchy. Laurie was informed that the findings of a group known as "Friends of the Earth" would run in the *Washington Post* in their Monday print edition and that a press conference would follow. She quickly realized Taco Bell could be the subject of negative media exposure. Although the workweek was rapidly coming to a close, Gannon had to prepare a response—the phone call seemed perfectly timed so that Taco Bell would have minimal time to react. Nevertheless, she moved quickly, first notifying several key executives within Taco Bell as well as those at Kraft of this breaking news. Her weekend was spent tracking down all available information on *StarLink*, the unapproved corn ingredient in question.

The Recall

In the past several years, there has been much debate surrounding the side effects, if any, of [genetically modified] foods. Since these foods are a relatively recent discovery, there has not been an opportunity to study the comprehensive long-term effects. Accordingly, some countries and organizations have taken a hard stance on these "frankenfoods" and have enacted strict guidelines against their use.[2] For instance, in 1999, the European Parliament imposed "tighter restrictions on the use of [genetically modified] products."[3]

This debate was the central argument by certain countries and nongovernmental organizations (widely known as NGOs) who publicly rallied against those who support the use of [genetically modified] ingredients. In August 2000, corn-based products became the focal point in this debate, as a series of tests had been conducted on 23 of the leading corn-based foods, including the Taco Bell *Home Originals* taco shells.[4] These tests had concluded that the taco shells contained the "Cry9c" protein, a pesticide that had been deemed unfit for human consumption.[5]

In less than a week after the group's findings became public, Kraft announced a voluntary recall of its entire line of Taco Bell *Home Originals* taco shells and taco kits. The recall consisted of:

- Taco Bell *Home Originals* 12 Taco Shells
- Taco Bell *Home Originals* 18 Taco Shells
- Taco Bell *Home Originals* 12 Taco Dinner (12 shells, sauce and seasoning)[6]

Kraft's September 22, 2000, press release read, "Kraft has pledged full cooperation with [the] FDA . . . [and Kraft] will discontinue production of the taco shell products until . . . [the] products are in full compliance with all regulatory requirements."[7] In another statement issued by Kraft, the company asserted, "We estimate that approximately 2.5 million to 2.9 million boxes of product containing taco shells are affected by the recall. Kraft's recall does not include any products sold in Taco Bell restaurants."[8]

Taco Bell Corporation

Taco Bell was founded in 1962 by Glen Bell in Downey, California. Mr. Bell's two taco stands quickly grew to become a popular restaurant concept, and in 1969, the company filed for a public offering. Growth continued at an unprecedented rate into the mid-1970s when Mr. Bell sold his 868 restaurants to PepsiCo, Inc., and became a major PepsiCo shareholder.[9] Since then, Taco Bell [has grown] both in terms of revenues and units. Currently, there are approximately 7,000 units in the Taco Bell system.

Taco Bell is considered a quick-service restaurant (QSR) concept and operates in a very competitive climate, evidenced by the industry's average annual growth rate of approximately 3 percent. QSRs are, therefore, compelled to grow their market share by stealing share from their competition.

In addition, growth is sustained through new product offerings and line extensions. Recent new product launches include the *Grilled Stuft Burrito*, the *Gordita,* and the *Quesadilla.* Examples of line extensions of these recent launches include the *Steak Grilled Stuft Burrito*, the *Cheesy Gordita Crunch,* and the *Monterey Jack Quesadilla.*

Operational efficiencies can also be realized. Currently, "multibranding" is a popular method to drive revenue and share. Multibranding exists where two distinct concepts (e.g., Taco Bell and Pizza Hut) are housed under one roof. This is typically a more profitable way to operate two restaurants, as opposed to operating two separate locations. According to Taco Bell's parent organization, "These [multibranded] restaurants generate more cash flow per unit than [do] single-brand facilities."[10]

Unofficially, Taco Bell seeks to position itself as a "left of center" restaurant concept.[11] While some competitors cater to primarily to youths or elder generations, Taco Bell prides itself on marketing primarily to the 18- to 24-year-old segment as these consumers help drive a large portion of the company's revenues.[12] In addition to its catchy marketing campaigns over the years, the company continually strives to generate "buzz" through creative advertising such as the April 1, 1996, fictitious purchase of the Liberty Bell and "free taco" giveaways.[13–15] Taco Bell serves more than 35 million consumers each week in nearly 6,500 restaurants in the United States. In 2001, the company generated nearly $5 billion in system-wide sales.[16]

Intrinsic to Taco Bell's rapid growth was the early establishment of franchises. From the company's first franchisee in 1964, these business partners and their respective restaurants have grown commensurate with the company, and as a result, the franchisees have developed into a powerful constituent within the Taco Bell system. To become a Taco Bell franchisee, one must first qualify by satisfying a series of financial and operational hurdles and later attend Taco Bell's "Setting the Pace" training program.[17,18]

Seeing the need to form a collective voice, the franchisees formed the Franchise Management Advisory Council. FRANMAC maintains a direct link with the Taco Bell executive team and regularly participates in business decisions, which include advertising, market development, and product offerings. In addition to [bimonthly] meetings of the FRANMAC leadership team, periodic "open FRANMAC" gatherings offer the franchisees, key vendors, and the Taco Bell executive team an opportunity to meet, talk, and resolve important issues. During those conferences, stakeholders are able to address issues surrounding the brand. By mid-2003, franchise units comprised approximately 80 percent of the Taco Bell system.[19]

Seeking to concentrate on their core business of beverages and snack foods, PepsiCo, Inc., in 1997, divested their ownership of Taco Bell and formed Tricon Global Restaurants, Inc., a separate operating company. Under Tricon, Taco Bell's president reports directly to the President and CEO of Tricon.

In 2002, Tricon changed its name to "YUM Brands, Inc." after acquiring additional restaurant concepts.[20] Yum Brands (NYSE: YUM) handles many of the company's shared services functions, including investor relations. Yum Brands is headquartered in Louisville, Kentucky.

Kraft Foods, Inc.

Founded in 1903, Kraft Foods, Inc., is the largest food and beverage company in North America and the second largest in the world.[21] From its modest beginnings as James L. Kraft's cheese business, the company has expanded to a global conglomerate, marketing many of the world's leading brands such as *Nabisco* crackers, *Oscar Mayer* meats, and *Post* cereals. In fact, an examination of Kraft's history requires a look at the history of the food industry in general.[22]

Mr. Kraft's early success was found via his innovative way of producing cheese in 3 1/2- and 7 3/4-ounce tins in an effort to meet customers' demands for longer shelf life. This production method was such a hit that Mr. Kraft obtained a patent for it in 1917 and began supplying cheese to the U.S. Army in World War I.[23] Thus, the momentum from Kraft's humble beginnings thrust it into the forefront of the food services industry as Kraft teamed up with other food industry pioneers throughout the twentieth century.

Acquired by Philip Morris in 1988, Kraft subsequently became united with many [food-service] companies, specifically *General Foods*, *Oscar Mayer*, and *Nabisco*.

General Foods Corporation, formerly Charles W. Post's "[Postum] Cereal Company," managed household brand favorites such as *Jell-O* pudding, *Maxwell House* coffee, *Tang* fruit drink, and *Cool Whip* whipped topping.[24] In 1981 General Foods expanded its product line by acquiring Oscar Mayer & Co., and with the 1985 Philip Morris acquisition, became part of Kraft Foods in 1988. In addition, Nabisco, manager of such brands as *Triscuit* wafers, *Ritz* crackers, *Honey Maid* graham crackers, and *Planters* nuts, became part of Kraft with Philip Morris's merger of the two food industry companies in 2001.

In June 2001, Philip Morris spun off its food service subsidiary in an Initial Public Offering. Since then, Kraft (NYSE: KFT) has leveraged the legacy of its well-known brands and the character of its founders to position itself at the forefront of the food industry.[25] Today, Kraft Foods manages more than 60 brands and—as company publications put it—Kraft continues the search for products that will fulfill the needs of families across the world.

The Taco Bell/Kraft License Agreement

On August 1, 1996, Taco Bell and Kraft announced the formation of a license agreement for Kraft to manufacture and distribute Taco Bell-branded taco shells in grocery stores.[26] Kraft had a strong reputation within this distribution channel, primarily through the many products the company currently offered.

Although terms of this deal remained confidential, many agree that it was a standard license agreement, whereby . . . Kraft (the licensee) would produce and distribute Taco Bell products, including the *Home Originals* line. Taco Bell (the licensor) would oversee the use of their logo and trademarks to ensure they are held to the highest standard. Representatives

from Taco Bell and Kraft meet periodically to discuss, among other things, quality, financial and operational aspects of the agreement. In addition, they would have final say as to the use of the Taco Bell name in the marketing of Taco Bell's products.[27]

With Kraft's superior distribution and national reach, this agreement is expected to help Taco Bell launch their brand on a national scale without Taco Bell bearing the entire cost of the rollout.[28] Outsiders speculate that Kraft remits between 4 percent and 6 percent of the taco shell revenues to Taco Bell.

Genetically Modified Foods

Genetically modified (GM) foods are produced from crop plants that are enhanced with molecular biology techniques. These plants have been modified in the laboratory to enhance desired traits such as increased resistance to herbicides or improved nutritional content.[29] Rather than create these advanced qualities through the time-consuming process of breeding, genetic engineering can produce specific traits or characteristics in a fast and accurate fashion. For example, plant geneticists can isolate a gene responsible for drought tolerance and insert that gene into a different plant. The new [genetically modified] plant will gain drought tolerance as well.[30] Furthermore, there exist certain naturally occurring bacteria that produce proteins that are lethal to insect larvae. The gene associated with this fatal protein can be transmitted into crops, thus enabling them to produce their own form of pesticide.

Some advantages of GM foods are associated with ensuring that enough food exists for the expanding population. Specific benefits include pest resistance, herbicide, temperature and drought tolerance; nutrition and pharmaceuticals.[31] According to the FDA there are more than 40 plant types that have completed the necessary requirements for federal authorization. Though GM foods are not as prevalent in grocery store fruits and vegetables, they are common in vegetable oils, breakfast cereals and processed foods.[32]

As one might expect, a certain amount of criticism also revolves around [the] notion of GM foods. Most concerns are associated with environmental hazards, human health risks and economic concerns as agribusiness is blamed for being driven by profit potential rather than health concerns.

Aventis and StarLink

Formed in December 1999 through the business combination of former pharmaceutical-chemical conglomerates Hoechst of Germany and Rhone-Poulence of France, Aventis is a world leader in life sciences. Focused on two core business areas—pharmaceuticals and agriculture—Aventis is dedicated to improving life through the discovery and development of innovative products in the fields of prescription drugs, vaccines, therapeutic proteins, crop production and protection, animal health and nutrition.[33]

The pharmaceuticals business of Aventis is comprised of three main areas, including prescription pharmaceuticals, human vaccines and therapeutic proteins. The company's agricultural arm, Aventis CropScience, focuses on the combination of crop protection, crop production and seeds businesses.[34] Aventis also has an animal health joint venture called "Merial" with Merck & Co.

StarLink, developed by Aventis, is a [genetically modified] strain of corn engineered to produce a toxin to ward off crop-harming pests. This toxin is actually a protein called "Cry9c" which the EPA granted registration as a "plant pesticide" in August of 1998. This approval also enabled the corn strain to be utilized only for commercial use as animal feed. However, Aventis must ensure that systems are in place to prevent StarLink from entering the human food supply.[35] In studies, this strain has withstood certain attributes that cause it to become "heat stable" such that it can withstand stomach acids and digestive enzymes. Accordingly, Cry9c is a potential allergen, the full symptoms of which are not known.[36] In April 1999, Aventis resubmitted a request to the EPA for approval of StarLink to be used amongst the human population, yet the EPA declined due to lingering concerns about allergens.

Aventis expanded the sale of StarLink globally, introducing the modified corn into the U.S. market in 1998. StarLink was first grown commercially in the United States in 1999, and by the year 2000, an estimated 2,000 farmers in 29 states planted the strain on 341,000 acres.[37]

Friends of the Earth and GEFA

Friends of the Earth was founded in San Francisco in 1969 and prides itself on being "at the forefront of high-profile efforts to create a more healthy, just world."[38] Friends of the Earth is a member of the Genetically Engineered Food Alert (GEFA) campaign. . . . GEFA "supports the removal of [genetically engineered] ingredients from grocery store shelves unless they are adequately safety tested and labeled. . . . The campaign is endorsed by over 250 scientists, religious leaders, doctors, chefs, environmental and health leaders as well as farm groups."[39]

GEFA is headquartered in Washington, DC, and has offices in Los Angeles, California. In addition to Friends of the Earth, the six other founding members of the GEFA include The Center for Food Safety, Institute for Agriculture and Trade Policy, National Environment Trust, Organic Consumers Association, Pesticide Action Network of North America, and the Public Interest Research Groups.

Government Regulators

Since the study of genetically engineered food products is still in its relative infancy, the United States government does not have a central agency to oversee the approval and use of [genetically modified] products. Three organizations within the United States federal government—the Environmental Protection Agency, the U.S. Department of Agriculture and the Food and Drug Administration—share oversight of [genetically modified] food to protect the public against genetically engineered organisms (including Cry9c).

The Food and Drug Administration (FDA)

The FDA evaluates food products when a new component is added to them. Although food and color additives undergo strict testing, genetically engineered foods have been exempted from these regulations and are not required to undergo any safety testing by the FDA. However, in 1992, the FDA decided before any products had reached the market that genetically engineered foods were "substantially equivalent" to traditionally bred conventional crops. Therefore genetically engineered foods are not required to undergo any mandatory premarket safety testing or labeling. The FDA authorizes and communicates recalls.

The Environmental Protection Agency (EPA)

The EPA is chartered with ensuring that these crops go through a pre-market approval process to assess potential health and environmental effects. However, the Agency often relies on research that is submitted by the applicant, which potentially compromises objectivity.

The United States Department of Agriculture (USDA)

The USDA is responsible for determining whether genetically engineered crops pose threats to the environment and then regulating the growth of these plants, as well as overseeing the testing of crops that have not been approved for commercial growth. In the past, the USDA has been criticized as being inadequate and for allowing potentially harmful plants to grow virtually unregulated. The *New York Times* reported in November 1999, that "part of the problem, scientists say, is that the [USDA] has set no scientific standards for proving the environmental safety of a plant."[40]

What Next?

When Laurie Gannon hung up the phone she realized that her weekend would not be spent with friends and family but, rather, in her office managing this situation. Staring at the telephone, she wondered how to go about informing all the affected parties. Gannon knew she had to act fast as the story was scheduled to break in just 48 hours. Whom should she contact first? What should Kraft Foods do to address the situation? Would the public associate the product recall with the food served in Taco Bell's restaurants? What would the risks be to the Kraft brand?

DISCUSSION QUESTIONS

1. Who are the affected stakeholders? Who is (are) the most important one(s)? Which stakeholder(s) should Ms. Gannon communicate with first? How should she go about doing this?

2. Since the study of genetically modified foods is not complete (i.e., no official conclusions on long-term effects have been identified), the use of genetically modified foods has become an emotional issue. How does Taco Bell manage these perceptions? Should Taco Bell continue to use approved genetically modified substances (i.e., tomatoes) in its food?

3. How should Taco Bell communicate with Kraft? What can Taco Bell do to ensure that Kraft manages the situation appropriately? What issues are present in regard to Taco Bell's relationship with Kraft? Has it been strained? What brand damage has been caused, if any? How can it be mitigated? Should Taco Bell contact media outlets regarding this issue or allow Kraft to take the lead given that it manufactured the corn shells? What communication channel(s) should be utilized?

WRITING ASSIGNMENT

Please respond in writing to the issues presented in this case by preparing two documents: a communication strategy memo and a professional business letter.

In preparing these documents, you may assume one of two roles: you may identify yourself as a Taco Bell senior manager who has been asked to provide advice to Laurie Gannon regarding the issues she and the company are facing. Or, you may identify yourself as an external management consultant who has been asked by the company to provide advice to Ms. Gannon. Either way, you must prepare a strategy memo addressed to Laurie Gannon that summarizes the details of the case, rank orders critical issues, discusses their implications (what they mean and why they matter), offers specific recommendations for action (assigning ownership and suspense dates for each), and shows how to communicate the solution to all who are affected by the recommendations.

You must also prepare a professional business letter for the CEO's signature. That document should be addressed to Taco Bell franchisees. If you have questions about either of these documents, please consult your instructor.

References

1. "Taco Bell: Drop the Biotech Corn," www.wired. com/news. Last visited: January 21, 2003.
2. "Banned Corn in Taco Shells," www.more. abcnews.go.com. Last visited: January 21, 2003.
3. "Europe Approves New GM Rules," news.bbc.co.uk/1/hi/world/europe/1167511.stm . Last visited: April 18, 2003.
4. "Banned Corn in Taco Shells," www.more. abcnews.go.com.
5. "Shell Shocked," www.more.abcnews.go.com. Last visited: January 21, 2003.
6. "Kraft Announces Voluntary Recall of All *Taco Bell* Taco Shell Products from Grocery Stores," www.kraft.com, September 22, 2000. Site last visited: January 21, 2003.
7. Ibid.
8. "Taco Shell Recall Focuses on Safety of Biotech Foods," www.mindfully.org/GE
9. www.tacobell.com. Last visited: April 18, 2003.
10. www.yum.com/investors/fact.htm. Last visited: April 23, 2003.
11. "Yeah Baby! Taco Bell and Mini-Me 'Power' Up for the Summer," www.tacobell.com. Last visited: January 21, 2003.
12. "New 'Age of Hedonism' Emerges in 18–24 Year Olds—Nationwide Survey Reveals Self-Indulgence Trend Has Reached All-Time-High with Younger Generation," www.tacobell.com. Last visited: April 18, 2003.
13. Taco "Liberty" Bell. www.painepr.com/ case_studies2.asp. Last visited: April 18, 2003.
14. "America Eats Free Tacos if World Series Home Run Hits Taco Bell Target," and "Free Tacos for U.S. If Mir Hits Floating Taco Bell Ocean Target," www.tacobell.com. Last visited: April 18, 2003.
15. "Taco Bell Chalupas Point Promotion for Los Angeles Lakers Fans Begins Sunday," www.tacobell.com. Last visited: April 18, 2003.
16. "Yeah Baby! Taco Bell and Mini-Me 'Power' Up for the Summer," www.tacobell.com. Last visited: January 21, 2003.
17. www.tacobell.com
18. "World Franchising: Taco Bell," www.world franchising.com/Top50/Food/TacoBell1.html. Last visited: April 23, 2003.
19. Telephone and e-mail correspondence with Michael Lim, Taco Bell Analyst. April 18–24, 2003.
20. "Tricon Global Restaurants to Acquire Long John Silver's and A & W All-American Food Restaurants to Drive Multibranding Leadership—Company Will Change Name From Tricon To 'Yum! Brands, Inc,'" www.yum.com. Last visited: April 18, 2003.
21. www.kraft.com/newsroom/anniversary/ history.html. Last visited: April 22, 2003.
22. Ibid.
23. Ibid.
24. Ibid.
25. Ibid.
26. "Kraft Foods Acquires Taco Bell Grocery Products Line," Kraft Foods, Inc. press release, August 1, 1996.
27. Interview with Laurie Gannon. April 18, 2003.
28. Bluth, Andrew. "Taco Bell Selling Its Grocery Line to Kraft," *The Orange County Register*, August 2, 1996.
29. www.csa.com/hottopics/gmfood/ overview.html. Last visited: April 21, 2003.
30. Ibid.
31. Ibid.
32. Ibid.
33. Aventis, "New World Leader in Life Sciences, Launched Today," www.archive.hoechst.com/ english/news/99/pm121599.html. December 15, 1999.
34. Ibid.
35. www.greenpeaceusa.org. Last visited: April 27, 2003.
36. www.for.gov. Last visited: April 18, 2003.
37. www.greenpeaceusa.org. Last visited: April 27, 2003.
38. www.foe.org. Last visited: April 18, 2003.
39. Ibid.
40. Madigan, Kate. "Risky Business—Financial Risks that Genetically Engineered Foods Pose to Kraft Foods, Inc. and Shareholders," *State Public Interest Research Group*, Appendix B: Regulatory Agencies. April 2003.

This case was prepared by Research Assistants Jared T. Hall and Michael P. Viola under the direction of James S. O'Rourke, Concurrent Professor of Management, as the basis for class discussion rather than to illustrate either effective or ineffective handling of an administrative situation.

Chapter 3

Communication Ethics

*Never suffer a thought to be harbored in your mind which you would not avow
openly. When tempted to do anything in secret, ask yourself if you would do it in
public. If you would not, be sure it is wrong.*
Letter from Thomas Jefferson to his grandson Francis Eppes, age 14, Monticello,
May 21, 1816

Pick up the *Wall Street Journal* or the *New York Times* any given morning and look through sections A and C. The news is not especially encouraging:

"AUCTION" BROKERS ARE CHARGED. Authorities Say Ex-Credit Suisse Employees Misled Investors. A federal grand jury in Brooklyn indicted two former Credit Suisse Group Brokers, alleging that they lied to investors about how $1 billion of their money was placed into short-term securities. The 12-page indictment describes how the brokers, Julian Tzolov and Eric Butler, allegedly misled corporate clients around the world, primarily through e-mails. The brokers made it appear as if the securities were backed by federally guaranteed student loans, when in fact they were tied to riskier mortgage products and other debt that earned the brokers higher commissions, according to the indictment.[1]

On other days, it's likely to be a story like this:

FORMER EXECUTIVE TO PAY $200 MILLION TO SETTLE S.E.C. FRAUD CHARGES. A former chief executive of the AremisSoft Corporation, a defunct software company, has agreed to pay $200 million to settle fraud accusations made by the Securities and Exchange Commission.

That is about the amount of the unlawful profit that the commission said he made trading AremisSoft stock in 2000. The executive, Roys Poyiadjis, also agreed to a lifelong ban on running a public company. He did not admit or deny wrongdoing. The S.E.C. said the settlement, which it announced yesterday, was among the largest it has made with an individual.

Mr. Poyiadjis and his fellow executive, Lycourgos Kyprianou, who is still a defendant in a civil lawsuit filed by the commission, issued at least three false statements about AremisSoft's financial condition from 1999 to 2001, the S.E.C. said.[2]

While the recent list of convictions ranges from investment fund director Bernard Madoff to Enron and WorldCom executives to Martha Stewart (good grief!), it's not always chief executives and senior corporate officers who find themselves in ethical and legal trouble. Often, it's a young college graduate, confronted with choices she wasn't required to think about in college.

AN EMPLOYEE ON WALL ST. IS ARRESTED. Said to Profit from Her Position of Trust. Prosecutors said yesterday that they had arrested a brokerage firm employee responsible for protecting market-sensitive information and charged her with using the information to profit from insider trading.

The employee . . . , an analyst in the legal department at Morgan Stanley, DeanWitter, Discover & Company, was arrested on Monday at work and charged on Tuesday with grand larceny, possession of stolen property, scheming to defraud, commercial bribe receiving, and securities fraud, the office of District Attorney Robert M. Morgenthau of Manhattan said. Investigators indicated at a news conference yesterday that they expected to make more arrests. . . .

[She] is said to have sold to other unnamed parties her advance knowledge of a revamping of Georgia Pacific, and—just last week—sold proprietary information about a Morgan Stanley analyst's forthcoming downgrade of Einstein Bagels stock. "Whenever you have a market as heated as this market is, there's a temptation for someone with inside information to trade on it," Mr. Morgenthau said.

[The employee] is a law school graduate who, according to one investigator, earned [a substantial salary] at Morgan Stanley. She lives on Manhattan's Upper East Side. . . .[3]

A day hasn't gone by in the past year without at least one news item dealing with allegations of misstatement, misappropriation, equivocation, or fraud. They're often printed alongside stories of people who have lied to their employers, to their customers and clients, to regulatory agencies, and to the courts. In other instances, they have simply deceived themselves.

What's going on here? Does this behavior represent a sudden outbreak of unethical conduct or confusion over appropriate uses of proprietary information in North American businesses? Or are investigation and prosecution techniques improving? While the latter may be true in part, it's hard to believe that managers have only recently begun to display illegal or unethical tendencies.

Many experts on this subject report that a surprising percentage of businesspeople seem to believe they can handle information in any way they see fit and can communicate (or fail to do so) with shareholders, clients, customers, competitors, regulatory agencies, legislative bodies, and other branches of government without regard to truth, fairness, equity, justice, and ethics.

The latest round of accounting scandals, executive misconduct, and deception on the part of corporate financial officers only serves to underscore the need for values and integrity throughout the corporate world. According to *BusinessWeek*'s John A. Byrne, "In the post-Enron bubble world, there's a yearning for corporate values that reach higher than the size of the chief executive's paycheck or even the latest stock price. Trust, integrity, and fairness do matter, and they are crucial to the bottom line."[4] In recent years, too many companies allowed performance to be disconnected from meaningful corporate values. "A lot of companies simply looked at performance in assessing their leaders," says Larry Johnson, CEO of Albertson's, Inc., the food retailer. "There have to be two dimensions to leadership: performance and values. You can't have one without the other."[5] And, according to Landon Thomas of the *New York Times*, "with regulatory scrutiny heightened after the collapse of Enron and other companies, corporations and their boards are adopting zero-tolerance policies. Increasingly, they are holding their employees to lofty standards of business and personal behavior." The result, he writes, "is a wave of abrupt firings as corporations move to stop perceived breaches of ethics by their employees that could result in law enforcement action or public relations disasters."[6]

THE ETHICAL CONDUCT OF EMPLOYERS

A recent National Business Ethics Survey discovered that employees care about the ethical conduct of their employers. What should be of serious concern is that employees are questioning the ethics of many of their managers today. The Hudson Institute and Walker Information, both located in Indianapolis, surveyed more than 3,000 workers from business and not-for-profit organizations across the United States about their experiences and attitudes. What was the most worrisome finding? Fewer than half of working Americans believe that their senior leaders are people of high integrity.[7]

Other findings in the Hudson–Walker survey may be cause for concern, as well. Only a third of employees feel comfortable reporting misconduct, in part because fewer than half feel that ethical or compliance problems are dealt with fairly and completely. Case in point: Thirty percent of employees know of or suspect ethical violations in their organizations in the past two years. However, the majority of these employees—six in ten—who have seen or know about a violation have not reported it. Why not? Three primary reasons were given for not reporting actual observed misconduct.

- Employees did not feel the organization would respond.
- There was a perceived lack of anonymous and confidential means of reporting.
- Fear of retaliation from management prevented workers from reporting the misconduct they had witnessed.[8]

Fast Company magazine reported recently that 76 percent of workers in a national survey had observed violations of the law or company standards during the preceding 12 months. Nearly two-thirds of those surveyed thought their company would not discipline workers guilty of an ethical infraction, and more than half said that "management does not know what type of behavior goes on in its company." Worse, nearly 40 percent said that "management would authorize illegal or unethical conduct to meet business goals."[9]

Do any of these findings—these attitudes about ethical behavior—have any effect on you? Virtually all business leaders say they do. Business—even in a free marketplace—is governed by rules. Those rules range from complex tax laws and restrictions on exports to broad, general notions of truth in advertising and reliance on a person's word. If competitors either break the rules or behave as though no rules exist, the free marketplace is jeopardized, expectations are destroyed, and trust is undermined.

If you behave in unethical ways, people will quickly realize that you cannot be trusted. Your performance will be seen as unreliable and self-centered. Aside from running afoul of the law, unethical behavior will eventually isolate you from the community of business practitioners who play by the rules and for whom trust is an important part of doing business.

DEFINING BUSINESS ETHICS

Raymond Baumhart, a former college president and ethicist, once asked a number of business managers what the word *ethical* meant to them. Half of the managers in his interviews defined *ethical* as "what my feelings tell me is right." Yet feelings are often an inadequate basis on which to make decisions. Twenty-five percent of his respondents defined *ethical* in terms of what is "in accord with my religious beliefs" and 18 percent defined the term as what "conforms to the golden rule." Religious authority has been devastatingly criticized, along with the "golden rule," as an inadequate foundation for ethical claims.[10]

For one thing, religion often requires an act of faith to accept guidelines, norms, dogma, or precepts. And the golden rule ("Do unto others, as you would have others do unto you") assumes that we each would wish for the same form of treatment. Our interests and preferences, in fact, may be substantially different. A supervisor's inquiry on behalf of an employee may be seen as a thoughtful, caring gesture by some and as intrusive snooping or prying by others. If such guides are helpful, but hardly definitive, how should we make ethical judgments? What does *ethical* mean to a business communicator?

Ethics most often refers to a field of inquiry, or discipline, in which matters of right and wrong, good and evil, virtue and vice, are systematically examined. Morality, by contrast, is most often used to refer not to a discipline but to patterns of behavior that are actually common in everyday life. In this sense, morality is what the discipline of ethics is about. And so business morality is what business ethics is about.[11]

The phrases "corporate social responsibility" and "corporate citizenship" are sometimes used as though they were synonymous with business ethics. Oil companies frequently advertise about how careful they are with the environment, and chemical companies proclaim their "good citizen" role of providing jobs, opportunity, and the chance to "do good things." However, these statements can be misleading if they imply that business ethics deals exclusively with the relationships between business organizations and what have come to be called their external constituencies, such as consumers, suppliers, government agencies, community groups, and host countries.

Even though these relationships define a large and important part of business ethics, they do not encompass the entire field. Important internal constituencies, such as employees, stockholders, boards of directors, and managers, are also involved, as well as ethical issues that do not lend themselves to constituency or stakeholder analysis. Thus, business ethics is a much larger notion than corporate social responsibility, even though it includes that concept.[12]

THREE LEVELS OF INQUIRY

The three most common concerns in the moral responsibilities, obligations, and virtues of business decision making have been the choices and characters of persons, the policies and cultures of organizations, and the arrangements and beliefs of entire social and economic systems, such as capitalism. Business ethics, then, is multileveled.

THE INDIVIDUAL For the individual businessperson, business ethics concerns the values by which self-interest and other motives are balanced with concern for fairness and the common good, both inside and outside of a company. The project leader who unfairly claims credit for a proposal that many of his subordinates worked on is clearly putting his own self-interest ahead of that of the organization and his fellow employees. It may not be illegal, but it's certainly unfair.

THE ORGANIZATION At the level of the organization, business ethics concerns the group conscience that every company has (even though it may be unspoken) as it pursues its economic objectives. This conscience is a reflection of both organizational culture and conduct. A real estate development firm that buys an entire city block filled with low-income housing may see only the benefits to be derived from demolishing the apartments and constructing offices, shops, and a parking garage. The people occupying the low-income apartments to be demolished may have great difficulty finding another place to live that they can afford. A failure to see them as an important part of the purchase and development plans, again, would not likely be against the law, but it would certainly be unjust.

THE BUSINESS SYSTEM Finally, at the level of the entire business system, ethics concerns the pattern of social, political, and economic forces that drives individuals and businesses—the values that define capitalism, for example. But even capitalism works within a system of ethical rules. For the government of one nation to decide that it will not enforce copyright laws or extend patent protection to products or intellectual property produced overseas is to invite chaos within the free-market system.[13]

THREE VIEWS OF DECISION MAKING

For business communicators and others who make business decisions, three points of view are available to assist in making those decisions. They include a moral point of view, an economic point of view, and a legal point of view.

MORAL POINT OF VIEW From this perspective, businesspeople ask, "Morally, what is the best thing to do?" Such questions would be separate from inquiries about economic decisions that seek to maximize shareholder wealth or legal decisions that ask what the law requires, permits, and forbids. According to many business ethicists, a moral point of view has two important features. The first is a willingness to seek out and act on reasons.

Second, a moral point of view requires the decision maker to be impartial: Decision makers must demonstrate a commitment to use reason in deliberating about what to do, constructing moral arguments that are persuasive to themselves and to others. They will also give all interests equal weight in deciding what to do. The problem with this point of view is that most ethical business issues aren't especially clear and, in many instances, decision makers don't have adequate information at the time they need it most.[14]

ECONOMIC POINT OF VIEW An economic point of view, by contrast, employs a free market model of capitalism in which scarce resources or factors of production are used to produce goods and services. The forces of supply and demand are used to allocate resources, and the structure of the marketplace determines what is in the best interests of the organization. Economic theory, however, is not entirely value-neutral. Certain assumptions about a free market underlie all business activities, including basic notions about honesty, theft, fraud, and the like.

In addition, it is important for business communicators to understand that companies are not merely abstract economic entities but large-scale organizations that involve flesh-and-blood human beings. Those same firms, further, must operate in a complex environment with many constituencies to please, some of which are often in conflict with others.[15]

LEGAL POINT OF VIEW A third point of view for ethical decision making in business is the legal viewpoint. Most business activity takes place within an extensive system of laws, so that all business decisions—especially those involving communication—must be made from a legal as well as an economic standpoint. Many businesspeople assume that "if it's legal, then it's morally okay." This attitude ignores a number of realities involving the law and decision making.

First, the law is inappropriate for regulating certain aspects of business activity. Not everything that is immoral is, in fact, illegal. Hiring a relative for a position that other, better qualified, applicants have applied for will certainly raise conflict-of-interest questions, but it may not be illegal. Second, the law is often slow to develop in new areas of concern. Technology, for example, not only presents new opportunities for unethical behavior but often outpaces legal restrictions.

The law often employs moral concepts that are not precisely defined, so it is often difficult to use the law to make decisions without also considering issues of morality. In addition, the law itself is often unsettled or in a state of evolution on many issues. Frequently, the notion of whether an action was legal or illegal must be decided case-by-case in the courts, with key issues often being decided higher within the appellate court system. The law cannot provide specific guidance for behavior in all possible instances. For example, the issue of whether a conversation among a few friends constitutes protected speech or is sexual harassment is one that courts must decide on the merits of the specific incident. Finally, the law is generally seen as an inefficient instrument, inviting expensive legislation and litigation where more efficient systems of decision making might do just as well in producing workable answers.[16]

AN INTEGRATED APPROACH

Many business ethicists advocate a decision-making process that integrates these three viewpoints, considering the demands of morality, economics, and the law together. Decisions, they say, can be made on the basis of morality, profit, and legality together to arrive at workable solutions that will take into account the best interests of all concerned, protect the investment of shareholders, and obey the law.

A company that elects voluntarily to remove a tainted or defective product from supermarket shelves considers the safety and welfare of its customers while, at the same time, avoiding lawsuits and protecting the company's good name and market share. Such decisions, though costly in the short run, almost always prove to be beneficial in the long run.

What about those cases in which neither the issue at hand nor the outcome of the decision is entirely clear? Some ethicists focus on the value of dialogue in arriving at an ethical answer. Michael G. Bowen and F. Clark Power write, "In this regard, our definition of the moral manager is a person willing to engage in a fair and open dialogue with interested stakeholders or their representatives."[17]

Making choices based on the input and ideas of those who are most affected by the outcome of your decisions can help to produce better decisions. Becoming an ethical business communicator may involve more than a simple willingness to talk about the issues with stakeholders, though. It might also include some knowledge of moral judgments and how they are made.

THE NATURE OF MORAL JUDGMENTS

Two basic types of judgments are normative judgments and moral judgments. Normative judgments are claims that state or imply that something is good or bad, right or wrong, better or worse, ought to be or ought not to be. Normative judgments, then, express our values. They indicate our attitudes toward some object, person, circumstance, or event. Non-normative judgments, on the other hand, are value-neutral. They describe, name, define, report, or make predictions.[18]

If I were to say, "These figures are mistaken," that would be normative. To say, "These figures do not match the auditor's," would be non-normative. Normative judgments are prescriptive, while non-normative judgments are descriptive. Moral judgments, then, are a special subset or category of normative judgments.

Ethics does not study all normative judgments, only those that are concerned with what is morally right and wrong or morally good and bad. When decisions are judged to be morally right or wrong, or morally good or bad, the underlying standards on which the judgment is based are moral standards. It would be immoral by such standards to short-weight a shipment of goods, for example, or to identify the contents of a package as containing "all natural ingredients," when, in fact, it does not.

Businesspeople use two types of moral standards to make decisions. Moral norms, on the one hand, are standards of behavior that require, prohibit, or allow certain kinds of behavior. Moral principles, on the other hand, are much more general concepts used to evaluate both group and individual behavior. A norm, for example, might permit rounding of figures to the nearest hundred or thousand in standard accounting procedure, while principles might deal with the general notion of full disclosure to interested stakeholders.

Alfred P. West, Jr., for example, believes that transparency is a moral principle fundamental to building trust among those involved in a business. West is founder and CEO of financial-services firm SEI Investments Company, which operates back-office services for mutual funds and bank trust departments. His goal of building an open culture of integrity, ownership, and accountability is a harbinger for what he believes organizations will look like in the future. "We tell our employees a lot about where the company is going," he says. "We over-communicate the vision and the strategy and continually reinforce the culture."[19]

DISTINGUISHING CHARACTERISTICS OF MORAL PRINCIPLES

Moral standards, in many respects, are like other standards. They provide direction, guidance, and counsel. They are guideposts or compass headings when decisions have to be made. They are different from other standards in several important respects, though.

THEY HAVE POTENTIALLY SERIOUS CONSEQUENCES TO HUMAN WELL-BEING Moral standards require distinguishing between things that matter and things that don't. Omitting small details about packaging or manufacturing from a product insert may be an important legal matter but is probably not a moral issue. Failing to reveal potential hazards of product use is certainly a moral issue.

THEIR VALIDITY RESTS ON THE ADEQUACY OF THE REASONS THAT ARE USED TO SUPPORT AND JUSTIFY THEM If the reasons you employ to support your decisions are not accepted by the society at large, or at least by a thoughtful group of people who have given the matter careful consideration, then you may wish to reassess just how adequate your standards are.

THEY OVERRIDE SELF-INTEREST Genuine moral standards transcend the interests of just one or a few people. They involve doing things for the greater good of society or people at large. Rather than asking, "How will this affect me?" you might wish to ask, "How will this decision affect the entire firm or the whole community?"

THEY ARE BASED ON IMPARTIAL CONSIDERATIONS Moral standards are devised from a universal standpoint and are clearly more objective than subjective. They don't bring harm or disruption to many simply to benefit a few.[20]

FOUR RESOURCES FOR DECISION MAKING

Four simple but powerful resources are available to every business communicator who is trying to make ethical decisions. They are observations, assumptions, value judgments, and proposals. Let's examine each of them independently.

OBSERVATIONS These descriptive statements tell about the situations. "Not all of the information about pending litigation against the company is revealed in the annual report to shareholders." Such statements rely on a correct presentation of the facts and can usually be verified through more research. The usefulness of observations can also be evaluated by the degree of objectivity they contain. The more objective the statement, the more likely it is to be an observation. A statement qualifies as an observation if contrary evidence can disprove it. If I observe, for example, that "an increasing number of product liability suits is jeopardizing our industry," I could verify or refute that statement with specific evidence.

Observations sometimes look like assumptions because they both appear to describe. An important difference is that observations are usually specific and empirical in nature. "Our product package insert does not reveal all of the potential hazards associated with this product's use." This statement is an example of an observation; a related assumption might be that revealing all potential hazards would be useful or instructive to our customers. An opposing assumption might be that revealing all potential hazards would only serve to frighten our customers because many of the hazards are extremely rare.

ASSUMPTIONS These *reflective statements* express world views and attitudes. "Our employees are honest." Statements such as this one rely on culture, religion, social, and personal history. They're usually taken for granted in day-to-day conversation and business correspondence, but they have theoretical roots in our attitudinal system. They can be evaluated by such criteria as relevance, consistency, and inclusiveness.

Table 3-1 summarizes the key differences among these resources. Proposals and value judgments, for example, are action oriented, telling the listener or reader what to do. Observations and assumptions, on the other hand, merely serve to describe. Proposals and observations tend to be specific in nature, focused on the action or situation at hand. Value judgments and assumptions, though, are more general in nature and provide broad guidance to a decision maker.

Table 3-1 Four Resources for Decision Making

	Action-Orientation	Descriptive-Orientation
Specific	Proposals	Observations
General	Value Judgments	Assumptions

Source: Adapted from Marvin T. Brown. *The Ethical Process: A Strategy for Making Good Decisions.* Upper Saddle River, NJ: Prentice Hall, Inc., 1996, p. 7.

VALUE JUDGMENTS These normative statements guide the actions of others. "Information that significantly affects a worker's schedule or position should be delivered in person by the supervisor." Such statements rely on assumptions and make the connection between a proposal and an observation. These statements, however, cannot be verified by empirical research. They can be evaluated by different ethical traditions.

Value judgments can also be asserted as *should statements*. Unlike proposals, which are usually specific, value judgments are general statements. "We should be fair in our dealings with customers." This statement does not indicate what we should do specifically in each instance with a customer. It is, rather, a general guideline for action.

PROPOSALS These prescriptive statements suggest actions. "We should develop a child care center for our company," would be an example of a proposal. It is a statement that relies on observations, value judgments, and assumptions but goes further. It suggests actions that people should take and that can be evaluated by examining supporting reasons. Proposals often reveal what people have been paying attention to (observations) and can frequently serve as a clue to their values and assumptions.

Proposals are often answers to questions. Good questions can generate good proposals. "Should we revise our performance review system?" The best questions are specific and action oriented, while the best proposals are specific responses to such questions. For example: "We should revise our performance review system to include semiannual peer feedback." The only missing element of this proposal is the underlying reasoning or the values that prompted it.[21]

MAKING MORAL JUDGMENTS

Moral judgments seem to depend on decision makers having and using four separate capacities: ethical sensibility, ethical reasoning, ethical conduct, and ethical leadership.[22]

ETHICAL SENSIBILITY An ethical sensibility is reflected in your capacity to impose ethical order on a situation—to identify aspects of the situation that have ethical importance. A person who is insensitive to the ethically important features of a situation is vulnerable to acting in ways that are improper.

Suppose you are working as a computer software consultant, and a local charitable group asks you to serve as a member of its volunteer advisory board. Sounds noble and worthwhile, right? Well, suppose further that the charitable group decides to accept bids on an information technology system that will assist in fund-raising. You're in a position to provide expert advice. Now what happens if your employer decides to bid on that IT system? Can you remain a member of that advisory board? Not if you recognize the conflict of interest that faces you. Your interests as a commercial software consultant conflict with your interests as an advisor to the charitable group. Ethical sensibility would make you aware of that conflict.

ETHICAL REASONING Recognizing the ethically important features of a situation is the first step toward dealing with them appropriately. The next step is to reason carefully about the situation to determine what kind of ethical problem you face: Is it bribery, an unfair labor practice, or consumer deception? Ethical reasoning then offers opportunities for solution: What would be fairest for all concerned? Is this problem similar to one we've seen in the past? Is a rule or policy applicable in determining our conduct in this case? If not, should we consider writing one? What's the basis for the argument I'm faced with?

Sometimes simple recognition of an ethical problem will point toward a solution. Let's say your job is to review advertising copy for your company's products. As you do so, you recognize a series of misleading claims in the proposed ad copy. Your solution is easy enough: Return the copy to the writing team with specific instructions to remove or correct the misleading claims. More often, however, the solution to an ethical problem involves conflicting values.

Let's say you are a manager who discovers that the production line presents potential hazards to the reproductive health of female workers. You also recognize that removing women from the line would be unfair. Two competing values in this instance—equal employment opportunity and keeping workers from harm—require some careful ethical reasoning in order to make an appropriate moral judgment.

ETHICAL CONDUCT Recognizing ethical dilemmas and reasoning your way to an appropriate solution are simply the first two steps in living an ethical life in business. It's one thing to know what you should do and quite another to do it. Lynn Sharp Paine of the Harvard Business School says, "Hypocrisy and cowardice, both reflected in discrepancies between professed beliefs and actual conduct, are the enemies of integrity."[23]

Recognizing that it would be wrong to file an inflated travel voucher following a business trip, you remind your colleagues that the company will gladly reimburse all necessary expenses but only for the amounts actually spent. Although you encourage and expect others to comply with that reasoning, you claim expenses in excess of what you actually spent and ask for reimbursement for expenditures that were not legitimate business expenses. In such a case, hypocrisy would best describe your behavior.

If you were witness to a fellow employee stealing supplies from your company but failed to speak with either him or your supervisor, you might well be guilty of cowardice. You recognized the problem and knew what the appropriate response would be but failed to act. Such situations require a certain amount of moral courage—the ability to stand up and do what is right, even though it won't be easy, profitable, or popular.

ETHICAL LEADERSHIP The capacity for ethical leadership, according to Professor Paine, "is associated with the highest levels of integrity." She quotes Confucius, saying "The superior person seeks to perfect the admirable qualities of others and does not seek to perfect their bad qualities. The lesser person does the opposite of this." She goes on to note that most business students will work in organizations in which they will have the power and responsibility not only to exercise their own ethical capacities but to influence the exercise of those capacities in others.[24]

Numerous researchers and commentators attribute critical importance to the ethical example provided by an organization's top officials. It seems unlikely that great integrity would emerge in an organization led by men and women lacking in basic integrity. Yet, without question, leadership is not confined to the chairman or chief executive officer of an organization. It extends directly to every organization's executives and senior managers.

Executive-search firm Russell Reynolds, along with personality-testing firm Hogan Assessment Systems, conducted psychological profiles of more than 1,400 managers in large U.S. companies. Each manager was given 28 true-or-false questions on rule compliance and interactions with others to gauge their level of integrity. The somewhat troubling result: One out of every eight responded in ways that may be seen as "high risk." According to Dean Stamoulis, an executive director at Russell Reynolds, the findings indicate that those managers are far more likely to break the rules than the others. "These are folks who believe the rules do not apply to them," he says.[25]

Ethical leadership also extends from those managers to their frontline supervisors. Day to day, these supervisors are responsible for setting examples and assisting those who work for them. Others in an organization will watch what you do, and if you're in a position of leadership or responsibility, an ethical obligation accompanies your management duties. If you let your employees know, directly or indirectly, that you condone industrial spying or the theft of competitive marketing data, they will assume that the company approves of this and that such acts are probably all right. The plain fact is, the moral education of those beneath you in an organization depends on your willingness to engage in and reward ethical behavior.[26]

APPLYING ETHICAL STANDARDS TO MANAGEMENT COMMUNICATION

Ethical business practice is a noble goal to which virtually all firms aspire. Many companies, however, fail to achieve this lofty ideal for a number of reasons. Increased levels of global competition, financial pressures, lack of communication throughout organizations, and the absence of moral leadership at the top levels are but a few of the most prevalent reasons.[27]

STATEMENTS OF ETHICAL PRINCIPLES

Perhaps the most important means of establishing moral leadership in a business organization—and demonstrating that leadership to employees, customers, clients, competitors, and the world at large—is through a formal statement of ethical principles. Developing and publishing a corporate statement of ethics certainly will not, by itself, make a company ethical, but it is certainly a good first step. To the question of why a company should have such a statement, Professor Patrick E. Murphy of Notre Dame offers this response:

> First, and most important, ethics statements denote the seriousness with which the organization takes its ethical commitments. Words are empty without some documentation. The written statement then serves as a foundation from which ethical behavior can be built. Corporate culture is often viewed as being more important than policies in setting the ethical climate for any organization. However, written ethical principles send a strong signal that ethics matters to the firm.[28]

> Once an organization's size, according to Murphy, goes beyond a handful of employees who interact regularly face to face, it becomes difficult to convey a sense of an organization's principles and values. An ethics statement makes expectations more concrete. Furthermore, developing such a document forces those engaged in the process, whether they be the founder or current management, to articulate their beliefs in a cohesive fashion and then set them down in writing for possible challenge by others.[29]

TYPES OF ETHICAL STATEMENTS Although ethics statements can be classified into several types, three appear to predominate. They include values statements, corporate credos (or sets of basic beliefs), and corporate codes of ethics.

The most prevalent form in which ethical principles are stated in U.S.-based corporations is a code of ethics. More than 90 percent of large organizations have one. At least half of those same companies also have a values statement. A corporate credo appears to exist in about one-third of all large U.S.-based firms. Interestingly, while fewer firms seem to have a corporate credo, many that do have such documents have had them in place for a long time.[30] A recent Conference Board survey of 124 companies in 22 countries found that more than three-quarters of all boards of directors are now setting ethical standards in those companies, up from just 41 percent a few years earlier. Executives at those companies see self-regulation as a way to avoid legislative or judicial intrusions in their business operations. The study also found that ethics codes help promote tolerance of diverse practices and customers while doing business overseas.[31]

Jacques Polet, in reviewing corporate ethical statements in both the United States and Europe, found that the most recurring principles are clarity, transparency, honesty, truth or objectivity (negative and unpleasant information must be communicated, as well as positive information), credibility, coherence, loyalty, and respect for human beings.[32]

In examining corporate ethical statements, the importance of communication, as well as many other behaviors, receives considerable attention. "In the same spirit," writes Polet, "communication must serve the company (its shareholders, staff, and customers) without prejudicing third parties or hurting respectable feelings. Basically, it should reflect the company project, expressing its goals, its strategy, and the corporate culture. . . ."[33] Thus, effective management communication is not only a means to an end (a way to convey the principles) but an end in itself (ethical communication is a fundamental principle guiding management behavior).

TENSION AND ETHICAL VALUES Many values, along with the roles and objectives that managers must follow, are in competition with one another, and a certain tension inevitably pulls first in one direction and then another. The value of transparency, or of not hiding from public view what the company really does and how it does it, may be in competition with the value of confidentiality. Employees expect a certain measure of privacy in the workplace, yet the demand for disclosure is ever-present. Managers must respond to these conflicts and to the tension that arises from them with caution, sensitivity, and a sense of fairness to everyone concerned.[34]

Every communication activity, from annual reports to general shareholder meetings, becomes a balancing act for executives and managers. To be honest with our employees and our shareholders, what and how much must we disclose? To preserve our competitive edge, what and how much shall we hold back? Ethical philosopher Gilles Lipovetsky, in *The Dawn of Duty*, captures the dialectical debate in this way:

> It is obvious: an ethics of company communication does not present itself in terms of a choice between Good and Evil (a question of Morality). In real life, there is a balance between "various more or less contradictory imperatives."[35]

THE VALUE OF CORPORATE VALUES A new emphasis on values at the corporate level has made it fashionable for many companies to make their values explicit. That's a change—quite a significant change—from corporate practices just a few years ago. At Xerox, former CEO Anne Mulcahy says that corporate values "helped save Xerox during the worst crisis in our history" and that "living our values" has been one of Xerox's five performance objectives for the past several years. These values are "far from words on a piece of paper," she says. "They are accompanied by specific objectives and hard measures."[36]

According to market and social trend analyst Daniel Yankelovich, the public's widespread cynicism toward businesses today is the third wave of public mistrust about corporations in the past 80 years. The first, set off by the Great Depression, continued until World War II; the second, caused in part by economic stagflation and the Vietnam War, lasted from the early 1960s until the early 1980s. In each of these periods, companies tended to be reactive, blaming "a few bad apples," dismissing values as "not central to what we do," or ignoring opportunities to improve.[37]

The current wave of disapproval began in 2001 with the bursting of the dot-com bubble, the ensuing bear market and financial scandals involving Madoff Investment Securities, Enron Corporation, WorldCom, Tyco, and others. This time, according to a recent survey, the response appears to be different. More and more companies are looking inward to see what has gone wrong and looking outward for answers. They are questioning the quality of their management systems and their ability to inculcate and reinforce values that benefit the firm, their stakeholders, and the wider world. And they are showing little patience with executives who place their businesses at risk by crossing the line from prudent to unethical behavior.

In their survey of 365 companies in 30 nations and five regions around the world, consulting firm Booz Allen Hamilton and the Aspen Institute found that ethical behavior is a core component of company activities. Of the 89 percent of companies that have a written corporate values statement, 90 percent specify ethical conduct as a principle. Further, some 81 percent believe their management practices encourage ethical behavior among staff employees. The study found that ethics-related language in formal statements not only sets corporate expectations for employee behavior but it also serves as a shield in an increasingly complex legal and regulatory environment.[38]

HOW ETHICAL STATEMENTS CAN HELP While the presence of an ethical statement will not automatically ensure ethical behavior on the part of corporate employees, such documents certainly can raise ethical awareness, create an atmosphere in which ethical behavior is expected and rewarded, and promote a companywide dialogue about the value of ethical behavior.

In 1982, seven people died in the United States after taking Tylenol capsules that had been poisoned with cyanide. Investigators eventually determined that some unknown person had tampered with the capsules after they had been placed on store shelves for sale. Even before Johnson & Johnson, which manufactures the product, had obtained all the information on the cause of the tragedy, and even before legal liability had been evaluated, the company assumed moral liability for it, immediately recalling 31 million bottles of Tylenol with a market value of $100 million. The company set up a toll-free help line to answer questions from the general public.[39] Johnson & Johnson chairman and CEO James Burke opened up the company's meetings to the news media and offered a reward of $100,000 to anyone able to supply information leading to the arrest of the culprit. According to Lipovetsky, "There is no doubt as to the ethical orientation of the operation. It was nonetheless a triumph of communication which managed to dramatize the firm's responsible action."[40]

The Tylenol crisis highlights the importance of personal ethical commitment of top management in a special way. In these periods of extreme tension, while managers may wish to do the right thing, it's not always immediately clear what the right thing to do is. Johnson & Johnson employees had worked with their credo, a broadly phrased statement of company ethics, since 1947. In the words of one Johnson & Johnson official during the crisis, "What we are doing here is not specifically mentioned in the Credo, but it is definitely generated by the Credo."[41]

Johnson & Johnson's Jim Burke had no hesitation in assuming direct responsibility for and control over the true spirit of the credo. As Laura Nash reports, "Jim Burke has often stated that the guidance of the Credo played the most important role in management's decision making during the crisis."[42] If anyone doubted that Burke and his president, David Collins, did the right thing, the proof is that 11 weeks after the start of the crisis, the Tylenol brand had recovered 80 percent of its initial market share and within two years had recovered all of it.[43]

HOW TO MAKE ETHICAL STATEMENTS WORK Professor Murphy offers a series of seven imperatives to follow when writing and living out the principles of a corporate ethics statement, code, or credo.

- **Write it.** Writing down the guiding philosophy or values of the firm makes it possible for management to communicate those ideas to all stakeholders, especially to the employees. A written document also signals to everyone concerned that the company is serious about its ethical views.

- **Tailor it.** Tailoring a statement of ethics to an organization's industry or line of business offers managers an opportunity to place special emphasis on those issues most likely to arise in the course of ordinary business and to address those matters that it regards as especially important.
- **Communicate it.** This step may be most important in ensuring that all stakeholders, external as well as internal, are aware of and understand the behavior that the company expects of them. Many authors note that this process must be ongoing for every company.
- **Promote it.** It is not enough to simply communicate the ethics document. It should be actively promoted at every opportunity through as many publications, events, and channels as possible.
- **Revise it.** Revising the document every few years will help to keep it current, reflecting changing worldwide conditions, community standards, and evolving organizational practices.
- **Live it.** The litmus test for any type of ethics document, according to Murphy and others, is whether members of the organization follow it on a daily basis. Top management must make a concerted effort to reward employees who follow the principles listed in the statement.
- **Enforce/Reinforce it.** For those who refuse to live by the principles, management must exact punishment. Sanctions and penalties must be enforced in a fair and evenhanded manner so that all stakeholders understand how they will be treated and exactly what will be the consequences of their behavior.[44]

For an ethics code to work, top management must convince employees that the company is not simply using the code to sidestep recent events and—even more important—they must act on what they say they value. Linda Klebe Trevino, a professor of organizational behavior at Pennsylvania State University, said that outlining appropriate or inappropriate behavior in a code with the intention of avoiding future problems "can be a healthy response. But if you create a code, especially in response to some problem, and it's inconsistent with the culture as employees perceive it, then it appears to be only window dressing and hypocritical," she added.[45]

"When management disciplines somebody, they're sending a very powerful signal," says Professor Trevino. "Most people are going about their business trying to do the right thing. When they see somebody engage in highly inappropriate behavior that everybody agrees is inappropriate and management doesn't do much about it, it devalues the norm and, in a sense their own status."[46]

THE "FRONT PAGE" TEST

In judging whether its policies or its actions are fundamentally sound, managers might simply apply what's come to be known as the "front page" test. Would you be pleased if the policies in your organization or the behavior of your employees were to appear in a story on the front page of the *Wall Street Journal* or, perhaps, your hometown newspaper? If not, then you might ask yourself, "Why not?" What are we doing wrong that I wouldn't want others to know about?

Do the methods and means of communication in your organization hold up to that test? Does your company deal honestly with its customers and clients, treating each of them fairly and with respect? Do you honestly and accurately disclose to regulatory agencies and governmental organizations all that they are entitled to know? Are your relations with the press and news media based on openness, honesty, and candor? If not, what can you do to improve them?

Are the rituals, ceremonies, and formal activities of your organization planned and conducted with a sense of inclusion, honesty, and equality? Do people in your organization know how they will be evaluated, by whom, and against which set of standards in their hopes for promotion or advancement?

Day in and day out, do you and others in your company speak, write, listen, and act with a sense that others will appreciate and respect? Do you treat people not simply as they might treat you, but in a way they prefer to be treated? In many ways, ethics and communication are not simply inseparable but are essential to the success of any business and at the heart of how human beings interact with one another. Striving for ethical perfection, both as you communicate and as you manage your business, is probably pointless. Striving each day to observe the best of ethical principles, to demonstrate a level of conduct that others can aspire to, and to lead by example, however, is not only possible but also unquestionably worthwhile.

For Further Reading

Allen, L. and Voss, D. *Ethics in Technical Communication: Shades of Gray.* New York: John Wiley & Sons, 1997.

Donaldson, T. and Werhane, P. *Ethical Issues in Business: A Philosophical Approach*, 8th ed. Upper Saddle River, NJ: Prentice Hall, 2007.

Ferrell, O. C. and Fraedrich, J. *Business Ethics: Ethical Decision Making and Cases*, 7th ed. Mason, OH: South-Western College Publishing, 2010.

Fritzsche, D. J. *Business Ethics: A Global and Managerial Perspective*, 2nd ed. New York: McGraw-Hill, 2004.

Gardner, H. "The Ethical Mind," *Harvard Business Review*, March 2007, pp. 51–56.

Hartman, L. P. *Perspectives in Business Ethics.* New York: McGraw-Hill, 2001.

Lancaster, H. "You Have Your Values: How Do You Identify Your Employer's?" *Wall Street Journal*, April 8, 1997, p. B1.

McCarthy, M. J. "Virtual Morality: A New Workplace Quandary," *Wall Street Journal*, October 21, 1999, pp. B1, B4.

Murphy, P. E. "Creating Ethical Corporate structures," *Sloan Management Review*, Winter 1989, pp. 81–87.

Paine, L. S. "Managing for Organizational Integrity," *Harvard Business Review*, March–April 1994, pp. 106–117.

Seglin, J. L. "In Ethics, It's the Thought That Counts," *New York Times*, December 19, 1999, p. BU-4.

Thomas, L. "On Wall Street, a Rise in Dismissals Over Ethics," *New York Times*, Tuesday, March 29, 2005, pp. A1, C4.

Trevino, L. K. and Nelson, K. A. *Managing Business Ethics: Straight Talk About How to Do It Right*, 4th ed. New York: John Wiley & Sons, 2006.

Van Lee, R., Fabish, L., and McGaw, N. "The Value of Corporate Values," *Strategy + Business*, 39, Summer 2005, pp. 52–65.

Velasquez, M. G. *Business Ethics: Concepts and Cases*, 6th ed. Upper Saddle River, NJ: Prentice Hall, 2005.

Weiss, J. *Business Ethics: A Stakeholder and Issues Management Approach*, 4th ed. Cincinnati, OH: South-Western College Publishing, 2005.

Endnotes

1. Efrait, A. and Randall Smith. "Auction Brokers Are Charged," *Wall Street Journal*, Thursday, September 4, 2008, p. C1. Copyright © 2008 by Dow Jones & Company, Inc. All rights reserved worldwide. Reprinted with permission.

2. Story, L. "Former Executive to Pay $200 Million to Settle S.E.C. Fraud Charges," *New York Times*, Friday, June 10, 2005, p. C3. Copyright © 2005 by The New York Times Company. Reprinted with permission.

3. Truell, P. "An Employee on Wall St. Is Arrested," *New York Times*, November 7, 1997, p. C8. Copyright © 1997 by The New York Times Company. Reprinted with permission.

4. Byrne, J. A. "After Enron: The Ideal Corporation," *BusinessWeek*, August 26, 2002, p. 68.

5. Ibid., p. 70.

6. Thomas, L. "On Wall Street, a Rise in Dismissals Over Ethics," *New York Times*, Tuesday, March 29, 2005, pp. A1, C4.

7. The 1999 National Business Ethics Survey. Indianapolis, IN: Walker Information, September 1999. A summary is available online at www.walkerinfo.com/.

8. Ibid.

9. "Conduct Unbecoming." *Fast Company*, September 2000, p. 96.

10. Baumhart, R. *An Honest Profit: What Businessmen Say About Ethics in Business*. New York: Holt, Rinehart, Winston, 1968, pp. 11–12.

11. Goodpaster, K. E. "Business Ethics," in L. C. Becker (ed.), *Encyclopedia of Ethics*. New York: Garland Publishing, Inc., 1992, p. 111.

12. Ibid., pp. 111–112.

13. Boatright, J. R. *Ethics and the Conduct of Business*, 5th ed. Upper Saddle River, NJ: Prentice Hall, 2006, pp. 6–7.

14. Ibid, pp. 7–9.

15. Ibid.

16. Ibid.

17. Bowen, M. G. and F. C. Power. "The Moral Manager: Communicative Ethics and the Exxon Valdez Disaster." *Business Ethics Quarterly*, February 1993, p. 10.

18. Velasquez, M. G. *Business Ethics: Concepts and Cases*, 6th ed. Upper Saddle River, NJ: Prentice Hall, 2005, pp. 8–16.

19. Byrne. "After Enron," p. 74.

20. Velasquez. *Business Ethics*, pp. 11–13.

21. Brown, M. T. *The Ethical Process: An Approach to Disagreements and Controversial Issues*, 3rd ed. Upper Saddle River, NJ: Prentice Hall, 2003, pp. 5–7.

22. Paine, L. S. "Ethics as Character Development: Reflections on the Objective of Ethics Education," in R. E. Freeman (ed.), *Business Ethics: The State of the Art*. New York: Oxford University Press, 1991, pp. 67–86.

23. Ibid., p. 81.

24. Ibid., p. 82.

25. Lavelle, L. "Another Crop of Sleazy CEOs?" *BusinessWeek*, August 26, 2002, p. 12.

26. Paine. "Ethics as Character Development," pp. 82–83.

27. Murphy, P. E. *Eighty Exemplary Ethics Statements*. Notre Dame, IN: University of Notre Dame Press, 1998, p. xiii.

28. Ibid., p. 1.

29. Ibid., p. 2.

30. "Global Ethics Codes Gain Importance as a Tool to Avoid Litigation and Fines," *Wall Street Journal*, August 19, 1999, p. A1. Reprinted by permission of the *Wall Street Journal*, Copyright © 1999 by Dow Jones & Company, Inc. All rights reserved worldwide.

31. Ibid.

32. Polet, J. "Company Communication: From the Ethics of Communication to the Communication of Ethics," in G. Enderle (ed.), *International Business Ethics: Challenges and Approaches*. Notre Dame, IN, and Hong Kong, China: The University of Notre Dame Press and the University of Hong Kong Press, 1998.

33. Ibid., p. 6.

34. Ibid., p. 7.

35. Lipovetsky, G. *Le Crepuscule du Devoir. L'Ethique Indolore des Noveaux Temps democratiques*. Paris: Gallimard, 1992, p. 248.

36. Mulcahy, A. M. Keynote Address, Business for Social Responsibility, Annual Conference. New York, November 11, 2004.

37. Yankelovich, D. "Making Trust a Competitive Asset: Breaking Out of Narrow Frameworks," a report of the Special Meeting of Senior Executives on the Deeper Crisis of Trust. New York, May 15–17, 2003. Available at www.viewpointlearning.com.

38. For a complete description of the study, see Van Lee, R., L. Fabish, and N. McGaw. "The Value of Corporate Values," *Strategy+Business* 39, Summer 2005, pp. 52–65.

39. Barton, L. *Crisis in Organizations: Managing and Communicating in the Heat of Chaos*. Cincinnati, OH: Southwestern Publishing Company, 1993, pp. 84–85.

40. Lipovetsky. *Le Crepuscule du Devoir*, pp. 269–270.

41. Nash, L. L. "Johnson & Johnson's Credo." In *Corporate Ethics: A Prime Business Asset*. New York: The Business Roundtable, 1988, p. 100.

42. Ibid., p. 97.

43. Lipovetsky. *Le Crepuscule du Devoir*, p. 270.

44. Murphy. Eighty Exemplary Ethics Statements, pp. 5–9.

45. Seglin, J. L. "An Ethics Code Can't Replace a Backbone," *New York Times*, April 21, 2002, p. BU-4. Copyright © 2002 by The New York Times Company. Reprinted with permission.

46. Ibid.

CASE STUDY 3-1

Excel Industries (A)

Background Note

The workforce in North America, particularly in the United States and Canada, is becoming increasingly female, reflecting a general trend toward two-paycheck families. According to a study from [the] Hudson Institute, an increasing number of women are entering the North American job market. Since 1990, approximately two-thirds of all new entrants to the workforce have been women. And, since about 2002, nearly two-thirds of all working-age women in the United States have entered the workforce. Other studies indicate that women in the United States have entered the job market more for economic than for professional reasons. While the number of women with college degrees and professional credentials is rising, so is the number of single-parent families headed by women. These families are, for the most part, well below average in income and education and are more likely than two-parent households to require public assistance.

At the same time, employers are coming to realize that what had formerly been seen as "women's issues"—including flexible scheduling, maternity and family leave, and daycare—are really "family issues," deserving serious attention from both the public and private sectors. Some of these matters have become the object of protracted and heated negotiation during collective bargaining. What once was regarded as a luxury or fringe benefit in many organizations is more frequently viewed by employees as an entitlement.

In North America, and especially in the United States, daycare for the children of working mothers is not seen as an entitlement to be provided by government. The U.S. federal government views itself as constitutionally excluded from issues related to management of education and child care, and state and local governments cite a lack of funding. Corporate America has increasingly come to see a social responsibility for the children of their employees, and employees have come to expect and depend on such corporate responsiveness to their needs.

This case deals with several aspects of these emerging family issues. Each employee has both a cost and a value to a business organization, and each employer has concomitant obligations and responsibilities to those employees. This case is about balance among those obligations and management decision making when obligations are in conflict or when responsibilities pull in opposite directions.

This case also involves corporate communication. The executives and management of every business enterprise operate in an environment that is information-rich, yet rife with rumor, misunderstanding, and misinformation. Business leaders must understand that every action, whether intended for public discussion or not, will have an effect on the public's perception of their business. Business leaders should also understand that, as they draft their corporate strategy and implement tactical moves in the marketplace, they will interact and communicate with a diverse and complex audience. Individuals who will see and hear of management's actions will have varying backgrounds, reading abilities, knowledge of the subject, political views, prejudices, and interests.

In many ways, the mass audience reached by radio, television, newspapers, magazines, and the Internet is actually many smaller audiences. It may be helpful to think of the larger audience as comprised of shareholders; customers; suppliers; competitors; politicians; local, regional, and national government officials; potential investors; prospective employees; neighbors; community members; and others.

In some cases, business leaders might well consider separate messages for separate audiences, designing their content for the backgrounds, needs, interests, inclinations, and potential reactions of each. Shareholders, for instance, might have a greater interest in knowing how an event or announcement will affect their investment than do members of the surrounding community. Employees might have a much keener interest in how an event will affect their jobs and their lives in the organization than would others.

A Manufacturer Moves into Child Care

In 1988, Excel Industries, Inc., a supplier of window systems to the automotive industry, purchased Nyloncraft, Inc., a $40 million injection molding company. Both firms were headquartered in northern Indiana, in the heart of the domestic automobile supply region. At the time of the acquisition, Nyloncraft was a highly regarded firm with great promise for growth and had exactly the sort of manufacturing capacity, equipment, and labor force that Excel Industries was looking for.

When the corporate takeover was executed, Nyloncraft, Inc., operated a daycare facility that was regarded as among the most innovative in the nation. *Money* magazine, *U.S. News & World Report,* and other business publications featured the facility, describing it as "one of the best-equipped 24-hour-a-day learning centers in the Midwest that is operated by a corporation for the benefit of its employees." James J. Lohman, chairman, president, and chief executive officer of Excel Industries, said "When the Learning Center was opened, it suited the needs of Nyloncraft very nicely. It was expensive, but it helped us to attract and retain a reliable workforce that would help the company grow. We had a number of female workers who were of child-bearing age and it made good sense for us to assist them with their child care needs. We knew from experience," he added, "that a first-class, on-site learning center would reduce turnover, absenteeism, and tardiness. It was good for business, it was good for our employees, and it was good for the kids."

When he said expensive, Lohman wasn't exaggerating. "When Excel acquired Nyloncraft, we immediately invested $200,000 in the Learning Center, improving it so that it met or exceeded all recommended standards for facilities of that type." The Center's annual budget was in excess of $400,000 to provide round-the-clock care and instruction for 162 children.

The Cost of Providing On-Site Child Care

"Within a few years," Lohman said, "we discovered that fewer and fewer of our employees had children enrolled in the Nyloncraft Learning Center, so we expanded enrollment to the community at large." By July 1988, employees' children accounted for about 45 percent of the enrollment at the Center. "By 1990," he said, "less than seven percent of those enrolled were children of Nyloncraft employees." And by then, he added, the annual subsidy had grown to nearly $300,000. All parents with children enrolled in the Learning Center, regardless of who their employer might be, received a substantial tuition discount, each paying just a fraction of what such care and instruction would be worth on the retail market.

"We weren't just looking after these children, as a baby-sitting service might," he added. "We provided state-certified instruction, professional preschool development programs, and we fed them. Our insurance, reporting, and oversight problems were growing by the day. It was becoming increasingly difficult to justify a subsidy that was well in excess of a quarter-of-a-million dollars for the children of only 10 Excel employees. The financial pressure was simply too great for us to continue the operation."

Excel tried unsuccessfully for nearly a year to find a buyer for the Learning Center. Failing that, they tried to find a management firm that would agree to take over the day-to-day operations of the facility. "No one would step forward to help us," he said. "We didn't want to close the Nyloncraft Learning Center. But, increasingly, I saw fewer alternatives open to us."

Lohman began to think carefully about the decision alternatives available to him and the audiences that would be most affected by his choice. Looking after the children of those few employees who still used the Learning Center would be neither difficult nor expensive. But how would others react to a management decision to close the facility? What other choice did the company have? What other choice did the parents have? Quality daycare was in short supply in the local area, and time was running out on Jim Lohman. The board of directors wanted an answer from him soon.

The two most troubling questions were deceptively simple: What should I do about the Learning Center, and how should we communicate our decision?

DISCUSSION QUESTIONS

1. What ethical obligations, if any, did Excel Industries have to the women who were employed there?
2. Is an employer obligated to provide daycare for its employees' children?
3. What obligations does the firm in this case have to the community? Having once opened its doors to the children of nonemployees, was the firm obligated in any way to continue caring for them?
4. Could a firm, such as Excel Industries, sidestep ethical issues associated with daycare altogether by recruiting either male employees or women past child-bearing age?
5. What responsibilities does Mr. Lohman have as chief executive officer to the shareholders and debtholders of Excel Industries, Inc.? Does his obligation to maximize shareholder wealth and minimize debtholder risk conflict with an obligation to provide a safe, comfortable working environment for female employees who may be concerned about child care?
6. Since it became apparent to Mr. Lohman that the Nyloncraft Learning Center could no longer be economically justified, what ethical obligations did he have to the women whose children were enrolled there? Do Mr. Lohman's responsibilities to employees of the firm exceed those to women who are not employed by Excel Industries?
7. What role should corporate public relations and the public news media play in communicating this decision to Excel Industries employees? What role should they play in communicating the decision to the community at large?
8. What vested interest do you suppose the community has in the continued operation of the Nyloncraft LearningCenter? Do any reciprocal obligations exist between the community and the employers for the proper care, feeding, and education of preschool children whose parents are employed in the community? Has Excel Industries violated any "unspoken pact" between management and its workers, or between the company and the community?

WRITING ASSIGNMENT

Please respond in writing to the issues presented in this case by preparing two documents: a communication strategy memo and a professional business letter. In preparing these documents, you may assume one of two roles: you may identify yourself as an Excel Industries manager who has been asked to provide advice to Mr. Lohman regarding the issues he and the company are facing. Or, you may identify yourself as an external management consultant who has been asked by the company to provide advice to Mr. Lohman.

Either way, you must prepare a strategy memo addressed to Jim Lohman that summarizes the details of the case, rank orders critical issues, discusses their implications (what they mean and why they matter),

offers specific recommendations for action (assigning ownership and suspense dates for each), and shows how to communicate the solution to all who are affected by the recommendations.

You must also prepare a professional business letter for Mr. Lohman's signature. That document may be addressed to parents of children attending the Nyloncraft Learning Center, addressing their concerns in the case. If you wish, you may write separate letters to parents who are Excel employees and to parents who are not employees of the company. If you have questions about either of these documents, please consult your instructor.

NYLONCRAFT Summary Balance Sheet December 1990	
Cash	97
Accounts Receivable	3,207
Inventory	7,308
Prepaid Expense	93
Total Current Assets	10,705
Fixed Assets, Net	8,585
Goodwill and Other Assets	3,691
Total Assets	22,981
Accounts Payable	1,897
Accrued Liabilities	1,232
Current Portion Ltd	413
Long Term Debt, Banks	1,800
Due to Parent/Equity	17,639
Total Liabilities & Equity	22,981

NYLONCRAFT Income Statement Year Ended December 1990	
Sales	36,730
Cost of Goods Sold	35,332
Gross Profit	1,398
Selling and Administrative Expense	2,697
Operating Income	(1,299)
Other Expenses	522
Loss Before Tax and Corp. Allocation	(1,821)

Note: Figures are given in thousands of dollars (U.S.).

This case was prepared from personal interviews and public sources by James S. O'Rourke, Concurrent Professor of Management, as the basis for class discussion rather than to illustrate either effective or ineffective handling of an administrative situation.

CASE STUDY 3-2

A Collection Scandal at Sears, Roebuck & Company

It was just 8:30 A.M. on a Sunday morning. While most of Chicago was either still asleep or out retrieving the morning paper, Arthur C. Martinez was meeting with a dozen of his company's top executives at their headquarters building in suburban Hoffman Estates. For a few moments, the room grew quiet as Martinez tried to digest what he had just been told. Lawyers for Sears, Roebuck & Company were explaining how employees had secretly violated federal law for nearly a decade.

Martinez couldn't believe what he was hearing: Sears attorneys and credit employees, according to a bankruptcy judge in Boston, had for years been dunning delinquent credit card holders who had filed for—and had been granted—bankruptcy protection. The newspapers and cable television news channels didn't have the story yet, but it would only be a matter of hours before they would. The company that Martinez, a former Saks Fifth Avenue executive, had struggled to turn around would quickly be mired in the worst legal and ethics scandal in its 111-year history.

The United States Department of Justice was already considering not only civil penalties, but also criminal prosecution. Worse, this wasn't simply a rogue operation or an honest misinterpretation of the law: Sears appeared to have been violating the rights of many of its customers systematically and intentionally. The company, the lawyers were suggesting, may even have put the illegal practice into its procedures manual.

How could such wrongdoing have gone unchecked for years? Martinez wanted to know. "Not one phone call about this? Ever?" he demanded. According to at least one participant in the meeting, it was a "sickening moment."

A "Half-Billion Dollar" Handwritten Letter

As an extensive investigation would later reveal, Sears struggled—first to understand and then to deal with criminal charges and an ethical lapse that would cost the company nearly $500 million. According to Sears' senior vice president Ron Culp, the collection scheme began to unravel in November 1996, when Francis Latanowich, a disabled security guard, hand wrote a letter on a yellow legal pad, begging the Boston Bankruptcy Court to reopen his case. Although Judge Carol Kenner had wiped out his debts, Sears later asked Latanowich to repay the $1,161 he owed for a TV, an auto battery, and some other merchandise. But the monthly payment, he wrote, "is keeping food off the table for my kids."

Sears, it turned out, had mailed Latanowich an offer. In return for $28 a month on his account, the company wouldn't repossess the goods he had bought with a Sears charge card before he went bankrupt. The practice of urging debtors to sign such deals, called reaffirmations, is legal and relatively widespread in the retail credit business, but many judges view them as unethical practices that keep people from getting a fresh start. Moreover, every signed reaffirmation must be

filed with the court so a judge can review whether the debtor can handle the new payment. Sears, Roebuck & Company hadn't filed this one with the court and Judge Kenner wanted to know why not.

At January 29, 1997, hearing, a Boston attorney working for Sears offered a convoluted technical excuse for not filing. Kenner's response: "Baloney." According to *Newsweek* magazine, there were hints from prior cases that Sears, both praised and feared nationwide as the most aggressive pursuer of reaffirmations, wasn't filing many of them with the court. If true, the company was using unenforceable agreements to collect debts that legally no longer existed. Judge Kenner pushed Sears for a list of such cases. Sears' response, delivered reluctantly in mid-March by a credit manager, was shocking: The company had apparently ignored the law nearly 2,800 times in Massachusetts alone. Martinez and his senior team could only imagine what the company was up to in the other 49 states.

Soaring Personal Bankruptcies

Between 1994 and 1998, personal bankruptcies in the United States rose from 780,000 to more than 1.3 million, leaving many retailers and credit card issuers awash in bad debt. Sears, as the nation's second-largest retailer, was in a particularly vulnerable position. That year, the company earned 50 percent of its operating income from credit, including charge cards held by more than 63 million households with Sears credit cards.

The problem, as Martinez would come to discover, [was] that too many of those new cardholders barely qualified for credit. In its zeal to attract new business, Sears became a lender to its riskiest customers. As the number of bankruptcies rose nationwide, so did the number of unpaid accounts at Sears. By 1997, more than one-third of all personal bankruptcies in the United States included Sears as a creditor. Companies heavily dependent on income from their credit cards chose to aggressively pursue bad debts, and Sears was just one of many to do so. The list included such prominent creditors as Federated Department Stores, the May Company, G. E. Capital, Discover Card, and AT&T.

As Martinez would also come to discover, the problem was neither isolated nor small. During the previous five years, some 512,000 customers had signed reaffirmation agreements with Sears, pledging to repay debts that totaled $412 million. Martinez suspected that his company's transformation from an exhausted, defeatist bureaucracy into "an aggressive, can-do company" had an unanticipated consequence: Managers simply wouldn't send bad news up the chain of command.

A culture of aggressively pursuing bad debts while filtering out bad news from top management had become part of the company's culture and official policy. Michael Levin, chief of Sears' law department, explained to his CEO that at least one outside law firm had told someone in the company that Sears' policy was questionable. But word of the alert, which might have triggered a broader investigation within the company, somehow never worked its way up through the bureaucracy.

Martinez leaned back and motioned to his executive assistant, "Call a meeting of the Phoenix Team," he said. "Eight o'clock tomorrow." That would mean 200 of Sears, Roebuck & Company's top executives would get the bad news directly from their CEO. It would also signal the start of Sears' response to the charges.

Martinez then turned to Ron Culp, Sears' senior vice president for public relations and government affairs, and Bill Giffen, vice president for ethics and business policy. "Give me your best thinking," he said. "Tell me what you think we should do."

DISCUSSION QUESTIONS

1. What is Sears' best strategy at this point? What would you advise Arthur Martinez to do?
2. As Ron Culp thinks about corporate communications and the events that have just unfolded in the board room, which audiences would you advise him to focus on first?
3. What do you suppose the interests will be for each of these audiences? Are they similar interests or are some of them in conflict with one another? What do they want to hear from Mr. Martinez?
4. As Bill Giffen examines Sears' credit collection policies and practices, what advice would you offer? How can Martinez keep a sense of enthusiasm and excitement in his company and still encourage people to report and disclose bad news?
5. Even though the reaffirmation agreements are perfectly legal and enforceable, if properly filed with the courts, is it ethical to try to extract money from people who have legally declared bankruptcy? What ethical obligations do those people in bankruptcy have toward companies who lent them credit, such as Sears?
6. Has the reward structure at Sears somehow affected the communication structure? What would you change if you could advise Mr. Martinez on restructuring either of those systems?

WRITING ASSIGNMENT

Please respond in writing to the issues presented in this case by preparing two documents: a communication strategy memo and a professional business letter. In preparing these documents, you may assume the role of the Vice President for Corporate Communication for Sears, Roebuck & Company. Your task is to provide advice to Mr. Arthur Martinez regarding the issues he and the company are facing. Or, you may identify yourself as an external management consultant who has been asked by the company to provide advice to Mr. Martinez.

Either way, you must prepare a strategy memo addressed to Arthur Martinez, Chairman and Chief Executive Officer of the company, that summarizes the details of the case, rank orders critical issues, discusses their implications (what they mean and why they matter), offers specific recommendations for action (assigning ownership and suspense dates for each), and shows how to communicate the solution to all who are affected by the recommendations.

You must also prepare a professional business letter for Mr. Martinez's signature. That document should be addressed to Sears' premium credit customers in good standing, explaining what happened and how the company intends to respond. If you have questions about either of these documents, please consult your instructor.

SOURCES

Cahill, Joseph B. "Sears's Credit Business May Have Helped Hide Larger Retailing Woes," *Wall Street Journal*, July 6, 1999, pp. A1, A8.

Culp, E. Ronald. Personal communication, November 1999–January 2000.

"Final Accord in G.E. Debt Collection," *New York Times*, January 23, 1999, p. B1.

McCormick, John. "The Sorry Side of Sears," *Newsweek*, February 22, 1999.

"Sears to Pay Fine of $60 Million in Bankruptcy Fraud Lawsuit," *New York Times*, February 10, 1999, p. C1.

Sparks, Debra. "Got an AT&T Credit Card? Don't Go Bankrupt," *BusinessWeek*, September 15, 1997.Weimer, De'Ann. "Is Sears Putting the Comeback on Its Card?" *BusinessWeek*, November 10, 1997.

This case was prepared from personal interviews and public sources by James S. O'Rourke, Concurrent Professor of Management, as the basis for class discussion rather than to illustrate either effective or ineffective handling of an administrative situation.

CASE STUDY 3-3

The Tiger Woods Foundation: When Values and Behavior Collide

Introduction

From the moment he stepped into the public spotlight as a two-year-old on The Mike Douglas Show, Tiger Woods was seen as the epitome of a hard-working athlete of strong character. The world viewed him as a model citizen who worked tirelessly not only to succeed on the golf course, but also to be a positive influence to the global community and a caring husband and father. The golfer, along with his late father, Earl Woods, founded the Tiger Woods Foundation to promote their family's values of integrity, honesty, discipline, responsibility, and fun.

Tiger's reputation changed suddenly in the early morning hours of November 27, 2009. At approximately 2:25 a.m., a neighbor of Tiger Woods dialed 911 to report that the golfer had crashed his 2009 Cadillac Escalade outside his Windermere, Florida, home. He was taken to the hospital in "serious condition," treated for minor injuries and released later that day. News reports throughout the day were fragmented and sometimes contradictory. There was a report about a neighbor finding Tiger shoeless and unconscious next to his crashed car. There was another report that Tiger's wife, Elin, smashed out the back window of his Cadillac Escalade with a golf club. Many of these rumors were never confirmed.

These reports left many unanswered questions. Where was Tiger going at 2:30 in the morning? How was he knocked unconscious when the accident was so minor that the air bags did not even deploy? Why was his wife smashing car windows? News reports began to connect this incident with an article published in the National Enquirer, a newspaper tabloid, which stated Woods was having an extramarital affair. It only got worse. With each passing day, more and more women stepped forward and claimed that they too had affairs with Tiger during his five-year marriage.

Within a few days, Woods' near-stellar reputation was shattered. No longer was he seen as a driven, hard working, family-oriented professional. He was now viewed by the public as a surreptitious philanderer and womanizer. As the founder and figurehead of the Tiger Woods Foundation, he had been responsible for much of the financial success and publicity the Foundation had garnered over the years. He seemed to embody all the values that the Foundation promoted. The revelation of his misdeeds gravely damaged his reputation and now put his image at odds with the core values of the Foundation. How was the Tiger Woods Foundation, which relied so heavily on the reputation and character of its figurehead, going to continue its mission? Would they still be able to leverage his celebrity to raise money and continue to improve the lives of youths?

About the Tiger Woods Foundation

The Tiger Woods Foundation was created as a 501(c)(3) nonprofit organization aimed at helping children develop character and explore potential careers. It is a philanthropic organization that partners with various corporations and other entities to support community-based programs, which work to improve the lives of youths, both in the United States and abroad. Over the course of its 14-year history, the Tiger Woods Foundation has established a number of events to raise money and awareness to various character-development causes. Tiger Woods is the founder of the Foundation, and has remained active as its figurehead. His father, Earl Woods, was a co-founder. His mother, Kultilda Woods, sits on the Board of Directors.

The Foundation is led by Gregory McLaughlin, President and CEO. Assisting the CEO are three vice presidents who are responsible for Events and Business Development, Communications and Marketing, and Programs and Administration. The Tiger Woods Foundation employs a total of 25 people.[1]

The Foundation's main priority is to provide the youth of America with access to critical development programs.[2] The Tiger Woods Foundation believes that providing the access to these programs will enable children to explore their own curiosity and thus, aspire to new careers and life goals that would not have otherwise been known or considered. In order for children to meet their full potential, the Foundation works to provide them with an outlet of character development programs. The Tiger Woods Foundation achieves this mission through a variety of events and programs of its own.

Tiger Woods Foundation History

The Foundation was established in November 1996. Tiger Woods and his father wanted to begin a charitable organization that promotes the Woods' family motto of "caring and sharing" to youths around the world. Throughout the late 1990's, the Tiger Woods Foundation began its fundraising efforts and held golf clinics throughout the country. The Tiger Woods Junior Golf Team was created in 1999.

While driving from St. Louis to Florida shortly after the terrorist attacks of September 11, 2001, Tiger Woods decided to embark upon building the Tiger Woods Learning Center (TWLC), which he envisioned as one of the cornerstones of the Foundation's work. This became a reality with the opening of the TWLC in 2006. By the end of 2001, the Tiger Woods Foundation reached the $1 million mark in grants awarded to youth charities. Earl Woods passed away in 2006, and shortly thereafter, the Earl D. Woods Scholarship was established in his memory.

By the end of 2006, the Tiger Woods Foundation had administered and contributed to programs that affected the lives of over 10 million youths. The Foundation continued to grow and was the recipient of fundraising efforts from new PGA Tour events, such as the AT&T National, which started in 2007.

Programs of the Tiger Woods Foundation

The Foundation administers and supports a variety of educational and character development causes, such as the Tiger Woods Learning Center, grants and scholarships, and various golf clinics and junior golf teams. Since 1996, the Foundation has also raised and distributed over $30 million toward local charity initiatives. In 2009, the Tiger Woods Foundation educated 5,000 children at the Tiger Woods Learning Center, distributed four-year college scholarships to 25 students, and provided 109 grants to youth-oriented organizations throughout the world.[3]

Grants and Scholarships

The Tiger Woods Foundation provides grants and scholarships to a variety of programs throughout the year. The grants focus on providing opportunities to underserved youth, ages 8–18. The typical grant sum ranges between $2,500 and $25,000. The grants are distributed to other local non-profit organizations with a mission for education or youth mentoring / tutoring organizations. In a given year, the Tiger Woods Foundation reserves the right to emphasize a certain geographical area for awards.[4] The Foundation also administers the Earl Woods Scholarship, which provides up to $5,000 for high school seniors who demonstrate financial need and a commitment to community service. In addition to the financial award, the Earl Woods Scholarship also provides recipients with mentoring and an internship during their college careers.[5] The funding for the scholarship is raised through donations from individuals around the world. Since its creation, donations have totaled $1 million. Tiger matched this amount, bringing the total to $2 million.[6]

Tiger Woods Learning Center

The Tiger Woods Learning Center, located in Anaheim, California, is a 35,000-square-foot, facility that sits on a 14-acre plot of land. The TWLC is a place where children in grades 5-12 can explore new careers with hands-on, interactive projects. The center was designed to provide a unique after-school program, with a curriculum designed by kids. The various programs, including a wide variety of topics such as biotechnology, marine biology, entrepreneurship and aerospace rocketry, were designed to provide opportunities that go beyond what children normally experience in school. The curricula emphasize career exploration and preparation.[7]

Tiger Woods Foundation National Junior Golf Team

The Tiger Woods Foundation National Junior Golf Team (TWFNJGT) was originally developed to provide underprivileged youths with the opportunity to participate in the Junior Golf World Championship. The Junior Golf World Championship is an international tournament for talented golfers under the age of 18.[8] Typically, young golfers within a specific age bracket must apply for selection into the tournament. The Tiger Woods Foundation worked with the Championship to reserve a number of exemptions within each age bracket for children who had been selected onto the TWFNJGT.

Tiger's Action Plan

Based on Earl Woods' book, Start Something, Tiger's Action Plan is a free program for children ages 8-17 that addresses character education, volunteer service and career exploration. Through the program, youths define a particular personal or career goal and learn how to achieve that goal while simultaneously giving back to their communities.[9]

International Programs

In order to increase its reach to all youths, the Foundation recently started an international program by funding six organizations around the world.[10]

Students In Free Enterprise (SIFE): Korea and Thailand

Dreams + Teams: Thailand

International Youth Foundation: China

Rural China Education Fund: China

ProLiteracy: China

Investments in three organizations in Thailand

Fundraising Efforts

The Tiger Woods Foundation relies on the donations of individuals, as well as partnerships with various corporations. The biggest corporate sponsors have included AT&T, Bank of America, Chevron, HSBC, Deutsche Bank, Chevron, Booz Allen Hamilton, TAG Heuer and Mercedes Benz.[11] In addition to this, the Foundation is the beneficiary of several annual fundraising events, which include PGA Tour events, benefit concerts and other events. For the fiscal year ending in 2007, the Tiger Woods Foundation had revenues totaling $12.8 million, of which $9.2 million came in the form of donations from corporate partners and individuals. In fiscal year 2008, the foundation had revenues totaling $10.6 million, of which $7.8 million came from donations.[12]

AT&T National

The AT&T National is a PGA tournament that began in 2007 and is hosted by Tiger Woods to benefit the Tiger Woods Foundation. It is typically held on the 4th of July Weekend. Approximately 120 PGA Tour professionals from around the world compete to win a share of the $6.2 million purse, as well as raise funds for the Foundation, local charities and pay tribute to men and women in the Armed Forces.

Chevron World Challenge

The Chevron World Challenge is another PGA Tour event, held each year in early December in Southern California. The tournament raises money for programs of the Tiger Woods Foundation, including the Tiger Woods Learning Center in Orange County. Programs developed and supported by the Tiger Woods Foundation all share a similar mission of empowering young people to dream big and to set specific goals to achieve their dreams.

Tiger Jam

The Tiger Jam is an annual benefit concert, held at the Mandalay Bay Resort and Casino in Las Vegas, to raise funds for the Tiger Woods Foundation. Since its inception in 1998, Tiger Jam has raised more than $10 million for the Tiger Woods Foundation and has attracted artists such as Bon Jovi, Sting, Stevie Wonder, Prince, Celine Dion and Christina Aguilera.

Block Party

The Block Party is an annual celebration of the community and youths served by the Tiger Woods Learning Center in Orange County. Each year, the Block Party raises over $1 million for the various programs at the Tiger Woods Learning Center.

Tiger Woods Biography

Impact

Tiger Woods is one of the most exceptionally gifted golfers the sport has ever seen. In addition to winning 71 tournaments on the PGA Tour, 14 of which were majors, he influenced the sport in several other ways, as well. As an individual of multi-ethnic heritage, he brought diversity to golf, a sport that had not historically appealed to minorities in the United States. He was also one of the youngest athletes ever to attain such success on the course. His intense focus on improvement led him to introduce a new level of fitness to the sport and to reconstruct his swing technique relatively late in his career. Tiger was also the first athlete to earn $1 billion throughout the course of his career.[13]

Personal Characteristics

Tiger has been known for his drive, determination, and mental toughness. It was his extensive training regimen, work ethic and lack of vacations, attention to detail, and relentless pursuit of improvement that caught the public's attention most. Tiger had become an American icon, an image of what can be accomplished through hard work and determination.

According to his official website, Tiger's typical day goes as follows:[14]

6:30 a.m.:	One hour of cardio. Choice between endurance runs, sprints or biking.
7:30 a.m.:	One hour of lower weight training, 60–70 percent of normal lifting weight, high reps and multiple sets.
8:30 a.m.:	High protein/low-fat breakfast. Typically includes egg-white omelet with vegetables.
9:00 a.m.:	Two hours on the golf course. Hit on the range and work on swing.
11:00 a.m.:	Practice putting for 30 minutes to an hour.
12:00 noon:	Play nine holes.
1:30 p.m.:	High protein/low-fat lunch. Typically includes grilled chicken or fish, salad and vegetables.
2:00 p.m.:	Three-to-four hours on the golf course. Work on swing, short game and occasionally play another nine holes.
6:30 p.m.:	30 minutes of upper weight training with high reps.
7:00 p.m.:	Dinner and rest.

In addition to being known for the qualities that help him win on the course, he was seen as laudable off the course, as well. The public viewed Tiger as a family man and an all-around good guy. Tiger was able to maintain this image through careful public management and leading a very private life, despite the fact that he was one of the most famous individuals in the sports world.

Biography

Tiger was coached by his father, and began to play golf as a very young child. He was introduced to the public at an early age. At the age of two, he appeared on both CBS News and Mike Douglas Show putting with Bob Hope. By age 13, he had appeared on the Today Show, Good Morning America, ESPN, CBS, NBC and ABC. At the age of 15 he was the youngest golfer ever to win the U.S. Junior Amateur Championship and was named Golf Digest Player of the Year.[15]

Tiger's most notable golf accomplishments include 95 tournament victories and 71 PGA tour victories. He has achieved the career "Grand Slam," having won all four major tournaments: the Masters, the U.S. Open, the British Open, and the PGA Championship.[16] Only five other golfers have accomplished this feat. At age 34, he is on pace to become the most successful golfer in the history of the game. Tiger married former Swedish model Elin Nordegren in October 2004. Elin gave birth to their first child in June 2007. Their second child was born in February of 2009.[17]

Endorsements

Tiger's broad-based market appeal resulted in numerous endorsements throughout the course of his career. His sponsors have included:[18]

    Nike

    Titleist

    General Mills

    American Express

    Accenture

    Buick

    TAG Heuer

    Tiger Woods PGA Tour series video games

    Electronic Arts, video game publisher

    Gillette

    Gatorade

The endorsements help clarify exactly what Tiger means to the public. An Accenture TV commercial begins with Tiger's alarm clock going off at 4:30 a.m. It states "To stay at the top, a high performer can never let up."[19] Many Accenture commercials end with the statement "High Performance. Delivered." However, Accenture has since ended its relationship with Woods. Other sponsors continue to actively promote Tiger Woods as a pitchman for their companies. Nike Golf, which had built its entire business around Tiger, continues to portray the golfer in its advertisements. A Nike advertisement includes Tiger's father discussing how he became the mentally toughest golfer in the world.[20] Another Nike commercial shows a series of aspiring children golfers saying "I'm Tiger Woods."[21] This particular commercial demonstrates the admiration that the American public had for Woods. He was seen as a strong role model that children could proudly imitate. Tiger's reputation for excellence and moral character was so strong that he was chosen to give a speech commemorating the military at "We Are One: The Obama Inaugural Celebration at the Lincoln Memorial."[22]

Future of the Tiger Woods Foundation

It is impossible at this point to predict the full ramification of Tiger's scandal and the impact it will have on his corporate partners. Some sponsors, such as Accenture, have ended their relationship with Woods entirely, indicating that Tiger Woods "is no longer the right representative for our advertising."[23] Others have significantly scaled back. AT&T, for instance, opted to end their sponsorship of Tiger Woods and the Tiger Jam benefit concert.[24] AT&T, however, is still under contract to sponsor the AT&T National golf tournament through 2014.[25]

Sponsors' continued support of Tiger and his Foundation relies largely upon his reputation and the extent to which sponsors can build their own brands through a relationship. Marketing analysts note that the commercial appeal of Tiger Woods was great because of the traits he possessed: athleticism, power and integrity. Now his only appeal is his great ability on the golf course.[26] Given the current circumstances, it could be very difficult for Tiger to reclaim his former brand identity. Corporate partners may be unwilling to link their own reputations with his.

It is too soon to know if donations have been adversely affected by Tiger's behavior and subsequent apology and absence from public life. Foundation president Gregory McLaughlin indicates that the Tiger Woods Learning Center has ample resources to continue its mission throughout Tiger's absence.[27] A recent study by University of California (Davis) economics professors Christopher Knittel and Victor Stango showed that companies maintaining sponsorship deals with Tiger Woods have lost between $5 billion and $12 billion in shareholder wealth since the news broke of Tiger Woods' scandal.[28]

There is a possibility that corporations that had once been eager to align themselves with Tiger and the various causes he champions will now seek out other outlets to give back to communities. " 'Character education' is one of the 'three priorities' of Tiger's Action Plan … [and] one of the great ironies of this program at present is that its existence could be the reason the Foundation backers cite if they decide to withdraw their support."[29] The Tiger Woods Foundation has worked for 14 years to help the youth of the world build character and achieve goals. The Foundation must now work to maintain its reputation and operational success, given the personal failures of its figurehead.

DISCUSSION QUESTIONS

1. How can the Foundation disassociate itself with Tiger's personal behavior, but still be able to leverage his celebrity status to bring funding and awareness to its causes?
2. Should the Foundation make any statements regarding the scandal?
3. What could the Foundation do to retain its sponsors?
4. How will the scandal affect public interest in the Foundation's services?
5. Should the Foundation disassociate itself entirely from Tiger?
6. Could Tiger improve his reputation by increasing his personal involvement in the Foundation?

WRITING ASSIGNMENT

Please respond in writing to the issues presented in this case by preparing two documents: a communication strategy memo and a professional business letter.

In preparing these two documents, you may assume one of two roles: you may identify yourself as an officer of the Tiger Woods Foundation who has been asked to provide advice to Gregory McLaughlin, President and CEO, regarding the issues he and the foundation are facing. Or, you may identify yourself as an external management consultant who has been asked by the foundation to provide advice to Mr. McLaughlin. Either way, you must prepare a strategy memo

addressed to him that summarizes the details of the case, rank orders critical issues, discusses their implications (what they mean and why they matter), offers specific recommendations for action (assigning ownership and suspense dates for each), and shows how to communicate the solution to all who are affected by the recommendations.

You must also prepare a professional business letter for the CEO's signature. That document must be addressed to one of the Tiger Woods Foundation's corporate sponsors. If you have questions about either of these documents, please consult your instructor.

This case was prepared by Research Assistants Danielle Van Dyk and Bill Rayball under the direction of James S. O'Rourke, Concurrent Professor of Management, as the basis for class discussion rather than to illustrate either effective or ineffective handling of an administrative situation. Information was gathered from corporate as well as public sources.

References

1. Tiger Woods Foundation, About the Foundation, Board & Staff http://web.tigerwoodsfoundation.org/aboutTWF/staff
2. Tiger Woods Foundation, About the Foundation, What We Do http://web.tigerwoodsfoundation.org/aboutTWF/whatWeDo
3. 2009 Tiger Woods Foundation Annual Report, http://web.tigerwoodsfoundation.org/aboutTWF/annualReport
4. Tiger Woods Foundation, TWF Grants, Overview http://web.tigerwoodsfoundation.org/programs/grants/index
5. Tiger Woods Foundation, TWF Scholarships, Steps for Success http://web.tigerwoodsfoundation.org/programs/scholarships/stepsForSuccess
6. Tiger Woods Foundation, TWF Scholarships, Earl Woods Scholarship Program http://web.tigerwoodsfoundation.org/programs/scholarships/index
7. Tiger Woods Foundation, Tiger Woods Learning Center, TWLC Programs http://web.tigerwoodsfoundation.org/programs/twlc/twlcPrograms
8. The 2010 Callaway Junior World Golf Championships, Eligibility Requirements for 2010 Championships http://www.juniorworldgolf.com/index.php?pg=dyn&bi=eligability
9. 2009 Tiger Woods Foundation Annual Report http://web.tigerwoodsfoundation.org/aboutTWF/annucaalReport
10. Tiger Woods Foundation, TWF Grants, International Programs http://web.tigerwoodsfoundation.org/programs/grants/internationalPrograms
11. 2009 Tiger Woods Foundation Annual Report http://web.tigerwoodsfoundation.org/aboutTWF/annualReport
12. Charity Navigator, Your Guide to Intelligent Giving, Tiger Woods Foundation, Revenue http://www.charitynavigator.org/index.cfm?bay=search.history&orgid=8100
13. Tiger Woods, (Eldrick Tont Woods), Wikipedia http://en.wikipedia.org/w/index.php?title=TigerWoods&oldid=345273017
14. Tiger Woods, Health & Fitness, Tiger's Daily Routine http://web.tigerwoods.com/fitness/tigerDailyRoutine
15. Tiger Woods, About Tiger Woods, Chronology http://web.tigerwoods.com/aboutTiger/chronology
16. Tiger Woods, About Tiger Woods, Biography http://web.tigerwoods.com/aboutTiger/bio
17. Tiger Woods, (Eldrick Tont Woods), Wikipedia http://en.wikipedia.org/w/index.php?title=Tiger_Woods&oldid=345273017
18. Ibid.
19. Accenture—High Performance. Delivered (TV Ad by Tiger Woods), February 18, 2009 http://www.youtube.com/watch?v=YM8FrX3b_Jo
20. Nike Golf-Never-Tiger Woods, June 14, 2008 http://www.youtube.com/watch?v=UTuk5Uloyjg
21. Tiger Woods first Nike commercial: I am Tiger Woods, March 13, 2008 http://www.youtube.com/watch?v=tAnlcW_ILyw&NR=1
22. Tiger Woods, (Eldrick Tont Woods), *Wikipedia* http://en.wikipedia.org/w/index.php?title=Tiger_Woods&oldid=345273017
23. Mark Ritson, "Tiger Economy in Jeopardy," *Marketing*, December 16, 2009 http://www.marketingritson.com/documents/ritson161209.pdf
24. Ken Belson, "AT&T Is the Latest to Drop Woods," *New York Times*, December 31, 2010 http://www.nytimes.com/2010/01/01/sports/golf/01tiger.html
25. Tim Dalhberg, "School's In, Despite Tiger's Many Woes," Associated Press, January 30, 2010 http://abcnews.go.com/Sports/wirestory?id=9707365&page=2
26. Sarah Skidmore, "Tiger the Pitchman Far from Out of the Woods," Associated Press, February 19, 2010 http://abcnews.go.com/Sports/wireStory?id=9890054

27. Tim Dahlberg, "School's In, Despite Tiger's Many Woes," Associated Press, January 30, 2010, http://abcnews.go.com/Sports/wireStory?id=9707365

28. News release, UC Davis News Service, "Tiger Woods Scandal Cost Shareholders up to $12 Billion," December 28, 2009

http://www.news.ucdavis.edu/search/news_detail.lasso?id=9352

29. Rick Horrow and Karla Swatek, "Who Benefits from Tiger Woods' Scandal?" *Business Week*, December 10, 2009 http://www.businessweek.com/lifestyle/content/dec2009/bw20091210_272903.htm

CASE STUDY 3-4

Google's New Strategy in China: Principled Philosophy or Business Savvy?

On January 12, 2010, David Drummond, Senior Vice-President of Corporate Development and Chief Legal Officer at Google, Inc. posted a message to Google's official blog, announcing that the company would no longer cooperate with the Chinese government's demands for limited censorship of Internet searches on its Google.cn portal and that it may withdraw from the Chinese market entirely. Drummond stated that Google suffered a "highly sophisticated and targeted attack on our corporate infrastructure originating from China" resulting in "the theft of intellectual property from Google."[1]

The mid-December 2009 cyber attack originated from six Internet addresses in Taiwan, a common diversion strategy used by Chinese hackers.[2] Google's internal investigation concluded that the attack targeted at least 20 other large U.S. companies in the technology, financial services, and media industries. The company indicated that the hackers were attempting to access its Gmail service in order to review data from e-mail accounts of various human rights protestors. In total, the hackers uncovered only two accounts and accessed minimal data from them. They were not able to read any actual e-mail messages.[3]

While it could not confirm that the government was complicit in the attacks, Google believed that China had violated the spirit of the parties' 2006 agreement, under which Google agreed to limit some content that the government deemed objectionable. Google believed that giving Chinese citizens access to most of the Internet was more desirable than giving them no access to the Internet.

Tensions have been building between Google and China in recent years. In 2009, the Chinese government accused the company of carrying pornography on its sites. In addition, YouTube, Google's popular video-sharing website, has been prohibited in most of China since March of that year. Industry insiders also note that Google's criticism of the attack is further fueled by its similarity to a recent breach affecting the computers of the Dalai Lama and a number of foreign embassies.

Google's History in China

In 1998, graduate students Sergey Brin and Larry Page founded the search engine company BackRub, Google's predecessor, in their dorm room. The company was immediately successful, and in 1999, Page and Brin secured more than $25 million in venture capital funding to grow the company to more than 60 employees. In 2001, Page and Brin appointed an experienced outsider, Eric Schmidt, as CEO, while the founders remained active as co-Presidents. Google's highly successful initial public offering (IPO) in 2004 valued the company in excess of $100 billion.

At the time of the IPO, the company released a letter from the founders. The letter asserted Google's mission: "We believe strongly that in the long term, we will be better served . . . by a company that does good things for the world even if we forgo some short-term gains. We aspire to make Google an institution that makes the world a better place." Google's popularity and rapid growth are often attributed, in part, to the company motto embodying these ideals: "Don't Be Evil."[4]

On January 25, 2006, Google, Inc. announced that it would provide access to the Internet through a new portal, Google.cn. Based on the huge growth potential in the world's most populous country, Wall

Street enthusiastically supported the new venture, as the company's share price rose 3.6% in just one day.[5] After extensive debate, Google executives agreed to censor all search results that included content considered objectionable by the Chinese government. Many stakeholders claimed that Google had set aside its "Don't Be Evil" philosophy in the pursuit of profits; however, Google's executives claimed that it would provide a greater disservice to the Chinese people if it provided no Internet search access than it would if it provided limited, filtered Internet access.

Although Google has operated in the country in compliance with censorship laws, tensions have been building between the company and the Chinese government in recent years. In 2009, China publicly admonished the company, accusing it of storing pornographic material on its sites. In March of the same year, China blocked Google's popular YouTube video sharing service from its citizens.[6] Despite offering many of the same search-based products popular in the United States, Google's communication platform is increasingly limited due to Chinese government control.

The Extent of the Suspected Attack

Although Google publicly indicated that the suspected Chinese hacking attempt affected 20 other companies, anonymous insiders familiar with the investigation believe that as many as 34 different entities were targeted. Google's decision to publicly address the attack on its infrastructure was an unusual move, given the technology sector's proclivity to shield data breaches from public scrutiny. In 1998, President Bill Clinton's administration made the first government attempts to collaborate with private companies with regard to sharing information about Internet threats. Sharing of this data, however, remains voluntary, and few companies report threats with any sense of urgency. Estimates indicate that businesses reported only 37% of the approximately 7,000 data breaches in 2009, and they only disclosed 10% involving sensitive information.[7]

The human rights issues connected to the Chinese attack resulted in a handful of other companies publicly addressing their involvement. Concurrent with Google's blog posting, a spokeswoman for Adobe Systems Inc., a design and web development software

company, announced that they, too, had experienced a similar breach.[8] Two days later, networking equipment manufacturer Juniper Networks Inc. joined the movement by stating that it was "currently investing a cyber security incident involving a sophisticated and targeted attack against a number of companies." In addition, the law firm of Gipson Hoffman & Pancione declared that it had been the target of a China-based cyber attack. The firm represents Cybersitter, LLC, which is engaged in litigation with the Chinese government over allegations of piracy of the company's filtering software. None of the companies that publicly announced their involvement in the hacking attempt acknowledged whether the breach was successful.[9]

Industry insiders believe that a number of other prominent companies have experienced a related cyber attack, although these businesses have not officially announced any association. A spokesman for Dow Chemical Co. indicated that federal law enforcement agencies reached out to the company regarding an Internet-based attack. Security experts also believe that Northrop Grumman Corp. and Symantec Corp. were also targets of the Chinese hackers.[10] Furthermore, experts indicated that Google's major rival, Yahoo Inc., also had its network compromised. After Google's announcement, Yahoo issued a statement indicating that it "aligned" itself with Google's corporate position. This angered Yahoo's Chinese partner, the Alibaba Group, which felt the statement was reckless given the lack of evidence in the matter.[11]

Censorship Philosophies

Even after the initial furor subsided following its entry into China in 2006, Google faced some internal division with respect to its participation in censorship activities. Its cofounder, Sergey Brin, emigrated from the former Soviet Union as a child and experienced firsthand the devastating effects of oppressive government rule there. At two consecutive annual meetings following Google's entrance into China, a bloc of shareholders brought to a vote a resolution ordering management to defy the Chinese government's censorship policies. Although neither motion had extensive popular support, Brin elected to abstain from the vote in protest, rather than actively oppose the measures, as did other members of Google's leadership.[12] Nevertheless, Brin clearly supported CEO Eric Schmidt's profitability goals. Schmidt continued to see enormous potential in the Chinese market as an increasing percentage of its population became active on the Internet with both computers and smartphones. In fact, in 2009 Schmidt believed that Chinese would replace English as the Internet's dominant language within five years.[13]

The Role of Government

Google could trace the source of the hacker attacks to servers within China; however, it could not prove unequivocally that the Chinese government was directly responsible or that it had granted tacit approval to third parties to do so. As a result, Google faced a delicate balance in sharply criticizing the government to achieve its policy objectives despite having limited evidence to back up those claims. If the government truly was not involved, Google risked compromising its business objectives in the country unnecessarily. Within 10 days following the report of the attack, the Chinese Ministry of Industry and Information Technology strongly denied the government's involvement; however, the credibility of this organization was somewhat suspect.[14] Realistically, Google believed that only the government would have the resources to execute such a sophisticated attack.

For many U.S. politicians, Google's response to the hacker attack quickly became a microcosm for various other long-running, larger political and ideological trade disputes between the two nations. In his 2008 Presidential campaign, then-Senator Barack Obama focused extensively on improving diplomatic relations and cooling heated rhetoric between the U.S. and China. As a result, Secretary of State Hillary Rodham Clinton rushed to Google's defense soon after the hacker attacks occurred, accusing the Chinese government of "hijacking technology to crush dissent and deny human rights."[15] The Chinese government bristled at the increased public criticism, however, and sharply criticized Google for escalating the issue. While Google appreciated the support of the U.S. government, it became increasingly concerned that its objectives could be lost amid issues such as the role of the Dalai Lama and arms sales to Taiwan.[16]

While the Chinese government disapproved of Google's focus on Internet freedom, it did have some interest in promoting the company's continued presence in the country. The developing nation had invested significant resources into educating and training a new generation of software and hardware engineers, in the hope that Western companies would look to China in the future as an outsourcing destination, as they had done with India in the past. Furthermore, the Chinese government hoped that new domestic firms could continue to emerge as legitimate competitors to (or collaborators with) the world's leading technology companies, moving forward. Google's continued presence in China could help legitimize the country's technology industry and help promote these goals.[17]

The Internet Search Market in China

The independent eMarketer Inc. estimated that there were approximately 330 to 400 million regular Web users in China as of 2010, a 232% increase over the 2006 level when Google entered the Chinese market. Estimates indicated that the number would likely rise to approximately 840 million users by 2013.[18] At the time of its controversial entry, Google's primary competitor was Baidu.com, which held a 48% market share. Google's chief US rival, Yahoo Inc. attempted to enter China in 1999. After years of struggling with restrictive Chinese policies, Yahoo transferred its operation to the Alibaba Group, a local Internet company, and paid $1B for a 40% stake in the company.[19] Google believed it would fare better, given its dominance of the US market, and because increasing foreign investment in China would encourage greater Internet openness.

The company's objective was to capture existing market share from Baidu and capitalize on the extensive growth of new users in the market. Despite nearly two years of effort, however, Google has been largely unsuccessful in its attempts to compete with Baidu. As the implicit favorite of the Chinese government, Baidu actually increased its market share by early 2010 to 63%, with Google far behind at 33%.[20] A handful of smaller search providers that are not major competitors to either firm comprise the remaining 4%. Google's departure would leave Baidu with an effective monopoly on the Internet search market in China. Many interest groups worried that Google's exit would cause Baidu, under the government's influence, to further restrict Internet content, and slow the process of innovation due to the lack of market competition.[21]

JP Morgan estimated that approximately $600 million, or 2.7% of Google's $22 billion in 2009 total revenue came from its Chinese operations.[22] Citigroup estimates that China will only contribute to 1% of Google's 2010 profits and that withdrawal from the country will have minimal impact in the near future.[23] Although Google's market share is much smaller than Baidu's, market research indicates that Google's customers are among the most desirable for advertisers: the youngest, wealthiest, and highest educated.[24] At the same time, many of these same users have expressed indifference toward Google's potential departure. "If Google leaves China, we'll lose one search engine. But we still have other choices," said 28-year-old Deng Zhiluo of Beijing.[25] Immediately following the hacker attacks, some non-profit organizations promoting Internet freedom expressed some hope that Google might be able to serve the Chinese market without restrictions from a location outside of the country.[26] By February 2010, however, such a solution had not materialized.

New Product Development Initiatives

Approximately 700 Google employees worked in China's Beijing, Guangzhou, Shanghai, and Hong Kong offices as of January 2010.[27] Regardless of whether it elected to discontinue its Google.cn search engine, Google expressed interest in maintaining its research and development center and keeping its advertising sales team active in China. Google hoped to continue to capture advertising contracts for its U.S. and European sites from Chinese countries with interests in exporting to those nations. Most significantly, however, Google needed to preserve its capability to develop and grow its Android operating platform for mobile smartphones that became popular in the United States in 2009. Google had planned a large-scale release of an Android-based phone in China in early 2010; however, it quickly postponed the release in light of the hacker attacks.[28]

Google's withdrawal from China threatened other technology partners as well. Analysts at Morgan Stanley estimated that the delay of the Android launch in China could reduce sales of Motorola's Android-based phone by 25% in the first quarter of 2010, which they estimated could lead to a loss of $160 million in

the same period.[29] Regardless of Google's decision, phone manufacturers such as Motorola and HTC likely would be able to release an Android-based product at some point; however, such phones would not include key functionalities such as Google Maps that could make them less desirable to Chinese consumers. Even before the hacker attacks, Motorola planned to include a Baidu-based search engine in its Android-based phone. Ironically, even the state-owned China Mobile planned to release an Android-based smartphone that could face difficulties if Google chose to withdraw from the country.[30]

Moving Forward

As Google navigated various news outlets through early 2010, the tone of their rhetoric became much less harsh. Google's management made few public statements and, instead, referred interested parties to its initial blog post of January 12. Nevertheless, company leaders expressed more optimism about the possibility of reaching a more effective agreement with the Chinese government regarding security and controls. While the government has made no public concessions, it is possible that its leaders may have adopted a more conciliatory approach in private.[31] Nevertheless, despite Google's aspirations, the two parties did not appear to be close to reaching a quick agreement. Despite its announcement a month earlier, as of February 12, 2010, Google had not yet made any change to its censorship policy.

Speaking at the World Economic Forum annual summit in Davos Switzerland, CEO Eric Schmidt said, "We like what China is doing in terms of growth … we just don't like censorship." Schmidt hopes that the company can be a catalyst for Chinese reform and stated, "We would very much like to stay in China. We would very much like the censorship we oppose to improve in China." At the TED Conference in Long Beach, California two weeks later in mid-February, Google co-founder Sergey Brin expressed his optimism for the situation despite past reservations. "We want to find a way to work within the Chinese system, but without having to censor political results. A lot of people might think I am naive and that might be true."[32]

DISCUSSION QUESTIONS

1. Was Google's 2006 decision to enter the censored Chinese compatible with the "Don't Be Evil" mantra?
2. Has Google's experience in the Chinese market been successful thus far?
3. What obligations did Google have to the human rights of the Chinese public:
   (a) Before its entry into China?
   (b) After its entry into China?
4. What commitments did David Drummond make on January 12, 2010 when he announced that Google would no longer cooperate with the Chinese government's demands for limited censorship?
5. Should Google have brought U.S. government authorities in to the situation as early as they did?
6. If Google's 2006 entry into the Chinese search engine market was a good (or bad) philosophy-based decision, is withdrawal necessarily a bad (or good) decision?
7. If Google's 2006 entry into the Chinese search engine market was a good (or bad) profit-based decision, is withdrawal necessarily a bad (or good) decision?
8. Can Google stay committed to its founders' "Don't Be Evil" philosophy, or should it adopt new motto? How would a change in its Chinese operations impact stakeholders' perceptions of Google?
9. How will a decision about Google's Chinese search engine presence affect its other domestic and foreign business ventures (i.e., phones)?
10. What is the appropriate role of Rachel Whetstone, Google's Vice President of Public Policy and Communications, in the situation moving forward?

This case was prepared by Research Assistants Ryan Hayes, Greg Trezise, and Neil Walther under the direction of James S. O'Rourke, Concurrent Professor of Management, as the basis for class discussion rather than to illustrate either effective or ineffective handling of an administrative situation. Information was gathered from corporate as well as public sources.

Appendix A – Blog Post

http://googleblog.blogspot.com/2010/01/new-approach-to-china.html

The Official Google Blog | Insights from Googlers into our products, technology, and the Google culture.

A new approach to China

1/12/2010 03:00:00 PM

Like many other well-known organizations, we face cyber attacks of varying degrees on a regular basis. In mid-December, we detected a highly sophisticated and targeted attack on our corporate infrastructure originating from China that resulted in the theft of intellectual property from Google. However, it soon became clear that what at first appeared to be solely a security incident--albeit a significant one--was something quite different.

First, this attack was not just on Google. As part of our investigation we have discovered that at least twenty other large companies from a wide range of businesses--including the Internet, finance, technology, media and chemical sectors--have been similarly targeted. We are currently in the process of notifying those companies, and we are also working with the relevant U.S. authorities.

Second, we have evidence to suggest that a primary goal of the attackers was accessing the Gmail accounts of Chinese human rights activists. Based on our investigation to date we believe their attack did not achieve that objective. Only two Gmail accounts appear to have been accessed, and that activity was limited to account information (such as the date the account was created) and subject line, rather than the content of emails themselves.

Third, as part of this investigation but independent of the attack on Google, we have discovered that the accounts of dozens of U.S.-, China- and Europe-based Gmail users who are advocates of human rights in China appear to have been routinely accessed by third parties. These accounts have not been accessed through any security breach at Google, but most likely via phishing scams or malware placed on the users' computers.

We have already used information gained from this attack to make infrastructure and architectural improvements that enhance security for Google and for our users. In terms of individual users, we would advise people to deploy reputable anti-virus and anti-spyware programs on their computers, to install patches for their operating systems and to update their web browsers. Always be cautious when clicking on links appearing in instant messages and emails, or when asked to share personal information like passwords online. You can read more here about our cyber-security recommendations. People wanting to learn more about these kinds of attacks can read this Report to Congress (PDF) by the U.S.-China Economic and Security Review Commission (see p. 163-), as well as a related analysis (PDF) prepared for the Commission, Nart Villeneuve's blog and this presentation on the GhostNet spying incident.

We have taken the unusual step of sharing information about these attacks with a broad audience not just because of the security and human rights implications of what we have unearthed, but also because this information goes to the heart of a much bigger global debate about freedom of speech. In the last two decades, China's economic reform programs and its citizens' entrepreneurial flair have lifted hundreds of millions of Chinese people out of poverty. Indeed, this great nation is at the heart of much economic progress and development in the world today.

We launched Google.cn in January 2006 in the belief that the benefits of increased access to information for people in China and a more open Internet outweighed our discomfort in agreeing to censor some results. At the time we made clear that "we will carefully monitor conditions in China, including new laws and other restrictions on our services. If we determine that we are unable to achieve the objectives outlined we will not hesitate to reconsider our approach to China."

These attacks and the surveillance they have uncovered--combined with the attempts over the past year to further limit free speech on the web--have led us to conclude that we should review the feasibility of our business operations in China. We have decided we are no longer willing to continue censoring our results on Google.cn, and so over the next few weeks we will be discussing with the Chinese government the basis on which we could operate an unfiltered search engine within the law, if at all. We recognize that this may well mean having to shut down Google.cn, and potentially our offices in China.

The decision to review our business operations in China has been incredibly hard, and we know that it will have potentially far-reaching consequences. We want to make clear that this move was driven by our executives in the United States, without the knowledge or involvement of our employees in China who have worked incredibly hard to make Google.cn the success it is today. We are committed to working responsibly to resolve the very difficult issues raised.

Update: Added a link to another referenced report in paragraph 5.

Posted by David Drummond, SVP, Corporate Development and Chief Legal Officer

Appendix B – Stock Price Data

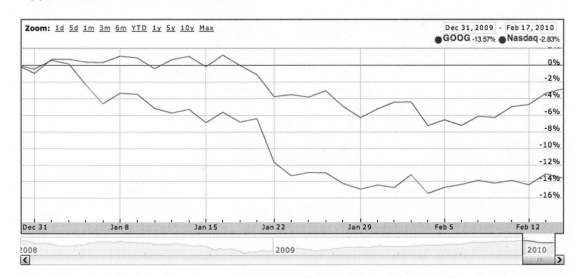

Source: Google Finance

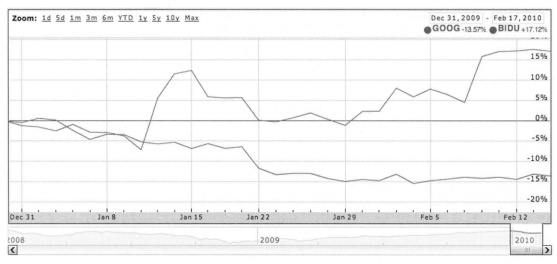

Source: Google Finance

References

1. David Drummond, "The Official Google Blog: A New Approach to China (Online)," (Jan. 12, 2010). http://googleblog.blogspot.com/2010/01/new-approach-to-china.html

2. Jessica E. Vascellaro, Jason Dean and Siobhan Gorman, "Google Warns of China Exit Over Hacking; Cyber Attack Targeted as Many as 34 Firms, Email of Human-Rights. Activists; Investigators Probe Link to Chinese Government," *The Wall Street Journal*, (Jan. 13, 2010), A1. http://online.wsj.com/article/SB126333757451026659.html

3. Michael Liedtke, "Google to End China Censorship After E-mail Breach," S*an Jose Mercury News (AP)* (Jan. 12, 2010). http://www.mercurynews.com/search

4. Google Corporate Information (Online). http://www.google.com/intl/en/corporate/index.html (Feb. 23, 2010)

5. Googling Oppression, *Ottawa Citizen*, Final Edition, (Jan. 28, 2006) B6.

6. Jessica E. Vascellaro, Jason Dean and Siobhan Gorman, "Google Warns of China Exit Over Hacking; Cyber Attack Targeted as Many as 34 Firms, Email of Human-Rights Activists; Investigators Probe Link to Chinese Government," *The Wall Street Journal*, (Jan. 13, 2010), A1. http://online.wsj.com/article/SB126333757451026659.html

7. Ben Worthen, "Private Sector Keeps Mum on Cyber Attacks," *The Wall Street Journal*, (Jan. 19. 2010) B4. http://online.wsj.com/article/SB10001424052748704541004575011113352790040.html

8. Jessica E. Vascellaro, Jason Dean and Siobhan Gorman, "Google Warns of China Exit Over Hacking; Cyber Attack Targeted as Many as 34 Firms, Email of Human-Rights Activists; Investigators Probe Link to Chinese Government," *The Wall Street Journal*, (Jan. 13, 2010) A1. http://online.wsj.com/article/SB126333757451026659.html

9. Ben Worthen, "Google Vs. China: Other Firms Acknowledge Being Target of Attacks," *The Wall Street Journal*, (Jan. 15, 2010) A6.

10. Jessica E. Vascellaro and Jay Solomon, "Corporate News: Yahoo Was Also Targeted in Hacker Attack," *The Wall Street Journal*, (Jan. 16, 2010) B5.

11. Jessica E. Vascellaro and Aaron Beck, "Fallout From Cyber Attack Spreads—Google Investigates China Employees; Rift Emerges

Between Yahoo and Alibaba," *The Wall Street Journal*, (Jan. 19, 2010) B1.

12. Michael Liedtke. "Google's Decision on China Traces Back to Founders," S*an Jose Mercury News (AP)* (Jan. 13, 2010). *http://www.mercurynews.com/search*

13. Ibid.

14. Edward Wong, Jonathan Ansfield and Sharon LaFraniere. "China Paints Google Issue as Non-Political," *The New York Times*, (Jan. 21, 2010) page 10. http://www.nytimes.com/2010/01/21/world/asia/21china.html

15. David M. Dickson, "Google Weighs Leaving China Over Attacks and Censorship," *The Washington Times*, (Jan. 25, 2010) A01. http://www.washingtontimes.com/news/2010/jan/25/google-weighs-leaving-china/

16. Chris Buckley, "China Steps Up Defense of Internet Controls," *Times of Oman (Jan. 26, 2010)*.

17. Joe McDonald and Michael Liedtke. "Google negotiating ways to keep China presence—Censorship fight puts search engine at risk," *The Commercial Appeal*, (Jan. 27, 2010) C4.

18. Michael Liedtke, "Google's Decision on China Traces Back to Founders," S*an Jose Mercury News (AP)* (Jan. 13, 2010). *http://www.mercurynews.com/search*

19. Jessica E. and Aaron Beck Vascellaro, "Fallout From Cyber Attack Spreads—Google Investigates China Employees; Rift Emerges Between Yahoo and Alibaba," *The Wall Street Journal*, (Jan. 19, 2010) B1.

20. David Barboza, "Baidu's Gain from Departure Could be China's Loss," *The New York Times*, (Jan. 14, 2010) B1. http://www.nytimes.com/2010/01/14/technology/companies/14baidu.html

21. Kit Eaton, "Did Google Just Worsen China's Human Rights Situation (Online)," (Jan. 13, 2010) http://www.fastcompany.com/blog/kit-eaton/technomix/google-china-censorship-human-rights

22. Michael Liedtke, "Google to End China Censorship After E-mail Breach," S*an Jose Mercury News (AP)*, (Jan. 12, 2010).

23. Andrew Peaple, "Google Takes Last Stand in China," *The Wall Street Journal*, (Jan. 14, 2010) C10. http://online.wsj.com/article/SB10001424052748704362004575000883673674598.html

24. Sharon LaFraniere, "China at Odds With Future in Internet Fight," *The New York Times*, (Jan. 17, 2010). http://www.nytimes.com/2010/01/17/world/asia/17china.html

25. Anita Chang, "Many Wired Chinese Unfazed at Possible Google Exit," *Associated Press Newswires* (Feb. 1, 2010) , 21:36.

26. Michael Liedtke, "Google to End China Censorship After E-mail Breach," *San Jose Mercury News (AP)* (Jan. 12, 2010). *http://www.mercurynews.com/search*

27. Joe McDonald and Michael Liedtke, "Google Negotiating Ways to Keep Presence in China," *San Jose Mercury News,* (Jan. 25, 2010).

28. Joe McDonald, "China says no limits on Google's Android," *Mail & Guardian Online,* (Jan. 27, 2010). http://www.mg.co.za/article/2010-01-27-china-says-no-limits-on-googles-android

29. Zhu Shenshen, "Phone Sellers Await Google Moves," *Shanghai Daily,* (Feb. 2, 2010). http://www.shanghaidaily.com/sp/article/2010/201002/20100202/article_427583.htm

30. Ibid.

31. Joe McDonald and Michael Liedtke, "Google Negotiating Ways to Keep Presence in China," *San Jose Mercury News*, (Jan. 25, 2010*)*.

32. Kara Swisher, "Google's Brin Says He Is 'Always Optimistic' About China Solution," *The Wall Street Journal: All Things Digital,* (Online). (Feb. 12, 2010). http://kara.allthingsd.com/20100212/googles-brin-says-he-is-always-optimistic-about-china-solution/

Chapter 4

Speaking

Your stomach is in a knot, you're sweating, turning, tossing, anxious. The room seems hot. How can that be? You got up ten minutes ago to turn down the thermostat. A glance at the clock reveals that it's 2:00 A.M. At this rate, you'll never get to sleep.

What's going on here? Is a bad meal keeping you up? Has a lumpy hotel mattress worked its magic on your back once again? Has a case of jet lag thrown your circadian rhythms off? Although any of these maladies is possible, it's much more likely that your sleeplessness and anxiety are caused by the greatest among human fears: The knowledge that you have a speech to give.

CBS News journalist Charles Osgood posed the question this way: "Have you ever been driving at night and come upon a deer frozen in the beam of your headlights? Here's my theory," says Osgood. "The deer thinks the lights are spotlights, and what has it paralyzed is stage fright. It imagines the worst: It has to give a speech."[1]

According to an often-cited study by market researchers, speaking before a group came in first among "worst human fears." Death was number 6, elevators number 12.[2] The reason, according to Osgood, is that we're all afraid of making fools of ourselves. The more important the speech, the more frightened we become.[3]

Those fears are not entirely unreasonable, either. Peter Shea, a plant controller for Imperial Chemical Industries, was asked to make a five-minute presentation on his value to the company. Shea wanted to capture the imagination of the 18 senior executives in the room, so he opened with a metaphor: His factory was like a race car and he wanted to keep it running fast. Bad idea. The executives cut him off after four sentences and asked him to leave the room. "I lost it," he said. "I wilted and died."[4]

He's not alone. Others have tried to be clever with a business presentation and flopped. Dave Jensen is an executive recruiter with Search Masters International, a search firm focused on the biotechnology industry. He was giving a presentation in San Diego to the Society for Industrial Microbiology and wanted to charge up the crowd. So he opened with a joke from a book of speaking tips. Bad idea. "It just died," he recalls. "It wasn't very funny. And industrial microbiologists aren't a funny group to begin with. When you lose something in the first two minutes of a talk, you just can't get it back."[5]

Darryl Gordon, an advertising manager from La Jolla, California, was invited to demonstrate the power of digital technology to 60 advertising agency presidents. So he decided to run his presentation on his laptop computer, complete with colorful slides, bright graphics, and sound. The one thing he hadn't checked before he began was the battery in his computer. Bad idea. When he pushed the power button, nothing happened. It took 15 minutes to load the presentation onto a spare machine. "Every second of that 15 minutes felt like a lifetime," he said. "I'll never forget it."[6]

The advice for people about to give a speech is simple: Preparation will help you overcome fear, whether that fear is reasonable or not. Really thorough preparation can set you up for success, help you achieve the goals you've set for yourself, and get the audience you fear so much to do exactly what you want them to do.

WHY SPEAK?

Often, we don't have a choice. As a manager, you'll find yourself preparing to speak to an audience you'd rather not meet on a topic you'd rather not talk about. Addressing the corporate executive committee on the subject of a quarterly budget shortfall is no one's idea of a good time, but you will do it because it's part of your management responsibility. Many speaking assignments are directive in nature. You do it because you're told to, or you do it because you must. These occasions are not easy, but they are certainly nothing to be afraid of.

Many speaking opportunities, however, are voluntary in nature. You give the talk because you choose to do so. You drop in on a group of employees to share the good news that the company has just landed a big contract they had worked hard to secure. You could have shared that information in an e-mail, but you'd rather see their faces, hear them cheer, and watch "high fives" around the room.

It might be another occasion, explaining to your daughter's elementary school class what you do for a living (come to think of it, that might be tougher than the employee meeting). You might also accept the invitation of a local Kiwanis Club to speak at their weekly luncheon. Each speaking opportunity you accept, each speech you give will increase your self-assurance and reinforce the idea that you are competent, confident, and capable of speaking in public (and speaking well).

Every speaking opportunity, even if it's involuntary, becomes an occasion for you to show what you know and to demonstrate your skills. Joan Finnessy, now vice president for finance at Fisher Scientific International in Pittsburgh, Pennsylvania, found that out firsthand in a prior job:

> A few years ago, I was working as a division controller for a company that held a worldwide conference for its controllers. All the controllers in the company were required to make a presentation at this conference. Our company had recently purchased another organization, but we were not aware that the company was planning to reorganize itself and reduce the number of controllers.
>
> Senior finance managers were, of course, in attendance. We all had our few minutes "in the spotlight." Some controllers did a very good job at displaying strong delivery skills and solid content. Others did not do as well. The assumed purpose of the presentations was to communicate information about our divisions for the benefit of others at the conference.
>
> Approximately a month later, however, those controllers who did not display good presentation skills found themselves in negotiations for severance packages.
>
> While nothing was ever said about a connection between poor presentations and terminations, only those individuals who did not present well were terminated.[7]

Even if you haven't been expressly told that you're being evaluated during a speech, one thing seems clear: You're being evaluated. Two keys to successful evaluation present themselves time and again in public speaking: taking control of the situation and preparing yourself to succeed.

HOW TO PREPARE A SUCCESSFUL MANAGEMENT SPEECH

Here are 15 ideas to prepare you for any speech, large or small, important or impromptu. Focus on these points, one at a time, and you're unlikely ever to develop sweaty palms on the podium again.

- Develop a strategy.
- Get to know your audience.
- Determine your reason for speaking.
- Learn what you can about the occasion for your talk.
- Know what makes people listen.
- Understand the questions listeners bring to any listening situation.
- Recognize common obstacles to successful communication.
- Support your ideas with credible evidence.
- Organize your thoughts.
- Keep your audience interested.
- Select a delivery approach.
- Develop your visual support.
- Rehearse your speech.
- Develop confidence in your message and in yourself.
- Deliver your message.

DEVELOP A STRATEGY

If you have no strategy, you probably shouldn't give a speech. So, what exactly is a strategy for public speaking? Simply put, it's a reason for speaking, a knowledge of who will hear your speech, and some sense of the context in which it will occur.

More than 2,300 years ago, Aristotle told his students they would have a greater chance for success as they prepared to deliver a speech if they would first consider three basic elements: audience, purpose, and occasion.[8]

GET TO KNOW YOUR AUDIENCE

Who are these people? What do you know about them? What do they know about you or your subject? How do they feel about it? Before you go any further in your preparation, perform a simple audience analysis that involves just two steps: (1) knowing something about the people you'll speak to and (2) knowing why people listen.

What should you know about your audience? Here are a few categories of information that might prove useful as you prepare your remarks.

AGE How old are they? Will they be familiar with the concepts you plan to speak about? What's their vocabulary range? What sort of life experiences have they had? Remember, if you're speaking to a group of 18-year-old college freshmen, you should know that they were born just as Bill Clinton came into office. They have no direct memory of the Berlin Wall coming down or Saddam Hussein invading Kuwait. And, just for the record, they have never "rolled down" a car window; they've grown up with bottled water; being "lame" has to do with being dumb or inarticulate, not disabled; and "off the hook" has never had anything to do with a telephone.[9] Make certain your references to events and ideas are both known to them and relevant to their concerns. Similarly, an older audience might have been around for certain events, but references to Napster, Foursquare, or an episode of *Aqua Teen Hunger Force* may well be lost on them.

EDUCATION Knowing the age of the audience will tell you something about how much education they have had but perhaps not as much as you would like to know. Speech content, including central themes and vocabulary, will certainly be influenced by the level and type of education of your audience.

PERSONAL BELIEFS What this group believes may well be more important than how old or how well educated they are. The reason is simple: What you believe defines who you are. Are these folks liberal or conservative? What's their political affiliation? Are they committed to a particular religious or social point of view? Do they have certain biases favoring or opposing such issues as red meat, cigar smoking, gun ownership, or parallel parking?

OCCUPATION What do these people do for a living? Are they students? As such, many of them may not do anything for a living but might hope to have occupations someday soon. Are they managers, professionals, or colleagues of yours? Knowing how people earn their living will tell you something about their educational background and their daily routines, as well as their motivations and interests.

INCOME Knowing how much money an audience makes may be of some help as you formulate your remarks. By knowing their income levels, you will have some idea of what their concerns are: The less they make, the more fundamental and basic are their concerns. Abraham Maslow nicely documented the Hierarchy of Human Needs, noting that it's difficult to sell people on self-actualization if they haven't enough to eat.

SOCIOECONOMIC STATUS This term describes where in the social/economic spectrum your audience is located. It is, of course, a direct function of other factors, such as income, education, occupation, neighborhood, friends, family, and more. Think of this as a single descriptor that explains just how much prestige your audience has in the eyes of others in society.[10]

ETHNIC ORIGIN This information may be worthwhile to know, but its value is limited. Its utility may lie in knowing which issues and positions are of greatest concern to members of a particular ethnic group. The limitation lies in knowing that you cannot reasonably stereotype the views of all members of such a group. Sensitivity to ethnic causes and issues, as well as language, should be sufficient as you prepare a speech.

SEX/GENDER Sex refers to the biological differences between males and females. Gender refers to the social and psychological expectations, roles, and views of men and women. Considerable evidence now indicates that sex/gender may be among the least useful pieces of information you might want to know about your audience. Why? Because study after study has shown no statistically significant difference in the responses of professional men and women to a wide range of stimuli. Clearly, knowing that your audience might be composed exclusively of one sex or another might alter your approach somewhat, but you would be unwise to assume that you would write one speech for men and another for women. Treat them as intelligent humans and you will get the response you're seeking.

KNOWLEDGE OF THE SUBJECT This category of information (along with the next) may be one for which you would be willing to pay in order to know more. A thorough knowledge of what your audience already knows about your speaking subject is useful in a number of ways. First, this would tell you where to begin. Don't speak down to them by explaining fundamentals they already understand. Similarly, don't start above their heads. Begin at a point they're comfortable with and move on from there.

ATTITUDE TOWARD THE SUBJECT Even more important than what they know about your subject is how they feel about it. What I know about the federal tax code is far less relevant than how I feel about it when I listen to a talk about tax reform. My emotions are not irrelevant as I approach a subject. Neither are yours. You certainly should know what the emotional response of your audience will be to the content and direction of your talk. The greater the degree of ego involvement (or emotional response) in a given topic, the narrower will be the range of acceptable positions. In other words, people are much more open-minded on topics they are indifferent about than they are on topics they care about passionately. What you don't know in this regard can hurt you.

DETERMINE YOUR REASON FOR SPEAKING

Knowing why you are speaking is almost as important as knowing to whom you will speak. Aristotle told his pupils that people rise to speak for three basic reasons: to inform, to persuade, or to inspire.[11]

Some authors have argued that all speaking is persuasive: You have chosen this topic as opposed to any other; you've selected this evidence, excluding all else. I'll accept that. However, it's especially important to know whether your audience expects you to take a position regarding the subject of your speech.

Let's say, for example, that your boss is thinking about purchasing a new color copying and printing system for the office and she has asked you to gather information about equipment available for sale or lease. She would also like you to present that information to members of the executive committee. You can find and organize such data easily. But should you take a position regarding which system to lease or buy? Should you become an advocate on behalf of one system or another? If the audience (your boss, in particular) expects information that will help her or the committee make such a decision, your views may be unwelcome. On the other hand, if you have been specifically asked to make your recommendations known, your speech would be seriously incomplete without them.

All public speaking should inform (without telling people what they already know). It should also inspire when appropriate to the occasion. Still, managers—young managers, in particular—should be careful to make certain they know the role that is expected of them as they rise to speak. Too often, young managers get into trouble with senior members of their organization by offering opinions on the topic at hand when the demand for such opinions is not especially brisk.

Keep in mind that you've been asked to speak to this audience for a particular reason: You know something they'd like to know more about. On the other hand, you can't simply step onto the platform and begin dumping data on your audience. Think about your speech in the form of a question: "If these people had money to invest, what would they want to know about this company?" Or, "If they were seeking employment in this industry, what would they want to know about this company?" Then, think of what you know as the answer to that question. You'll need to spend the first few minutes of your speech asking that question—more if the question is not well understood by the audience, less if it is. You're there to share what you know and to help them understand it from their own perspective.[12]

LEARN WHAT YOU CAN ABOUT THE OCCASION

In addition to knowing who will hear your talk and the reasons for which you will speak, it may also be useful for you to know something about the occasion. Many occasions simply call for a polite, informative presentation. Others, however, will ask that you incorporate some theme into your speech that arises from the moment. Certain holidays lend a clear and useful tone to your talk, such as Christmas ("Peace on Earth, goodwill toward all"), Thanksgiving ("We are grateful for what we have been given and mindful of those who have less"), or Independence Day ("The price of freedom is eternal vigilance").

Other occasions call for different themes. Graduations, commencements, or rites-of-passage events call for a focus on the future and the responsibilities and opportunities that lie ahead. As a manager, you know you will have the opportunity to welcome new employees into the organization or, perhaps, the sad task of saying farewell to them. Your audience will pay close attention to your words, to the tone of your speech, and to your approach to the subject. You are in charge and they expect you to say the right thing. It won't always be immediately clear what the right thing to say is, but your audience will know it when they hear it.

KNOW WHAT MAKES PEOPLE LISTEN

Consultant and speech critic Sonya Hamlin says that people listen to speeches for three basic reasons: their own self-interest, who is telling the story, and how it is told.[13] If you know your audience, you will know what their interests are. You can't have much effect on their views about you, at least before you speak, but you certainly can have some influence on how the speech is delivered. In terms of control, two of the three reasons people listen are well within your grasp.

POSITIVE SPEAKING STYLES Numerous studies of public speaking have shown that people react positively to speaking styles they regard as positive. Read the following list of words and see whether you can think of a public speaker whose style fits many, if not most of them.

Warm	Honest
Friendly	Exciting
Interesting	Knowledgeable
Organized	Creative
Confident	Inspiring
Open	Authentic

NEGATIVE SPEAKING STYLES Not surprisingly, audiences react negatively to speakers whose style is the opposite of those words you just read. Consider this list of words and think of your reaction to certain speakers you heard (or were forced to listen to). What was your reaction?

Pompous	Vague
Unenergized	Complex
Patronizing	Unsure

Formal	Irrelevant
Stuffy	Monotonous
Closed	Nervous

The advice in response to these research findings is simple: Make your speaking style positive, embracing all those attributes described as positive. And, do what you can to eliminate or avoid those speaking styles described as negative.[14]

UNDERSTAND THE QUESTIONS LISTENERS BRING TO ANY LISTENING SITUATION

As the members of your audience take a seat in the auditorium or conference room, each has questions about you, your message, the situation, and the consequences of this speech for them. Here are seven basic questions you should be prepared to answer, either directly or in the course of your talk to them.

DO YOU KNOW SOMETHING I NEED TO KNOW? No matter who you are, people will listen if you know something they need to know. Obviously, the more you know about them, the better prepared you will be to answer this question. The more you can do for them, personally and professionally, the more they will reward you with their attention.

CAN I TRUST YOU? Trust is not simply given or demanded. It's earned. You must show your audience that you are trustworthy by providing accurate information, useful points of view, and reliable evidence. It may well prove to be the most important question any audience has about a speaker.

AM I COMFORTABLE WITH YOU? Audiences feel more comfortable with people who are like them, or who have experiences similar to their own, or whose values and beliefs parallel their own. What can you do to show them who you are, to raise their comfort level?

HOW CAN YOU AFFECT ME? More sophisticated audiences think about outcomes. How can you influence my decisions, my career, my life? What can you do for me? If you can show them, in concrete or tangible terms, what you can do for them, they will tune in directly to what you say.

WHAT'S MY EXPERIENCE WITH YOU? If your audience has no experience with you, they may not trust you. Similarly, if they have had an unfortunate experience with you, they may not trust you. What you can do is to put them at ease, assure them that you are here to speak for their benefit.

ARE YOU REASONABLE? The question of how you *affect* people deals with their feelings. This question, on the other hand, deals with *reason* or *logic*. Does the content of your speech reveal that you are a reasonable person? Does your argument make sense? Are you open-minded at all, particularly to viewpoints that may be shared by members of the audience?

WHOM DO YOU REPRESENT? This question is often tricky and difficult, especially when you are speaking on behalf of an organization or other people. If the audience knows that you represent a particular cause or point of view, it may be difficult for them to see you as open-minded, reasonable, or unbiased. Declaring your interests early in a speech may be one way to assure them of your purpose. Acknowledging their interests may be another.[15]

RECOGNIZE COMMON OBSTACLES TO SUCCESSFUL COMMUNICATION

Every manager faces barriers to success as a speaking occasion arises. Some barriers are fairly mundane: Am I available that evening? Can I reschedule another obligation? Will I be able to gather the information I need to answer their questions? Other barriers, though, are more serious and can present great difficulty for a speaker. Obstacles to success appear to fall broadly into the following five categories.

STEREOTYPES Stereotyping ascribes to all members of a group or class those characteristics or behaviors observed in just one or a few. The word was coined by social scientist Walter Lippmann in 1921 when he wrote about why people so readily imagine how other people are, or why they behave as they do, even in the face of ready evidence to the contrary.[16]

The fact is people are comfortable with stereotypes. They help to explain the world around us, don't require much effort to construct, and give us ready categories into which we can insert new experiences, new people, and new ideas. Treating each one as unique or different is much more difficult and requires a great deal more reasoning and work on our part. Stereotypes may be useful as a starting point from which to understand groups and their members, but they can be damaging when we fail to acknowledge differences within those groups or when we fail to admit that not all people act or think in the same ways.

To succeed as a speaker, you must put aside whatever stereotypical views you may hold of your audience and try with an open mind to treat them as individuals. If you are both successful and fortunate, they may do the same for you.

PREJUDICE The word *prejudice,* derived from Latin, means "to judge before knowing." We do it all the time. In fact, it's not necessarily bad. We have little prejudices that serve us well: the food we eat, the stores we shop in, our taste in clothing. Often, as managers, we are forced to judge before we have all the facts. We simply don't have the time or the resources to gather more information. We must act now.

As we speak to others, though, it's best that we acknowledge we are working with incomplete data. It's useful to admit that we don't know as much as we might like or, perhaps, that we simply didn't have time to gather information that might have been easily available to us. We don't want others making judgments about us too quickly. The best way to encourage that sort of careful thinking in others is to lead by example and admit to our prejudicial thinking whenever possible.[17]

FEELINGS Keep your emotions in check. Control your anger. Don't display your contempt for others and their ideas in public. Good advice, but it's all easier said than done. Our emotions and those of our audience can easily get in the way of an objective look at the facts. They can blur the important distinctions that exist between factual data and our affective interpretation of what they mean.

The best advice is simply to acknowledge that we have feelings and then use them to advance our cause. We must also recognize, however, that the people in our audience will have feelings— about us, our subject, and our evidence—and those feelings may be at odds with our own. Acknowledge that, and then move on to make your case as best you can.[18]

LANGUAGE You probably know from a basic communication course that words don't have meaning; people do. People assign meaning to the words they hear and read, and you should know that people with different backgrounds, different education, and different life experiences will assign much different meanings to the words you speak. This will happen during the course of a single speech. Various audience members will hear the same words at precisely the same moment, spoken by the same person, yet they will assign different meaning to those words and leave the speech with different impressions of what the speaker meant.

Work around the difficulties inherent in language by offering multiple examples to illustrate your key points. Often a graph, table, or visual display can convey more meaning than whole paragraphs. Give your audience several ways to understand what you mean: repeat yourself, rephrase your intentions, tell stories, and give examples.[19]

CULTURE No two of us are the same, not only because of genetic individual differences, but also because we each have been enculturated in different ways. We tend to think of culture as an expression of entire nations or civilizations, but it's really much more specific than that. If culture is everything we have, say, think, or do as a people, then folks who live in the country are different in important ways from those who live in the city. Those who live in one state are culturally different from those who live in another.

We have other experiences as we grow up, become educated, find our life's work, and live out our lives. The experiences of one generation are not the same as those of another. Customs, habits, and preferences in food and music are different from one ethnic group to another. If you look carefully, you can also see the cultural differences that exist among various corporations and business organizations. Some show a preference for informality, while others prefer more structure. Various habits from the use of titles to the use of time distinguish us from one another. Your response to the cultural habits and preferences of others is a mark of your respect for them and an acknowledgment that they are not only different but that those differences are important.[20]

COMMUNICATION OBSTACLES CAN PROVOKE NEGATIVE REACTIONS When people feel threatened, intimidated, lost, or confused, a number of things can happen. During a speech, people may stop listening. They may discover how much they don't know, which can lead to frustration, anger, and hostility toward the speaker and the ideas being discussed. If the speaker has made them feel sufficiently dumb, they may withdraw entirely.

Begin with the familiar and move to the unfamiliar. Start with what the audience already knows and then move on to ideas that are a logical extension or outcome of those they are familiar with. Don't intimidate or confuse your audience; do everything you can to make them feel that they are just as smart as you are. The reward, once again, is their attention and their willingness to think about your ideas.

SUPPORT YOUR IDEAS WITH CREDIBLE EVIDENCE

Even though your reputation or the subject you are planning to speak about may keep an audience with you for awhile, you have a much better chance of convincing them of the value in your ideas if you support your talk with current, believable, easy-to-understand evidence.

Where to begin? Well, it's probably best to begin with your own experience, knowledge, and interests. If you are genuinely interested in the ideas you plan to present, your audience will pick up on that and respond accordingly. You will also know where to look for the most interesting, most believable support. If you like a particular subject, chances are good that you know which publications to read, know which experts are cited most often, and know a great deal about the latest developments. The confidence that comes with all of this will not be lost on your audience.

Secondly, consider new ideas, information, and techniques. You and your audience may together know a great deal about the subject of your talk, but they may not know about the latest information. Here is where your interests can help them. Bring them up-to-date on the subject; share the latest innovations and developments.

Next, as you consider how to support your speech, think about the availability and quality of support material. You may have a special interest that you simply can't support because you will not have access to the right information by the time you must speak.

Talk to some experts. Not all credible evidence is found in books, magazines, journals, newspapers, or on the Internet. Some of the most interesting, compelling evidence comes in the form of direct testimony from people who are genuine experts on the subject. Where can you find them? They're all around you. A punch-press operator working on a factory shop floor may not seem especially expert, but if he's been at his job for a number of years, chances are good that he knows a great deal about the machinery, the materials, and the processes involved in the job. Ask him a few questions. You might be surprised how much you can learn if you listen carefully.

Know how much time is available. You can't include large amounts of detail if you have only a few minutes to speak. Because you know you must respect the time limits imposed on your talk, consider carefully how much information, and in what level of detail, you'll be able to include. You'll have some idea of whether you need more or less information once you rehearse the speech. As you begin, of course, it's always better to have too much than too little. You can easily edit a speech later on; it's much tougher to go back and begin your research again as the speaking date approaches.

ORGANIZE YOUR THOUGHTS

Based on a number of public speeches you've already listened to, you know that a well-organized talk is easy to follow, sensible in its patterns, and has a feeling of coherence. In other words, the parts fit together and flow along nicely. At the risk of dwelling on the obvious, you should know that each speech has an introduction, a main body, and a conclusion. If the talk is especially well written and delivered, you may not even be aware of these separate parts, but they each exist to serve a number of important purposes.

YOUR INTRODUCTION A well-crafted introduction will help you to get the audience's attention and allow them to settle in and focus on your topic and your reason for speaking to them. Unless you have a good reason for not doing so (several good reasons do exist), you should disclose your purpose right up front. Telling an audience what your objectives are will build both credibility and interest. When should you withhold your real purpose in speaking to them? The research in this area tells us that you may safely delay stating your intentions if doing so would confuse your audience, if you plan to ask them for money, or if you know the audience initially disagrees with your position.

A good introduction will also recognize and involve the audience in some way. A reference to the occasion or to people who are likely to be known to the audience may help.

HOW SHOULD YOU BEGIN? Many proven methods are available to you as you begin a speech. Consider the following approaches:

> **An anecdote.** Tell a story. People have loved listening to stories since they were kids, waiting for bedtime. Ronald Reagan's success as a speaker, in part, was due to his ability to "spin a yarn." Even those who disagreed with his politics acknowledged the importance storytelling played in his political life.

Humor. People love to laugh, but be careful. Humor is great, unless you're not funny. Foremost among the occasions when you are likely not to be funny is when the joke is on the audience or someone they hold in high regard. Spontaneous, contemporary humor tends to work best. Stay away from set-piece jokes and "amusing" stories you have heard recently.

A prediction. Can you offer, based on the evidence you have gathered, a prediction that is likely to interest, amuse, frighten, or arouse your audience? Make sure you can support your contentions. Also make sure the evidence on which they are based is readily available and easily understood.

A dramatic forecast. This is similar to a prediction but longer-range in nature and usually involving extended or more complex events.

A striking example. This is just one form of an illustration or brief anecdote. If you can make your point by citing an example, do so. Just make sure you are not citing a notable exception to prove your point.

A climactic moment. Interesting speeches often base their central premise on an event or a particular moment in time. Audiences often find such examples powerful and easy to understand.

A suitable quotation. You can find quotes everywhere. Rather than look in the usual sources (*Bartlett's Familiar Quotations, The Oxford Dictionary of Quotations*, or some similar volume or Web site), why not pick up the phone and talk with someone close to the subject? Get a reaction from a friend, family member, participant, or person who knows the events you are trying to describe. Internet search engines will turn up quotes for you by topic or by source. *Conner's Unfamiliar Quotations* is available on the Internet by typing. http://home.comcast.net/~connect_2/quotes.html.[21]

A reference to the occasion. A brief explanation about why you are glad to be there or why the occasion is special might generate interest in your talk while helping to humanize you to the audience.

A provocative question. If you cannot predict the future with any measure of certainty, perhaps you can pose the issue in the form of a rhetorical question. If you are actually hoping for answers from the audience, remember that you must be prepared for any response, including no response at all.

A description. One effective way to introduce a topic to an audience is to describe in vivid, even lurid detail exactly what you mean. Get the audience to visualize objects or events they cannot see. Use imagery and imaginative language to involve them in the process.

A statement of opinion. This method may work, although it is important that you reveal the source of the opinion and that the source be both well known to and respected by the audience. An opinion from someone they hold in low repute will do little to bolster your cause; it may actually damage your own credibility.

Current or recent events. Audiences usually respond well to information that is fresh out of the newspaper or right off the Internet. An anecdote or detail taken from a breaking news story or from a conversation with a well-respected person gives an audience a feeling that they are receiving current, inside information that others don't have or won't receive.

HOW SHOULD YOU STRUCTURE YOUR SPEECH? Regardless of which pattern you select for your speech, research indicates that your strongest or most important point should be placed either first or last for emphasis. Don't bury your best ideas. For an overall pattern of organization, consider one (or more) of the following:

Chronological order. Time is the controlling pattern here. Start at the beginning and move to the end. Start with a particular event and move backward in time. Be consistent, giving your listeners plenty of timing cues so they will stay with you.

Topical organization. When one issue is no more important than any other, you may want to organize them by topics, one after another.

Cause and effect. This pattern is good if you hope to establish a likely outcome from a particular known cause or if you hope to trace the cause of a known event or effect.

Problem solution. This pattern examines the nature of a problem, poses alternative solutions, and then weighs those solutions according to a set of values the speaker provides. Speeches using this pattern usually offer the listener a particular solution favored by the speaker.

Geographic. Compass points are the controlling motif here. The talk moves from east-to-west, north-to-south, or in some other readily identifiable direction.

Spatial. Where compass points are inappropriate, you may wish to organize a talk from a front-to-back, left-to-right, top-to-bottom, inside-to-outside, stem-to-stern, or other non-geographic pattern.

ANY ADVICE BEYOND STRUCTURE? Yes, several bits of forensic wisdom may be helpful to you.

Keep it simple. After a long church service, or so the story goes, President Calvin Coolidge's wife asked him what the sermon had been about. "Sin," said Coolidge. "What did the preacher say about it?" she wanted to know. "He was against it," Coolidge replied.[22]

Your audience is going to come away with one or two of your main ideas—one or two—not ten or fifteen. If you can't express in a sentence or two what you intend to get across, then your speech isn't focused well enough. If you don't have a clear idea of what you want to say, you can be sure your audience won't.

Keep it brief. President Bill Clinton's State of the Union addresses were notoriously long, some of them more than 80 minutes. According to the *Wall Street Journal*, Congress was "begging for mercy" after an hour. "If you can do it in 20 minutes, you have the best shot at the minds of the people present," says Kevin R. Daley, the president and CEO of Communispond, Inc. "Sixty minutes is suicide. You should commit it—or they will."

At New York's Union League Club a few years ago, a prominent steel company chief ended a 90-minute presentation before 400 of his executives and managers by striding from the stage and down the middle aisle. No one applauded until he was halfway out of the room. "They didn't know he was finished," a critic recalls. "They hadn't been attentive enough to recognize that."

Offering some free advice to speakers, former New York Governor Mario Cuomo says, "When you can hear them coughing, stop whatever you are doing and get out." During his unsuccessful reelection effort a few years ago, Mr. Cuomo was losing a crowd at a late-night event but won them back when he suddenly broke into the song, "Boulevard of Broken Dreams."[23] Clever, but he'd have been better off with a shorter speech.

Talk, don't read. Scripted speeches, particularly those written by someone other than the speaker, almost never sound authentic or convincing. I once wrote to a number of *Fortune 500* executives asking for video samples of speeches they had given in the previous year. A friend who is a senior executive at PepsiCo said, "I hope you don't intend to use those speeches as teaching examples. Most chief executives," he said, "are terrible speakers simply because they won't give up the script." They bury their heads in the text, ignore the audience, and hope for the best. It rarely comes off the way they hope it will.

Relax. Comedian Robert Klein, in his routine about the Lamaze method of natural childbirth, points out that the husband's principal role seems to be to remind the wife to breathe.[24] That's good advice, actually. Breathing steadily and naturally will help you focus, relax, and deliver a convincing, entertaining, and interesting speech. If you fall into a pattern of rapid, shallow breathing and can't seem to finish a sentence or a paragraph, just stop for a moment. Breathe deeply, then exhale. Bring your breathing under control once more and then continue.

HOW SHOULD YOU CONCLUDE? Conclusions are among the more important (and most welcome) portions of a public speech. Why are they important? Well, to begin, they represent one more opportunity to put your best evidence or most important ideas before your audience. They represent one last chance to say what you really mean, to reinforce your purpose for speaking, and to ask for their support or compliance.

Be certain you clue people in to the fact that your speech is coming to an end. Don't leave them wondering whether there's more to come. Cue them both verbally and nonverbally to the fact that you're just about done speaking. Above all else, leave them with a clear, simple, unambiguous message. Don't let them leave the room wondering what this speech was all about.

KEEP YOUR AUDIENCE INTERESTED

If you are worried about keeping your audience involved as you speak, think about these ideas as you prepare your remarks.

PROVIDE ORDER, STRUCTURE If your audience is forced to work in order to follow your argument, they may lose interest. Make it easy for people to follow what you are saying: Provide a structure for them to follow, an easy-to-understand structure that will carry them from one point to another.

GIVE THEM SOMETHING THEY CAN USE Even the most charitable and altruistic among us is, from time to time, selfish. We ask ourselves, "What's in it for me?" Often, if we think a speech or a conversation holds nothing of interest for us, we'll excuse ourselves and go do something else. Your audience may be polite enough to stay in their seats, but they may not pay close attention to your talk if they cannot see their self-interests being served. Give them something they can take to the bank, some ideas or information they can put to work as soon as they leave the room.

MAKE IT LOGICAL Not everyone is influenced by logic. Many of us, in fact, can be convinced by an entirely illogical argument that contains just the right type and amount of emotion. For most of your audience members, however, logic and rationality are particularly important considerations. The more logically sound your arguments are, the greater the chance your listeners will understand and adopt your viewpoint.

MAKE IT REASONABLE A number of important psychological studies have shown that adults will not routinely engage in behavior that they regard as unreasonable. Now, what's reasonable to one person may seem totally unreasonable to another, but the vast majority of people will remain consistent in their definitions of what is and is not reasonable. If you know your audience well and can determine how they would characterize "reasonable behavior," you have a much better chance of convincing them to adopt your viewpoint, as long as what you ask of them falls within the limits they establish for themselves.

MAKE IT CLEAR One reason many managerial speeches fail is that the audience simply has no idea what the speaker wants. The main point may be unclear, the supporting evidence may not be well understood, or the conclusion may be incomprehensible. Even when ambiguity may be a deliberate communication goal in some instances, consider this statement from a chief executive officer: "This firm will take all measures afforded by the law to seek the objectives we have outlined." What does that mean? Well, not only is the listener uncertain, so is the speaker. The speaker has deliberately chosen to be ambiguous, perhaps because he doesn't really know what he intends to do. Unless ambiguity is a deliberate part of your communication strategy, do what you can to make your message, your evidence, and your intentions clear to your listeners.

USE WORDS THEY UNDERSTAND Plain English will go a long way toward winning friends and influencing people. Former U.S. Securities and Exchange Commission Chairman Arthur Levitt, in speaking to people who write financial disclosure documents, recently said the following:

> The benefits of plain English abound. Investors will be more likely to understand what they are buying and to make informed judgments about whether they should hold or sell their investments. Brokers and investment advisors can make better recommendations to their clients if they can read and understand these documents quickly and easily.
>
> Companies that communicate successfully with their investors form stronger relationships with them. These companies save the costs of explaining legalese and dealing with confused and sometimes angry investors. Lawyers reviewing plain English documents catch and correct mistakes more easily. Many companies have switched to plain English because it's a good business decision. They see the value of communicating with their investors rather than sending them impenetrable documents. And as we depend more and more on the Internet and electronic delivery of documents, plain English versions will be easier to read electronically than legalese.[25]

Chairman Levitt was speaking specifically about the language used in written documents given to potential investors. But, if plain English works for written financial disclosure documents and has the support of a large and complex government agency like the Securities and Exchange Commission, it will probably work for you and your employer. Frankly, unless you are writing or speaking with the hope that no one will understand you, plain English is the only sensible approach.

KEEP IT MOVING Your audience will be patient with you for just so long. Don't try their patience and good nature by dragging the pace of your speech or dawdling on minor points. If your talk moves along briskly, chances are good that you'll maintain audience interest.

ANSWER THEIR QUESTIONS Every audience has questions. Your task is to determine what they are and to answer them to their complete satisfaction. (See the section earlier in this chapter, entitled "Understand the Questions Listeners Bring to Any Listening Situation.") If you are unwilling to address those questions, your audience may be unwilling to pay attention to or buy into your argument.

ALLAY THEIR FEARS Everyone in your audience is afraid of something. Find out what it is. Some may be afraid that you will be asking things of them that they'll be unwilling to do. Others may be afraid they won't understand the implications of your request. If you cannot deal with their fears, no audience will accept your point of view. Fear is a powerful emotion, and when people feel frightened, they are usually unwilling to take risk or to try something new. Social psychologist Robert Cialdini suggested that persuasive speakers deal with emotions by channeling fear into excitement. Rather than simply asking an audience to calm down or not to worry, he suggests redirecting the energy inherent in audience fear into excitement for the speaker's proposals.[26]

RESPECT THEIR NEEDS Everyone in your audience has specific psychological needs. Each of them gathers and organizes information in slightly different ways, and each of them takes a slightly different approach to decision making. If you understand and respect their needs, they'll reward you. Some may have a need for details—show them the numbers. Others may have a need to understand where this idea fits in the larger scheme of things—show them the big picture. Still others may have a need to know who else has tried or approves of this idea—show them the celebrity endorsements. If I have a specific need—say, a strong desire to know the source of your information—and you don't deal directly with my need, I'm unlikely to adopt your viewpoint or do as you ask.

SELECT A DELIVERY APPROACH

You have four options for delivering a speech. You probably shouldn't depend on more than just one or two of them.

Memorized speeches are delivered verbatim, word-for-word just as the authors wrote them. The problem with memorized speeches is that, unless you are a trained actor, you cannot deliver them with any level of conviction. They sound wooden, contrived, and artificial. Worse yet, you may forget where you are and have to start over. Unless you're doing Shakespeare from the stage, forget about memorized talks.

Manuscripted speeches are far more common among managerial and executive speaking events. The problem with speaking from a manuscript is that it sounds *read.* The impression from the audience is almost always negative: "Why am I here? He could have e-mailed this to me." Reading a fully scripted speech ensures that you will include each key point and resist the temptation to ad lib, but without a TelePrompTer, you lose eye contact with the audience and seem distant or remote to them. Unless you have no other choice, don't work with a verbatim manuscript. If you must, rehearse carefully and try looking up frequently, making regular contact with the audience.

Extemporaneous speeches are, perhaps, the best among your alternatives. These speeches are thoroughly researched, tightly and sensibly organized, well rehearsed, and delivered either without notes or with visual aids to prompt your memory. They are especially convincing to an audience because you make and maintain eye contact, you look at them rather than at a script, and you speak (seemingly) from the heart and not from a set of prepared notes. This is really the effect you are striving for.

Impromptu speeches are delivered without any preparation at all. Someone in charge usually asks you to stand up and "offer a few remarks." This is not the best approach to public speaking, obviously, because you prepared no evidence and have not rehearsed. You may not even have a topic or an idea worth hearing. The good news is that the audience's expectations are low. They will applaud for nearly anything as long as it's brief and not insulting to them.

What do you do when someone asks you to stand up and "offer a few remarks"? Modesty usually dictates that you say little, but protocol usually demands that you say something. Here are a few ideas that may help.

MAINTAIN YOUR POISE Just smile, thank your host for the opportunity to speak, and take advantage of the moment.

DECIDE ON YOUR TOPIC AND APPROACH Speak briefly about something that you understand and that will be of interest to those listening. Select a pattern of organization: past, present, future; advantages, disadvantages; risks, benefits; reasons favoring an idea, reasons opposing. Once you have your pattern, stick to it. Don't get inventive as you go along.

DO NOT APOLOGIZE People know you didn't prepare a speech. Just talk to them.

SUMMARIZE YOUR POINT AND POSITION In one sentence, or two at the most, underscore your key points and reiterate why they are important or worthwhile.

BE SINCERE, HONEST, AND DIRECT Nothing impresses an audience more profoundly than an honest person. Convey the impression that you have nothing to hide and nothing ulterior in your motives for speaking. They will reward you by considering your ideas and applauding your delivery.

DEVELOP YOUR VISUAL SUPPORT

In preparing a speech, managers will often ask if they even need visual support. To answer this question properly, you should consider whether visual support will help to explain, reinforce, or clarify your position or your evidence. If you can't *say* it easily, you may be able to *show* it.

Graphs, charts, tables, and photographs are usually helpful, but not always. If you clutter the screen with unreadable or unnecessary detail, you may confuse your audience. On the other hand, if your graphics are crisp, clear, and uncluttered, your audience may gain insights they might otherwise miss.

Some people are visual-attenders, while others are aural-attenders. Give each group an opportunity to hear and see your key points. One should reinforce the other. Don't show them something you don't plan to talk about. Similarly, if you choose to use visual support, don't talk at length about things you can't show or reinforce visually.[27]

Other research shows that 30–40 percent of people are *visual learners*, and about 20–30 percent are *auditory learners*, but a substantial number of others learn best through physical activity. This group, sometimes referred to as *kinesthetic learners*, is often overlooked in business presentations. The key here, according to Harvard's Nick Morgan, is to get your listeners doing something. "Get them involved early and often," he says, "through role-playing, games, working with models, even creating charts and physical representations of what you want them to learn."[28]

WHEN DO VISUALS WORK BEST? Visual information is often at its best when you are working with new data, complex or technical information, or a new context. Visual aids can help you with numbers, facts, quotes, and lists. They are also frequently good for side-by-side comparisons, emphasizing similarities or differences. Geographical or spatial patterns will also frequently benefit from some form of visual illustration.[29]

Good visuals will . . .

- Be simple in nature
- Explain relationships
- Use color effectively
- Be easy to set up, display, and transport
- Reinforce the spoken message

CAN I SPEAK WITHOUT VISUALS? Yes, of course. That's the basic difference between a narrator and a public speaker. Some speaking situations call for visual aids and you want to make certain you've done your best to illustrate the content of your speech appropriately. Other speaking occasions either don't require visual support or would be better served without it. I can't imagine John F. Kennedy, Martin Luther King, Jr., or Winston Churchill using PowerPoint to illustrate a talk. They were, of course, political orators, not businessmen. But the point is the same: Don't overdo the visual aids.

Some executives have been known to ban PowerPoint entirely from their company presentations. That may seem like an overreaction, but it's easy to understand how those feelings came about. A colleague showed me some written critiques of a presentation he gave to a supervisory development course not long ago, and they weren't encouraging: "Overhead avalanche," read one. "Death by PowerPoint," said another. My advice to him was simple: Use fewer slides, make sure they reinforce only key points, and make certain you do not overdo the basics, including color, transitions, type fonts, motion, or sound effects. It can pretty quickly get to be too much for the audience.

Keep in mind that you may be the best visual of all. "Good leaders understand that *they* are the best visual," says Judith Humphrey, the president of The Humphrey Group, a Toronto-based firm that specializes in executive speech training. "They instinctively know that their message will come through best if the audience looks at them and listens to them—with no distractions."

Her recommendations include stepping out from behind the podium and making yourself a focal point of the speech. "If you are committed and engaged, the audience can see it in your face, in your gestures, in the way you walk, in the way you stand, in the way you hold your head high."[30]

"Here's the key," says Humphrey. "Great speaking is really about great thinking. People can be persuaded by the passion you have for your ideas, but only if they can see you." In a darkened room, she says, the audience is focused on the slides and not on you. "But, if you're willing to step forward, look them in the eyes, and show your conviction for those ideas, people will be more inclined to believe you." You could e-mail those slides to your audience, but when you speak to them in person, you become an important part of the speech itself. "If so much information is processed visually," she adds, "that's all the more reason to make yourself visual."[31]

That may mean inserting an occasional blank slide in your PowerPoint deck, just to create an opportunity for you to explain the main point of your talk or show why it might be particularly important for your audience to act on what you've just told them. It may mean stepping forward, out of the shadows, so that your audience can see you. At a basic level, it means taking advantage of the opportunity to create a personal bond between you and at least a few selected members of the audience who can act as proxies for the rest. The more personal and human that bond, the greater the chance your audience will understand your commitment to the ideas in the speech and respond in the way you hoped they would.

REHEARSE YOUR SPEECH

SHOULD YOU PRACTICE? Absolutely! Don't even consider giving a speech you haven't rehearsed—several times. Why should you practice? Rehearsal will do at least three things for your speech.

First, it will limit timing. You will know after a run-through or two whether you have too much, too little, or just enough to say. Second, rehearsal will improve your transitions. As you practice your speech, you will have an opportunity to identify the rough spots and work on movement from one main point to another and from one part of the speech to another. Finally, rehearsal will polish your delivery and build confidence. When the day to deliver the speech finally comes, you will step to the podium with the knowledge that you know this stuff inside and out. A well-rehearsed speech contains no surprises.

Not convinced? Apple CEO Steve Jobs is considered to be among the most masterful, persuasive speakers in business today. How did he get that way? According to *Fortune* magazine's Adam Lashinsky, "A key Jobs business tool is his mastery of the message. He rehearses over and over every line he and others utter in public about Apple, which authorizes only a small number of executives to speak publicly on a given topic. Key to the Jobs approach is careful consideration of what he and Apple say—and don't say."

SHOULD YOU USE NOTES? The best speakers seem to deliver their speeches extemporaneously, or "from the heart." Such speeches aren't really memorized word-for-word, but rather are thoroughly researched, well rehearsed, and professionally supported. Many extemporaneous speakers will use their visual support to prompt their memories, as if giant notecards had been placed on the wall for them and their audience to see.

If you do choose to use notecards, here are some suggestions. At a minimum, they should be:

- Simple
- Compact
- Easy-to-follow
- Easy-to-handle
- Numbered
- Readable

Having put your notecards together in this way, reconsider once again why you need them. Speech coaches and public speaking experts in the United States are nearly unanimous in their disapproval of notecards. Instead, use your projected visuals to prompt your memory.

DEVELOP CONFIDENCE IN YOUR MESSAGE AND IN YOURSELF

It's one thing to know your material. It's another matter entirely to believe that you can get up on stage and speak with confidence to a group of strangers. Understanding your message and knowing that you have both quality support and a well-organized speech are important to your success, but so is self-confidence.

Rehearsal will help. Simply knowing that you've been through the contents of your speech more than once is reassuring. The knowledge that you personally arranged and rehearsed the talk will give you confidence. And, as you work on your self-assurance, consider this thought: You're the expert. This audience asked for you to speak on this subject because they want to hear what you have to say. They are interested in your expertise and your viewpoint. Chances are good that you know more about your subject than anyone else in the room (though you can never be completely certain). Use your interest, your expertise, and your background to your advantage.

The more confident you are, the more credible you are. If you seem uncertain, the audience may be reluctant to believe you. Just approach this speech as you would any other managerial task, knowing that you have the ability, the intelligence, and the confidence to get it done. The more professional, sincere, and capable you seem, the more likely the audience is to believe you and buy into your message.

DELIVER YOUR MESSAGE

BEFOREHAND Before you begin your talk, make certain you've checked on all of the most important details:

Date, time, and location. Where are you supposed to be? When is your talk scheduled to begin? If you are unfamiliar with the location, do your best to find out all about it in advance.

Room layout. It's never wise to walk into the room with no idea of how it will be organized. Don't depend on others to do it to your satisfaction, either. If you can arrange it, be there in advance and set things up the way you'd like them to be. It's your speech; take charge of the room.

Microphone and acoustics. Try out the sound system in advance. If you will be wearing a wireless mike, find out exactly what you need to do to make it work. Decide in advance whether you are willing to speak without a sound system if it fails or wait for someone to repair it.

Visual aids. Check out the screen, the placement of your projector, and the system you plan to use to support your talk. Make sure it's focused, centered, and visible to the people in the back row.

Stage. Take a moment to find out how to get on and off the stage, where the sound projection limits are, and where the trapdoors, cables, and high-risk footing might be.

Time limits. Double-check with your host on the time limits for your talk and then abide by them. Don't disappoint by saying less than you had promised, and don't disappoint by speaking beyond your allotted time.

Lectern. Find out where you will speak and, if possible, whether you'll be able to move beyond a lectern and walk around the front of the room.

Notes. Don't trust anyone else with your speech. If you're working from a script or detailed notes, hang onto them personally. Review them beforehand, but don't make a point of poring over them just as your host is about to introduce you.

Lights. Determine whether the overhead lighting will wash out a projected image on the screen. Are the lights bright enough for people to see you and whatever handouts you provide for them? Are they dim enough to allow them to see your visual aids?

TRY IT OUT Use the microphone, check out the projector, walk across the stage, examine the effect of your visual aids from the back of the room. See if you can be seen and heard in all parts of the room. Gain some confidence by knowing where you'll be and what it feels like before you actually begin.

AS YOU SPEAK Consider these ideas to keep your audience interested.

• Step up to the lectern, breathe deeply, smile, think positively, and speak.
• Do your best to be one of them (unless it's obvious you are really not).

- Use humor where it may be appropriate (unless you are not funny).
- Share your own experiences, values, background, goals, and fears.
- Focus on current local events and other issues known to the audience.
- Begin by moving from the familiar to the unfamiliar.
- Talk process first, then detail.
- Blueprint the speech: Tell them where this talk is going.
- Visualize and demonstrate.
- Use interim summaries, transitions.
- Give examples.
- Humanize and personalize.
- Tell stories, dramatize your central theme.
- Use yourself, involve them.

As you approach the challenge of becoming a speaking professional (as opposed to a professional speaker), keep in mind a few basic ideas. No one is born with great public speaking ability. Language is the habit of a lifetime, and your ability to speak with conviction and sincerity is a function of your willingness to work at it. If you work, one speech at a time, to improve your skills, chances are quite good that others in a position of influence will notice and reward you for your effort.

For Further Reading

Arredondo, L. *Business Presentations: The McGraw-Hill 36-Hour Course.* New York: McGraw-Hill, 1994.

Booth, D., Shames, D., and Desberg, P. *Own the Room: Business Presentations that Persuade, Engage, and Get Results.* New York: McGraw-Hill, 2009.

Hauer, N. and Martley, E. *The Practical Speech Handbook.* Burr Ridge, IL: Irwin Mirror Press, 1993.

Hindle, T. *Making Presentations.* New York: DK Publications, 1998.

Hofmann, T. M., Womack, D. F., and Shubert, J. *Effective Business Presentations.* Cambridge, MA: Harvard Business School Publications, 1990. HBS Note 9-391-011.

Koegel, T. J. *The Exceptional Presenter: A Proven Formula to Open Up and Own the Room.* Austin, TX: Greenleaf Book Group Press, 2007.

O'Rourke, J. S. *The Truth About Confident Presenting.* Upper Saddle River, NJ: Financial Times Press, 2008.

Endnotes

1. Osgood, C. *Osgood on Speaking.* New York: William Morrow and Company, 1989.

2. Suskind, R. and J. S. Lublin. "Critics Are Succinct: Long Speeches Tend to Get Short Interest," *Wall Street Journal*, January 26, 1995, pp. Al, A8. Reprinted by permission of the *Wall Street Journal*, Copyright © 1995 Dow Jones & Company, Inc. All rights reserved worldwide.

3. Osgood, *Osgood on Speaking.*

4. Matson, E. "Now That We Have Your Complete Attention . . .," *Fast Company*, February 1997, pp. 124–126.

5. Ibid.

6. Ibid.

7. Finnessy, J. M. Personal communication with the author. June 16, 2000.

8. Cooper, L. (ed.) *The Rhetoric of Aristotle.* Upper Saddle River, NJ: Prentice Hall, 1960, pp. 141–142.

9. For a selected list of people, concepts, and ideas that have never been part of young people's lives, see the Beloit College Mindset List at http://www.beloit.edu/mindset/ Accessed August 21, 2011 at 3:24 P.M.

10. National Center for Education Statistics, Institute of Education Sciences, U.S. Department of Education. Retrieved from http://nces.ed.gov/programs/coe/glossary/s.asp on Wednesday, July 9, 2008, at 11:15 A.M.

11. Cooper. *The Rhetoric of Aristotle*, pp. 16–17.

12. For a thorough review of preparation for public speaking, see "The Basic Presentation Checklist," *Harvard Management Communication Letter*, October 2000, pp. 4–5.

13. Hamlin, S. *How to Talk So People Will Listen.* New York: Harper and Row, 1989, p. 23.

14. Ibid., pp. 26–29.

15. Ibid., p. 30.

16. Lippmann, W. *Public Opinion.* New York: The Free Press, 1965, pp. 53–68.

17. For an excellent discussion of the emotional foundations of prejudice and prejudicial thinking, see Bem, D. J. *Beliefs, Attitudes, and Human Affairs.* Belmont, CA: Brooks/Cole Publishing, 1970, pp. 40–44.

18. For a thorough review of current research on human emotion and the management of human feelings, see Goleman, D. *Emotional Intelligence: Why It Can Matter More Than IQ.* New York: Bantam Books, 1995.

19. Borden, G. A. *An Introduction to Human Communication Theory.* Dubuque, IA: William C. Brown, 1971, pp. 81–87.

20. Hoecklin, L. Managing Cultural Differences: Strategies for Competitive Advantage.

Reading, MA: Addison-Wesley, 1995, pp. 23–49.

21. Bilodeaux, J. "Use the Net to Catch Quotes," *The Toastmaster* 64, no. 5 (May 1998): 15.

22. Osgood. *Osgood on Speaking.*

23. Suskind and Lublin. "Critics Are Succinct."

24. Osgood. *Osgood on Speaking.*

25. Smith, N. (ed.). *A Plain English Handbook: How to Create Clear SEC Disclosure Documents.* Office of Investor Education and Assistance, U.S. Securities and Exchange Commission, August 1998, p. 4.

26. Cialdini, R. B. *Influence: The Psychology of Persuasion*, rev. ed. New York: Quill/William Morrow, 1993.

27. Ingersoll, G. M. *The Effects of Presentation Modalities and Modality Preferences on Learning and Recall.* Doctoral dissertation, Pennsylvania State University. Ann Arbor, MI: University Microfilms, 1970. No. 71-16615.

28. Morgan, N. "Presentations That Appeal to All Your Listeners," *Harvard Management Communication Letter*, June 2000, pp. 4–5.

29. For a thorough and useful discussion of visual support for business presentations, see Bailey, E. P. *A Practical Guide for Business Speaking.* New York: Oxford University Press, 1992, pp. 36–78, 111–125.

30. Humphrey, J. Telephone interview with the author, July 29, 2002.

31. Ibid. p. 98.

32. Lashinsky, A. *Fortune*, November 23, 2009, p. 98

CASE STUDY 4-1

A Last Minute Change at Old Dominion Trust

"It was a quarter to four on Friday afternoon," said Rob Leonard. "I was just closing out my accounts and trying to clear up a few more issues before the end of the business day. Then along came my division vice president. Since my desk is in the center of the mortgage banking division, I could tell long before he got to me that I was the one he was looking for. And, frankly, the folder he dropped on my desk was the last thing in the world I expected to see."

Rob Leonard is a 26-year-old assistant broker in the mortgage banking division of Old Dominion Trust, a relatively small interstate bank located in the mid-Atlantic region. Rob's branch has regional responsibility for home mortgages in Northern Virginia and the Washington, DC, area. Although he had joined Old Dominion Trust following graduation four years earlier, he was still among the more junior people in his branch.

"The boss came directly to my desk and asked if I had a minute. Of course I have a minute," said Leonard, "Who hasn't got a minute for the Branch V.P.?" Brian Lorigan was senior vice president,

Mortgage Banking for Old Dominion, and executive vice president for the Annandale branch office. He was not only Leonard's supervisor but his mentor and partner in several important projects.

"Mr. Lorigan and I had been working on a new, federally funded mortgage program that would permit low-to-middle-income, first-time home buyers to obtain financing at very low rates. It was an important project that would require both thorough explanation to the community and careful screening of each of the applicants." Leonard went on to explain that the program has been more than six months in development and would require the cooperation of state and local officials if it were to work. It was an impressive attempt, Leonard thought, on the bank's part to provide mortgage financing to people who would otherwise never qualify for a home loan.

"I thought he would want to review the screening procedures we'd been working on, or perhaps talk about the software I planned to use to help set up the program," said Leonard. "What he had in mind frightened me a lot more. He said that Dick Gidley, his principal assistant, had been scheduled to speak to a Capitol Hill neighborhood group about the federally assisted home loan program." Unfortunately, Dick was in Philadelphia and had just been 'bumped' from his return flight to Washington.

"Mr. Lorigan asked if I would fill in for Dick at the neighborhood group meeting this evening and speak about the new loan program. 'The details are all in this package,' he said. I got a phone number, a set of street directions to a renovated fire station on Rhode Island Avenue, and the name of the woman who would introduce me. The rest of the information would have to come from documents I had prepared for the bank and for the select committee that had prepared the legislation." Leonard was philosophical about the request. "It wasn't that I minded canceling dinner plans I had for that evening. It was just that I wasn't sure I was ready to stand up in public and explain a bank loan program that I wasn't in charge of. After Mr. Lorigan shook my hand and said thanks, I looked at my watch. It was five minutes to four, and this thing in Washington was scheduled for seven o'clock."

DISCUSSION QUESTIONS

1. Assuming you are in Rob Leonard's position, what would you do? Would it be a good idea to tell Mr. Lorigan you're just not ready (or willing) to give that speech?
2. What would you want to know about the audience that you don't already know? Where could you find that information?
3. What would you want to know about the occasion and speaking situation that you don't already know?
4. Is there anything you think you should know about the physical layout of the room or the arrangements in the fire station that you'll be speaking in?
5. How would you go about preparing your notes for this speech?
6. What else would you bring with you for this event? Do you have time to get visual aids or flip charts made? Is that a good idea?
7. How should you dress for this occasion?
8. What do you think your principal message should be for these people?

This case was prepared by James S. O'Rourke, Concurrent Professor of Management, as the basis for class discussion rather than to illustrate either effective or ineffective handling of an administrative situation.

CASE STUDY 4-2

Preparing to Speak at Staples, Inc.

As Elizabeth Allen pulled into her parking spot at Staples, Inc., headquarters in Framingham, Massachusetts, she knew the next three days would be a challenge. "This is a huge opportunity," she thought to herself. It would be visible, risky, and filled with snares. "On the other hand," she thought, "this really should be fun." Ms. Allen was thinking about a speech manuscript she had been preparing for her chairman and chief executive officer. Less than 72 hours from now, he would give one of the most important talks in his professional career across the country in California.

"Technology and the Internet are clearly the most powerful communication media available to any company today," says Elizabeth Allen. "But on some occasions, there is just no substitute for face-to-face interaction and a personal statement from a senior official of the company." The statement Allen envisioned would be powerful, important to shareholders and the community, and seen by literally millions of people on television, both as it happened and later on news programs nationwide.

Elizabeth Heller Allen was vice president for corporate communication at Staples, Inc., and had primary responsibility—among her many other duties—for preparing members of the Staples senior team for press conferences, speeches, and public appearances. The ten most senior people in the company were known as the Point Team, and Allen's corporate communication staff worked very hard to prepare them for a wide range of public appearances, including the one her CEO would make the day after tomorrow. Staples, Inc., is the number-two office supply superstore company in the United States, with market capitalization of $13.5 billion and annual revenues of $8.3 billion. They sell office products, furniture, computers, and photocopying services at more than 1,000 stores, primarily in the United States and Canada but also in Germany, the United Kingdom, the Netherlands, and Portugal. With more than 21,500 employees, the company sells some 8,000 different office products to small and medium-sized businesses through their retail stores, a catalogue, and an e-commerce site.

"Speaking opportunities are important at any business," says Allen, "but they are especially important at a company like Staples because the current CEO, Thomas G. Stemberg, is the company founder. Like Herb Kelleher at Southwest Airlines, Bill Gates at Microsoft, or Jim Barksdale at Netscape, the founder of a company has special visibility in the marketplace, and it's very important for shareholders, employees, and other stakeholders that we take best advantage of that."

According to Allen, speaking styles and preparation for speeches will vary greatly. "Some members of the Point Team will ask that every single word of a speech be written out in advance. They rehearse, they work from a manuscript, and—if one were available—they would ask for a TelePrompTer. Others will say, 'Send me an outline 24 hours in advance. I'll wing it.'" For each of her senior executives, Allen found [different challenges] as they prepared for a public speech. The more important the venue or the audience, the more important the text, rehearsal, and detailed preparation become. "If a lot of people are going to see and hear this speech—even fragments of it on videotape—it's all the more important that we spend time and energy in getting the speaker ready." Frequently, that means a complete manuscript, even though most executives would prefer to speak extemporaneously.

"Most of the Point Team would rather have a few key points, some supporting detail, and a couple of closing thoughts to work from," says Allen. "These are important people—supremely confident—who got to their current positions by being comfortable in front of a crowd." Her preference is to prepare such people with information about who will be in the room, the occasion on which they'll be speaking, and the business objective of the talk itself. Beyond that, delivery and rehearsal are up to the individual speaker.

"There is a value to a complete manuscript, though," she says. "We not only like to know what someone said to a particular audience on a given occasion, but my staff can get substantially greater mileage out of a speech if I can share a copy of the script with the press." Advance copies of a speech may induce a journalist to attend the talk, or inspire a reporter who couldn't attend to include direct quotes in a news story. Either way, the company and the message in the executive's speech receive greater exposure.

That morning, Elizabeth Allen had just such an opportunity as her CEO prepared for a speech on the West Coast. "Staples had an agreement to purchase the naming rights for a new basketball and hockey arena in Los Angeles," she said. "A press conference was scheduled to reveal the identity of the naming-rights company." According to Allen, the event was preceded by considerable advance media coverage and speculation throughout the L.A. basin. "Many people thought the name would be a local, California company. And, of course, we did nothing to discourage the attention given to the event." It was a closely guarded secret. And Staples was about to pay $100 million for the privilege—the highest sum ever paid for the right to name an athletic venue.

"I know several things about this event," said Allen. "First, I know that it's being covered not by the business press, but the sports press. From the news media's point of view, this isn't a business story. It's a sports story." She also knew who would be in the room. "Dave Taylor of the Los Angeles Kings and Jerry West of the LA Lakers—both general managers—will be there." Civic officials, investors, reporters, and many others would be watching and listening. "This five-minute speech of Tom Stemberg's will have huge marquee value," said Allen. Elizabeth Allen also knew that this was more than just another corporate investment in professional sports. "This is a Boston company putting its name on a Los Angeles landmark. I know there are cultural factors at work here, and political factors as well as business factors." For Allen, this speech—brief as it would be—had to be flawless. "No faux pas," she said. "This has got to be perfect."

DISCUSSION QUESTIONS

1. If you were assisting Ms. Allen with this event, what would you want to know that you don't already know?
2. As she drafts Mr. Stemberg's remarks, what issues should Ms. Allen pay especially careful attention to?
3. Can you think of any references, issues, or remarks that Ms. Allen might want her CEO to avoid?
4. What sort of pre-event information would you want to brief Mr. Stemberg about? What sort of detail does he need about the event, the audience, and the occasion?
5. Others will certainly speak on this occasion. Would it be helpful for Ms. Allen to know who they are? Would it be important for her to know what they intend to say? Why? How can she go about obtaining that information?

This case was prepared by James S. O'Rourke, Concurrent Professor of Management, as the basis for class discussion rather than to illustrate either effective or ineffective handling of an administrative situation.

Chapter 5

Writing

Business writing isn't simply a way to move information from one office to another. Nor is it just another storage mechanism for business decisions. Business writing, at its best and at its worst, is an expression of the values and beliefs of an organization. A peek inside the file drawers and out-baskets of any business will reveal a great deal about what's important to an organization, as well as how the people in that organization think about their work, their customers and clients, and themselves.

Business writing is important because, as you saw in Chapter 1, the most important projects and decisions in the life of a business end up in writing. Writing is a way of thinking about business, a way of organizing. It provides analysis of and justification for our best ideas. It also provides documentation and discipline for an organization.

Writing is also a career sifter. Managers do most of their own writing and editing, relying on the assistance and advice of others only on occasion. If you can't write at a minimally effective level, others in positions of influence will notice and you'll be looking for work elsewhere. At the very least, an inability to express yourself effectively on paper can stop a career dead in its tracks.

Why is most business writing so bad and what makes it that way? Well, most business writing isn't terrible—some is, of course—but much of it is just badly organized, passive, not parallel in structure, littered with jargon and obscure terminology. Some business writers pay little attention to the conventions of spelling and punctuation. Others just keep writing until they've told their readers *everything* they know about the subject. Sentences run on and paragraphs take up entire pages.

Most business writing isn't bad for just one reason. It's a result of a series of reasons, and heading the list is this: Writers simply are not writing for the benefit of their readers. They don't craft a memo, a proposal, a report, or a letter with the needs and interests of their readers in mind. If they did, we would see fewer documents written like this mutual fund prospectus paragraph:

> Maturity and duration management decisions are made in the context of an intermediate maturity orientation. The maturity structure of the portfolio is adjusted in the anticipation of cyclical interest rate changes. Such adjustments are not made in an effort to capture short-term, day-to-day movements in the market, but instead are implemented in anticipation of longer term, secular shifts in the levels of interest rates (i.e., shifts transcending and/or not inherent to the business cycle). Adjustments made to shorten portfolio maturity and duration are made to limit capital losses during periods when interest rates are expected to rise. Conversely, adjustments made to lengthen maturity for the portfolio's maturity and duration

strategy lie in analysis of the U.S. and global economies, focusing on levels of real interest rates, monetary and fiscal policy actions, and cyclical indicators.[1]

Ordinary human beings who read that paragraph will recognize that it's grammatically correct and syntactically sound. Each sentence has a verb. The capital letters are used correctly. For the most part, people will recognize the words, but when words are put together like that, we read and feel confused. What can this mean? What's the writer trying to say here?

When Berkshire Hathaway Chairman Warren Buffett saw that paragraph, he got out a yellow legal pad, a ballpoint pen, and drafted another version:

> We will try to profit by correctly predicting future interest rates. When we have no strong opinion, we will generally hold intermediate-term bonds. But when we expect a major and sustained increase in rates, we will concentrate on short-term issues. And, conversely, if we expect a major shift to lower rates, we will buy long bonds. We will focus on the big picture and won't make moves based on short-term considerations.[2]

The first paragraph was written by a mutual fund manager with one of several ideas in mind. He may have been insecure and eager to show his boss and the customers how many big words and important business phrases he knew. Or he may have been deliberately trying to disguise the mutual fund's lack of an investment strategy. If the prospectus isn't entirely clear, how can the fund manager be held accountable for failing to live up to the aims of his strategy?

I have another suggestion about that paragraph you just read: The fund manager who wrote it was probably modeling his writing after thousands of other mutual fund prospectus documents he's seen in his career. He's following a well-trodden path to obscurity, hoping his writing will look just like that of so many other successful managers.

Let's give him the benefit of the doubt and assume that his intentions were good but his mentors were not. Times are changing, though, and that fund manager will never again be able to write dense, impenetrable prose and get away with it. Former U.S. Securities and Exchange Commission Chairman Arthur Levitt recently struck a blow in favor of plain English:

> Whether you work at a company, a law firm, or the U.S. Securities and Exchange Commission, the shift to plain English requires a new style of thinking and writing. We must question whether the documents we are used to writing highlight the important information investors need to make informed decisions. The legalese and jargon of the past must give way to everyday words that communicate complex information clearly.[3]

Warren Buffett responded by saying:

> Chairman Levitt's whole drive to encourage "plain English" . . . [is] good news for me. For more than forty years, I've studied the documents that public companies file. Too often, I've been unable to decipher just what is being said or, worse yet, had to conclude that nothing was being said.
>
> One unoriginal but useful tip: write with a specific person in mind. When writing Berkshire Hathaway's annual report, I pretend that I'm writing to my sisters. I have no trouble picturing them: though highly intelligent, they are not experts in accounting or finance. They will understand plain English but jargon may puzzle them. My goal is simply to give them the information I would wish them to supply me if our positions were reversed. To succeed, I don't need to be Shakespeare; I must, though, have a sincere desire to inform. No sisters to write to? Borrow mine: Just begin with "Dear Doris and Bertie."[4]

Workplace Writing Is a "Threshold Skill"

A recent survey of 120 American corporations employing nearly 8 million people concludes that in today's workplace writing is a "threshold skill" for hiring and promotion among salaried (i.e., professional) employees. Survey results indicate that writing is a ticket to professional opportunity, while poorly written job applications are a figurative kiss of death.

People who cannot write and communicate clearly, the study found, will not be hired and are unlikely to last long enough to be considered for promotion. The National Commission on Writing, a panel established by the College Board, concluded that two-thirds of salaried employees in large American companies have some writing responsibility, and 80 percent or more of the companies in the service and finance, insurance, and real estate sectors now assess writing during hiring.

A similar dynamic is at work during promotions. Half of all companies take writing into account when making promotion decisions. "You can't move up without writing skills," said one respondent.

More than half of all responding companies report that they "frequently" or "almost always" produce technical reports (59%), formal reports (62%), and memos and correspondence (70%). Communication through e-mail and PowerPoint presentations is almost universal. "Because of e-mail," said one executive, "more employees have to write more often. Also a lot more has to be documented."

The study also found that more than 40 percent of firms offer or require training for salaried employees with writing deficiencies, and it appears that such training now costs American companies as much as $3.1 billion annually.

Source: "Writing: A Ticket to Work...Or a Ticket Out," Report of The National Commission on Writing, September 2004. Available in PDF form at www.writingcommission.org/report.html.

AN INTRODUCTION TO GOOD BUSINESS WRITING

Good business writing is simple, clear, and concise. It's virtually "transparent." By not calling attention to itself, good writing helps the reader focus on the idea you are trying to communicate rather than on the words that describe it.

Good writing, in business and elsewhere, is a pleasure to read. Ideas become clear, the writer's intentions are undisguised, and the evidence used to support those ideas is readily understandable.

No one I know thinks writing is easy. Good writing—that is, writing with power, grace, dignity, and impact—takes time, careful thought, and revision. Such writing is often the product of many years of training and practice. And, to be sure, the language we bring to the task is the product of a lifetime of use. Even though writing seems like hard work to many of us, I know for sure that you can learn to do it well.

No teacher of writing can lay much claim to original thinking on this subject. Instead, we each have built on the good ideas given to us by those who have written, taught, and observed organizational and business writing before us. If you can put some of this advice to work in your own writing, your reward will be the approval of your readers.

FIFTEEN WAYS TO BECOME A BETTER BUSINESS WRITER

Here are 15 guidelines for better writing—a supplement, if you will, to the rules of grammar, syntax, and punctuation you learned in school. These were crafted by writing consultant Jean Paul Plumez and will help you bring simplicity and clarity to your writing and power and vitality to your ideas.[5]

- **Keep in mind that your reader doesn't have much time.** Memos often travel to senior managers who have tight schedules and much to read. Your memo must be clear on first reading. The shorter it is, the better chance it has of being read and considered.

- **Know where you are going before you start writing.** Start with a list of the important points you want to cover, then put them into an outline. If you are composing a memo, write the Overview section first. It should contain your purpose for writing and the keys to understanding the rest of what follows. Then, write the most important paragraphs before you get to details and supplementary material.

- **Don't make any spelling or grammatical errors.** Readers who find bad grammar and misspelled words will perceive the writer to be careless or uneducated. They will not put much stock in the writer's ideas.

- **Be responsive to the needs of the reader.** Don't be accused of missing the point. Before you write, find out what the reader expects, wants, and needs. If you must deviate from these guidelines, let the reader know why early in the memo.

- **Be clear and specific.** Use simple, down-to-earth words. Avoid needless words and wordy expressions. Avoid vague modifiers like *very* and *slightly*. Simple words and expressions are clearer and easier to understand. They show confidence and add power to your ideas.

- **Try to use the present tense.** Be careful not to slip from the present to the past tense and back again. Select one tense and stick to it. Use the present tense when possible to add immediacy to your writing.

- **Make your writing vigorous and direct.** Use active sentences and avoid the passive voice. Be more positive and definite by limiting the use of the word "not." Avoid long strings of modifiers.

- **Use short sentences and paragraphs.** Send telegrams, not essays! Vary length to avoid monotonous-looking pages, but remember that short sentences and paragraphs are more inviting and more likely to get read.

- **Use personal pronouns.** Don't hesitate to use *I*, *we*, and *you*, even in formal writing. The institutional references can be cold and sterile, while personal pronouns make your writing warm, inviting, and more natural.

- **Avoid clichés and jargon.** Tired, hackneyed words and expressions make your writing appear superficial. Find your own words and use them.

- **Separate facts from opinions.** The reader should *never* be in doubt as to what is fact and what is opinion. Determine what you *know* and what you *think* before you start writing. Be consistent about facts and opinions throughout the memo.

- **Use numbers with restraint.** A paragraph filled with numbers is difficult to read, and difficult to write. Use a few numbers selectively to make your point. Put the rest in tables and exhibits.

- **Write the way you talk.** Avoid pompous, bureaucratic, and legalistic words and expressions. Use informal, personal human language. Write to others the way you would talk to them. Read your memo out loud—if you wouldn't talk that way, change it.

- **Never be content with your first effort.** Revising and editing are critical to good writing. Putting some time between writing and editing will help you be more objective. Revise your memo with the intent to simplify, clarify, and trim excess words.

- **Make it perfect!** Seek out and eliminate factual errors, typos, misspellings, bad grammar, and incorrect punctuation. Remember, if one detail in your memo is recognized as incorrect, your entire line of thinking may be suspect.

WRITING A BUSINESS MEMO

Memos are, for the most part, *internal* documents. They are used to pass information, ideas, and recommendations to other people in the same organization. They have the advantage of not requiring an inside address, a salutation line, and perfunctory opening lines that greet the reader, inquiring about matters unrelated to the subject of the document.

Good memos get to the point, focus on just one issue, and support the writer's central ideas with coherent, relevant, convincing evidence.

The best of business memos are concise, written in plain English, and sensibly organized. That's true of business letters as well, but it's especially true of memos. They say what they must without using any more words than necessary. They present your ideas at something less than the upper reaches of bureaucratic formality, and they are organized with headings, subheadings, and parallel structure so that they are easy to read, easy to follow, and easy to understand.

Your ability to write a crisp, clean, no-nonsense memo will mark you as someone who contributes to the organization—someone worth keeping, watching, and promoting. Will a good memo get you promoted? That's unlikely. A series of bad memos—poorly crafted, disorganized, and densely expressed—however, may stop your career in its tracks. Writing, after all, is a career sifter. Good writers move up; bad writers get left behind.

THE SIX COMMUNICATION STRATEGIES

Before you begin writing, begin thinking. Give some careful thought to your reader, to your objectives, and to the strategy you will employ to achieve your objectives. The content and pattern of organization will follow from those. When you are sure you know what you want to achieve and what you want your reader to learn from your writing, you will need a communication strategy.

Here are six basic strategies, three designed to convey information and three designed to promote action.[6]

Information Strategies	Action Strategies
To confirm agreement	To request assistance
To provide facts	To give direction
To provide a point of view	To seek agreement

WRITING AN OVERVIEW PARAGRAPH

The opening or Overview paragraph of any memo should reveal a communication strategy for the entire document. By writing it first, you will identify your purpose and main ideas. This approach will give you perspective and direction that will guide the development of the memo, letter, or report.

Your reader will benefit as well. That Overview paragraph provides perspective on what's coming and what's important, much like the topic sentence of a well-constructed paragraph.

An Overview paragraph should simply and clearly tell the reader:

- **Purpose:** Why are you writing the memo?
- **Main idea:** What do you want to tell the reader? Or what do you want the reader to do?
- **Opinion:** What is your point of view on the subject?

In addition, the Overview should begin to establish the tone of the document for your reader. As the first paragraph a reader will see and, without question, one of the most important elements of a memo, the Overview should display a number of important basic qualities.[7] It should:

- **Be clear and simple.** Remember that the reader is trying to get oriented. The Overview provides perspective on what is coming. Keep the words simple and the sentences short. Think about your audience and what the various readers know. Anyone who receives the document should be able to understand it.
- **Be brief.** The Overview paragraph acts as an executive summary of the memo that follows. This summary is not the entire memo packed into a paragraph or two. Stick to the main ideas.
- **Deal with the what, not with the how.** *What* is the recommended course of action in a proposal or the main conclusion in an information memo. Avoid *how*, or implementation, at the early point in your memo. Readers have trouble dealing with implementation until they understand and agree with what should be done.
- **Include and identify the writer's point of view.** Go beyond the facts—interpret, conclude, and recommend. Then take responsibility up front for what you believe by stating your point of view in the Overview. This helps convey confidence and a sense of leadership.
- **Reflect the needs of the reader.** The Overview is geared to the knowledge and skill level of the reader. It takes into account what the reader needs and wants to know.
- **Be thorough and complete.** Although brief, the Overview should be able to stand on its own. It does not tell the reader everything in the memo; it contains key highlights. The best test of a good Overview: Can the reader say yes without reading further?

SAMPLE OVERVIEWS

Here are several Overview paragraphs that will help the reader to better understand what the writer is saying and what the writer wants from the reader. Pay careful attention to the length and structure of these Overviews. Note how compact and cogent each of them is.

1. This memo recommends the establishment of an on-site exercise and health club facility in the corporate headquarters complex. An initial investment of $475K in remodeling an existing, little-used storage facility will provide significant health insurance claim savings and will result in measurably greater employee productivity and morale.
2. This memo provides a summary of the GrillMaster II's market performance in each sales region for the first quarter of FY2011.
3. This memo *urgently* recommends a product design review for the DiceOmatic Plus. Warranty claims, field reports, and customer complaints about this product indicate a possible defect in the blade shield. Failure to review the design may result in significant liability exposure for the firm and may irreparably damage the brand reputation.
4. This memo recommends a 30-day continuation of the Pria Classic customer rebate program in Region 5. Initial response to the rebate coupons at retail level has exceeded market projections by 135 percent.
5. This memo recommends the addition of a Level-3 administrative assistant in the Information Technology Division. Launch of the company's new intranet and our new wireless PDA system have increased technician workloads and created a 25-day backlog in customer assistance requests. An additional administrative assistant would help solve this and other related problems.

6. This memo provides guidance and instructions for complying with the company's new Conflict-of-Interest Disclosure policy. Step-by-step instructions and frequently asked questions are included, along with contact information if you encounter difficulty.

THE INFORMATIVE MEMO

Interoffice memos have two purposes: to inform or to persuade. If your purpose is to document, record, or inform, here are some things to think about as you write.

- **Make your reasons for writing clear to the readers.** Explain, right up front, in the Overview paragraph why you're writing. Use boldface headings and subheadings to label and describe the information you're providing.
- **Write about just one subject.** Don't confuse your readers with information about more than one subject in a memo. If you must write about several subjects, either give your memo a more general, abstract subject line or (preferably) write several memos.
- **Begin with the big picture first, then move to the details.** Don't simply download data on your readers and expect them to figure out what it means. Show your readers where this information fits into the big picture and then organize it in a way that makes sense to them.
- **Provide just as much detail as you think your reader will need.** The problem, of course, is that some readers want all sorts of detail. Others just want the bottom line or main point. There's nothing wrong with either of those groups; that's just the way they are. In order to satisfy the needs of as many readers as possible, you should provide the most important information first, explaining what it is, what it means, and why it's important. You might then direct those who want additional detail to a paper appendix attached to your memo or, perhaps, to an intranet or Web site where they can read or download what they want.
- **Group similar information together.** Read through your first draft and look for similar bits of information that appear in multiple paragraphs. Eliminate redundant sentences or paragraphs in which you've become repetitious.
- **Provide a point-of-contact for your readers.** If the people reading your memo have questions or concerns about the information you have provided, whom should they contact? Helpful informative memos will include not only a return address but telephone numbers, e-mail addresses, and (if you're willing) the name of a person who can assist with questions.
- **Avoid gratuitous use of the first-person singular.** Address the reader as "you" or write in the third person. By doing so, you will reduce the temptation to include your own opinion with such phrases as "I think . . . ," "In my opinion . . . ," or "It is clear to me that. . . ." If you must write in the first person, use the plural form. It should be clear to the readers that we're all in this together.
- **Stick to the facts.** Distinguish clearly between fact and opinion and omit those things about which you are not sure. If you must include assumptions, please label them as such: "Assuming that interest rates do not rise by more than half a basis point during the next six months . . ." Finally, ask yourself how you know that this information is current and accurate. What's the source of your confidence for all of this?

THE PERSUASIVE MEMO

Writing a persuasive memo is much like constructing a winning argument. The document must provide a complete, logical argument with which the reader cannot disagree. It must anticipate all questions and responses—and deal with them. Procter & Gamble vice president G. Gibson Carey offers this advice on persuading others by memo.[8]

- **Consider your objective against the reader's attitudes, perceptions, and knowledge of the subject.** Be sure you know exactly what you want to accomplish with your memo. Do a careful assessment of the reader's mind-set at the beginning. What will it take to get the reader to say yes?
- **Outline on paper, focusing on the Situation Analysis and Rationale sections.** This will help you construct a complete, logical argument. An outline also helps identify missing information.
- **Include a plan of action.** A well-thought-out implementation section adds credibility and practicality to your ideas. It gives the busy reader added incentive to consider your proposal. Even if you are awaiting approval to develop a detailed plan, include an outline of the plan to demonstrate that your concept can be accomplished.
- **Don't lose your argument in the Situation Analysis.** Your proposal should flow naturally from the problem or opportunity described in the Situation Analysis. The reader who disagrees with anything in this section of the memo cannot buy your proposal. Avoid controversial issues, opinions, and unsupported assertions in the Situation Analysis. Stick to the facts.
- **Use the direct approach.** Present your Recommendation and Rationale before you discuss other options that you have considered and rejected.
- **Always lead from strength.** Start your proposal with a strong, confident Overview paragraph. Bring the important ideas to the beginning of each section. In the Rationale section, always present your arguments in order of importance.
- **Use precedent to make your proposal appear less speculative.** Managers seek to avoid risk and error. Relevant precedent is the most effective way to reduce the perceived risk in a recommended action.
- **Gear your argument to the reader's decision criteria.** Know how your reader's mind works. Ask yourself if your argument is persuasive given the reader's interests and motivations.

STANDARD FORMATS FOR MEMOS

Putting your ideas on paper helps you evaluate them. It forces you, the writer, to think through the issues carefully. Good ideas are invariably strengthened on paper and weak ideas are exposed for what they are.

Having a format in mind for the memo or report as you move forward with any project can eliminate one of the common stumbling blocks to sound thinking and good communication. The format becomes an organization plan for your ideas. It ensures that you think logically and that you don't overlook anything relevant to the project.

A standard format helps you organize information and concepts quickly. You don't have to think about where to put everything each time you start writing. If something is missing, it is immediately evident.

A standard format helps readers too. They don't have to figure out how your mind was working each time they get a document from you. They know immediately where to find the pieces and how they fit together, which saves time and promotes understanding.

A document can be organized or put together in a variety of ways. Always be certain your case is developed in a logical and persuasive manner. Consider using a format with which your readers are familiar, to increase their comfort level. However, don't compromise on clarity, simplicity, and logical flow to do so.

You'll find a suggested format for a Business Strategy Memo in Appendix D at the end of the book. The format suggested there is appropriate for just about any memo, regardless of how long or complex. Many companies have adopted this format (or variations of it) because it works particularly well when communication is moving up to senior management. A sample business letter format appears in Appendix C. A sample business letter format appears in Appendix C. You'll also find a suggested communication strategy memo format at the end of this chapter.

If you work for an organization that has a detailed correspondence manual, you need only to follow the directions it provides. If your employer doesn't provide such guidance, your task is simple: Find a writing format that best suits your reasons for writing, the needs of your readers, and the organization that you work for.

Note that the format suggested here separates the contents of a memo into six or seven sections, each no more than a paragraph or two, and each clearly marked with an all-caps, boldface heading.

MEETING AND CONFERENCE REPORTS

The purpose of a conference or meeting report is to record decisions made at the meeting. Avoid long descriptions of what was discussed or presented, restatements of arguments, praise, or blame. Use a standard format that includes the name of the group, persons attending, and subjects covered.

Report briefly on:

- What was discussed or presented.
- What was decided and why.

Focus your report on:

- What action is required.
- Who is responsible.
- What the timing will be.

PROJECT LISTS

Many businesses keep track of current and proposed activities with project lists. These lists are nothing more than simple descriptions of what the organization is doing to achieve its goals or serve its customers. Project lists usually take more time to prepare than they are worth, so try to keep them simple. Simplicity will save time and actually make them more useable documents.

Separate each project by category, then list projects in order of priority or importance. Each project on your list should include a title and brief description, status, next steps, responsible parties, and due dates.

If your project list is long, consider adding a cover page to highlight key projects that require management attention.

Projects should never just disappear. Completed or terminated projects should be shown as such the following month, with a brief notation about why the project will not appear on future project lists.

MAKE YOUR MEMOS INVITING AND ATTRACTIVE

A good document is both inviting and easy to read or easy to use as a reference.[9] Here are some ideas on how to write a good memo:

- **Grab attention up front.** A strong Overview section gives the reader perspective on what's coming and makes any memo easier to read and understand. Don't open the memo with unimportant details or information the reader already knows.
- **Vary sentence and paragraph length, but keep them short.** Short paragraphs and short sentences are inviting because they are easier to deal with. If all your sentences or paragraphs are the same length, however, the memo will seem monotonous.
- **Use headings.** The reader will understand your organization plan for the memo. Headings also make it a better reference document.
- **Use bullets and numbers to identify groupings.** This approach helps break up long paragraphs and is another way to indicate how the memo is organized.
- **Use parallel structure for lists (as this one does).** Keep things with things, actions with actions, do's with do's, "don't's" with "don't's", and so on.
- **Underline or use boldface type to focus on topic sentences, key words, and phrases.** Don't overdo it though; too much underlining makes a document look cluttered and busy.
- **Leave adequate margins.** Lots of white space makes any document more inviting. Use tables, charts, and exhibits. Paragraphs full of numbers are difficult to read. Presenting the same information in a table or chart makes it easier to understand and easier to refer to.
- **Don't settle for sloppy or illegible duplication.** Make it a quality document.

EDITING YOUR MEMOS

Good writing requires rewriting. The overall purpose of editing is to trim, clarify, and simplify. Put the document aside for a while—overnight if possible—before revising. This break helps you step back, look at the memo through the eyes of the reader, and be more objective.

Before revising your memo, quickly review the guidelines provided in the opening section. Then put yourself in the reader's place and go through the document several times, each time asking yourself these seven basic questions:

- **Is it clear?** Is the flow of the memo logical? Will the reader understand the development of your thesis? Are the words simple and concrete? Will the reader understand technical terms? Is every sentence clear, unambiguous, easy to read?
- **Is it complete?** Will the reader understand your purpose? Does the Situation Analysis have all the background information the reader needs to know? Are all the key numbers in the body of the memo? Have all necessary agreements been spelled out?
- **Is it persuasive?** Does your Rationale section lead from strength? Are your arguments in order of importance? Have you anticipated potential responses and questions, and dealt with them? Have you avoided exaggeration and provided a balanced, rational argument?
- **Is it accurate?** Are opinions and facts separated and clearly labeled? Is every number correct?
- **Is it concise?** Do you have too many arguments? Did you waste words telling readers what they already know? Do you have unnecessary words, phrases, or sentences?
- **Is it inviting to read?** Should any large blocks of type be broken up? Did you leave adequate margins? Is the memo neat, clear, and legible?

- **Is it perfect?** Does the memo contain any typos, misspellings, or grammatical errors that could cast doubt on the quality of your thinking?

WRITING GOOD BUSINESS LETTERS

Business letters, unlike memos, are primarily external documents, though managers will occasionally use a letter format to correspond with subordinates and executives. Like memos, good letters are crisp, concise, spoken in tone, and organized so that readers can follow and understand with a minimum of effort. They are easy to follow and don't read like a mystery story.

Nearly 40 years ago, writing consultant Rudolph Flesch offered a set of basic precepts for writing good business letters. They are as useful today as they were back then.[10]

- **Answer promptly.** Answer the mail within three business days. If you don't have an answer, must speak with someone else before you can formulate a reply, or need additional information, drop your reader a note to say "I'll have a more complete reply in a few days, but for now please understand that I am working on a solution to the problem."
- **Show that you are genuinely interested.** The person writing to you obviously thought the issue was important enough to write about; you should think so, too. The problem or matter at hand may seem trivial in your world, but in theirs it is not. Show by your words and actions that you care about them and the issue they have written about.
- **Don't be too short, brief, or curt.** We preach brevity, but you can overdo it. Make sure your reader has enough information to understand the subject. Make certain you include each issue relevant to the subject, and that you explain the process, the outcome, or the decision to the satisfaction of the reader. If you were receiving the letter, would it contain enough information for you to act on? Are you satisfied that the writer (and his or her employer) has taken you seriously?
- **If it's bad news, say you are sorry.** With bad news, use phrases such as, "I am sorry to tell you that . . ." or "I regret to say that we'll be unable to refund your money because. . . ." You can soften the blow that accompanies bad news by saying that you're sorry it happened, you regret the outcome, or some similar selection of words. If it's bad news and your reader thinks you don't care (or, worse, that you are amused by it all), you may be in for further trouble.
- **If it's good news, say you are glad.** With good news, use phrases such as, "I am delighted to tell you that . . ." or "You will be pleased to learn that. . . ." Now and again, the word *congratulations* may be in order. Go ahead and share in your reader's good fortune and joy.
- **Give everyone the benefit of the doubt.** Don't automatically assume that the person corresponding with you is doing so for the purpose of fleecing or cheating you (or your company). If it's not clear whether product failure or customer misuse is to blame, for example, give the other person the benefit of whatever doubt may exist. In the vast majority of instances, you will have done the right thing.
- **Never send off an angry letter.** Venting your spleen in an angry, hostile reply to someone may feel good, but it's almost *never* a good idea to mail such a letter. One real danger with e-mail is that you may compose a vicious reply to someone and click the send button well ahead of the arrival of rational thought. Cool down before you compose a letter and, if you have written something you are not sure about, wait until tomorrow before re-reading it. Chances are, you will think twice about posting that letter.
- **Watch out for cranks.** Occasionally, a certifiable goofball will cross your path. The advice is simple: Be polite, do your job, and they will usually go away. If they persist, be firm but professional in responding. After the second letter, if you really are dealing with a whacko,

you may be able to ignore their correspondence. If the tone is threatening, turn it over to security.

- **Appreciate humor.** If someone makes (or attempts) a joke, play along. Show that you have a sense of humor. Racist, sexist, or profane humor is never appropriate, but ordinary self-deprecating or directionless humor can often lighten or improve a difficult situation.
- **Be careful with form letters.** A one-size-fits-all approach to writing with many recipients is a real recipe for disaster. Make sure your letter answers all (or virtually all) of the questions your audience is likely to have; respond to their fears, doubts, and concerns. Once you have written a form letter and had an opportunity to edit it, why not test-market the document? Show it to several people who are (or have been) members of the audience you are writing for. Ask them to suggest improvements. Think about maps, diagrams, lists, references, and ways your readers might learn more about the subject you are writing to them about.

WHEN YOU ARE REQUIRED TO EXPLAIN SOMETHING

If you find yourself in the position of explaining something in writing to someone else, a few bits of common sense seem appropriate.[11]

- **Nothing is self-explanatory.** This may all seem self-evident to you, but that's because you've been thinking about and working on the subject for some time. Explain in simple, ordinary English what you want your reader to know. Don't assume anything.
- **Translate technical terms.** It's perfectly all right for you to use scientific or technical terminology. You just have to explain or define it first. Writing to one person you know quite well is much easier than writing to many people whom you don't know because you cannot be sure your readers will share your vocabulary.
- **Go step-by-step.** Be sequential in your explanations, moving step-by-step through processes that are complex. Don't skip anything, even steps in the process that seem absolutely self-evident to you. Your readers may be encountering this subject for the first time.
- **Don't say too little.** Your reader probably doesn't know as much about this subject as you do (that's why you are writing). Make certain you provide enough information to answer questions, allay fears, and quell doubts.
- **Don't say too much.** Don't overdo it. You can bury your readers in details that will eventually confuse, frighten, anger, or bore them. Provide enough detail to satisfy their curiosity but not so much that you put them off.
- **Illustrate.** If you can't explain it, perhaps you can show it. Illustrations can take the form of examples, anecdotes, or explanations. Additionally, you may wish to include drawings, maps, schematics, or a process flow chart.
- **Answer expected questions.** Put yourself in your reader's position. What would you most want to know? What questions are likely to arise? Which areas of this subject are likely to raise the greatest doubt, confusion, or misunderstanding?
- **Warn against common mistakes.** If it's easy to misunderstand, misread, or get this subject wrong, caution your readers. Explain the pitfalls, snares, and traps they can easily fall into by not reading your words carefully.

WHEN YOU ARE REQUIRED TO APOLOGIZE

If your job requires that you apologize to someone—most likely a customer or a client—for something that you or the company has done wrong (or not done at all), here are four basic guidelines to consider:

- **Take the complaint seriously.** Once again, you may not see the issue at hand as serious or important, but it's important to the person with the complaint. The sooner you act as if it's a big deal, the sooner you will satisfy the frustration or hostility that prompted the complaint in the first place.
- **Explain what happened and why.** People with complaints often seem irrational; some really are. For the most part, though, people will calm down and adopt a more understanding attitude if you can simply explain what happened and tell them why. For one thing, they will feel that they have more control over the circumstance. When you explain what's happened, they will be more likely to accept your answer.
- **Don't shift the blame.** Blaming everything on someone else is generally a bad idea. Even if someone else is at fault, your readers don't want to hear about it. Just accept responsibility for what's happened and offer a solution. Shifting the blame to "the computer system" or "those geniuses over in shipping" is simply unacceptable.
- **Don't just write, do something.** All the soothing, sympathetic words you can muster will do little to make your reader feel better if you don't offer to fix the problem. "Thanks for your input" is not enough. Telling your reader that you'll share the information with higher management is a good first step, but they may want more. Most people who have taken the time and effort to write to you will expect some sort of action. Don't disappoint them.[12]

A FEW WORDS ABOUT STYLE

Your success as a business writer depends, in large measure, on your ability to convince others that what you have written is worth their attention. A considerable amount of research on this subject has shown that your writing will be better received if it meets three basic criteria: It ought to be *compact*, it should be *informal*, and it absolutely must be *organized*.

Why compact, informal, and organized writing? Three things seem to depend on writing that meets those criteria: organizational efficiency, personal productivity, and your career. Large and complex organizations have shown time and again that the less time their employees spend at the keyboard composing correspondence, the more time they have to think about and accomplish other (presumably important) things.

If you spend less time both *writing* and *reading* what's been written for all employees in your organization, you become more personally productive. And, of course, important people—those in a position to influence your career—will notice. They will notice whether you are someone who can be counted on to draft, edit, and improve written communication, or someone who struggles with the written word. In other words, they will know whether you are part of the problem or part of the solution.

MAKE YOUR WRITING EFFICIENT

You must somehow find a way to deal with a number of different problems that appear consistently in letters, memos, reports, proposals, staff studies, and other business documents. In addition to those memo-writing issues we discussed earlier, here are a dozen of the most common problems:

- **Big words.** If you want a few laughs from readers sensitive to language, use pompous substitutes for small words. Don't *start* things; *initiate* them. Don't *end* a program; *terminate* it. Readers know that *utilize* means *use* and *optimum* means *best*, but why force them to translate? You sell yourself and your ideas through your writing. Come across as a sensible person, someone who knows that good writing begins with plain English.

- ———— -wise. Another no-no: words ending in *-wise*. Rather than write, "Marketwise, this firm should engage in sustained efforts to effect an improvement in our understanding of events and forces," you might consider "We need to know much more than we do about market forces."

- **Doublings.** Words that have the same or nearly the same meaning are known as *synonyms*. Select the one which most closely approximates what you really intend for your reader to know. Why write about a project's "importance and significance" when *importance* will do?

- **Noun modifiers.** Some writers insist on using one noun to modify another, when just one would do. "She is now in an important leadership position with the company" could be rewritten as "She is now a leader in this company." Look through your correspondence. You will see these noun-pairs everywhere: *management capability, market situation, habit patterns.*

- **It is.** Few words do more damage than the innocent-looking *it is.* These words stretch sentences, delay your point, encourage passives, and hide responsibility. Unless *it* refers to something definite mentioned earlier, try to write around *it is.* "It is recommended that you revise . . ." becomes "We recommend that you revise," or "You should revise."

- **Legalese.** Avoid legal-sounding language like *hereto* and *aforesaid.* Such pompous and wordy language doesn't give a writer any added authority; it simply shows that his or her writing style—and perhaps his or her thinking—is outdated. Why say "Attached *herewith* is the report"? Instead, say, "Here's the report. . . ." And rather than write, "It is incumbent upon supervisors . . . ," just say "Supervisors must. . . ." If your writing reads like a fire-and-casualty policy or a mutual fund prospectus, you may want to think twice about your style.

- **Missing hyphens.** Two-word modifiers may need hyphens when the two words act as one. Don't hyphenate if the first word ends in *-ly:* "*Fairly* recent change." Otherwise, consider it. "Three day trips" (three trips, each for a day) differs from "three-day trips" (trips, each for three days). If you are sensitive to how hyphens work, you will see what happens when they are left out of a sentence: "We're looking for a *short term accountant.* . . ." A CPA under 5'4", perhaps?

- **Smothered verbs.** Express ideas involving action with specific verbs. Weak writing relies on general verbs, which take extra words to complete their meaning. When you write general verbs such as *is, give,* and *hold,* see if you can replace them by turning nearby words into specific verbs. Don't *make a choice; choose.* Don't *provide guidance; guide.* I have loaded the next two sentences with common smothered verbs: "The committee members *held a meeting* (*met*) to *give consideration to* (*consider*) the plan. They *made the decision* (*decided*) to *give their approval to* (*approve*) the product launch." Get the idea? *Make use of* (*use*) specific verbs!

- **Specialized terms.** Try to avoid specialized terms with outsiders and use them no more than you must with insiders. Acronyms, jargon, and verbal shorthand unique to your organization can really confuse people who don't share the vocabulary. Are technical or specialized terms forbidden? Not at all. If you must use a technical term and you are reasonably sure that some of your readers won't understand, define it—tell them what it means and how it's used. They will show their appreciation by reading (and understanding) what you have written.

- **That and which.** More often than not, *that* and *which* don't help the meaning or flow of a sentence so use them sparingly. Sometimes you can just leave out these words; sometimes you will have to rewrite slightly. Consider this sentence: "We think (*that*) the changes (*which*) they have asked for will cost too much." Rather than writing "A system *which* is unreliable," you could say "An unreliable system." Read the sentence aloud and ask if you need *that* or *which* for meaning or flow. If not, try a revised sentence without those words.
- **The ──── ion of . . .** Shorten this ponderous *-ion* construction whenever the context permits. Instead of saying "I recommend *the adoption of* the plan," say "I recommend *adopting* the plan." And, instead of saying "We want *the participation of* all concerned," say "We want all concerned *to participate.*" You add life to your writing by favoring the verb (action) form over the noun (static) form.
- **Wordy expressions.** Wordy expressions don't give writing impressive bulk; they litter it by getting in the way of the words that carry meaning. So simplify these sentence stretchers. The longer it takes you to say something, the weaker you come across. *In order to* means *to*. *For the purpose of* usually means *to*. *In the near future* could be rephrased as *soon*. *In the event that* can be rewritten as *if*.[13]

SPEAK WHEN YOU WRITE

To escape from outdated, excessively formal writing styles, try to make your writing more like your speaking. I'm not suggesting that you include snorts, grunts, and rambling stream-of-consciousness monologues in your correspondence. We all know people who speak no better than they can write. Still, the basic principle holds: Because people "hear" writing, the most readable writing sounds like one person talking to another. Begin by imagining your reader is in front of you and then use these ideas to guide you.

- **Write with personal pronouns.** Use *we*, *us*, and *our* when speaking for the company. Use *I*, *me*, and *my* when speaking for yourself. Either way, be generous with *you*. Avoiding these natural references to people is false modesty. Besides, the alternatives to personal pronouns are awkwardness ("Your support is appreciated," which doesn't work as well as "We appreciate your support") and hedging ("It was decided" in place of "I decided"). Stamp out "untouched by human hands" writing.
- **Use contractions (occasionally).** Write with the ones we speak with, such as *I'm*, *we're*, *you'd*, *they've*, *can't*, *don't*, and *let's*. Not all your writing has to sound like a telephone conversation, but it certainly won't hurt if some of it does. If contractions come easily to you, then you've mastered spoken writing. If contractions seem out of place, don't remove them; deflate the rest of what you say. Also, don't overlook the advantages of negative contractions for instructions; they soften direct orders and keep readers from skipping over the word *not*.
- **Reach out to your reader occasionally by asking questions.** A request gains emphasis when it ends with a question mark. In a long report, a question can be a welcome change. Do you hear how spoken this next sentence is? Rather than write, "Please advise this office as to whether the conference is still scheduled for February 21," you might simply ask, "Is the conference still scheduled for February 21?"
- **Prefer short, spoken transitions over long, bookish ones.** Use *but* more than *however*, *also* more than *in addition*, *still* more than *nevertheless*, *so* more than *consequently* or *therefore*. Use formal transitions only for variety. And, yes, you can start a sentence with words like *but*, *so*, *yet*, *and*, and *or*.

- **A preposition is a word you can end a sentence with.** Don't rework a sentence just to shift a preposition from the end. You'll lengthen, tangle, and stiffen the sentence. Common prepositions include *after, at, by, from, of, to, up, with.*
- **Keep sentences short, about 20 words on average.** Use some longer and shorter sentences for variety. Short ones won't guarantee clarity, but they will prevent many of the confusions common to longer ones. Try the eye test: Average about two typed lines a sentence. Or try the ear test: Read your writing aloud and break apart any sentence you can't finish in one breath.[14]

HOW TO MAKE PASSIVE VERBS ACTIVE

Passive sentences are deadly in business memos and letters for several reasons. First, they obscure responsibility by omitting a subject or human actor from the sentence. Second, they are almost always longer—one-quarter to one-third longer than active sentences. Finally, they delay discussion of the subject. The real action in a passive sentence or paragraph comes at the end.

The best advice: Use as few passives as possible. They're not grammatically wrong, but they are really overworked in most business writing. To write actively, remember this simple rule: *Put the doer before the verb.* By leading with the doer, you'll automatically avoid a passive verb. Consider these examples:

> **Passive:** "It has been determined that more purchase decisions should be made by local managers."

> **Active:** "The director decided that local managers should make more purchase decisions."

The passive version of that sentence (double passive, actually) contains 14 words. The active version contains just 11. Better yet, the active version tells the reader who made that decision—an important element missing from the passive sentence.

You can spot passive sentences by checking for these characteristics:

- The receiver of the verb's action comes before the verb. In the passive example, *it* is the receiver.
- The verb has these two parts: any form of *to be,* either simple (such as *are* or *was*) or compound (such as *is being, have been, will be,* or *must be*), plus the past participle of a main verb (most end in -en or -ed). In the preceding example, *has been decided* is the verb.
- If the doer appears at all, it follows the verb and usually has *by* just before it. But unlike active sentences, passive ones are complete without doers: *It has been determined* (by whom?).

Passive sentences may be useful in one of three circumstances:

- *When the doer is obvious*: "Barack Obama was elected President of the United States in November of 2008." How did *that* happen, you ask? Well . . . the explanation is complex, and you may not have time for the answer. Just leave it in the passive.
- *When the doer is unknown*: "My uncle was mugged in the park." Who mugged him? We don't really know; the mugger didn't leave a business card.
- *When the doer is unimportant*: "The parts were shipped on January 8." We don't really care who shipped them; we just know that they were sent on the eighth of January.

If you use passive sentences when you might just as easily write sentences with active verbs, your writing will be wordy, roundabout, and (as the word *passive* implies), a bit sluggish. Worse, because passive sentences don't always show who is doing the action, you may forget to include important information. The result may be confusing to the reader.

- "All requests must be approved beforehand." By whom? It doesn't say because it's a passive sentence. The active version: The regional manager must approve all requests beforehand.
- "The figures were lost." Who lost them? Again, we don't know because it's cast in the passive. The active version: "We lost the figures."

The best advice: Write actively whenever you can. If you decide to cast a sentence in the passive voice, do so only after considering what the active version would look like.[15]

MAKE YOUR BOTTOM LINE YOUR TOP LINE

Open with your main point, the one sentence you'd keep if you could keep just one. You can often put that sentence in its own paragraph for added clarity. Give directions before reasons, requests before justifications, answers before explanations, conclusions before details, and solutions before problems.

A poorly organized letter reads like a mystery story. Clue by clue, it unfolds details that make sense only toward the end. Try the approach used in newspaper articles. They start with the most important information and taper off to the least important.

You might delay the main point to soften bad news or to remind your reader of an old conversation, for example, but avoid delaying for long. Readers, like listeners, are put off by people who take forever to get to the point. They need to know the main point at the start so they can appreciate the relevance of whatever else you may say.

If no single sentence stands out, you probably need to create one to keep from drifting aimlessly. Occasionally, as in a set of instructions or a reply to a series of questions, all your points may be equally important. In this case, create a starting sentence that tells your readers what to expect: "Here's the information you asked for."

To end most letters, just stop. When writing to persuade rather than to routinely inform, you may want to end strongly, perhaps with a forecast, appeal, or implication. When feelings are involved, you may want to exit gracefully with some expression of goodwill. When in doubt, offer your help and encourage the reader to call or write back to you.[16]

Here are three ideas that will help you to better organize your letters.

- **Use headings and subheadings.** Boldface headings or italicized subheadings can help to organize your writing. When topics vary widely in one document, they let readers follow at a glance. Use them in recurring reports, proposals, and even short business letters when you need to catch a reader's eye or break up long, complex paragraphs.
- **Keep paragraphs short.** Average roughly four or five sentences in each paragraph. For lists and instructions, try using subparagraphs. You make reading easier by adding white space.
- **Don't clutter up the first paragraph.** It's the most important paragraph in your letter; don't waste the prime space and impact of that paragraph with endless references to letters you've exchanged, previous reports, regulatory documents, or other pieces of paper. Put your reason for writing—your most important point—right up front.

HOW TO ENCOURAGE AND DEVELOP GOOD WRITERS

Every manager has a responsibility—in some respects, a moral obligation—to improve the skills of his or her subordinates. Writing skills are no exception. Too often, people get frustrated because assignments are given with careless direction, and comments about writing are vague and difficult to understand.

Working effectively with subordinates is not easy. It takes knowledge, experience, and patience. Surprisingly, it doesn't take much time. It does take a willingness to sit down and review your expectations and their performance in specific terms. Here are some ideas to consider as you work with your people on improving communication.

- **Show your people you want clear, concise writing by example.** Give them samples of good writing and explain why it works. Sit down with new people and discuss your writing guidelines.
- **Know what you want before giving assignments.** Discuss projects with subordinates before they head off in the wrong direction. Be as specific as you can.
- **When projects are difficult or complex, break up the assignment into manageable parts.** Start with an Overview section to identify purpose and main ideas. Then have the writer prepare an outline of the document. Review this work before the writer tackles a first draft. This approach will save time and eliminate the frustration of trying to deal with a disaster.
- **Read and review before discussing a memo.** When a memo is submitted for your review, spend some time reviewing it before meeting with the writer. Be sure you understand what's wrong and how it can be fixed.
- **Try to see the big picture first.** When you review a memo, start with big issues such as strategy, logic flow, and conclusions versus facts. Then move to smaller issues like grammar and appearance. Do not rewrite the memo, but be specific about areas that need work. And do remember to be positive.
- **Be certain the writer understands—and agrees with—your comments.** Make sure your writer can repeat, in his or her own words, what you want so that you're sure you are both on the same page.
- **Don't force writers to parrot your style and expressions.** Give your people flexibility and freedom to develop their own style.[17]

For Further Reading

Alred, G. J., Brusaw, C. T., and Oliu, W. E. *The Business Writer's Companion*, 6th ed. Boston, MA: Bedford/St. Martin's Press, 2011.

Flintoff, J. P. "Companies Seek Help from a Man of Letters," *The Financial Times*, June 7, 2002, p. 12.

Hall, D. and Birkets, S. *Writing Well.* Boston, MA: Addison-Wesley-Longman, 1997.

Holcombe, M. *Writing for Decision Makers: Memos and Reports with a Competitive Edge.* New York: Lifetime Learning, 1997.

Oliu, W. E., Brusaw, C. T., and Alred, G. J. *Writing That Works: Communicating Effectively on the Job*, 10th ed. Boston, MA: Bedford/St. Martin's Press, 2009.

Roman, K. and Raphaelson, J. *Writing That Works: How to Improve Your Memos, Letters, Reports, Speeches, Resumes, Plans, and Other Business Papers.* New York: HarperCollins, 1995.

Smith, N. *A Plain English Handbook: How to Create Clear SEC Disclosure Documents.* Washington, DC: The U.S. Securities and Exchange Commission, August 1998. You can obtain a copy of this document by calling the Office of Investor Education and Assistance toll-free information service at 1-800-SEC-0330, or download a PDF from www.sec.gov.

Stott, B. *Write to the Point: And Feel Better About Your Writing.* New York: Columbia University Press, 1991.

Strunk, W. and White, E. B. *The Elements of Style*, 3rd ed. New York: Macmillan Publishing Company, Inc., 1979.

Williams, J. *Style: Ten Lessons in Clarity and Grace*, 9th ed. New York: Longman, 2006.

Zinsser, W. *On Writing Well: The Classic Guide to Writing Nonfiction*. New York: HarperCollins, 1998.

Endnotes

1. *USA Today*, October 14, 1994, p. C1. Reprinted with permission.
2. Ibid.
3. Smith, N. *A Plain English Handbook: How to Create Clear SEC Disclosure Documents*. Washington, DC: Government Printing Office, 1998, pp. 5–6.
4. Ibid., p. 4.
5. Plumez, J. P. *Leadership on Paper*, 1996, pp. 1–2. Personal communication with the author, August 8, 2002, from Larchmont, NY. Used by permission.
6. Ibid.
7. Ibid., pp. 4–5.
8. Carey, G. G. Personal communication with the author, August 20, 2002, from Cincinnati, OH. Used by permission.
9. Ruch, W. V. and M. L. Crawford. *Business Reports: Written and Oral*. Boston, MA: PWS-Kent, 1999, p. 203.
10. Flesch, R. *On Business Communication: How to Say What You Mean in Plain English*. New York: Harper & Row, 1974, pp. 100–112.
11. Ibid., pp. 113–126.
12. Ibid., pp. 139–151.
13. Murawski, T., P. Luckett, J. Mace, and J. Shuttleworth. *The United States Air Force Academy Executive Writing Course*. Colorado Springs, CO: HQ USAFA, Department of English, 1983.
14. Ibid.
15. Bailey, E. *The Plain English Approach to Business Writing*. New York: Oxford University Press, 1993, pp. 93–101.
16. Murawski, et al. The United States Air Force Academy Executive Writing Course.
17. Plumez, *Leadership on Paper*, p. 16.

CASE STUDY 5-1

Cypress Semiconductor Corporation

Background Note

Trusted senior managers are often called upon by executives to provide advice regarding relations with important and sensitive publics. Relations with customers, employees, suppliers, vendors, affiliates, shareholders, market analysts, and others may well depend on the quality of advice managers are able to provide to the senior leadership of their organization.

Much of the contact that a chief executive officer may have with such groups, along with others in the world outside the company, is subject to filtering by front-office staff and executive support personnel. Frequently, CEOs won't even see a letter of complaint or other correspondence from small-lot shareholders, minor customers, or members of public interest groups seeking donations, favors, or support of some sort. In such cases, mid-level managers are often delegated to respond on the executive's behalf.

Depending on company size and the personality of the CEO, however, some correspondence from external sources may very well land on the chief executive's desk. Some CEOs enjoy responding to selected correspondents personally; others delegate the task of preparing a reply. In both cases, the tone and style of a response is central to [the] success of the letter or message. Trusted managers are frequently asked to review the executive's correspondence for accuracy, completeness, and appropriateness of the response.

The Case At Hand

T. J. Rodgers, Chairman and CEO of Cypress Semiconductor Corporation, has received a letter from a Catholic nun, suggesting he appoint qualified women and minorities to his company's board of directors. Rodgers has responded to the one-page form letter (attached) with a six-page reply (also attached), blasting Sister Doris for the "political correctness" which seemed to motivate her letter. The scathing retort that he proposes to send to Sister Doris tells her ". . . to get down from your moral high horse." "Choosing a board of directors based on race and gender is a lousy way to run a company," he writes, [adding,] "Cypress will never do it." And for good measure, Rodgers suggests that "bowing to special-interest groups is an immoral way to run a company."

As vice president for investor relations, you are, frankly, not surprised at either the tone or length of Rodgers's response. Once known as the "bad boy of Silicon Valley," Rodgers, who is now 48 years old, often makes a habit of publishing provocative, editorial-style articles on everything from proposed immigration restrictions to federal support of high-tech industries—he is opposed to both. His attack on Sister Doris, however, has stirred some concern among senior managers and the executive support staff at Cypress. Mr. Rodgers has circulated a draft version of his proposed reply to the corporate senior team and asked for comment.

In addition to a response to Sister Doris in Philadelphia, Rodgers has proposed sending his letter to all Cypress shareholders and a select group of sympathetic veterans of the affirmative-action debate. Cypress Semiconductors is an international producer and distributor of computing chips with about US$600 [million] in annual sales. The company's headquarters and principal production facilities are located in Palo Alto, California. Mr. Rodgers began the company when he was 35 years old, developing a gruff management style that earned him a place on *Fortune* magazine's list of the country's toughest bosses. He is not, however, an altogether unreasonable man, and you may assume that your working relationship with him is amiable, personal, and sound. He listens when you speak, though he doesn't always do as you suggest.

Your Task

Rodgers has asked for your opinion of the two letters attached to this case. He wants to send a response to Sister Doris within 48 hours, providing copies of his letter to shareholders and selected analysts. His memo to you explains that the "arrogance" of Sister Doris's letter spurred him to action. "It was Friday night and I got it and I said, 'It's time.' Then, I looked down and . . . she didn't even sign the . . . thing." Rodgers also acknowledged that he "was kind of pumped, so I really let her have it."

The CEO trusts your judgment and, in particular, your ability to advise him when he's gone too far. In response to his request, please prepare two documents: a memo responding to his appeal for your thoughts and a draft letter to Sister Doris that you believe to be appropriate. You may take whichever position regarding [Sister] Doris's request you care to—just be certain to justify your approach. Simply agreeing with the boss is insufficient. Mr. Rodgers, after all, has said repeatedly that he "can't stand 'yes men.'"

Your memo to Mr. Rodgers should be confidential and for his eyes only. The proposed reply to Sister Doris should be in final form and ready for dispatch.

May 23, 1996
The Sisters of St. Francis of Philadelphia
Our Lady of Angels Convent—Glen Riddle
Aston, Pennsylvania 19014
(610) 459-4125
Fax (610) 558-1421

Dear _____

The Sisters of St. Francis of Philadelphia, a religious congregation of approximately 1,000 women, is the beneficial owner of _____ shares of stock in _____ Corporation.

    We believe that a company is best represented by a Board of qualified Directors reflecting the equality of the sexes, races, and ethnic groups. As women and minorities continue to move into upper level management positions of economic, educational, and cultural institutions, the number of qualified Board candidates also increases. Therefore, our policy is to withhold authority to vote for nominees of a Board of Directors that do not include women and minorities.

    It appears from the proxy statement, which does not include pictures, that _____ Company has no women or minority Directors. We have voted our proxy accordingly, and we urge you to enrich the Board by seeking qualified women and members of racial minorities as nominees.

Sincerely,

Doris Gormley, OSF
Director, Corporate Social Responsibility

Doris Gormley, OSF
Director, Corporate Social Responsibility
The Sisters of St. Francis of Philadelphia
Our Lady of Angels Convent—Glen Riddle
Aston, PA 19014

Dear Sister Gormley:

Thank you for your letter criticizing the lack of racial and gender diversity of Cypress's Board of Directors. I received the same letter from you last year. I will reiterate the management arguments opposing your position. Then I will provide the philosophical basis behind our rejection of the operating principles espoused in your letter, which we believe to be not only unsound, but even immoral, by a definition of that term I will present.

    The semiconductor business is a tough one with significant competition from the Japanese, Taiwanese, and Koreans. There have been more corporate casualties than survivors. For these reasons, our board of directors is not a ceremonial watchdog, but a critical management function. The essential criteria for Cypress board membership are as follows:

- Experience as a CEO of an important technology company.
- Direct expertise in the semiconductor business based on education and management experience.
- Direct experience in the management of a company that buys from the semiconductor industry.

    A search based on these criteria usually yields a male who is 50-plus years old, has a master's degree in an engineering science, and has moved up the managerial ladder to the top spot in one or more corporations. Unfortunately, there are currently few minorities and almost no women who chose to be engineering graduate students 30 years ago. (That picture will be dramatically different in 10 years, due to the greater diversification of graduate students in the 1980s.)

Bluntly stated, a "woman's view" on how to run our semiconductor company does not help us, unless that woman has an advanced technical degree and experience as a CEO. I do realize there are other industries in which the last statement does not hold true. We would quickly embrace the opportunity to include any woman or minority person who could help us as a director, because we pursue talent—and we don't care in what package that talent comes.

I believe that placing arbitrary racial or gender quotas on corporate boards is fundamentally wrong. Therefore, not only does Cypress not meet your requirements for boardroom diversification, but we are unlikely to, because it is very difficult to find qualified directors, let alone directors that also meet investors' racial and gender preferences.

I infer that your concept of corporate morality contains in it the requirement to appoint board of directors with, in your words, "equality of sexes, races, and ethnic group." I am unaware of any Christian requirements for corporate boards, and your views seem more accurately described as "politically correct," than "Christian."

My views aside, your requirements are—in effect—immoral. By immoral, I mean "causing harm to people," a fundamental wrong. Here's why:

- I presume you believe your organization does good work and that the people who spend their careers in its service deserve to retire with the necessities of life assured. If your investment in Cypress is intended for that purpose, I can tell you that each of the retired Sisters of St. Francis would suffer if I were forced to run Cypress on anything but a profit-making basis. The retirement plans of thousands of other people also depend on Cypress stock—$1.2 billion worth of stock—owned directly by investors or through mutual funds, pension funds, 401(k) programs, and insurance companies. Recently a fellow 1970 Dartmouth classmate wrote to say that his son's college fund ("Dartmouth, Class of 2014," he writes) owns Cypress stock. Any choice I would make to jeopardize retirees and other investors from achieving their lifetime goals would be fundamentally wrong.
- Consider charitable donations. When the U.S. economy shrinks, the dollars available to charity shrink faster, including those dollars earmarked for the Sisters of St. Francis. If all companies in the United States were forced to operate according to some arbitrary social agenda, rather than for profit, all American companies would operate at a disadvantage to their foreign competitors, all Americans would become less well off (some laid off), and charitable giving would decline precipitously. Making Americans poorer and reducing charitable giving in order to force companies to follow an arbitrary social agenda is fundamentally wrong.
- A final point with which you will undoubtedly disagree. Electing people to corporate boards based on racial preferences is demeaning to the very board members placed under such conditions, and unfair to people who are qualified. A prominent friend of mine hired a partner who is a brilliant, black Ph.D. from Berkeley. The woman is constantly insulted by being asked if she got her job because of preferences: The system that creates that institutionalized insult is fundamentally wrong.

Finally, you ought to get down from your moral high horse. Your form letter signed with a stamped signature does not allow for the possibility that a CEO could run a company morally and disagree with your position. You have voted against me and the other directors of the company, which is your right as a shareholder. But here is a synopsis of what you voted against.

- Employee ownership. Every employee of Cypress is a shareholder and every employee of Cypress—including the lowest-paid—receives new Cypress stock options every year, a policy that sets us apart even from other Silicon Valley companies.
- Excellent pay. Our employees in San Jose averaged $78,741 in salary and benefits in 1995. (That figure excludes my salary and that of Cypress's vice presidents; it's what "the workers" really get.)

- A significant boost to our economy. In 1995, our company paid out $150 million to its employees. That money did a lot of good: It bought a lot of houses, cars, movie tickets, eyeglasses, and college educations.
- A flexible health care program. A Cypress-paid health care budget is granted to all employees to secure the health care options they want, including medical, dental, and eye care, as well as different life insurance policies.
- Personal computers. Cypress pays for half of home computers (up to $1,200) for all employees.
- Employee education. We pay for our employees to go back to school and we offer dozens of internal courses.
- Paid time off. In addition to vacation and holidays, each Cypress employee can schedule paid time off for personal reasons.
- Profit sharing. Cypress shares its profits with its employees. In 1995, profit sharing added up to $5,000 per employee, given in equal shares, regardless of rank or salary. That was a 22 percent bonus for an employee earning $22,932 per year, the taxable salary of our lowest-paid San Jose employee.
- Charitable work. Cypress supports Silicon Valley. We support the Second Harvest Food Bank (food for the poor), the largest food bank in the United States. I was chairman of the 1993 food drive, and Cypress has won the food-giving title three years running. (Last year, we were credited with 354,131 pounds of food, or 454 pounds per employee, a record.) We also give to the Valley Medical Center, our Santa Clara–based public hospital, which accepts all patients without a "VISA check."

Those are some of the policies of the board of directors you voted against. I believe you should support management teams that hold our values and have the courage to put them into practice. So, that's my reply. Choosing a board of directors based on race and gender is a lousy way to run a company. Cypress will never do it. Furthermore, we will never be pressured into it, because bowing to well-meaning, special-interest groups is an immoral way to run a company, given all the people it would hurt.

We simply cannot allow arbitrary rules to be forced on us by organizations that lack business expertise. I would rather be labeled as a person who is unkind to religious groups than as a coward who harms his employees and investors by mindlessly following high-sounding, but false, standards of right and wrong. You may think this letter is too tough a response to a shareholder organization voting its conscience. But the political pressure to be what is euphemized as a "responsible corporation" today is so great that it literally threatens the well-being of every American. Let me explain why.

In addition to your focus on the racial and gender equality of board representation, other investors have their pet issues, for example, whether or not a company:

- is "green," or environmentally conscious.
- does or does not do business with certain countries or groups of people.
- supplies the U.S. Armed Forces.
- is involved in the community in appropriate ways.
- pays its CEO too much compared with its lowest-paid employee.
- pays its CEO too much as declared by self-appointed "industry watchdogs."
- gives to certain charities.
- is willing to consider layoffs when the company is losing money.
- is willing to consider layoffs to streamline its organization (so-called downsizing).
- has a retirement plan.
- pays for all or part of a health care plan.
- budgets a certain minimum percentage of payroll costs for employee training.
- places employees on its board of directors (you forgot this one).
- shares its profits with employees.

We believe Cypress has an excellent record on these issues. But that's because it's the way we choose to run the business for ourselves and our shareholders, not because we run the business according to the mandates of special-interest groups. Other companies, perhaps those in older industries just trying to hold on to jobs, might find the choices our company makes devastating to their businesses and, consequently, their employees. No one set of choices could be correct for all companies. Indeed, it would be impossible for any company to accede to all of the special interests because they are often in conflict with one another. For example, Cypress won a San Jose Mayor's Environmental Award for water conservation. Our waste water from the Minnesota plant is so clean we are permitted to put it directly into a lake teeming with wildlife. (A game warden station is the next-door neighbor to that plant.) Those facts might qualify us as a "green" company, but some investors would claim the opposite because we adamantly oppose wasteful, government-mandated, ride-sharing programs and believe car-pool lanes waste the time of the finest minds in Silicon Valley by creating government-inflicted traffic jams while increasing pollution, not decreasing it, as claimed by some self-declared "environmentalists."

The May 13, 1996, issue of *Fortune* magazine analyzed the "ethical mutual funds" which invest with a social-issues agenda and currently control $639 billion in investments. Those funds produced an 18.2 percent return in the last 12 months, while the S&P 500 returned 27.2 percent. The investors in those funds thus lost 9 percent of $639 billion, or $57.5 billion in one year, because they invested on a social-issues basis. Furthermore, their loss was not simply someone else's gain, the money literally vanished from our economy, making every American poorer. That's a lot of houses, food, and college educations that were lost to the "higher good" of various causes. What absurd logic would contend that Americans should be harmed by "good ethics"?

Despite our disagreement on the issues, the Sisters of St. Francis, the ethical funds, and their investors are merely making free choices on how to invest. What really worries me is the current election-year frenzy in Washington to institutionalize "good ethics" by making them law—a move that would mandate widespread corporate mismanagement. The "corporate responsibility" concepts promoted by Labor Secretary Reich and Senator Kennedy make great TV sound bites, but if they were put into practice, it would be a disaster for American business that would dwarf the $57 billion lost by the inept investment strategy of the "ethical funds." And that disaster would translate into lost jobs and lost wages for all Americans, a fundamental wrong.

One Senate proposal for "responsible corporations," as outlined in the February 26 issue of *BusinessWeek,* would grant a low federal tax rate of 11 percent to "responsible corporations," and saddle all other companies with an 18 percent rate. One seemingly innocuous requirement for a "responsible corporation," as proposed by Senators Bingaman and Daschle, would limit the pay of a "responsible" CEO to no more than 50 times the company's lowest-paid, full-time employee. To mandate that a "responsible corporation" would have to limit the pay of its CEO is the perfect, no-lose, election-year issue. The rule would be viewed as the right thing to do by voters who distrust and dislike free markets, and as a don't-care issue by the rest. But the following analysis of this proposal underscores the fact that the simplistic solutions fashioned by politicians to provoke fear and anger against America's businesses often sound reasonable—while being fundamentally wrong.

Consider the folly of the CEO pay limit as it applies to Intel: the biggest semiconductor company in the world, the leader of America's return to market dominance in semiconductors, the good corporate citizen, the provider of 45,325 very high-quality jobs, the inventor of the random-access memory, the inventor of the microprocessor, and the manufacturer of the "brains" of 80 percent of the world's personal computers. Suppose that Intel's lowest-paid trainee earns $15,000 per year. The 50 to 1 CEO salary rule would mandate that the salary of Intel's co-founder and CEO, Andy Grove, could be no more than $750,000. Otherwise, Intel would face a federal tax rate of 18 percent rather than 11 percent. Last year, Andy Grove earned $2,756,700, well over that $750,000 limit, and Intel's pretax earnings were $5.6 billion. Seven percentage points on Intel's tax rate translates into a whopping $395 million tax penalty for Intel. Consequently, the practical meaning of this "responsible corporation" law to Intel would be this gun-to-the-head proposition. "Either cut the pay of your Chief Executive Officer by a factor of four from $2,756,700 to $750,000, or pay the federal government an extra $395 million in taxes."

The Bingaman–Daschle proposal would limit the pay of the CEO of the world's most important semiconductor company to less than that of a second-string quarterback in the NFL. That absurd result is not about "responsible corporations," but about two leftist senators, out of touch with reality, making political hay, causing harm, and labeling it "good." Their plan is particularly immoral in that it would cause the losses inherent in practicing their newly invented false moral standard to fall upon all investors in American companies, even though the government itself had not invested in those companies.

Meanwhile, my current salary multiple of 25-to-1 relative to our lowest-paid employee would qualify Cypress as a "responsible corporation," only because we are younger and not yet as successful as Intel—a fact reflected by my lower pay. If Cypress had created as much wealth and as many jobs as Intel, and if my compensation were higher for that reason, then, according to the amazingly perverse logic of the "responsible corporation," Cypress would be moved from the "responsible" to the "irresponsible" category for having been more successful and for having created more jobs! A final point: Why should either Intel or Cypress, both companies making 30 percent pretax profit, be offered a special tax break by the very politicians who would move on to the next press conference to complain about "corporate welfare"?

How long will it be before Senators Kennedy, Bingaman, and Daschle hold hearings on the "irresponsible corporations" that pay tens of millions of dollars to professional athletes? Or, are athletes a "protected group," leaving CEOs as their sole target? If not, which Senate Subcommittee will determine the "responsible" pay level for a good CEO with 30 percent pretax profit, as compared to a good pitcher with a 1.05 earned run average? These questions highlight the absurdity of trying to replace free market pricing with the responsible-corporation claptrap proposed by Bingaman, Daschle, Kennedy, and Reich.

In conclusion, please consider these two points: First, Cypress is run under a set of carefully considered moral principles, which rightly include making a profit as a primary objective. Second, there is fundamental difference between your organization's right to vote its conscience and the use of coercion by the federal government to force arbitrary "corporate responsibilities" on America's businesses and shareholders.

Cypress stands for personal and economic freedom, for free minds and free markets, a position irrevocably in opposition to the immoral attempt by coercive utopians to mandate even more government control over America's economy. With regard to our shareholders who exercise their right to vote according to a social agenda, we suggest that they reconsider whether or not their strategy will do net good—after all the real costs are considered.

Sincerely,

T. J. Rodgers
President/CEO
TJR/cxs

This case was prepared from public sources by James S. O'Rourke, Teaching Professor of Management, with the assistance of Ellen Jean Pollock of *The Wall Street Journal* as the basis for class discussion rather than to illustrate either effective or ineffective handling of an administrative situation.

CASE STUDY 5-2
CARNIVAL CRUISE LINES:

Fire Aboard a Stranded Cruise Ship

"During the next 10 minutes I kept talking to the guests reminding them to stay in their cabins and did my best to keep them calm. I also spoke to the crew, telling them to remember their training and to also stay calm. And they did, both the guests and the crew did exactly what I asked of them and meanwhile I waited for the captain to tell me what was next. And what was next was that the smoke was so intense and so thick that, even with breathing apparatus on, the teams could not get close to the source."[1]

These were the words of Cruise Director John Heald as he reflected on the events that transpired during the early hours of Monday, November 8, 2010. Thick smoke was billowing from the aft engine room of Carnival Splendor, one of the largest vessels owned and operated by Carnival Cruise Lines, and none of the ship's fire squads could stay in the engine room long enough to determine the cause of the smoke.

As Cruise Director, Heald was responsible for keeping the guests informed of any emergencies during the cruise, and to do so calmly, reassuringly, truthfully, and as often as possible. Thus, with limited information and a sense of urgency, Heald began making frequent updates to guests regarding the "smoke" situation. Little did he know that the thick smoke was the product of a debilitating fire that would leave the Carnival Splendor without electrical power 200 miles off the coast of California. The next three days would prove to be among the most trying experiences in the company's history as John Heald and Tim Gallagher, Carnival Cruise Lines' Vice President of Corporate Communications, attempted to control the situation and ensure the safety and well-being of all passengers onboard the stranded cruise ship.

Carnival Cruise Lines

Carnival Cruise Lines was founded in 1972 by entrepreneur Ted Arison with the vision of making cruising, a vacation experience once reserved for the rich, available to the average. Carrying more passengers than any other cruise line, Carnival has become the largest cruise line in the world, and in 1987, earned the distinction, "The Most Popular Cruise Line in the World." Carnival operates 1,400 voyages per year with a fleet of 22 ships, and serves approximately four million passengers per year.[2]

Carnival has 3,800 shoreside employees and 33,500 shipside employees. It operates voyages ranging from three-to-sixteen days in length to some of the most popular vacation destinations in the world, including The Bahamas, Caribbean, Mexican Riviera, Alaska, Hawaii, Canada, Europe, the Panama Canal and Bermuda.[3] The company prides itself on providing an entertaining and relaxing experience for all guests onboard its "Fun Ships." Carnival builds all its ships with one goal in mind: "to make sure that every time you walk up the gangway, you get the sense that you're crossing over into a whole new world of fun."[4]

Carnival Cruise Lines is the flagship brand in a portfolio operated by its parent company Carnival Corporation & plc. Carnival Corporation has headquarters in Miami, Florida and London, England and is publicly traded under the ticker symbol CCL on the New York and London Stock Exchanges. Carnival Corporation & plc is the only group in the world to be included in both the S&P 500 and the FTSE 100 indices.[5]

Operating many of the world's best known cruise brands including Carnival, Princess, Holland America, Seabourn, Cunard, and P&O, Carnival Corporation & plc is a global cruise company. As one of the largest vacation companies in the world, the corporation's mission is to deliver exceptional vacation experiences that cater to a variety of different geographic regions and lifestyles, while delivering outstanding value.[6] The corporation maintains its top position in the industry by leveraging its cruise lines to penetrate a variety of markets. For instance, Carnival Cruise Lines and Princess both target families, retirees, and other upper middle class customers with competitively priced cruise packages whereas the Seabourn brand provides its upscale travelers with luxury cruises to exotic destinations.[7] Carnival Corporation has a decentralized operating structure and each of its brands has its own headquarters and operating team. The company believes this system helps create the ownership culture it believes to be an important driver of performance.[8]

The company maintains a strong balance sheet with the goal of investing in new and innovative ships, a strategy the company feels is critical in strengthening the leadership position of its brands. Across all brands, Carnival Corporation operates 98 ships and plans to add two to three ships annually in 2012 and beyond. Carnival Cruise Lines operates approximately 18% of Carnival Corporation's total passenger capacity of 191,464 cabins, while serving approximately four million of Carnival Corporation's 8.5 million guests annually.[9]

To fuel its future growth and fill its expanding inventory of cruise ships, Carnival Corporation has expanded its number of home ports to move its cruises closer to its customers. In addition, it has invested heavily in marketing, especially targeting those consumers who have never before sailed. Since 2009, the firm has been moving away from print media and expanding its efforts in social media, such as Facebook, YouTube, Twitter, Flickr, and Podcasts. For instance, Carnival Cruise Lines manages its own "Funville" blog through its website, with the goal of engaging in two-way conversations with potential customers about the experience of cruising. Through such tools, Carnival hopes to attract new guests and create brand fans to continue its reign as the world's largest cruise operator.[10]

During the fiscal year ending November 30, 2010, Carnival Corporation reported earnings of $2.47 per share diluted on nearly 14.5 billion dollars in total revenue.[11] Following the engine fire on the Splendor, in a press release dated November 16, 2010, the company estimated that the total impact from voyage disruptions for the Carnival Splendor and related repair costs will result in an approximate $0.07 reduction in the company's 2010 fourth quarter earnings per share. The company stated that impact of voyage disruptions in the first quarter of 2011 is not expected to be material to the company's 2011 earnings.[12]

The Cruise Line Industry

According to the Carnival Corporation's 2010 Annual Report, "The multi-night cruise industry has grown significantly [over the past decade], but still remains relatively small compared to the wider global vacation market, which includes a variety of land-based travel destinations around the world. For example, there were only about 215,000 cabins in the global cruise industry on November 30, 2010, which is less than the 265,000 rooms in just two North American vacation destinations: Orlando, Florida and Las Vegas, Nevada. Within the wider global vacation market, cruise companies compete for the discretionary income spent by vacationers. Within that context, a recent Nielsen Global Confidence Survey found that after providing for savings and living expenses, the number one global spending priority is for vacations." [13]

As a result of these factors and other favorable cruise industry characteristics, Carnival Corporation believes that the cruise industry exhibits opportunities for growth. The industry's customers have increased at a compound annual growth rate of 5.7% from 2005 to 2010. In 2010, the global cruise industry marketed capacity of 423,000, with Carnival Corporation & plc representing 44% of this capacity. The cruise industry points to exceptional value proposition, wide appeal, low market penetration, positive guest demographics, and high guest satisfaction rates as positive growth dynamics that demonstrate the high potential within the industry.[14]

Trouble at Sea

The cruise industry has experienced its fair share of crises at sea. Facing issues that range from pirates to virus outbreaks to fires, cruise ships must develop and practice extensive contingency plans and drills that meet the International Maritime Organization (IMO) and U.S. Coast Guard standards. The Cruise Lines International Association (CLIA) states that these standards are internationally mandated and govern the design, construction, and operation of cruise vessels. To ensure compliance with both international and U.S. regulations, the U.S. Coast Guard examines all new cruise vessels and thereafter inspects each quarterly. If any deficiencies are discovered, the U.S. Coast Guard may require correction before allowing any passengers aboard the ship.[15]

Despite comprehensive precautionary measures, crises aboard cruise ships still occur regularly. One of the most notable occurred on August 4, 1991 when the cruise ship Oceanos sank off the coast of South Africa. The disaster could have been avoided had the ship not been in a "state of neglect," with loose hull plates, missing valves, and a hole in what was supposed to be a watertight bulkhead.[16] Although all 571 guests and crew survived, the captain and crew were widely ridiculed as cowardly and irresponsible for being among the first to leave the sinking vessel.[17]

Unlike the Oceanos incident, which was attributed to human neglect, many cruising hazards originate outside of the cruise line's direct control. Cruise ships are subject to a dangerous movement known as roll, which is a nautical term for rotation about the ship's longitudinal (front to back) axis, when encountering rogue waves or making sharp turns. On April 21, 2010, sixty passengers were injured aboard Carnival Ecstasy when the ship rolled twelve degrees after suddenly turning to avoid a drifting buoy that could have caused a hole in the ship's hull upon impact.[18] In 2008, a P&O cruise ship operated by Carnival Corporation caught in severe storms off the coast of New Zealand sent passengers and furniture flying as waves lashed up as high as the fifth deck, injuring 42 people.[19] More recently, on March 3, 2010, two guests were killed and six others injured when three abnormally high waves up to 26 feet high smashed glass windows in a public lounge in the forward section of Louis Majesty, sailing near the French Mediterranean port of Marseilles.[20] Such an incident could have been avoided if only the crew had instructed passengers to remain in their cabins during the storm.[21]

A cruising vacation may also be ruined by an outbreak of norovirus, a one-to-two day infection often transmitted through food that causes diarrhea, vomiting, nausea, and stomach cramping. The Centers for Disease Control and Prevention (CDC) warns that the norovirus can spread rapidly from person to person in crowded, closed areas such as cruise ships.[22] Since neither a vaccine nor a treatment exists for the norovirus, many cruise ships have found themselves helpless in the face of an outbreak once a ship has already left port. If presence of the norovirus is discovered early enough in the trip, the crew may altogether cancel - or cut short the cruise as in the case of the Holland America cruise liner ms Oosterdam operated by Carnival Corporation in March of 2009[23]

Depending on the geographic area of cruising, pirate attacks may pose a significant threat. In November of 2005, Seabourn Spirit, a ship operated by the Carnival Corporation subsidiary Seabourn Cruise Line, was chased and attacked by Somali pirates. The cruise ship was able to repel the two speedboats carrying the pirates without returning fire by using an on-board loud acoustic bang to create the illusion of gunfire. None of the 151 terrified passengers was injured, and the cruise line spokesmen were pleased that their safety measures worked.[24] According to the International Maritime Bureau (IMB) Annual Report 2010, a total of 445 actual and attempted pirate attacks occurred around the world, with a strong concentration of the attacks around Africa.[25] The IMB, a non-profit division of the International Chamber of Commerce created to fight against maritime crime and malpractice, advises all mariners to exercise caution and take all necessary precautionary measures when operating in certain areas [26]

Finally, fires pose a serious concern for anyone sailing hundreds of miles from land. In 2006, Star Princess, another ship owned by Carnival Corporation, was set ablaze as it sailed toward Jamaica. Believed to be caused by a cigarette left on a passenger balcony, the fire killed one guest, injured 11 others, and damaged 150 cabins before the crews could douse the flames.[27] As a result, additional sprinklers were installed on balconies and the ship had fewer designated smoking areas.[28]

Carnival Splendor Sets Sail

Carnival Splendor, a 113,300 ton, 952-foot long behemoth, is one of the largest vessels owned by Carnival Cruise Lines. With 13 passenger decks, Splendor's 1,503 guest staterooms can accommodate over 3,000 guests per voyage.[29] A ship the size of Splendor requires six diesel engines, three of which are housed in the aft engine room and the other three in the forward engine room. Two electric switchboards are connected to each engine's generator by electric cables.[30]

Cruise ships are governed by the laws of the country under which each ship is registered. Since Splendor is registered in Panama, any issues that arise at sea would be under the scrutiny of the Panamanian government. However, small countries like Panama are usually reluctant to conduct strenuous investigation into any mishaps at sea because that could result in the ship operator being required to make costly improvements, which would hurt Panama's flag of convenience business.[31]

Carnival Splendor departed Long Beach, California on Sunday, November 7, 2010 for a weeklong cruise of the Mexican Riviera. The ship's normal itinerary included stops in Puerto Vallarta, Mazatlan, and Cabo San Lucas, Mexico. The seven-day, six-night cruise was scheduled to arrive back in Long Beach with its 3,299 guests and 1,167 crew on Saturday, November 13 until a crisis struck during the first leg of its journey.[32]

Fire!

By early morning on Monday, November 8, 2010, the ship was sailing in calm seas 200 miles south of San Diego, California. At 6:00 a.m., a fire started in the aft engine room and passengers reported smelling smoke and seeing it billow out of the rear of the ship. The blaze was extinguished within a few hours by crew members with the aid of the built-in fire-suppression system. No passengers or crew members were injured as a result of the engine fire.[33]

Engineers were unable to restore ship power and auxiliary generators had to be used. Though the ship was designed by reputable Italian shipbuilders to ensure that damage to a single generator and switchboard wouldn't inhibit the rest of the ship's engines, the fire unexpectedly disabled all power generation onboard Splendor. The intense heat of the fire severely damaged the power lines housed in the ceiling of the aft engine room, which consequently made the forward engine room also inoperable. As a result, the destruction caused by the fire was much more widespread.[34] The ship had previously been regularly inspected by the Coast Guard and other maritime regulators and found in regulatory compliance.[35]

The initial speculation about the cause of the fire was that one of the generators for an aft engine ignited and damaged its accompanying switchboard. The damage to the switchboard and overhead power lines prevented electrical transmission to propulsion, communication, and other operating systems, leaving the ship dead in the water.[36] Gerry Cahill, CEO of

Carnival Cruise Lines, later confirmed that the fire was a result of a catastrophic failure in one of six diesel generators. Cahill said he doubted that any of the other ships in the company's fleet were at risk.[37]

Because the ship was registered in Panama, the Panamanian government would be responsible for probing into the official cause of the fire. However, because most of the passengers traveling on the Splendor were American citizens, Panama agreed to allow the U.S. Coast Guard and the National Transportation Safety Board, an independent U.S. federal agency charged with determining the probable cause of transportation accidents and promoting transportation safety, to join the investigation. The three parties would conduct a full examination into the causes of the fire after first ensuring the safety of the passengers and the crew.[38]

At 6:30 a.m. on Monday, passengers were awakened by a message transmitted over the ship's public address system from Splendor Cruise Director John Heald. Guests were initially instructed to remain in their cabins but were soon evacuated to the ship's upper deck.[39] Although passengers were later allowed to return to their cabins, many spent the majority of the remainder of the voyage on the upper levels of the ship. By the afternoon, the U.S. Coast Guard had dispatched three cutters and an airplane to provide aid and medical assistance to Splendor. The Mexican navy also responded with aircraft and relief boats.[40] Ongoing announcements from Heald about the fire, decisions, and progress kept passengers informed about the situation.

The "Circus" Aboard Carnival

In one of his first public statements about the incident, CEO Gerry Cahill acknowledged that the passengers endured "an extremely trying" situation aboard Carnival Splendor. He publicly apologized for the distress and inconvenience of the passengers. Guests endured challenging circumstances including no electrical power, no Internet service, no refrigerated food, very long lines to obtain food, sanitation problems, and boredom. Air conditioning and hot food service were also unavailable, and the disabled elevators due to the lack of electrical power meant that passengers would have to climb as many as 13 floors to get to the food. Some passengers reported that plumbing was almost to capacity and that the odor in sections of the ship smelled like vomit.[41]

Cahill admitted that after 35 years of business, nothing like the Splendor situation had happened before.[42] The Cruise Director, John Heald, tried to keep passengers' spirits up with frequent announcements from the bridge using the ship's PA system. Heald, an avid blogger of johnhealdsblog.com, a blog featured on Carnival Corporation's website, told his eight million readers in a post on Wednesday, November 10 that he didn't know how his attempts to add humor in his announcements were being received by the guests. Heald praised the passengers saying, "...the guests have been magnificent and have risen to the obvious challenges and difficult conditions onboard."[43]

After the fire, Carnival Splendor was some 200 miles south of San Diego and dead in the water. Originally scheduled as a seven-day cruise from Long Beach to Puerto Vallarta, the new objective was to safely transport the passengers to a port as soon as possible. Within two hours of the fire, Gallagher had opened and fully staffed the crisis command center at the Carnival corporate office and worked collectively to aid the Splendor crew and passengers.[44] Their initial plan was to tow Splendor to the Mexican port of Ensenada;[45] however, the crisis response team soon decided to change the destination to San Diego.[46] The rationale was that passengers would be more comfortable onboard the ship and that the new plan would not require the customers to go through the difficult customs process in Mexico.[47]

The Mexican navy sent multiple tugboats to the aid of Splendor, one of which had to turn back because it wasn't powerful enough. The tug boats reached the cruise ship midday on Tuesday, November 9, 2010.[48] In addition, to the good fortune of Carnival Cruise Lines, the U.S. Navy was conducting regularly scheduled training in the area. At the request of the Coast Guard, the U.S. Navy resupplied the ship on Tuesday with 70,000 pounds of bread, canned milk, and other food including Pop Tarts and Spam, and supplies that had been flown from North Island Naval Station in Coronado. The supplies were then ferried by helicopter from the USS Ronald Reagan (CVN-76), an aircraft carrier diverted from maneuvers nearby.[49] According to Navy officials, maritime tradition, customs, and treaties demand that ships in the area must respond to ships in distress whenever possible.[50]

Toilet service to all public bathrooms and most cabin rooms, as well as cold running water, was restored late Monday night much to the relief of uncomfortable passengers.[51] One passenger considered the voyage a "diet cruise" because of the lack of hot food. Instead of the fine dining expected aboard any cruise line, passengers were served salads, fruit, small sandwiches, and canned crab meat. First-time Carnival guest Peg Fisher said, "This could be the only cruise ever where people lost weight instead of gaining weight."[52] With no power, swimming pools were closed due to lack of filtration and casinos were also closed. Interior state rooms were pitch black and stuffy due to the lack of electricity and air flow. Passengers passed the time with live music, scavenger hunts, trivia contests, and card games. However, bars were open and did offer free drinks.[53]

Less than one day after the engine fire, Carnival Cruise Lines announced that they would offer all passengers a full refund for the cruise and a credit equal to the price they paid for a future Carnival cruise. In addition, Carnival arranged and paid for all necessary hotels and flights for passengers arriving in San Diego.[54] The ship was expected to arrive in San Diego the morning of Thursday, November 11, more than 62 hours after the fire disabled Splendor. Initially, it was unknown how long the ship would be out of service while necessary repairs were being made.

News and Social Media Response

The events on Monday and Tuesday happened outside of cellular phone service range. In addition, Internet service was knocked out due to the loss of power. Passengers were unable to personally update friends and family of their safety until the ship got closer to the coast on Wednesday, November 10, 2010.[55] On Wednesday, individuals could finally assure loved ones of their safety and share their experiences on the cruise. Passengers called home and sent text messages to communicate with friends and family about arrival in San Diego.[56] Witnesses tweeted pictures and messages about the ships arrival.[57] In addition, national news outlets began interviewing passengers aboard the ship via cell phones and their reports covered the evening news.

Carnival used Twitter, Facebook, and its Funville blog primarily as push mechanisms to provide factual updates about the cruise.[58] John Heald also used his personal blog to provide a brief update to readers about the cruise ship on Wednesday, November 10. Passengers had been taking pictures and videos throughout the cruise and many videos were uploaded to YouTube following arrival.[59] The increasing volume of social media that mentioned the Carnival Splendor created significant buzz on the Internet.

After learning about the delivery of Spam to the Splendor, some media outlets used "Spam Cruise" as a tagline for articles about the event. Carnival attempted to use Twitter to address the incorrect view that Spam was served to its passengers: "Despite media reports to the contrary, Carnival Splendor guests were never served Spam!"[60] However, news and social media outlets continued to embrace the Spam angle, and a new phrase, "Spamcation" emerged online. As passengers departed the ship on Thursday, November 11, they were eager to buy $20 T-shirts emblazoned with the phrase: "I survived the 2010 Carnival Cruise Spamcation."[61]

Decision Point

As Carnival Splendor approached the San Diego port at 8:30 a.m. on the morning of Thursday, November 11, Gerry Cahill and Tim Gallagher knew that their work was just beginning. Carnival Cruise Lines had already announced that all guests would receive reimbursement for the trip and travel costs. Cahill and Gallagher had been working around the clock to coordinate the arrival of the ship by arranging transportation and hotels for all guests. But unless Gallagher and his team could quickly address the other issues, Carnival Cruise Lines was at risk of losing a lot more than simply one week of cruise revenues.

- Should the company have done anything differently in their communication efforts while the ship was being brought back to port?
- Who are the key stakeholders? Who, in your opinion, is (are) the most important stakeholder(s)?
- What channels of communication should Carnival Cruise Lines use and what should the message be? What audiences do they need to address?
- How does Carnival Cruise Lines manage its brand reputation in the aftermath of this event? What damage, if any, has been caused? How can it be mitigated? What measures of reputation should the company use?
- What should Carnival Cruise Lines do to prepare for similar situations in the future? What, if any, performance issues does Carnival Cruise Lines need to address?
- How may this situation impact future business for Carnival Cruise Lines and the entire cruising industry?

WRITING ASSIGNMENT

Please respond in writing to the issues presented in this case by preparing two documents: a communication strategy memo and a professional business letter.

In preparing these documents, you may assume one of two roles: you may identify yourself as a Carnival Corporation senior manager who has been asked to provide advice to Mr. Gerry Cahill regarding the issues he and his company are facing. Or, you may identify yourself as an external management consultant who has been asked by the company to provide advice to Mr. Cahill.

Either way, you must prepare a strategy memo addressed to Gerry Cahill, President and CEO, Carnival Cruise Lines, that summarizes the details of the case, rank orders the critical issues, discusses their implications (what they mean and why they matter), offers specific recommendations for action (assigning ownership and suspense dates for each), and shows how to communicate the solution to all who are affected by the recommendations.

You must also prepare a professional business letter for Mr. Cahill's signature. That document should be addressed to all *Carnival Splendor* cruisers who have been inconvenienced or disappointed by the events described in the case.

References

1. Heald, John. "Smoke on the Water: Part 1," *John Heald's Blog*, 12 Nov. 2010. Accessed 28 Feb. 2011. http://johnhealdsblog.com/2010/11/12/smoke-on-the-water-part-1/.

2. McWhirter, Cameron. "U.S. News: Aided by Tugs, Stranded Cruise Ship Heads to San Diego," *Wall Street Journal*, 11 Nov. 2010: A.7.

3. "Carnival Cruise Lines Fact Sheet," *Carnival Cruise Lines*, 8 July 2009. 12 Feb. 2011. http://carnivalpressroom.wordpress.com/2009/07/08/carnival-cruise-lines-fact-sheet/.

4. "Carnival Fun Ships," *Carnival Cruise Lines*, 26 Feb. 2011. http://www.carnival.com/FunShips.aspx.

5. "Investor Relations," *Carnival Corporation & plc*, 12 Feb. 2011. http://phx.corporate-ir.net/phoenix.zhtml?c=140690&p=irol-irhome.

6. "10-K," *Carnival Corporation & plc*, 31 Jan. 2010, 12 Feb. 2011, Page 4. http://phx.corporate-ir.net/phoenix.zhtml?c=140690&p=irol-sec

7. "Carnival Corporation: Overview," *Hoovers*, delivered via ProQuest, 12 Feb. 2011. http://cobrands.hoovers.com/global/cobrands/proquest/overview,xhtml?ID=11803.

8. "10-K," *Carnival Corporation & plc*, 31 Jan. 2010. 12 Feb. 2011, Page 4. http://phx.corporate-ir.net/phoenix.zhtml?c=140690&p=irol-sec

9. "10-K," *Carnival Corporation & plc*, 31 Jan. 2010. 12 Feb. 2011, Page 3. http://phx.corporate-ir.net/phoenix.zhtml?c=140690&p=irol-sec.

10. "Carnival Corporation: Overview," *Hoovers*, Delivered via ProQuest, 12 Feb. 2011. http://cobrands.hoovers.com/global/cobrands/proquest/overview,xhtml?ID=11803.

11. "10-K," *Carnival Corporation & plc*, 31 Jan. 2010. 12 Feb. 2011, Exhibit 13, page F-1. http://phx.corporate-ir.net/phoenix.zhtml?c=140690&p=irol-sec.

12. "Carnival Corporation & plc Reports Financial Impact of Voyage Disruptions in the 4th Quarter," *Carnival Corporation & plc*, 16 Nov. 2010. 12 Feb. 2011. http://phx.corporate-ir.net/phoenix.zhtml?c=200767&p=irol-newsArticle&ID=1497049&highlight.

13. "10-K," *Carnival Corporation & plc*, 31 Jan. 2010. 12 Feb. 2011, Page 5. http://phx.corporate-ir.net/phoenix.zhtml?c=140690&p=irol-sec.

14. "10-K," *Carnival Corporation & plc*, 31 Jan. 2010. 12 Feb. 2011, Page 6. http://phx.corporate-ir.net/phoenix.zhtml?c=140690&p=irol-sec.

16. Walker, Jim. "Top Five Worst Cruise Ship Disaster Videos," *Cruise Law News*. 23 Jan. 2011. 20 Feb. 2011. http://www.cruiselawnews.com/2011/01/articles/rough-weather-1/top-five-worst-cruise-ship-disaster-videos/.

17. Chua-Eoan, Howard G. "Disaster: Going, Going...," *Time.com*, 24 Jun. 2001. 20 Feb. 2011. http://205.188.238.109/time/magazine/article/0,9171,157677,00.html.

18. Gavazzi, Debbie. "Carnival Ecstasy Cruise Ship Tilts and Injures Passengers," Associated Content from Yahoo!, 23 Apr. 2010. 20 Feb. 2011. http://www.associatedcontent.com/article/2927054/carnival_ecstasy_cruise_ship_tilts.html?cat=16.

19. Pickup, Oliver. "P&O cruise ship horror: CCTV footage captures moment when severe

storm sends passengers and furniture flying," Mail Online, 8 Sept. 2010. 20 Feb. 2011. http://www.dailymail.co.uk/travel/article-1310056/P-O-Pacific-Sun-cruise-ship-caught-storm-New-Zealand-coast.html.

20. Garrison, Linda. "Two Killed When Rogue Wave Hits Louis Majesty Cruise Ship in the Mediterranean," *About.com*, 3 Mar. 2010. 20 Feb. 2011. http://cruises.about.com/b/2010/03/03/rogue-wave-mediterranean.htm.

21. Walker, Jim. "Top Five Worst Cruise Ship Disaster Videos," *Cruise Law News*, 23 Jan. 2011. 20 Feb. 2011. http://www.cruiselawnews.com/2011/01/articles/rough-weather-1/top-five-worst-cruise-ship-disaster-videos/.

22. "Prevent the Spread of Norovirus," Centers for Disease Control and Prevention, 20 Feb. 2011. http://www.cdc.gov/Features/Norovirus/.

23. "Virus Hits Cruise Ship on First Day at Sea," *ConsumerAffairs.com*, 2 Mar. 2009. 20 Feb. 2011. http://www.consumeraffairs.com/news04/2009/03/cruise_illness.html.

24. "Cruise ship repels Somali pirates," *BBC News*, 5 Nov. 2005. 20 Feb. 2011. http://news.bbc.co.uk/2/hi/4409662.stm.

25. "Piracy and Armed Robbery Against Ships Annual Report 2010," *ICC International Maritime Bureau*, 20 Feb. 2011, Page 6. http://www.simsl.com/Downloads/Piracy/IMBPiracyReport2010.pdf.

26. "Piracy Prone Areas and Warnings," *ICC International Maritime Bureau*, 20 Feb. 2011. http://www.icc-ccs.org/piracy-reporting-centre/prone-areas-and-warnings

27. Nguyen, Daisy, and John Rogers. "Troubled Cruise Shows Unpredictability of the Sea," Associated Press, *ABC News*. 13 Nov. 2010. 12 Feb. 2011. http://abcnews.go.com/Business/wireStory?id=12135725.

28. Martin, Timothy. "U.S. News: Thousands Stranded on Disabled Cruise Liner --- Navy Delivers Food to 4,500 Passengers, Crew Off Mexican Coast After Fire Cripples Ship; Carnival Offers Refund, Free Trip," *Wall Street Journal*, 10 Nov. 2010: A.6.

29. "Carnival Splendor," *Carnival Cruise Lines*, 5 Feb. 2011. http://www.carnival.com/cms/fun/ships/carnival_splendor/default.aspx.

30. Stroller, Gary. "Carnival Splendor stranding baffles marine experts," *USA Today*, 12 Nov. 2010. 12 Feb. 2011. http://www.usatoday.com/

travel/cruises/2010-11-12-cruise-inside_N.htm?loc=interstitialskip.

31. Nguyen, Daisy, and John Rogers. "Troubled Cruise Shows Unpredictability of the Sea," Associated Press, *ABC News*. 13 Nov. 2010. 12 Feb. 2011. http://abcnews.go.com/Business/wireStory?id=12135725.

32. Ruiz, Mary. "Updates Carnival Splendor," *Carnival Cruise Lines*, 8 Nov. 2010. 12 Feb. 2011. http://www.carnival.com/Funville/forums/p/140814/730198.aspx.

33. Vercammen, Paul; Martinez, Michael and Gast, Phil. "Crippled cruise ship expected in San Diego Thursday," *CNN*, 11 Nov. 2010. 12 Feb. 2011. http://edition.cnn.com/2010/TRAVEL/11/10/cruise.ship/?hpt=T2.

34. Telephone interview with Tim Gallagher, Carnival Cruise Lines' Vice President of Corporate Communications, 1 Mar. 2011.

35. Stroller, Gary. "Carnival Splendor stranding baffles marine experts," *USA Today*, 12 Nov. 2010. 12 Feb. 2011. http://www.usatoday.com/travel/cruises/2010-11-12-cruise-inside_N.htm?loc=interstitialskip.

36. Ibid.

37. Spagat, Elliot. "Travelers Disembark 'Nightmare' Cruise Amid Cheers," Associated Press, *ABC News*, 11 Nov. 2010. 12 Feb. 2011. http://abcnews.go.com/Business/wireStory?id=12122689.

38. McWhirter, Cameron. "U.S. News: Aided by Tugs, Stranded Cruise Ship Heads to San Diego," *Wall Street Journal*, 11 Nov. 2010: A.7.

39. La Ganga, Maria L., and Perry, Tony. "Stranded cruise ship offers lesson in huge vessels' vulnerabilities," *Los Angeles Times*, 10 Nov. 2010. 12 Feb. 2011. http://articles.latimes.com/print/2010/nov/10/local/la-me-cruise-ship-20101110.

40. La Ganga, Maria L., and Tony Perry. "Stranded cruise ship offers lesson in huge vessels' vulnerabilities," *Los Angeles Times*, 10 Nov. 2010. 12 Feb. 2011. http://articles.latimes.com/print/2010/nov/10/local/la-me-cruise-ship-20101110.

41. Vercammen, Paul; Martinez, Michael and Gast, Phil. "Crippled cruise ship expected in San Diego Thursday," *CNN*, 11 Nov. 2010. 12 Feb. 2011. http://edition.cnn.com/2010/TRAVEL/11/10/cruise.ship/?hpt=T2.

42. Ibid.

43. Heald, John. "Here I Am," *John Heald's Blog*, 10 Nov. 2010. 12 Feb. 2011. http://johnhealdsblog.com/2010/11/10/here-i-am-2/.

44. Telephone interview with Tim Gallagher, Carnival Cruise Lines' Vice President of Corporate Communications, 1 Mar. 2011.

45. Heald, John. "Update on the Carnival Splendor," *John Heald's Blog*, 8 Nov. 2010. 12 Feb. 2011. http://johnhealdsblog.com/2010/11/08/update-on-the-carnival-splendor/.

46. Heald, John. "Latest Carnival Splendor Update," *John Heald's Blog*, 9 Nov. 2010. 12 Feb. 2011. http://johnhealdsblog.com/2010/11/09/latest-carnival-splendor-update/.

47. Watson, Julie, et al. "Carnival CEO apologized to stranded cruisers," *MSNBC Travel News*, 11 Nov. 2010. 12 Feb. 2011. http://www.msnbc.msn.com/id/40084109/ns/travel-news/.

48. Ibid.

49. Perry, Tony. "Tugboats, Navy copters head for cruise ship damaged by fire off Mexico," *Los Angeles Times*, 9 Nov. 2010. 12 Feb. 2011. http://latimesblogs.latimes.com/lanow/2010/11/tugboats-navy-copters-head-for-cruise-ship-damaged-by-fire-off-mexico.html.

50. McWhirter, Cameron. "Disabled Cruise Ship Reaches San Diego Harbor," *Wall Street Journal* (Online), 11 Nov. 2010. http://online.wsj.com/article/SB10001424052748703848204575608381063993198.html

51. Heald, John. "Latest Carnival Splendor Update," *John Heald's Blog*, 9 Nov. 2010. 12 Feb. 2011. http://johnhealdsblog.com/2010/11/09/latest-carnival-splendor-update/.

52. Spagat, Elliot. "Travelers Disembark 'Nightmare' Cruise Amid Cheers," Associated Press, *ABC News*, 11 Nov. 2010. 12 Feb. 2011. http://abcnews.go.com/Business/wireStory?id=12122689.

53. Watson, Julie, et al. "Carnival CEO apologizes to stranded cruisers," *MSNBC Travel News*, 11 Nov. 2010. 12 Feb. 2011. http://www.msnbc.msn.com/id/40084109/ns/travel-news/.

54. Martin, Timothy. "U.S. News: Thousands Stranded on Disabled Cruise Liner --- Navy Delivers Food to 4,500 Passengers, Crew Off Mexican Coast After Fire Cripples Ship; Carnival Offers Refund, Free Trip," *Wall Street Journal*, 10 Nov. 2010: A.6.

55. Vercammen, Paul, Michael Martinez, and Phil Gast. "Crippled cruise ship expected in San Diego Thursday," *CNN*, 11 Nov. 2010. 12 Feb. 2011. http://edition.cnn.com/2010/TRAVEL/11/10/cruise.ship/?hpt=T2.

56. Sloan, Gene. "Carnival Splendor passengers disembark in San Diego," *USA Today*, 11 Nov. 2010. 12 Feb. 2011. http://www.usatoday.com/travel/cruises/2010-11-11-1Acruise11_CV_N.htm.

57. Benabia, Jeff. "Carnival Splendor cruise ship being towed back home (from my balcony)," *Twitter*, 11 Nov. 2010. 12 Feb. 2011. http://twitter.com/dermdoc/status/2751684606431234.

58. Schaal, Dennis. "Carnival Splendor and 1-way social media response from Carnival," *tnooz*, 10 Nov. 2010. 12 Feb. 2011. http://www.tnooz.com/2010/11/10/news/carnival-splendor-and-1-way-social-media-response-from-carnival/.

59. Hoffer, Steven. "Footage Gives Peek into Cruise Ship Ordeal," *AOL News*, 12 Nov. 2010. 12 Feb. 2011. http://www.aolnews.com/2010/11/12/passenger-footage-gives-inside-look-at-carnival-splendor-cruise/.

60. Sloan, Gene. "Carnival: No spam was served on Carnival Splendor during crisis," *USA Today*, 11 Nov. 2010. 12 Feb. 2011. http://travel.usatoday.com/cruises/post/2010/11/carnival-splendor-cruise-ship-fire-spam-/130847/1.

61. Spagat, Elliot. "Travelers Disembark 'Nightmare' Cruise Amid Cheers," Associated Press, *ABC News*, 11 Nov. 2010. 12 Feb. 2011. http://abcnews.go.com/Business/wireStory?id=12122689.

CASE STUDY 5-3
ANTENNAGATE:
Apple's Loss of Signal (A)

Shattered Illusions

On June 24, 2010, Steve Jobs should have been basking in his recent success. With the day's highly anticipated release of the iPhone 4, Apple had taken enormous strides forward in smart-phone technology. Based on pre-order data, Apple was expecting to sell almost two million phones in the first few days. If Merrill Lynch's prediction in March was correct, over 55 million iPhones would be sold worldwide by the end of the year since the first iPhone's release nearly three years ago. These sales not only provided Apple with a tidy profit through hardware, but also through the highly lucrative exclusive service contract with AT&T, for which Apple receives a generous cut, and increased business to the iTunes App Store, of which Apple receives a 30% royalty.

Apple's successful sales had come despite new competitors mimicking the innovative features built into the iPhone that initially made the product so popular. Products such as the Motorola Droid had been met with great enthusiasm, and had the support of Google to produce streamlined software to optimize Internet and mobile app performance. It was reassuring to see that sales had remained strong, in no small part due to Apple's avid supporters.

Despite this success, Jobs had reason to be cautious. Several users had already complained of reception problems due to the phone's new antenna configuration, and some of the specialty blogs had begun to take notice. Consumers reported that the phone would lose its signal if held in a certain way. Jobs knew that this could erupt into a huge problem, and that something needed to be done. The only question was: what?

Phones Have Antennas?

At the highly-anticipated June 2010 press conference to unveil the iPhone 4, Apple CEO Steve Jobs went out of his way to herald the phone's revolutionary design and the "brilliant engineering" behind the phone's antenna, which is actually built into the stainless steel band around the edge of the phone. When an iPhone 4 was leaked to the tech blog Gizmodo a few months prior, skeptics singled out a series of black lines, or breaks in the stainless steel band as proof that the phone was a fake. Steve Jobs made a point of addressing those concerns as part of his press event:

> "People have asked, 'What's this?' Some have even said, 'This doesn't seem like Apple.' What are these lines in this beautiful stainless steel band? Well, it turns out there's not just one of them, there's three of them. And they are part of the entire structure of this phone… It turns out this is part of some brilliant engineering, which actually uses the stainless steel band as part of the antenna system. And so, one piece is Bluetooth, WiFi, and GPS, and the other is UMTS and GSM. So it's got these integrated antennas right in the structure of the phone. It's really never been done before and it's really cool engineering." [1]

The stainless steel band on the iPhone 4 acts as the phone's antenna, and is separated into three parts in order to service three different types of antenna frequencies.

Almost immediately after iPhone 4 units began shipping in June, tech blogs and Apple call centers began receiving reports of signal problems when making calls. A pattern emerged among the complaints that focused on a so-called "death grip" caused by holding the phone in a manner that covered the black lines Steve Jobs was so proud to discuss days earlier. If the user's hand was not covering the black lines, service as indicated by the reception bars was normal. As soon as the black lines were covered, the signal bars immediately fell and the active call was often dropped. Dozens of YouTube videos and first-hand accounts were able to replicate the issue.

Signal Attenuation Comparison in dB - Lower is Better				
	Cupping Tightly	**Holding Naturally**	**On an Open Palm**	**Holding Naturally Inside Case**
iPhone 4	24.6	19.8	9.2	7.2
iPhone 3GS	14.3	1.9	0.2	3.2
HTC Nexus One	17.7	10.7	6.7	7.7

Courtesy Anandtech.com: http://www.anandtech.com/show/3794/the-iphone-4-review/2

Signal issues are certainly not a new phenomenon when it comes to cell phones. Covering almost any phone's internal antenna is bound to cause some signal loss, as explained by Dr.Richard Gaywood, a wireless network planning expert from Cardiff University. In his analysis of the iPhone 4, however, he explains that such signal attenuation (or loss of signal) is far worse for Apple's new device, particularly when the incoming signal is weak.[2]

Just as holding an AM/FM radio antenna with your bare hand will cause the sound quality to drop, holding the stainless steel antenna on an iPhone 4 with your bare hand will cause the call quality to drop, as the conductive nature of human skin naturally causes interference. This problem is amplified further when bare skin covers the black gap between the antennas on the iPhone's band, as it causes a kind of short-circuit that leads to significantly reduced call strength.

A popular theory for how this problem may have slipped through the cracks is that Apple employees who were testing the iPhone had to use it in a plastic case to disguise it as an iPhone3G. Because they were not field-testing the iPhone 4 with their bare hands, they would not have experienced the attenuation issue.

Breaking the Bad News

By the time Apple officially released the iPhone 4 on June 24, complaints about the highly anticipated product had already begun to bubble to the surface. With some pre-ordered phones having been delivered as early as June 22, customers had begun using and analyzing the new phone days before the official launch.

On June 23, Fame Foundry, a Charlotte-based website design company, posted a YouTube video demonstrating the loss of signal strength bars upon touching the antenna. The initial video compared the signal strength obtained when the phone was lying on a table untouched to when it was held by the metal antenna band or by the glass on the front and back. The video clearly showed the signal strength dropping from five bars to zero bars only when the user held the phone by the antenna band. The video was soon posted to MacRumors, where it elicited over 60 responses in the first hour and 1000 in the first twelve hours.

The rumors and videos quickly became viral, spreading to technology websites such as Gizmodo, Engadget, and AppleInsider. On June 24, the day of the official launch, website Engadget sent an e-mail regarding the matter to Apple and received a response that stated:

"Gripping any mobile phone will result in some attenuation of its antenna performance, with certain places being worse than others depending on the placement of the antennas. This is a fact of life for every wireless phone. If you ever experience this on your iPhone 4, avoid gripping it in the lower left corner in a way that covers both sides of the black strip in the metal band, or simply use one of many available cases."[3]

The response by Apple was immediately met with disappointment, as Apple had a long history of providing products that excelled in both form and function. The article on Engadget drew such comments as, "I find that explanation to be not only unsatisfactory, but down-right wrong" and "they need to adjust to the customer." Customers felt that Apple was blaming "a bit of bad design"[4] on user error.

Within a week, Nokia made an attempt to capitalize upon the iPhone 4's antenna problems. Nokia created an entry on their corporate blog demonstrating the many ways that Nokia users were able to hold their phones. The entry illustrated four common holding styles, all of which are "both comfortable and … offer no signal degradation whatsoever." According to the entry, "the key function on any Nokia device is its ability to make phone calls … when making a phone call, people generally tend to hold their phone like a - well, like a phone."[5]

On June 30, Motorola made its own attempt to exploit Apple's antenna issue by featuring its new Droid X in a full-page ad in *The New York Times*. The ad showcased the features of the Droid X and finished by stating that "most importantly, it comes with a double antenna design. The kind that allows you to hold the phone any way you like and use it just about anywhere to make crystal clear calls."[6]

History of Apple

The Founding

Apple was formed on April 1, 1976 by Steve Wozniak and Steve Jobs, with the sale of 50 Apple I computers to The Byte Shop at an initial cost of $500.00. The successful sale of these computers enabled the pair to continue development of what would arguably become one of the first financially successful examples of a personal computer. While the concept of a computer built for the average person met some initial resistance, Wozniak and Jobs were able to cosign for a $250,000 loan with Mike Markkula to continue their development.[7]

With this investment, Wozniak and Jobs went on to make several significant technological breakthroughs that established Apple's reputation for innovation. This included such achievements as the first graphical user interface (GUI), significant improvements to the floppy drive, and the introduction of the Macintosh computer. In 1980, Apple launched its IPO, which at the time became the second largest IPO in history behind Ford's 1956 IPO. In 1983, John Sculley was hired as CEO, leaving his position as president at Pepsi-Cola. While Sculley was responsible for growing the company from an $800 million company to an $8 billion company by the end of his tenure in 1993, he notably limited Jobs from spending on innovation. By the end of 1985, Steve Jobs left Apple following a failed attempt to regain control of the company from Sculley. Steve Wozniak had left months earlier due to a serious car accident.

The Return of Steve Jobs

Steve Jobs returned to Apple in 1997 as an advisor, and later as interim CEO. While the company had partially been brought back to life by the CEO Gil Amelio through organizational restructuring, the company had struggled since Jobs's departure. Upon his return through an acquisition of NeXT, Jobs immediately began implementing change. Jobs made his first appearance as the keynote speaker at the 1997 MacWorld Convention, and would continue to use this forum as an opportunity to announce the release of all of Apple's biggest products. Most notably, with the return of Steve Jobs came a revived passion for innovation.[8]

The iPhone

The idea for the iPhone can be traced to the Apple Newton, one of the first true personal digital assistants, or PDAs. While the Newton was eventually discontinued by Steve Jobs, the device can be seen as an important forerunner for the iPhone.

The actual idea for the iPhone evolved from the successful launch of the iPod in 2002. Steve Jobs knew that phones posed a threat to the iPod due to the fact that customers would likely rather carry one device that could both place calls and play music. In 2004 Jobs entered negotiations with Motorola and Motorola's carrier, Cingular, to produce software that would incorporate iTunes on the successor to Motorola's popular RAZR phone. The deal was tenuous from the start, as there was much debate among the three companies on how much of the phone's limited hardware capabilities would be dedicated to Apple's software. What resulted was the ROKR. Released in 2005, the ROKR paled in comparison to the iPhone that would be released only a short time later, as it was less visibly appealing and had a fraction of the functionality.[9]

The relative failure of the ROKR and the difficulties Jobs experienced in getting his partners to agree on the phone's functionality convinced Jobs that Apple needed to produce its own phone. After successfully negotiating a deal with Cingular's executives for exclusivity priorto AT&T's acquisition of the company, Jobs successfully set the foundation for the launch of the phone. After only one year of production, more than 5.4 million phones had been sold. More than 33.7 million phones were sold world-wide by the end of Q4, 2009.

The Apple/AT&T Marriage

Since the first iPhone was released in 2007, AT&T has been the sole US wireless carrier to provide the iPhone. This relationship has not come without its issues, however. The number of iPhones and the amount of data use by iPhone users was initially underestimated and has continued to be a problem as AT&T has struggled to keep up with demand. Dropped calls are frequent for many iPhone users, especially in larger cities such as New York and San Francisco where there are more users.

Other problems that the companies have faced together in conjunction with the iPhone include activation issues and pre-order system malfunctions. Activations of previous generations of the iPhone have taken days in some cases because of the large numbers of phones that have been trying to activate on the release date. Additionally, in the case of the iPhone 4 pre-order on June 15, AT&T systems crashed and requests were unable to be processed, enraging many of Apple's faithful customers.[10] These issues and the demand from customers using other services have been the basis for debates on whether or not Apple should continue exclusivity with AT&T.

Apple's contract with AT&T expires in 2010. Thus, Apple's problems with the iPhone antenna and any resulting damage to its image come at a critical time for the company as they explore new options. Apple's exclusive contract with AT&T had been extremely lucrative for the company. As Apple negotiates with AT&T and expands its negotiations to other carriers, scandals such as Antennagate could amount to the loss of billions during negotiations, especially in the face of growing competition.

Rise of Competing Smartphones

So-called "smartphones" are defined as mobile phones that can access the internet, have larger screens, and can run installed applications. In 2010, estimated smartphone sales accounted for two-thirds of new mobile phone sales revenue and roughly one third of unit sales[11] (the discrepancy explained by the significantly higher per-unit sales price of smartphones). This is a category that the iPhone helped define and has long since dominated, at least in terms of "buzz" and public perception.[12] But recent trends have competing devices showing a legitimate threat to iPhone's crown.

Sales of devices with Google's open-source Android OS topped the iPhone in the second quarter of 2010 and are on track to overtake Research In Motions (RIM)'s Blackberry OS for the first time by the end of the year. This meteoric rise brings Android's install base from 1.8% to17.2%.[13] Nokia still holds the global lead, mainly due to its large presence in Europe. Android presents the most direct threat to the iPhone because it is seen as the most equivalent competitor, with primarily touch-screen controls and a vast library of third-party apps to enhance the use of the phone. Unlike the iPhone OS, Android is available to any phone manufacturer and all major carriers.

RIM's Blackberry devices, available on all major carriers in the US, is also a direct competitor to the iPhone, but with a target focused more directly on business contracts and integration with corporate IT infrastructures. RIM manufactures their own devices and does not license the operating system to other phone makers; however, third-party developers were allowed to make apps that integrate with the OS starting in March of 2009.[14]

Early entrants in the smartphone platform category, including Palm, Nokia (Symbian), and Windows Mobile, have largely fallen from popularity due to less favorable third-party app offerings and their presence on slower, older-generation phones.

Of grave concern to Apple in the wake of Antennagate is the possibility of this snafu speeding adoption of competing smartphone platforms.

DECISION POINT

Within a week after the iPhone 4 release, reported antenna problems had been bandied about tech blogs and Apple enthusiast websites. The extent of the problem, at least in regards to the actual number of consumers being affected, seems fairly small.

1. What, if any, reaction should Apple have to the reported Antenna issues?
2. Who are the key stakeholders?
3. What does Apple "owe" its customers?
4. Through what channels should Apple address consumers' concerns?

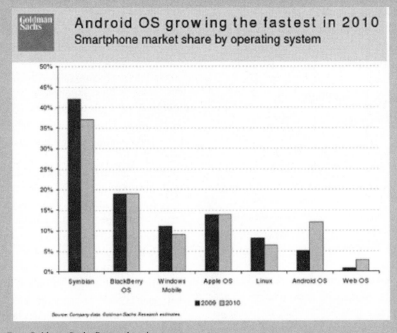

Source: Company Data Goldman Sachs Research estimates

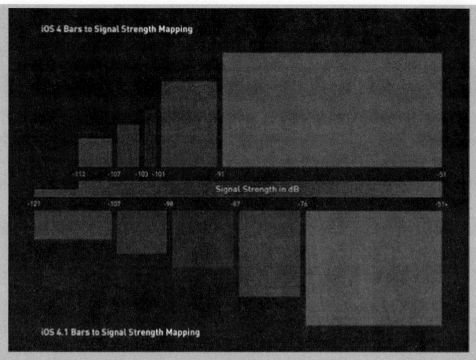

Source: "The iPhone 4 Redux: Analyzing apples's iOS 4.0 Signal Fix & Antenna Issue," AnandTech, July 15,

2010 http://www.anandtech.com/show/3821/iphone-4-redux-analyzing-apples-ios-41-signal-fix

There's a weird subtext about transparency and victimization through all of this, too. A sense of, "See what happens when we're transparent?" … As a journalist, this is laughable: Apple has one of the most opaque and impregnable walls of PR people in the industry. Apple's silence, enforced by PR staff who will clam up at the slightest hint of someone going off-message, are legendary

--Matt Buchanan, *Gizmodo*

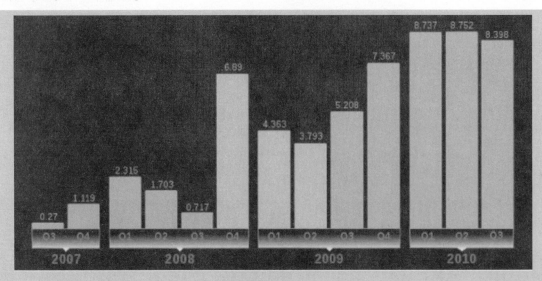

Source: "File: Iphone sales per quarter simple.svg," Wikipedia.

http://en.wikipedia.org/wiki/File:IPhone_sales_per_quarter_simple.svg

WRITING ASSIGNMENT

Please respond in writing to the issues presented in this case by preparing two documents: a communication strategy memo and a professional business letter.

In preparing these documents, you may assume one of two roles: you may identify yourself as an Apple, Inc., senior manager who has been asked to provide advice to Mr. Steve Jobs regarding the issues he and his company are facing. Or, you may identify yourself as an external management consultant who has been asked by the company to provide advice to Mr. Jobs.

Either way, you must prepare a strategy memo addressed to Steve Jobs, Chairman and CEO, Apple,

Inc., that summarizes the details of the case, rank orders the critical issues, discusses their implications (what they mean and why they matter), offers specific recommendations for action (assigning ownership and suspense dates for each), and shows how to communicate the solution to all who are affected by the recommendations.

You must also prepare a professional business letter for Mr. Jobs's signature. That document should be addressed to all Apple customers who are concerned about the events described in the case.

References

1. Business Insider, "The Saddest Part Of The Whole iPhone 4 Antenna Fiasco Is How Proud Steve Jobs Was When He Introduced It," *Gizmodo*, July 14, 2010 < http://gizmodo.com/5586855/the-saddest-part-of-the-whole-iphone-4-antenna-fiasco-is-how-proud-steve-jobs-was-when-he-introduced-it>.

2 "I Phone4 Antenna: Letter of Apple Decoded," Eastern News, July 3, 2010 http://www.easternews.net/371/iphone-4-antenna-letter-of-apple-decoded/

3 Topolsky, Joshua, "Apple responds to iPhone 4 reception issues: you're holding the phone the wrong way," *Engadget*, Accessed October 7, 2010 http://www.engadget.com/2010/06/24/apple-responds-over-iphone-4-reception-issues-youre-holding-th/

4 Ibid.

5 "How do you hold your Nokia," *Nokia Conversations: The Official Nokia Blog*, Accessed October 7, 2010

<http://conversations.nokia.com/2010/06/28/how-do-you-hold-your-nokia>.

6   Slattery, Brennon, "Verizon's Droid X Ad Takes Aim at iPhone 4," *PCWorld*, Accessed October 7, 2010,http://www.pcworld.com/article/200520/verizons_droid_x_ad_takes_aim_at_iphone_4.html?tk=rel_news

7   "How the Founders of Apple Got Rich," *www.mac-history.net* http://www.mac-history.net/the-history-of-the-apple-macintosh/how-the-founders-of-apple-got-rich

8   "Steve Jobs," *Wikipedia*, last modified 6 October, 2010, http://en.wikipedia.org/wiki/Steve_Jobs

9   Vogelstein, Fred, "The Untold Story: How the iPhone Blew Up the Wireless Industry," January 9, 2008,http://www.wired.com/gadgets/wireless/magazine/16-02/ff_iphone?currentPage=all#ixzz0zcF91jfI

10 Alanesius, Chloe, "Apple Apologizes, Nets 600,000 iPhone 4 Pre-Orders," *PCMag.com*, June 16, 2010,http://www.pcmag.com/article2/0,2817,2365167,00.asp

11 Mintel report, "Segment Performance," *Mobile Phones – US – June, 2010*

12 Mintel report, "Social Media Buzz about OS and App Stores," *Mobile Phones – US – June, 2010*

13 Sandstrom, Gustav, "Google's Android Gains Ground on Rivals," *The Wall Street Journal*, August 13, 2010 < http://online.wsj.com/article/SB100014240527487044078045754246939543842462.html>

14. Mies, Ginny, "BlackBerry App World open for business," *PC World*, April 1, 2009 <http://www.pcworld.com/article/162349/first_look_blackberry_app_world_open_for_business.html>

This case was prepared by Research Assistants Jonathan Retartha, Brian Riordan, Joseph Tingey and Kevin Vega under the direction of James S. O'Rourke, Teaching Professor of Management, as the basis for class discussion rather than to illustrate either effective or ineffective handling of an administrative situation. Information was gathered from corporate as well as public sources.

Chapter 6

Persuasion

"A baseline of trust must exist in order to effectively persuade people to accept a different point of view or participate in an activity that may vary from the status quo. People need to be informed and engaged," said Susan Hoff, "before you can change their behavior." Ms. Hoff is senior vice president and chief communications officer for Best Buy Company, a *Fortune* 500 retailer based in Richfield, Minnesota. "At Best Buy," she said, "we use a variety of communication techniques to move people to the desired outcome."[1]

Every communications plan developed and implemented at Best Buy includes a set of key messages, as well as elements focused on what Ms. Hoff calls "the head, the heart, and the hands of the stakeholders we are trying to reach." The head refers to the facts: "Our actions must be based on research." The heart assures that the company's messages resonate in a personal, emotive way with the audience. And the hands are the direction to "specific actions that we want the stakeholder to take." This head/heart/hands approach is used in the company's employee communications activities, as well as those with external stakeholders.[2]

"As a retailer, we must persuade customers to come into our stores each day," said Hoff. "As an employer, we must persuade potential employees that Best Buy is a great place to work, and work to retain them. As a publicly traded entity, we must persuade shareholders that Best Buy is a viable growth company that merits their continued investment. As a newcomer into a community, we must persuade our neighbors that we will be a good and thoughtful corporate citizen. And, every time we interact with a member of the news media, we must persuade them to take the time to listen to our point of view." Persuasion, she says, is not about selling or spinning. It's about building a level of trust so that people will be open to a new perspective.[3]

Virtually all elements of organizational communication include some element of persuasion. It might be an interpersonal communication, such as a manager approaching an employee with a stretch goal or the opportunity to work on a new project. Or it could be a much larger, more structured communication related to a major corporate initiative.

For example, Best Buy recently decided to outsource its information systems function to Accenture. The challenge for Ms. Hoff and her communications team was to persuade 600 Best Buy employees to transition their employment to Accenture. "This was a significant cultural shift that required trust," she noted, "as well as frequent and transparent communications that were grounded in our company values."[4] Using the head/heart/hands approach, they employed a variety of two-way communications to move employees along the change curve—including everything from information sessions and department meetings to brown bag seminars, employee roundtables, and a special transition Web site—all to ensure that they acknowledged employees' questions and concerns.

"It was essential," said Hoff, "that our key messages (what we said) matched our actions and behaviors (what we did). With that baseline of trust and credibility, we were able to successfully persuade our employees to transition to Accenture, with a higher-than-expected retention rate of 98%."[5] What Susan Hoff and her team faced was the daunting task of convincing others—many different people in this instance—that an important portion of their business had changed and why restructuring would be inevitable. It amounted to persuading them that cooperating with her was really in their own best interest.

THE HUMAN BELIEF SYSTEM

What we believe defines, in so many important ways, *who* we are. Yet what we believe—or hold to be true—is not simply a function of what we know. It is a product of how we were raised, who educated us, and the lives we led when we were young.

We were each raised by different people, in different places, at different times. We were educated, coached, and enculturated by many different people, each of whom had some influence on who we would ultimately become. Our potential, combined with our personality preferences and our life experiences, results in unique individuals. No two of us believe exactly the same things. And no two of us have precisely the same interests, attitudes, or feelings about life and the world around us. We are, in so many ways, different from one another.

The human attitudinal system—that collection of beliefs, attitudes, and opinions that makes us who we are—is a rich and interesting mixture of education, experience, and inventiveness. Our attitudinal systems constantly undergo re-evaluation and change. We add new information each day; we reinforce existing beliefs; we remove old ideas and concepts; and we frequently challenge new assumptions.

TWO SCHOOLS OF THOUGHT

For as long as people have been trying to influence others, the focus has been squarely on human behavior. Two old aphorisms have it that "actions speak louder than words" and that "talk is cheap, but action has value." What conventional wisdom has been telling us for thousands of years is that we cannot often tell what people are thinking, but we can certainly observe their behavior. And, such wisdom tells us, behavior is a much surer measure of a person's real intentions.

BEHAVIORISM One school of thought, behaviorism, contends that human behavior will most clearly reveal what a person is thinking and that persuasion is most effectively exercised at the behavioral level. Learning theory that dominated educational psychology during the first half of the twentieth century was mainly behaviorist in nature and represented an approach to psychology that emphasized observable, measurable behavior and discounted the role or value of mental activity. Learners were viewed by behaviorists as passively adapting to their environment, and instruction focused on conditioning a learner's behavior. Learning, thus, is indicated by a measurable change in the frequency of observable events. These changes are the result of a strengthening of the relationship between cue and behavior, driven by a pattern of consequences, called reinforcement (which may come in the form of rewards or punishment). This shaping of behavior, with enough practice, can create a link so strong that the time between cue and behavior gets very small.[6]

John B. Watson published an early paper promoting the view that psychology should be concerned only with the objective data of behavior.[7] Professors B. F. Skinner of Harvard and Stanley Milgram of Yale later underscored what Ivan P. Pavlov had so famously demonstrated a generation earlier: Behavior is conditioned by its consequences. If human behavior can be conditioned to respond to external influences, an internal change in attitudes and beliefs *may* result.

COGNITIVISM On the other hand, cognitivism, which emerged in the 1950s and 1960s, represents a different view of learning. Many theorists disagreed with the strict focus on observable behavior, arguing that it was entirely possible to learn something without changing the learner's behavior. The cognitivist school basically went inside the head of the learner to see what mental processes were activated and changed during the course of learning. In cognitive theories, knowledge is viewed as symbolic mental constructs in the learner's mind, and the learning process is the means by which the symbolic representations are committed to memory.[8] Changes in behavior are observed, but only as an indicator to what is going on inside the learner's head. Even though our actions may be informed and motivated by our beliefs, cognitive psychologists have come to see the human attitudinal system in a different way. They look at what psychologist Howard Gardner calls "the contents of what we think about—concepts, theories, stories, and skills—and the formats in which our mind/brain does that thinking."[9]

Among the early cognitivists, the work of Milton Rokeach at Michigan State University stands out as particularly important to our understanding of how human beings think and behave. In a landmark work entitled *Beliefs, Attitudes, and Values: A Theory of Organization and Change*, Rokeach explored the human attitudinal system. Among other things, he examined the relationship among the elements that comprise our beliefs and the factors associated with attitudinal assimilation and behavioral change. His work also includes a description of the basic ways in which we each organize and structure what we know and what we believe. Figure 6-1 is a simplistic adaptation of Rokeach's work, but it may help us to understand the relationship between those constructs that are fundamental to our beliefs and that, in so many important ways, help to define who we are, and less important, less central attitudes that may, nonetheless, guide or inform our behavior.[10]

In Rokeach's view of the human attitudinal system, three components help to define what we believe, how we organize those beliefs, and how they influence our day-to-day behavior.

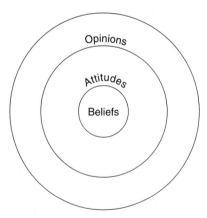

FIGURE 6-1 A Conceptual View of the Human Attitudinal System

BELIEFS At the core of the system and acquired early in life, beliefs are the most fundamental component of our values. They come to us from highly trusted sources, including our parents, close relatives, teachers, coaches, religious instructors, and other authority figures. Because young children are generally unable to form what psychologists call higher cognitive structures, they are not able to reason in the way that adults are able to.[11] They tend to respond to emotional needs and direct instruction from their elders. We come to believe the world is a particular way because that's what we've been told by those who feed, house, instruct, and care for us. Preadolescent children, thus, form a view of the world around them largely because they have few other choices.[12] These basic beliefs encompass everything from an understanding of God, to our relationship with nature, or our views about health and nutrition.

Our most basic beliefs don't necessarily follow, one from another, nor are they carefully aligned. They generally represent some sense of balance and consistency, though, even if some beliefs contradict others. A basic belief about nutrition, for example, might be that "eating healthy is good for me, and the occasional consumption of red meat is fine." Others (particularly vegetarians) might disagree with you or try to convince you to give up eating meat, but for now let's assume you're comfortable with your position.

ATTITUDES As outgrowths of our beliefs, our attitudes are dependent on them and tend to be consistent with them. The term *attitude* is really a navigational term describing your position relative to the rest of the world. Thus, our attitudes about a particular topic will influence not only how we perceive the world around us but how we are perceived by others. One belief may give rise to literally dozens of attitudes, each of which may have an important role to play in how we organize and live out our lives.[13]

Your views about meat, for example, might give rise to the idea that an occasional steak or beef burrito would be a nice addition to your diet. That attitude doesn't say much about why you believe it's good or about where to eat, just that you enjoy an occasional beef dish for dinner. (By way of disclosure: I am the grandson of a Montana cattle rancher, so it's easy to see how I came by my own beliefs about the role of beef in my diet.)

OPINIONS At the very fringes of our belief system, our opinions are among the least stable. Rokeach and others believe that opinions, in fact, are the structures in our belief system most susceptible to persuasion. They are the outgrowths of many different attitudes (themselves not as stable and central to our view of the world as our core beliefs); they are dependent on little more than preference, and can easily be shifted, modified, created, or done away with entirely.

My views about what to have for dinner, as we have just seen, are guided by my fundamental belief that it's okay for me to include red meat in my diet (even though others whom I respect and admire don't agree with me), and that one attitude (among many) tells me that an occasional beef burrito might be just fine. My opinion about where to eat or who makes the best beef burritos in town may be less stable, less enduring, and more quickly and easily subject to change than those attitudes and beliefs that support it. A bad experience at one particular Mexican restaurant might easily cause me to switch my preference for where I dine. Similarly, a good experience at a new restaurant might establish a new loyalty—all based on the underlying, positive attitude about beef burritos.

THE ROLE OF BELIEFS, ATTITUDES, AND OPINIONS As we noted, beliefs change slowly—if at all—over the course of a lifetime, while attitudes are more easily shaped by life experience, education, and current events. Opinions are completely ephemeral; they come and go, seemingly with the next piece of evidence that arrives. The human attitudinal system is governed by a number of other principles, as well.

- *Change in one layer may expose a more fundamental layer to reexamination, but will require no change in the more basic layer.* If I have a bad fish dinner at one restaurant, it may cause me to rethink the wisdom of ordering fish in Indiana, though it will not require that I change my views about the role of seafood in my diet.

- *Change in a basic layer will require change in all higher attitudinal layers.* If I should decide to stop smoking because it's bad for my health (and those around me), the attitudes I've developed about when and where to smoke, along with the opinions about brand selection are all out the window. My basic change in belief (from "smoking is cool" to "smoking is harmful") will mandate changes in all attitudinal structures dependent on that belief.

- *The more basic the change, the more profound the reordering throughout the system.* G. K. Chesterton once wrote, "When a man stops believing in God, he doesn't start believing in nothing. He starts believing in anything."[14] Our beliefs are among the most basic and stable of our values, and to alter or cast aside any of them is to invite confusion and instability in our belief system.

- *The less rational the basis for adoption, the more difficult is the basis for change in a given belief or attitude group.* Emotionally charged attitudes are especially difficult to change because they were not rationally acquired. As such, they are particularly resistant to rational attempts or the use of logic to change them. I may see the merit or value in what the Chicago White Sox do each summer, but I'll never be a fan, even if you tell me they're doing great things for the neighborhood and the city of Chicago. I'm a Cub fan. And, of course, that loyalty involves enough emotion to fill the rest of this book.

- *The closer a structure is to the center of one's belief system, the more central it becomes to one's self-concept.* Such beliefs, thus, become self-defining.[15] If you are a committed environmentalist, you will most likely identify yourself as such, describing your beliefs, views, and actions in personal terms. These beliefs can define who you are and how you live your life each day.

THE OBJECTIVES OF PERSUASION

In seeking to influence the views of others, most psychologists tell us that we have three general aims in mind: to reinforce positive opinion, to crystallize latent or unformed opinion, and to neutralize hostile opinion.

REINFORCING POSITIVE OPINION A particularly useful and productive approach to persuasion is to reinforce positive opinion because it offers the speaker or writer the advantage of addressing people who already think the same way, believe the same things, and who are likely to respond in a positive, enthusiastic way to the messages they receive. The second, often hidden advantage of "preaching to the choir" is that people who are already on your side, who believe as you do, will offer their reinforced views to others who may not yet have formed an opinion. Reinforcing positive opinion not only helps to prevent backsliding on the part of those who agree with you; it may also help to influence those who are not yet informed or convinced on this topic.

CRYSTALLIZING LATENT OPINION Some instruction and, perhaps, some extensive explanation are required for this purpose. To convince someone with no background on the subject at hand, and no emotional link to either the topic or your position, often requires an extended effort. For most purposes, you don't really need to convince everyone in town of your views, you only need to reach the few who matter—those in a position to influence the outcome of a debate or controversy. Often, though, if we ignore the vast, uninformed masses, we risk allowing someone hostile to our position to reach them first. In the absence of accurate information about your position or views, the uninformed may make up their minds with the first bit of useful information that comes along.

NEUTRALIZING HOSTILE OPINION The task of neutralizing hostile opinion is never easy and never-ending. Those whose views are diametrically opposed to your own are likely never to be convinced that you're actually correct, that you're right about a particular issue or idea. The point is not to convert these people; you can't. Who they are is often the polar opposite of who you are. The best you can hope for is to prevent them from reaching the uninformed before you or your allies do. Your best weapons are the truth; a solid, rational argument; an emotional connection to the topic; and speed. The sooner you reach those who have yet to form an opinion, the sooner you'll have an opportunity to change their minds. Don't worry about converting those who disagree.

OUTCOMES OF THE ATTITUDINAL FORMATION PROCESS

Any attempt at persuasion must first consider the goals and objectives of the persuader: Why are you communicating with this particular group or person? What do you hope to achieve as a result? Is your purpose to raise awareness or to influence behavior? Any persuasive attempt must also consider the goals and objectives of the audience: Why would they agree to read, listen, or pay attention to this communication? Do they want information? Are they seeking encouragement for a decision? What do they hope for as a result of this interaction?

In general, the outcomes of persuasion—or the attitudinal formation process—include the following:

- **Reinforcement of existing attitudes.** As you've already seen, your first task in persuasion is to reinforce the views of those who agree with you. This reinforcement not only helps to prevent backsliding but will expand the number of people who can help you reach the uninformed.
- **Modification or shifting of existing attitudes.** This outcome is a bit more difficult but certainly possible. Attitudes will move in one direction or another with the arrival of new evidence from credible sources, but this process happens slowly. New evidence that doesn't fit our frame of reference is likely to be rejected, but over time, enough new evidence from sources we trust might tip the balance and cause us to rethink our position.
- **Creation of new attitudes.** Perhaps the most difficult goal of persuasion is the creation of entirely new attitude sets. This task is best done by linking the position we hope to create to an existing belief (or beliefs) in our audience. Advertisers often try to get consumers to switch brands by showing how a new product is more economical, cleaner and kinder to the environment, or safer than existing brands. An extended instructional task may be involved as you attempt to construct new attitudes, but if done properly, the result may be a useful, enduring viewpoint.

THE SCIENCE OF PERSUASION

"A lucky few have it," says Professor Robert Cialdini, "most of us do not. A handful of gifted 'naturals' simply know how to capture an audience, sway the undecided, and convert the opposition."[16] How is it that such masters of persuasion are able to work their magic on an audience? What techniques or principles do they apply that others do not? Is some science at work here, or is it all high artistry beyond the grasp of ordinary mortals? As it happens, and as Cialdini has shown, managers and executives can improve their abilities to persuade by turning to science.

"For the past five decades, behavioral scientists have conducted experiments that shed considerable light on the way certain interactions lead people to concede, comply, or change. This research," he writes, "shows that persuasion works by appealing to a limited set of deeply rooted human drives and needs, and it does so in predictable ways. Persuasion, in other words, is governed by basic principles that can be taught, learned, and applied."[17]

Cialdini has identified six scientific principles that ordinary business writers and speakers can apply each day to win concessions, cut deals, or secure consensus.

- **Liking.** We tend to like those who like us, but we also tend to like those who *are* like us. Making friends with others may help us to influence them. Uncovering real similarities and offering genuine praise can help us to persuade others.
- **Reciprocity.** The Japanese call this principle *giri*, a kind of mutual indebtedness. It means that people repay in kind and expect to receive what they give. If what you want from your colleagues and coworkers is their time and help with your problems, then you must be prepared to share your time and help with them.
- **Social proof.** People follow the lead of similar others when they're asked to do something. If you can show that you have the support of neighbors, friends, colleagues, and others known to those you hope to influence, you'll have a better chance of success. Testimonials from satisfied customers, surveys, and opinion polls can all have a powerful effect on a person's decision, particularly if that support comes from key opinion leaders admired by your audience.
- **Consistency.** If nothing else, people genuinely enjoy being consistent. They do what they say they will and they appreciate staying within their own "comfort zone." People align with their clear commitments, particularly if those are both public and voluntary. That campaign button on your lapel is not intended to get me to vote for your candidate. It's designed to prevent you from voting for someone else. If you've publicly said you're voting for a candidate, you're unlikely to back away from that position or do something else.
- **Authority.** If you can't convince people that their friends and neighbors support your position, then perhaps you can show them an expert who does. People readily defer to experts, and you can use this ready inclination in two ways. You can explain your own expertise (people often don't recognize or appreciate your experience), or you can find someone whose expertise they do understand.
- **Scarcity.** The value of an object often rises as fewer of them become available. The odd thing is that people often want something simply because it is scarce. To claim something is rare, unavailable, or in short supply when it's actually not would be unethical. "This deal is only good until 5:00 o'clock," says the salesman. Chances are, he'll have a similar deal tomorrow. To apply this principal ethically, you should highlight unique benefits of what you advocate or offer exclusive information unavailable elsewhere.[18]

SUCCESSFUL ATTEMPTS AT PERSUASION

Most successful attempts at persuasion involve four separate yet related steps. Following these steps won't guarantee success with any particular audience, but they will set the conditions for attitudinal assimilation and behavioral change to follow.

GAINING THE ATTENTION OF YOUR AUDIENCE The marketplace is crowded. The in-box is full. People are clamoring for your attention in the media, on the phone, and in the workplace. Attention serves as a human gate-keeping function. Each day we are exposed to so many stimuli—sight, sound, taste, touch, and smell—that our senses would quickly be overloaded if we were not selective in what we pay attention to. Psychologists refer to this ability as *selective perception*. In other words, we select—often subconsciously—what we will pay attention to, take in, think about, and act on. And we selectively ignore virtually everything else.[19]

It's clear that a stimulus we choose to pay attention to has an advantage over one that we ignore. Whatever controls our attention tends to produce action. What we choose to pay attention to is hardly accidental. Two factors are at work in our selections: First, people pay attention to stimuli that contain inherent attention-getting factors (bright lights, noise, motion, color, and so on). And, second, people respond to stimuli that relate to their needs and goals. Restaurant signs seem more obvious to us when we're hungry, and by contrast, we are less likely to notice "help wanted" ads unless we're looking for work.

PROVIDING THE APPROPRIATE MOTIVATION FOR YOUR AUDIENCE The persuasive writer or speaker is one who can lead an audience to believe in what he or she is advocating and to encourage some form of behavior that is consistent with that belief. This approach amounts to giving good reasons for what you believe. Rhetorician Karl R. Wallace goes even further to say that these shouldn't simply be reasons that *you* think are good. They must be reasons that your audience will think are good. Of course, that means you must know your audience well, long before you write or speak to them.[20] Research in behavioral psychology has shown three broad, general categories of motivators for human behavior:

- **Human needs as motivation.** Psychologist Abraham Maslow offered a theory, widely known as the Hierarchy of Needs, in which he describes a set of five needs, the most basic of which must be satisfied first, followed by the need to feel secure, a need to belong, a need to be loved or admired, and finally, self-actualization needs. He observed that people have various kinds of needs that emerge, subside, and emerge again as they are met or not met. For example, the need for food and water emerges and then recedes as we eat or drink. Maslow argued that these needs have a *prepotency*—that is, they are linked together so that weaker, higher needs emerge only after stronger, more basic needs have been met and satisfied.

  Figure 6-2 is only a model and the divisions between the various levels are not as distinct as the lines might suggest. Also, it's important to note that higher needs are not necessarily superior to or more important than lower ones. They're simply weaker and less likely to emerge until our basic needs have been met.

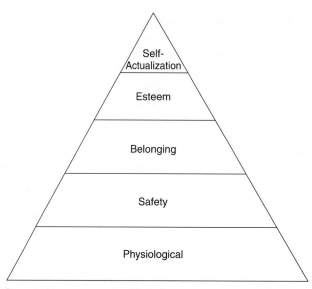

FIGURE 6-2 Maslow's Hierarchy of Human Needs

- *Basic needs* include the most fundamental of physiological requirements for human life: air, food, water, sleep, and elimination of waste. Until these needs are met, we cannot concern ourselves with other, higher needs. The basic needs are simply too strong to be forgotten in favor of other needs.
- *Security needs* are on the second level of Maslow's hierarchy, and they deal with our feelings of well-being and confidence. Our insecurities may range from fears of becoming a crime victim to fears about our jobs, our families' well-being, and our future. This need is relatively constant, and even when it is satisfied, it frequently redefines itself and is, thus, present to some extent in our lives.
- *Belonging needs* follow those related to security. Once we feel secure, we become aware of needs at a third level. Humans have a relatively strong desire for association or affiliation with other humans. We are social animals who continue to form relationships and associate with other humans in groups. Belonging, being a part of the group, being accepted by others is a powerful motivation for most people, even for those who say they don't care what others think about them. Deep inside, we each long for the company of others.
- *Love or esteem needs* are one step up from belonging, in level four of Maslow's hierarchy. We each want to feel loved, wanted, and admired by other people, especially those closest to us. Humans frequently are disappointed with themselves when they encounter failure, not so much because their own self-image has suffered, but because they have disappointed or "let down" a close friend or member of the family. If we find that we are loved and needed by our family, the need for esteem does not disappear; it is a reemerging need. We seek approval and acceptance from others, including friends and coworkers. The more of this need we satisfy, the less powerful it becomes, but it is never fully satisfied.
- *Self-actualization needs'* position at the top of Maslow's hierarchy suggests that each person cannot really become all that he or she could be unless each of the four lower needs is first satisfied. Only with satisfaction of all lower needs, said Maslow, can people then truly begin to live up to their full potential. Later in life, Maslow rethought some of his earlier writing on this subject and amended his thinking to include the idea that people can self-actualize early in life, long before they have met and satisfied all four levels of their needs. He described "peak

experiences" in which people learn to be self-reliant, perform to the maximum of their ability, and live up to their potential at various stages of their lives. Maslow's later thinking does not contradict any of his earlier writing but amends it to demonstrate that we needn't live out our lives entirely or be promoted to president of the company before we can begin to self-actualize.[21]

ERG THEORY OF MOTIVATION Psychologist Clayton Alderfer has developed another need-based approach called *ERG theory*. It involves a streamlining of Maslow's classifications and some different assumptions about the relationship between needs and motivation. The name *ERG* comes from Alderfer's compression of Maslow's five-category system into three categories: existence, relatedness, and growth.

- *Existence needs* are satisfied by some material substance or condition and might include the need for such things as food, shelter, pay, and safe working conditions.
- *Relatedness needs* are satisfied by open communication and the exchange of thoughts and feelings with other human beings, including friends, family members, and coworkers.
- *Growth needs* are fulfilled by strong involvement in work, education, and personal development. They often involve not only the full use of a person's skills and abilities but the development of new ones.

In many ways, Alderfer's theory is similar to Maslow's, with three broad classifications substituting for five in Maslow's Hierarchy of Human Needs. According to Alderfer, an apparently satisfied need can act as a motivator by substituting for an unsatisfied need. ERG theory's contribution to our understanding of human motivation rests on two basic premises: First, as more lower-level needs are satisfied, more higher-level need satisfaction is desired. And, second, the less higher-level needs are satisfied, the more lower-level need satisfaction is desired. The value of this theory, along with Maslow's work, for a business communicator is that both can tell us something about what motivates people. Knowing which needs have been satisfied in a particular target audience will help in formulating messages to prompt further behavior.[22] Figure 6-3 shows how the theories of Abraham Maslow and Clayton Alderfer are closely related and provide similar insights into human motivation.

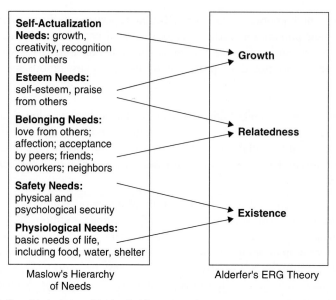

FIGURE 6-3 The Relationship between Maslow's Hierarchy of Human Needs and ERG Theory

EIGHT HIDDEN NEEDS In the late 1950s, author and critic Vance Packard gathered and published motivational research done on behalf of advertisers in a book called *The Hidden Persuaders*. In the results of a series of complex psychological tests measuring the motivation for consumer goods purchases of a large number of people, Packard found eight "compelling needs" that were frequently used in selling products with a motivational research approach. More than 50 years later, many advertisers still rely on these findings, though in a more sophisticated way.

- *Need for emotional security*. We need to be reassured that everything will be okay, that we will be secure and safe. Everything from disease to terrorists can threaten our sense of well-being.
- *Need for reassurance of worth.* No matter who we are or what we do for a living, we need reassurance that we have personal value, that we're worth something as an individual. We like to know that people understand and appreciate us.
- *Need for ego gratification.* We need to be told that we're not only worth something but that we are actually special or—in some ways—better than other people at certain things. Compliments, public recognition, and awards confirm this worth.
- *Need for creative outlets.* We each feel the need to assemble, craft, configure, or create on our own. When mom adds an egg to her boxed cake mix, she's "creating" dessert for her family. Powdered eggs in the cake mix would leave the housewife with nothing to add and no sense of creative accomplishment.
- *Need for love objects.* In addition to being loved, we have a strong need to love others. Everyone (and everything) from movie stars, royalty, and celebrities to family pets can fulfill our need to extend love.
- *Need for a sense of power.* A feeling of power can come in different ways for different people. For a young man, the roar of a motorcycle engine that responds to his command will convey a sense of power. For women, power can mean something entirely different: They may look for control or decision authority as a source of power satisfaction in their lives.

- *Need for roots.* In a society that moves frequently and often over vast distances, the need for roots can be powerful. Reminders of home, family experiences, "old-fashioned" products, and middle-class values are often used to motivate consumer purchases ranging from long-distance telephone calls to fast-food hamburgers.
- *Need for immortality.* We often like to think we can exert influence on others even after we're dead. Life insurance policies, trust funds, and other products appeal to this need. A continuing emphasis on youth in advertising appeals to our fears about growing old. Immortality and youth, we are told, can be bought from a jar.[23]

RELATING NEEDS THEORY TO PERSUASIVE MESSAGES In an affirmative appeal, a writer might argue that if the reader accepts his or her proposal, a need not now being satisfied will be met or a need being met will be satisfied more fully, more efficiently, or quickly. The human resources group in your company might argue, for example, that opening an on-site exercise center will help to improve employee fitness and health, boost morale, and give the firm an edge in recruiting new employees.

In a threat or fear appeal, a writer might pose a threat to the continued satisfaction of a need and then argue that if the reader follows the advice, the threat will be neutralized or avoided. A group of industrial tenants might argue, for instance, that building management must increase security in their facilities. If management doesn't comply, the tenants say, they will relocate their businesses at the end of their lease agreements.

Some research on fear appeals shows that:

- A highly credible source gets a good response from a fear appeal. If the audience knows and trusts the message source, they're much more likely to comply.
- If a strong fear appeal threatens the welfare of a loved one, it tends to be more effective than if it threatens the members of the audience themselves.
- A strong fear appeal may be related to personality characteristics of the audience; that is, uneducated people and those with poor self-esteem may be easily influenced by a direct threat.
- The arousal of fear in an audience seems to depend on the speaker's ability to convince the audience of the probability that the threat will materialize and the magnitude of the consequences. It's much easier to sell home fire insurance or automobile accident coverage than it is to sell asteroid collision insurance to a home owner. Even if the probability of an event is fairly high (say, bad breath in the morning), the writer must still convince the reader that the consequences of such an event are serious.[24]

MOTIVATING BY APPEAL TO RATIONALITY AND CONSISTENCY In addition to being motivated by their fulfillment needs, people are also motivated to be reasonable in their behavior by the traditions of society. We are constantly urged to be rational, to behave consistently. Thus, consistency theories assume that people try to avoid incongruent or inconsistent beliefs, attitudes, and actions.

These theories all say that the greater the dissonance or imbalance in our inner mental states, the greater the motivation to resolve it. Dissonance is nothing more than inner tension created when we come into contact with information that is at odds with what we already know and believe. Because we are uncomfortable with that tension, we're highly motivated to resolve the problem and relieve the tension. For example, let's assume you have done business with a supplier for a number of years and enjoy a good working relationship. Now you discover that he's been implicated in a corruption scandal involving illegal kickbacks and bribes in his business dealings. How do you respond to that news? Most likely, you'll dismiss the information as untrue or the work of your supplier's competitors. If you should discover highly credible evidence from reliable sources that the charges are true, however, it's likely that you'll resolve the dissonance by buying supplies from someone else.[25]

As you attempt to apply such theories, you must first show your audience how the position you advocate—along with its subsequent actions and behavior—is consistent with their existing beliefs. Or you must show them how alternative positions, advocated by your competitors or opponents, are inconsistent with their current beliefs.

SOCIAL CONFORMITY AS MOTIVATION A number of important social forces shapes each of us as human beings, including the following:

- *Admired individuals:* Parents, teachers, entertainers, politicians, professional athletes, friends, relatives, teachers, coaches, religious leaders, and many others.
- *Peer groups:* Early in life, people identify most closely with those of their own age, race, ethnic group, social status, and common interests. Pressure from such groups to conform can be powerful.
- *Societal norms:* Standards of behavior are imposed by our social groupings and social interactions with other people, even if we are not conscious of group affiliation with them. These norms are so widely accepted by society as a whole that they tend to become invisible prescriptions for behavior. They include everything from language use to how we dress to the food we eat to personal mannerisms.[26]

As managers, we must look for ways to motivate those whom we're trying to communicate with. Human needs, rational and consistent behavior, and social conformity can be powerful tools to persuade others to think and act as we would like them to. Whether they are customers, suppliers, shareholders, employees, supervisors, or people we work with, each will react in separate ways to our attempts to motivate them. The key is to know your audience.

CHANNELING THE MOTIVATION OF YOUR AUDIENCE TO TAKE ACTION Once your audience has begun to pay attention to your message and has been given some appropriate and powerful motivation to believe in the message, you must provide them with a channel or an outlet for action. This motivation comes in two basic forms:

- *Recommend a specific proposition or proposal.* A specific proposal allows your audience to adopt it in order to attain the satisfaction you've promised. In other words, tell them specifically what you want them to do, as well as when and how they're to do it. "Sign up for ride-sharing Monday through Friday of this week at the main reception desk or in the first-floor cafeteria and receive close-in parking for the next 12 months."
- *Show the high probability that the satisfactions will be forthcoming.* Your audience is looking for some assurance that what you've promised will actually come true if they do as you've asked. "If you are not completely satisfied, we will refund your money anytime within 30 days of purchase."

INDUCING RESISTANCE IN THE AUDIENCE TO COUNTERPERSUASION Information decays quickly. So do the positions assumed by your audience in response to your persuasive message. Emotional appeals, in particular, are ephemeral or transitory. If you've convinced someone to donate money to your cause based on an emotional appeal, you must find a way to collect the donations quickly, before the fervor of the moment passes. Much impulse buying is dependent on actions taken before the buyer's motivation changes.

To help assure that those who are persuaded by your message will remain believers, you must induce in each of them a resistance to counter-persuasion and counter-arguments. Several ways are available to you:

- ***By stating opposing arguments and refuting them.*** If you know your audience will hear the arguments of your competitors, it might not be a bad idea to present at least part of their argument to the audience and then explain what's wrong with it, refute it, or show where it's flawed.
- ***By encouraging audience commitment in some tangible or visible way.*** As we explained a few pages ago, it's much more difficult to back away from a position or an idea for which we've publicly proclaimed our support. George Bush the elder greatly regretted using the phrase, "Read my lips. No new taxes." Just 18 months after that public declaration, he was maneuvered by his political opposition into raising taxes and was then roundly criticized for it.
- ***By warning the audience that others will attempt to get them to change their minds.*** If you know your audience will be exposed to your competitor's message, it's not a bad idea to warn them that others are out for their money, their votes, or their commitment. Some popular advertisements warn against look-alikes: "Accept no substitutes, ask for the real thing when you place your order."

SHOULD YOU USE A ONE- OR TWO-SIDED ARGUMENT?

People often wonder if they should even mention the other side (or sides) of an argument, or whether it's best to simply leave it alone. Will the discussion of another point of view make it easier for your opponent to influence the audience, or would it be better for you to raise and refute that argument? When is a two-sided argument most effective, and when is it best to simply leave the opposition's ideas alone? Again, behavioral scientists looked at this question and conducted experiments, and here's what their evidence suggests:

One-sided arguments work best when:

- ***The audience initially agrees with your position and your aim is simply to intensify agreement.*** If you know they're already on your side, there's no need for a complicated, multifaceted argument. Simply tell them what you believe and why you think it's important, and boost their confidence in your position.
- ***The audience is not well-educated or has relatively low self-esteem.*** In some instances, people may not have the education or background to fully understand an issue. Young children, the elderly, and others may respond best to a persuasive presentation that offers just one side of the issue.
- ***The audience will not later be exposed to any form of counter-persuasion.*** If you know that this argument is the only one your audience will be exposed to and you're asking for the equivalent of a one-time purchase, a one-sided argument may work best.

Two-sided arguments work best when:

- ***The audience initially disagrees with your proposal.*** For example, if you intend to explain why it's unwise for employees to bring food into the company computer lab—and most of your audience already agrees with you—a simple, one-sided presentation of the factors and your reasons for the decision will suffice. If you advocate eliminating all food and refreshments from the building—and most of your audience disagrees with you—it may be more effective to present both sides of the story: reasons for having food in the workplace and reasons for eliminating it.

- *You know the audience will be exposed to subsequent counter-persuasion or propaganda.* Regardless of the audience's initial attitude, a two-sided presentation is usually best when you are certain your audience will hear the other side of the argument. If you are selling products or services to a customer who will receive sales calls from your competitors, it may be a good idea to present all the facts—including those your competition will raise—before making the case for why your products or services are best.

- *The audience has a low level of knowledge or personal involvement with the topic.* If your intended audience doesn't know much about the subject at hand, or when the position you take is widely different from their views, a two-sided presentation is usually most effective. A neighbor rang our doorbell recently with a petition to prevent the construction of a 24-hour convenience store in a nearby residential neighborhood. Because most of the people he spoke with had little involvement in or information about the subject, our neighbor constructed a brief but careful two-sided argument, for and against the new store, concluding with the reasons why it shouldn't be built in our neighborhood.

- *You hope to produce more enduring results.* A two-sided presentation seems to ensure that any change in attitude provided by your message will endure longer than if the attitude change is secured by a one-sided message. If you want long-term commitment from the people you communicate with, they will want to know the underlying arguments and reasons for your position. Give them both sides of the argument before presenting your persuasive position.[27]

Keep in mind that you may face an ethical need to disclose both sides of an argument. If you have an agreeable, yet poorly educated, audience that is not likely to learn about possible counter-arguments—but who might possibly benefit from knowing them—you should consider disclosing all aspects as you underscore the value of your own position.

Finally, remember that you have an obligation to be honest with your audience. If you misrepresent the facts or if you don't tell the truth, you will eventually be found out—perhaps not immediately, but eventually. Your credibility can and will be harmed. Be logical, organize your material carefully, and use evidence that is consistent, believable, and up-to-date.

Not All That We Remember Is Actually True

What we believe to be true often simply isn't so. During the early stages of the War in Iraq, numerous press accounts offered conflicting reports, some of which were later proven to be untrue and subsequently retracted by various news organizations. But new research suggests that even with a public correction of the record, readers of the original report may continue to believe the now-discredited story. The research, published in *Psychological Science*, a journal of the American Psychological Society, suggests that once you've seen a news report, you may go on believing it even if later information shows it to have been false.[28]

"People build mental models," explains Stephan Lewandowsky, a psychology professor at the University of Western Australia, who led the study. "By the time they receive a retraction, the original misinformation has already become an integral part of that mental model, or world view, and disregarding it would leave the world view a shambles." He concludes that "people continue to rely on misinformation, even if they demonstrably remember and understand a subsequent retraction."[29]

This finding comes as no surprise to memory researchers. Time and again, lab studies show that people have an astonishing propensity to recall things that never happened. If you read a list of words such as *pillow*, *bed*, and *pajamas*, and later asked whether the word *sleep* was there, a remarkable number of people would recall that word as having been on the list.[30]

The task of changing minds under such circumstances can be daunting. Influencing what people believe to be true, even when it's not, is a difficult but manageable task. It amounts to showing people why change is both possible and desirable and then offering incentives to make the change, first in attitude and then in behavior.

MANAGING HEADS AND HEARTS TO CHANGE BEHAVIORAL HABITS

Managing change in a business organization is never easy. Most people will say they're eager for change, but they're not really. They're simply trying to look cooperative, like team players helping the organization along. The vast majority of us prefer things the way they are: It's easier, simpler, more familiar, and less stressful to continue doing business just as we always have. The status quo has powerful support.

However, as a business school dean once said, "There is no status in the status quo."[31] The pressure for businesses to change is enormous and inexorable, mostly because the competition is changing, and so is the marketplace. Most management strategists agree that there is no such thing as a permanent strategic advantage. If that's true, then virtually all advantage in business is temporary and subject to change. So how can you compete when all about you are changing? The answer, of course, is change itself. To set the stage for change in the attitudes and behaviors of those responsible for an organization's success, three conditions must be present.

- *You must create a new frame of reference through which information and messages are interpreted.* We don't operate on facts, figures, or data as much as we work with stories, narratives, and ideas that help us to see and understand the world we live in. These frames of reference are the touchpoints for any new information or persuasive messages that we receive. When new employees start at W. L. Gore & Associates, the maker of Gore-Tex fabrics, they often refuse to believe that the company doesn't have a hierarchy with job titles and bosses. It just doesn't fit their frame of reference. It often takes several months for new hires to begin to understand Gore's reframed notion of the workplace, which relies on self-directed employees making their own choices about joining one another in egalitarian small teams.[32]
- *You must manage the emotions and expectations of your audience.* To convince others of the value of your viewpoint, you must evoke the appropriate emotion both in them and in yourself. As author and psychologist Daniel Goleman has shown in *Emotional Intelligence*, "The goal is balance, not emotional suppression: every feeling has its value and significance. A life without passion would be a dull wasteland of neutrality, cut off and isolated from the richness of life itself. But," says Goleman, "as Aristotle observed, what is wanted is *appropriate* emotion, feeling proportionate to circumstance."[33]
- *You must provide constant reinforcement to prevent backsliding.* The opinions that motivate behavior are ephemeral, fleeting, and subject to change on a moment's notice. Even though attitudes are a bit more enduring, they too can shift, modify, or vanish with enough evidence and motivation. To prevent such losses in your audience, continual reinforcement of the position you advocate is often necessary. Harvard Business School professors David Garvin and Michael Roberto describe the problem this way: "Without a doubt, the toughest challenge faced by leaders during a turnaround is to avoid backsliding into dysfunctional routines— habitual patterns of negative behavior by individuals and groups that are triggered

automatically and unconsciously by familiar circumstances or stimuli. In our studies of successful turnarounds," they write, "we've found that effective leaders explicitly reinforce organizational values on a constant basis, using actions to back up their words. Their goal is to change behavior, not just ways of thinking."[34]

BEING PERSUASIVE

Ultimately, your ability to persuade people that your point of view is correct, moral, optimal, desirable, just, or simply preferable may come down to a few, simple precepts about how other people feel, think, and react to you and your argument.

- **Know your audience.** Aristotle was right; it's really *all* about them. The more you know, the greater your chance for success. You have little incentive and almost no excuse for failing to do your homework on what the audience knows and how it feels about the subject on which you're trying to persuade them.
- **Know what you want and what they want.** Part of knowing your audience means an understanding of their goals and objectives. The extent to which you know what they want is the degree to which you can offer ideas and evidence that will help you to get what you want. If you can't give them something they want or can use, you have little hope of persuading them to change behaviors.
- **Select your evidence carefully.** Not all evidence is equally persuasive, and not all audiences will approach the same argument in the same way. Make sure you understand the sources your audience will respect and the frame of reference through which they will interpret what you say. Logic and rationality may work for some, but emotion or source credibility may appeal more to others.
- **Keep the argument simple.** The more complex your argument, the lower the probability it will be acknowledged, understood, internalized, and acted on. Simplicity, underscored by a cogent, brief presentation, will carry the day far more often than not.
- **Listen before you speak.** It's difficult to know what they're thinking, what they want, or what they're afraid of if you won't listen. You must listen carefully for content, emotion, and intention. If you can tune into their thoughts and feelings before you speak—and convince them that you've done so—your chances for success are greater.
- **Manage your emotions as well as theirs.** Keep your own emotions under control and you'll have a greater opportunity to manage those of your audience. If you let their hopes and fears run away with the discussion, an "emotional hijacking" can ruin your chances at persuading them of your position.
- **Connect with your audience on a personal level.** Finally, although your audience cares in a general sense about the nature of your evidence and the organization of your argument, they care a lot more about how it will affect them. Answer their basic questions: "Can I trust you?" "What do I know about you?" "Do you know something I need to know?" "Can you help me?" and you'll find yourself rewarded with their attention and their agreement with your ideas.

Endnotes

1. Hoff, S., Senior Vice President and Chief Communications Officer, Best Buy Company, Richfield, MN. Personal interview, May 27, 2005.
2. Ibid.
3. Ibid.
4. Ibid.
5. Ibid.
6. Buell, C. *Behaviorism*. Available online: web.cocc.edu/cbuell/theories/behaviorism. Retrieved July 4, 2005.
7. Watson, J. B. *Psychology as the Behaviorist Views It*. Available online from York University of Canada: psychclassics.yorku.ca/Watson/views.htm. Accessed July 10, 2008 at 2:20 P.M.
8. For an extensive description of cognitivism, see Wikipedia's online discussion at: en.wikipedia.org/wiki/Cognitivism_ (psychology).
9. Gardner, H. *Changing Minds: The Art and Science of Changing Our Own and Other People's Minds*. Boston, MA: Harvard Business School Press, 2004, p. 42.
10. Rokeach, M. *Beliefs, Attitudes, and Values: A Theory of Organization and Change*. San Francisco, CA: Jossey-Bass, 1968. See also Rokeach, M. *The Open and Closed Mind: Investigations into the Nature of Belief Systems and Personality Systems*. New York: Basic Books, 1960, pp. 3–27.
11. Travers, R. M. W. "Piaget's Approach to Learning and the Development of the Intellect." In *Essentials of Learning*, 4th ed. New York: Macmillan Publishing, 1977, pp. 147–203.
12. Bem, D. "The Cognitive Foundations of Beliefs." In *Beliefs, Attitudes, and Human Affairs*. Belmont, CA: Brooks/Cole Publishing, 1970, pp. 4–13.
13. Ibid, pp. 14–23.
14. Chesterton, G. K. *The American Chesterton Society*. An extended discussion of the origins of this quote is available online: http://www.firstthings.com/onthesquare/2005/12/rjn-123005-one-more-word
15. Bem, D. "Our most fundamental primitive beliefs are so taken for granted that we are not apt to notice that we hold them at all; we remain unaware of them until they are called to our attention or are brought into question by some bizarre circumstance in which they appear to be violated. For example, we believe that an object continues to exist even when we are not looking at it; we believe that objects remain the same size and shape as we move away from them even though their visual images change; and, more generally, we believe that our perceptual and conceptual worlds have a degree of orderliness and stability over time. These are among the first beliefs that a child learns as he interacts with his environment, and in a psychological sense, they are continuously validated by experience. As a result, we are usually unaware of the fact that alternatives to these beliefs *could* exist, and it is precisely for this reason that we remain unaware of the beliefs themselves. We shall call primitive beliefs of this fundamental kind 'zero-order' beliefs. They are the 'nonconscious' axioms upon which our other beliefs are built." *Beliefs, Attitudes, and Human Affairs*, pp. 5–6.
16. Reprinted by permission of *Harvard Business Review* from Cialdini, R. B. "Harnessing the Science of Persuasion," *Harvard Business Review*, October 2001, pp. 72–79. Copyright © 2001 by the Harvard Business School Publishing Corporation; all rights reserved.
17. Ibid, p. 74.
18. Cialdini, R. B. *Influence: Science and Practice*, 4th ed. Boston, MA: Allyn & Bacon, 2000.
19. Ross, R. S. *Understanding Persuasion*, 3rd ed. Englewood Cliffs, NJ: Prentice Hall, 1990, pp. 79–80.
20. Wallace, K. R. "The Substance of Rhetoric: Good Reasons." In R. Johannesen (ed.), *Contemporary Theories of Rhetoric: Selected Readings*. New York: Harper and Row, 1971, pp. 357–370.
21. Larson, C. U. *Persuasion: Reception and Responsibility*, 6th ed. Belmont, CA: Wadsworth, 1992, pp. 159–163.
22. Johns, G. *Organizational Behavior*, 2nd ed. Glenview, IL: Scott, Foresman, 1988, pp. 158–159. See also Alderfer, C. P. "An Intergroup Perspective

on Group Dynamics." In J. W. Lorch (ed.), *Handbook of Organizational Behavior*. Englewood Cliffs, NJ: Prentice Hall, 1987, p. 211.

23. Packard, V. *The Hidden Persuaders*. New York: Pocket Books, 1964.

24. Cho, H. and White, K. "A Review of Fear-Appeal Effects." In J. S. Seiter and R. H. Gass (eds.), *Perspectives on Persuasion, Social Influence, and Compliance Gaining*. Boston, MA: Allyn & Bacon, 2004, pp. 223–235.

25. Larson. *Persuasion*, pp. 71–73.

26. Ibid, pp. 71–73.

27. Minnick, W. C. *The Art of Persuasion*, 2nd ed. Boston, MA: Houghton Mifflin, 1968, pp. 263–264.

28. Lewandowsky, S., W. G. K. Stritzke, K. Oberauer, and M. Morales. "Memory for Fact, Fiction, and Misinformation," *Psychological Science* 16, no. 3 (2005): 190–195.

29. "People Believe a 'Fact' That Fits Their Views Even If It's Clearly False," *Wall Street Journal*, February 4, 2005, p. B-1. Reprinted by permission of Dow Jones & Company, Inc.

Copyright © 2005 Dow Jones & Company, Inc. All rights reserved worldwide. License number 1280830699090.

30. Roediger, H. L., III, and K. B. McDermott. "Creating False Memories: Remembering Words Not Presented in Lists," *Journal of Experimental Psychology: Learning, Memory, and Cognition*, 21 (1995), pp. 803–814. See also Roediger, H. L., III. "Memory Illusions," *Journal of Memory and Language* 35 (1996): 76–100.

31. Keane, J. G., former dean, Mendoza College of Business, University of Notre Dame. Personal interview, June 21, 2005.

32. Deutschman, A. "Making Change," *Fast Company*, May 2005, pp. 54–62.

33. Goleman, D. *Emotional Intelligence*. New York: Bantam Books, 1995, p. 56.

34. Garvin, D. A. and M. A. Roberto. "Change Through Persuasion," *Harvard Business Review*, February 2005, p. 111.

35. Deutschman, A. "Change or Die," *Fast Company*, May 2005, p. 55.

CASE STUDY 6-1

The United States Olympic Committee

Persuading Business to Participate in the Olympic Movement

"We don't receive government funds," said Lynne Cribari, "so corporate funds and private donations provide the bulk of our support. And, in asking for corporate sponsorship, we walk a very fine line between encouraging enthusiasm for and participation in the Olympic spirit on the one hand, and crass over-commercialization on the other."

Lynne Cribari is Manager of Corporate Participation for the United States Olympic Committee (USOC), and works in the USOC's headquarters in Colorado Springs, Colorado. She received a political science degree from The Colorado College and, following a brief career in media relations and local television, joined the USOC as assistant director of broadcasting. Today, her task is to assist the Director of Marketing and the Executive Director of the USOC in securing corporate sponsorship for United States athletes training for and participating in the Olympic Games.

"Asking for corporate sponsorship is a difficult task," she said, "because we maintain exclusivity in each product category and we must negotiate separately with each corporation for the rights to use our marks and logos." Exclusivity, she explained, means that only one sponsor will be permitted to use the U.S. Olympic Committee's logotypes, including the universally recognized five-ring Olympic symbol.

Current sponsors include such corporate giants as IBM, Bausch & Lomb, Eastman Kodak, VISA Cards International, and Anheuser-Busch Brewing.

"Our task is to create an environment in which the marks are used appropriately," Cribari said, "and that means that we're directly involved in what's known as 'cause-related marketing.' If you use your VISA card to make a purchase, for example, VISA will contribute a certain amount to the U.S. Olympic Committee."

Cribari said the persuasive challenge in her job is to create a partnership in which both the Olympic Movement and the corporate sponsor will benefit. "We have a $600 million budget for the current four-year period and, as you can imagine, the costs involved in training and preparing an Olympic team for the coming games are enormous. We're proud of the fact that 85 cents from every dollar contributed will go directly to our primary purpose: training athletes."

"We usually ask our sponsors for cash," she explained, "but some provide us with 'value in kind.' " For example, 97 percent of the food fed to athletes in our Colorado Springs Training Center is "value in kind" and comes from corporate sponsors in the food business. These contributions are not trivial, though. "On average," she said, "we receive about $60 million from each sponsor. As you can see, this represents a huge investment for these companies, because they'll probably spend twice that amount on advertising and promotion in order to use our [trademarks] and logos."

How does the U.S. Olympic Committee approach a potential sponsor and ask for that much money? "Well," said Cribari, "we look at these partnerships from a value-added viewpoint. Altruism only goes so far; at a certain point, we must show them how their sponsorship of Olympic athletes will pay off in greater sales and increased corporate revenues."

"We usually begin with some historical data about the Olympic movement," she explained, "and then demonstrate how association with the movement has helped drive sales for other firms. Once a potential sponsor understands how the association works, we'll help them develop a marketing plan that will make the most effective use of our marks."

Cribari cited the case of Kraft General Foods as an example. "We helped them develop a fully integrated persuasive campaign," she said. "Kraft wanted to change the public perception of processed cheese. The public impression was that their products weren't in sync with a health-conscious diet, so they began using the phrase, 'Kraft sets the U.S. Olympic training table.' We worked with Kraft to develop their campaign, because we insist [on] truth in advertising, accuracy, and the use of actual athletes in their commercials. It's been a successful partnership for both of us," she added.

The campaign involves more than just the use of the Olympic rings, however. "A typical arrangement with a corporate sponsor will include help with advertising, promotions, product packaging, and such things as point-of-purchase giveaways." In the case of Kraft, the USOC helped produce a number of Olympic training table recipes using Kraft products, a cookbook that consumers could receive by mail, and a number of in-store appearances by Olympic athletes.

"As we formulate persuasive messages," Cribari said, "we must keep in mind that we're accountable to the public, to our sponsors, and to the Congress of the United States. As a result, we insist on truthfulness and accuracy and we work

very hard to establish and maintain long-term relationships with prestigious, reliable sponsors." Coca-Cola, for example, has been an Olympic partner for more than 75 years.

"Our persuasive task doesn't end with a signed agreement for corporate sponsorship," Cribari explained. "After we've convinced a sponsor that association with the Olympic movement will help them sell products, we must convince them to use the logos and marks appropriately, and to remain both ethical and true to the spirit of the Olympic movement. Our relationship is unique to each sponsor," she added, "and it's an [ongoing], evolving matter for us."

What's the single greatest challenge in all of this for the USOC? "No question about it," Cribari replied. "We're competing for corporate sponsorship in a market that includes the NFL, the NHL, the NBA, and Major League Baseball. We're after limited sponsorship dollars and it's up to us to show how the Olympic movement is useful, productive and worthwhile for a corporate sponsor. If we succeed," she added, "it's a win-win situation for all of us: for the sponsor, for the USOC and the Olympic movement, and for U.S. athletes who'll compete for the gold in the Olympic games."

DISCUSSION QUESTIONS

1. Are Ms. Cribari and her colleagues at the U.S. Olympic Committee following the basic theories of persuasion in any way? Can you identify in their work any of the steps discussed earlier in this chapter?
2. What sort of attention-getting device is she employing?
3. What's the principal motivation for corporate sponsors to pay such large sums of money for the use of the Olympic name and logos?
4. Do you see resistance to [counter-persuasion] in any of their work?
5. Who are Ms. Cribari's main competitors?
6. What do you suppose is the reason for exclusivity in each product category?
7. Can you imagine some product categories the USOC would not be interested in securing sponsorship for?

WRITING ASSIGNMENT

Please respond in writing to the issues presented in this case by preparing two documents: a communication strategy memo and a professional business letter.

In preparing these documents, you may assume one of two roles: you may identify yourself as an external marketing consultant who has been asked to provide advice to the U.S. Olympic Committee, or you may assume the role of Ms. Lynne Cribari, Manager of Corporate Participation for the USOC.

Either way, you must prepare a strategy memo, addressed to Dr. Harvey Schiller, Executive Director of the U.S. Olympic Committee, that identifies a corporate sponsorship prospect and suggests ways in which the USOC might convince that firm to participate in the Olympic movement, either with sponsorship in cash or sponsorship in kind (goods and/or services).

Your memo should explain something about the company you have chosen as a prospect, what industry they compete in, their size, as well as their business model. Your discussion of the company should identify the principle(s) of persuasion you think will be most effective in convincing the company's leadership to become an Olympic sponsor, in addition to the reasons why such an arrangement would be in their best interest.

You must also prepare a professional business letter for Dr. Schiller's signature. That document should be addressed to an officer of the corporation you have selected and must offer to open a dialogue on the advantages of participation in the Olympic movement. If you have questions about either of these documents, please consult your instructor.

This case was prepared from personal interviews by James S. O'Rourke, Concurrent Professor of Management, as the basis for class discussion rather than to illustrate either effective or ineffective handling of an administrative situation.

CASE STUDY 6-2

An Invitation to Wellness at Whirlpool Corporation

"We know there is a direct correlation between employee wellness and the use of insurance benefit dollars. Employees who are well spend less of the company's money. They feel better. They're more productive. And, of course, they lead healthier, happier lives."

Dana Donnley is Director of Employee Communication for Whirlpool Corporation, a $12.1 billion appliance manufacturer and marketer with assets placing it 143rd on *Fortune* magazine's list of 500 largest business organizations. With corporate headquarters in Benton Harbor, Michigan, Whirlpool has more than 39,000 employees in the United States and 30 foreign nations.

"During the month of his or her birthday," Donnley said, "we offer each employee in the headquarters a free mini-physical. Our company health nurse sends a letter to each employee sometime toward the end of the month before their birthday, inviting that person to participate." Is this letter persuasive or directive in tone? "Oh, it's persuasive," Donnley replied. "The program is entirely voluntary. We pick up the cost and certainly encourage each employee to participate, but we can't make them do it. We've got to persuade them that it's in their best interest to have a physical at least once a year."

"The biggest objection," said Donnley, "usually revolves around confidentiality. People are concerned about that and sometimes have questions regarding how the information will be used. We do our best in that letter, and in personal conversations, to convince them that the results of these physicals are entirely confidential. The company doctor will see the results and then mail them to the employee. We don't keep any records—the employee gets the original and no copies are made."

What's involved in the physical? "Well, it's fairly comprehensive. The nurse records each employee's height, weight, blood pressure, and vital signs. A routine exam is performed, testing various functions and reflexes, providing each employee with a relatively complete work-up."

What's the doctor looking for? "This is a screening program designed to let our employees know the general condition of their health. A number of different illnesses and diseases can develop without any outward symptoms. And, of course, if he catches something early—before it has a chance to progress very far—it's all to the employee's benefit. In such cases," she added, "we'll recommend that the employee contact his or her family physician and seek appropriate treatment."

Does Whirlpool have trouble getting people to participate? "Not really," said Donnley. "Most people are eager to be involved. That hasn't always been the case, though, and it's taken a concerted effort on our part to persuade them that this wellness program benefits them at least as much as it benefits the company. This year, in fact, we've opened the program to spouses of our employees, as well." The task of convincing a husband or wife to participate, according to Donnley, is really a two-step process. "First, we've got to sell each employee on the idea. Then, they've got to go home and convince their wife or husband to get involved."

Is that important to Whirlpool? "Listen," she replied, "an employee with a healthy spouse is more likely to have healthy diet and exercise habits. They're certainly more conscious of what's involved in a personal wellness program. And that," she added, "is good for all of us."

DISCUSSION QUESTIONS

1. Why do you suppose employees at Whirlpool Corporation might be concerned about confidentiality in these physical examinations?

2. What could Ms. Donnley do to reassure Whirlpool employees that exam findings and test results would be kept confidential?

3. If you were hoping to persuade Whirlpool employees to sign up for a physical examination, would you say something different in person than you might say in a letter?

4. What would you choose to say first to those employees in a letter? How long should the letter be?

5. What's the value of the company's offer to an employee? What's the value of such a program to the company?

6. What means of persuasion are available to Ms. Donnley, other than a letter to each employee? What else would you choose to do?

WRITING ASSIGNMENT

Please respond in writing to the issues presented in this case by preparing two documents: a communication strategy memo and a professional business letter.

In preparing these documents, you should identify yourself as an Employee Communication Manager at Whirlpool Corporation who has been asked to provide communication advice to Ms. Donnley. Your strategy memo should be directed to her, providing analysis of the business problem, the relevant background details, critical issues, audience factors, options for action, and your specific recommendations. Think broadly and

provide comprehensive advice for Ms. Donnley regarding the Whirlpool Corporation Employee Wellness Program.

You must also prepare a professional business letter for Ms. Donnley's signature. That document should explain directly to Whirlpool employees the purposes of the program, the reasons for their participation, and the benefits you expect them to derive from doing so. If you have questions about either of these documents, please consult your instructor.

This case was prepared by James S. O'Rourke, Concurrent Professor of Management, as the basis for class discussion rather than to illustrate either effective or ineffective handling of an administrative situation.

CASE STUDY 6-3

Kraft Foods, Inc.: The Cost of Advertising on Children's Waistlines

The room fell silent as Dr. Ellen Wartella, Dean of the College of Communications at the University of Texas at Austin, gave Kraft executives her opinions on a presentation they had just made regarding Kraft and advertising to children. Wartella characterized Kraft's online marketing as "indefensible" and concluded that Kraft's claim that it was not advertising to children under the age of six was "at best disingenuous and, at worst, a downright lie."[1] The executives in the room were visibly shaken by her comments.

In late 2003, Kraft formed the Worldwide Health & Wellness Advisory Council, composed of ten nutritionists and media experts, including Wartella, to investigate allegations that Kraft had been knowingly advertising unhealthy foods and to help address the rise

in obesity among other health issues.[2] The pressure for Kraft to review its advertising policies came amidst increasing criticism from congressional panels, parent groups, and other concerned citizens that food corporations, such as Kraft Foods and McDonald's Corporation, have been knowingly targeting young children (up to age 12) in their advertising campaigns. The concern surrounding childhood obesity stems from statistics showing a 200 percent increase in childhood obesity since the 1980s. Between the 1960s and the 1980s, the percentage of overweight children hovered around 6 percent, but in the last two decades, this rate has leapt to 16 percent.[3] Despite this, Kraft decided to keep marketing to children under 12. One Kraft executive admitted, "We didn't want to give up the power of marketing to kids."[4]

This "power" is villainizing the company, however. Currently, Kraft is a trusted brand, but that reputation is already slipping. According to the Reputation Quotient study conducted in 2005 by research firm Harris Interactive, Kraft is ranked in the 50th slot.[5] While this is a small drop from the 48th spot Kraft held the previous year, it is a far distance from the 8th position occupied by competitor General Mills. This survey is based on consumer perception of various factors, including a company's quality of products and services, social responsibility, and vision and leadership. Depending on what Kraft chooses to do about its food marketing issue, the company may rise higher in the subsequent Reputation Quotient studies, or it may fall further down.

Kraft Foods is a company that values quality and safety in its products. One of Kraft's key strategies is to "build superior consumer brand value" through "great-tasting products, innovative packaging, consistent high quality, wide availability, helpful services and strong brand image."[6] With products in more than 99 percent of U.S. households, Kraft certainly has earned the trust of its consumers.[7] With the recent feedback from the Health and Wellness Advisory Council and public concerns about childhood obesity due to aggressive food marketing, however, Kraft must take action before it loses consumers' loyalty and trust in its products.

Kraft Foods, Inc.

Kraft Foods, Inc., the largest food and beverage company in North America, has grown considerably from its humble beginnings in 1903. With only $65, a rented wagon, and a horse named Paddy, J. L. Kraft started the company by purchasing cheese from a wholesale market and reselling it to local merchants.[8] These cheeses were packaged with Kraft's name. A decade later, Kraft improved the cheese by processing the product, which prolonged its shelf life. The processed cheese became such a success that a patent for the "Process of Sterilizing Cheese and an Improved Product Produced by Such Process" was issued to Kraft in 1916.[9] Over the years, the company went on to create other new cheese products that are familiar to homes today including *Velveeta* and *Cheez Whiz*, as well as expanding beyond cheese to introduce salad dressings, packaged dinners, barbecue sauce, and other products.

Tobacco giant Philip Morris acquired General Foods Corporation in 1985 and then Kraft three years later for $12.9 billion.[10] Through the acquisition of these two major food companies, Philip Morris formed Kraft General Foods, which put products such as

Velveeta, *Post* cereals, *Oscar Mayer*, and *Jell-O* pudding all under the same food division. Kraft General Foods further expanded its household reach by acquiring Nabisco, home of well-known brands including *Oreo* cookies, *Ritz* crackers, and *Planter*s nuts, in 2000. The next big step for Kraft occurred in 2001 when Philip Morris conducted an Initial Public Offering of Kraft's shares (NYSE: KFT). The following year, Philip Morris shareholders accepted a proposal to change the company's name to Altria Group. As of January 27, 2003, Altria Group became the parent company to Kraft Foods.

Kraft's Troubles in Advertising

There are many reasons why Kraft should be concerned about further criticism of its advertising practices. As a leader in the food industry, Kraft is both large and very visible, and the company has experienced repeated controversy and criticism of its advertising campaigns over the years. A few recent issues include:

- Kraft's advertisement of *Post* cereal in *National Geographic Kids* was not focused on the food but rather on the premium of Postokens instead, which is a violation of The Children's Advertising Review Units' Self-Regulatory Guidelines for Children's Advertising.[11]
- Kraft had previously announced its intention to reduce portion size and then later backed out of that commitment, saying that consumers wanted to choose their portion sizes for themselves.[12]
- Kraft pulled an Oreo commercial directed at teenagers that promoted a "sloth-like" lifestyle because the company realized that such an ad would hurt its image and instead opted for promoting "a more active lifestyle."[13]

Obesity in the Courts: The McLawsuit

The food industry became visibly worried about food marketing and childhood obesity in 2002. It was then that McDonald's Corporation faced a lawsuit, *Pelham v. McDonald's Corporation*, in which the company was charged with marketing food products that contribute to the rise of obesity in children and teenagers. Although the judge threw out the class-action lawsuit against McDonald's, he made it very clear that he supports the plaintiffs' position. He encouraged them to redraft and refile the suit with stronger evidence, and went so far as to provide advice on what to look for. One of his recommendations was to show how McDonald's advertising campaigns encouraged over-consumption by promoting its food products for "everyday" eating.[14]

McDonald's Corporation still stands behind their standards in marketing to children. According to David Green, Senior Vice President of Marketing for McDonald's, even though 20 percent of McDonald's commercials are targeted at children, the company follows a strict set of guidelines. The Golden Arches Code, according to company spokesmen, "conforms with the major network Broadcasting Standards and the guidelines of the Children's Unit of the National Advertising Division Council of Better Business Bureaus, Inc., as well as establishing additional standards applicable only to McDonald's advertising."[15] Green says that the Golden Arches Code "states that in our advertising we should never promote the sale of food items to children that might be too large for them to consume realistically at one sitting nor should children be depicted as coming to McDonald's on their own, as they must always be accompanied by an adult."

A month prior to *Pelham v. McDonald's Corporation*, Sam Hirsch, the attorney who filed the suit for the overweight children and teenagers, had filed another class-action suit against McDonald's and other leading fast-food establishments.[16] This suit was filed not only against McDonald's Corporation, but also Burger King, Kentucky Fried Chicken, and Wendy's. Observers speculated the driving force behind these two suits was the prospect of a large financial settlement. Hirsch remained adamant about his clients' intentions, saying "we are not looking to get rich from a large money settlement. We are proposing a fund that will educate children about the nutritional facts and contents of McDonald's food."[17] These suits intensified fears in the food industry of a future of "tobacco-like" litigation against restaurants and food manufacturers.[18]

In January 2005, the Second U.S. Circuit Court of Appeals reinstated claims that McDonald's falsely advertised the health benefits of its fast food, a

violation of the New York Consumer Protection Act.[19] Unquestionably, the plaintiffs had the full attention of quick service restaurant operators and food manufacturers worldwide.

Studies Show. . .

Fewer Ads. In July 2005, the Federal Trade Commission (FTC) released its findings that children today watch fewer food commercials than they did almost three decades ago. Children today watch 13 food advertisements on television per day, a significant reduction from the 18 television commercials per day in 1977.[20] The FTC also reported that kids today are exposed to fewer ads for cereal, candy, and toys but more ads for restaurants and fast-food chains, other television shows, movies, video games, and DVDs. Wally Snyder, President of the American Advertising Federation, believed this study was proof that food marketing is not culpable for the rise of obesity in children, which he blamed on a "lack of exercise and moderation in the diet."

More Ads. A year earlier in 2004, the Kaiser Family Foundation released a study with contrary information, claiming "the number of ads children see on TV has doubled from 20,000 to 40,000 since the 1970s, and the majority of ads targeted to kids are for candy, cereal and fast food."[21] The study suggested that this increase in food advertising was correlated to the rise in obesity in children aged 6–11. From 1963 to 1970, only 4.2 percent of children in this age group were listed as overweight compared to 1999–2000, when the number spiked to 15.3 percent.

The Tie-Breaker. Perhaps because of the conflicting findings or because of rising concerns about food marketing to children and its effects, Congress requested a study of its own from the National Academy of Sciences, which was created by the federal government to advise on scientific issues.[22] In December 2005, the Institute of Medicine (IOM), a private, nongovernmental division of the National Academy of Sciences, released the latest study on the subject, *Food Marketing to Children and Youth: Threat or Opportunity?* Based upon individual findings, the IOM committee responsible for the study came to the following five conclusions:

Broad Conclusions

- Along with many other intersecting factors, food and beverage marketing influences the diets and health prospects of children and youth.
- Food and beverage marketing practices geared to children and youth are out of balance with healthful diets, and contribute to an environment that puts their health at risk.
- Food and beverage companies, restaurants, and marketers have underutilized potential to devote creativity and resources to develop and promote food, beverages, and meals that support healthful diets for children and youth.
- Achieving healthful diets for children and youth will require sustained multi-sectoral, and integrated efforts that include industry leadership and initiative.

Public policy programs and incentives do not currently have the support or authority to address many of the current and emerging marketing practices that influence the diets of children and youth.[23]

The study also suggested there was "strong evidence" that food marketing influences the preferences, purchase requests, and short-term consumption of children between the ages of 2 and 11. This information combined with the fact that a "preponderance of television food and beverage advertising relevant to children and youth promotes high-calorie and low-nutrient products, it can be concluded that television advertising influences children to prefer and request high-calorie and low-nutrient foods and beverages."[24] Wartella, who served not only on Kraft's advisory council but also as a member of the committee that produced the IOM study, said "We can't any more argue whether food advertising is related to children's diets. It is."[25]

The Institute of Medicine's recommendations for the food industry included promoting and supporting healthier products and working with government, public health, and consumer goods "to establish and enforce the highest standards for the marketing" of food and beverage products to children.[26] In general, many food companies had already started programs to promote healthier products. The problem was with the later recommendation in marketing standards. IOM believed this meant licensed characters should be "used only for the promotion of foods and beverages that support healthful diets for children and youth."[27] Most companies, Kraft included, were reluctant to give this up. Licensed characters were typically familiar faces to children. How does a company replace a spokesperson or promoter that already has the trust of the audience, is affordable, and will never get into any real-life trouble?

The Announcement

In January 2005, Kraft announced that it would stop advertising certain products to children under 12. These products include regular *Kool-Aid* beverages, *Oreo* and *Chips Ahoy* cookies, several *Post* children's cereals and some varieties of its *Lunchables* lunch packages.[28] These favorites will still be found in stores, but Kraft said it will no longer be targeting children with television, radio, and print ads for these products. The initial cost of implementing these new guidelines, included an estimated $75 million in lost profits, thought this figure continued to change several times.[29] While this estimate may seem high, Michael Mudd, a member of Kraft's obesity strategy team said, "If the tobacco industry could go back 20 or 30 years, reform their marketing, disarm their critics, and sacrifice a couple of hundred million in profits, knowing what they know today, don't you think they'd take that deal in a heartbeat?"[30] Kraft, learning the lessons of Philip Morris, was eager for the deal.

Shortly after Kraft made its announcement, however, the company joined competitors General Mills and Kellogg to form a lobbying group to keep the government from regulating food marketing to children. The group's mission statement states its belief that "there is not a correlation between advertising trends and recent childhood obesity."[31] General Mills had always argued for this point. In fact, instead of stopping ads to children, Tom Forsythe, General Mills vice president, announced that the company "launched a vigorous defense of cereal," to support its health benefits.[32] The company also decided to promote "balanced moderation and exercise," believing that such lifestyle choices affect obesity as much as food selection.[33] Thus, General Mills' participation in this group was expected, but for Kraft, joining this group appeared to be a hypocritical move. David S. Johnson, Kraft's Chief of North America, defended the action,

"We believe self-regulation of the marketing of food products can and does work, and we are collaborating with the industry to strengthen efforts in this area."[34]

Conclusion

Since the announcement, Kraft has still struggled with child advertising and obesity issues. Margo G. Wootan, Director of Nutrition for the Center for Science in the Public Interest, has called Kraft's new marketing plan only "a really good step forward."[35] The problem is there will always be critics who will demand for more.

For instance, although Kraft has taken a huge leap in minimizing television, radio, and print ads, the company has yet to act on Wartella's criticism for its online advertising.

Kraft has spent a great deal of time responding to critics and potential threats of government regulation. What Kraft really needs at this point is to put the focus back on its customers and communicate with them. The question is how to go about doing this without appearing to go back on its promised of not saturating the market with advertisement.

DISCUSSION QUESTIONS

1. What are the critical issues of this case? Who are the stakeholders (primary, secondary, and indirect)?
2. What should Kraft do to maintain the already declining trust of the consumers?
3. Can the public believe in Kraft's commitment to control food marketing to children?
4. What are Kraft's options concerning its marketing tactics?

5. What media should Kraft use to communicate to its customers?
6. Who should Kraft's key audience be: critics, agencies, parents, children, nonparent adults, or others? Should the company even target a particular audience?

WRITING ASSIGNMENT

Please respond in writing to the issues presented in this case by preparing two documents: a communication strategy memo and a professional business letter.

In preparing these documents, you may identify yourself as a Kraft Foods senior manager who has been asked to provide advice to Ms. Perry Yeatman, Senior Vice President, International Corporate Affairs and Global Issues Management, regarding the issues she and the company are facing. Or, you may identify yourself as an external management consultant who has been asked to provide advice to Ms. Yeatman. Either way, you must prepare a strategy memo addressed to Ms. Yeatman that summarizes the details of the case,

rank orders critical issues, discusses their implications (what they mean and why they matter), offers specific recommendations for action (assigning ownership and suspense dates for each), and shows how to communicate the solution to all who are affected by the recommendation.

You must also prepare a professional business letter for the signature of Ms. Irene Rosenfeld, Kraft CEO. That document may be addressed to Kraft retailers, customers, investors, or another key stakeholder group. If you have questions about either of these documents, please consult your instructor.

References

1. Ellison, Sarah. "Why Kraft Banned Some Food Ads," *Wall Street Journal*, November 1, 2005.
2. http://164.109.46. 215/newsroom/09032003. html.
3. http://www.childstats.gov/americaschidren/ index.asp.
4. Ellison. "Why Kraft Banned Some Food Ads."
5. http://www.foodprocessing.com/ industry news/2006/018.html.
6. http://kraft.com/profile/comany_ strategies.html. "Grow, Oreo Tries a New Twist," *Chicago Tribune*, August 22, 2005.
7. http://www.altria.com/about_altria/ 01_00_01_kraftfoods.asp.

8. http://kraft.com/profile/factsheet.html.

9. http://kraft.com/100/founders/JLKraft.html.

10. http://www.altria.com/about_altria? 1_2_5_1_altriastory.asp.

11. http://www.caru.org/news/2004/kraft.asp.

12. Callahan, Patricia and Alexan, Delroy. "As Fat Fears."

13. Ibid.

14. Weiser, Benjamin. "Your Honor, We Call Our Next Witness: McFrankenstein," *New York Times*, January 26, 2003.

15. "McLibel" Case—Green, David B., Witness Statement, http://www.mcspotlight.org/people/ witnesses/advertising/green.html.

16. Summons, http://news.findlaw.com/cnn/docs/ mcdonalds/barbermcds72302cmp.pdf.

17. Wald, J. "McDonald's Obesity Suit Tossed," CNNmoney.com, February 17, 2003 onathan, http://money.cnn.com/2003/01/22 news/companies/mcdonalds/.

18. Reuters article: http://onenews.nzoom.com/ onenews_detail/0,1227,218579-1-6,00.html.

19. http://www.law.com/jsp?id=1106573726371.

20. Mayer, Caroline E. "TV Feeds Kids Fewer Food Ads, FTC Staff Study Finds," *Washington Post*, July 15, 2005.

21. "Ads Rapped in Child Obesity Fight," http://www.cbsnews.com/stories/2004/02/24/he alth/main601894.shtml.

22. http://www.iom.edu/?id=5774.

23. Institute of Medicine. "Food Marketing to Children and Youth: Threat or Opportunity?" 2006, Box 7-1, p. 317.

24. Institute of Medicine, p. 322.

25. Ellison, Sarah and Adamy, Janet. "Panel Faults Food Packaging for Kid Obesity," *Wall Street Journal*, December 7, 2005.

26. Institute of Medicine. "Food Marketing to Children and Youth," pp. 325–326.

27. Ibid., p. 326.

28. "Kraft to Curb Some Snack Food Advertising," Associated Press, January 12, 2005, http://msnbc.msn.com/id/6817344/.

29. Ellison, Sarah. "Why Kraft Decided to Ban Some Food Ads to Children," *Wall Street Journal*, November 1, 2005.

30. Ibid.

31. Callahan and Alexan. "As Fat Fears Grow, Oreo Tries a New Twist."

32. Ellison and Adamy. "Panel Faults Food Packaging for Kid Obesity."

33. Ellison, Sarah. "Divided, Companies Fight For Right to Plug Kids' Food," *Wall Street Journal*, January 26, 2005.

34. Callahan and Alexan. "As Fat Fears Grow, Oreo Tries a New Twist."

35. Mayer, Caroline E. "Kraft to Curb Snack -Food Advertising," *The Washington Post*, January 12, 2005.

This case was prepared by Research Assistants Pauline Hwa and Timothy Housman under the direction of James S. O'Rourke, Concurrent Professor of Management, as the basis for class discussion rather than to illustrate either effective or ineffective handling of an administrative situation. Information was gathered from corporate as well as public sources.

Chapter 7

Technology

It seemed like such an innocent act: hitting the "Forward" button on the e-mail toolbar. For 19 employees of the brokerage firm Edward Jones & Co., it cost them their jobs. Following an investigation, management asked workers to admit whether they had sent inappropriate files or off-color jokes to others over the company's e-mail system. When they lied about having done so, they were fired. Another 41 who came forward were disciplined but allowed to stay on.[1]

They're not alone. Employees were recently fired at the New York Times Company, at Morgan Stanley, and a number of other organizations for abusing the communication systems provided by their employers.[2]

The "Forward" button isn't the only source of trouble, apparently. A few years ago, an insurance company manager, working with an internal mailing list devoted to his customers, replied to an office e-mail. His response focused on the company's strategy for selling a particular policy, but the message wasn't sent to just one person—it was sent to the entire listserv. He had clicked "Reply All" and, buried in that huge list was the address of the customer they were working with. That manager's crass language and arrogant approach went directly to his customer and, not surprisingly, he didn't make the sale.

How can such wonderful technology be the source of so much frustration? Isn't information technology (IT)—including e-mail, voice mail, video conferencing, desktop computing, instant messaging, text messaging, cell phones, and handheld wireless devices—supposed to make our lives easier? Aren't we all more productive as a result? Even though the inventors and manufacturers of all this technology can fairly claim great things for us personally and professionally, the new world in which we live is not without its dark side. Every opportunity has its risks, and communication technology is no exception.

LIFE IN THE DIGITAL AGE

When MIT media technology professor Nicholas Negroponte told us in 1995 that "being digital" is not simply a way of communicating but a new way of living, only the propeller-heads, IT gurus, and technology buffs were enthusiastic. But nearly two decades later, just about everyone realizes that he was right. It's quicker, cheaper, and easier to ship electrons (as in e-mail attachments) than it is to ship atoms and molecules (as in FedEx overnight packages). Some things still must move around physically, but so much more can move electronically.[3]

We can create files anywhere, store them in the cloud (online), access them from an iPad or wireless Blackberry, insert graphics and hyperlinks, and pass them on to someone else. Or with the use of shareware and collaborative software platforms such as eProject and CommuniSpace, multiple authors can work on the same document at once from different locations, edit the content, discuss the changes, and assure themselves of document version control.

The way we work and live has changed. We can find information quickly, check the nannycam at our children's daycare center on the Internet, manage inventory, control cash flow, and follow the stock market simultaneously. We can find just about anyone with a smart phone or personal computer in a matter of seconds. Since the advent of PCs just over 25 years ago, more than 1.3 billion have been sold worldwide.[4] According to the Gartner Group, the industry shipped more than 300 million units in 2009, up more than 5 percent from the year before, as the price of desktop computing has dropped steadily to less than $1,000 apiece.[5]

By 2011, more than 80 percent of all U.S. households had access to at least one personal computer, and 66 percent had in-home access to broadband connections.[6] It will take a few years before literally everyone has access to computerized word processing, spreadsheet technology, e-mail, social media and the Internet, but that day is coming. And as Professor Negroponte told us in the mid-1990s, it is changing the way we live.

COMMUNICATING DIGITALLY

Professor Carolyn Boulger, in *e-Technology and the Fourth Economy*, shows how the movement from hunting and gathering to an economy based on agriculture and then industrial production made civilization possible. But a fourth economy, based entirely on mindwork—an exchange of ideas— creates possibilities previously undreamt of. No longer must we follow the herds, depend on the growing seasons, or own the means of production in order to create a life for ourselves. The means of production are now in our minds, in our hands, and on our desktops.[7]

Along with all of the advantages that this new technology brings to our homes, our businesses, and our personal and professional lives, it also brings complications. More than 20 million households in the United States do not have access to the Internet. Even more surprising, perhaps: nearly one-third of U.S. households have never used a computer to create a document.[8] Those who do have access to computing and the Internet tell us they're not necessarily better off. "I see these people on airplanes, in building lobbies, and in restaurants," says a friend, "and they're all pounding away on their laptops, entering data in a Blackberry, or making client calls on a cell phone. There is absolutely no distinction anymore between work and home." Another put it more succinctly: "If I drag my notebook computer on the road with me, I feel as if I'm on the wrong end of some sort of electronic dog-leash."

Technology, it seems, is a two-edged sword with the potential to make us more productive or to drain away our time. A typical information worker who sits at a computer all day turns to his e-mail program more than 50 times and uses instant messaging 77 times, according to RescueTime, a company that analyzes computer habits. The company, which draws its data from 40,000 people who have tracking software on their computers, found that an average worker also stops at 40 Web sites over the course of the day. The fractured attention comes at a cost. In the United States, more than $650 billion a year in productivity is lost because of interruptions and inattention.[9] Vault.com reports that an astonishing 37 percent of the employees it surveyed say they constantly surf the Web at work for personal reasons.[10] And, according to SexTracker, a service that monitors Internet traffic, "On most pornographic Web sites, up to 70 percent of traffic takes place during work hours."[11]

A recent survey in the United Kingdom revealed that nearly a third of all workers in Britain use e-mail at work to gossip about rivals and flirt with colleagues.[12] E-mail has already created multiple problems for businesses in this country and abroad, including legal liability, confidentiality breaches, damage to reputation, lost productivity, network congestion, downtime, and court orders demanding that e-mail records be turned over to trial judges.[13]

Any thoughtful person will tell you those aren't the only problems technology brings in the door with it. Managers must now rely on fewer nonverbal and visual cues to gather meaning. They work across time zones and with geographically dispersed groups and teams. Often, they're asked to work electronically with people they've never met and don't really know. People say they're virtually buried in e-mail some days. "If you get 35 messages a day," says a colleague, "it means that when you return from a three-day trip, you have more than a hundred messages to deal with." For some, it's voice mail ping-pong that drives them crazy. For others, it's the loss of privacy and the sense that they're no longer in control of their lives.

This chapter examines e-technology, workplace behaviors and the policies that guide them, as well as workplace privacy and employer monitoring. We also look at how companies use telecommuting and virtual workgroups to increase productivity. You will find some new rules of etiquette, along with a brief look at social media and three case studies that focus directly on how these issues affect you.

ELECTRONIC MAIL

What began as a method for sharing scientific and technical information among Defense Department and university researchers more than 30 years ago is now an everyday fact of life. Electronic mail, or e-mail to most people, is a global means of staying in touch, passing data and graphics, and managing the moment-to-moment flow of information needed to run a business. It's also a gateway for the unwanted: unsolicited spam and mass advertising, scam artists, grifters, predators, pornographers, viruses, hackers, and thieves. E-mail is an unlatched doorway into your computer and into the innermost secrets of your personal and professional life.

Properly managed, though, e-mail can become a productivity booster, a link to distant markets, and an essential tool for managing everything from employee communication to customer relations. It requires some forethought, discipline, and planning, though. Let's begin with some personal issues and then move to the policies and procedures you should think about as you try to make e-mail work for you.

For a growing number of people, just keeping up with e-mail is a battle they can't seem to win. Consider these statistics:

- **6 trillion** business e-mail messages send annually worldwide.
- **49 minutes** spent managing e-mails each day by the average office worker.
- **4 hours** spent managing e-mails by senior management workers.
- **80:** the percentage of e-mails sent which are actually "spam"—unsolicited advertisements, many of which are fraudulent or otherwise illegal.
- **62:** the percentage of workers in industrialized nations who check business e-mails while at home or on vacation.
- **10:** the points fall in IQ experienced by workers distracted by e-mail (more than twice that found in cannabis studies).
- **20:** the percentage of workers who are stressed.[14]

Another study from the Gartner Group reveals that nearly half of all American e-mail users (more than 100 million of us) check e-mail on vacation. Nearly one in four looks for messages every weekend.[15] "I was addicted to e-mail," says Sabrina Horn, CEO of Horn Group in San Francisco. "I lived for the little bell that would go *ding*! when a new message arrived. I got sucked into using e-mail to try to figure out where in the organization I could best focus my attention," she said. As a result, "I had this nagging feeling that I was never getting anything done at the office. I went home every day completely frustrated. I knew what was going on at work, but I didn't actually *do* anything."[16]

To manage the growing problem of e-mail in your life, here are a few suggestions you can act on now.

ADMIT YOU HAVE A PROBLEM Mark Elwood, author of *Cut the Glut of E-Mail*, calculates that white-collar workers waste an average of three hours a week just sorting through junk mail. If you spend more time than that, you have a problem.[17]

SEND LESS, GET LESS If you send less e-mail, you'll reduce the volume of return mail in your in-box. Think carefully about whether you really need to draft new messages or respond to those you've received. Misty Young of KPS3 Advertising in Reno, Nevada, says, "Unless I get an error message, I assume it got through. I don't need someone to send a 'Thank you for keeping me in the loop' or 'Is there anything else you need?' or 'Have a really great day.'"[18]

ESCAPE THE ENDLESS REPLY LOOP Silence in response to an e-mail message is often thought of as rude. "It's like walking out on someone who is still talking to you," says Kaitlin Sherwood, who writes about the problem at overcomeemailoverload.com. She suggests that you finish a message with "No reply needed" or follow a request with "Thanks in advance." If you're fulfilling a request, you might conclude with "Hope this helped." Even though it may be helpful to anticipate questions that could arise, you should avoid asking questions you really don't want the answers to.[19]

CHECK THE "TO" FIELD BEFORE YOU CLICK "SEND" Make sure you're sending this message to the address you intend. Double-check to make absolutely certain you haven't clicked "Reply All" or are sending it to people and places you shouldn't.

DON'T COPY THE WORLD Think twice about the people you put on your CC list. If they all respond, then how bad will your message backlog be? Mailing lists can also create problems for you and for all those family members, school chums, and business contacts included on them. When you reply to mailing list messages, make sure you reply only to the sender, not the whole list. A colleague of mine (unnamed) sent an e-mail message to a list of folks on campus about a faculty meeting. Minutes later, another colleague (also unnamed) replied to the entire list, thinking she was corresponding only with the sender: "Thanks for the update. By the way, you left your keys on the kitchen counter when you left this morning. I'll drop them at your office this afternoon." Uh-oh. Who knew they were an item? Well . . . now the whole campus does.

PICK A SUBJECT (ALMOST) ANY SUBJECT Some people leave the subject line of their e-mails blank. This is baffling because it will take more than curiosity to get me to open a message from someone I don't know. Crafting a relevant subject line will prompt people to open your messages and act on them quickly. Capital One, where employees average 40 to 50 e-mail messages a day, is trying to make their existing system better by teaching employees to write better messages. "It turns out that stronger subject lines help recipients better understand why they received an e-mail" and it also makes it easier to find the message later, if they decide to store it. Instead of writing, "here's what you asked for," as the subject line, it would be more effective to say "here's the 2009 staffing model." Using bullet points and underlining or bolding major points also makes the text more effective.[20]

THINK BEFORE REPLYING If you respond to e-mail messages immediately, you establish the expectation in your readers' minds that you will always respond quickly. The old rule about responding was simple: Return phone calls the same day; respond to postal service mail within three working days. If people expect an instant response, they'll be upset when you take longer to reply. Tell them to call if it's really urgent.

THINK AGAIN BEFORE REPLYING If you're angry, upset, or irritated at something you've just read in an e-mail message, give yourself a day—or at least a few hours—to cool down before responding. You may end up saying something you'll regret. The same goes for dumb jokes, criticism of supervisors or coworkers, off-color remarks, or any other smart-aleck responses you probably wouldn't offer up in person.

BE CAREFUL WITH CRITICISM E-mail—even with those clever emoticons and smiley faces that clutter up the message—eliminates virtually all of the important nonverbal cues we're accustomed to seeing and hearing as we judge a message sender's intent. E-mail can seem especially cold and inhumane if you're delivering criticism. The mother who puts her arm around you and smiles before saying, "The Thanksgiving turkey was a bit dry" probably won't cause many hurt feelings. But the mother who writes an e-mail that says, "Too bad about that overcooked turkey" may set off a family feud that lasts until next year.[21]

HANDLE EACH MESSAGE JUST ONCE If it's unimportant or irrelevant, hit the delete key. If it's something you'll need to respond to, decide whether to do it now or later, when you have the time and information you need. If you can discipline yourself to check e-mail folders, you may wish to file each message as it comes in and keep your in-box clean.

DON'T CHECK YOUR E-MAIL CONSTANTLY Have the self-discipline to check it at regular intervals, such as first thing in the morning, once after lunch, and again before going home. If you leave your e-mail system open and running constantly, at least turn off the chime.

DON'T IGNORE THE CONVENTIONS OF CORRESPONDENCE Even though e-mail seems more like a conversation than a letter, you should not write to people in all–lower case letters, ignore punctuation, or abandon conventional spelling. The same goes for sentence and paragraph structure. The more organizational structure and cues you include in your writing, the easier it will be for your recipients to read.

AVOID ABBREVIATIONS AND CYBERJARGON PC users have their own shorthand language that uses expressions designed to save typing, such as IMHO (in my humble opinion) or TTYL (talk to you later). Most business professionals, however, find these abbreviations unintelligible. *PCWorld*'s Laurianne McLaughlin says, "You can't assume everyone is familiar with the endless acronyms circulating out there. WIDLTO: When in doubt, leave them out."[22]

BREVITY IS THE SOUL OF WIT AND WISDOM If your messages go much beyond two or three paragraphs, perhaps you need to have a conversation on the phone or in person. If that's not possible, consider drafting your remarks separately as a text file and attaching them to a one-sentence cover message. Send them in as many forms (MS Word and Corel WordPerfect) as you think your readers will need. If you're sending a one-line response, consider using the subject line to carry the whole message, if it fits. That way, the recipient doesn't have to open your e-mail. For example: "Got your package today, everything fine. Thanks (no msg)."

MAKE URLS USEFUL When you refer people to a Web site, include the complete address on a line of its own. For example:

You'll find more information about our organization at this Web site: www.nd.edu/~fanning

Don't put any punctuation before or after the URL (universal resource locator). If you do, it may prevent your recipients from simply clicking on the URL and having the Web page open in their browser window.

BE CAUTIOUS ABOUT ATTACHMENTS Sending unsolicited attachments can quickly turn you into an e-mail outcast. Don't attach documents, pictures, or spreadsheets to your messages unless you're certain the recipient wants or needs to see them. Business journalist Scott Kirsner suggests it may be more convenient for your readers if you simply post documents to an easily accessible intranet site and send an e-mail with a pointer to their location. And if you're sending out three or more attachments, you may want to send each as a separate message, using the subject line to alert the recipient to the contents of the file you're attaching.[23] If you're still keen on sending a large attachment, consider compressing the file with WinZip or another file compression program.

INCLUDE A SIGNATURE FILE Your outgoing e-mail should automatically include a signature file. This feature is available on virtually all e-mail software and will append your name and contact data to every message you send. Many people like to include an inspirational phrase or humorous quote with their signature file. Resist. Such things will not win you any friends.

CHECK YOUR TIME/DATE STAMP Make sure your computer—and your company's e-mail server—are set to the correct time and date. Messages with an incorrect time or date can show up in the wrong place in a recipient's e-mail in-box and can be misfiled or overlooked.

GET HELP WHEN YOU NEED IT Senior managers should allow administrative assistants to wade through their in-boxes. An assistant can open, read, and organize e-mail messages before you respond. You may also wish to manage the flow of e-mail with an auto-response that informs those sending e-mail to you that you are out of the office or on vacation. That way, they won't expect a response until you return.

Despite the fact that e-mail is part of a new technology that has changed the ways in which we communicate, many of the old rules still apply. According to Bob Rozakis of the Alpha Development Group, "A business communication is business, period. As a result, a certain degree of formality is required. Just because e-mail tends to be more immediate and personable, it can't be casual. Business e-mail must be businesslike. You'll be judged by the quality of your writing, so spelling and grammar do count." He goes on to say, "All forms of business communication you send reflect on you, affecting your chances for advancement. Sending e-mail riddled with misspellings is the same as wearing a shirt spattered with catsup. Sloppy e-mail gets tongues wagging about the writer's literal failings."[24]

PRIVACY AND WORKPLACE MONITORING

If you draft a quick e-mail message to a friend on your computer at work, that's your own private property, isn't it? What about the Web sites you visit online at the office? As long as you do it on your lunch hour, that's okay, isn't it? And those Instant Messenger notes flying around the office among friends and coworkers? Those are private, too, aren't they?

"Privacy is dead," says Sun MicroSystems CEO Scott McNealy. "Deal with it."[25] Even though your e-mail account may be password-protected, it isn't private. If your account is provided by your employer, it isn't even yours. E-mail and other forms of electronic communication, as so many people have discovered, are vulnerable to invasion and snooping. And although some of it is plainly illegal, many of those folks looking through your in-box and sent files are perfectly within their rights to do so.

J. D. Biersdorfer of the *New York Times* says, "You would probably do well to abide by an old rule of thumb when it comes to the privacy of e-mail: never put anything in an e-mail message that you wouldn't write on a postcard."[26] Between the time you click the send button and it arrives in the in-box of the recipient, a typical e-mail message travels through at least a couple of mail servers, routers, and other computers. Hackers don't often target mail servers, but that's no guarantee that someone won't open, read, and save what you've written.

It's much more likely, in fact, that the person reading your e-mail will be your employer. About 55 percent of companies retain and review e-mail, according to a recent survey by the American Management Association and the e-Policy Institute, up from 47 percent four years earlier. About a quarter of them have fired workers for e-mail abuse.[27]

More than one-third of companies with 1,000 or more employees now employ staff to read or otherwise analyze outbound e-mail, according to a study by Proofpoint, an e-mail security firm. The main concern is leakage of trade secrets. Here are a few more of the company's findings in a survey of e-mail decision makers at large companies:

- Leaks of proprietary information and valuable intellectual property are the top e-mail concerns of large companies.
- Almost one in four outgoing e-mails contains content that poses a legal, financial, or regulatory risk.
- More than one in four companies have terminated employees for violating e-mail policies in the past 12 months.
- More than one in three companies have investigated a suspected e-mail leak of confidential or proprietary information in the same time frame.
- More than 10 percent of companies were ordered by a court or regulatory body to produce employee e-mail in the past year.
- Seventy percent of companies say they are "concerned" or "very concerned" about Web-based e-mail as a conduit for exposure of confidential information.[28]

Just about all workplace communication experts agree: There is no such thing as private e-mail on a company-owned system. "Legally, they're not required to tell you if they're monitoring the e-mail," says Shari Steele of the Electronic Frontier Foundation. "The equipment you're using when at work belongs to the employer. And, therefore, the employer can do anything [it wants to] with the equipment."[29]

Businesses can customize the software to identify senders and scan for keywords that send up a red flag. They can also choose from a set of keywords associated with viruses or unsolicited e-mail, or spam. Once a policy is established, your employer can choose what happens next: to save the e-mail for review, divert it, or send it to the trash.

WHY DO EMPLOYERS MONITOR? Reasons for tracking everything from e-mail to Internet use are often justified by four basic considerations:

- *Security.* Every business, no matter what industry or which part of the marketplace it competes in, has information that it wants kept confidential. Prerelease information, research and development efforts, patented or copyrighted items, bid or proposal data, or contractual negotiations are just a few of the categories that every business hopes to protect.
- *Productivity.* Employees who spend a substantial portion of their workday surfing the Net, sending e-mail to family and friends, or abusing the technology on their desktops are a drain on productivity and profits. More than one-third of all lost productivity is attributed to Internet abuse at work.[30]
- *Protection.* Many companies faced with costly lawsuits are monitoring e-mail, voice mail, Twitter, and other communication systems to uncover and discipline workers who harass, demean, threaten, or intimidate others in the workplace. In a recent survey of large firms, almost 10 percent report having received a subpoena for employee e-mail. "Almost every workplace lawsuit today, especially a sexual harassment case, has an e-mail component," says Nancy Flynn, executive director of the ePolicy Institute. Some records may be kept on file indefinitely.[31]
- *Industry Regulation.* State and federal regulatory agencies have published numerous rules requiring businesses of many sorts to hang onto all of their e-mail, just as they would retain their paper-based correspondence. The U.S. Securities and Exchange Commission, for example, has extensive and strict requirements for e-mail retention in the financial services industry. Brokerages and trading firms have been fined for failing to keep the electronic exchanges between brokers and their clients and between brokers and the back-office staff who execute trades.

DOES AN EMPLOYEE HAVE A RIGHT TO PRIVACY? The answer to this question is yes, but it's not as extensive as you might imagine (or wish for). Several considerations are important in examining any concerns about privacy in the workplace. First, no federal law covers all aspects of an employee's right to privacy on the job. Instead, a patchwork of federal and state laws regulates everything from electronic monitoring to visual surveillance, drug testing, and locker searches.

Employees really do not have a right of privacy in e-mail communication on their employer's system unless the employer consistently acts in a manner giving rise to a reasonable expectation of privacy.

Such expectations may be created deliberately or inadvertently. For example, an employer can possibly create an expectation of privacy if he or she is aware of the use of the company's e-mail system for personal communications among employees and allows the system to be used for that purpose.

The Electronic Communication Privacy Act of 1986, as amended, protects e-mail messages from interception by and disclosure to *third parties*. Electronically stored communications are also protected, but the law does not prohibit employers from monitoring e-mail system activities and message content. Your boss can open your messages, read them, store them, and use them to make an employment decision about you. She just can't give them to someone else unless ordered by a court to do so.[32]

Congress clearly intended to provide broad privacy protection to the individual, both inside and outside of our homes. What is less clear is the extent to which, or even whether, Congress intended to protect individuals in their capacity as employees from privacy invasions by their employers. When employers access stored data for reasons other than system maintenance, corporate security, or suspicion of illegal conduct, they may become vulnerable to invasion of privacy claims. And data captured for a legally permissible purpose, such as system maintenance or monitoring against theft, may not necessarily be used for other purposes.[33]

Even though employees do have limited privacy rights in the workplace—mostly related to issues concerning modesty and nonbusiness matters—employers clearly have the upper hand in this struggle. Employers have both rights and expectations regarding the use of company-owned systems. Here are a few basic considerations:

Employer rights. An employer has the right to:

- Intercept and review e-mail messages generated, transmitted, stored, or received on a company-owned or leased system.
- Conduct an e-mail audit to determine how the system is being used, when, and under what conditions, for what purposes, and by whom.
- Disclose certain e-mail content to third parties if an appropriate authority (postmaster or system administrator) suspects or discovers illegal or unauthorized use.
- Require employee training in e-mail system use.
- Receive employee acknowledgment of training and understanding of e-mail system policy guidelines, restrictions, and limitations.[34]

Employer expectations. An employer may reasonably expect that:

- Company-owned e-mail systems will be used principally or exclusively for official business purposes.
- Employees will not use company-owned e-mail systems for profit, private gain, or personally owned businesses.
- Employees will not use company-owned systems for illegal purposes.
- Employees will not use company-owned systems for unauthorized disclosure of proprietary data or confidential information.
- Employees will not use company-owned systems to send inappropriate messages, including rude or discourteous messages, sexually harassing messages, sexist or racist language, profane language, obscene language or graphic images, or correspond with unauthorized addresses.[35]

Here are a few common questions most employees have regarding workplace monitoring and their rights to privacy:

- **Can my employer listen to my phone calls at work?** In most instances, yes. For example, employers may monitor calls with clients or customers for training purposes to assure quality control. Federal law, however, which regulates phone calls with people outside the state, does not allow unannounced monitoring for business-related calls.

    An important exception is made for personal calls. Under federal case law, when an employer realizes the call is personal, he or she must immediately stop monitoring the call. However, when employees are told not to make personal calls from specified business phones, the employee then takes the risk that calls on those phones may be monitored.[36]

- **Can my employer obtain a record of my phone calls?** This type of monitoring is easy. Telephone numbers dialed from phone extensions can be recorded by a device called a pen register. It allows an employer to see a list of phone numbers dialed by your extension and the length of each call. Cellular service providers now routinely offer calling logs for a small monthly fee.

    A programming concept called "presence awareness" is able to determine whether a PC, cell phone, or wireless device is turned on or in use. A new system now permits tracking technology such as global positioning systems (GPS) to detect the location of a person whose cell phone or PDA is turned on or in use. Parents may see this technology as extremely valuable, while teenagers or employees who'd like to spend the day at the ballpark may be less enthusiastic.[37]

- **Can my employer watch my computer terminal while I work?** Generally, yes. Because your employer owns the computer network and terminals, he or she is free to use them to monitor employees. Most employees are given some protection from electronic monitoring under certain circumstances. Union contracts, for example, may limit an employer's right to monitor. If employers state in a written document that they do not monitor their employees, they are bound by the agreement, with just a few limited exceptions.[38]

- **What sort of things can an employer monitor?** All kinds of stuff. Inexpensive software and easy-to-operate hardware make it possible for almost any employer to know who has company-provided Internet access, who's online, what they're watching, how often, and for how long. Most firms keep a Top 10 "Hit Parade" of most popular sites frequented by their employees. New software will now permit an employer to follow what's happening on each employee's computer screen as it happens. It's a useful technology when you need technical support: An IT specialist can simply "reach out" to your screen, control your mouse movements, and address the problem you've encountered. The software permits an employer to follow literally everything you do, keystroke-by-keystroke, and keep a record of it even if you never save it or send it anywhere. Many employers see that capability as a valuable security feature. Many employees think it's just creepy.

- **How can I tell if I am being monitored?** You can't. Most computer monitoring equipment allows employers to monitor without an employee's knowledge. Some employers, however, do notify their workers that monitoring takes place. That sort of information may be contained in memos, employee handbooks, union contracts, on a user information screen that appears when your computer boots up, or on a sticker attached to your computer. Look carefully. Even though they are not legally required to do so, most employers will tell you if they are monitoring your work. The reason? If you know they're watching, you're more likely to behave yourself.

- **Is my voice mail private?** Not really. Voice mail and e-mail are regarded as being nearly the same in the eyes of the law (and your employer). The telephones, switching equipment, and the computer hard drives on which the voice mail is stored are the property of the company that employs you and the company can access, store, and listen to anyone's voice mail. A Cincinnati, Ohio, newspaper got into big trouble a few years ago when one of its reporters hacked into the voice mail system of Chiquita Brands, the banana importer. Many folks were surprised at how easily an outsider could listen to other people's passcode-protected voice messages.

- **Is there any way I can keep my e-mail and other work private?** Yes, but your employer may not like it. He may, in fact, forbid it. You could encrypt personal e-mail messages before you send them. Most encryption programs will translate your message into gibberish and require the same program and a password to decipher the text on the other end. You can purchase commercial encryption software to work with your e-mail program or download a copy of the freeware version of the Pretty Good Privacy program from the link at http://www.pgp.com.[39] Other companies, including ziplip.com, offer similar programs.[40] Liquid Machines of San Francisco now makes the equivalent of an e-mail shredder that automatically destroys e-mail in 30 minutes or 30 days. When the detonation time is reached, the encryption key inserted into the messages is voided, making all copies of the e-mail permanently unreadable, including forwarded copies.[41]

- **How about instant messages? There's no way they can monitor those . . . is there?** By now, you should have figured out that your employer can monitor just about anything, and that includes AOL Instant Messenger. At the annual meeting of Sonalysts, a software and consulting company in Waterford, Connecticut, systems analyst Randy Dickson recently drove home the point that even a few quick remarks flying among instant messages could be picked up by the company's computer surveillance. He displayed a document that showed a conversation between two employees whose names were blacked out. With only a few lines of text, the gist was clear. Here were the words of two employees using what Mr. Dickson called "less than professional" language to talk about a colleague. "Instant messaging is very loose and chatty, almost like a conversation," he said. Those exchanges were evidence that people divulge more than they should—and that without persistent monitoring, the company could be at risk. Secret projects could be leaked and offensive language could be forwarded inside and outside the office.[42]

Instant messaging (IM) is invading and changing the workplace. Employees started to sneak instant messaging into the office in the late 1990s, but now companies are endorsing it. Faster and more casual than e-mail, IM can foster broader collaboration among employees even as it further blurs the boundaries between work and life. Roughly one-third of U.S. employees use instant messaging at work. Tech consultant Gartner Inc. projects that IM will be the "de facto tool for voice, video and text chat" for 95 percent of employees in big companies within five years.[43]

As any corporate IM user will tell you, however, instant messaging has its trade-offs. If people know you're in the office or working from home and logged-on, maintaining privacy and avoiding distractions becomes much more difficult. In many workplaces, failing to respond quickly to an IM is considered rude, so workers have an incentive to sign out when they leave the office or show themselves as "busy" when they know they can't reply for a while.

With most systems, others must agree to be on your buddy list. "Presence," says Microsoft product manager Chris Niehaus, "has to be managed." At some companies, though, anyone on IM can be added to the buddy list. At IBM, for example, some 220,000 employees worldwide are registered for instant messaging. Users can search for in-house experts on subjects such as database integration or designing Web ads and see which of them are available for a quick IM question.[44]

One other by-product of instant messaging is beginning to appear in the nation's elementary and secondary schools. Do you recognize this list: *u, r, ur, b4, wuz, cuz, 2*? These IM shortcuts are creeping into student papers and, to say the least, teachers are not impressed. "Kids should know the difference," says Jacqueline Harding, an eighth-grade English teacher at Viking Middle School in Gurnee, Illinois. "They should know where to draw the line between formal writing and conversational writing."[45] The conventions of instant messaging are an important part of how students communicate and—in that context—nearly everyone agrees it's not wrong, it's just part of how IM works. The important issue students and others who use instant messaging regularly must understand is that the expectations of the reader will govern which style to use. For paper-based interoffice memos, an informal style will work, but readers still expect conventional punctuation, spelling, and paragraph organization. For business letters sent outside the organization, the standard is even higher because business relationships are won and lost on the impressions that readers gather from the documents they receive.

THE INTERNET AND ONLINE BEHAVIOR

Andy Perez uses the library at Rice University in Houston for the quiet, not the books. He does his research online. Edell Fiedler taps into the Internet to register for classes and check grades at Minnesota State University, Mankato, sometimes saving her the 60-mile drive to school. And Rakesh Patel regularly uses e-mail to ask his professors at Chicago's DePaul University questions about assignments.[46]

These stories are increasingly common, as the generation that grew up with the personal computer is now heavily wired on campus and relies on the Internet in almost every dimension of college life. The findings of a large-scale survey by the Pew Internet and American Life Project confirm what many have suspected for some time: The Internet has become an integral part of college life, and not just for studying. The survey of college students across the country found that 94 percent use the Internet, compared with just 66 percent of the overall U.S. population.[47]

"Today's college students were born around the time the first PCs were introduced to the public and they have grown up with these technologies," said Professor Steve Jones, lead author of the study and head of the department of communication at the University of Illinois at Chicago. "To them, the Internet and e-mail are as commonplace as telephones and television—and equally as indispensable."[48]

If it's true that more than 90 percent of all college students surveyed say they use the Internet more than the library for research, and if 86 percent check their e-mail each day, wouldn't you expect those behaviors to continue once they've graduated? Two-thirds say they think the Internet has improved their relationships with classmates, and more than half think e-mail has enhanced their relationships with professors. These habits are clearly likely to continue once students enter the workforce and begin communicating in a professional setting.

The Internet has become central to the way college students conduct research for their courses; communicate with their professors, friends, and family; post updates to social networking sites; gather information about everything from sports to the stock market and the weather; and, finally, make important short-notice purchases of gifts, clothing, and airline tickets. The trend is clear: When college students enter the workforce, online retrieval and storage of information and continual communication with others who are important to them will already have become daily and lifelong habits. The workplace of the twenty-first century will adjust to accommodate those habits and, in many ways, become more productive and interesting. The news is not all good, however, because technology and social behavior are often at odds with business goals.

TEXT MESSAGING

For anyone who doubts that the texting revolution is upon us, consider this: The average 13 to 17-year old sends and receives 3,339 texts a month—more than 100 per day, according to the Nielsen Co., the media research firm. Adults are catching up, though. People from ages 45 to 54 sent and received 323 texts a month during 2010, up 75 percent from a year earlier, Nielsen says.[49]

Behind the texting explosion is a fundamental shift in how we view our mobile devices. Nielsen recently analyzed the cellphone bills of 60,000 mobile subscribers and found that adults made and received an average of 188 mobile phone calls a month during 2010, down 25 percent from three years earlier. Average "talk minutes" fell 5 percent compared with 2009; among 18 to 24-year olds, the decline was 17 percent.[50]

Text messages—also known as SMS (Short Message Service)—take up less bandwidth than phone calls and cost less. A text message's content is so condensed that it routinely fails, even more than e-mail, according to the *Wall Street Journal* writer Katherine Rossman, to convey the writer's tone and affect. The more we text, the greater the opportunity for misunderstanding.

A recent survey of 2,000 college students asked about their attitudes toward phone calls and text-messaging and found the students' predominant goal was to pass along information in as little time, with as little small talk, as possible. "What they like most about their mobile devices is that they can reach other people," says Naomi Baron, a professor of linguistics at American University in Washington, D.C., who conducted the survey. "What they like least is that other people can reach them."[51]

Part of what's driving the texting surge among adults is the popularity of social media. Sites like Twitter, with postings of no more than 140 characters, are creating and reinforcing the habit of communicating in micro-bursts. And these sites are also pumping up the sheer volume. Many Twitter and Facebook users create settings that alert them, via text message, every time a tweet or message is earmarked for them.[52]

Texting's rise over conversation is changing the way we interact, social scientists say. We default to text to relay difficult information. We stare at our phone when we want to avoid eye contact. Rather than make plans in advance, we engage in what Rich Ling, a professor at IT University in Copenhagen, Denmark, calls micro-coordination—"I'll txt u in 10mins when I know wh/restrnt."

Of course, phone conversations will never be completely obsolete. Deal makers and other professionals still spend much of the day on the phone. Researchers say people are more likely to use text-based communications at the preliminary stages of projects. The phone comes into play when there are multiple options to consider or binding decisions to be made.[53]

SOCIAL MEDIA

Social media is a term widely used to include a number of Internet-based platforms for connecting with other people as individuals and as members of a social community. Some writers have referred to such media as "Web 2.0," meaning an online source that not only provides information but interacts with users, as well.

Several important categories of social media are worth noting:

- **Social bookmarking**. (Del.icio.us, Blinklist, Simpy). These sites interact by tagging Web sites and searching through Web sites bookmarked by other people.
- **Social news**. (Digg, Propeller, Reddit). These interact by voting for articles by most popular, most read, and most e-mailed, and commenting on them.
- **Social networking**. (Facebook, MySpace, LinkedIn, Hi5, Last.FM). These sites interact by adding friends, commenting on profiles, joining groups, and holding discussions.
- **Social photo and video sharing**. (YouTube, Flickr). These interact by sharing photos or videos and commenting on user submissions.
- **Wikis**. (Wikipedia, Wikia). And, finally, these interact by adding articles and allowing users to edit existing articles online.[54]

Facebook now has more than 500 million users worldwide. Twitter has nearly 200 million visitors per month, generating 65 million tweets a day.[55] Dozens of minor players in the social media market are vying for your time and attention, as well, offering messaging services, connection with people you know (and might like to know), photo sharing, music downloads, shopping, and a rapidly growing set of reasons to spend much of your time online, connected with other people.

Businesses are beginning to figure out how to use social media, primarily for marketing purposes, but for reputation management and corporate communication, as well. There is, in fact, no shortage of public relations counselors ready and eager to provide business advice on the most profitable use of social media.

On your own time, though, social media can be helpful for boosting your career and, of course, connecting with friends. Be careful how much you log on at work, as some office computers can track how much time you spend on different sites and even what you type online. It's best to log on from a private computer or smart phone (iPhone, Blackberry), and if you do use your desktop computer, do it during break times.

Remember that there is still a risk when you post on publicly accessible sites such as Facebook. Don't trash your boss or coworkers, complain too severely about your work, or post photos on your profile of yourself doing something illegal or scandalous. Make sure that only the friends you approve of can see photos or more private information, and don't be reluctant to adjust privacy settings so that your boss or anyone who isn't your friend can't just click through your profile to see what you're up to on weekends.[56]

ETIQUETTE AND OFFICE ELECTRONICS

The distinction between home and office has virtually disappeared. And so have many of the instincts that govern our behavior when we work, relax, and socialize. Communication behaviors somehow seem to top the list of issues that puzzle, irritate, and (yes) aggravate everyone from members of our family to coworkers and clients. Here are a few suggestions for managing new technology and the expectations of those around us:

CELL PHONES They are an astounding invention, but one with the power to enrage as well as reassure. The basic problem with cellular telephones is that so many people have them and many of them feel compelled to use them literally everywhere. According to industry analysts, more people own cell phones than computers, and today more than 5 billion mobile phones are in use around the globe.[57] In the United States, more than 260 million people had cellular telephone subscriptions by 2011.[58] That translates to about 85 percent of Americans owning a mobile phone.[59] What guidelines might govern their appropriate use? With some important exceptions, the following rules apply:

- Unless it's an absolute emergency, turn your phone off while you're driving. It's not simply a distraction, it's downright dangerous.
- Unless you're a doctor or employee-on-call, turn it off when you're in a restaurant, theater, concert, religious service, or any other location where people expect some measure of privacy and quiet. If you must leave it on, switch your phone to vibrate and leave the immediate area before you answer or return the call.
- Don't assume everyone else within 500 meters is interested in hearing your half of the conversation. Lower your voice and respect other people's need for peace and quiet.
- Don't assume that because your employees own a cell phone they are available (or eager) to talk business 24 hours a day, 7 days a week. They have lives outside of the office and would like to live them without talking to you.

A scientific poll commissioned by online wireless retailer LetsTalk found that, in the past five years, the percentage of Americans who are willing to use their cell phones in public places, including movies, restaurants, and public transportation, decreased significantly. The study, conducted by Wirthlin Worldwide, also found that less than half of Americans find it acceptable to use their cell phones while in a car and only 10 percent find it appropriate to use a cell phone while at school. Surprisingly, 28 percent said it was acceptable to take a call while in a restaurant.[60]

"Despite an overall increase in cell phone usage," said Delly Tamer, President and CEO of LetsTalk, "Americans appear to be much more cognizant of their cell phone etiquette. It's important to recognize that Americans are beginning to self-police their wireless etiquette, especially as leaders evaluate the pros and cons of banning cell phone usage in public places."[61]

VOICE MAIL If you do not have an administrative assistant or someone to answer the phone for you while you're out, voice mail can be especially helpful. It's most helpful when you learn to use it properly:

- Keep your outgoing message brief: "This is Jim O'Rourke in the Fanning Center. Please leave a message and I'll get back to you soon." Note the somewhat vague use of the word *soon*. If people are required to listen to more than 10–15 seconds of greeting, or are required to listen to more than three "press 1 now" options, they'll grow frustrated and may simply hang up.
- Related to the overly long greeting is the new-greeting-everyday approach: "Today is Monday, September 9th. I'll be in the office today, but have meetings at nine thirty, eleven fifteen, and three o'clock. I appreciate your business and am very sorry I'm not here to take your call. However, if you leave your name, number, and a message, I'll return your call just as quickly as I can." Those five sentences are not much more helpful than just saying, "Leave a message and I'll call you back." One outgoing message will do the trick, unless you plan to be gone for a week.
- Tell people how to get past the outgoing message. Every voice mail system has a command that lets callers bypass the message. If your outgoing message has a number of options for listeners, just say, "You can skip this message by pressing the pound key" or whatever command your system uses for that purpose.
- If you're leaving a voice mail message, identify yourself, give your callback number, and explain *briefly* why you're calling. Don't leave a 5-minute message when you can leave a 30-second message. And before you hang up, give the listener your number one more time.
- Unless you can shut the door to your office, don't listen to your voice mail messages on the speaker phone. Pick up the receiver, download your messages, and give others in the office a chance to concentrate on their own work.

E-MAIL We already spoke at length about the risks and responsibilities involved in using electronic mail. Here are a few suggestions for making the system more civilized:

- Don't send e-mails that make angry demands. "I must have an answer by 2 p.m. tomorrow. Repeat, by 2 p.m." You have no idea what's happening in the life of the message recipient and can only guess at how he'll react to your demands. Such demands are better if they are toned down and written in the conditional: "Unless I hear from you by tomorrow, we may not be able to ship your order on time. If it's convenient, could you let me know of your selections?"
- Don't waste our time with the latest "jokes du jour," sent to hundreds of e-mail addresses, including mine. In fact, if that's all you send, please rethink the value of an e-mail address book.

- Please don't order people to visit your Web page. Ask nicely and your readers may think about it. Tell them about the interesting and useful information they'll find there, and they may see the logic in your request.
- Please don't write to anyone in all lower case letters, or SHOUT AT YOUR READERS IN ALL-CAPITAL LETTERS. Please include proper punctuation, conventional spelling, and customary paragraph and document structure, which may include headings and subheads, bulleted items, or numbered lists. Make your message brief, clean, and inviting to read.
- Do not ever insult, malign, harass, or demean your readers or anyone else in the e-mail messages you write. Please don't spread rumors or say things that you know to be untrue. You just never know who's going to save your message and later use it to your detriment.
- Please include a salutation, complimentary close, and—in the first paragraph or two—a statement of purpose. Tell your readers why you've written to them. Be polite and treat them with respect.[62]

WORKING VIRTUALLY

"I can't figure out how people could operate a business today without virtual teams," says Elizabeth Allen, the vice president for corporate communication at Dell Computer. From the corporate headquarters in Round Rock, Texas, Ms. Allen talks with her global communication team by teleconference every working day. On others, they will schedule a videoconference. Her e-mail is open constantly, providing a link to employees, clients, journalists, colleagues, and other executives in the firm.[63]

Everyone uses e-mail, the telephone, and many of us participate in the occasional videoconference. So what makes Dell different from so many other organizations? For one thing, the company actively discourages the possession and storage of paper. "I have a lovely office," said Ms. Allen, "but it has no filing cabinets, no lateral files, and not much of anywhere to put paper. We do just about everything electronically here, and we have plenty of storage space for that—online and on disk." She also mentioned that postal service mail gets delivered once a week at Dell. "If you're expecting something, you'll have to walk down to the mail room and pick it up. The incentives here to use e-mail and electronic storage are huge."[64]

Many firms are working in different ways today for obvious reasons. "When we talk, 'virtual organizations,' " says Dana Meade, retired chairman and CEO of Tenneco, "we are really talking about dramatically different ways of organizing capital, technology, information, people, and other assets than we utilized in the past."[65] Professor Sandra Collins documents the trend in her book, *Communication in a Virtual Organization*, noting that organizations, groups, and teams have moved from a physical environment to a virtual environment to save money, increase efficiency, raise productivity, and span everything from organizational boundaries to international time zones.[66]

Managing work with virtual tools is growing rapidly in popularity. An estimated 23.6 million Americans telecommuted in 2001. That number was an increase from just 4 million in 1990, and grew to 44 million by 2011.[67] Worldwide, the Gartner Group now estimates that some 100 million people telecommute to their place of employment.[68] Some were in the next cubicle as they connected with virtual teammates around the world. Others stayed home and logged on to a company server to do their work. Still others drove to a nearby telework center to avoid a long or costly trip into a central metropolitan area.[69]

ADVANTAGES The advantages of working virtually may be grouped into three basic categories: cost, productivity, and access.

- **Cost.** Paying less for office space and employee support is certainly among the most obvious of cost advantages. Jack Heacock is a member of the International Telework Association and Council's executive committee. "At 10:45 a.m. on any particular day, 40–60 percent of employees are somewhere other than their offices. Walk around and see for yourself," he says. "Then ask yourself why you are investing in real estate space you don't need."[70]
- **Productivity.** Efficiency and productivity can easily increase when people are offered the opportunity to work from home, to contact the office when they're traveling, or to work whenever or wherever they may have the opportunity. Professor Collins documented reduced absenteeism and increased employee retention as results of telecommuting.[71] Merrill Lynch implemented telecommuting nearly twenty years ago and today has more than 3,500 employees who work from home one to four days a week. Managers at Merrill report that they saw an average of 3.5 fewer sick days per year and a 6 percent decrease in turnover among the telecommuters during the first year of the program.[72] Merrill Lynch also saw a 10–50 percent increase in productivity with its telecommuters, while other organizations, including IBM, AT&T, and American Express, have reported similar gains.[73]
- **Access.** Among the most important benefits to a company can be access, not only to its own employees at unusual times and places but to others as well. The ability to delegate work to part-time employees or free agents who can assist in project management or work against specified deadlines means that regular employees can be free to work on issues that may require face-to-face contact with coworkers. John Byrne of *BusinessWeek* magazine says that the emergence of a virtual workforce means that "many outfits will depend on free agents and outside contractors to develop products faster than ever."[74]

DISADVANTAGES If telecommuting, Web-based organizations, and virtual teams provide so many obvious advantages, why aren't more people taking part in them? The answers vary, but generally touch on one of several issues: costs, technology, culture, and people.

- **Costs.** The initial outlay to purchase equipment can be significant. Equipping each worker with a laptop, printer, phone lines, and software can easily exceed several thousand dollars.[75] "When everyone works from a centralized location," says Professor Collins, "all of the most expensive equipment can be shared. Not so with off-site workers."[76]
- **Technology.** Managers have concerns about providing technical support to remote workers and, as you very likely already know, there are only so many problems that an IT specialist can help you with over the phone. When the printer jams, you either fix it yourself or work on something else.
- **Culture.** In many organizations, telecommuting is appreciated, valued, and rewarded. In others, it is not. "Out of sight, out of mind," may mean that telecommuters aren't given the same opportunities for training, advancement, or promotion. In still other organizations, managers may be reluctant (or forbidden) to let an employee leave the building with sensitive or confidential data. Client records, government research, or products-in-development may require that they and the people working on them remain in the office.
- **People.** Finally, it's easy to see why some people just wouldn't want to work from home. Many people develop a sense of their own self-worth from the location in which they work. They take pride in their office, enjoy socializing and interacting with their coworkers and colleagues, and find the climate in their work locations energizing and inspiring. Sitting at home in your bathrobe, thinking of all the housework (or other things) you could be doing may not prove either inspirational or productive. Issues ranging from frequency of communication to the development of trust may depend on having a workforce located in the same place.[77]

TELECONFERENCING

The idea of teleconferencing, or using the basics of telephone and television technology to conduct a meeting with people in distant locations, has been around for many years. Educators have used low-cost video cameras and codec (coder-decoder) systems since the 1960s to link people to courses distributed from a central location. Businesses with geographically separated offices and production facilities have used teleconference systems to share everything from marketing plans to high-tech expertise across time zones and oceans.

The problem for so long with teleconferencing, however, was twofold: high cost and low quality. Fuzzy, streaky images flipped across the screens of hideously expensive two-way telecom systems. Speakers sounded as if they were trapped in a barrel, and visual aids such as flipcharts, 35-mm slides, and overhead transparencies were risky at best. During the flush years of a good economy in the 1980s and 1990s, flying people here and there didn't seem expensive or difficult. After 2001, many firms began to rethink the value of teleconference meetings.

Recently, prices for relatively high-quality visual images have come down from $50,000 to $5,000, and telecom providers have begun to develop both expertise and marketing approaches that have made teleconferencing easy (well, *easier*) and much less expensive. With the advent of desktop, Internet Webcasting (such as WebEx), many firms have discovered that they can push images from a central location to a corporate server that employees can access from anywhere on earth. Inexpensive desktop cameras and easy-to-use software now make the average manager a potential teleconference participant in a matter of minutes. According to 3M Corporation's Michael Begeman, "The only ones who could afford videoconferencing a few years ago were really big companies." Begeman manages 3M's meeting network and now thinks that declining costs have "suddenly put videoconferencing into the price range of small companies."[78]

The technology isn't foolproof, though. It's still difficult to get everyone you hope to include in a meeting on the same page at the same time of day. It's still easy to lose your connection with one or more of the locations in a conference. And neither the equipment nor the software is as inexpensive or simple as a cell phone, but they're rapidly getting more sophisticated and more attractive. The day when we can all connect with desktop dial-up, simply by double-clicking a teleconference icon, isn't far off (think: FaceTime on your iPhone).

To make the teleconference meetings, interviews, and training sessions you are almost certain to participate in during the next few years as productive as possible, consider the following suggestions.

First, plan carefully. As you will read in Chapter 12 of this book, business meetings are time-consuming, troublesome to plan and execute, and a lot more expensive than you might imagine. That includes teleconference meetings, as well. The most basic rule of meetings is simple: Don't ever schedule a meeting if you can achieve your communication goals in some other way. If e-mail or paper will work better, do it. If a voice mail message will convey your thoughts less expensively and more effectively, don't ask people to take an hour of their day to sit and listen to you speak.

That said, on some occasions meetings are unavoidable. If a teleconference will assist in achieving your goals, please think about the following ideas before you make the arrangements with your long-distance provider:

- *Identify the purpose of your teleconference meeting.* Explain to people what they will be doing and why. Be clear about your objectives in asking for their time.
- *Identify the person who will chair the meeting.* A leaderless teleconference will often end in confusion and disaster. Name one person who will be responsible for starting, stopping, and

running the conference. That person should be someone known to all or most of the participants and someone who can follow the agenda and keep things moving.

- *Plan the agenda.* Meetings frequently veer off-course when the organizer decides to "wing it" or just gather the participants and see what happens. A specific agenda with easy-to-accomplish items listed first will always help, as long as the conference leader can keep the group focused on those issues.
- *Distribute the agenda.* Give participants a chance to plan for the meeting by telling them in advance what you plan to discuss. They may wish to gather information or share key documents with others before the meeting.
- *Schedule the teleconference.* Select a time and date when you know for sure that all (or the majority) of your participants can dial in or show up at a conference center. Make certain that all of your indispensable participants are aware of the schedule and have agreed to be available.
- *Confirm the teleconference with the participants.* Planning for meetings of this sort often takes place days or weeks in advance of the event. It's easy for participants to forget when it will take place, where they should be, or what the access codes are. Send more than one reminder as the day and time approach.
- *Share important resource materials with participants.* Send another copy of the agenda, along with materials you think are important for everyone to have before the meeting begins. Don't waste teleconference airtime as people read through key documents or learn for the first time what the data mean and why they matter. Posting such information on a company intranet and sending a Web link in your reminder e-mail may be helpful.

Planning a teleconference and actually conducting one are two separate issues. No one can guarantee that your participants will all show up, will have read the materials you sent, or will be in agreement with the agenda, or will even care about the subjects you plan to discuss, even if you have planned meticulously. In order to give your teleconference a better chance for success, consider these ideas.

- *Get to the conference site early.* If you're in charge of a teleconference, make sure you have an opportunity to check out the setting, meet the support technician (if you have one on site), and learn what your responsibilities for the equipment will involve. Once you walk into a room for a videoconference, avoid idle talk or unguarded comments. Assume that someone is watching and listening.
- *Watch what you wear.* Avoid lots of white, red, or black. White reflects too much light, causing your face to appear dark. Black clothing causes the face to appear overexposed, and red tends to smear. Consider a light blue shirt instead of white, and choose solid colors over complex patterns. Mr. Begeman of 3M advises people to stay away from small prints, thin stripes, and plaids. Bulky or baggy clothing can make you look heavier on screen, and tinted eyeglasses give you raccoon eyes. Glittery or dangling jewelry is distracting.[79]
- *Act as if people are watching you.* Quirky mannerisms that may go unnoticed in a face-to-face meeting are magnified in a videoconference and can detract from the image you are trying to project. Avoid playing with your hair, your eyeglasses, a pencil, or your nose. Rocking back and forth in your chair can be equally distracting. If you behave as though you are onstage, you're more likely to project the professional image you're hoping others will see.
- *Start on time.* Make a promise to your participants about time and keep it. If you begin on time, every time, you will encourage others to be there precisely as you begin. Reward those who are there at the start of the meeting with important or useful information. Explain to

latecomers that they can catch up on what they've missed by accessing the intranet site devoted to the group's activities or by downloading an e-mail attachment you will send as a follow-up to the conference.

- *Take control of the conference.* Being in control does not mean talking all the time. It merely means providing others with an opportunity, at appropriate moments, to share what they know, ask questions, and make comments. Your goals for the meeting should include widespread participation from all of those invited to join you.

- *Ask participants to introduce themselves as you begin.* Give each participant an opportunity to explain who and where they are. And as you do, be careful to mention anyone who may be in the room but out of camera range. Knowing that your boss is watching, unseen from the back of the room, could be useful information for people in other locations.

- *Jot down people's names and locations.* Knowing who is participating in the teleconference by name, title, and location will be helpful as you call on them or ask for their participation.

- *Ask participants to identify themselves when they speak for the first time.* Even with high-resolution video cameras, not everyone will recognize or know everyone else. A simple introduction ("This is John Kamp in Washington") will let everyone know who is speaking.

- *Speak a bit more slowly to ensure that everyone can understand you.* Videoconferencing systems are not as sophisticated as television broadcast studios, and many people are tempted to speak at once. As you develop a little more confidence and know that people are paying attention, you can resume a more conversational pace.

- *Avoid side conversations.* Conversations among two or three participants at one location can be distracting. First, not all participants are aware that everyone can hear what they say (or see what they do), and second, mute buttons are provided for occasions when you must speak to someone else privately.

- *Be patient if the system includes a slight delay.* Some videoconferencing systems feature a slight delay in the transmission of voice and picture images. Check out the system before your meeting begins, and if you discover that it has such a delay, explain its effect to the participants as you begin. Be prepared for overlapping dialogue and long pauses. Speak more slowly, let people know when you are finished talking so they can have their turn, and try not to interrupt.

- *Try to make eye contact with the camera.* You should do your best to look at the camera lens at least half (or more) of the time you are speaking. If you are responding to a difficult or sensitive question, you'll enhance your credibility dramatically if you focus squarely on the camera. Participants at other locations will feel more comfortable if it appears you are addressing them directly.

- *Don't read a speech or prepared statement.* Such statements are something you can share with people in advance unless the information is confidential or embargoed for release at a specific time.

- *Summarize key issues as you move along.* Interim summaries can serve as transitional devices. Refer to the agenda and remind people of elapsed time as you move from point to point.

- *Establish what's next for the group.* Tell participants if you expect them to be a part your next teleconference. Ask them to make a note of the time and date if you have already established those. Summarize the issues discussed and remind the group of any actions they may have agreed to.

- *Stop on time.* If you specified a one-hour meeting, don't let it run for 75 minutes. Keep this promise, just as you kept your promise to start on time. Time is clearly among the most valuable (and limited) commodities your colleagues have. Be respectful of how you use it.
- *Prepare and distribute minutes of the teleconference.* Ask or appoint someone (yourself, perhaps) to take notes and provide a brief summary of what happened and what the participants agreed to. Share those notes with all participants promptly—within a few days—of the meeting, if only as a reminder of the business goals you hoped to achieve by gathering everyone together.

For Further Reading

Argenti, P. and Barnes, C. M. *Digital Strategies for Powerful Corporate Communications.* New York, NY: McGraw-Hill, 2009.

Belson, K. "Four Score and . . . Mind If I Take This?" *The New York Times,* Sunday, September 30, 2007, p. WK-5.

Byron, K. "Carrying Too Heavy a Load? The Communication and Miscommunication of Emotion by E-mail," *Academy of Management Review,* January 2008.

"Facebook, Instant Messaging and Twitter Are Most Popular Social Media Tools," *PR Newswire.* August 4, 2010.

Lohr, S. "Slow Down, Multitaskers; Don't Read in Traffic," *The New York Times,* March 25, 2007. Retrieved from http://www.nytimes.com on March 25, 2007 at 10:25 P.M.

Mamberto, C. "Instant Messaging Invades the Office," *The Wall Street Journal,* July 24, 2007, pp. B1–B2.

Mindlin, A. "You've Got Someone Reading Your E-Mail," *The New York Times,* June 12, 2006. Retrieved from http://www.nytimes.com on June 12, 2006 at 8:35 P.M.

Richtel, M. "Digital Devices Deprive Brain of Needed Downtime," *The New York Times,* August 25, 2010, p. B1.

Robinson, J. "Blunt the E-Mail Interruption Assault," Entrepreneur.com, March 12, 2010. Retrieved from http://www.msnbc.msn.com/id/35689822

Sharma, A. and Vascellaro, J. E. "Those IMs Aren't as Private as You Think," *The Wall Street Journal,* October 4, 2006, p. D1.

Shellenbarger, S. "A Day Without Email Is Like . . .," *The Wall Street Journal,* October 11, 2007, pp. D1–D2.

Shipley, D. and Schwalbe, W. *Send: The Essential Guide to Email for Office and Home.* New York: Alfred A. Knopf, 2007.

Villano, M. "E-Mail in Haste, Panic at Leisure," *The New York Times,* September 3, 2006, p. BU-10.

Weber, Larry. *Sticks & Stones: How Digital Business Reputations Are Created Over Time and Lost in a Click.* Hoboken, NJ: John Wiley & Sons, 2009.

Wortham, J. "Everyone Is Using Cellphones, but not so Many Are Talking," *The New York Times,* May 14, 2010, pp. A1, B4.

Endnotes

1. Farrow, C. "E-mail Abuse Leads to Firings," *South Bend Tribune,* May 9, 1999, p. Bl.
2. Carrns, A. "Those Bawdy E-mails Were Good for a Laugh—Until the Ax Fell," *Wall Street Journal,* February.
3. Negroponte, N. *Being Digital.* New York: Alfred A. Knopf, 1995.
4. Mattocks, Julian. "Number of PCs Worldwide to Double by 2010," *NewsFox Press Distribution.* http://www.newsfox.com/pte.mc?pte=041216011. Accessed January 3, 2011 at 1:09 P.M.
5. Number of Computers Sold Worldwide in 2009 Rose—Gartner. Retrieved from http://www.fortune500global.com/news/number-of-computers-sold-worldwide-in-2009-rose-gartner/. on January 3, 2011 at 1:05 P.M.
6. *Home Broadband 2010.* Pew Internet and American Life Project. Full report available

online at http://pewinternet.org/Reports/2010/
Home-Broadband-2010.aspx?r=1

7. Boulger, C. A. *e-Technology and the Fourth Economy*. Cincinnati, OH: Thomson South-Western, 2003.

8. "Digital Chasm: 18% of U.S. households are netless; 30% have never used PC to create a document," WRAL.com. Retrieved from http://localtechwire.com on July 10, 2008 at 4:29 P.M.

9. Richtel, M. "Lost in E-Mail, Tech Firms Face Self-Made Beast," *The New York Times*, June 14, 2008, pp. A1, A14.

10. Ibid, p. 29.

11. Ibid, pp. 6, 8.

12. "New Study Says E-Mail May Cost British Companies Worktime," Reuters News Service. Online at: www.msnbc.com/news/614783.asp. Retrieved August 20, 2001.

13. "E-mail Policy: Why Your Company Needs One," Email-policy.com. Online at: www.email-policy.com. Retrieved August 29, 2002.

14. Campbell, Denis. "Email Stress—The New Office Workers' Plague," *Guardian.co.uk/The Observer*. Retrieved from http://www.guardian.co.uk/technology/2007/aug/12/news/print on Monday, January 3, 2011 at 1:54 P.M.

15. Taylor, C. "12 Steps for E-Mail Addicts," Time.com. Online at: www.time.com/time/columnist/printout/0,8816,257188,00.html. Retrieved June 3, 2002.

16. Canabou, C. "A Message About Managing E-Mail," *Fast Company*, 49 (August 2001), p. 38.

17. Taylor. "12 Steps for E-Mail Addicts," p. 2.

18. Cohen, J. "An E-Mail Affliction: The Long Goodbye," *New York Times*, May 9, 2002, p. C5. Copyright © 2002 by The New York Times Company. Reprinted with permission.

19. Ibid.

20. Brown, Paul B. "After E-Mail," *The New York Times*, August 18, 2007, p. B5.

21. McLaughlin, L. "Essentials of E-Mail Etiquette," PCWorld.com. Online at: http://www.pcworld.com/article/80624/essentials_of_email_etiquette.html. Retrieved August 11, 2002.

22. Ibid., p. 2.

23. Kirsner, S. "The Elements of E-Mail Style," www.darwinmag.com, October 2001, p. 22.

24. Rozakis, B., L. Rozakis, and R. Maniscalco. *The Complete Idiot's Guide to Office Politics.*

New York: Pearson/MacMillan Distribution, 1998.

25. Meeks, B. "Is Privacy Possible in the Digital Age?" MSNBC.com. Online at: www.msnbc.com/news/498514.asp. Retrieved January 22, 2002.

26. Biersdorfer, J. D. "Privacy Can Be Elusive in the World of E-Mail," *New York Times*, July 27, 2000, p. D4. Copyright © 2000 by The New York Times Company. Reprinted with permission.

27. "2005 Electronic Monitoring and Surveillance Survey," American Management Association and the e-Policy Institute. Online at: www.amanet.org/research/index.htm.

28. "Outbound e-Mail Security and Content Compliance in Today's Enterprise, 2005," Results from a survey by Proofpoint, Inc., fielded by Forrester Consulting on outbound e-mail content issues, May 2005. Reprinted by permission. Online at: www.proofpoint.com/outbound. Retrieved on August 4–5, 2005. See also: "Many Firms Snooping on Work-Related E-mail," MSNBC. June 2, 2006. Retrieved from http://www.msnbc.msn.com on July 6, 2006 at 3:35 P.M.

29. Hattori, J. "Workplace E-Mail Is not Your Own," CNN.com. Online at: www.cnn.com/2002/TECH/internet/06/03/e.mail.monitoring/index.html. Retrieved June 3, 2002. Retrieved August 4–5, 2005.

30. Conlin, M. "Workers, Surf at Your Own Risk," *BusinessWeek*, June 12, 2000, p. 105.

31. Hawkins, D. "Lawsuits Spur Rise in Employee Monitoring," *U.S. News & World Report*, August 13, 2001, p. 53.

32. Hartman, D. B. and K. S. Nantz. *The 3 Rs of E-Mail: Rights, Risks, and Responsibilities*. Beverly Hills, CA: Crisp Publications, 1996, pp. 68–79.

33. Ibid.

34. For a more thorough discussion of employer rights and corporate-owned electronic mail systems, see Hartman and Nantz, *The 3 Rs of E-Mail*, pp. 51–79.

35. Ibid.

36. "How Much Snooping Can the Boss Really Do?" MSNBC.com. Online at: www.msnbc.com/news/498495.asp. Retrieved January 22, 2002. Used by permission. See also the Privacy Rights Clearinghouse at www.privacyrights.org.

37. Guernsey, L. "You Can Surf, but You Can't Hide," *New York Times*, February 7, 2002, p. D1. Copyright © 2002 by The New York Times Company. Reprinted with permission.

38. Ibid.

39. Biersdorfer. "Privacy Can Be Elusive in the World of E-Mail," p. D4.

40. Guernsey, L. "Free Service Is a Way to Keep Prying Eyes Off Your E-Mail," *New York Times*, July 15, 1999, p. D3. Copyright © 1999 by The New York Times Company. Reprinted with permission.

41. Byron, E. "Omniva Lets E-Mail Disappear Without a Trace," *Wall Street Journal*, September 6, 2001, p. B7. Reprinted by permission of *The Wall Street Journal*, Copyright © 2001 Dow Jones & Company, Inc. All rights reserved worldwide.

42. Guernsey, L. "Keeping Watch Over Instant Messages," *New York Times*, April 15, 2002, p. C4. Copyright © 2002 by The New York Times Company. Reprinted with permission.

43. Mamberto, C. "Instant Messaging Invades the Office," *Wall Street Journal*, July 24, 2007, pp. B1, B2. Reprinted by permission of *The Wall Street Journal*, Copyright © 2007 Dow Jones & Company, Inc. All rights reserved worldwide.

44. Bulkeley, W. M. "Instant Message Goes Corporate: 'You Can't Hide.'" *Wall Street Journal*, September 4, 2002, pp. B1, B4. Reprinted by permission of *The Wall Street Journal*, Copyright © 2002 Dow Jones & Company, Inc. All rights reserved worldwide.

45. Lee, J. S. "I Think, Therefore IM. Text Shortcuts Invade Schoolwork, and Teachers Are not Amused," *New York Times*, September 19, 2002, pp. E1, E4. Copyright © 2002 by The New York Times Company. Reprinted with permission.

46. Associated Press, "Pew Survey: College Net Use at 86%." Online at: from www.msnbc.com/news/8708450.asp. Retrieved September 15, 2002.

47. Kvavik, R. B. "Convenience, Communications, and Control: How Students Use Technology." EDUCAUSE Center for Applied Research and University of Minnesota, Twin Cities. Available online at http://www.educause.edu/Resources/EducatingtheNetGeneration/Convenience CommunicationsandCo/6070 Accessed Saturday, August 27, 2011 at 2:17 P.M. (est).

48. Ibid.

49. Rossman, Katherine. "YU Luv Texts, H8 Calls," *Wall Street Journal*, October 14, 2010, p. D1-D2.

50. Ibid.

51. Ibid.

52. Ibid.

53. Ibid. See also: Wortham, Jenna. "Everyone Is Using Cellphones but not so Many Are Talking," New York Times, May 14, 2010, pp. A1, B4.

54. Nations, Daniel. "What Is Social Media?" About.com. Retrieved from http://webtrends.about.com/od/web20/a/social-media.htm on January 3, 2011 at 3:40 P.M.

55. Schonfeld, Erik. "Costolo: Twitter Now Has 190 Million Users Tweeting 65 Million Times a Day," TechCrunch.com. Retrieved from http://techcrunch.com/2010/06/08/twitter-190-million-users/# on January 3, 2011 at 3:46 P.M

56. "Social Media and Internet." Retrieved from http://www.onlineuniversities.com/career-counselor/office-etiquette/social-media-and-internet on January 3, 2011 at 3:59 P.M.

57. "Number of Cell Phones Worldwide Hits 4.6 B," Associated Press. Retrieved from http://www.cbsnews.com/stories/2010/02/15/business/main6209772.shtml on January 4, 2011 at 12:29 P.M.

58. Hernandez, Fabiola, "Top 5 Countries with Most Cell Phone Subscribers," Associated Content from Yahoo!. Retrieved from http://www.associatedcontent.com/article/1764 228/top_5_countries_with_most_cell_phone. html on January 4, 2011 at 12:37 P.M.

59. Ibid. See also: "Cell Phones," Center on Media and Health, Children's Hospital Boston. Retrieved from http://www.cmch.tv on Friday, July 11, 2008 at 4:00 P.M.

60. "Research Updates Americans' View on Cell Phone Etiquette," press release, September 3, 2002. Online at: www.letstalk.com/company/release_090302.htm. Retrieved October 3, 2002. Quotation used by permission.

61. Ibid. See also Leland, J. "Just a Minute Boss. My Cellphone Is Ringing: The Workplace Is the Last Frontier for Cell Etiquette. Expect Hang-Ups," *New York Times*, July 7, 2005, pp. El, E2. Copyright © 2005 by The New York Times Company. Reprinted by permission.

62. Baldrige, L. "E-Etiquette," *New York Times*, December 6, 1999, p. A29. Copyright © 1999

by The New York Times Company. Reprinted by permission.

63. Allen, E., personal communication by telephone with Professor Sandra D. Collins, June 24, 2002.

64. Allen, E., personal communication with the author, Armonk, New York, May 6, 2002.

65. Mead, D. G. "Retooling for the Cyber Age," *CEO Series 42*, September 2000. Online at: csab.wustl.edu/csab/. August 4, 2005.

66. Collins, S. D. *Communication in a Virtual Organization*. Cincinnati, OH: South-Western College Publishing, 2003.

67. Lister, K. "How Many People Telecommute?" Telework Research Network. Retrieved from http://www.teleworkresearchnetwork.com/research/people-telecommute Accessed Saturday, August 27, 2011 at 2:56 P.M. (est).

68. Van Horn, C. E. and D. Storen. "Telework: Coming of Age? Evaluating the Potential Benefits of Telework," *Telework and the New Workplace of the 21st Century*. Online at: www.dol.gov/asp/telework/p1_1.html. See also: Rhoads, C. and Silver, S. "Working at Home Gets Easier," *Wall Street Journal*. December 29, 2005. Available from http://www.online.wsj.com. Retrieved on July 14, 2008 at 11:43 A.M.

69. Hafner, K. "Working at Home Today?" *New York Times*, November 2, 2001, p. D1. Copyright © 2001 by The New York Times Company. Reprinted by permission.

70. Verespej, M. A. "The Compelling Case for Telework," *Industry Week*, September 2001, p. 23.

71. Collins. *Communication in a Virtual Organization*, pp. 9–11.

72. Wells, S. J. "Making Telecommuting Work," *HR Magazine*, 46 (2001), pp. 34–46.

73. Lovelace, G. "The Nuts and Bolts of Telework: Growth in Telework," *Telework and the New Workplace of the 21st Century*. 2000. Online at: www.dol.gov/asp/telework/p1_2.html. August 5, 2005.

74. Byrne, J. A. "Management by Web," *BusinessWeek*, August 28, 2000, p. 92.

75. Cascio, W. "Managing a Virtual Workplace," *Academy of Management Executive*, March 2000, pp. 81–90.

76. Collins. *Communication in a Virtual Organization*, p. 12.

77. Jarvenpaa, S. and D. Leidner. "Communication and Trust in Global Virtual Teams," *Organization Science: A Journal of the Institute of Management Sciences*, 10 (1999), pp. 791–846.

78. Lawlor, J. "Videoconferencing: From Stage Fright to Stage Presence," *New York Times*, August 27, 1998, p. D6. Copyright © 1998 by The New York Times Company. Reprinted by permission.

79. Ibid.

CASE STUDY 7.1

Cerner Corporation: A Stinging Office Memo Boomerangs

We are getting less than 40 hours of work from a large number of our KC-based EMPLOYEES. The parking lot is sparsely used at 8 a.m.; likewise at 5 p.m. As managers—you either do not know what your EMPLOYEES are doing; or YOU do not CARE.

I will hold you accountable. You have allowed this to get to this state. You have two weeks. Tick, tock.

NEAL L. PATTERSON,
CEO CERNER CORPORATION

The only things missing from the office memo were expletives. It had everything else. There were lines berating employees for not caring about the company. There were words in all capital letters like "SICK" and "NO LONGER." There were threats of layoffs and hiring freezes and a shutdown of the employee gym.

The memo was sent by e-mail on March 13 by the chief executive of the Cerner Corporation, a health care software development company based in Kansas City, Mo., with 3,100 employees worldwide. Originally intended only for 400 or so company managers, it quickly took on a life of its own.

The e-mail message was leaked and posted on Yahoo! Its belligerent tone surprised thousands of readers, including analysts and investors. In the stock market, the valuation of the company, which was $1.5 billion on March 20, plummeted 22 percent in three days. Now, Neal L. Patterson, the 51-year-old chief executive, a man variously described by people who know him as "arrogant," "candid," "passionate," says he wishes he had never hit the send button.

"I was trying to start a fire," he said. "I lit a match, and I started a firestorm."

That is not hard to do in the Internet age, when all kinds of messages in cyberspace are capable of stirring reactions and moving markets. In the autumn of 2000, for example, a young California investor pleaded guilty to criminal charges that he made $240,000 by sending out a fake news release that resulted in a sharp drop in the stock of Emulex, a communications equipment manufacturer.

In Mr. Patterson's case, this is what the world saw: "We are getting less than 40 hours of work from a large number of our KC-based EMPLOYEES. The parking lot is sparsely used at 8 a.m.; likewise at 5 p.m. As managers—either you do not know what your EMPLOYEES are doing; or YOU do not CARE. You have created expectations on the work effort which allowed this to happen inside Cerner, creating a very unhealthy environment. In either case, you have a problem and you will fix it or I will replace you. NEVER in my career have I allowed a team which worked for me to think they had a 40-hour job. I have allowed YOU to create a culture which is permitting this. NO LONGER."

Mr. Patterson went on to list six potential punishments, including laying off 5 percent of the staff in Kansas City. "Hell will freeze over," he vowed, before he would dole out more employee benefits. The parking lot would be his yardstick of success, he said; it should be "substantially full" at 7:30 a.m. and 6:30 p.m. on weekdays and half-full on Saturdays.

"You have two weeks," he said. "Tick, tock."

For Cerner Corporation, the message apparently promoted a market upheaval. On March 22, the day after the memo was posted on the Cerner message board on Yahoo!, trading in Cerner's shares, which typically runs at about 650,000 a day, shot up to 1.2 million shares. The following day, volume surged to four million. In three days, the stock price fell to $34 from nearly $44. It closed at $30.94 on April 4, 2001.

"While the memo provided some much-needed laughter on Wall Street after a tough week, it probably got overblown as an issue," said Stephen D. Savas, an analyst with Goldman, Sachs who rates the stock a market performer, which is relatively low. "But it did raise two real questions for investors. One: Has anything potentially changed at Cerner to cause such a seemingly violent reaction? And two: Is this a CEO that investors are comfortable with?"

Mr. Patterson said that the memo was taken out of context and that most employees at Cerner understood that he was exaggerating to make a point. He said he was not carrying out any of the punishments he listed. Instead, he said, he wanted to promote discussion. He apparently succeeded, receiving more than 300 e-mail responses from employees.

Glenn Tobin, the chief operating officer at Cerner, said he had read several. "Some people said, 'The tone's too harsh, you've really fouled this one up,'" he said. "Some people said, 'I agree with your point.'" Mr. Patterson, who holds an MBA from Oklahoma State University and worked as a consultant at Arthur Andersen before starting Cerner with two partners in 1979, attributes his management style to his upbringing on a 4,000-acre family wheat farm in northern Oklahoma. He spent day after day riding a tractor in the limitless expanse of the fields with only his thoughts for company, he said, and came to the conclusion that life was about building things in your head, then going out and acting on them. "You can take the boy off the farm," he said, "but you can't take the farm out of the boy."

And his directness with subordinates is not necessarily a management liability. Cerner is a fast-growing company that had $404.5 million in revenue in 2000 and met earnings projections for the first three quarters of 2001. The company made *Fortune* magazine's lists in 1998 and 2000 of the "100 Best Companies to Work for in America."

The Day of the Memo

March 13 began like any other day. Mr. Patterson said he woke up at 5:00 a.m. and did some work at home. He then drove the 30 miles to Cerner's corporate campus, seven brick-and-glass buildings, surrounded by 1,900 parking spaces atop a hill in northern Kansas City. In the elevator, he spoke with the receptionist, a woman who had been with the company for 18 years. She remarked that the work ethic had been declining at the company, he said, reinforcing his own fears.

At 7:45 a.m., he walked into his sixth-floor office and typed up a draft of the memo. He met with a client downstairs, then had two managers and his assistant read over the memo. At 11:48 a.m., he sent it. The memo went up on the Yahoo! message board a week later. Analysts began getting calls from investors. They, in turn, called Cerner to verify the authenticity of the memo, then exchanged a flurry of phone calls and e-mail messages, trying to divine the tea leaves of Mr. Patterson's writings.

"The perception was that they have to work overtime to meet their quarter," said Stacey Gibson, an analyst with Fahnestock & Company, who rated the company's stock a "buy" and was among the first to post a warning on Thomson Financial/First Call about the memo. "Whether that's true or not, I don't know," she said. "This is how it was taken on the Street."

Some analysts say that other factors could have contributed to the drop in stock price. The overall market was shaky. There were investors who wanted to sell the stock short, betting that it was ready for a fall. One analyst was especially bearish about the company. But even Mr. Patterson acknowledged that his memo "added noise" to what was already out there.

At the end of the week, as the stock fell, Mr. Patterson sent out another e-mail message to his troops. Unlike the first memo, it was not called a "Management Directive," but rather a "Neal Note." It began this way: "Please treat this memo with the utmost confidentiality. It is for internal dissemination only. Do not copy or e-mail to anyone else."

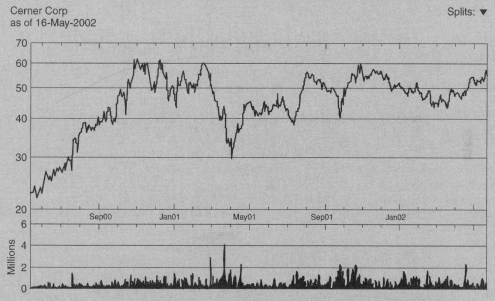

FIGURE 7-1 Cerner Corporation Stock Performance, June 2000 to May 2002
Source: Yahoo Finance. Used by permission.

DISCUSSION QUESTIONS

1. What's the principal business problem here?
2. From the company's perspective, what would an optimal outcome look like?

3. Who are the key stakeholders in this case?
4. If Mr. Patterson were to ask for your counsel on this matter, what would you advise?

5. Which actions would you encourage him to take first? What measure would you use to determine success in resolving the business problem identified in question number one?

6. What sort of problems did Mr. Patterson create for himself when he chose e-mail as his communication medium?

7. How should discussions of this sort be conducted?

WRITING ASSIGNMENT

Please respond in writing to the issues presented in this case by preparing two documents: a communication strategy memo and a professional business letter.

In preparing these documents, you may assume one of two roles: you may identify yourself as a Cerner Corporation senior manager who has been asked to provide advice to Mr. Neal Patterson regarding the issues he and his company are facing. Or, you may identify yourself as an external management consultant who has been asked by the company to provide advice to Mr. Patterson.

Either way, you must prepare a strategy memo, addressed to Neal Patterson, Chairman and Chief Executive Officer of the company, that summarizes the details of the case, rank orders the critical issues, discusses their implications (what they mean and why they matter), offers specific recommendations for action (assigning ownership and suspense dates for each), and shows how to communicate the solution to all who are affected by the recommendations.

You must also prepare a professional business letter for Mr. Patterson's signature. That document should be addressed to all Cerner Corporation employees. If you have questions about either of these documents, please consult your instructor.

From: Patterson, Neal.
To: DL_ALL_Managers.
Subject: MANAGEMENT DIRECTIVE: Week #10_01: Fix it or changes will be made.
Importance: High.

To the KC-based managers:

I have gone over the top. I have been making this point for over one year. We are getting less than 40 hours of work from a large number of our KC-based EMPLOYEES. The parking lot is sparsely used at 8 a.m.; likewise at 5 p.m. As managers—you either do not know what your EMPLOYEES are doing; or YOU do not CARE. You have created expectations on the work effort which allowed this to happen inside Cerner, creating a very unhealthy environment. In either case, you have a problem and you will fix it or I will replace you.

NEVER in my career have I allowed a team which worked for me to think they had a 40-hour job. I have allowed YOU to create a culture which is permitting this. NO LONGER. At the end of next week, I am planning to implement the following:

1. Closing of Associate Center to EMPLOYEES from 7:30 a.m. to 6:30 p.m.
2. Implementing a hiring freeze for all KC-based positions. It will require Cabinet approval to hire someone into a KC-based team. I chair our Cabinet.
3. Implementing a time clock system, requiring EMPLOYEES to "punch in" and "punch out" to work. Any unapproved absences will be charged to the EMPLOYEES vacation.
4. We passed a Stock Purchase Program, allowing for the EMPLOYEE to purchase Cerner stock at a 15% discount, at Friday's BOD meeting. Hell will freeze over before this CEO implements ANOTHER EMPLOYEE benefit in this Culture.
5. Implement a 5% reduction of staff in KC.
6. I am tabling the promotions until I am convinced that the ones being promoted are the solution, not the problem. If you are the problem, pack your bags.

I think this parental-type action SUCKS. However, what you are doing, as managers, with this company makes me SICK. It makes me sick to have to write this directive. I know I am painting with a broad brush and the majority of the KC-based associates are hard-working, committed to Cerner success and committed to transforming health care. I know the parking lot is not a great measurement for "effort." I know that "results" is what counts, not "effort." But I am through with the debate.

We have a big vision. It will require a big effort. Too many in KC are not making the effort.

I want to hear from you. If you think I am wrong with any of this, please state your case. If you have some ideas on how to fix this problem, let me hear those. I am very curious how you think we got here. If you know team members who are the problem, let me know. Please include (copy) Kynda in all of your replies.

I STRONGLY suggest that you call some 7 a.m., 6 p.m. and Saturday a.m. team meetings with the EMPLOYEES who work directly for you. Discuss this serious issue with your team. I suggest that you call your first meeting—tonight. Something is going to change.

I am giving you two weeks to fix this. My measurement will be the parking lot. It should be substantially full at 7:30 a.m. and 6:30 p.m. The pizza man should show up at 7:30 p.m. to feed the starving teams working late. The lot should be half full on Saturday mornings. We have a lot of work to do. If you do not have enough to keep your teams busy, let me know immediately.

Folks this is a management problem, not an EMPLOYEE problem. Congratulations, you are management. You have the responsibility for our EMPLOYEES. I will hold you accountable. You have allowed this to get to this state. You have two weeks. Tick, tock.

Neal Patterson
Chairman & Chief Executive Officer
Cerner Corporation
www.cerner.com
2800 Rockcreek Parkway
Kansas City, Missouri 64117
"We Make Health Care Smarter"

This case was prepared by James S. O'Rourke, Concurrent Professor of Management, as the basis for class discussion rather than to illustrate either effective or ineffective handling of an administrative situation. Information was gathered from corporate as well as public sources.

CASE STUDY 7.2

Johnson & Johnson's Strategy with Motrin:

The Growing Pains of Social Media

"Wearing your baby seems to be in fashion ... plus it totally makes me look like an official mom. And so if I look tired and crazy, people will understand why. Motrin® We feel your pain."

An online ad created by Taxi Advertising and Design, an advertising agency headquartered in Toronto,

Ontario with these words appeared on the Motrin website as an effort to target mothers who developed pain from carrying their babies around in slings. On Friday, November 14, 2008, 45 days after the ad was posted to the site, an influential mommy blogger with a significant Twitter following noticed the ad and began tweeting about her offense to the suggestion that moms use baby slings as fashion statements.[1] Other influential mommy bloggers picked up on the thread, and from Friday into Saturday, the Motrin ad became one of the most tweeted about topics on Twitter, even amidst the highly-publicized 2008 presidential election of Barack Obama.[2]

On Saturday and Sunday, continual negative reactions appeared on Twitter. The conversation was tracked on Twitter by utilizing the hashtag "motrinmoms" that helped interested groups to closely follow the conversation.[3] The message moved into the blogosphere where several bloggers called for a boycott of Motrin, and harsh comments flooded message boards. Some angry consumers even created counter ads that they posted on YouTube.[4] The messaging of the tweets and outcry was strong, and stated that the Motrin ad "trivialized women's pain and the method of carrying babies."[5] As uproar spread through the various social media channels, the messaging shifted from "shame on" Johnson & Johnson to "where is a response" from Johnson & Johnson?[6]

The Opportunities of Social Media

Global brands have continually been increasing their social media activation in advertising and marketing, as companies recognize social media's cost effectiveness and their ability to generate deep customer engagement as the consumer dictates on his or her own terms. Companies continue to realize that customer advocates are the most powerful marketing channel available, as people trust and listen to what others say most of all. The most difficult challenge for brands to succeed at this is to recruit the appropriate and influential advocates and leverage these associations; this has been notoriously difficult to achieve through traditional media. Social media provide a vehicle for a brand to learn and understand the way that customers respond and interact with a company's products and services. Social media also provide forums, such as chat rooms, for customer communities to develop.[7]

Social media outreach also provides the opportunity to learn more about the company's customer. As consumers continue to become more deeply involved with multiple social media channels, customer-volunteered information begins to further flesh out the consumer profile for the company. With more complete information, marketers are better able to facilitate messaging and placement toward a target customer group. Social media provide companies with the opportunity to better and more effectively engage customers on a meaningful basis.[8]

Johnson & Johnson History

Johnson & Johnson was founded in 1885 by two brothers, James and Edward Mead Johnson, as a medical products company in New Brunswick, New Jersey. One year later, their brother, Robert, joined the company to make the antiseptic surgical dressing that he had developed. In 1921, Johnson & Johnson introduced two of its classic products that still exist today, the Band-Aid and Johnson's Baby Cream.[9]

J&J purchased McNeil Labs in 1959, which launched Tylenol in 1960 as an over-the-counter drug. Throughout the 1970s, the company continued to focus on consumer products, with Tylenol becoming the top-selling painkiller. In 1982, crisis struck when Tylenol capsules were laced with cyanide, killing eight people. The company immediately recalled 31 million bottles and redesigned the packaging to prohibit tampering–a response that cost the company $240 million but ultimately saved the Tylenol brand. J&J's response has become well-known and is often used as a model for proper damage control and corporate best practices. In the 1990s, J&J continued its acquisition and diversification strategy and acquired Neutrogena in 1994 to further bolster its consumer product lines. The company bought the over-the-counter rights to Motrin in 1997 from Pharmacia, which is now Pfizer. In 2006, the company acquired Pfizer's consumer products business for $16.6 billion, which added approximately 40 brands to J&J's portfolio. The company announced a major restructuring in 2007, trimming costs and executing job cuts mainly within its Pharmaceuticals segment and reinvesting in other areas.[10]

Johnson & Johnson now operates within three segments through more than 250 operating companies in approximately 60 countries. J&J's Pharmaceuticals division produces drugs for a variety of ailments including autoimmune diseases, neurological conditions, blood disorders and pain. Its Medical Devices and Diagnostics division offers monitoring devices, surgical equipment, orthopedic products, contact lenses and a variety of other products. The third division, J&J's Consumer segment, makes over-the-counter drugs and assorted products for skin, baby and oral care, and first aid and women's health. In 2009, Johnson & Johnson was ranked #33 in the Fortune 500 and reported nearly $62 Billion in sales and 115,500 employees.[11]

The company is renowned for its decentralized operating structure, with management teams having wide latitude in their decision-making. Johnson & Johnson has a strong drug development pipeline to address the competitive challenge of patent expiration, which is increasingly relevant as some of the company's major products have recently lost patent protection. While the company's Pharmaceuticals and Medical Devices segments each account for more than 35% of company sales, challenges within these segments led to recent restructuring efforts by the company. Additionally, Johnson & Johnson's Consumer segment has been growing through acquisitions, and offerings include brands such as Neutrogena, Tylenol, Listerine, Benadryl, Lubriderm, Rolaids, Sudafed, and Splenda.[12]

A Short History in Social Media at Johnson & Johnson

Johnson & Johnson has always set the standard for communication in the corporate world, so it should be no surprise that it has an extensive social media network in place to reach its many customers. With the onslaught of new social media platforms, Johnson & Johnson has kept up to speed on all interfaces.

Ray Jordan joined Johnson & Johnson in 2003 as Vice President of Public Affairs and Corporate Communication. Responsible for corporate communications and public affairs for the company, Jordan oversees the Public Affairs responsibilities and activities of the entire family of Johnson & Johnson operating companies.[13] Jordan recognized that there were new groups in social media that were influencing online dialogue and Johnson & Johnson needed to develop relationships with these bloggers. Jordan created an environment where the Corporate Communication team could explore the various social media networks.[14]

Kilmer House

Johnson & Johnson's first attempt to enter the social media market was through the creation of Kilmer House. Created in 2006 by Corporate Communication team member Margaret Gurowitz, Kilmer House was Johnson & Johnson's first attempt at a blog. Named after Dr. Fredrick Kilmer, the company's first scientific director, Kilmer House serves as a history blog for the Johnson & Johnson Company.[15] This was a safe and conservative way to enter the blogosphere without causing any controversy.

Gurowitz still runs the blog as the company historian and she tries to reach out to groups interested in the history of Johnson & Johnson who want to better understand the company. Within four years of posts, the blog summarizes: "One of the best ways to understand Johnson & Johnson is to know the Company's history and the things that make it unique."[16] Gurowitz has covered topics over a wide spectrum including: the people who established Johnson & Johnson, some of its unusual products, early science and technology, the Johnson & Johnson community, anniversaries, advertising, iconic products, innovations and trivia. At the bottom of every blog, readers are able to interact with the company by leaving comments which J&J can respond to in order to clarify questions that readers might pose.

Kilmer House allowed Johnson & Johnson to develop a comfort level with its own legal and regulatory department on how to manage new issues that could arise in the blogosphere.[17] This blog set the stage for all of Johnson & Johnson's social media platforms by developing ways to manage content created by Johnson & Johnson, as well as content created by its readers.

JNJ BTW

Kilmer House had allowed Johnson & Johnson to experiment with the voice it could establish online in addition to the development of a two-way dialogue with its customers. In early 2007, approximately six months after Kilmer House had launched, Marc Monseau, Director, Corporate Communication, Social Media, created a new blog called Johnson & Johnson By The Way, or JNJ BTW. The blog summarizes its purpose by stating:

Everyone else is talking about our company, so why can't we? There are more than 120,000 people who work for Johnson & Johnson and its operating companies. I'm one of them, and through JNJ BTW, I will try to find a voice that often gets lost in formal communications.

This is a big step for us as a company. Anyone working for a large corporation will appreciate that there are many internal limitations on what we say and how we say it.

I've been reading blogs for only a few months now, but already it's clear to me how important it is not just to watch, but to join in productively. Doing that will take some unlearning of old habits and traditional approaches to communicating — and I will have to find my own voice.

On JNJ BTW, there will be talk about Johnson & Johnson — what we are doing, how we are doing it and why. There will be comment on the news about our company and the industry — occasionally correcting any mistakes (not that that ever happens!) or simply providing more context. I hope and expect that some of my colleagues will eventually join me on this blog.[18]

Johnson & Johnson needed a way to engage these bloggers and respond with its own story. JNJ BTW was purposely designed to allow Johnson & Johnson to discuss corporate topics, company strategy, emerging issues, and good works happening within the company in a slightly more informal manner.[19]

An example of this was when Jordan posted on JNJ BTW about Johnson & Johnson's decision to sue the American Red Cross. Being well aware that suing the American Red Cross could backfire and cause injury to the company, Jordan used JNJ BTW as a platform to discuss why J&J came to this final decision. Jordan explained how the company tried almost every other remedy before pursuing legal action. His blog post not only tempered the anger in the blogosphere, but also created advocates that posted positive reactions on JNJ BTW and went as far as re-posting Jordan's comments on their own blogs. Jordan's post changed the entire attitude of the discussion online and worked exactly how Johnson & Johnson had hoped.[20]

JNJ YouTube Health Channel

A few months after Monseau launched the JNJ BTW blog, Rob Halper, Director of Video Communication, launched the Johnson & Johnson health channel on YouTube. With the concept of

"videos to promote a better understanding of health,"[21] the Johnson & Johnson health channel posts videos that provide context and information about health issues and health topics. These videos do not deal with specific Johnson & Johnson products or brands. They offer general information on popular health topics, such as the long term effects of obesity, how to live with diabetes, bipolar disorder family support, and Alzheimer's disease.

Facebook and Twitter

Following the relatively quick launches of two blogs and a YouTube channel, Johnson & Johnson opened a Facebook account in 2008. The Facebook account provided yet another channel of communication between Johnson & Johnson and its stakeholders. In 2009, Johnson & Johnson created a Twitter account to provide up-to-date information to consumers as well as to gather information. Johnson & Johnson now has three corporate Twitter accounts to its name. Monseau tweets for the JNJCOMM twitter account. Monseau will post on topics he finds interesting and topics that are being discussed on Johnson & Johnson's other social media platforms.[22]

Johnson & Johnson Uses Social Media

The Motrin case of 2008 prompted Johnson & Johnson to think about becoming more involved with Twitter. The company noticed a large group of Twitter users were of interest to the company, due to the consumers' buying power and influence. Johnson & Johnson wanted to use Twitter as a medium not only to engage its online stakeholders, but also to gather information from them, share thoughts with them, and give the stakeholders an informal way to talk with the company. As Monseau tried to figure out what kind of Twitter account to create, he grouped all Twitter accounts into five different categories:

Customer Service: The company viewed the JetBlue Twitter account as a perfect example of a customer service account. JetBlue uses Twitter to keep customers up-to-date on flight delays and cancellations and allows passengers to file complaints about lost luggage.

Expert Source: The accounts can provide information and key insights by an official who is knowledgeable both from within the company and out in public.

News Gatherer: The account can take information about one's business and the industry the company is a part of, gather the information, and provide it to customers as a news source.

Suggestion Box: The account can solicit input and ideas from Twitter followers that can be redistributed to all interested parties.

Special Offers: The account can be a location to distribute coupons and provide special offers.

Monseau and the social media team at J&J wanted to use Twitter to provide information as an Expert Source and News Gatherer.[23]

Johnson & Johnson wanted to increase its ability to listen, respond, and engage with its customers through the use of Twitter. In order to do this effectively, Monseau and his team had to ensure there was a system of processes in place that would enable the right people in the company to speak to each of their areas of expertise. In order to allow these subject matter experts to respond quickly, J&J had to grant its employees a degree of flexibility and trust to answer questions in a timely manner with the understanding that the responders knew their limitations of what can and cannot be posted. Monseau likes to refer to these understood limitations as guardrails:

"We have specific guardrails that have been set up where we are allowed to drive all over the road and say certain things and publish different topics. If there is a topic that goes beyond those guardrails, we have to get approval for it, go through an approval process, and get sign off for it. We all have to keep in mind and be aware of where those limits are, where those guardrails fit, and if we go outside of them we have to make sure the company understands what direction we are going in."[24]

Without this flexibility and trust, J&J would not be able to post information fast enough to meet consumer needs. This would pose a challenge for the company because customers would look elsewhere for their information, and J&J would no longer be the information provider.

Johnson & Johnson Responds

On Sunday, November 16, 2008, Johnson & Johnson became aware of the outraged discussion regarding the Motrin online advertisement. The company was well aware that a significant number of mommy bloggers had worked in the areas of advertising and media, and the possibility for a media firestorm was sizeable.[25] Monseau and the social media team at J&J knew that a response was in order.

Additionally, Monseau and his team would need to assess the expectations and plans for Johnson & Johnson's social media outreach. The team must also evaluate what opportunities to pursue in the future and how its social media strategy aligns with the company's business objectives as a whole. Finally, as social media continues to grow in its applications and consumer involvement, Monseau must gauge if the size and the composition of his corporate social media team is sufficient.

DISCUSSION QUESTIONS: JOHNSON & JOHNSON RESPONDS TO THE MOTRIN CASE

1. How should Johnson & Johnson respond to the crisis?
2. What audience should the company reach out to?
3. What member(s) of the company should engage the audience?
4. What does the company offer to those offended by the ad?
5. How does Johnson & Johnson track the success of its response?

DISCUSSION QUESTIONS: JOHNSON & JOHNSON ASSESSES SOCIAL MEDIA STRATEGY

1. What will Johnson & Johnson's social media strategy be moving forward?
2. What other social media platforms should J&J utilize?

3. Is the social media team big enough or should J&J grow it?
4. What metrics should the social media team utilize to measure the success of its social media outreach?
5. How can J&J link the social media objectives to the overall company's business objectives?

WRITING ASSIGNMENT

Please respond in writing to the issues presented in this case by preparing two documents: a communication strategy memo and a professional business letter.

In preparing these documents, you may assume one of two roles: you may identify yourself as a Johnson & Johnson corporate communication manager who has been asked to provide advice to Mr. Ray Jordan, Vice President for Public Affairs and Corporate Communication, regarding the issues he and the company are facing. Or, you may identify yourself as an external management consultant who has been asked by the company to provide advice to Mr. Jordan.

Either way, you must prepare a strategy memo addressed to Mr. Jordan that summarizes the details of the case, rank-orders critical issues, discusses their implications (what they mean and why they matter), offers specific recommendations for action (assigning ownership and suspense dates for each), and shows how to communicate the solution to all who are affected by the recommendations.

You must also prepare a professional business letter for the signature of Mr. William Weldon, the CEO. That document may be addressed to a specific stakeholder group, such as customers, investors, or government regulators. If you have questions about either of these documents, please consult your instructor.

This case was prepared by Research Assistants Kathryn Eisele and Patrick Fishburne under the direction of James S. O'Rourke, Concurrent Professor of Management, as the basis for class discussion rather than to illustrate either effective or ineffective handling of an administrative situation. Information was gathered from corporate as well as public sources.

References

1. Wheaton, K. (2008, December), "Middle road in Motrin-gate was right choice for J&J. Advertising Age," 79(44), 12, Retrieved September 20, 2010, from ABI/INFORM Global (Document ID: 1611223211).
2. Telephone conference with Marc Monseau, Johnson & Johnson, New Brunswick, New Jersey, 21 September 2010
3. Anonymous, "All companies simply must get up to speed on Twitter," (2008, November). PRweek, 11(46), 6, Retrieved September 20, 2010, from ABI/INFORM Trade & Industry (Document ID: 1665581141)
4. Zerillo, N., (2008, November), "J&J reaches out to mothers to apologize for its Motrin ad," PRweek, 11(46), 1, Retrieved September 20, 2010, from ABI/INFORM Trade & Industry (Document ID: 1665581021)
5. Shirley S. Wang, (2008, November 18), "J&J Pulls Online Motrin Ad After Social-Media Backlash," Wall Street Journal (Eastern Edition), p. B.4, Retrieved September 20, 2010, from ABI/INFORM Global (Document ID: 1596949231)
6. Telephone conference with Marc Monseau, Johnson & Johnson, New Brunswick, New Jersey, 21 September 2010
7. Plimsoll, S., & Thorpe, A., (2010, July), "Find and target customers in the social media maze," Marketing: Road to recovery, 10-11, Retrieved from ABI/INFORM Global (Document ID: 2109794771)
8. Ibid.
9. Johnson & Johnson Medical Ltd., (15 September), Hoover's Company Records, 135526, Retrieved September 26, 2010, from Hoover's Company Records. (Document ID: 769857951)
10. Ibid.
11. Ibid.

12. Ibid.
13. JNJ BTW blog, "Contributing Authors," http://jnjbtw.com/jnj-btw-authors/
14. Telephone conference with Marc Monseau, Johnson & Johnson, New Brunswick, New Jersey, 21 September 2010.
15. Kilmer House blog, "About Kilmer House." http://www.kilmerhouse.com/about/
16. Ibid.
17. Telephone conference with Marc Monseau, Johnson & Johnson, New Brunswick, New Jersey, 21 September 2010
18. JNJ BTW Our People and Perspectives blog, "About JNJ BTW," http://jnjbtw.com/about-jnj-btw/
19. Telephone conference with Marc Monseau, Johnson & Johnson, New Brunswick, New Jersey, 21 September 2010
20. Ibid.
21. Johnson & Johnson Health Channel http://www.youtube.com/user/jnjhealth
22. Telephone conference with Marc Monseau, Johnson & Johnson, New Brunswick, New Jersey, 21 September 2010
23. e-Patient Connections Conference, "How J&J Joined the Twittersphere," Presentation by Marc Monseau, October 27, 2009
24. Telephone conference with Marc Monseau, Johnson & Johnson, New Brunswick, New Jersey, 21 September 2010
25. Wheaton, K., (2008, December), "Middle road in Motrin-gate was right choice for J&J," Advertising Age, 79(44), 12, Retrieved September 20, 2010, from ABI/INFORM Global. (Document ID: 1611223211)

CASE STUDY 7.3

Facebook Beacon (A): Cool Feature or an Invasion of Privacy?

I made a purchase yesterday for my wife for Christmas . . . when my wife logged onto Facebook, there was an entry in her news feed that I had bought a ring from Overstock. It had a link to the ring and everything. Christmas ruined.[1]

These were the words of Sean Lane shortly after his 14k White Gold 1/5 Diamond Eternity Flower Ring from overstock.com became common knowledge to his social network on Facebook. Lane's purchase was supposed to be a surprise Christmas present for his wife. Instead, news of the purchased ring wound up not only as a story on the News Feed of his wife's profile, but his classmates, coworkers, and acquaintances as well.[2]

On November 6, 2007, Mark Zuckerberg, founder and CEO of Facebook, announced a new and innovative approach to advertising by way of a feature named Beacon.[3] Initially, Beacon created 44 advertising partner relationships for Facebook.[4] It also essentially turned its users into advertisers by displaying their purchases on News Feed. On November 19, political and civic action organization, MoveOn, launched a public campaign against Beacon which included a petition to make Beacon an opt-in feature. MoveOn, though, was not the only form of negative response to Beacon.[5] Thousands of users also joined "Facebook groups" such as "Petition: Facebook, stop invading my privacy!"[6]

Incidentally, the Beacon uproar was not the first time Facebook had faced such criticism for privacy issues regarding a new feature. On September 5, 2006, Facebook launched a feature called News Feed.[7] News Feed revolutionized the way Facebook worked by consolidating a user's recent activities so friends could more efficiently keep track of each other. Users strongly disapproved of the feature, although all of the information in News Feed could actually be found with enough searching. Much like News Feed, Beacon led Facebook into another privacy frenzy.

History of Facebook

Facebook was launched from Mark Zuckerberg's dorm room on February 4, 2004.[8] The online social networking site became an instant hit at Harvard within the first few weeks.[9] Zuckerberg then began expanding Facebook to other colleges and gained extensive popularity along the way. Originally, the business plan of Facebook focused solely on college campuses across the nation. The strategy was to provide a social network that would allow students to communicate and share information with each other via a profile. It was, in a sense, a grown-up and parent-free universe connected only to friends.[10] A key difference for Facebook, in comparison to competitors such as MySpace or friendfinder, is that it acts as a closed community. Originally, it was set up solely for the use of college students which Facebook had established networks with and the site did not allow outsiders to view any profiles.[11] For example, a student at Notre Dame could view a fellow profile of a Notre Dame student, but could not view a Harvard student's profile unless they accepted each other's friendship. By May 2004, Facebook had spread to the rest of the Ivy Leagues and a few other schools.[12] For Facebook, this would only prove to be the tip of the iceberg.

In the summer of 2004, Zuckerberg moved his ideas and staff to Palo Alto, California.[13] There they received $500,000 of financial backing from Peter Thiel, co-founder of PayPal.[14] Venture capital firms soon thereafter began investing millions of dollars into Facebook while the social network expanded rapidly to almost every college across the nation.[15] On September 5, 2005, Facebook began allowing high schools to participate in the network.[16] Much like the success and popularity Facebook found at the college level, the social platform took off with high schools across the nation. A year later, on September 11, 2006, Facebook expanded its user base by allowing anyone with a valid email address to become a user on the site, so long as they were over the age of 13.[17] Users could now become part of a network based on colleges, high schools, employer, or geographic region. By September 2006, the company was believed to be worth over $100 million thanks to its 9 million users who spent an average of 18 minutes on the site per day.[18] Since 2006, Facebook has resisted several take-over attempts and is persistent on maintaining itself as a private company. In October 2007, Microsoft purchased a 1.6 percent share in the company for 240 million dollars that ultimately valued the company at $15 billion with over 50 million users. Users now average over 20 minutes per day on the site.[19] The online student directory that once took Harvard by storm became a commonality across the nation.

Facebook Applications and Features

Facebook, originally known as thefacebook.com, originated as a very simplistic social networking site which offered individuals the opportunity to develop and maintain their own personal profile.[20] Shortly thereafter, the developers of Facebook began expanding the functionality of the Web site. For instance, users were given the ability to create events, messages, and groups.[21] Facebook began rapidly developing additional applications and features. Each additional application or feature provided incentive for outsiders to join the Facebook network. At the same time, current Facebook users employed the applications and features to further develop their own networks and connections. As of February 2008, more than 15,000 applications had been built on Facebook Platform and roughly 140 new applications are added on a daily basis.[22] Some of the most recognized applications and features on Facebook include photos, Walls, News Feed, and Mini-Feed.

Walls

Before the Wall was introduced, the communication between friends actually taking place on Facebook was limited. When the Wall feature became available in September of 2004, each user received a space on their profile page dedicated to displaying comments left by others. For example, a user could access the Wall of any his or her friends and leave a message on their Wall. Likewise, that user could receive Wall messages from any of his or her friends. In addition, options and settings gave users the power to remove comments from their Wall, restrict who could view their Wall, and even turn off the Wall feature entirely.

Photos

There was once a time when a Facebook user's profile picture was the only picture they could upload to the Web site. In October of 2005, Facebook launched the Photos application which allowed each user to upload an unlimited number of photos.[23] In order to help with the organization of such photos, it was possible to create albums for each user's various groups of pictures. Users could also tag the people in each photo for identification purposes or to alert others that a picture of a particular user had been uploaded. Finally, privacy settings for each album gave users the ability to determine which networks and friends could view their photos.[24] The combination of these features resulted in an overwhelming number of pictures being uploaded. By Spring of 2008, more than 14 million photos were uploaded each day.[25] As a result, Facebook not only became the number one photo sharing application on the Web, but it attracted more than twice the traffic of the next three sites combined.[26]

News Feed and Mini-Feed

Early in September of 2006, Facebook launched yet another two features called News Feed and Mini-Feed.[27] The reaction to these features, however, was unlike any other reaction Facebook had received before. Ruchi Sanghvi, the product manager for Feed at Facebook, addressed the new features on September 5 at 4:03 a.m. in a Facebook blog. She expressed excitement for the features which highlighted the activities which had "recently taken place in your social circles." News Feed focused on every friend within a user's networks, while Mini-Feed would display that user's recent activities on their profile page. All of the information displayed by the two features was already accessible throughout Facebook.[28] What News Feed and Mini-Feed did was to centralize everyone's recent activity and make it much more noticeable upon logging in.

There was an instant backlash from Facebook users on seeing the change in their social networking site. Ironically, Facebook users responded by expressing their anger and disapproval in Facebook designed groups. One of the first groups formed, "Students Against Facebook News Feed (Official Petition to Facebook)," generated more than 200,000 supporters in the first 24 hours and would eventually grow to more than 700,000 members.[29] The general consensus was that the privacy of Facebook users had been compromised.

At 1:45 a.m. on September 6, Mark Zuckerberg left a post on the Facebook Blog titled "Calm down. Breathe. We hear you." In his post, Zuckerberg acknowledged the overwhelming amount of concern expressed by its users. He also explained that News Feed and Mini-Feed were intended to prevent people from missing the things going on in their friends' lives. Facebook agreed with its users in saying "stalking isn't cool."[30] The final message appeared to show no intention of eliminating News Feed and Mini-Feed. Rather, Facebook was willing to improve the product by listening to the suggestions and feedback of its users.

Two days later, Zuckerberg left yet another post on the Facebook Blog. The first sentence of this post simply said, "We really messed this one up." Zuckerberg went on to acknowledge that Facebook did a "bad job of explaining what the new features were and an even worse job of giving you control of them." To remedy the situation, Facebook quickly established a better set of privacy controls. They also created a group called "Free Flow of Information on the Internet" where users and Facebook employees could meet to discuss the mishap surrounding News Feed and Mini Feed.[31]

Social Media and Competitors

Since the advent of the Internet and enhanced communication through open platforms, social networking has taken off. Popular social networking sites include, but are not limited to MySpace, YouTube, Flickr, and Match.com. Each of these sites attracts users for their own specific reasons. For example, although MySpace is designed very similarly to Facebook, it offers a different feel and can become quite a complex atmosphere. YouTube is known for its ability to share a wide array of videos across users. Flickr is recognized for its ability to allow users to share pictures amongst each other. Finally, Match.com and numerous similar Web sites have focused on connecting people for dates and potentially long-term relationships. Each one of these social networks offers a service that has the potential to intrude on their users' privacy. Currently, a lack of regulation leaves many users unprotected when considering user privacy. It can only be expected that individuals, groups, and businesses will continue to test the social networking waters and push the limits. As Facebook matures, sites such as Google and Yahoo are being viewed as direct competitors. Some even believe tasks commonly completed on Google or Yahoo will soon be more easily or efficiently completed on Facebook. For instance, someone looking to purchase a particular item may look for direct reviews and ratings from friends on Facebook, rather than turning to corporate advertisements and other sources.

Privacy Concerns

The release of News Feed and Mini-Feed certainly shed light on the privacy issues that accompany a social networking site such as Facebook. Judging from the reaction of its users, the Facebook staff did a sufficient job in tweaking the controversial features and regaining a sense of comfort with its users. Of course, this would not be the last privacy concern Facebook would have to deal with. Just over a year later, Facebook released a new feature called Beacon which ultimately led Facebook and its users down an all-too-familiar path.

Beacon

On November 6, 2007, Facebook released a feature called Beacon which would allow users to share their online activities outside of Facebook with their friends.[32] Activities primarily included online purchases and surveys. Through advertising partnerships with 44 companies, Facebook began gathering and posting data about its users' activity on other Web sites.[33] For example, if a user was logged onto Facebook and simultaneously made an online purchase through one of Facebook's advertising partners, the details of that purchase would soon be sent to Facebook.[34] Facebook would then take this information and display it within its users' homepage and profile via News Feed and Mini-Feed.[35] Messages which were intended to inform users that information was being sent or had been sent to Facebook didn't appear to be sufficient.

Although Beacon was one way in which Facebook could generate revenues through advertisement partnerships, Facebook expressed that its intentions were to help people better share information with others. Instead, users were alarmed by the personal information that was quickly becoming public knowledge. As a result, Facebook users responded both quickly and negatively under the premise that Beacon was a complete invasion of privacy. A petition through MoveOn.org and anti-Beacon groups on Facebook were just two of the ways user opinions were expressed.[36]

The Future of Facebook

By no means are social networking sites a simple business to manage. Facebook has discovered this firsthand. This case has highlighted the significant pushback Facebook experienced from its users following the introduction of Beacon. Facebook's relationships with its users have certainly been affected. Facebook has even lost advertising partners after they observed the reactions of users. With both of these issues in mind, Mark Zuckerberg must figure out a way to regain the trust and confidence of its users and advertising partners. Facebook has recovered from mishaps before, but this situation has taken on a life of its own. The last thing Facebook needs now is to experience a serious setback after being on such a prosperous path for the last four years.

DISCUSSION QUESTIONS

1. What are the critical issues in this case and who are the stakeholders?
2. Is there a need for Facebook to deliver a message? If so, what should the content of the message be, to whom should it be delivered, who should send the message, and what would the best delivery medium be?
3. Should modifications be made to Beacon? If so, what changes should be made and how should they be made?

4. Should Facebook be concerned about preventing a similar situation in the future? If so, how can they prevent similar situations from occurring?
5. Does Facebook need to establish a communications department or an executive communication position?
6. Should Mr. Zuckerberg be concerned about reactions from his business partners and potential investors?

WRITING ASSIGNMENT

Please respond in writing to the issues presented in this case by preparing two documents: a communication strategy memo and a professional business letter.

In preparing these documents, you may assume one of two roles: you may identify yourself as a Facebook senior manager who has been asked to provide advice to Mr. Elliot Schrage regarding the issues he and the company are facing. Or, you may identify yourself as an external management consultant who has been asked by the company to provide advice to Mr. Schrage.

Either way, you must prepare a strategy memo addressed to Elliot Schrage, Vice President, Global

Communications, Marketing, and Public Policy, that summarizes the details of the case, rank orders the critical issues, discusses their implications (what they mean and why they matter), offers specific recommendations for action (assigning ownership and suspense dates for each), and shows how to communicate the solution to all who are affected by the recommendations.

You must also prepare a professional business letter for Mr. Mark Zuckerberg's signature. That document should be addressed to all Facebook users, explaining the company's reaction to the events described in the case.

References

1. "Does Facebook Hate Christmas?" *Valleywag: Silicon Valley's Tech Gossip Rag*. February 8, 2008. http://valleywag.com/tech/your-privacy-is-an-illusion/does-facebook-hate-christmas-327664.php.
2. Nakashima, Ellen. "Feeling Betrayed, Facebook Users Force Site to Honor Their Privacy." *Washington Post Online*. November 30, 2007. http://www.washing-tonpost.com/wp-dyn/content/article/2007/11/29/AR2007112902503.html?hpid=topnews.
3. "Press Room: Press Release & Announcements." *Facebook.com*. February 9, 2008. http://www.facebook.com/press/releases.php?p=9166.
4. Mattocks, Julian. "Number of PCs Worldwide to Double by 2010," NewsFox Press Distribution. http://www.newsfox.com/pte.mc?pte=041216011.
4. Ibid.
5. Catone, Josh. "Is Facebook Really Ruining Christmas?" *Read Write Web*. November 21, 2007. http://www.readwriteweb.com/archives/facebook_moveon_beacon_privacy. php.
6. Adam G., Daniel, Marika, Eli, Wes, Karin, and the MoveOn.org Civic Action Team. "Join Our Facebook Group." November 20, 2007. http://civ.moveon.org/facebookprivacy/071120email.html.
7. "The Facebook Blog: Facebook Gets a Facelift." *Facebook.com*. February 14, 2008. http://blog.facebook.com/blog.php?blog_id=company&m=9&y=2006.
8. "Facebook." *Wikipedia: The Free Encyclopedia*. February 14, 2008. http://en.wikipedia.org/wiki/Facebook.
9. Ibid.
10. Graham-Felsen, Sam. "The Facebook Rebellion: New 'Feature' Has Users Upset." *CBSNews.com*. September 7, 2006. http://ww.cbsnews.com/stories/2006/09/07/opinion/main1982347.shtml.
11. Ibid.
12. "Facebook." *Wikipedia: The Free Encyclopedia*. February 14, 2008. http://en.wikipedia.org/wiki/Facebook.
13. Ibid. org/wiki/Facebook.
14. Ibid.
15. Ibid.
16. Ibid.
17. Ibid.
18. Graham-Felsen. "The Facebook Rebellion."
19. "Press Room: Statistics." *Facebook.com*. February 12, 2008. http://www.facebook.com/press-/info.php?statistics.
20. "The Facebook Blog." *Facebook.com*. February 9, 2008. http://blog.facebook.com/blog.php?blog_id=company&m=8&y=2006.
21. Ibid.
22. "Press Room: Statistics." *Facebook.com*.
23. "Press Room: Company Timeline." *Facebook.com*. February 14, 2008.

http://www.facebook.com/press/info.php?
timeline.

24. "Press Room: Product Review." *Facebook.com.*
February 14, 2008. http://www.facebook.com/
press/product.php.

25. "Press Room: Statistics." *Facebook.com.*

26. Ibid.

27. "Press Room: Company Timeline."*Facebook.
com.*

28. "The Facebook Blog: Welcome to Facebook
Everyone." *Facebook.com.* February 11, 2008.
http://blog.facebook.com/blog.php?blog_id=
company&m=9&y=2006.

29. Aslani, Layla. "Users Rebel against Facebook
Feature." *The Michigan Daily.* February 11,
2008. http://blog.facebook.com/blog.php?blog_id
=company&m=9&y=2006.

30. "The Facebook Blog: Facebook Gets a
Facelift." *Facebook.com.* February 14, 2008.

http://blog.facebook.com/blog.php?blog_id=
company&m=9&y=2006.

31. Ibid.

32. "Facebook Beacon." *Wikipedia: The Free
Encyclopedia.* February 14, 2008. http://
en.wikipedia.

33. Ibid.

34. Palmer, Shelly. "Facebook's Beacon of
Despair." February 14, 2008. http://
forum.ecoustics.com/bbs/messages/
34579/410909.html.

35. Ibid.

36. Adam G., Daniel, Marika, Eli, Wes, Karin, and
the MoveOn.org Civic Action Team. "Join Our
Facebook Group." November 20, 2007.
http://civ.moveon.org/facebookprivacy/
071120email.html.

This case was prepared by Research Assistants William R. Borchers and Brett W. Lilley, under the direction of James S. O'Rourke, Concurrent Professor of Management, as the basis for class discussion rather than to illustrate either effective or ineffective handling of an administrative situation. Information was gathered from corporate as well as public sources.

Chapter *8*

Listening and Feedback

Two highly accomplished lawyers are sitting at the bar at Sparks Steakhouse in New York. One is a fellow named Tom, the other is Tom's law partner, Kevin. They're having a leisurely drink, waiting for their table to open up. Sparks is a landmark steakhouse where a handful of New York's rich, powerful, and glamorous are in attendance most nights. This particular night includes superstar attorney David Boies, who argued the U.S. government's antitrust case against Microsoft. He makes a beeline to the bar to say hello to Kevin, whom he knows from previous cases, and joins Tom and Kevin for a drink. A few minutes later, Kevin gets up to make a phone call outside.

Mr. Boies remains at the bar, talking to Tom for 30 minutes. "I'd never met Boies before," Tom said. "He didn't have to hang around the bar talking to me. And I have to tell you, I wasn't bowled over by his intelligence, or his piercing questions, or his anecdotes. What impressed me was that when he asked a question, he waited for the answer. He not only listened, he made me feel like I was the only person in the room."[1]

In showing interest, asking questions, and listening for the answers without distraction, Boies was simply practicing the one skill that has made him inarguably great at relating to people. "The only difference between us and the super-successful among us," says business journalist Marshall Goldsmith, "is that the greats do this all the time. It's automatic. There's no on-off switch for caring, empathy, and showing respect. It's always on."[2]

AN ESSENTIAL SKILL

We have all grown to understand how valuable communication is to the success of any business. And few of us would argue with the value of being skilled as a communicator on a personal level. We make friends, establish relationships, pass ideas, and accomplish the work that earns our living each day. Yet, strangely, the communication skill most central to our success—personally and professionally—is the one we're least likely to study in a formal way.

According to Professors Nichols and Stevens of the University of Minnesota, the average person spends about 70 percent of each day engaged in some type of communication. More specifically, researchers report that of all the time we spend communicating each day, 45 percent is spent listening, 30 percent speaking, 16 percent reading, and only 9 percent writing.[3]

More recent studies show that adults now spend more than half their daily communication listening to someone else speak. Even though it's clearly a crucial skill, few people, according to Professor James Floyd, know how to do so efficiently and effectively.[4] Nichols warns, however, that "listening is hard work. It is characterized by faster heart action, quicker circulation of the blood, a small rise in bodily temperature." The implication is simple: If you are not motivated to work at listening, you are not likely to improve.[5]

Studies of listening skill repeatedly show that the average North American adult listens at an efficiency rate of just 25 percent. Your mother was right: For most of us, literally three-quarters of what we hear goes in one ear and out the other. We retain and understand just a fraction of what's going on around us.[6]

The difference between hearing and listening is substantial. Hearing is merely an involuntary physical response to the environment. Listening, on the other hand, is a process that includes hearing, attending to, understanding, evaluating, and responding to spoken messages. It's a sophisticated communication skill that can be mastered only with considerable practice. It is fair to emphasize, however, that while improving one's listening skills is difficult, demanding, and challenging, it can be immensely rewarding.[7]

Why have most of us become so resistant to careful listening? "It's because of our fast-paced world," says Kathy Thompson of Alverno College. "We're always in a hurry. Mentally we're saying, 'Get to the point.' We don't have time to hear the whole story. We're running from house to job to store to church. Good listening takes time."[8]

That's part of it, according to Wick Chambers, a partner in Speechworks, an Atlanta communications-training firm. "But also, people think listening is boring; it's more fun to talk." Still others blame TV, radio and the Internet, which allow people to combine listening with so many other activities that simply listening—to music, for example—seems like a waste of time.[9]

"When you watch television," says Sheila Bentley, a Memphis, Tennessee, communications consultant, "you're listening in a way that doesn't require you to retain anything and doesn't object if you leave the room. And because it's interrupted by commercials, you don't have to develop sustained attending skills. With people spending six hours a day doing that kind of listening, it's no wonder there's concern that we're becoming a nation of poor listeners."[10]

WHY LISTEN?

Poor listening can cause disasters, as it did in the 1977 runway collision at Tenerife Airport in the Canary Islands, when misunderstood instructions caused 583 deaths. But more often, poor listening results in millions of little time-wasting mistakes a day—the wrong coffee order, credit card charge, or telephone number. Ms. Bentley spends hours with medical managers because of the massive liability awards doctors and hospitals can pay in response to poor listening. "People are realizing," she says, "that a lot of mistakes we attributed to other things are actually listening problems."[11]

At Starbucks Coffee Company stores, where a customer can order a "double-shot decaf grande iced half-skim vanilla dry cappuccino," employees are taught a procedure for hearing and calling orders developed by the company five years ago. It systematizes the sequence of words describing the drink—size, flavoring, milk, decaf—with automatic defaults. Then the person making the drink echoes the order aloud. "We expect our employees to listen," says Alan Gulick, a Starbucks spokesperson. "It's an important component of customer service."[12]

Listening is the central skill in the establishment and maintenance of interpersonal relationships. No matter what type of relationship—professional, personal, neighborly, romantic—listening is the skill that forms the bond and keeps the relationship moving forward. Harvard psychologist Daniel Goleman says, "Listening is a skill that keeps couples together. Even in the heat of an argument, when both are seized by emotional hijacking, one or the other, and sometimes both, can manage to listen past the anger, and hear and respond to a partner's reparative gesture."[13]

THE BENEFITS OF BETTER LISTENING

James J. Floyd, who has taught and written on this subject for many years, offers four specific benefits you'll obtain from becoming a better listener: increased knowledge, job success, improved interpersonal relations, and self-protection.[14]

Scholars of human behavior have shown a steady tendency during the past 50 years in the United States toward more passive learning techniques and more passive leisure activities. As a society, we spend more time watching television, movies, and videos, and less time reading. Coincidentally, we also spend more time these days listening to CDs, tapes, radio, and MP3s.

A study conducted by UNISYS Corporation reported that students spend 60–70 percent of their time in a classroom listening.[15] Professors Nichols and Stevens found in their studies at the University of Minnesota that every group of students receiving instruction in listening improved by at least 25 percent, while some groups improved by as much as 40 percent.[16] Without some instruction in listening improvement, however, it appears that the listening abilities of most people actually decline from elementary school on.[17]

A number of other good reasons exist for you to improve your listening:

- **Listening demonstrates acceptance.** The very act of listening to another person demonstrates that you value him or her and care about what he or she is saying. If you show that you *don't care* about others, they'll quit talking to you. Good, perhaps, in the short run, but disastrous in the long term.
- **Listening promotes problem-solving abilities.** Good managers are often asked to do what bartenders, cab drivers, and counselors have done for years: allow someone the time and attention to talk through a problem. Rather than providing advice and solutions right away, most successful managers encourage employees to arrive at solutions on their own. By listening carefully and reflectively, a supervisor can guide a subordinate to a solution that has a greater chance for success and substantially greater levels of employee buy-in.
- **Listening increases the speaker's receptiveness to the thoughts and ideas of others.** The best ideas don't always come from yourself or your immediate staff and colleagues. Often, you'll find great ideas where you least expect them. They may come from your customers, your employees, your suppliers and business partners, and (interestingly) from people who refuse to do business with you. You might be genuinely surprised at what your competitor's customers are saying about you, if only you'd take the time to listen to them.
- **Listening increases the self-esteem of the other person.** You are not personally responsible for the self-esteem of everyone in your organization, but think about it for a moment. Isn't it easier to come to work, concentrate on the tasks at hand, and compete successfully if you feel good about yourself? Sales managers have known intuitively for years that self-esteem is crucial to a sales representative's ability to succeed. They hear "no" so often that they come to accept failure as an inevitable part of the job. Having a manager who'll listen to them willingly and uncritically can be enormously helpful.
- **Listening helps you overcome self-consciousness and self-centeredness.** A little instruction and some practice in active listening can help talkers to shut up and the self-consciously shy to open up. Working more toward the center of the "listening-talking" continuum can be especially helpful to junior managers who are inclined to offer opinions when the demand for them is not especially brisk.
- **Listening can help to prevent head-on emotional collisions.** If you concentrate on your own needs to the exclusion of other people's needs and interests, you will find that others will return the favor: They will focus on their own interests and not yours. The key to preventing

the sort of emotional train wrecks that are destructive to any organization is to put other people's needs ahead of your own. Find out what their concerns and interests are first—by listening carefully to them—and you will likely get what you want sooner and with substantially less angst.

By taking responsibility for successful communication through active and reflective listening, you can become more successful at those activities that depend on communication, including your personal and professional life. You can learn more, improve your relationships with others around you, and increase your chances for success. Careful listening is no guarantee, of course, but it's a wonderful place to start.

THE ROLE OF INEFFECTIVE LISTENING HABITS

Ralph Nichols, followed by a number of other researchers, was early to discover that many of us employ listening habits that are ineffective and may interfere with learning. The problem is not that we *can't* listen or *don't* listen. It's far more likely that we've learned to listen *haphazardly* and in ways that are simply counterproductive.

The first step in becoming a more effective listener, both in the workplace and in our personal lives, is to identify the poor listening habits we've developed over a lifetime and replace them with effective, productive habits.

AN INVENTORY OF POOR LISTENING HABITS

Here, then, are a few habits that hinder rather than help as we try to listen to what others are telling us:

BEING PREOCCUPIED WITH TALKING, NOT LISTENING The most successful CEOs, board chairs, military generals, university presidents—that handful of enormously talented high achievers who run large and complex organizations—without exception are far more interested in listening to what others have to say than they are in talking. When they talk, they invariably ask questions—to gather information, to solicit opinions, to "take the pulse" of the organization. When they speak, the sentences tend to be brief, cogent, and terse. They succeed by gathering up what others know and sharing what they know selectively.

CALLING THE SUBJECT UNINTERESTING We've all done it. You can probably recall doing it in algebra class or, perhaps, during a lecture on a subject you had little interest in knowing anything about. Many have paid dearly for this error by declaring that everything from cost accounting to microeconomics just "isn't especially interesting." If you declare a subject to be dull, you virtually guarantee that you'll learn nothing about it. Some subjects may be a bit duller than others, but in order to learn anything at all, you'll have to be somewhat selfish and tell yourself, "This may not be fascinating, but there's something in here that's important for me to know." Taking an interest in the subject is the first step.

LETTING BIAS OR PREJUDICE DISTORT THE MESSAGES YOU HEAR We all have biases. They are an important, almost inescapable part of who we are and the kind of lives we've led. By filtering incoming messages through these biases, stereotypes, or prejudices, however, we put another speaker's intentions at risk. We hear what our biases tell us to hear and not what's being said. The best advice is not to rid yourself of your preferences but simply to know what they are. Don't let your views on a particular subject or about a particular speaker interfere with what you're hearing.

OVERSIMPLIFYING ANSWERS OR EXPLANATIONS This form of uncritical listening comes from an all-too-understandable desire to reduce the complex to something simpler, to eliminate detail, to tighten up arguments that depend on important detail. Listen carefully to what's being said and later examine those parts of the explanation or answer that may be eliminated, keeping what's most valuable or useful.

YIELDING TO EXTERNAL DISTRACTIONS It's certainly easy to be distracted. If you work in a cubicle rather than a private office, you may be exposed to a half-dozen or more conversations at once. Carol Hymowitz of the *Wall Street Journal* says, "In this open-space era, aimed at flattening hierarchies and promoting teamwork, managers . . . have to adapt to less privacy and more contact, to being constantly seen and heard as they make decisions and deals." Learning to focus on the task at hand, whether it's a phone conversation or a face-to-face meeting with an employee, is crucial to success as a listener.[18]

YIELDING TO INTERNAL DISTRACTIONS These can come from anywhere, even (or especially) when you're isolated and trying to concentrate. Put aside your personal concerns—everything from car payments to your next appointment—and devote just a few minutes to the listening task at hand, and you will find far fewer problems in your life. A few minutes spent concentrating on the words you are hearing will pay big dividends all week.

AVOIDING DIFFICULT OR DEMANDING MATERIAL This problem is akin to an earlier one we talked about—it's just as bad to say that a subject is difficult as it is to say it's dull or uninteresting. By staying with subjects and material you know and are already comfortable with, you limit your ability to grow intellectually. Any debate or forensics coach will tell you that listening is a skill, just like putting in golf or a free throw in basketball. If you are unwilling to work at it, you are unlikely to get any better.

RATIONALIZING POOR LISTENING We all can point to various people or circumstances to blame poor listening habits on: "No one taught me how to do this." "This office is filled with noise and distractions." "I've never paid much attention to listening as a skill." Don't give up. And don't accept that 25 percent efficiency rate as something you can't do anything about. Effective, active listening is important and you can improve.

CRITICIZING THE SPEAKER'S DELIVERY Rather than focus on the speaker's accent, pacing, or phrasing, concentrate instead on the message they carry. Look for both cognitive and emotional content, but give the speaker a break. Most people haven't had much formal training in public speaking and, in the course of casual conversation, directional changes and fluency breaks are common. Concentrate on *what's* being said rather than *how* it's said.

JUMPING TO CONCLUSIONS Formulating a response prematurely may disrupt the speaker's thoughts, may take the conversation in an unintended direction, or may reveal that you do not understand what the speaker has been trying to say. Rather than predicting the direction or outcome of a conversation, give your partner an opportunity to get to the point. Relax and let him or her talk for a little while.

GETTING OVERSTIMULATED If you're more concerned about your response than about what's being said to you, chances are good that you will miss much of what you are hearing. "There's the old joke," says communications consultant Wicke Chambers. "The opposite of talking isn't listening. It's waiting to talk. That's what a lot of people do," she says. "They just wait to talk." The advice? Take it all in, think about it, then formulate a response. Go one step at a time.

ASSIGNING THE WRONG MEANING TO WORDS This habit sounds remarkably simple, but we do it every day, at home, at work, and at school. Some words have specific meaning and you can, in fact, look them up. (*Enormity* meaning "excessive wickedness" or "beyond all moral bounds," rather than "largeness" or "big.") Others require interpretation. ("The customer says he needs this right away." Does that mean 20 minutes from now? By the close of business? Or will sometime this week be okay? You'd better ask.)

LISTENING ONLY FOR THE FACTS On the face of it, this habit doesn't sound like such a bad idea. ("I wish he'd get to the point.") The problem, however, is that if we listen *only* for the facts, all we'll have is facts. We won't have any real understanding of why the issue is important, how it's linked to other issues, or what the implications or outcomes may be. Along the way, you have to listen for context, connections, and those rhetorical ligatures that link facts to human experience.

TRYING TO MAKE AN OUTLINE OF EVERYTHING WE HEAR Because so little of what we'll hear from one day to the next is really organized in any systematic way, forcing it into an outline is not a good idea. Not many extemporaneous speeches and few impromptu conversations are based on any sort of organized outline. Don't force what you hear into artificial patterns. Just take it in, sort it out as you go along, and try as best you can to make sense of what the speaker is saying.

FAKING ATTENTION TO THE SPEAKER This skill, learned in high school and college classrooms all over the country, later develops as a high art form in business meetings everywhere. You don't want to seem impolite, so you smile and nod. The speaker thinks you not only understand but also agree! The fact is, you haven't heard a word that's been said, but you've given the impression that you have. As a direct result, the speaker is unlikely to repeat any information, offer additional examples or illustrations, or seek questions from those who might appear confused or curious.

LETTING EMOTION-LADEN WORDS THROW US OFF THE TRACK Most intelligent speakers know well enough to avoid racist, sexist, or profane language precisely because it is offensive to so many people. But what about words or phrases that have some emotional attachment for you that a speaker would have no clue about? Sometimes the attachment is personal (a date or a song title, for example); more often, it's a topic or subject reference that can set you off (taxes, for instance). It's easier said than done, but stay in control of your emotions and pay attention, at least until the conversation or speech is finished.

RESISTING THE TEMPTATION TO INTERRUPT One of the by-products of the imbalance between talkers and listeners is interruption, with three or four people talking and no one listening. "We have become a nation of interrupters," says Prof. Kathy Thompson. It's as true at home as it is in business, where several people may be vying for the boss's attention, and none much cares what his or her competitors are saying. According to Sam Nelson, director of debate at the University of Rochester, "People want to take credit for things. If you're the first person to get it out, it's yours. So you go into the meeting thinking, 'I'm going to get this out if it kills me.' " That also helps explain the disappearance of the pause from many people's speech. Many experts see the value of pausing, however, saying that it signals a sense of confidence. If you are confident in your ideas, confident in your position, it will probably pay for you to wait your turn and avoid interrupting others.

WASTING THE DIFFERENTIAL BETWEEN THE RATE AT WHICH WE SPEAK AND THE RATE AT WHICH WE THINK If all this weren't bad enough, biology also works against attentive listening. Most people speak at a rate of 120–150 words a minute, but the human brain can easily process more than 500 words a minute, leaving plenty of time for what Cynthia Crossen calls *mental fidgeting.* "If the speaker also happens to be slow, monotonal and wordy," she adds, "it requires a heroic effort to stay tuned instead of simply faking it."[19]

DEVELOPING GOOD LISTENING HABITS

Researchers at UNISYS Corporation identified ways in which you can review your ineffective habits, identify those you should replace, and substitute more effective strategies for listening, learning, and remembering. In fact, they described more than a dozen habits you may wish to consider for your own inventory of communication skills.

STOP TALKING This approach doesn't occur to many people, but it is effective.

ONE CONVERSATION AT A TIME You can't talk on the phone and have a conversation with someone in the room at the same time. Choose the conversation you most want to have and tell the other person you'll be available in a few minutes.

EMPATHIZE WITH THE PERSON SPEAKING Put yourself in his or her shoes; try as best you can to see it from the other person's point of view. It's not easy to listen empathetically, but it's important to try.

ASK QUESTIONS If you are confused, lost, or need information, ask for clarification. Simple questions that seek data, positions, or intentions can be especially helpful.

DON'T INTERRUPT Asking questions may be useful, but initially at least it may be more helpful simply to let your conversation partner talk for a bit. If the conversation has any substance at all, it won't be long before you have an opportunity to react.

SHOW INTEREST Demonstrate complete interest in what's being said to you. Look the talker in the eyes, show interest with your facial expression, and maintain an open and nonthreatening posture. Show that you care.

GIVE YOUR UNDIVIDED ATTENTION If you can, close the door, hold your calls, and give all of your attention to whomever is speaking. If privacy isn't possible, at least put aside what you're working on, reading, or doing. If you really need some conversational privacy and your office isn't set up for that sort of thing, you might consider going for a walk. Low tones and a steady pace will usually provide you with an opportunity to speak in confidence.

EVALUATE FACTS AND EVIDENCE Listen critically. Ask yourself (and, perhaps, your conversation partner) how you know this information is true. What's the source of your confidence in the data? Ask whether the evidence is recent, reliable, accurate, and relevant to the subject.

REACT TO IDEAS, NOT TO THE SPEAKER It's tough to separate the message from the messenger, but give it a try. We often choose to believe what we hear based on who we hear it from. Wherever possible, look beyond your assessment of the speaker to the ideas contained in the speech.

WISHING DOESN'T MAKE IT SO Just because you want to hear it doesn't mean it is what the speaker is saying. Shakespeare's phrase "The wish is father to the thought" means simply that we don't listen carefully because we're often engaged in a great deal of wishful thinking.

LISTEN FOR WHAT IS NOT SAID If you expect to hear something and don't, perhaps it's time to ask why you haven't. Match your expectations of the speaker's content against what you actually hear, and think carefully about what hasn't been said.

LISTEN TO HOW SOMETHING IS SAID We told you earlier not to criticize the speaker's delivery and that's still a useful rule. You should consider listening, however, for the emotional content, for hints of sarcasm, cynicism, or irony in what you hear. Often a speaker will downplay criticism or make light of a key point simply with a shift in his or her tone of voice. Tune in to the speaker's mood and intention, as well as the content of the speech.

SHARE THE RESPONSIBILITY FOR COMMUNICATION It's not entirely the speaker's responsibility to make sure you understand what's being said. You have an obligation to seek out information that's useful or important to you. Focus, concentrate, ask questions, pay attention to what's going on.[20]

THE FIVE ESSENTIAL SKILLS OF ACTIVE LISTENING

To become an effective, empathetic, and skilled listener, you must participate in the dialogue. This process is much more active than the one you use when listening to speeches, lectures, or in meetings. The dialogue process involves you and one or two other people engaged in direct conversation. To increase your probability of success, here are five skills you should practice and master.

PARAPHRASE OTHERS AS THEY SPEAK From time-to-time in a conversation, it will be useful for you to summarize what others are saying. It's helpful to use your own words to do this, but you must do it to their satisfaction in order to convince them you are really listening. Such summaries often begin with a phrase similar to this: "If I understand you correctly, what you're saying is . . . ," or "In other words, you're telling me that. . . ."

REFLECT FEELINGS Some managers will look intently for the meaning in a spoken sentence without paying much attention to the emotional load attached to it. Try, as best you can, to grasp the affective intent of the speaker. Summaries that reflect feeling might sound like this: "You're not very confident about this, are you?" or "You seem determined to see this through."

REFLECT MEANING It's always helpful for a manager to focus on the cognitive or logical content of a discussion—the facts at hand, how they're organized, and how they bear on the topic being discussed. Consider this reflection of a conversation's meaning: "When you say you will need help with this project, am I correct in assuming you mean you will require additional support staff, particularly in the start-up phase?"

REFLECT CONCLUSIONS Discussions can ramble far and wide and can include a great deal of information that may not be directly relevant. It's often useful to review what you have agreed to or concluded, particularly as a conversation is drawing to a conclusion. A summary reflecting the conclusion of a conversation might sound like this: "So, considering the cost of the upgrade and our other immediate needs, am I right in assuming you are not in favor of the purchase?"

FOLLOW THROUGH Important as listening is, follow-through is even more so. Calvin Morrill, a professor of sociology at the University of Arizona, cautions that once you have asked for feedback, "unless you take steps that show your employees that you've listened to them and intend to take action, they will never speak again. In cases like those," he says, "the manager would have been better off never having asked at all."[21]

A SYSTEM FOR IMPROVING YOUR LISTENING HABITS

The time you spend preparing for your quarterly or semiannual performance review might be a good time to review your communication habits in general and your listening habits in particular. If you're serious about becoming a better listener, consider this four-step process.

1. **Review your listening inventory.** Make a few notes about those habits and behaviors that dominate your communication from day to day. Think, in particular, about those that you most often use and which seem to work best or work least for you.
2. **Recognize your undesirable listening habits.** If you display, even occasionally, any of those habits we have listed above as undesirable, make a note of them: which ones, how often, and under what circumstances (i.e., one-on-one conversations with employees, during meetings with colleagues and coworkers, and so on).
3. **Refuse to tolerate undesirable habits.** Even if the undesirable habits you list are infrequent and don't seem particularly serious, refuse to tolerate them as a part of your communication skill inventory. Tag them for removal and get to work on them.
4. **Replace undesirable habits with effective ones.** For every unproductive, undesirable, or negative listening habit you have, identify a positive habit or skill to replace it. Don't simply tell yourself you won't daydream during a lecture; work out a system to use the spare time effectively.[22]

Becoming a good listener carries some risks. Talkers can attach themselves to you like barnacles to a boat, and detaching them isn't easy. Good listeners can also find themselves on the receiving end of other people's problems, even when they may have little to offer in the way of support or counsel. But the rewards can be enormous for developing this skill, both for you as an individual and for the organization that employs you. Remember: Putting other people's needs ahead of your own may seem counterintuitive, but doing so will help both you and others achieve your goals sooner, more efficiently, and less stressfully. It's in your best interest to care about how well you listen.

Child psychologist Robert Coles, who teaches psychiatry and medical humanities at Harvard Medical School, cautions that listening is more than a set of cognitive skills—it's an approach to life and other people that involves the whole person. "I think real listening is something you do with your whole self," he says. "You have to hear what people are really saying beneath all the words. You have to pick up the messages that have a certain urgency and then respond to these nuances with further questions. Over the years," he notes, "I've learned that really attentive listening requires conversational responsiveness. You have to try to listen in such a way that you can respond with your own ideas and feelings and aspirations—so that you can show the speaker you've truly been paying attention."[23]

GIVING AND RECEIVING FEEDBACK

When he was mayor of New York City, Ed Koch frequently walked the streets of his hometown asking his constituents, "How am I doing?" The question wasn't simply rhetorical; nor was it a ritualistic greeting for his faithful supporters. He asked the question of friend and foe alike. He cared about the responses he received because his ability to perform as that city's mayor depended on *feedback*—direct, honest, current, unfiltered feedback. If he wasn't doing well, New Yorkers let him know about it. When he performed to their satisfaction, they told him. For a public official, honest feedback is almost as important as campaign contributions. It is no less important to a manager in the private sector.

Kent Thiry is a prime example of an executive trying to avoid one of the most common and dangerous traps of corporate leadership: the higher an executive climbs, the easier it is for him to distance himself from problems. Top company officials are often surrounded by people who filter out bad news. They then convince themselves their strategies are working, even when they're not.

Mr. Thiry is the chief executive of DaVita of El Segundo, California, a large dialysis-treatment operator, who starts worrying that he is out of touch when all he hears is good news. He recently mingled with employees at an annual staff gathering, learning all he could about the company's buyout of Gambro Healthcare. When several people told him they thought it was "a fun process," he realized people were just telling him what he wanted to hear, rather than the truth. His efforts to build a truth-telling culture that provides honest feedback for executives is beginning to pay off: The company has reduced turnover by 50 percent and grown revenues by more than $5 billion. How do top executives know they're getting accurate feedback? Some comes from worker surveys, but much of it is culled at town hall meetings. Mr. Thiry holds about 20 a year and tells each of his vice presidents to convene one whenever they are with at least seven "teammates" or employees. "Most important," says Mr. Thiry, "is for executives who seek frank feedback to be candid about their own shortcomings."[24]

Good feedback doesn't just happen. It's the product of careful, deliberate communication strategies, coupled with good interpersonal communication skills. You can significantly increase the probability of communication success if you understand the role of feedback in both personal and professional communication.[25]

GUIDELINES FOR CONSTRUCTIVE FEEDBACK

Now that you have improved your listening skills, it may be time to focus on how and when to provide feedback to others. Here are a few suggestions.

ACKNOWLEDGE THE NEED FOR FEEDBACK The first thing we each must recognize as communicators is the value of giving and receiving feedback, both positive and negative. Feedback is vital to any organization committed to improving itself, because it is the only way for managers and executives to know what needs to be improved. Giving and receiving feedback should be more than just a part of an employee's behavior; it should be a part of the whole organization's culture.

You will need high-level feedback skills to improve your organizational meetings and, more generally, interactions between employees. These skills will also help you communicate more effectively with customers and suppliers. In fact, you will find many opportunities to apply these skills across your working environment.

GIVE BOTH POSITIVE AND NEGATIVE FEEDBACK Many people take good work for granted and give feedback only when they encounter problems. This policy is counterproductive; people will more likely pay attention to your complaints if they have also received your compliments. It is important to remember to tell people when they have done something well.

UNDERSTAND THE CONTEXT The most important characteristic of feedback is that it always has a context: where it happened, why it happened, what led up to an event. You should never simply walk up to a person, deliver a feedback statement, and then leave. Before you give feedback, review the actions and decisions that led up to the moment. Every communication event exists in a context and if you don't understand the context to the events you're thinking of criticizing, your comments are unlikely to have a positive effect on others.

PROVIDE DEFINITIONS Don't assume that the person you are counseling or offering feedback to will understand the words, phrases, or terms you're using. Make certain that the language you use is both acceptable to the person you're speaking with and appropriate for the circumstances. More to the point, make sure you're using words whose meaning you both clearly understand and agree on. A simple example may help: *The American Heritage Dictionary of the English Language* lists 93 separate and distinct meanings for the word *get*. When you use that word in conversation, what do you mean? Some scholars now say the 500 most commonly used words in our language have more than 14,000 dictionary definitions. The fact is, the more meanings assigned to a word, the less it means. Make sure people understand you by providing definitions, examples, and illustrations. You may even need to provide exceptions and limits. Make sure people understand the language you're using as you provide feedback to them.[26]

USE A COMMON LANGUAGE Don't speak in a language that your conversation partner is likely to misunderstand, misconstrue, or misinterpret. Use words, phrases, terms, and ideas that are in line with what you know about that person. If you are sure he understands an acronym or company jargon, it's probably okay to use it, but if you're dealing with someone who doesn't share the same frame of reference you do, avoid language that will cause confusion.

DON'T ASSUME Making assumptions invariably gets you into trouble. During interpersonal communications, it is dangerous to make the assumption that the other person either thinks or feels as you do at that moment. Communication consultant Tony Alessandra says, "The other person may have a frame of reference that is totally different from your own. She reacts and perceives according to what she knows and believes to be true, and that may be different from your own reactions, perceptions and beliefs." To avoid the problems inherent in assumptions, ask for direct feedback, check on facts, examine underlying assumptions, and use a healthy dose of skepticism before you say, "I know exactly what you mean."

FOCUS ON BEHAVIOR RATHER THAN PEOPLE When people receive feedback, especially feedback from a supervisor or superior, they are often defensive, fearful, and likely to take anything you say as a personal assault. Defuse the hostility, minimize the fear, and depersonalize the conversation by focusing your comments on the behavior involved and not the people. Saying "These trip reports need additional information," is substantially less threatening than saying, "Why can't you fill out a trip report correctly?"

KNOW WHEN TO GIVE FEEDBACK Before deciding to offer feedback, determine whether the moment is right. You must consider more than your own need to give feedback. Constructive feedback can happen only within a context of listening to and caring about the other person. If the time isn't right, if the moment isn't appropriate, you can always delay briefly before offering your thoughts. Don't wait too long or you'll find that feedback won't be helpful, but choose your moments wisely.

Deborah Lake is a manager at SC Johnson who moved from a traditional office to a cubicle last year at the company's Commercial Markets headquarters. She quickly figured out that she had to unlearn advice on speaking forcefully in business conversations. Everyone, in fact, had to lower their voices in the open space to preserve their privacy and avoid disturbing the person in the adjacent cubicle. She doesn't hesitate to speak loudly, however, when giving positive feedback. "I want others to hear if I tell someone they've done a wonderful job, because I want that person to be recognized," she says. But if it's negative feedback, she speaks quietly.[27]

KNOW HOW TO GIVE FEEDBACK Providing constructive, useful feedback involves more than simply responding to people as they speak to you. Effective feedback involves an understanding of the language, people's intentions as they speak (or choose not to speak), the context in which the communication takes place, and your objectives as a manager.

KNOWING WHEN NOT TO GIVE FEEDBACK

You shouldn't attempt to give feedback to another person when:

- You don't know much about the circumstances of the behavior.
- You don't care about the person or will not be around long enough to follow up on the aftermath of your feedback. Hit-and-run feedback is not fair.
- The feedback, positive or negative, is about something the person has no power to change.
- The other person seems low in self-esteem.
- You are low in self-esteem.
- Your purpose is not really improvement but to put someone on the spot ("gotcha!") or demonstrate how smart or how much more responsible you are.
- The time, place, or circumstances are inappropriate (e.g., in the presence of a customer or other employees).

KNOWING HOW TO GIVE EFFECTIVE FEEDBACK

Most of us would prefer a trip to the dentist than a performance review session with an employee who isn't performing up to company standards. The irony is that while many managers will do all they can to avoid giving face-to-face feedback to an employee, they'll gladly complain about it in detail to their colleagues and peers.

Jamie Resker, the founder and president of Employee Performance Solutions, says we often steer clear of challenging feedback sessions with employees because we don't know what to say.

"The employee is due to retire in two years anyway . . . I'm worried about the employee's reaction . . . What if I make things worse?" she says. Resker offers three steps to reducing defensive reactions to feedback: first, identify the performance issue. "It's clear that the key reason managers avoid giving feedback is not because they don't understand the problem, but rather because they don't know how to craft a message that is 'sayable' and 'hearable.' "

The second step is to be specific about the desired change. The more detailed and precise the description of what you want, the greater the chance your employee will understand you and begin to visualize the behavior you're asking for. Finally, Resker advises managers to detail the benefits of making the change. Show your employees the value of what you're asking for and explain how their lives and the company's performance will improve.[28]

The following suggestions should make it easier for you to provide feedback that works for another person.

BE DESCRIPTIVE Relate, as objectively as possible, what you saw the other person do or what you heard the other person say. Give specific examples, the more recent, the better. Examples from the distant past are more likely to lead to disagreement over the facts.

BE OBJECTIVE Objectivity may not be possible, but it's worth trying anyway. Do what you can to remove subjectivity from your discussions with others when you're providing feedback, at least at the beginning of the discussion. When it's time to offer personal opinions or subjective observations, identify them as such and explain that "it's only my view." Wherever possible, stick to the facts and focus on what you know for sure.

DON'T USE LABELS Be clear, specific, and unambiguous. Words such as *immature*, *unprofessional*, *irresponsible*, and *prejudiced* are labels we attach to a set of behaviors. Describe the behavior and drop the labels. For example, say "You missed the deadline we had all agreed to meet," rather than "You're being irresponsible and I want to know what you're going to do about it."

DON'T EXAGGERATE Be exact. To say "You're always returning late from your lunch break" is probably untrue and, therefore, unfair. It invites the feedback receiver to argue with the exaggeration rather than respond to the real issue.

DON'T BE JUDGMENTAL Or at least don't use the rhetoric of judgment. Words such as *good*, *better*, *bad*, *worst*, and *should* place you in the role of a controlling parent. This approach invites the person receiving your comments to respond as a child. When that happens, and it will most of the time, the possibility of constructive feedback is lost.

SPEAK FOR YOURSELF Don't refer to absent, anonymous people; don't attempt to speak for your supervisor or for people much higher up the line. Avoid such references as "A lot of people here don't like it when you. . . ." Don't allow yourself to be a conduit for other people's complaints. Instead, encourage others to speak for themselves. You must take responsibility for your own job, but don't attempt to speak on others' behalf.

TALK FIRST ABOUT YOURSELF, NOT ABOUT THE OTHER PERSON Use a statement with either the word *I* or the word *we* as the subject, not the word *you*. This guideline is one of the most important and one of the most surprising. Consider the following examples regarding lateness:

1. "You are frequently late for meetings."
2. "You are not very prompt for meetings."
3. "I feel annoyed when you are late for meetings."
4. "We appreciate your coming to meetings on time."

The first two statements begin with second-person pronouns. People can become defensive when criticism begins with *you* and may be less likely to hear what you say when feedback is phrased as direct criticism. The last two statements begin with first-person pronouns and can help to create an adult/peer relationship. People are more likely to remain open to your message when the criticism does not appear to be aimed directly at them. Even if your rank is higher than the feedback recipient's, strive for an adult/peer relationship. Try using first-person statements (*I* or *we*) so the effectiveness of your comments is not lost in the accusation.

PHRASE THE ISSUE AS A STATEMENT, NOT AS A QUESTION Contrast "When are you going to stop being late for meetings?" with "We can't begin the meeting on time when you are late." The question is controlling and manipulative because it implies "You, the responder, are expected to adjust your behavior to accommodate me, the questioner." Most people become defensive and angry when spoken to in this way. On the other hand, I or we statements imply, "I think we have an issue we must resolve together." The I statement allows the receiver to see what effect the behavior had on you.

ENCOURAGE PEOPLE TO CHANGE Feedback must focus on things the recipient has the power to change. Most people can't change such basic personality preferences as shyness or a preference for openness over closure. But they can change the behavioral outcomes that affect the workplace. Leaving a set of sensitive documents scattered across a desktop is an outcome that a manager can focus on regardless of personality preferences. Focus on those issues that are both important to improvement and well within the power of the other person to change.

RESTRICT YOUR FEEDBACK TO THINGS YOU KNOW FOR CERTAIN Don't present your opinions as facts. Speak only of what you saw and heard and what you feel or think. If you're not sure or can't say so with certainty, hold your comments. Feedback based on speculation or second-hand information may be far more destructive than you imagine. Make sure of what you know and then act on it.

BUILD TRUST Although people occasionally learn valuable lessons from those they don't get along with, feedback is always more readily accepted if it comes from a trusted source. The psychological research on trust has shown that persuasive messages from a trusted source always produce greater impact and longer-lasting results. Skillful managers will use each opportunity for feedback to establish useful working relationships and build long-term trust.

HELP PEOPLE HEAR AND ACCEPT YOUR COMPLIMENTS WHEN GIVING POSITIVE FEEDBACK Many people feel awkward when told good things about themselves and will fend off the compliment ("Oh, it wasn't that big a deal. I just helped another manager put together a proposal.") Sometimes they will change the subject. It may be important to reinforce the positive feedback and help the person hear it, acknowledge it, and accept it.[29]

KNOWING HOW TO RECEIVE FEEDBACK

At times you may receive feedback from someone who does not know feedback guidelines. In these cases, *help your critic refashion the criticism* so that it conforms to the rules for constructive feedback ("Tell me what we can do to improve the conditions in your department."). When reacting to feedback:

BREATHE Our bodies are conditioned to react to stressful situations as though they were physical assaults. Our muscles tense. We start breathing rapidly and shallowly. We need to follow some simple advice: Take full, deep breaths to force our bodies to relax and allow our brains to maintain greater alertness.

LISTEN CAREFULLY Don't interrupt. Don't discourage the feedback-giver. You can't benefit from feedback you don't hear.

ASK QUESTIONS FOR CLARITY You have a right to receive clear feedback. Ask for specific examples. ("Can you describe what I do or say that makes me appear hostile to you?") If you don't understand terminology or references, request an explanation.

ACKNOWLEDGE THE FEEDBACK Paraphrase the message in your own words to let the person know you have heard and understood what was said. Don't simply sit there silently. Provide the other person with both verbal and nonverbal indicators that you've heard and understand what's been said. Remember, this situation isn't any easier for the other person than it is for you.

ACKNOWLEDGE VALID POINTS Agree with what is true. Agree with what is possible. Acknowledge the other person's point of view ("I understand how you might get that impression") and try to understand their reaction. Agreeing with what's true or possible does not mean you agree to change your behavior. You can agree, for instance, that you sometimes jump too quickly to a conclusion without implying that you will slow down your conclusion-making process. Agreeing with what's true or possible also does not mean agreeing with any value judgment about you. You can agree that your work has been slow lately without agreeing that you are irresponsible.

DON'T BE DEFENSIVE Most of us don't take direct criticism well. We often spend part of the conversation planning our response (or defense), rather than listening carefully to what's being said. Don't listen *passively*; ask questions, inquire about issues that you don't understand or that aren't clear to you. But avoid the temptation to draw your sword and do battle then and there. Most feedback provided to you by a superior is carefully thought out in advance and is designed with your best interests and improvement in mind. Take it for what it's worth: an opportunity to improve your performance and chances for success.

TRY TO UNDERSTAND THE OTHER PERSON'S OBJECTIVES Whether you're listening to your subordinates or to your own boss, you'll never fully understand what they're saying unless you set aside your own goals and objectives and focus on theirs. Try to see the world from their viewpoint and appreciate what motivates their comments.

TAKE TIME OUT TO SORT OUT WHAT YOU HEARD You may need time for sorting out or checking with others before responding to the feedback. It is reasonable to ask the feedback-giver for time to think about what was said and how you feel about it. Make a specific appointment for getting back to him or her. Don't use this time as an excuse to avoid the issue.[30]

Communication is clearly a two-way process. People who serve in management positions must accept the responsibility for both providing and seeking out information that will be useful in correcting and improving the processes involved. The place to begin is with the recognition that feedback is both a useful and productive part of communication. With careful application of productive listening skills as you interact with others in the workplace, your chances for success are greater.

For Further Reading

Adler, R. and Towne, N. *Looking Out, Looking In.* Fort Worth, TX: Harcourt Brace, 1999.

Barker, L. L. and Watson, K. "The Role of Listening in Managing Interpersonal and Group Conflict." In D. Borisoff and M. Purdy (eds.), *Listening in Everyday Life*, pp. 139–162. New York: University Press of America, 1991.

Collins, S. and O'Rourke, J. S. (ed.). *Interpersonal Communication: Listening and Responding*, 2nd ed. Mason, OH: Cengage South-Western, 2008.

Crossen, C. "Blah, Blah, Blah," *Wall Street Journal*, July 10, 1997, pp. A1, A6.

Fuhrmans, V. "Bedside Manner: An Insurer Tries a New Strategy: Listen to Patients," *Wall Street Journal*, April 11, 2006, p. A1.

Jackman, J. M. and Strober, M. H. "Fear of Feedback," *Harvard Business Review*, April 2003, pp. 101–107.

Morse, G. "Feedback Backlash," *Harvard Business Review*, October 2004, p. 28.

Nichols, M. P. *The Lost Art of Listening: How Learning to Listen Can Improve Relationships.* New York: The Guilford Press, 2009.

Prospero. M. "Leading Listener," *Fast Company*, October 2005, p. 53.

Wilson, G. L. *Let's Talk It Over*, 5th ed. Needham Heights, MA: Pearson, 2000.

Wolvin, A. and Coakley, C. (eds.). *Perspectives on Listening.* Norwood, NJ: Ablex, 1993.

Endnotes

1. Goldsmith, M. "The One Skill That Separates," *Fast Company*, July 2005, p. 86. Reprinted by permission.
2. Ibid.
3. Nichols, R. G. and L. Stevens. *Are You Listening?* New York: McGraw-Hill, 1957.
4. Floyd, J. J. *Listening: A Practical Approach.* Glenview, IL: Scott, Foresman, 1985, pp. 2–3.
5. Nichols, R. G. "Listening Is a 10-Part Skill," in Huseman R. C., et al. (eds.), *Readings in Interpersonal and Organizational Communication.* Boston, MA: Holbrook Press, 1969, pp. 472–479.
6. Crossen, C. "The Crucial Question for These Noisy Times May Just Be: 'Huh?' " *Wall Street Journal*, July 10, 1997, p. A1. Reprinted by permission of *The Wall Street Journal.* Copyright © 1997 Dow Jones & Company, Inc. All rights reserved worldwide.
7. Wolvin, A. D. and C. G. Coakley. *Listening.* Dubuque, IA: Wm. C. Brown, 1982.
8. Crossen. "The Crucial Question," p. A1.
9. Ibid.
10. Ibid.
11. Ibid.
12. Ibid.
13. Goleman, D. *Emotional Intelligence.* New York: Bantam Books, 1995, p. 145.
14. Floyd. *Listening: A Practical Approach*, pp. 2–8.
15. Sperry Corporation. *Your Personal Listening Profile*, 1981.
16. Nichols and Stevens. *Are You Listening?* p. 15.
17. Landry, D. L. "The Neglect of Listening," *Elementary English* 46 (1969), pp. 599–605.
18. Hymowitz, C. "If the Walls Had Ears, You Wouldn't Have Any Less Privacy," *Wall Street Journal*, May 19, 1998, p. B-1. Reprinted by permission of *The Wall Street Journal.*

Copyright © 1998 Dow Jones & Company, Inc. All rights reserved worldwide.

19. This collection of ineffective listening habits was assembled from ideas presented in Nichols and Stevens, *Are You Listening?* "Listening is a 10-Part Skill," pp. 472–479; and Floyd, *Listening: A Practical Approach*, pp. 2–3. See also Alessandra, A. and P. Hunsaker. *Communicating at Work.* New York: Simon & Schuster, 1993, pp. 54–68.

20. This collection of effective listening habits was assembled from ideas presented in Sperry Corporation, *Your Personal Listening Profile.* See also Floyd, *Listening: A Practical Approach*; and Alessandra and Hunsaker, *Communicating at Work*, pp. 54–68.

21. Carvell, T. "By the Way . . . Your Staff Hates You," *Fortune*, September 28, 1998, pp. 200–212.

22. Floyd. *Listening: A Practical Approach*, pp. 34–43.

23. Reprinted by permission of *Harvard Business Review* from "Different Voice: The Inner Life of Executive Kids," *Harvard Business Review*, November 2001, pp. 63–68. Copyright © 2001 by the Harvard Business School Publishing Corporation; all rights reserved.

24. Hymowitz, C. "Executives Who Build Truth-Telling Cultures Learn Fast What Works," *Wall Street Journal*, June 12, 2006, p. B1.

25. For a discussion of the role feedback plays in theoretical communication models, consult Rogers, Everett M. *A History of Communication Study.* New York: The Free Press, 1997, pp. 396–399.

26. Claiborne, R. *Our Marvelous Native Tongue: The Life and Times of the English Language.* New York: Times Books, 1983, pp. 3–24.

27. Hymowitz. "If the Walls Had Ears," p. B1.

28. Resker, J. "3 Keys to Reducing Defensive Reactions to Feedback," HR.com, July 4, 2008. Retrieved from http://www.hr.com on July 15, 2008 at 1:31 P.M.

29. For an extended discussion of feedback technique and applications, see Wolvin and Coakley, *Listening*, pp. 97–99, 214–219, and 223–238.

30. For a discussion of feedback applications in the workplace, see Alessandra and Hunsaker, *Communicating at Work*, pp. 79–90.

CASE STUDY 8-1(A)

Earl's Family Restaurants

The Role of the Regional Sales Manager

Among the more difficult to master, yet less obvious of human communication skills is that of listening. For many managers, listening often seems more of a luxury than a necessity. Time is short, pressures to accomplish work goals are substantial, and communication takes on a one-way character: It's my job to speak; it's your job to listen.

As managers rise from junior to more senior positions in an organization, they gradually discover that more and more of their time is spent in interpersonal communication, face-to-face with subordinates, peers, and superiors. They are less task-oriented, more process-oriented. Gathering information is far less difficult than figuring out what it means.

The key to many management problems often lies in another's perspective. Finding out what others think of an issue, how they view the matter at hand, is frequently useful to a manager. The danger lies in wasted time or misspent effort in such conversations. Somehow learning to make listening a more structured, productive activity becomes increasingly important to managers who have the talent and the will to succeed.

Listening and hearing are not the same thing. Surprisingly, most North American adults listen at an efficiency rate of no more than 25 percent. Yet much of what we need to make decisions, to understand our circumstances, and to solve the problems we face comes to us in an aural form.

Becoming an active listener, a reflective, skilled communicator, is not easy, but it's certainly within reach for the average manager. Acknowledging bad listening habits is a good way to begin the process, systematically replacing such habits with productive, useful listening skills. Knowing that it's possible to become more skilled in this process makes listening one of the central talents that managers must concentrate on early in their careers.

The case of Earl's Family Restaurants involves two roles, each played from a different perspective. One is the regional sales manager for a food service manufacturing firm in the Midwestern United States; the other is the chief buyer for a midsized chain of restaurants, also in the Midwest.

The facts of this case are the same for both participants. As is usual, though, both people see the facts through slightly different eyes. Each has a perspective unique to the position he or she occupies, and each has a set of objectives and goals that accompany the job. As you read the relevant facts in this case and assume your role, keep in mind that you are evaluated by your supervisor on the extent to which you can achieve those job-related goals. Keep in mind, as well, that communication may be one of the tools you can use to reach your objectives.

Your Task

Please read and familiarize yourself with the information in this case. You have been selected to participate in a role-playing exercise designed to demonstrate the importance of communication skills in practical, everyday human interaction. Your portion of this exercise involves only the role of the regional sales manager for Exceptional Food Products, Inc.

Make whatever assumptions you need to in order to play your role, but be convincing as you create your character. The other person involved in this exercise knows many of the same facts about the incident but may have a different perspective on those facts. Do your best to communicate effectively.

The Facts of the Case

You are the regional sales manager for Exceptional Food Products, Inc., of Chicago. You have seven territorial sales representatives who work directly for you, covering a five-state area in the Midwestern United States. Your region includes Illinois, Wisconsin, Iowa, Michigan, and Indiana. Your seven-person team handles more than 200 accounts; you have reserved several, special accounts for yourself, and you handle those customers personally.

Among your more important accounts, both in dollar volume and in years of service, is Earl's Family Restaurants. Your grandfather, who established

Exceptional Food Products, Inc., was a personal friend of Mr. Earl Tolliver of Indianapolis, the founder of Earl's Family Restaurants. Your two families have been doing business together for many years.

About six weeks ago, because of the growing volume of work in your office, you felt it safe to assign the account to your most successful territorial sales representative. This individual is relatively new to restaurant food sales but seems bright, energetic, and eager to succeed. He took the account gladly and, for the moment at least, appears to be doing well with it.

Exceptional Food Products, Inc., provides a full range of packaged goods to restaurants, clubs, schools, institutions, and military installations throughout the country. Your region is one of the more important to the firm and, occasionally, your team leads the nation in sales volume. Your team regularly leads in market penetration. In recent months, however, problems have begun to arise. Customers have complained to delivery people, to your territorial sales representatives, and lately, to you.

Institutional complaints have not been as frequent or as great as restaurant complaints, but they're growing. Among the more routine complaints is one that alleges customers aren't getting what they ordered. On occasion, delivery people will leave a substitute product or two without notifying the restaurant or seeking permission to do so. Deliveries have been late in recent days to a number of customers; your boss tells you a Teamster's job action (a work-to-rule slowdown) in the transportation division and some maintenance problems have slowed things down. That should improve soon, though, he says.

You have lost some customers in recent months to several new market entrants. They seem strongly customer-oriented and are working hard to take away your business. One of the top people in finance at Exceptional Food Products, Inc., tells you that your top new competitor is now a subsidiary of a very large firm, Cub Foods, Inc., that is engaging in a deliberate policy of undercutting you on price. They're willing to lose money for an unspecified period of time in order to push you out of several lucrative markets. Frankly, this is a worrisome development.

The chief buyer for Earl's Family Restaurants has called and asked to meet with you. He is concerned about a number of things that have happened recently and he concludes the phone conversation with this: "Look, if you guys can't do any better than you've done over the past six weeks, we may just have to look somewhere else for a supplier."

Your objective in meeting with the buyer from Earl's is to save that account for Exceptional Food Products and, if possible, convince him that you will be able to beat the competition on both price and service

before long. You simply cannot afford to lose this account—it means nearly 15 percent of total sales for the region.

From your perspective, the problems in this case are primarily—though not entirely—about cost. You are under pressure to cut costs yet deliver the most competitively priced products possible to restaurants that face narrow margins and tough competition.

CASE STUDY 8-1(B)

Earl's Family Restaurants

The Role of the Chief Buyer

Among the more difficult to master, yet less obvious of human communication skills is that of listening. For many managers, listening often seems more of a luxury than a necessity. Time is short, pressures to accomplish work goals are substantial, and communication often takes on a one-way character: It's my job to speak, it's your job to listen.

As managers rise from junior to more senior positions in an organization, they gradually discover that more and more of their time is spent in interpersonal communication, face-to-face with subordinates, peers, and superiors. They are less task-oriented, more process-oriented. Gathering information is far less difficult than figuring out what it means.

The key to many management problems often lies in another's perspective. Finding out what others think of an issue, how they view the matter at hand, is frequently useful to a manager. The danger lies in wasted time or misspent effort in such conversations. Somehow learning to make listening a more structured, productive activity becomes increasingly important to managers who have the talent and the will to succeed.

Listening and hearing are not the same thing. Surprisingly, most North American adults listen at an efficiency rate of no more than 25 percent. Yet much of what we need to make decisions, to understand our circumstances, and to solve the problems we face comes to us in an aural form.

Becoming an active listener, a reflective, skilled communicator is not easy, but it's certainly within reach for the average manager. Acknowledging bad listening habits is a good way to begin the process, systematically replacing such habits with productive, useful listening skills. Knowing that it's possible to become more skilled in this process makes listening one of the central talents that managers must concentrate on early in their careers.

The case of Earl's Family Restaurants involves two roles, each played from a different perspective. One is the regional sales manager for a foodservice manufacturing firm in the Midwestern United States; the other is the chief buyer for a midsized chain of restaurants, also in the Midwest.

The facts of this case are the same for both participants. As is usual, though, both people see the facts through slightly different eyes. Each has a perspective unique to the position he or she occupies, and each has a set of objectives and goals that accompany the job. As you read the relevant facts in this case and assume your role, keep in mind that you are evaluated by your supervisor on the extent to which you can achieve those job-related goals. Keep in mind, as well, that communication may be one of the tools you can use to reach your objectives.

Your Task

Please read and familiarize yourself with the information in this case. You have been selected to participate in a role-playing exercise designed to demonstrate the importance of communication skills in practical everyday human interaction. Your portion of this exercise involves *only* the role of the chief buyer for Earl's Family Restaurants.

Make whatever assumptions you need to in order to play your role, but be convincing as you create your character. The other person involved in this exercise knows many of the same facts about the incident, but may have a different perspective on those facts. Do your best to communicate effectively.

The Facts of the Case

You are the chief buyer for Earl's Family Restaurants of Indianapolis. Your 54-restaurant chain extends throughout the Midwestern United States, with most of your establishments concentrated in Illinois, Indiana, Michigan, and Wisconsin. You have a few restaurants in Kentucky and Ohio. Your firm is publicly held, but the majority shareholder is Earl Tolliver, III, grandson of the restaurant chain's founder. You have been closely associated with the family for many years and have been employed with the firm since you left business school.

Exceptional Food Products, Inc., of Chicago is one of your principal suppliers of packaged goods. You buy most of your condiments, table supplies, canned and packaged restaurant supplies from them. They have done well for you and your firm for many years. Lately, though, you've had some trouble with Exceptional Food Products.

For one thing, your account was assigned about six weeks ago by the regional sales manager at Exceptional Food Products to a territorial sales representative. This person is loud, obnoxious, rarely available, and doesn't seem to know your business particularly well. This sales rep is new to the area and has been in the food business for just three years.

You could put up with this new salesperson if it were just the personality that seemed to get in the way of a good working relationship. After all, there is no interaction with your customers; the only contact is with you and your central buying office. Lately though, other, more serious problems have arisen. Shipments have been late. Often, Exceptional Food Products will show up late on Fridays at your restaurants in Northern Indiana and Southwest Lower Michigan, just in the nick of time to restock for the weekends. Friday nights,

Saturdays, and Sunday breakfasts are typically your busiest times, both in volume and cash flow.

On several occasions, Friday deliveries in South Bend, Benton Harbor, Grand Rapids, and Fort Wayne have simply been postponed until Monday. Last weekend, your Benton Harbor restaurant ran out of several crucial condiments and had to telephone the South Bend restaurant and ask for an emergency transfer by automobile.

Lately, Exceptional Food Products has pulled another clever stunt on you by leaving substitute brands that you didn't order. When your restaurant managers confront the delivery person, he simply says: "Look, here's what's on the invoice. I got no control over what the invoice says or what they load on my truck. I'm just here to deliver what they tell me to deliver."

Your restaurant managers have been stuck with generic labels and off-brands when they clearly specified the national brand of several products. Worse, you've been billed for the national brand. You regard that as a kind of double-whammy: inferior products at name-brand prices.

Your contacts with the new territorial sales representative have been entirely unsatisfactory. You'd really like to do business with the regional sales manager once again, but have had trouble getting together. You have called Exceptional Food Products, Inc., and asked for a meeting with the regional sales manager from Chicago.

Your objective is to let these people know, in no uncertain terms, that their behavior has been unacceptable. You've spent far too much time and money straightening out the account with them and you want them to know that Exceptional Foods is causing more grief than your restaurant managers need.

From your perspective, the problems are entirely about the relationship between the supplier and your company and are focused on deficiencies in service.

Exceptional Foods' task, in your view, is to make life easier for your managers, not harder. If things don't turn around soon, you're considering taking your business to another supplier. The fact that you have been doing business with Exceptional Foods for longer than anyone can remember makes no difference to you or to the Tolliver family. Business is business.

One last item: Don't let the sales manager go until you get an apology from their firm for their behavior. You want their service (and their prices) to improve, but you really want them to recognize what they've done to your business, and an apology is in order.

CASE STUDY 8-1(C)

Earl's Family Restaurants

The Role of the Observer

Among the more difficult to master, yet less obvious of human communication skills is that of listening. For many managers, listening often seems more of a luxury than a necessity. Time is short, pressures to accomplish work goals are substantial, and communication often takes on a one-way character: It's my job to speak, it's your job to listen.

As managers rise from junior to more senior positions in an organization, they gradually discover that more and more of their time is spent in interpersonal communication, face-to-face with subordinates, peers, and superiors. They are less task-oriented, more process-oriented. Gathering information is far less difficult than figuring out what it means.

The key to many management problems often lies in another's perspective. Finding out what others think of an issue, how they view the matter at hand, is frequently useful to a manager. The danger lies in wasted time or misspent effort in such conversations. Somehow learning to make listening a more structured, productive activity becomes increasingly important to managers who have the talent and the will to succeed.

Listening and hearing are not the same thing. Surprisingly, most North American adults listen at an efficiency rate of no more than 25 percent. Yet much of what we need to make decisions, to understand our circumstances, and to solve the problems we face comes to us in an aural form.

Becoming an active listener, a reflective, skilled communicator is not easy, but it's certainly within reach for the average manager. Acknowledging bad listening habits is a good way to begin the process, systematically replacing such habits with productive, useful listening skills. Knowing that it's possible to become more skilled in this process makes listening one of the central talents that managers must concentrate on early in their careers.

The Case at Hand

The case of Earl's Family Restaurants involves two roles, each played from a different perspective. One is the regional sales manager for a food service manufacturing firm in the Midwestern United States; the other is the chief buyer for a midsized chain of restaurants, also in the Midwest.

The facts of this case are the same for both participants. As is usual, though, both people see the facts through slightly different eyes. Each has a perspective unique to the position he or she occupies, and each has a set of objectives and goals that accompany the job. As you read the relevant facts in this case and assume your role, keep in mind that you are evaluated by your supervisor on the extent to which you can achieve those job-related goals.

Your Task

Please read and familiarize yourself with the information in this case. You have been selected to observe a role-playing exercise that is designed to demonstrate the importance of communication skills in practical everyday human interaction. Your task is to observe what happens during the conversation between two people playing the roles of the Chief Buyer for Earl's Family Restaurants and the Regional Sales Manager for Exceptional Food Products, Inc.

Observe and take note of as much as you can during the conversation. Pay particular attention to both verbal and nonverbal communication issues. Note the direction and pace of the conversation. Who takes the lead in speaking? Who responds? What's the general tone of the exchange? Is this a conversation among friends? Are these people colleagues or business partners in a successful enterprise? What's the nature of the relationship between these two people? Does either participant emerge from the conversation having achieved the goals they had set for themselves in advance? Does this exchange between two people involve winners and losers, or are they able to accommodate each other's needs to reach a satisfactory compromise?

The Perspective of the Regional Sales Manager

The regional sales manager for Exceptional Food Products, Inc., manages the work of seven territorial sales representatives over a five-state area in the Midwestern United States. That seven-person team handles more than 200 accounts. Among the more important of those accounts, both in dollar volume and in years of service, is Earl's Family Restaurants.

About six weeks ago, because of growing volume, the regional sales manager assigned the Earl's Family Restaurant account to a successful territorial sales representative. This individual is new to restaurant food sales, but seems bright, energetic, and eager to succeed. From the sales manager's perspective, the new rep seems to be doing well with the account.

Exceptional Food Products, Inc., provides a full range of packaged goods to restaurants, clubs, schools, institutions, and military installations throughout the country. The Midwestern region is one of the more important to the firm and, occasionally, leads the nation in sales volume. This sales team, in fact, regularly leads in market penetration. In recent months, however, problems have begun to arise. Customers have complained to delivery people, to sales reps, and lately, to the sales manager.

Institutional complaints have not been as frequent or as great as restaurant complaints, but they're growing. Among the more routine complaints is one that alleges customers aren't getting what they ordered. On occasion, delivery people will leave a substitute product or two without notifying the restaurant or seeking permission to do so. Delivery truck drivers seem to feel that an occasional substitution is preferable to not delivering a much-needed product.

Deliveries have been late in recent days to a number of customers; the regional sales manager has been told by the national sales manager that a Teamsters job action (a work-to-rule slowdown) in the transportation division and some maintenance problems have slowed things down. According to company officials, that should improve soon.

The company has lost some customers in recent months to new market entrants. They seem strongly customer-oriented and are working hard to take away business. A top new competitor is a subsidiary of a very large firm, Cub Foods, Inc., and they're engaging in a deliberate policy of undercutting Exceptional Food Products on price. They're willing to lose money for an unspecified period of time in order to push Exceptional Foods out of several lucrative markets. This is a worrisome development.

The chief buyer for Earl's Family Restaurants has called and asked to meet directly with the regional sales manager for Exceptional Food Products. He is concerned about a number of things that have happened recently and he concludes the conversation with this: "Look, if you guys can't do any better than you've done over the past six weeks, we may just have to look somewhere else for a supplier."

From the regional sales manager's perspective, the problems are entirely about cost. The sales manager is under pressure to cut costs yet deliver the lowest-priced products possible to restaurants that face narrow margins and tough competition.

The Perspective of the Chief Buyer

The chief buyer for Earl's Family Restaurants resides in Indianapolis and supervises purchasing for a 54-restaurant chain located throughout the Midwestern United States. The firm is publicly held, but the majority shareholder is Earl Tolliver, III, grandson of the company's founder. The chief buyer, incidentally, is married to a member of the Tolliver family and has been with the company since graduating from college.

Exceptional Food Products, Inc., of Chicago is one of the company's principal suppliers of packaged goods. The company buys most of its condiments, table supplies, canned and packaged restaurant supplies from them. They've done well for Earl's Family Restaurants for many years. Lately, though, the company has experienced trouble with Exceptional Foods.

One bone of contention is the assignment of a new sales representative at Exceptional Foods to the account. For many years, the regional sales manager had personally overseen the Earl's account. And, from the perspective of Earl's chief buyer, the new sales rep is loud, obnoxious, never available when needed, and doesn't seem to know the restaurant business particularly well. The new sales rep, in fact, has been in this business for just three years.

Lately, more serious problems have arisen. Shipments have been late. Often, Exceptional Food Products will show up late on Fridays at Earl's restaurants, just in the nick of time to restock for the weekends. Friday nights, Saturdays, and Sunday breakfasts are typically the company's busiest times, both in volume and cash flow. On several occasions, deliveries have been postponed until Monday.

One other contentious issue is the delivery of generic labels and off-brands when the customer clearly specified the national brand of several products. Worse, Earl's has been billed for the national brand. The chief buyer has heard and seen enough and has asked for a personal meeting with the regional sales manager for Exceptional Foods.

From the chief buyer's perspective, the problems are entirely about the relationship between the supplier and the restaurant chain, and are focused on deficiencies in service.

This case was prepared from public sources by James S. O'Rourke, Concurrent Professor of Management, as the basis for class discussion rather than to illustrate either effective or ineffective handling of an administrative situation. Personal and corporate identities have been disguised.

CASE STUDY 8-2(A)

The Kroger Company

The Role of the Store Manager

Among the more difficult to master, yet less obvious of human communication skills is that of providing feedback to others in the workplace. For many managers, feedback must often wait for specified, formal counseling occasions, such as a performance review. Time is short, pressures to accomplish work goals are substantial, and communication often takes on a one-way character: Feedback is used, not to improve communication, but to correct job-related performance issues.

As managers rise from junior to more senior positions in an organization, they gradually discover that more and more of their time is spent in interpersonal communication, face-to-face with subordinates, peers, and superiors. They are less task-oriented, more process-oriented. Gathering information is far less difficult than figuring out what it means.

The key to many management problems often lies in another's perspective. Finding out what others think of an issue, how they view the matter at hand, is frequently useful to a manager. The danger lies in wasted time or misspent effort in such conversations. Somehow learning to make feedback a more structured, productive activity becomes increasingly important to managers who have the talent and the will to succeed.

Feedback is more than simply sending messages or issuing orders. Often, the process involves soliciting information from others so that you can first understand their perspective or point of view. Then, under planned and carefully controlled conditions, information regarding both performance and communication can assist both managers and subordinates in achieving organizational goals.

Knowing that it's possible to become more skilled in this process is the first step. Recognizing that, managers must concentrate early and often on improving their ability to both solicit and provide feedback.

The Role of the Store Manager

This case involves two roles, each played from a different perspective. One is the manager of a midsized] Kroger store in the Louisville Kroger Marketing Area.

The other is the sales manager for a local Pepsi-Cola bottler.

The facts in this case are the same for both participants. As is usual, though, both people see the facts through slightly different eyes. Each has a perspective unique to the position he or she occupies, and each has a set of objectives and goals that accompany the job. As you read the relevant facts in this case and assume your role, keep in mind that you are evaluated by your supervisor on the extent to which you can achieve those job-related goals. Keep in mind, as well, that communication may be one of the tools you can use to reach your objectives.

Your Task

Please read and familiarize yourself with the information contained in this case. You have been selected to participate in a role-playing exercise designed to demonstrate the importance of communication skills in practical everyday human interaction. Make whatever assumptions you need to in order to play your role, but be convincing as you create your character. The other person involved in this exercise knows many of the same facts about the incident, but may have a different perspective on those facts. Do your best to communicate effectively.

The Facts of the Case

You are the manager of the Rosewater, Kentucky, Kroger store, a midsized store that's been in operation for seven years. The store is profitable and has shown strong sales growth over the past three years, despite competition from two other regional chains, one of which opened a year ago, and another that has been in place for five years.

You have been in the retail food business for 11 years, serving as manager of the Rosewater store for the past three months. This is your first store manager's job and you are determined to show the Louisville marketing director that you have management potential.

Soft drink vendors have long been difficult to deal with for several reasons: First, they supply you with high-turn items that are nationally advertised and very popular with your customers; second, they are in constant competition with their rivals for display and shelf space; and, finally, soft drink vendors are often under great pressure from their distributors to push the product.

The local Pepsi-Cola sales manager is a fellow named Roger Willis. He works for a company called Southland Beverages, Inc., and is well known within the company for moving high volumes of product, but for his temper, as well. His drivers rarely speak back to him and are under considerable pressure to comply with his tight schedules, large delivery loads, and nearly impossible quotas. You have spoken with Mr. Willis several times on the telephone but have not yet met him in person.

You can deal with the drivers; after all, they have to earn a living, too, and most of them do a fine job of keeping your store stocked with fresh products at regular intervals. The local Pepsi vendor, however, is another story. Over the past six months his drivers have routinely dropped products you don't want on your loading dock, they're often late with deliveries, they have left quantities you can't sell, and they have been entirely uncooperative with your receiving staff on the dock. Often, they're just rude.

As you ask one of your department heads what happened last Friday, he tells a story that other Kroger employees regard as familiar. "We had a new route man for Pepsi last week and this guy just wouldn't listen to us."

"How so?" you ask. "What'd he do?"

"Well," your employee replies, "in the first place, he dropped nine flats, instead of the three that we asked for. Most of the order was 12-packs, and we're running low on 6-packs. And he arrived right at a shift change, so nobody was really able to spend much time with him."

"What did you say?"

"When I saw nine flats, I asked him 'Why so many?' He just said, 'I'm stocking you up for the weekend.' Man, I'm tellin' you, we couldn't sell nine flats in a week, much less by Monday." You pause for a moment, then ask, "Did you ask him to reload six of those flats on the truck?" Your department head replies, "I sure did, but he said 'Look, here's what's on the invoice. I got no control over what the invoice says or what they load in my truck. I'm just here to deliver what they tell me to deliver. Besides, it'd take me half the night to reslot all this stuff back in the warehouse.'"

"Well," you say, "I think we can fix this."

"That's not all," your employee adds. "He installed that new Pepsi endcap display a week early. The Coke guy saw it this morning and had a fit. He's upset and wants to talk with you about it." "A couple more phone calls to make," you think to yourself. "I think it's time I met Roger Willis."

Your Meeting with Mr. Willis

Your objective is to let Mr. Willis know, in no uncertain terms, that their behavior has been unacceptable. You have spent too much time already dealing with the antics of his drivers. You really want three things from him: First, you want his unconditional assurance that his employees will quit delivering more product than you order and will begin complying with your request for an appropriate product mix.

Second, you want him to arrange for a Southland Beverages, Inc., employee to disassemble the endcap display today. Their special promotion isn't scheduled for another week and the display space belongs to another vendor just now. Finally, you want an apology from them for the way they have behaved. Being an assertive businessperson is one thing; being rude and arrogant is another. You want his service to improve, but you also want him to recognize what he is doing to your store, and an apology is in order.

CASE STUDY 8-2(B)

The Kroger Company

The Role of the Pepsi-Cola Sales Manager

Among the more difficult to master, yet less obvious of human communication skills is that of providing feedback to others in the workplace. For many managers, feedback must often wait for specified, formal counseling occasions, such as a performance review. Time is short, pressures to accomplish work goals are substantial, and communication often takes on a one-way character: Feedback is used, not to improve communication, but to correct job-related performance issues.

As managers rise from junior to more senior positions in an organization, they gradually discover that more and more of their time is spent in interpersonal communication, face-to-face with subordinates, peers, and superiors. They are less task-oriented, more process-oriented. Gathering information is far less difficult than figuring out what it means.

The key to many management problems often lies in another's perspective. Finding out what others think of an issue, how they view the matter at hand, is frequently useful to a manager. The danger lies in wasted time or misspent effort in such conversations. Somehow learning to make feedback a more structured, productive activity becomes increasingly important to managers who have the talent and the will to succeed.

Feedback is more than simply sending messages or issuing orders. Often, the process involves soliciting information from others so that you can first understand their perspective or point of view. Then, under planned and carefully controlled conditions, information regarding both performance and communication can assist both managers and subordinates in achieving organizational goals.

Knowing that it's possible to become more skilled in this process is the first step. In recognizing that, managers must concentrate early and often on improving their ability to both solicit and provide feedback.

The Role of the Pepsi-Cola Sales Manager

You are the territorial sales manager for Southland Beverages, Inc., a nonunion regional Pepsi-Cola bottler. While your firm handles other products—including Mountain Dew and Dr. Pepper—Pepsi-Cola, Diet Pepsi, and Pepsi One are clearly your most important products and account for nearly two-thirds of your company's revenues.

The soft drink business isn't easy. After all, you're in constant competition with the local Coca-Cola bottler, the RC Cola vendor, and another beer and soft drink distributor who sells Seven-Up products. Your margins are narrow, largely because of your cost structure. Most of your expenses come from delivery operations: ownership, maintenance, and operation of your delivery fleet and your wage structure. To cut your fixed costs just a bit, you have convinced your general manager to let you implement a program of driver incentives. Their hourly wages are lower by one-third, but they get a percentage of every product flat (a term used to describe a shipping container) they deliver.

Your general manager likes the idea of driver incentives and is pushing you to lower your costs even further with less frequent deliveries. Fewer stops at each retail outlet, combined with longer stock leads will mean lower costs and more profit for Southland. In general, the drivers are happy with the scheme, but they have encountered some resistance from store managers with limited storeroom and loading dock space.

"Keep it up, Roger," says your boss. "You're doin' a great job. I'm really pleased with the way we've been able to get control of our delivery costs."

"Thanks," you say. "I was pretty sure this system would work. Not everybody's happy, but, hey, that's

life. Right?" Just as your general manager departs and closes the door to your office, the intercom beeps. It's your assistant, Darleen.

"Mr. Willis? It's Pat Hanson from Kroger on line two."

"Thanks," you say. "Hello. This is Roger Willis."

"Mr. Willis," says the voice on the other end, "this is Pat Hanson in the Rosewater Kroger Store. If you have a few minutes today, I'd really like to meet with you about some problems we've been having. I'd also like to show you something in your Pepsi display area. Can we get together today?"

"I suppose," you say. "How does four o'clock sound? I can be there by four, but I don't have much time."

"This won't take long," Hanson replies. "I'll see you at four."

CASE STUDY 8-2(C)

The Kroger Company

The Role of the Instructional Facilitator

This case involves two roles, each played from a different perspective. One is the manager of a midsized Kroger store in the Louisville Kroger marketing area. The other is the sales manager for a local Pepsi-Cola bottler.

Please read and familiarize yourself with the issues addressed in the background note, as well as the facts contained in both roles. The facts in this case are the same for both participants. As is usual, though, both people see the facts through slightly different eyes. Each has a perspective unique to the position he or she occupies, and each has a set of objectives and goals that accompany the job. As you read the relevant facts in this case and assume your role, keep in mind that you are evaluated by your supervisor on the extent to which you can achieve those job-related goals. Keep in mind, as well, that communication may be one of the tools you can use to reach your objectives.

Your Task

Your task is to facilitate a role-playing exercise designed to demonstrate the importance of communication skills in practical everyday human interaction. Make whatever assumptions you need to in order to assist the role players, but be flexible as they create their characters and play out the details of the case. Each person involved in this exercise knows basically the same facts about the incident, but each has a slightly different perspective on those facts.

Before the Role-Play Begins

Select two members of the class who would be willing to participate in a role-playing exercise. You can either ask the class as a whole for volunteers or you can select two people based on your knowledge of their personality, cooperativeness, and communication skill.

Give one copy of the store manager's role to one person and one copy of the Pepsi-Cola sales manager's role to the other. Have each person read their roles separately. If possible, give out the roles the day before you plan to conduct this exercise.

Please ask the two students who have agreed to participate in this exercise not to read the other role player's role. Ask that they confine their reading only to the role they've been assigned, and to play the role with sincerity and conviction. Please ask them, as well, not to collaborate or to share information with each other. The success of this exercise depends, in part, on each person seeing the communication situation from his or her own perspective.

As the Role-Play Begins

Tell all members of the class that two of their classmates have volunteered (or were selected) to participate in a communication exercise. Ask them all to observe carefully and, if they care to, take notes on what they see and hear. Then, tell the two role players to simulate the first meeting between the Kroger store manager and the Pepsi-Cola sales manager, beginning with introductions.

As the two role players begin, step back and observe the interaction carefully. They shouldn't be reading from their case instructions, but should assume the manners and actions of their character directly. Let the interaction go on for as long as you think it is productive. Most volunteers will play the character roles with enthusiasm and conviction and will carry the meeting through to some logical conclusion. If your players become frustrated, angry, or confused, step in and stop the role-play.

When the Role-Play Concludes

Take control of the classroom once again and, before you do anything else, thank the players for their time, effort, and talent. A small round of applause usually makes each of them feel better about the experience. Then, ask the class as a whole about several issues.

1. **Cognitive listening.** What facts arose during the discussion? Did the players come to the meeting with differing assumptions? Where did the discussions begin? Did either player ask the other to back up and review any details?

2. **Affective listening.** What emotions arose during the discussion? Were either of the players angry, frustrated, or upset? Did each maintain a professional manner? Were they courteous to one another? Did either player change his or her emotional tone as a result of the meeting?

3. **Nonverbal listening.** What was the body posture and gesturing like during the interaction? Did both players exhibit open posture with arms unfolded, palms open, or uplifted? Was the nonverbal communication essentially negative: arms folded, body posture at an angle, head down? What happened with eye contact during the meeting? Did both players look directly at each other, or did one search the ceiling or floor during the conversation? How close were they to one another? Did one of them back away from the other at some point? Did one interrupt the other at any point?

4. **Listening for meaning.** Did each player understand the other? Did they work from the same set of intentions? Did both players reach some sort of mutually satisfactory agreement by the end of the meeting? What could each of them have done to make the meeting more successful? Give each member of the class an opportunity to comment and then observe that, while no two conversations are ever the same (different people, different subjects, different moments), a number of basic considerations can make each of us more effective listeners and, ultimately, communicators.

5. **Quality of feedback.** Look for the quality of feedback provided by each participant in the exercise. Is the information being exchanged of any real value to the other participant in the conversation? Does emotion contribute to success in the exercise or hinder success? Is each participant saying and doing those things that will most likely lead to a successful resolution of the dispute?

CASE STUDY 8-3

Three Feedback Exercises

Organize the class into groups of three people each. Two people in each group will play roles defined for them in the exercises. The third person in each group will serve as the observer/recorder. The instructor should take 3 to 4 minutes to explain the role-playing exercise and assign roles to each of the participants.

Participants should take 10–12 minutes to read the exercise requirements and play their respective roles. Each group observer/recorder should then take 2 to 3 minutes to brief their observations to the entire class.

Feedback Exercise 1: The Disgruntled Analyst

Relationship: A supervisor and an employee who reports directly to him or her.

Context: You are an employee who joined the company 18 months ago as an entry-level analyst. You have a bachelor's degree in finance and some prior work experience in sales. You had other job offers but accepted this one because you thought it would offer the greatest challenge and most opportunity for growth and advancement. You are now no longer the most junior employee in the organization; others with similar education but less experience are assigned to your division.

The Analyst: You feel that you are stuck doing all of the most basic grunt work in the division: gathering and organizing data sets that everyone uses, dealing with ground-level maintenance problems, and producing report documents that newer employees can claim credit for but contribute less to.

The Supervisor: You think the analyst is doing acceptable work, but it's far from top-level performance. During the past 30 days, you have had to counsel this individual twice about late "after market" reports and misrouted reports. You think this person might eventually make a good trader, but first must "grow up" and begin accepting responsibility on the job.

Feedback Exercise 2: The Withholding Coworker

Relationship: Two coworkers who report to the same supervisor.

Context: You and a coworker are members of the same marketing department in a *Fortune* 500 firm. You have worked closely with this other person for the past eight months and have developed a casual relationship outside of working hours. You both enjoy your work, seem to like the company and the industry, and are dedicated to seeing your organization succeed. One of the reasons you like the work is that others who have preceded you in these positions have quickly moved on to "bigger and better things" within the company.

Issue: You feel that your coworker does not share information with you that is essential for you to be an effective department member. You suspect, in fact, that your coworker may occasionally withhold information (e.g., changes in team meeting times and locations, scheduling details, feedback from field visits) so that you don't look as good in the eyes of your supervisor.

You have asked to meet with your coworker to talk about this situation.

Feedback Exercise 3: The Imperiled Line Extension

Relationship: Two coworkers who report to different supervisors.

Context: You and another employee who is about your age work in different divisions of a large packaged-goods firm. You have been assigned to work on a product line extension together. Your target launch date is eight months from now. Needless to say, a considerable amount of time, effort, and money are being devoted to the success of this project.

Issue: You feel that your coworker (from another division) has simply not cooperated with you in gathering the information you'll need to make your launch window. Unless you can secure the cooperation of this person, key issues, including packaging, transportation, advertising and promotion, and retailer incentives, may be in jeopardy. You have asked to meet with your coworker to talk it over.

These exercises were prepared from public sources and personal interviews by James S. O'Rourke, Concurrent Professor of Management, as the basis for class discussion rather than to illustrate either effective or ineffective handling of an administrative situation. Personal and corporate identities have been disguised.

Chapter 9

Nonverbal Communication

Getting dressed for work used to be a snap for executive Ron Demczak. Then his company went casual—every day. With 30 suits and little else in his closet, Demczak spent several thousand dollars buying a new, sporty wardrobe. He learned to call ahead to clients to make sure he didn't wear corduroys when they were wearing suits. And he dreaded the mornings.

"I hated it because every morning I had to have my wife match new outfits to wear," said Demczak. He is the liaison for U.S. customers of drugmaker Warner-Lambert. "Now," he adds, "I'm getting a little better at it."[1]

He's not alone. Robert Park is a manager at Ernst & Young, LLP, in northern California. For his firm, the switch to full-time casual dress was spurred by a desire to blend in. In that region, the accounting firm's clients were mostly from Silicon Valley, where software engineers and other young techies practically invented casual office wear. "We used to stick out like sore thumbs, being the only ones in suits and ties," he said. "Everybody knew we had to be the accountants or the bankers."

Still, Park keeps a traditional wardrobe for use when meeting outsiders who expect suits and ties. Some managers even stow suits in their cars so they won't be uncomfortably surprised. "That's when it gets complicated," said Wendy Liebmann, President of WSL Strategic Retail consultants. "Do I go by my code or theirs?"[2] Managers who are accustomed to wearing more formal business attire may be comforted by recent studies that indicate suits and ties are making a comeback.[3] Still, many of them struggle each day with the uncertainty of knowing exactly what to expect.

Why would managers feel uncomfortable in casual clothes? What's so complicated or difficult about being dressed differently from others you're doing business with? The answers to these and thousands of other questions about how humans interact with one another are related directly to how we communicate. For Ms. Liebmann, Mr. Park, and everyone else in the workplace, the questions they are asking have little to do with language and a great deal to do with *nonverbal communication.*

If I look you directly in the eyes while we're speaking, is that a sign of respect or defiance? If you stare at a new employee while she's eating lunch, is that a sign of affection or harassment? When you speak with a friend, how far apart should you stand? How close should you be when the boss asks you a question? If the boss reaches out to pat you on the shoulder, would it be acceptable for you to reciprocate?

Some workplaces, like the commodities exchange, encourage people to speak up and raise their voices. Others demand quiet. Some offices provide private space with doors that close, while others simply push desks together in huge, open rooms. In many instances, understanding what coworkers mean when they speak depends on your ability to understand whether they're being serious, sarcastic, or humorous.

How can so much information be conveyed without using language? And, perhaps more importantly, how can one person possibly understand all the rules? What means one thing here may very well mean something else there, and what's seen as harmless in one company may be strictly forbidden in another. Clearly, understanding nonverbal communication is not simply useful for a manager. It's essential.

A FEW BASIC CONSIDERATIONS

Communication experts have established the fact that less than a third of the meaning transferred from one person to another in a personal conversation comes from the words that are spoken. The majority of meaning comes from nonverbal sources, including body movement; eye contact; gestures; posture; and vocal tone, pitch, pacing, and phrasing. Other messages come from our clothing, our use of time, and literally dozens of other nonverbal categories. Learning how to read and understand such wordless messages isn't easy, but may be essential to understanding everyone from your customers to your supervisor to your spouse.

Nonverbal communication is widely regarded as the transfer of meaning without the use of verbal symbols. That is, *nonverbal* refers in a literal sense to those actions, objects, and contexts that either communicate directly or facilitate communication without using words.[4] As communication professionals and casual observers alike will testify, though, separating the effects of verbal and nonverbal behavior is never easy, largely because they tend to reinforce each other, contradict each other, or are in some way *about* each other.

It's also important to note that, with the exception of emotional displays and certain facial expressions, virtually all nonverbal communication is culturally based. That is, we learn to behave and communicate in certain ways, and to interpret the meanings of those behaviors, as we grow up in our culture. Being *enculturated*, as we will see in the next chapter, means acquiring values, beliefs, possessions, behaviors, and ways of thinking that are acceptable to others and, in fact, expected of us as members of our society. So what may be strictly forbidden in one culture—exposing an adult woman's face to strangers in public—may be perfectly normal in another. As members of a global community, we must not only learn and abide by the rules of the society we grew up in but also come to understand and appreciate the rules of other societies.

NONVERBAL CATEGORIES

In a series of early studies of nonverbal communication,[5] communication researchers outlined three basic categories of nonverbal language.

SIGN LANGUAGE Gestures as simple as the extended thumb of the hitchhiker or as complex as the complete system of sign language for the deaf are all part of sign language.

ACTION LANGUAGE Movements that are not used exclusively for communicating are part of action language. Walking, for example, serves the functional purpose of moving us from one place to another, but it can also communicate, as when we decide to get up and walk out of a meeting.

OBJECT LANGUAGE All objects, materials, artifacts, and things—ranging from jewelry, clothing, and makeup to automobiles, furniture, and artwork—that we use in our daily lives are considered object language. Such things, including our own bodies, can communicate, whether we intend them to or not.

THE NONVERBAL PROCESS

Nonverbal communication is really a three-step process involving a cue, our own expectations, and an inference.

CUE We look first for a wordless cue—a motion, perhaps, or an object. On arriving at work, you notice a coworker who is glum, sullen, and withdrawn. You say "Good morning," but he doesn't reply.

EXPECTATION We then match the cue against our expectations, asking what seems reasonable or what seems obvious, based on our prior experiences. If your coworker is normally cheerful, talkative, and outgoing, are your expectations at odds with the cue you've just perceived?

INFERENCE Having picked up the cue and measured its importance and meaning against our expectations, we *infer* meaning. Because we can't see an attitude or intention directly, we must draw an inference based on the nonverbal cue and our own expectations. Given the cue and our expectations of this particular coworker, we conclude that he's unhappy, upset, or depressed for some reason. Note that this conclusion is based on observation alone and not an exchange of verbal information between two people. If we are careful and observant, we can learn a great deal without the use of language. We should be careful, though, because our confidence often exceeds our ability when it comes to accurately interpreting nonverbal cues.

READING AND MISREADING NONVERBAL CUES

"The great majority of us are easily misled," says Dr. Paul Ekman, a psychologist at the University of California at San Francisco. "It's very difficult, and most people just don't know what cues to rely on." To be sure, research shows that people can usually read someone else's feelings from the facial expression. "Most of us are fairly accurate in the rough judgments we make based on nonverbal cues," says Dr. Miles Patterson, editor of the *Journal of Nonverbal Behavior* and a psychologist at the University of Missouri at St. Louis.[6]

The new research, however, points to areas where people's confidence in reading nonverbal cues outstrips their accuracy. Recently, Dr. Robert Gifford reported finding specific nonverbal clues to such traits as aloofness, gregariousness, and submissiveness. His report, which appeared in the *Journal of Personality and Social Psychology*, also found that even though reliable clues about character are present, "people read much into nonverbal cues that just isn't there, while missing much that is," says Dr. Gifford.[7]

People are right about their reading of character some of the time, especially for more obvious traits like gregariousness; the problem, according to Dr. Gifford, is that they are overly confident and assume that they are equally adept at reading more subtle aspects of character when they are actually misjudging. For example, in a recent study of people applying for a job, Dr. Gifford asked 18 seasoned interviewers, most of them personnel officers, to evaluate videos of the applicants.

Before going for their interviews, each applicant had taken tests that gauged their degree of social skills and how highly motivated for work they were. The test for motivation, for instance, asked such questions as how willing they would be to work unusual hours if it were necessary. The interviewers were far more accurate about the applicants' self-evident social skills than about their motivation, a more subtle trait important in employment decisions.

The nonverbal cues that made the interviewers decide whether an applicant had high motivation included smiling, gesturing, and talking more than other applicants. In fact, though, none of those nonverbal patterns was a true indicator of motivation. The practical result of such mistakes is that many people are hired on a misreading of their personality traits, only to disappoint their employers. "Social skills are far more visible than motivation, but coming across well in your job interview is no guarantee of other traits that might matter in your day-to-day job performance," Dr. Gilford said. "People are being hired for some of the wrong reasons." A clever applicant might make a point of smiling, gesturing, and talking a lot during a job interview, but a savvy interviewer would be cautious about reading too much into that show of outgoingness.[8]

FUNCTIONS OF NONVERBAL COMMUNICATION

Nonverbal communication can serve any number of important functions in our lives, but researchers identify the following six major functions.

ACCENTING Nonverbal communication often highlights or emphasizes some part of a verbal message. A raised eyebrow might accompany an expression of surprise; a wagging finger might underscore an expression of disapproval.

COMPLEMENTING Nonverbal communication also reinforces the general tone or attitude of our verbal communication. A downcast expression and slumping posture might accompany words of discouragement or depression; upright posture, a smile, and animated movement might reinforce a verbal story about winning a recent promotion.

CONTRADICTING Nonverbal communication, on the other hand, can contradict the verbal messages we send, sometimes deliberately, sometimes unintentionally. Tears in our eyes and a quiver in our voices might involuntarily contradict a verbal message telling friends and family that we're doing all right. A wink and a nod might deliberately send the nonverbal message that what we're saying just isn't so. The fact is, when verbal and nonverbal messages contradict, we tend—for a number of reasons—to believe the nonverbal. In the last analysis, it's simply much easier to lie than it is to control a range of nonverbal reactions: our facial expression, pupil dilation, tension in our vocal cords, pulse rate, sweating, muscle tone, and many others. Control of such things is, for most of us, well beyond our voluntary reach.

REGULATING Certain nonverbal movements and gestures are used to regulate the flow, the pace, and the back-and-forth nature of verbal communication. When I want you to speak to me, I'll face you, open my eyes, open my arms with hands extended and palms facing upward, and look expectantly into your eyes. When I want you to stop speaking so I can either talk or think of what I'm about to say, I will turn slightly away from you, fold my arms, put one hand out with palm facing forward, and either close my eyes or turn them away from yours.

REPEATING Nonverbal messages can also repeat what verbal messages convey. With car keys in hand, coat and hat on, I can announce: "I'm leaving now," as I walk toward the door. You might hold up three fingers as you ask: "Is that the best you can do? I've gotta buy three of them."

SUBSTITUTING Nonverbal communication can also substitute for, or take the place of, verbal messages, particularly if they're simple or monosyllabic. As a youngster looks toward a parent on the sidelines during an athletic contest, a quick "thumbs up" can substitute for words of praise or encouragement that might not be heard from a distance or in a noisy crowd.[9]

PRINCIPLES OF NONVERBAL COMMUNICATION

After 50 years of research and 5,000 years of human experience with nonverbal communication, we have identified six principles that are thought to be universally true.

1. **Nonverbal communication occurs in a context.** Just as context is important to the meaning of verbal messages, so is context important to our understanding of nonverbal messages. Folded arms and laid-back posture may mean disinterest or boredom on one occasion, but may signify introspective thought on another. Professor Joseph DeVito of Hunter College says, in fact, that "Divorced from the context, it is impossible to tell what any given bit of nonverbal behavior may mean. . . . In attempting to understand and analyze nonverbal communication . . . it is essential that full recognition be taken of the context."[10]

2. **Nonverbal behaviors are usually packaged.** Nonverbal behavior, according to most researchers, occurs in *packages* or *clusters* in which the various verbal and nonverbal messages occur more or less simultaneously. Body posture, eye contact, arm and leg movement, facial expression, vocal tone, pacing and phrasing of vocal expressions, muscle tone, and numerous other elements of nonverbal communication happen at once. It's difficult to isolate one element of the cluster from another without taking all of them into account.

3. **Nonverbal behavior always communicates.** All behavior communicates, and because it is literally impossible not to behave in some way, we are always communicating, even when we aren't speaking with or listening to others. Even the least significant of your behaviors, such as your posture, the position of your mouth, or the way you've tucked (or failed to tuck) in your shirt say something about your professionalism to others around you. Other people may not interpret those behaviors in the same way, or in the way you might want them to, but like it or not, you're always communicating, even if you're just sitting there "doing nothing." Doing nothing, in fact, may communicate volumes about your attitude.

4. **Nonverbal behavior is governed by rules.** The field of linguistics is devoted to studying and explaining the rules of language. And just as spoken and written language follow specific rules, so does nonverbal communication. A few forms of nonverbal behavior, such as facial expressions conveying sadness, joy, contentment, astonishment, or grief, are universal. That is, the expressions are basically the same for all mankind, regardless of where you were born, raised, educated, or enculturated. Most of our nonverbal behavior, however, is learned and is a product of the cultures in which we are raised. A motion or hand gesture that means one thing in my culture may well mean another in yours. Touching the thumb and forefinger to form a circle is often raised in North America to signify everything is "A-Okay." In Latin America, that same gesture is used to illustrate the anal sphincter muscle and is employed as a powerful insult.

5. **Nonverbal behavior is highly believable.** Researchers have discovered what we have known individually for quite some time: We are quick to believe nonverbal behaviors, even when

they contradict verbal messages. When an employee's eyes dart away quickly, or search the floor as he thinks of an answer to a supervisor's question, most of us would suspect the employee is not telling the truth. Try as we might, there are many nonverbal behaviors we cannot fake. We might convincingly write or speak words that are untrue, but it's much more difficult to behave nonverbally in ways that are false or deceptive.

6. **Nonverbal behavior is metacommunicational.** The word *meta* is borrowed from Greek and means "along with, about, or among." Thus metacommunication is really communication about communication. The behaviors we exhibit while communicating are really about communication itself, and nonverbal communication occurs in reference to the process of communicating. Your facial expression reveals how you feel about the meal you've just been served; your handshake, vocal tone, and eye contact tell us what you think about the person you've just been introduced to.[11]

DIMENSIONS OF THE NONVERBAL CODE

When we talk about nonverbal communication, we're really talking about the codes we use to encrypt our messages and the signals that contain them. The code we use in verbal communication is language, and through thousands of years of human interaction, we've established rules to guide us and a structure for employing and interpreting the messages that language permits us to send and receive. With nonverbal communication, however, the code is neither as clear nor is it as precise, primarily because the meaning of our messages must be inferred without the benefit of feedback.

The code itself is divided into more than a dozen dimensions, each with the power to encode and carry messages from one person to another. Each has different characteristics: Some appeal to just one sense, while others appeal to several; some have a limited range of possible meanings, while others have a huge span of subtleties for encoding human intentions; some belong to the environment—both its physical and psychological aspects—of the communication event, while others belong to the participants in those events.

THE COMMUNICATION ENVIRONMENT

The communication environment refers to that collection of nonhuman factors that can, and often do, influence human transactions. People often change environments in order to accomplish their communication goals: the choice of a restaurant for a business meeting or a resort hotel to conduct a conference. Often, people will simply say, "Let's go somewhere quiet where we can talk." This category concerns those factors that can influence a human relationship but are not, in Professor Mark Knapp's words, "directly a part of it," and includes elements such as the furniture, architectural style, interior decorating, lighting conditions, colors, temperature, background noise, or music. It may be something as small as a dish left on a table you plan to use or something as grand as the city in which you are meeting.[12]

BODY MOVEMENT

The study of human motion in communication, often referred to as kinesics or kinesiology, is concerned primarily with movement and posture. The way we walk, sit, stand, move our arms, hands, head, feet, and legs tells other people something about us. This dimension also includes such areas of interest as facial expression, eye contact, and posture. The five basic categories of human movement include:

1. **Emblems.** These nonverbal acts have a direct verbal translation or dictionary definition, sometimes a word or two or a brief phrase. The thumbs-up sign, the extended middle finger, and the hitchhiker's thumb are three well-known examples.
2. **Illustrators.** These gestures often complement our verbal signals, helping to illustrate what's being said verbally. We can count off the number of items we want on our fingers or measure distance with the space between our hands.
3. **Affect displays.** These behaviors indicate the type and intensity of the various emotions we feel. Facial expressions, as well as hand and arm movements, are commonly used to communicate emotional or affective states of mind.
4. **Regulators.** These body movements help to control the flow of communication. Hand movement, arm positioning, and eye contact can easily maintain or regulate the back-and-forth nature of personal conversation, for example.
5. **Adaptors.** These movements or behaviors involve personal habits and self-expressions. They are methods of adapting or accommodating ourselves to the demands of the world in which we live. We usually engage in these behaviors in private, but sometimes under pressure we will resort to twisting our hair, scratching, adjusting our glasses, or perhaps, picking our noses if we think no one's looking.

From a workplace perspective, a trend toward incivility is fostering a backlash, especially in response to unwelcome or rude nonverbal behavior. During tense talks in Chicago courts, Southwest Airlines Chief Executive Herb Kelleher crouched and slowly flipped his middle finger toward a pilots' union lawyer. "It was a joke," he explained. But other companies are cracking down on crude nonverbal behavior. Cleveland-based American Greetings Corporation has banned obscene talk and gestures. And an official of Roadway Services, an Akron, Ohio, freight hauler, says truckers are told to practice restraint.[13]

EYE CONTACT

This human behavior is really a part of kinesics, but often deserves separate attention because of the importance it plays in human interaction. Direction, duration, and intensity of gaze are often seen as indicators of interest, attention, or involvement between two people. Keep in mind, however, that nonverbal mannerisms are culturally based, and eye contact is just one example of a human behavior that can vary from one society to another.

In Japan, for instance, looking a supervisor directly in the eyes is a sign of defiance, even insubordination. In the United States and Canada, supervisors expect direct and frequent eye contact as a sign of respect. A senior leader in a large organization once remarked, "I won't hire a person who won't look me in the eye." Why would he feel that way? Largely because in this culture we draw inferences about honesty and integrity from eye contact; if people look down or look away when we're speaking to them, we assume they are ashamed or being untruthful. Honesty and eye contact are, of course, unrelated behaviors, but people in our society make judgments about them, nonetheless.[14]

A COMMUNICATOR'S PHYSICAL APPEARANCE

This area is not concerned with movement, as kinesics is, but with aspects of our bodies and appearance that remain relatively unchanged during the period of interaction. Such things as body type (ectomorph, mesomorph, or endomorph), height, weight, hair, and skin color or tone are included. Some researchers also focus on physical attractiveness and people's reaction to personal appearance. A number of studies, in fact, show that people readily attribute greater intelligence, wit, charm, and sociability to those people whom they judge to be very attractive.[15]

Another new study found that good looks can yield substantial rewards. Economists Daniel Hamermesh of the University of Texas and Jeff Biddle of Michigan State University found that education, experience, and other characteristics being equal, people who are perceived as good looking earn, on average, about 10 percent more than those viewed as homely.[16] Being overweight can hurt your income as well, particularly if you're a highly educated woman. A study conducted in 2004 in Finland has shown that obese women with good educations earn about 30 percent less than normal-weight or even plump women. Obesity had little or no effect on pay if women were poorly educated, manual workers, or self-employed and, surprisingly, no significant effect at all on men's pay.[17]

Naomi Wolf, author of *The Beauty Myth*, agrees with Hamermesh and Biddle's conclusions but argues that women often face greater discrimination when it comes to appearance. One recent study looked at earnings of MBA graduates over their first 10 post-degree years. Ratings of beauty based on school photographs correlated positively with starting and subsequent salaries for men. No relationship was evident between the starting salaries of women and their beauty, but attractive women experienced faster salary growth. Dr. Hamermesh suggests that better-looking people may have high self-esteem—from years of compliments—that translates into better performance on the job.[18]

Independent of such studies, conventional wisdom tells us that others make judgments about us based on our appearance, including everything from hairstyle to body weight, clothing style to skin tone. How you perform on the job may well be the most important aspect of your behavior in the workplace, but if you don't make a favorable first impression, you may not be given the chance to show what you can do. On the other side of that coin, judging a coworker or prospective employee by appearance may seem intuitive and useful but may also prove inaccurate. Even though you can make some judgments about a book by its cover, you may wish to withhold judgment until you have an opportunity to gather more information.

ARTIFACTS

Artifacts are objects that are human-made or modified. The number and kind of things we might call *artifacts* is enormous, ranging from clothing, jewelry, and eyeglasses to the objects we own and decorate our offices with. Certainly the way we dress denotes how we feel about an occasion or those we're with. Every family, for instance, has at least one cousin who will show up at a wedding wearing a corduroy sport coat. It's not that he can't afford dinner clothes or a tuxedo; it's just that he's thumbing his nose at the rest of the family.

People in the business world make judgments about those they deal with as a result of the artifacts they see in their offices and in the communication environment. A friend once asked if I would trust a stockbroker who drove a '97 Toyota to work each day. The implication was that a "successful" broker would have enough money to buy and drive an expensive automobile. And even though investment success and taste in motor cars are not necessarily related, the majority of adults in the marketplace make such judgment links with great regularity.

TOUCH

Among the more widely discussed and, perhaps, least understood aspects of human behavior is touch. Numerous studies have shown that physical contact is essential to human existence. Adults need it for social and psychological balance; children need it for stimulation, security, and reassurance. Many infants, in fact, will fail to thrive if they're not regularly offered the reassuring warmth of human touch. Needless to say, touch is conducted on many levels and for many reasons by each of us, with functional, professional, social, and sexual implications for each kind of touch. Perhaps more than any other dimension of the nonverbal code, touching is a culturally determined, learned behavior. The relationship between the two people touching and the norms of the society in which they live—or were enculturated—will determine the length, location, intensity, frequency, acceptability, and publicness of their haptic behavior.

A recent study in the *Journal of Personality and Social Psychology* revealed that a number of important aspects of your personality can easily and accurately be detected during a handshake. Characteristics of a handshake, such as strength, vigor, completeness of grip, and accompanying eye contact can determine whether a person makes a favorable first impression. More surprisingly, evaluators could surmise a number of other key traits, such as confidence, shyness, or neuroticism. Lead researcher William Chaplin said that women should not worry about seeming too aggressive, because the firmer their handshake, the more favorably they are judged. Men, on the other hand, should have some concerns about creating bad impressions with weaker grips and lack of eye contact.[19]

The *rules* regarding touch in the North American workplace have changed in recent years from liberal to conservative—from frequent touch to little or no touch. Backslapping, arm-grabbing, and other forms of behavior that ranged from affectionate friendship to adolescent horseplay are now widely banned in most businesses, largely from a fear of lawsuits. A colleague who returned to work following a maternity leave was cheerfully welcomed by friends and coworkers in her office, but no one would touch her until she spoke up, "It's alright to give me a hug. I would appreciate that."

The best advice regarding touch is to assume that if people extend their hand, it's probably alright to shake it. Touching any other parts of their bodies would be considered inappropriate unless you're specifically given permission to do so. These developments are largely the result of abusive behavior in the workplace, mostly aimed at women. Such developments are particularly unfortunate in view of numerous recent studies presented to the Society for Neuroscience finding that touch, or direct human contact, can have a positive influence on the production of a hormone affecting the body's reaction to stress. Subnormal levels of the hormone, in fact, have been linked to changes in a part of the brain involved with learning and memory.[20] The value of human touch is undisputed. The issue for managers is one of exhibiting good sense and good manners when touching others.

PARALANGUAGE

The term *paralanguage* refers, very simply, to *how* something is said and not to *what* is said. It deals with the whole range of nonverbal vocal cues involved in speech behavior, including voice qualities, vocal characterizers, vocal qualifiers, and speech segregates, and sometimes referred to as *vocalics*.[21]

Often, the only real clues we have to a person's actual intent as we listen to him or her speak are found in paralanguage. If your supervisor approaches you just before lunch one day and says, "Lisa, we need to talk about the LaSalle account," your reaction to those words may depend on a number of factors, including the communication environment and context, as well as your expectations. But your sense of urgency—how quickly you offer to set up a meeting, whether you postpone a lunch date to talk about the account—may well depend on *how* those words were spoken. Your cue is often contained in your interpretation not of the words themselves but of the pacing, phrasing, tone, pitch, and intensity of your supervisor's delivery.

Vocal qualifiers are contained in the speech of every human and are an integral part of every spoken word. They are, in fact, our principal cue to identifying and interpreting sarcasm and cynicism. When you ask a coworker in a meeting if he thinks a new cost-control measure will work and the response is, "Oh yeah, you bet, no problem with *that* plan," you're faced with a brief dilemma. Was your coworker being sarcastic just then, or does he genuinely believe that plan will succeed? Your reaction to his words will depend entirely on how you interpret the tone of his voice.

Paralanguage not only serves to help listeners identify emotional states in the speaker but also plays an important role in conversational turn-taking. People often signal others in a conversation that it's their turn to talk or that they would like a turn to speak or that they aren't yet done speaking. Much of the signaling is done nonverbally through vocalics: rate, pacing, pitch, tone, and other vocal, subverbal cues.[22]

SPACE

The study of how humans use space, including the areas in which we work, live, socialize, and conduct our lives, is often referred to in the research literature as *proxemics*. We know intuitively that space communicates in many ways in the business world, especially when we examine the subject of office space. Professor Joseph DeVito says, "We know, for example, that in a large organization, status is the basis for determining how large an office one receives, whether that office has a window or not, what floor of the building the office is on, and how close one's office is to the head of the company."[23]

Workers in large organizations have faced two interesting, sometimes discouraging, trends in the allocation of office space: shrinking cubicles and disappearing personal space. With office space becoming more expensive per square foot, facility managers have looked for increasingly creative ways of dealing with the demand for workspace and privacy. The trend over the past 25 years away from huge office spaces with many desks and no privacy brought portable wall dividers known as *cubicles* into the workspace. The arrangement provided for a minimum of privacy, or in some cases, an illusion of privacy.[24]

Every couple of weeks, Michael McKay, a 33-year-old business analyst with a Santa Clara, California, Internet-services company, finds his concentration totally disrupted when three colleagues who sit near his workstation hop onto the same conference call—all on speakerphones. "You get this stereophonic effect of hearing one person's voice live, and then hearing it coming out of someone else's speakerphone two or three cubes over," he says. The obvious solution to incessant phone-ringing, very personal conversations, and rising noise levels would seem to be private offices. Don't count on it, says Jane Smith, a Manhattan office architect. "The open plan is here to stay."[25]

Julie Nemetz, a writer for a popular teen magazine, planned her wedding recently from under her desk. "It's quieter down there," she says. Nearly three-quarters of all U.S. and Canadian workers now do business in open plan or bullpen office space. And the average office space per person has shrunk steadily since the late 1990s, down by about 13 percent according to the International Facility Management Association. Do workers have a right to expect private space at their employers' expense? Legally no, it's a "fringe benefit," says Robert Ellis Smith, publisher of *Privacy Journal.* But given that more employees are putting in 60-plus hour weeks, he adds, "It's in employers' interests to make these accommodations for personal housekeeping."[26]

A second trend has developed in recent years, known as *hoteling*, to provide office space on demand for workers who have an infrequent need for private or semiprivate space. Greg Bednar is an audit partner in the accounting firm of Ernst & Young, LLP in Chicago. "We began 'hoteling' several years ago," Bednar said, "but expanded the program dramatically." The entire Chicago office of Ernst & Young, according to Bednar, including more than 3,000 people and 500,000 square feet of office space between the 11th and 17th floors were affected.[27]

"It seemed like a great idea at first," he said, "because we were able to save so much money. We got an instant economic benefit from giving up 100,000 square feet of workspace. We also wanted a more technology-literate workforce. People had to be plugged into the system and into our clients. Additionally, we were hoping to develop a more flexible workforce." What Ernst & Young got was a huge, temporary saving on office space rental but a workforce that felt disenfranchised from the company.[28]

Each morning, Ernst & Young employees report to work by checking in at the concierge desk in the outer lobby. Once properly identified, they receive access to a cubicle, known as a "four pod," so called, because four workers occupy one workspace about 20 feet square. They each have a desk and chair, a telephone, and a network connection for their laptop computers. The cubicle offers no overnight storage space, no opportunity to put up pictures, bookshelves, or personal items, and virtually zero privacy.[29]

"It's become a morale issue," said Bednar. "What we've gained in revenue by renting less floorspace, we've lost in teaming, mentoring, and social interaction. We have no 'water cooler chats,' and very little informal interaction with each other. Frankly, no one knows where anyone else is on any given day." Wayne Ebersberger, also a partner in Ernst & Young's Chicago office, says, "The loss of this personal space is an important matter. It isn't just a workspace or productivity issue any longer. We're losing some of the fabric of our culture."[30]

THE EFFECT OF SPACE ON COMMUNICATION Not long ago, Tom Allen, a professor at MIT, did a study determining the relationship between communication and distance in the workplace. For six months, he examined the communication patterns among 512 employees in seven organizations. He found that at a distance of 30 feet or less, the quality of communication is five times better than it is at a distance of 100 feet. Allen's research also showed that beyond 100 feet, distance is immaterial because communication is simply ineffective. In other words, ease of communication is largely dependent on physical location.[31]

CATEGORIES OF PERSONAL SPACE Cultural anthropologist Edward T. Hall has observed and classified four categories of distance, each of which helps to define the relationship between the communicators.

- *Intimate.* This ranges from actual touching to a distance of about 18 inches. At this distance, the presence of other individuals is unmistakable: Each individual experiences the sound, smell, even the other's breath. To be given permission to position yourself so closely to another implies a personal relationship involving considerable trust. Often, though, we're forced to stand or sit next to someone, perhaps actually touching them, without really wanting to do so—in an elevator, a subway car, or an airline seat. Most North Americans feel some level of discomfort at such closeness when they don't really know the other person. People try to avoid eye contact at this distance, focusing instead on distant or nearby objects.[32] Although most people feel uncomfortable at this distance from strangers or casual acquaintances, most are willing to briefly tolerate such closeness in order to get what they need—a trip to the top floor in an elevator, transportation to the next subway stop, or lunch in a crowded café.

- *Personal.* Each of us, according to Dr. Hall, carries a protective bubble defining our personal distance, which allows us to stay protected and untouched by others. In the close phase of personal distance, about 18 to 30 inches, we can still hold or grasp each other but only by extending our arms. In the far phase (about 30 inches to 4 feet), two people can touch each other only if they both extend their arms. This far phase, according to Professor DeVito, is "the extent to which we can physically get our hands on things; hence, it defines, in one sense, the limits of our physical control over others."[33] The common business phrase "arm's-length relationship" comes from the definition of this distance, meaning that a proper relationship with customers, suppliers, or business partners might be one in which we are not so close as to be controlled or unduly influenced by them.
- *Social.* At a distance of about 4 to 12 feet, we lose the visual detail we could see in the personal distance, yet we clearly are aware of another's presence and can easily make eye contact. You would have to step forward, however, in order to shake hands. Note that during most business introductions, people do just that: step forward, make eye contact, shake hands, then step back. The near phase of social distance (4–7 feet) is the range at which most business conversations and interactions are conducted. In the far phase (7–12 feet), business transactions have a more formal tone and voices are raised just slightly. Many office furniture arrangements assure this distance for senior managers and executives, while still providing the opportunity for closer contact if participants decide it's necessary.[34]
- *Public.* In the close phase of public distance, about 12 to 15 feet, we feel more protected by space. We can still see people, observing their actions and movements, but we lose much of the detail visible at closer distances. We can move quickly enough to avoid someone and are not forced to make eye contact with people we do not know. In the far phase, more than 25 feet, we see people not as separate individuals but as part of the landscape or scene in the room. Communication at this distance is difficult, if not impossible, without shouting or exaggerated body movement.[35]

Our use of space varies greatly, depending on where we live and how we were raised, but it varies even more from one culture to another and is a frequent source of difficulty for people who move to another culture as adults. The next chapter, which deals with international and intercultural communication, will explain more about how U.S. business managers adapt to changes in such important nonverbal behaviors as proxemics.

TIME

Our use of time and how we view its role in our personal and professional lives speaks volumes about who we are and how we regard others. This concept, too, is culturally determined to a large extent because the use of time involves extensive interaction with other people in our societies.

In North America, we place considerable importance on punctuality and promptness, announcing to anyone who'll listen that "time is money." U.S. and Canadian, and to a lesser extent European, society see time as a commodity that can be saved, wasted, spent, or invested wisely. Mediterranean, Latin, and Polynesian cultures, on the other hand, see time in a much more seamless fashion, moving past them in an inexorable stream. Lateness in South American nations is not only acceptable but often fashionable—a view that regularly frustrates North American businesspeople who experience it for the first time.[36]

Anthropologists have demonstrated how people from various parts of the world view time in different ways. Edward T. Hall has written at length about people who see the world in monochronic ways, that is, with one kind of time for everyone, while others see the world in polychronic ways, with many kinds and uses of time. U.S. and Canadian citizens, as well as those who live in Germany, Switzerland, and the industrialized nations of the G8, tend to work in precise, accountable ways with an emphasis on "saving time" and being "on time" for appointments and meetings.

People who live and work along the Mediterranean, in Latin America and the Middle East, and in more traditional, developing economies often view time from a multifaced or polychronic perspective. Although being on time for a business meeting may be important in Latin America, it's probably not *more important* than a conversation with a friend who has been ill or whom you haven't seen in some time. Additionally, the pace of life as well as business in such societies can vary considerably but is invariably slower than the pace of activity in Western Europe or North America.[37]

COLOR

Color, shading, and hue as subtle and powerful message-senders have a long and, well, colorful history. We signal our intentions ("This project has the green light"); reveal our reactions ("That move prompted red flags throughout the organization"); underscore our moods ("I'm feeling a little blue today"); and call our emotions to the surface ("She was green with envy"). We coordinate and carefully select (for the most part) the colors we use in our offices, our homes, our automobiles, our clothing, and even our hair. We even use color to stereotype and categorize others ("She's that blonde from marketing," and "He's one of the original graybeards in this company").

New marketing research has shown what we have suspected for some time: that color plays an important role in our perceptions of food packaging and food purchase decisions. According to Cooper Marketing Group in Chicago, health-conscious consumers are likely to think that any food, from cookies to cheese, is probably good for them as long as it comes in green packaging. A trip down the fat-free food aisle in your local supermarket will confirm those findings: The top brands, from Snackwell's cookies to Healthy Choice meals, use green packaging. Hershey Foods spokeswoman Natalie Bailey says, "Green is becoming recognized as a low-fat color." Elliot Young of Perception Research Services adds, "It's a risk not to use green. It makes it easier for the shopper to distinguish low-fat items."[38] Throughout much of the twenty-first century, green has also been used in advertising and political discourse to reflect an "environmentally friendly" approach to everything from marketing to public policy.

"Color serves as a cue," according to Dr. Russell Ferstandig, a psychiatrist whose company, Competitive Advantage Consulting, advises marketers about the hearts and minds of consumers. "It's a condensed message that has all sorts of meanings." Some are no more than fads, such as clear drinks like Crystal Pepsi or Coors' Zima, while others are more enduring, including everything from raspberry Jell-O to traditional school colors.[39]

Food companies are usually aware of the meanings they send and tend to rely on certain colors until circumstances require a change. According to color researchers, no colors are inherently good or bad; the context affects the meaning. White, for instance, is seen as a good color but no longer in bread, where brown is becoming preferred because of its more healthful and natural connotations. In packaging, the most popular colors have been red and yellow, according to John Lister, a partner in the New York design firm of Lister Butler. "People tend to be attracted to the warmth of these colors," he added. "They are cheery and friendly."[40]

SMELL

A primitive perceptive capability, smell is a powerful communicator reaching far and wide throughout human emotion and experience. Though it is less understood and more subtle than most other dimensions of the nonverbal code, our sense of smell plays an important part in our ability to communicate. According to the Sense of Smell Institute, the average human being is able to recognize approximately 10,000 different odors. What's more, people can recall smells with 65 percent accuracy after a year, whereas the visual recall of photos sinks to about 50 percent after only three months.[41]

We wear perfume, cologne, and after-shave lotions to signal others that we are freshly scrubbed and desirable. We use deodorants and antiperspirants to mask natural body odors. We use breath mints to cover the smell of bacteria growing in our mouths, and we use room fresheners to disguise the odors of everyday living trapped in our homes, cars, and offices. Smells can be highly evocative and emotional, in part because they're associated with one of our most primitive and least-developed sense organs. Everything from the aroma of mom's pot roast or apple pie cooking in the kitchen to the scent of leather seats in a new Mercedes can have an emotional effect on each of us.[42]

From a marketing perspective, human response to aromas is personal and highly emotional. According to Dr. Trygg Engen, a professor at Brown University, "Aromas are learned in association with a moment and remain inextricably linked to the mood of that moment."[43] Researchers found that a whiff of baking bread is enough to transport many people back to an idealized childhood. Others are perked up by the smell of lemon or lulled by jasmine. Still others report allergic reactions to smells.

During a recent weekend in New York, shoppers on the prowl for digital electronics unwittingly stumbled into a research project related to olfaction. Riding up the escalator to the third floor of the Shops at Columbus Circle, they encountered a scent like that of a young man or woman primed for a night on the town—a unisex, modern fragrance along the lines of Calvin Klein's cK one.

The scent wasn't emanating from one of the many tourists cruising the shops, however. Nor was it escaping from a promotional event at the nearby Aveda store. It was the seductive smell of consumer electronics. Samsung, the Korean electronics giant was conducting a test of its new signature fragrance in its *Samsung Experience* concept store. Researchers stopped shoppers leaving the store to ask them about whether they thought the scent was "stylish," "innovative," "cool," "passionate," or "cold," and—more important—whether the scent made them feel like hanging around the shop a little longer. According to Dr. Alan R. Hirsh, founder and neurological director of the Smell & Taste Treatment and Research Foundation in Chicago, "If a company can associate a mood state with a smell, it can transfer that happy feeling to the product." Those who don't lock in that connection risk being left behind, he warns.[44]

Aromatic mood manipulation is an area of increasing interest among productivity consultants, moving well beyond mom's spice jar and the romantically scented candle. Junichi Yagi, a senior vice president of Shimizu Technology, says, "If you have a high-stress office environment, you want to soothe and stimulate alertness. In a hotel, you might want to create a relaxed mood." To perk people up, Mr. Yagi has experimented with central air circulation systems to alter or enhance the moods of everyone from office workers to shopping mall customers. Peppermint, lemon, rosemary, eucalyptus, and pine have been shown to increase alertness, while lavender, clove, floral, and woodlands scents create a relaxing effect. Experiment participants described feeling refreshed in the presence of a light citrus mixture.[45]

From a workspace perspective, most personal scents are deemed acceptable if they are insufficiently powerful to extend beyond intimate distance. Employees, customers, and others have complained—and in some cases succeeded in court—about being exposed to various odors including food, perfumes, tobacco smoke, and unvented product odors. To protect themselves against unwanted and expensive litigation, many business organizations have published policies asking employees to be respectful of others with whom they must share the workspace, keeping colognes, perfumes, and other personal scents to a minimum.

TASTE

Closely related to our sense of smell is our ability to taste. It's limited to a small grouping of sensations that include salty, sweet, bitter, and other tastes located in a collection of small, flask-shaped sensors in the epithelium of the tongue. It's a complex response system that involves our abilities to see and smell as well, and one—much like color and touch—that is highly subjective in nature. What is "bitter" to some is "rich and full bodied" to others. For still others, such things as espresso coffee, broiled asparagus, and scotch whiskey are "acquired tastes." Our appreciation for the taste of various food and drink is a function of both age and enculturation and, like our use of space, can pose problems when we move from one culture to another.

As the demographic makeup of our society changes, it's important to note that our taste in food is changing along with it. Picante sauce now outsells catsup, and commercially prepared food ranging from fine dining to takeout is available in cuisines ranging from Mexican to Italian, Greek to French, and Thai to Szechuan.[46]

SOUND

The study of acoustics and its effects on communication is now an important part of nonverbal research. Public speakers are particularly conscious of whether they can be heard by everyone in the room, and those who use amplification and public address systems are involved in a constant struggle with audio system feedback, acoustical bounce, and other peculiarities of microphones, amplifiers, and speakers.

Sound comes in other forms, too, including the melodic ranges of the human voice, the sounds produced by nature as well as mankind and our machines (e.g., jets, trucks, and jackhammers,), and of course, there's music. Culture and, more often, subculture can determine our reaction to musical compositions and performances. The melodies of a big band or an orchestra may be attractive to some but sappy and dull to their grandchildren, whose tastes in music may run to salsa, reggae, or hip-hop.

SILENCE

The absence of speech or sound may be used to communicate as powerfully and directly as any verbal code. Some researchers liken silence to acoustics in the same way that facial expressions are related to kinesics. Silence can be used both positively and negatively: to affect, to reveal, to judge, or to activate. Asian cultures, in particular, make extensive use of silence during business meetings and contract negotiations.

Research in interpersonal communication has revealed that silence may serve a number of important functions.

- *To provide thinking time.* Silence can offer an opportunity for you to gather your thoughts together, to assess what's just been said by others, or to weigh the impact of what you might say next. U.S. Ambassador Mike Mansfield once observed that he carried his pipe and tobacco with him for so many years because they gave him something to do while the room grew quiet. "I was never at a loss for words," he said. "I was just reluctant to say the first few that came to mind."[47] Somehow guests or colleagues were more willing to tolerate the tobacco smoke than the silence.

- *To hurt.* Some people use silence as a weapon to hurt others. Giving someone the silent treatment can be particularly powerful, especially if they expect to hear from you and speak with you. In many business organizations, a drop-off in communication can be an early indication of trouble; often, the recipient of the silent treatment is being eased out of the decision-making processes and, perhaps, the company itself.

- *To isolate oneself.* Sometimes silence is used as a response to personal anxiety, shyness, or threats. If you feel anxious or uncertain about yourself or your role in an organization, particularly if you are new to the company or are junior in rank to others in the group, silence is a common response. Eventually, even the most junior or introverted of managers will be asked to speak up on important issues. The key is knowing when to speak and how much to say.

- *To prevent communication.* Silence may be used to prevent the verbal communication of certain messages. An executive may impose a "gag order" on employees to prevent them from discussing sensitive information with others inside or outside an organization. In other circumstances, silence may allow members of a negotiating team or collective bargaining group time to "cool off." If words have the power to inspire, soothe, provoke, or enrage, then silence can prevent those effects from occurring.

- *To communicate feelings.* Like the eyes, face, or hands, silence can also be used to communicate emotional responses. According to Professor DeVito, silence can sometimes communicate a determination to be uncooperative or defiant. "By refusing to engage in verbal communication," he says, "we defy the authority or legitimacy of the other person's position." In more pleasant situations, silence might be used to express affection or agreement.[48]

- *To communicate nothing.* Although it remains true that you "cannot *not* communicate," it is equally true that what you wish to communicate on occasion is that you have nothing to say. Keep in mind that receivers in the communication process will interpret silence, just as they interpret words, motion, and other forms of communication, in their own way. They, not you, will assign meaning to what you are not saying, to whom you are not saying it, and the occasion on which you are not saying anything. From a manager's perspective, it may be a good idea to call someone and say, "I don't have an answer for you yet, but I'll find one and get back in touch with you before the end of the week." That statement might be preferable to no contact at all. A customer might think you don't care about him or her; a supplier might think you have lost interest in doing business; an investment analyst might believe you have something to hide if you're not talking.

THE EFFECTS OF NONVERBAL COMMUNICATION The following six general outcomes are important for every manager to know.

- *Nonverbal cues are often difficult to read.* During the 1970s, a number of popular books introduced the general public to nonverbal communication. One popular volume, *Body Language,* written by a journalist, described the nonverbal studies of several researchers.[49] That bestseller was followed by others that simplified and popularized research in this area;

many of them, however, oversimplified the behavioral science behind the findings in the interest of making a sale, detecting a liar, attracting members of the opposite sex, and so on.

According to Professor Mark Knapp, "Although such books aroused the public's interest in nonverbal communication . . . readers too often were left with the idea that reading nonverbal cues as *the* key to success in any human encounter; some of these books implied that single cues represent single meanings. Not only is it important to look at nonverbal *clusters* of behavior but also to recognize that nonverbal meaning, like verbal, rarely is limited to a single denotative meaning."[50]

- *Nonverbal cues are often difficult to interpret.* What may mean one thing in one context, culture, or circumstance may mean something entirely different in another. Professor Knapp goes on to say, "Some of these popularized accounts do not sufficiently remind us that the meaning of a particular behavior is often understood by looking at the context in which the behavior occurs; for example, looking into someone's eyes may reflect affection in one situation and aggression in another."[51] The importance of reading context, just as we would with verbal expression, is especially critical. The meaning of all communication, after all, is context driven.

- *Nonverbal behaviors are often contradictory.* Our posture and vocal tone may say one thing, but our eyes may say another. We try to stand up straight and portray a dominant, confident posture, but our hands fidgeting with a pen may say something entirely different. Nonverbal behaviors do come "packaged" together, and we must often examine several behaviors before we begin to discern a coherent picture of the person before us. The problem with such packages or clusters of behaviors is that they're not always consistent and not always complementary. Which one should we believe?

- *Some nonverbal cues are more important than others.* As we examine several behaviors clustered together—vocal pace, tone, and pitch; body posture; pupil dilation; arm and hand movement—it often becomes clear to careful observers that some cues are more important than others. For the most part, the relative importance of a given cue is dependent on habits and usual behaviors of the speaker. In other words, are the behaviors I'm observing usual or unusual for this person? If they're unusual, do they contradict verbal portions of the message? And, finally, it is important to note that some portions of our anatomy are simply easier to control than others: Even a nervous person can sit still if she makes a determined effort to do so, but few among us can control the dilation of our pupils. Many can control facial expression, but few can determine when tears will flow or when our voices will choke with emotion.

- *We often read into some cues much that isn't there and fail to read some cues that are clearly present.* We often look for cues that seem most important to us personally: whether a person will look us directly in the eyes as we speak or which direction they've crossed their legs. Such cues may be meaningless. We can also misread cues if we have insufficient information on which to base a judgment. Business leaders seen nodding off in a conference may be judged as indifferent by their hosts; in reality, it may be jet lag that's caught up with them.

- *We're not as skilled at reading nonverbal cues as we think we are; our confidence often exceeds our ability.* Caution is the byword in dealing with nonverbal communication. Even though a substantial portion of what we learn from a human transaction (between two-thirds and three-quarters of all meaning) comes from nonverbal cues, we simply aren't as skilled at this as we'd like to be. It's easy to misinterpret, misread, or misunderstand someone. It's equally easy to jump to conclusions from just a few bits of evidence. The best advice for any manager would be to withhold judgment as long as possible, gather as much verbal as well as nonverbal information as possible, and then reconfirm what you think you know as frequently as possible. The stakes are high in business transactions, almost as high as the chances for error in decoding nonverbal cues.

For Further Reading

Archer, D. and Akert, R. "Words and Everything Else: Verbal and Nonverbal Cues in Social Interaction." *Journal of Personality and Social Psychology* 35 (1978), pp. 443–449.

Argyle, M. *Bodily Communication*, 2nd ed. London, UK: Methuen, 1998.

Buck, R. "A Test of Nonverbal Receiving Ability: Preliminary Studies." *Human Communication Research* 2 (1976), pp. 162–171.

Christensen, D., A. Farina, and Boudreau, L. "Sensitivity to Nonverbal Cues as a Function of Social Competence." *Journal of Nonverbal Behavior* 4 (1980), pp. 146–156.

McConnon, A. "You Are Where You Sit: How to Decode the Psychology of the Morning Meeting," *BusinessWeek*, July 23, 2007, pp. 66–67.

Leathers, D. G. *Successful Nonverbal Communication: Principals & Applications*. Boston, MA: Allyn & Bacon, 1996.

Morris, D. *Bodytalk: The Meaning of Human Gestures*. New York: Random House, Inc., 1994.

Morris, D. *The Naked Ape: A Zoologist's Study of the Human Animal*. New York: Delta Publishing, 1999.

Rogers, E. M. (ed.). *A History of Communication Study: A Biographical Approach*. New York: The Free Press, 1994.

Endnotes

1. Jackson, M. "Some Workers Uncomfortable with Trend Toward Casual Clothes," *South Bend Tribune*, January 8, 1998, p. C7. See also Lee, L. "Some Employees Just Aren't Suited for Dressing Down," *Wall Street Journal*, February 3, 1995, pp. A1, A6.

2. Jackson, "Some Workers Uncomfortable," p. C7. See also Berger, Joseph. "Black Jeans Invade Big Blue: First Day of a Relaxed IBM," *Wall Street Journal*, February 7, 1995, pp. A1, B4; and Bounds, W. and J. Lublin. "Will the Client Wear a Tie or a T-Shirt?" *Wall Street Journal*, July 24, 1998, pp. B1, B8. Reprinted by permission of *The Wall Street Journal*, Copyright © 1998 Dow Jones & Company, Inc. All rights reserved worldwide.

3. Critchell, S. "Men Move Toward More Dressy Clothes," *South Bend Tribune*, Sunday, April 28, 2002, p. F4. See also Jenkins, H. "Uptight Is Back in Style," *Wall Street Journal*, Wednesday, November 21, 2001, p. A15; Kaufman, L. "Return of the Suit Tentatively: Some Men Are Dressing Up Again, but Casual Still Lives," *New York Times*, Tuesday, April 2, 2002, pp. B1, B11; and Kaufman, L. "Casual Dress on the Way Out?" *Office Professional*, July 2002, p. 6.

4. Knapp, M. and J. Hall. *Nonverbal Communication in Human Interaction*, 3rd ed. Fort Worth, TX: Holt Rinehart and Winston, 1992, pp. 5–6.

5. Ruesch, J. and W. Kees. *Nonverbal Communication: Notes on the Visual Perception of Human Relations*. Los Angeles, CA: University of California Press, 1956.

6. Goleman, D. "Non-Verbal Cues Are Easy to Misinterpret," *New York Times*, September 17, 1991, p. B5. Copyright © 1991 by The New York Times Company. Reprinted with permission.

7. Ibid.

8. Ibid., pp. B5–6. See also, "Dated Suit, Dirty Nails Can Tip the Balance if You're Job Hunting," *Wall Street Journal*, Tuesday, June 1, 2004, p. B1. Reprinted by permission of *the Wall Street Journal*, Copyright © 2004 Dow Jones & Company, Inc. All rights reserved worldwide.

9. Eckman, P. "Communication Through Nonverbal Behavior: A Source of Information

About an Interpersonal Relationship." In Tomkins, S. S. and C. E. Izard (eds.), *Affect, Cognition and Personality*. New York: Springer and Co., Publishers, 1965.

10. DeVito, J. *The Interpersonal Communication Book*, 12th ed. Boston, MA: Allyn & Bacon, 2009, p. 215.

11. Ibid., pp. 214–226.

12. Knapp and Hall. *Nonverbal Communication*, pp. 13–16.

13. "Be Civil: There Is a Clampdown on Obscene Gestures in the Office and on the Field," *Wall Street Journal*, July 5, 1994, p. A1. Reprinted by permission of *The Wall Street Journal*, Copyright © 1994 Dow Jones & Company, Inc. All rights reserved worldwide.

14. Rubinkam, M. " 'Voice Stress' May Betray Suspects' Lies," *South Bend Tribune*, February 11, 2002, p. B7.

15. Varian, H. R. "A Beautiful Mind Is Not Enough When It Comes to Evaluating Teachers," *New York Times*, Thursday, August 28, 2003, p. C2. Copyright © 2003 by The New York Times Company. Reprinted with permission.

16. Harper, L. "Good Looks Can Mean a Pretty Penny on the Job, and 'Ugly' Men Are Affected More Than Women," *Wall Street Journal*, November 23, 1993, p. B1. See also Brody, J. "Ideals of Beauty Are Seen as Innate: The Ideal Face Transcends Culture, Study Says," *New York Times*, March 21, 1994, p. A6; Schoenberger, C. "Study Says the Handsome Turn Handsome Profits for Their Firms," *Wall Street Journal*, Thursday, August 12, 1997, p. B1; and Coy, P. "Thinner Paychecks for Obese Women?" *BusinessWeek*, October 30, 2000, p. 16.

17. "Fat Can Hit Women in the Wallet," *CBS News*. Online at: www.cbsnews.com/stories/2004/03/03/health/main603825.shtml. Retrieved July 28, 2008.

18. Ibid., p. B1. See also Newin, T. "Workplace Bias Ties to Obesity Is Ruled Illegal. Federal Judges Back a 320-Pound Woman." *New York Times*, November 24, 1993, p. A10. Copyright © 1993 by The New York Times Company. Reprinted with permission.

19. Brown, A. "Get a Grip—A Firm One: Handshakes Tell All," *U.S. News & World Report*, July 17, 2000, p. 48.

20. Rubin, R. "The Biochemistry of Touch," *U.S. News & World Report*, November 10, 1997, p. 62.

21. Knapp and Hall. *Nonverbal Communication*, p. 16.

22. DeVito. *Interpersonal Communication*, p. 265.

23. Ibid., p. 247.

24. Hymowitz, C. "If the Walls Had Ears, You Wouldn't Have Any Less Privacy," *Wall Street Journal*, May 19, 1998, p. B1. Reprinted by permission of *The Wall Street Journal*, Copyright © 1998 Dow Jones & Company, Inc. All rights reserved worldwide.

25. Rich, M. "Shut Up So We Can Do Our Jobs! Fed-Up Workers Try to Muffle Chitchat, Conference Calls and Other Open-Office Din," *Wall Street Journal*, Wednesday, August 29, 2001, pp. B1, B8. Reprinted by permission of *The Wall Street Journal*, Copyright © 2001 Dow Jones & Company, Inc. All rights reserved worldwide.

26. Bounds, G. "I Can't Really Talk, I'm Here in the Office. But Did You Know . . .?" *Wall Street Journal*, Wednesday, July 10, 2002, p. B1. Reprinted by permission of *The Wall Street Journal*, Copyright © 2002 Dow Jones & Company, Inc. All rights reserved worldwide.

27. Bednar, G., partner, Ernst & Young, LLP, Chicago, in a telephone interview with the author, August 17, 1998.

28. Ibid.

29. Ibid.

30. Ebersberger, W., partner, Ernst & Young, LLP, Chicago, in a telephone interview with the author, August 17, 1998. See also Pristin, T. "A New Office Can Mean Making Do with Less," *New York Times*, Wednesday, May 26, 2004, pp. Cl, C6.

31. Allen, T. J. *Managing the Flow of Technology*. Cambridge MA: The MIT Press, 1977, pp. 234–265.

32. For an excellent extended discussion of the role of space in social interaction, see Hall, E. T. *The Hidden Dimension*. New York: Doubleday, 1982.

33. DeVito. *Interpersonal Communication*, p. 248.

34. Ibid., p. 249.

35. Ibid., pp. 249–250.

36. Ferraro, G. *The Cultural Dimension of International Business*, 3rd ed. Upper Saddle River, NJ: Prentice-Hall, 1998, pp. 93–95.

37. For an excellent discussion of the role of time in human affairs, see Hall, E. T. *The Dance of Life.* New York: Doubleday, 1989.

38. Reiss, T. "Hey, It's Green—It Must Be Healthy," *BusinessWeek*, July 13, 1998, p. 6.

39. Hall, T. "The Quest for Colors That Make Lips Smack," *New York Times*, November 4, 1992, p. A13. See also Fountain, H. "Proof Positive that People See Colors with the Tongue," *New York Times*, March 30, 1999, p. D5.

40. Ibid., p. A19.

41. Tischler, L. "Smells Like Brand Spirit," *Fast Company*, August 2005, pp. 52–59. See also Laurent, G. "Olfaction: A Window into the Brain," *Engineering & Science*, California Institute of Technology, 68, no. 1–2 (2005).

42. Hall. *The Hidden Dimension*, pp. 45–50.

43. Tischler. "Smells Like Brand Spirit," p. 52.

44. Engen, T. *Odor Sensation and Memory.* New York: Praeger, 1991.

45. O'Neill, M. "Taming the Frontier of the Senses: Using Aroma to Manipulate Moods," *New York Times*, April 4, 1993, pp. B2, B6. Copyright © 1993 by The New York Times Company. Reprinted with permission.

46. Willoughby, J. "The Tip of Your Tongue Knows the Bitter Truth: Flavor Can Be Painful," *New York Times*, April 27, 1994, pp. B1, B5. Copyright © 1994 by The New York Times Company. Reprinted with permission.

47. Mansfield, M. United States Ambassador to Japan, in a personal interview with the author in the U.S. Embassy in Tokyo, May 1983.

48. DeVito. *Interpersonal Communication*, pp. 258–261.

49. Fast, J. *Body Language.* New York: M. Evans, 1970.

50. Knapp and Hall. *Nonverbal Communication*, p. 27.

51. Ibid.

CASE STUDY 9-1

Olive Garden Restaurants Division General Mills Corporation

Managers occupying junior- to middle-level positions in large organizations are often called upon to resolve disputes. Some of these are disagreements between lower-level supervisors and employees; some are disputes with suppliers or distributors; others, like the dispute in this case, are between the organization and a customer.

Every customer has a value to an organization, and every customer has a price to that organization. Customers are, of course, the lifeblood and source of revenue to a business, but not all customers are worth saving. Some, in fact, may be more trouble and expense to maintain than they are worth.

Dealing with customers—or with anyone else who is in disagreement with your organization—requires patience, tact, and a certain measure of skill. A variety of response modes is open to the manager who faces an angry customer, along with a range of options in dealing with the case.

This case requires two documents in response: a one-page communication strategy memo and a letter to the customer. The strategy memo should be directed to the president of the Olive Garden Restaurants Division and should describe in some detail how you plan to handle this case and why. The letter to the customer explains what you have chosen to do.

Assume that you are the director of customer service and report through the vice president for sales and marketing to the president. Your memorandum and customer letter should be in finished form, ready to transmit.

[Dated Three Days Ago]
51588 River Forest Dr.
South Bend, IN 46617

Mr. Ronald N. Magruder
President, Olive Garden Restaurants Division
General Mills Corporation
5900 Lake Ellenor Drive Orlando, FL 33809

Dear Mr. Magruder:

Last week, my family and I had a genuinely unpleasant experience in an Olive Garden Restaurant. My first instinct was to dismiss it as another example of bad customer service and forget about it. The truth is, I can't forget about it. The experience was bad enough that I thought you should hear about it.

On Tuesday evening of last week, I selected the Olive Garden Restaurant at 6410 Grape Road in Mishawaka, Indiana, for a mid-evening meal with my father and two daughters. We've had good experiences and great food in Olive Garden Restaurants before and, in fact, think your facilities are generally well run.

We arrived at the restaurant about 8:15 P.M. and were surprised to discover that very few customers were seated for dinner. No one was waiting in the entryway to greet us—something we have come to expect at Olive Garden. After waiting more than ten minutes for a hostess, I went into the bar and asked if someone could seat us. A hostess, clearly annoyed at the prospect of additional customers, offered us a table in an area my father couldn't walk to. He is an amputee and walks, with great difficulty, on crutches.

After an extended discussion about why we couldn't take a table in the upper seating area, the hostess showed us a table (not cleaned off) and left the menus. We discovered that I had a luncheon menu and there were no children's menus available.

Our next challenge was finding a waiter. After an extended wait (10–12 minutes), a young man appeared and wanted to know if we had been helped. He indicated that this table wasn't "in his station," but offered to take our orders anyway. We ordered our meals and I asked for a glass of wine. Twenty minutes later (nearly 45 minutes after our arrival), our meals arrived (cold) and I was told that the bar was out of wine. Two additional requests produced silverware and napkins.

When we sampled our meals and discovered they were cold, I asked to see the manager—a large, officious man who was equally annoyed with the prospect of customers at that hour. The meals were prepared exactly as we had ordered and were fine, except that our waiter had forgotten about them. My cannelloni was cold—there is no other way to describe it. My father's meal was the same but he asked me not to complain. The girls simply ate their meals (equally cold) and didn't want to become involved in a verbal exchange with the manager. Please keep in mind that I haven't sent back a meal twice in the past 30 years. I'm not a complainer.

I was given a second plate of cannelloni and the waiter departed—apparently for the evening. We never saw him again. We finished our meals and waited—it was nearly ten o'clock in the evening on a Tuesday with just one other couple seated in the dining room. Coffee and dessert were out of the question. I just wanted a check and, if possible, a brief discussion with the manager about what had happened.

Mr. Ronald N. Magruder
[Dated Three Days Ago]
Page Two

Again, I had to go into the bar to find an employee and wait—5 to 7 minutes—for my check. The manager was absolutely confrontational when I told him what I have just related to you. "What do you want me to do about it?" he said. "Tell your employees that I'm a customer and not a nuisance in their evening," I answered. Then, unbelievably, he asked "Are you lookin' for a free meal or somethin'?" I was stunned.

I signed the American Express charge slip and turned to leave. Your manager mumbled, just loud enough for me to hear, "No tip, huh?" I turned and said to him, "I've got a tip for you, friend. Get out of the food business."

It's been nearly a week since the event and I'm still upset, partly because of his behavior and the experience my father and children went through, and partly because I genuinely like Olive Garden Restaurants. I must tell you, in all honesty, I cannot now imagine returning to that one.

Thanks for listening to my story. I know it's not easy to listen to a customer with a "bad service" story, but I feel better having shared it with you.

Sincerely,

Martin A. Wallace, M.D.

This case was prepared from public sources by James S. O'Rourke, Concurrent Professor of Management, as the basis for class discussion rather than to illustrate either effective or ineffective handling of an administrative situation. Personal and corporate identities have been disguised.

CASE STUDY 9-2

Waukegan Materials, Inc.

Managers are often called on to recognize the achievements and accomplishments of their employees and others within their organizations. Public acknowledgment of exceptional work, career milestones, and special events in people's lives are important, not only to those being recognized, but also to others who carefully observe how the organization treats its people.

Those who have worked in and for large, complex organizations will often acknowledge that it's difficult to monitor and properly appreciate individual achievements. Many financial, sales, production, and profit goals are predicated on group activities; individuals often are made to bask in the reflected glory of group membership.

Among the more useful observations regarding letters of appreciation are these: If it isn't worth writing as a personal, individual document, it isn't worth receiving. Generic, one-size-fits-all letters are frequently the subject of employee scorn. Letters of appreciation, in general, should be brief, warm, and specific. They should probably not extend beyond two or three paragraphs, they should reflect a controlled enthusiasm for the message recipient, and they should comment specifically on the achievements or accomplishment for which the receiver is being recognized.

Waukegan Materials, Inc., is a regional distributor in the building and construction industry.

They conduct both wholesale and retail operations and are a nonunion firm. You may assume that you are general manager of the Lakefront Division. This case requires two documents: a one-page transmittal memorandum and a letter of appreciation to an employee. The memo should be directed to the company president and should respond to the president's questions posed in the case. Both documents should be in final form and ready to dispatch.

Waukegan Materials, Inc.
3400 Sheridan Road
Waukegan, Illinois 60620

DATE:　　　　[Today's Date]
TO:　　　　General Manager, Lakefront Division
FROM:　　　Paul Magers, President, Waukegan Materials, Inc.
SUBJECT:　Employee-of-the-Quarter Awards

Your suggestion that Waukegan Materials, Inc., begin a program of employee recognition was a good one. As you know, we have had more than two dozen nominations for the first of our quarterly employee recognition awards, and it's been difficult to select just one who is more deserving than the others for this honor. After several long and very trying sessions, the awards committee has selected our first recipient.

The Waukegan Materials Employee-of-the-Quarter is Mr. Delbert R. Finch of our roofing supplies branch. Finch is an all-around good fellow with a very impressive work record. In fact, he hasn't missed a day's work in the nine years he has been with Waukegan. He tracks the ordering of materials in our roofing supply branch, arranges for shipment to retailers and construction contractors, supervises stock assortment and reshelving operations, and generally keeps an eye on things in the Lakefront Warehouse.

Please help me and the committee by providing us with a letter to recognize Mr. Finch's good work. I would like to present him with the letter and some sort of appropriate gift or memento at our quarterly supervisors' luncheon next month. I don't want to spend a fortune on this program, but I do want the gift to be both appropriate and suitable. The letter should be a good one, too; I'm thinking about having it framed for him and giving a copy to the local newspapers.

Tell me what you plan for us to give him, what this will cost, and how much you think we should spend annually on the program. Please draft a letter today acknowledging his achievements. I'd like to see something by the close of business. Thanks for your help.

- PM -

This case was prepared from public sources by James S. O'Rourke, Concurrent Professor of Management, as the basis for class discussion rather than to illustrate either effective or ineffective handling of an administrative situation. Personal and corporate identities have been disguised.

Chapter *10*

Intercultural Communication

The world you inhabit in the twenty-first century is becoming a vastly different place from the one your parents knew as a child of the twentieth century. The industrialized nations of the world are experiencing change of an unprecedented sort, and the United States is gradually but inevitably becoming different from the nation your parents and grandparents lived and worked in.

What will be different in the days ahead? Almost everything, from the food you eat to the technology you use to the work you do. The organizations that will employ you are changing, restructuring, and transforming themselves. The products and services they provide are changing, as are the skills needed to produce them. The community in which you live will change, as will the people who live there.

The people who inhabit this nation, in fact, will change more profoundly and more quickly than at any previous time in our history, bringing with them fundamental cultural shifts that will redefine what it means to be an American, what *work* is, what *business* means, and what we mean by a *family*. In sum, life in the twenty-first century will not be "business as usual."

Let's look first at some areas we know will change dramatically in the years just ahead and then examine what we mean by culture and diversity. If you understand the circumstances you are likely to face as you tackle the task of managing a business in a highly competitive, global business environment, your chances for success are greater. And more than anything else—more than technology, science, law, the environment, or systems of government—the social norms and new rules of our society will affect how your business will operate and the challenges you will face as a manager.

INTERCULTURAL CHALLENGES AT HOME

ETHNICITY According to the U.S. Census Bureau, profound shifts in the next few decades will leave this country older and far more ethnically diverse than ever before. By the middle of the twenty-first century, the United States will no longer have a "majority" race, but instead will be a nation of multiple ethnic groups. Non-Hispanic whites will account for just half of our population. Hispanics will comprise about one-quarter of this country's people, and African Americans will grow slowly to just over 13 percent. Asian Americans are projected to become about 8 percent of the nation's citizens.[1]

POPULATION GROWTH The current U.S. population of 312 million is projected to reach about 325 million in 2020 and more than 400 million by mid-century. That increase may sound huge, but it will actually reflect an all-time *low growth rate* after the year 2025. Put simply, the large group of aging baby boomers—those 76 million Americans born between 1946 and 1964—will begin dying faster than new Americans are born, reducing net population increases.[2]

IMMIGRATION Offsetting some of that decline is a surge in immigration that has brought the number of foreign-born residents to the highest level in this nation's history. The most recent census figures available show that the number of foreign-born residents and their children grew from 34 million in the 1970s to more than 56 million. A comprehensive study of the census data shows that, on average, foreign-born residents are much more likely to live in or around a handful of large cities than are people born in the United States. That same study also shows the near impossibility of generalizing about immigrants and their experience here. For example, while just one-third of those residents over 25 who were born in Mexico had completed high school, more than 95 percent of those born in Africa had. And although median household income for those born in Latin American was well under $29,000 annually, it was more than $51,000 for those from Asia, well above that of the native U.S. population.[3]

Census Bureau figures show that the immigrant population is becoming younger, a shift likely to foster more tolerance for diversity and perhaps accelerate assimilation. Those figures also show that immigration trends are forming a unique generational divide: those immigrants over 40 are largely white, whereas those under 40 are increasingly Hispanic, Asian, and from other minority groups. By the second decade of this century, half of all Hispanics were under age 27, and one of every 5 children under age 18 in the United States was Hispanic. Most impressive, Hispanics account for about half of the overall population growth in the United States since the turn of the century.[4]

AGE In the next decade alone, the number of people in the United States over the age of 50 will increase by half. In July 1983, the number of Americans over the age of 65 surpassed the number of teenagers. And with continuing improvements in lifestyle and medical technology, the over-65 population in this country is likely to be more than 86.7 million by the year 2050—a figure that represents between one-fourth and one-fifth of our population. From 2010 through 2030, some 78 million "baby boomers" in the United States will turn 65 at the rate of 7,000 a day.[5] Today, in fact, more than 65,000 Americans are over the age of 100. And by the middle of the twenty-first century, that number may be more than 800,000.[6]

At the same time that the average ages of the population and the workforce are rising, the pool of young workers entering the labor market is shrinking. The average worker's age in the United States in 1987 was 36. By 2010, that average would be nearly 41. And workers in the 16- to 24-year-old age group will shrink by several million, or nearly 8 percent of the population.

FAMILIES The shape, size, and even the definition of American families have changed over the past 30 years. Since 1970, they have become smaller; more of them are led by just one parent; and more have mothers who work outside the home. According to Ken Bryson of the U.S. Census Bureau, "In the 1970s and 1980s, we had a big shift from married couples with children to one-parent families and people living alone."[7] A recent study that he supervised found that the number of married couples with children under 18 shrank from 40 percent of all households to 25 percent. Divorce rates have soared, and the number of single-person households has climbed from 17 to 25 percent.[8]

WOMEN IN THE WORKFORCE More women are entering the workforce than at any time since the end of World War II. Since 1998, two-thirds of all new workers in the United States have been female. And by 2010, nearly two-thirds of all working-age women were employed. Today, the United States has a workforce that is about 46 percent female, compared with smaller figures in Japan and Mexico but larger percentages in Sweden and Denmark. A U.S. Labor Department study shows that women hold 43 percent of all executive, administrative, and managerial jobs in the United States. By comparison, women hold just 17 percent of all managerial positions in Sweden and less than 10 percent in Japan.[9]

Noteworthy as well is that even though working women in the United States are doing better in terms of opportunity and advancement than the vast majority of their counterparts in other nations, they are still paid about 75 percent of what men in comparable positions receive. In addition, working women still bear a disproportionate share of the burden of child care and household duties. Some 42 percent of working moms, in fact, have children under seven years of age.[10]

CULTURAL CHALLENGES ABROAD

A NEW WORLD ORDER Among the more important events of the twentieth century was the fall of the Berlin Wall in 1988. In the decades that followed the collapse of communism and the disintegration of the Soviet Union, we have witnessed a flowering of freedom in Eastern Europe, the establishment of a single European currency, and a lowering of restrictions on the movement of capital, labor, and finished goods. The world has seen its exchanges and bourses integrate into a seamless, global marketplace for money. Jobs flow to areas with lower-priced, competent labor. Capital flows to investment opportunities that best balance risk with return. And the definition of "made in America" now depends on which part of the product or process you examine. In the early decades of the twenty-first century, the market never sleeps. The manager who plans to participate only in a domestic economy will have few places left to work.

International business is a fact of life today as never before. And in order to succeed, whether as a manager in a transnational corporation, or as an entrepreneur in a small business hoping to sell goods and services to people in other nations, you will need a thorough understanding of the people in your company, your industry, and the global marketplace. The key to understanding them is an understanding of their culture.

CUSTOMS AND CULTURE ABROAD In Hungary, men customarily walk on the left side of women or anyone of greater status, like a boss. It's considered intrusive to ask a man from the Middle East about his wife or female members of his family. It's also considered impolite for a woman to serve wine in Italy. Why? Well, as you will discover, different cultures promote different ways of thinking and behaving. What's considered customary for you at home may well be unacceptable overseas. And, of course, what's perfectly natural for people—even professional businesspeople—in other countries may be considered peculiar or offensive here.

Some mistakes can be worse than embarrassing. Anthropologist Margaret Nydell tells of an American woman in Saudi Arabia who slid into the front passenger seat of a car and planted a friendly kiss on the cheek of the man at the wheel. Public displays of affection don't play well there. The gesture was spotted by a captain of the Saudi National Guard who demanded to know if the couple was married. They were, but not to each other. As a result, the woman was expelled from the country and the man, who argued with the guardsman, spent some time in jail.[11]

Nonverbal communication can be as much a source of misunderstanding as verbal, according to American business consultant, Elizabeth Ulrich. "The classic example is the 'A-OK' gesture which is positive in the United States," she says, "but obscene in much of the rest of the world." That same gesture in France means "worthless." It is impolite to point to people in Japan or to give the split-fingered "victory" sign knuckles out in England. It is offensive to use the "thumbs-up" sign in Nigeria or to eat with your left hand in most Arab countries.[12]

Mary Murray Bosrock, author of a series of international etiquette books, says showing up on time for a dinner party in South America could be a disaster—no one expects anyone to be less than half-an-hour to an hour late. She says you are liable to find your host or hostess still getting dressed if you actually arrive at the hour printed on the invitation.[13]

In many Asian cultures, particularly Japan, saying no is considered very impolite. In fact, it's unusual to the point of being rare, particularly in business negotiations. According to Philip R. Harris, an international business consultant, and Robert T. Moran, a professor of international management, indirect and vague approaches are more acceptable than direct and specific references. "Sentences are frequently left unfinished so that the other person may conclude them in his or her own mind. Conversation often transpires within an ill-defined and shadowy context, never quite definite so as not to preclude personal interpretation."[14]

Japanese businesspeople are reluctant in the extreme to say no to a direct question, even when the answer is, in fact, no. Instead, you may hear, "These things often take much time," "Issues of this sort, as you understand, are sometimes difficult," or "We are sorry that things have developed in such a fashion." Often, a Japanese businessperson will simply change the subject or direct an unrelated question back to you. In the most extreme conditions, if you ask for a yes or no response, you will receive only silence, usually accompanied by head nods, tightened lips, and a break in eye contact with you. A senior, experienced Japanese trade negotiator puts it this way: "It is true that we Japanese try diligently to prevent any situation from becoming what we call *tairitsu*, a confrontation, whether in our personal lives or in business and politics."[15]

Being culturally sensitive is essential to your success. In Japan, for example, the presentation of a business card is done with reverence, almost like an intricate dance. Cards, which represent the person's importance to the company and personal identity within the community, are gently presented with two hands and accomplished with a bow. Businesspeople exchanging cards always face each other, holding their cards on the upper two corners. The recipient is expected to take the card and, with studied seriousness, examine it thoroughly before carefully and respectfully putting it in a cardholder. During business meetings, cards are often kept out in the open and used respectfully as a reference point during conversations.[16]

In the United States, according to Roger E. Axtell, former marketing vice president for Parker Pen Co., "We just stuff them in our pockets or even write on them." During a business trip to Japan, Axtell saw an American businessman picking his teeth with a business card. "I thought, 'Hey, that's my personal identity there!' "[17]

One further caution regarding business cards: Bring enough for everyone. You'll find that not only do the principals in a meeting want your card—everyone in the room expects one. Americans traveling in Asia should expect to hand out 200 cards a week. You'll get bonus points if your card is translated into the local language on the reverse side. To make absolutely certain the translation is precise and correct, ask your U.S. Chamber of Commerce contact for advice on having your cards printed on the backside before you arrive.

You've undoubtedly heard or read about the elaborate rituals of gift giving in Japan, where just about every business occasion demands an exchange of gifts. You know some numbers are unlucky in China or that some colors are inappropriate for gifts or flowers in the Middle East. But the rules are many and varied, so if you are traveling to a new part of the world to try to make money—or even as a tourist—you are well advised to learn something of the culture and the local customs.

BUSINESS AND CULTURE

Whether you are dealing with issues of marketing, management, finance, or even the details of accounting for a firm's assets and business activities, the success or failure of your company abroad will depend on how effectively your employees can exercise their skills in a new location. That ability will depend on both their job-related expertise and each individual's sensitivity and responsiveness to a new cultural environment. Among the most common factors contributing to failure in international business assignments, according to Professor Gary P. Ferraro of the University of North Carolina, "is the erroneous assumption that if a person is successful in the home environment, he or she will be equally successful in applying technical expertise in a different culture."[18]

Research has shown that failures in an overseas business setting most frequently result from an inability to understand and adapt to foreign ways of thinking and acting, rather than from technical or professional incompetence. At home, U.S. businesspeople equip themselves with vast amounts of knowledge about their employees, customers, and business partners. Market research provides detailed information on values, attitudes, and buying preferences of U.S. consumers. Middle- and upper-level managers are well versed in the intricacies of their organization's culture, and labor negotiators must be highly sensitive to what motivates those on the other side of the table. Yet when North Americans begin doing business abroad, they frequently are willing to work with customers, employees, suppliers, and others about whom they know and understand very little.[19]

In the last few years, a growing number of Americans in their 20s and 30s have been heading to China for employment, lured by its faster-growing economy and lower jobless rate. Their Chinese coworkers are often around the same age. But the two groups were raised differently. The Americans have had more exposure to free-market principles. "Young Americans were brought up in a commercial environment, said Neng Zhao, 28, a senior associate at Blue Oak Capital in Beijing. We weren't. So the workplace is a unique learning process for my generation."[20]

It is imperative for Americans working in China to adjust, according to Michael Normal, senior vice president at Sibson Consulting. "In the West, there is such a premium on getting things done quickly, but when you come to work in China, you need to work on listening and being more patient and understanding local ways of doing business." The Chinese now rising in the workforce were raised and educated in a system that tended to prize obedience and rote learning. Their American counterparts may have had more leeway to question authority and speak their minds, and this can affect workplace communication.[21]

Communication styles, according to Professor Vas Taras of the University of North at Greensboro, can create workplace challenges. "Americans often perceive the Chinese as indecisive, less confident and not tough enough, whereas the Chinese may see Americans as rude or inconsiderate."[22]

DEFINITIONS OF CULTURE

So what exactly is culture and how does it affect the way we do business? *Culture is everything that people have, think, and do as members of their society.* Culture affects and is a central part of our society, our economy, and the organizations that employ us. Culture is, thus, composed of material objects; ideas, values, and attitudes; and expected patterns of behavior.

MATERIAL OBJECTS Everything you own, lease, borrow, or use is defined as a part of your culture, from the automobile you drive to the clothing you wear. We make judgments each day, often without even being aware we are doing so, about the people we meet and do business with. Many, if not most, of those judgments depend on what we think about the way people are dressed, whether their shoes are polished, how their offices are furnished, the sort of wristwatch they wear or briefcase they carry, and so on. People, in turn, judge us by the material objects we use and surround ourselves with.

IDEAS, VALUES, AND ATTITUDES We also tend to categorize people according to the ways they think, the ideas they believe, or the basic values they hold to be true. Sometimes the categories are easily described, such as *liberal* or *conservative*. Other ideas, including religious beliefs, or fundamental ideas about family, society, and self are not so easy to categorize.

EXPECTED PATTERNS OF BEHAVIOR Every society has certain cultural norms regarding behavior. In the United States, women expect equal treatment under the law, but in many Middle Eastern nations, such as Saudi Arabia, women do not have voting privileges and are not permitted to drive an automobile. Cultural norms in that part of the world are very closely tied to Islamic religious doctrine and prescribe a wide span of expected behaviors ranging from what clothing is permissible to when and with whom a woman might be away from her home.

In many ways, culture defines how we look at life in general, and it guides how we respond to characteristics such as race, ethnicity, physical attributes, age, social class, education, and many other factors. It also shapes our responses to these qualities, both within ourselves and in other people.[23] At the broad social level, culture tells us who we are (what groups we belong to), tells us how we should behave, and "gives us attitudes about 'them,' the people who are different from us. It tells us what should be important as well as how to act in various situations."[24]

Culture surrounds us so completely, and from such an early point in life, that we are often unaware of other ways of dealing with the world, that others may have a different outlook on life, a different logic, or a different way of responding to people and situations.[25]

SOME PRINCIPLES OF CULTURE

Here, then, are a few ideas about culture that have been shown to be true across time and across both national and cultural boundaries.

CULTURE IS LEARNED In 1861, Giuseppe Garibaldi played a pivotal role in uniting a collection of feudal kingdoms and principalities into the modern nation-state of Italy. As the populace of southern Italy acclaimed Garibaldi as their ruler, he told the cheering throngs, "Now that we have founded the nation of Italy, we must all learn to be Italian."[26] Few of us would give a moment's thought to *learning* how to be American, Italian, Mexican, or any other culture. If you were born into a culture, you learn from the moment you begin to see, hear, and breathe. Our first culture is so closely defined with each of us that we're barely aware we *have* one. Learning a second culture, though, is clearly more difficult. The older we become, the closer to impossible the task becomes.

CULTURE IS UNIVERSAL TO HUMAN SOCIETY Everyone has a culture, regardless of where they were born, raised, educated, and civilized. For some among us, the idea of a *specific* culture is not as easy as it may look. My college roommate was born and raised in Syracuse, New York. His wife, Mary, was born and raised in northern California. Following their marriage in the 1970s, they moved overseas and have lived in the Philippines, Kenya, Greece, Italy, and England.

No matter where they move, however, and no matter how many different cultures they're exposed to, they'll always be thoroughly American. Their vocabulary and preferences in food have changed a bit, but not their basic culture. For their two boys, Jim and John, culture is a different matter. Even though they grew up with U.S. passports and American parents, they lived in societies different from those their parents grew up in. They were educated in British schools and, for all intents and purposes, they've really become British by culture and "citizens of the world" by experience.

All societies exhibit an interest in passing along cultural values and norms to their children. It's really the similarity of those values and norms that collectively creates and defines a culture. Thus, no matter where you travel, you'll find people with cultures of their own that are interesting, diverse, and rich, but different from the one in which you grew up.

CULTURE IS CONSTANTLY UNDERGOING CHANGE Among the basic truths about culture is that none is ever static. The clothing people wear, the transportation they use, the books they read, the topics they talk about, the food they eat, the music they listen and dance to, all will change over time. Compare the lives your grandparents led to the life you are leading, and you'll get some sense of how your own grandchildren will look at you. Change is the constant in every culture. Some will insist that whatever is new in a culture (what sort of music is your little brother listening to?) is inferior to whatever came before. True or not (and, usually, it's a matter of opinion about whether change is an improvement), the elements that make us who we are will constantly remain in flux.

Cultures change because of *internal forces*, such as discovery, invention, and innovation. They also change because of *external forces*, including the diffusion of innovation across space and time and borrowing the traits, habits, or customs of another culture.

SOME CULTURES CHANGE MORE QUICKLY THAN OTHERS Some societies are isolated by geography, such as vast oceans or tall mountain ranges. Others are isolated by preference. The more keenly tuned-in a society is to the interests and preferences of other cultures, the more quickly change will come. If fashions change quickly in Paris or Milan each spring, can New York and Los Angeles be far behind in producing copies? Life in parts of the American Midwest and South change more slowly, in part because of geography and in part because of preference. Some people prefer things as they are and try to preserve life as they know it; others prefer change and will move to cities or other nations in search of that change.

Los Angeles, California, is nearly 3,000 miles from New York City, but culturally the two cities are not vastly different. Residents will point to a faster pace in New York and a more laid back style in Los Angeles, but they are both metropolitan centers of business, politics, media, publishing, fashion, food, and much more. Needles, California, is just over 400 miles from Los Angeles, but culturally it's light years away. The pace of life, the food available in local restaurants, the clothing worn there, and everything else from entertainment to commerce are vastly different. The people of Needles proudly point to the fact that not much has changed in their little town over the past 50 years, and they like it that way. Life in Los Angeles can, and probably will, change in significant ways before you have lunch tomorrow.

Five factors influence the *rate* of change as well as the *kind* of change a culture may experience. These factors include:

- *Relative advantage.* Is it superior to what already exists? If the change isn't superior in some way to existing habits, the innovation is unlikely to catch on (think: 3-D television).
- *Compatibility.* Is it consistent with existing cultural patterns? Some changes are superior to current practices but they may be at odds with existing culture patterns. If what's new is not compatible with the ways in which the majority of people think and behave, change may be slow to occur.
- *Complexity.* Is it easily understood? Desktop computers represent a clearly superior means of communicating and processing both text and data, but their general complexity held back widespread adoption for the better part of a decade in our society.
- *Trialability.* Is it testable? Can we try it out experimentally? The difference between hair dye and a tattoo is that while one is temporary, the other is permanent. Cultural change comes more quickly when people can experiment a bit without making irrevocable decisions.
- *Observability.* Are the benefits clearly visible to those affected by change? If you can't see its value, you may be unwilling to try it.[27]

CULTURE IS NOT VALUE-NEUTRAL The diversity movement in this country, for all the good and positive change it has brought to American business and higher education, has passed along one subtle *untruth* that is frequently repeated: "We must respect all other cultures because our culture is really no better than theirs. Ours is simply different."

Our culture certainly *is* different from others, but that's not the same as saying that all cultures are equally moral, equally fair, or equally humane. Amnesty International annually publishes a list of cultures in which people are denied basic human rights. And Transparency International develops a list of nations each year that are rank ordered according to level of corruption. The United States, by the way, is among the least corrupt nations on earth but is still some distance from the top of the list. In 2010, Denmark was listed as the least corrupt among nations.[28]

With human rights and corrupt behavior as basic considerations, we must also understand that many factors from ancient tradition to religious belief can produce human behavior that you and I may well regard as offensive or outrageous. In the second decade of the twenty-first century, women are still not allowed to vote or own property in many nations, and in other nations they are often ritualistically mutilated or sold into slavery. The fact that such practices are accepted in those societies and simultaneously shock us is a sign that our values and theirs aren't the same. Our cultures may well be quite different from one another, but they are neither equal nor interchangeable in all respects. Culture, in fact, is *not* value-neutral.

NOT ALL CULTURES ARE EQUALLY COMPLEX Because of size, geography, distance from great population centers, and other factors, some cultures are simpler in their patterns of organization, behavior, and belief than others. Vast sections of sub-Saharan Africa, the Polynesian islands of the South Pacific, the dense interior of South America's jungles and rain forests, and the frozen tundra of the Arctic have developed cultures that are both ancient and rich in their heritage but not terribly complex. Many still depend on barter to survive and small councils of elders for adjudicating legal problems. The modern G-8 nations have legal systems and tax codes so complex that no lawyer or accountant could claim expertise in all of them.

VIRTUALLY ALL CULTURES PERMIT THE DEVELOPMENT OF SUBCULTURES Within each culture, small groups of people inevitably develop separate and specialized interests: hikers, bikers, baseball fans, gourmet cooks, Bible readers, bird-watchers, and volunteer firefighters. The list is potentially endless as people gather together in the same room, on the telephone, or on the Internet to pursue their common interests. The tolerance of some societies is not endless, however. Highly repressive cultures permit little in the way of deviation from doctrine. Cuba, for example, banned the celebration of Christmas from 1959 until 1998. Even the United States officially bans certain activities by hate groups even though the U.S. Constitution protects their right to exist. The more complex the culture, the greater the likelihood that subcultures will flourish, and the greater their number is likely to be.

CULTURE CAN INFLUENCE BIOLOGY AND BIOLOGY CAN INFLUENCE CULTURE This concept may not seem self-evident at first, but culture can, and does, have an enormous influence on human biology. The most striking example can be seen in the dramatic increase in average height and body weight of the Japanese people during the past 50 years of the twentieth century. Men in their third decade of life now weigh substantially more than their grandfathers did and are, on average, several inches taller. The gains in women's physiognomy are equally impressive.

Other illustrations abound, from facial scars and body adornment in West Africa to breast implants and plastic facial surgery in the United States. Even such issues as fat content in our diets can affect how big we grow and how fit we are. The United States, to counterbalance a culture that had grown soft and averse to exercise, has actively portrayed exercise and fitness as desirable and worthwhile. Not only have many people worked themselves into generally better physical condition, several new industries have grown up around them, offering sportswear, exercise machines, high-tech shoes, and high-energy diets.

FUNCTIONS OF CULTURE

Cultures universally respond to human problems and challenges by developing systems to deal with them. Most successful cultures develop economic systems, marriage and family systems, educational systems, and supernatural belief systems. These systems are more complex and intricate in some cultures than in others, but for the most part, people collectively establish rules for economic value and trade, systems for assigning responsibility, for establishing and raising families, for educating children, and for a belief in God or an afterlife. Individual beliefs may vary somewhat, but it is the culture itself that establishes how most people in a society think, believe, and behave.[29]

ETHNOCENTRISM

All cultures, to one degree or another, display *ethnocentrism*, or the tendency to evaluate a foreigner's behavior by the standards of one's own culture and to believe that one's own culture is superior to all others. We take our culture for granted. We're born into it, live with its rules and assumptions, day in and day out. We quickly come to believe that the way we live is simply "the way things should be."

As a result, we see our behavior as correct and others' as wrong. Keep in mind what we've said about culture *not* being value-neutral. We have good reasons for believing and behaving as we do, but that doesn't necessarily mean that others are "wrong."

All cultures are ethnocentric, some more so than others. Ethnocentrism, in fact, can enhance group solidarity within a society and is often used by corrupt national or ethnic leaders as a means of building or consolidating power and excluding outsiders. Clearly, ethnocentrism can foster prejudice, contempt, stereotypes, and conflict.[30]

CROSS-CULTURAL COMMUNICATION SKILLS

One set of skills essential to success in a global economy, then, is the ability to communicate across cultures. According to a number of authors on this subject, the skill set you need involves several personal capacities:

- *The capacity to accept the relativity of your own knowledge and perceptions.* We each tend to judge people, events, and ideas against our own education, background, and beliefs. Simply recognizing that some of these are bound to be different from those of other cultures is a useful starting point.
- *The capacity to be nonjudgmental.* Make personal judgments, if you wish. Just keep them to yourself.
- *A tolerance for ambiguity.* Accept the fact that you'll never understand everything about another culture; you can still appreciate and function within that culture satisfactorily.

This skill set, then, involves the capacity to communicate respect for other people's ways, their country, and their values without adopting or internalizing them. These skills also include the capacity to display empathy, to be flexible (particularly under conditions of high ambiguity or uncertainty), to take turns (or wait your turn, if you're uncertain of the protocol), and the humility to acknowledge what you do not know or understand.

Clearly, understanding what motivates the people you hope to do business with will be crucial to your success. Technical competence in your line of work is important, but so is an understanding of the culture, customs, norms, and beliefs of others, whether domestically or internationally. Curiously, as we find the world's economy becoming more global and interdependent, we also find our own nation undergoing similar changes. The only constant in the years ahead, it seems, will be change itself.

For Further Reading

Beamer, L. and Varner, I. *Intercultural Communication in the Global Workplace*, 4th ed. Boston, MA: McGraw Hill Irwin, 2007.

Binns, C. "American Can't Step Into Shoes of Others; Individualism Stops People from Seeing Others' Viewpoints, Study Suggests," MSNBC.com. Updated: 1:48 P.M. ET July 18, 2007. Retrieved from http://www.msnbc.msn.com/id/19832287/from/ET/.

Brinkley, C. "Where Yellow's a Faux Pas and White Is Death," *Wall Street Journal*, December 6, 2007, pp. D1, D8.

Ely, R. J., Meyerson, D. E., and Davidson, M. N. "Rethinking Political Correctness," *Harvard Business Review*, September 2006, pp. 79–87.

Ferraro, G. P. *Global Brains: Knowledge and Competencies for the 21st Century.* Charlotte, NC: Intercultural Associates, Inc., 2001.

Harrison, L. E. and Huntington, S. P. *Culture Matters: How Values Shape Human Progress.* New York: Basic Books, 2000.

Jandt, F. E. *An Introduction to Intercultural Communication: Identities in a Global Community.* Thousand Oaks, CA: Sage, 2003.

Javidan, M. "Forward-Thinking Cultures," *Harvard Business Review*, July–August 2007, p. 20.

Kenton, S. and Valentine, D. *CrossTalk: Communicating in a Multicultural Workplace.* Upper Saddle River, NJ: Prentice Hall, 1997.

Nagourney, E. "East and West Part Ways in Test of Facial Expressions," *New York Times*, March 18, 2008, p. D5.

Tierney, J. "As Barriers Disappear, Some Gender Gaps Widen," *New York Times*, Tuesday, September 9, 2008, pp. D1, D4.

Tuleja, E. A. *Intercultural Communication for Business*, 2nd ed. Mason, OH: Cengage South-Western, 2008.

Urich, E. *Speaking Globally: Effective Presentations Across International and Cultural Boundaries.* Exeter, NH: Kogan Page, 1998.

Walker, D. M., Walker, T., and Schmitz, J. *Doing Business Internationally: The Guide to Cross-Cultural Success*, 2nd ed. New York: McGraw Hill Trade, 2002.

Endnotes

1. Friedman, D. and K. Pollack. "Ahead: A Very Different Nation," *U.S. News & World Report*, March 25, 1996, p. 8.
2. U.S. Census Bureau, "National Population Projection (Summary Files)," available online at http://www.census.gov/population/www/projections/natsum-T1.html. Retrieved on July 16, 2008 at 1:43 P.M. See update: http://2010.census.gov/2010census/data/index.php retrieved on January 6, 2011 at 12:03 P.M.
3. Scott, J. "Foreign Born in U.S. at Record High: Census Puts Number at 56 Million, with Mexico Chief Supplier," *New York Times*, February 7, 2002, p. A18. See also Swarns, R. L. "Hispanics Resist Racial Grouping by Census," *New York Times*, October 24, 2005, pp. 1, 18.
4. Files, J. "Report Describes Immigrants as Younger and More Diverse," *New York Times*, June 10, 2005, p. A11. Copyright 2005 © by The New York Times Company. Reprinted with permission.
5. Marshall, Barbara. "With Boomers Turning 65, Retirements Turns from Slo-Mo to Go-Go," *The Austin Statesman*, December 31, 2010. Retrieved from http://www.statesman.com/news/nation/with-boomers-turning-65-retirement-turns-from-slow-1156635.html. on January 6, 2011 at 12:15 P.M.
6. The Los Angeles Gerontology Research Group. "Official Tables," updated July 15, 2008. Available online at http://www.grg.org/calment.html. For additional current figures and trends, see http://www.census.gov.
7. Kilborn, P. T. "Shifts in Families Reach a Plateau, Study Says," *New York Times*, November 27, 1996, p. B1. Copyright 1996 © by The New York Times Company. Reprinted with permission.
8. Ibid.
9. Thomas, P., V. Reitman, D. Solis, and D. Milbank. "Women in Business: A Global Report Card," *Wall Street Journal*, July 26, 1995, p. B1. Reprinted by permission of *The Wall Street Journal*. Copyright © 1995 Dow Jones & Company, Inc. All rights reserved worldwide.
10. Ibid.
11. Maxa, R. "How to Avoid Cultural Blunders: For Business Travelers, a Few Rules Can Go a Long Way," MSNBC. Available online at: www.msnbc.com/news/224480/asp. Retrieved on December, 23, 1998.
12. Adams, D. "Don't Get Upset If Foreign Executive Holds Your Hand," *South Bend Tribune*, December 20, 1998, p. B5.
13. Bosrock, M. M. *Put Your Best Foot Forward.* Minneapolis, MN: International Educational Systems, 1995.
14. Harris, P. R. and R. T. Moran. "Doing Business with Asians—Japan, China, Pacific Basin, and India," in *Managing Cultural Differences: High Performance Strategies for a New World of Business*, 6th ed. Houston, TX: Gulf Publishing Company, 2004, pp. 393–406.
15. Barnlund, D. *Communicative Styles of Japanese and Americans: Images and Realities.* Belmont, CA: Wadsworth Publishing Company, 1989, pp. 156–157.
16. Adams. "Don't Get Upset," p. B5.
17. Ibid.
18. Ferraro, G. P. *The Cultural Dimension of International Business*, 5th ed. Upper Saddle River, NJ: Prentice-Hall, Inc., 2005, p. 7.
19. Seligson, H. "For American Workers in China, a Culture Clash," *New York Times*, Thursday, December 24, 2009, pp. B1, B2.
20. Ibid, p. B2.

21. Ibid, p. B2.
22. McCartney, S. "Teaching Americans How to Behave Abroad," *Wall Street Journal*, April 11, 2006, p. D1.
23. Harvey, C. and M. J. Allard. *Understanding Diversity: Readings, Cases, and Exercises.* New York: HarperCollins, 1995, p. 7.
24. Simons, G. *Working Together: How to Become More Effective in a Multicultural Organization.* Los Altos, CA: Crisp Publications, 1989, p. 5.
25. Harvey and Allard. *Understanding Diversity*, p. 7.
26. See Harris, W. H. and J. S. Levey. *The New Columbia Encyclopedia.* New York: Columbia University Press, 1975, p. 1046. See also Trevelyan, G. M. *Garibaldi and the Making of Modern Italy*, 1911, reprinted 1948.
27. Ferraro. *The Cultural Dimension*, pp. 25–30.
28. Transparency International, "Corruption Perceptions Index 2010." Available online at http://www.transparency.org/policy_research/surveys_indices/cpi/2010. Retrieved on January 6, 2011 at 1:30 P.M.
29. Ferraro. *The Cultural Dimension*, pp. 22–25.
30. Lustig, M. and J. Koester. *Intercultural Competence: Interpersonal Communication Across Cultures*, 4th ed. New York: Addison Wesley Longman, 2002, pp. 146–149.

CASE STUDY 10-1

Oak Brook Medical Systems, Inc.

Jacqueline Harris has been an employee of Oak Brook Medical Systems for about 12 years. For the past 18 months, she has been director of strategic planning for the Hospital Supply Division, a segment of Oak Brook Medical Systems, which has grown at the phenomenal rate of nearly 35 percent per year over the past three years.

The division is relatively new, having been formed just seven years ago as a result of changes in the healthcare marketplace. The division's growth has been the direct result of good products, solid customer service, and the quality-focused people the company has managed to attract. The people working for the Hospital Supply Division are, for the most part, self-starters—entrepreneurial, competitive types who are dedicated and hardworking. The people in Jackie's division and the corporate leadership pride themselves on making things happen for their customers.

Jackie is considered a very valuable asset to her division and is widely credited with developing the strategy that resulted in a $40 million business for the company. She is also considered a no-nonsense, results-oriented manager with a history of being able to get things done. Jackie is also known for her directness and, on several occasions, has had problems interacting with her colleagues. According to friends and coworkers, she is known to be curt with colleagues as well as subordinates.

Jackie's Colleagues and Coworkers

Others in the division see her as being defensive and, at times, overwhelming. They say she overwhelms people with data when presenting an idea or making a point. Another person has been quoted as saying that "I feel like I am being talked down to when I have a conversation with her." As a result of these perceptions, some feel that she is unapproachable and tough to work with. In the last couple of years, her difficulty in communicating with colleagues has been a greater concern during discussions of her future in the division. To date, however, no one has brought this to her attention directly.

Jackie has experienced the difficulty of communicating with her colleagues, but she considers this simply to be a part of getting the job done. In fact, she thinks she is behaving in a manner comparable to the successful people who have preceded her. Jackie has grown increasingly frustrated, though, because of a lack of attention from senior management.

Despite her highly successful performance with the strategic plan, no one seems to be talking with her about a promotion, and she cannot understand why she is being overlooked. Increasingly, she thinks it is a result of her manager (a division vice president) and the president of the division not wanting to promote her because she is African American. She won't say it aloud, but she is beginning to suspect that subtle forms of racism are holding her back.

This frustration has grown more acute, at least to her thinking, because she has always known success. She graduated in the top 10 percent of her engineering class at a large, well-known Midwestern university. She was in the top 5 percent of her MBA class in the Sloan School of Management at MIT. Jackie has always taken pride in her work and has always worked toward excellence in whatever tasks she took on. She selected this division of Oak Brook Medical Systems, in fact, because it was fast-paced, results-oriented, and the market was growing dramatically for its products and services. This was an industry and a company, Jackie thought, that could provide job opportunities for people who could do good work and produce results.

This division, however, has had very little representation of women and people of color in its management ranks. At first, Jackie thought this would work to her advantage, creating opportunities for her to move up quickly. Now she was beginning to suspect that there were few women and no people of color in division upper management because those in power don't want them.

Both Jackie and other senior management officials recognized the shifting demographics in their customer base and the positive implications of having someone in the division who could identify with such customers and bring a different perspective to the business. With this in mind, she decided to remain with the division. Before long, though, it became plain to those around her that she was not happy.

WRITING ASSIGNMENT

This assignment requires two documents: a professional business memo and a professional business letter. Please assume that you are Vice President of the Hospital Supply Division and were promoted to that position 90 days ago from another division in the company. Please cast your reply to the issues addressed in this case in the form of a proposal memo to your division president. At a *minimum*, in your response to this case, please identify the following:

- Business and management issues
- Legal issues
- Cultural issues

The Need for Action

As her manager, how would you approach Ms. Harris with your concerns about her problems in communicating with others? How would you help her with her professional development and career growth within the division? In assisting her, you may wish to consider these questions:

1. What are the assumptions being made about Ms. Harris by her colleagues and managers?
2. What growth opportunities do you see for Ms. Harris that could address the issue of communication with other employees?
3. What do you see as obstacles that could get in the way of Ms. Harris's growth and development in the Hospital Supply Division? How do you think the environment in the division may have contributed to the difficulties she is experiencing?
4. What should you as her manager do to provide support and communicate that support to her? How would you go about challenging your assumptions about her? What would you do to confront her assumptions about others in the division?
5. If you would find it helpful, describe some examples of the sort of feedback you might provide for Ms. Harris regarding her work and her interactions with others in the division.

In your response to this case, you *must* also answer two additional questions:

- What must I do *right now* to solve the problem? What actions do I take immediately?
- What advice would I offer to senior management about this matter? Have any company policies (or lack of policies) contributed to the events described?

Please address your business letter to all employees in the Hospital Supply Division, explaining what's happened and what you and the company's leadership have decided to do about it.

CASE STUDY 10-2

LaJolla Software, Inc.

Todd Batey returned from lunch with high hopes for a productive afternoon. Two large, long-term projects had just been completed and this would be his opportunity to dig through that stack of unopened mail, deferred memos, file folders, journals, and magazines he simply hadn't found time to read.

Among the larger, more important projects Batey had worked on during the past several months was a new product launch in the company's enterprise software division. At the same time, he had been working with LaJolla Software's senior team on a highly confidential and potentially profitable strategic alliance: LaJolla executives were targeting several Japanese firms for a joint venture that would permit the company to distribute its famous "S-4" supply chain management software in Japan and, perhaps, throughout much of Asia.

Company Background

LaJolla Software, Inc., is a small but rapidly growing firm located outside of Silicon Valley in LaJolla, California. This quirky back-bedroom start-up had grown from $8 million in capital with no revenues just five years ago to a $150 million, publicly held firm that specializes in enterprise software, customized applications, and innovative thinking in systems integration and supply-chain management. Chad Lucas and his college roommate, Joshua Flynn, had converted an interest in management information systems into a successful business long before most of their classmates had paid off their college loans.

Virtually all of their efforts had been internal, however. Lucas and Flynn hired half-a-dozen of the smartest young programmers and systems engineers in Southern California and began developing a product line. Perhaps their brightest move was to hire Todd Batey, a recent Santa Clara graduate who specialized in marketing. Piece by piece, the team of Lucas and Flynn had put together a very strong business, but now things were beginning to move much more quickly. If they were to take advantage of the window of opportunity now open in the Far East, they would need more than bright programmers and a young marketing director. They would need a business partner who knows the territory.

Opportunity Knocks

As Batey tossed his soft drink cup in the recycling bin, one of the interns stuck her head in Todd's cubicle. "Chad and Josh need to see you."

"What's up?" he asked.

"No clue," she replied. "I just know something's happening and you're next on the agenda."

Batey grabbed his Palm Pilot and headed down the hallway. With just 75 employees, LaJolla Software didn't take up much space: two floors of a modern office building where Torrey Pines Road meets the I-5. On a nice day (and they were almost all nice) you could see Pacific Beach from the windows in Batey's cubicle. Not much privacy, but a great view.

Batey walked into Chad Lucas's office without knocking. Formality was about as common around LaJolla Software as neckties. "You need to see me?" he asked.

"Hey, Todd," came the reply, "have a seat."

"We just got a fax from Masahiro," said Lucas. "Our endless series of trips to Tokyo has finally paid off." The fax in question was from Masahiro Fudaba, a senior vice president with Ichi Ban Heavy Industries of Japan. "Really?" asked Batey.

"Finally." said Flynn. "We're going into partnership with Ichi Ban to form a joint venture. Their shareholders, business partners, bankers, and Keiretsu executives have finally bought off on the deal." He paused for a just a moment. "Looks like LaJolla is headed for Japan."

"First, though, we're going to have some Japanese visitors," said Lucas. "The word from Masahiro is that Kazushi Yakura and a team of eight Japanese managers will be here next week to begin the process of organizing our new, jointly owned company. Apparently Mr. Yakura will be here for just a few days. The transition team, however, is planning to stay until we have all the details worked out."

"How can I help?" asked Batey.

"Well," said Flynn, "we're engineers. You're the marketing guy, so we figured you would be the logical person to help make these folks feel welcome."

"More to the point," said Lucas, "we need to help the people on Ichi Ban's transition team understand a bit more about us. They know our business, our market, and our industry, but I'm not sure how much these guys know about the United States,

about California, or about doing business with Americans. According to Masahiro," he added, "only Mr. Yakura has been to the United States. Most of the others have never been out of Japan."

"Interesting," said Batey. "What else do we know about them?"

"Here's a list of people they've identified for the visit," said Lucas. "We have ages, job titles, and a little bit of background, including education and prior work experience, but not much else."

"What do you want them to know?" asked Batey.

"It's clear to me that we have to reduce their anxieties, eliminate their fears, and raise the level of mutual trust," said Flynn. "I know that you understand something about intercultural communication, so we'll leave the details up to you." He paused for a moment, then said. "Let's make it more than a Padres' game and a day at the Zoo."

"No problem," said Batey. "I'll have a preliminary plan worked up for you by the close of business tomorrow."

Lucas and Flynn thanked the young marketing manager and expressed complete confidence in his ability to make the Japanese managers' visit productive and successful. Todd left Lucas's office and, heading down the hallway, thought to himself, "No problem? Maybe there is a problem here. What are we gonna *do* with these guys?"

DISCUSSION QUESTIONS

1. Assume that your cubicle is near Todd Batey's and he has asked you for some advice on this subject. What would you say to him?
2. What objectives or measurable outcomes should Batey specify for his immersion into American culture for these visitors?
3. What American concepts can you safely assume these managers know and understand? What concepts do you think they absolutely must understand in order for the joint venture to succeed?
4. How would you go about showing them what the United States is all about? Where would you take them? What would you show them?
5. How can you be sure what your visitors will understand when they're ready to go home?
6. What sort of budget would you need for this program?
7. How much do you suppose other LaJolla Software employees understand about Japan and Japanese culture? Should any of them be involved in your effort to introduce North America to your new Asian business partners?

WRITING ASSIGNMENT

Please respond in writing to the issues presented in this case by preparing two documents: a communication strategy memo and a professional business letter.

In preparing these documents, you may assume one of two roles: you may identify yourself as an external management consultant who has been asked to provide advice to the officers of LaJolla Software or you may assume the role of Todd Batey.

Either way, you must prepare a strategy memo addressed to Chad Lucas and Joshua Flynn that summarizes the details of the case, rank orders critical issues, discusses their implications (what they mean and why they matter), offers specific recommendations for action (assigning ownership and suspense dates for each), and shows how to communicate the solution to all who are affected by the recommendations.

You must also prepare a professional business letter for Mr. Lucas's signature. That document may be addressed to Kazushi Yakura, addressing his concerns in the case. Or if you wish, you may address a letter from Mr. Lucas to all LaJolla Software employees, responding to their concerns and explaining what the company is doing to address the situation at hand. If you have questions about either of these documents, please consult your instructor.

This case was prepared by James S. O'Rourke, Concurrent Professor of Management, as the basis for class discussion rather than to illustrate either effective or ineffective handling of an administrative situation. All names are fictional and identities have been disguised for purposes of case discussion.

Chapter *11*

Managing Conflict

The workplace of the twenty-first century is filled with tension and strife. In a recent Gallup Poll, 40 percent of American workers said they were never angry at work, down from 51 percent in the mid-1990s.[1] Conflicts arise under pressure-cooker deadlines, increased workloads, fear of layoffs, and the unrelenting demand for higher productivity. Under such stress, workplace violence has been increasing. And even in calm settings, routine business negotiations often turn ugly.[2]

Some organizations don't seem interested in peace. General Motors Corporation lost more than $2.2 billion trying to win a labor struggle with the United Auto Workers union in the late 1990s. According to one industry analyst, "GM and the UAW are like oil and water. They just cannot get along." Threats, intimidation, walkouts, lockouts, and inflexible positions have characterized their relationship over the years. "GM ought to have learned from this strike that it can't win labor showdowns," says auto analyst Maryann Keller. "They've had 24 strikes since 1990, and it hasn't solved anything."[3] Bankruptcy in 2010 and reorganization in 2011–2012 demonstrated the price of conflict and a lack of collaboration. Ford Motor Company, by contrast, had fewer strikes, better cooperation, and didn't accept a government bailout seen as essential to save GM and Chrysler.

Others have seen organizational conflict exact a much greater price. Alan Krueger and Alexandre Mas of Princeton University examined the effect of labor relations on product quality and concluded that a disproportionate number of dangerously flawed Firestone tires were made at the firm's Decatur, Illinois, plant when labor and management were battling each other. Labor strife, they say, appears to be a major contributor to the production of faulty tires—killing more than 100 and injuring more than 500 people—and not, as the union argues, because strikebreakers hired by the company were incompetent. "It appears likely to us," say the researchers, "that something about the chemistry between the replacement workers and recalled strikers . . . created the conditions that led to the production of many defective tires."[4]

Conflict can arise from a variety of sources, but many experts see it as a function of such workplace variables as personality, personal and professional relationships, cultural differences, working environments, demands of the marketplace, and of course, competition. "Workers today compete for schedules and projects, for money and training," says Marilyn Moats Kennedy, a career coach in Wilmette, Illinois.[5] And as organizations move increasingly to teams and teamwork to accomplish specific objectives, differences among team members can lead to conflict.

"A lot of people are in workplaces where they are being emotionally abused and bullied and that can take a toll," says Paul Spector, a professor of industrial and organizational psychology at the University of South Florida in Tampa. "It's becoming much more socially acceptable to be mean and nasty to others." Anna Maravelas, a psychologist in St. Paul, Minnesota, says she regularly sees anger, hostility, rudeness, and general inhumanity in the workplaces where she consults. A corporate vice president, for example, told her, "I pay my people well; I don't have to appreciate them too." And a bank employee said, "Being nice here is seen as a weakness."[6] Spector said his research has found that 2-to-3 percent of people admit to pushing, slapping, or hitting someone at work. With roughly 100 million in the U.S. workforce, he said, that's as many as 3 million people.[7]

"Conflict in any endeavor that requires the input of two or more people is a real possibility," says Jeanne Gulbranson, President of Key Performance International in Las Vegas, Nevada. "As the scope of a project increases, the likelihood of differences in opinion and approach increases as a function of the number of tasks involved and the amount of time spent by the staff in the resolution of the project." These conflicts, according to Gulbranson, may arise because of people's natural resistance to change, scheduling pressures, perceived difficulties in reporting procedures, or simply because things aren't working well.[8]

Not all conflict within an organization is unhealthy, but conflict between and among people within an organization can quickly become counterproductive, divisive, and destructive if not properly managed. In some quarters, most notably high-tech companies, conflict is actually encouraged as a catalyst for creativity. An idea is turned loose on the company's intranet, and other employees begin to examine it for flaws. In the best of circumstances, a good idea can be turned into a great idea with creative input and reflective critical thinking from those who must take ownership of the project. At its worst, such conflict can encourage predators in the electronic jungle to "flame" the idea's creator with derisive e-mail messages, and the struggle for idea supremacy begins.[9]

In its most basic form, conflict driven by stress can be unsettling and even dangerous to an organization and its employees. Office workers, frazzled by long hours, excessive e-mail, unrealistic deadlines, and demanding supervisors, feel the effects directly. In a pair of recent surveys, Integra, a New York–based property valuation firm, discovered that an increasing number of people have witnessed workplace violence, abuse, or emotional outbursts. Labeling the phenomenon "desk rage," the studies cite a number of sources for the behavior, including office layout and managerial insensitivity to the problem (see Table 11-1).

According to another, more recent study by Christine Porath, a management professor at the University of Southern California, conflict in the workplace can cost an organization time, effort, and talent. More than 90 percent of nearly 3,000 people surveyed said they had experienced incivility at work. Of these, 50 percent say they lost work time worry about the incident, 50 percent contemplated changing jobs to avoid a recurrence, and 25 percent cut back their efforts on the job. One in eight said he had left a company because of a rude incident.[10]

Table 11-1 "Desk Rage" in the Workplace	
Witnessed yelling or other forms of verbal abuse	42%
Yelled at coworkers themselves	29%
Cried over work-related issues	23%
Seen someone purposely damage machines or furniture	14%
Seen physical violence in the workplace	10%
Struck a coworker	2%

Source: Integra Realty Resources, 2000/2001 survey of 1,305 adults 18 and older. Online at: www.irr.com.

A DEFINITION OF CONFLICT

Not surprisingly, we have even seen conflict over how to define conflict.[11] Most experts agree, however, that while opposition, incompatibility, and interaction are important ingredients in conflict, a perception of conflict is essential. In other words, if no one thinks a conflict exists, there probably isn't one.[12]

We can define conflict, then, as a process that begins when someone perceives that someone else has negatively affected, or is about to negatively affect, something that the first person cares about. In practical terms, says Erik Van Slyke of HR Alliance, a Greensboro, North Carolina, consulting firm, "conflict is any time we disagree to the point where we can't go forward." Unchecked, he thinks, small matters can quickly mutate from a business conflict to a personality issue.[13] And from there, everything from productivity to working relationships to share price can suffer.

CONFLICT IN ORGANIZATIONS

THE TRADITIONAL VIEW This perspective assumed that all conflict was bad. Conflict in an organizational setting was viewed negatively and was often used synonymously with words such as *violence*, *destruction*, and *irrationality* to reinforce the negative image. Conflict was assumed to be the result of poor communication, a lack of openness and trust between workers and management, and a failure on the part of managers to be responsive to the needs and aspirations of their employees.[14] Naturally, good managers would do all in their power to avoid conflict. A workplace without conflict was assumed to be a happy, productive workplace.

THE HUMAN RELATIONS VIEW Popular from the 1940s to the 1970s, this viewpoint assumed that conflict was a natural occurrence in all groups and organizations. Because conflict was inevitable, industrial and labor psychologists argued in favor of simply accepting conflict. They rationalized its existence: It can't be eliminated; it may even be beneficial. Embrace it, they said. It's a natural part of every organization.

THE INTERACTIONIST VIEW This perspective, which emerged in the social science literature during the 1980s and 1990s, was a bit more radical than its predecessors. The interactionist approach actually *encourages* conflict on the grounds that a harmonious, peaceful, tranquil, and cooperative group may become static, apathetic, and unresponsive to a need for change and innovation. Without a minimum level of conflict, they reason, no organization can change, adapt, and survive the rigors of the marketplace.[15]

In theory, the idea of ongoing minor conflict as a stimulus to creativity sounds good. But does it work in practice? Is it really a good idea to have people at each other's throats just for the sake of a few new market initiatives? "Never underestimate the power of a good idea," says business journalist Michael Warshaw. "Most people in most companies want to do the right thing. Give them an opportunity to make a positive contribution and chances are that they will." Warshaw, who writes for *Fast Company* magazine, also thinks people will work hard in order to leave their mark on a project or an organization. But, "most new-idea champions aren't in a position to order people to participate in their projects," he says.[16] Often, resources are scarce, values compete, and colleagues are looking for visibility in the company. The result is conflict. Properly managed, however, conflict *can* have a beneficial effect on a business. The important questions concern *why* conflict arises and *how* the process should be managed.

SOURCES OF CONFLICT IN ORGANIZATIONS

Conflict may develop over any number of issues or factors, but these five appear regularly in the social psychology literature.

LIMITED RESOURCES People in organizations large and small often confront one another over resources that are either scarce or dwindling. These issues might include managerial responsibility, supervision of other employees, office or storage space, budget, tools and equipment, training, and access to superiors. If one person perceives another to have some advantage (fair or not), conflict may arise over that perception. It may be something as simple as whose copier budget is bigger or as complex as who will lead the organization in a new, high-visibility product launch.

VALUES, GOALS, AND PRIORITIES Confrontation often occurs because of differences in specialty, training, or beliefs. Karen A. Jehn of Pennsylvania's Wharton School demonstrated in a series of experimental field studies that if people share the same basic values they're less likely to experience conflict, regardless of task or working conditions.[17]

POORLY DEFINED RESPONSIBILITIES Conflict may result from differences between formal position descriptions and informal expectations on the job. "The book" says one thing, but "the job" demands another. In many instances, job design problems arise from ill-defined, vague, or imprecise descriptions that are linked to everything from scheduling to compensation to performance review systems.

CHANGE Among the few constants in organizational life is change itself. Everything, including annual budgets, organizational priorities, lines of authority, limits of responsibility, restructuring, mergers, divestitures, and layoffs can induce anxiety, uncertainty, and conflict in a business.

HUMAN DRIVES FOR SUCCESS Conflict may also be a by-product of the natural sense of goal orientation that every human experiences. Virtually every organization, even those in the not-for-profit sector, produces competition among its members by employing many competitors striving for very few rewards. The greater the imbalance between competitors and rewards, the greater the potential for conflict. In a retail establishment, access to walk-in customers may produce significant conflict if compensation schemes are linked directly to sales. In a military organization, where salaries are determined by rank and seniority, competition develops for fewer and fewer available promotions as competitors move up the chain of command.

SENSING CONFLICT

It doesn't take a social psychologist to find conflict in a business. Conflict takes many forms and manifests itself in a number of ways—most of them easily visible, others not. Each manager in a business must assume responsibility for identifying conflict, both potential and actual, within the work environment and using appropriate means for managing or resolving differences that are unhealthy to the life of the organization.

As we have seen, conflict can be potentially healthy or destructive to a business. Social psychologists draw a distinction between *functional* and *dysfunctional* conflict. A healthy disagreement about when to act, how much to spend, whom to hire, or which path to take is essential to the survival of a business. Conflict becomes dysfunctional, however, when it impedes or prevents managers and their employees from achieving the organization's business objectives. Here are some ways to sense day-to-day conflict in the workplace.

VISUALIZE Try to visualize or imagine how your actions or those of others might cause, or are causing, conflict. Ask yourself the sort of questions a journalist might ask in reporting a news story: *Who? What? When? How? Why?* Sometimes those self-inquiries begin with if: "*If* I were to change the production schedule to assist the folks in shipping, how would *my* crew react?" You can't always know the answers, but knowing what questions to ask can help prevent serious conflict before it begins.

GIVE FEEDBACK The amount, accuracy, and timeliness of information that you can provide to an employee will help you to understand his or her point of view. Sharing your thoughts and feelings first, in a nonthreatening way, often encourages others to tell you what's on their minds. Your employees may not like a particular set of circumstances, but they are likely to be more accepting if they think they know the whole story.

GET FEEDBACK Take the time to find out what your associates are thinking and feeling. Don't wait until the last moment to discover that you have trouble. Probe for more information by asking questions such as: How so? In what way? Why? Can you tell me more? The quality of the feedback you receive, particularly from subordinates and those who are not in your reporting chain, will be a direct function of the level of mutual trust you are able to establish. Harvard professor Linda Hill concludes that balancing advocacy with inquiry is essential. "Managers are trained to be advocates," she says. "They are rewarded for being problem solvers—for figuring out what should be done, putting forth plans for action, and influencing others to adopt them. By contrast, inquiry skills—the ability to ask questions—have gone relatively undeveloped and unrecognized. But as managers rise in their organizations and the issues they confront become more complex and divergent from their personal experiences, inquiry skills become essential. Managers need to access and embrace the diverse expertise and perspectives of other people. They need to learn how to balance advocacy and inquiry to promote mutual learning."[18]

DEFINE EXPECTATIONS Meet regularly with your associates to determine priorities for the day ahead or the coming week. Any major discrepancies or misunderstanding between your expectations and theirs will alert you to potential conflict. Managers often discover that, as they define their expectations for employees in clear, easily understood terms, they will receive information in return about what team members and associates expect. Such conversations may be among the few opportunities for supervisors and subordinates to exchange both objective and subjective views of the workplace and the tasks at hand.

REVIEW PERFORMANCE REGULARLY When supervisors and employees communicate openly about how they are (or are not) working together, they reduce the opportunity for serious conflict and help to build stronger working relationships. Most businesses require annual performance reviews for managerial employees and more frequent reviews—semiannual or quarterly—for hourly employees. Experts say that when such reviews are seen by all participants as fair, objective, and professional, morale and workplace satisfaction are likely to be high.

THE BENEFITS OF DEALING WITH CONFLICT

Both you and the organization you work for will benefit if you deal directly with conflict. For you, personally, the benefits are important.

- **Stronger relationships.** You will be able to build stronger interpersonal relationships as a result of being comfortable expressing your true thoughts and feelings.
- **Increased self-respect.** You will be able to feel good about yourself and learn not to take every small bit of criticism personally. A key element in the definition of a professional is that he or she is able to accept feedback and handle criticism in a professional, rather than personal, manner. It's not about *you*. It's about the organization, the task at hand, and serving those who depend on you.
- **Personal growth and development.** When you break down some of your own invisible barriers and become more assertive in resolving or preventing conflict, you will invariably learn more and gain support from others. And if others in the organization come to know that they can depend on you when it really counts, team bonds are strengthened and success is that much easier to realize.

Dealing professionally with conflict in the workplace benefits not only you but the organization that employs you. Those benefits might include the following:

- **Improved efficiency and effectiveness.** Employees will be able to do their jobs more effectively, and probably with greater levels of efficiency and productivity, by focusing their efforts where they will produce the greatest results. Rather than wasting time and energy on workplace conflict, they can do what they were hired to do in the first place.
- **Creative thinking.** By encouraging people to share and learn from their mistakes, the organization will reap the benefits of creative thinking and a dramatically improved learning curve. By confronting potential conflict before it has an opportunity to paralyze the organization, managers can lower the level of apprehension and fear in the workplace, as well. An important consideration for any employee who is thinking about looking for work elsewhere is whether his work is valued over the long term by management. Advertising the fact that your organization is not a "one-mistake outfit" can help people become less fearful of making mistakes and more confident in trying new ideas and new ways of thinking.
- **Synergy and teamwork.** Managers and associates will be able to focus on serving customers and clients by helping each other. We often hear in the United States that "the customer is number one." In many Asian societies, however, executives have come to realize that "the employee is number one." By taking care of your employees, developing a sense of teamwork and organizational loyalty, you can be assured that they, in turn, will take care of your customers. And those customers, whose loyalty and business you've worked so hard to earn, will take care of your shareholders.

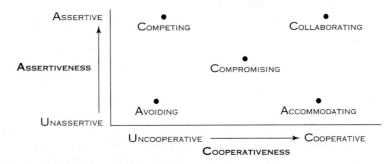

FIGURE 11-1 Five styles of Conflict Management
Source: Adapted from Thomas, K. "Conflict and Negotiation Processes in Organizations," in
M. D. Dunnette and L. M. Hough (eds.), Handbook of Industrial and Organizational Psychology, 2nd ed., Vol. 3.
Palo Alto, CA: Consulting Psychologists Press, 1994.

STYLES OF CONFLICT MANAGEMENT

Not everyone approaches conflict in quite the same way. Some welcome the opportunity for a good dust-up. Others duck into the shadows and do their best to avoid confrontation. The style you adopt should reflect a deliberate, thoughtful view of the reasons why people may be in conflict, the culture of your organization, and the personalities of those involved. Figure 11-1 represents author Kenneth Thomas's view of conflict management arrayed along two separate dimensions: *cooperativeness* and *assertiveness*. Thomas defines cooperativeness as the degree to which one person tries to satisfy another person's concerns, whereas assertiveness is seen as the degree to which one person tries to satisfy his/her own concerns.

With cooperativeness arrayed from low to high along the horizontal axis and assertiveness arrayed from low to high along the vertical axis, these two dimensions form a matrix that can be used to plot a manager's conflict response style. The "conflict-handling intentions," as he calls them, are *competing, collaborating, avoiding, accommodating,* and *compromising.*[19]

COMPETING This style of conflict management involves people who are both assertive and uncooperative. People who try to satisfy their own interests at the expense of others involved are regarded as competitive. It's a strategy that works when dealing with other participants in the marketplace, but it's often seen as counterproductive inside an organization. Internal competition often produces impressive results, but it certainly does not promote teamwork or the cooperative behaviors required of teammates. This approach clearly produces winners and losers.

COLLABORATING This style involves people who are assertive but cooperative. If those involved in a situation with the potential for conflict express a desire to fully satisfy the concerns of all others, we're likely to see cooperation and a search for mutually beneficial outcomes. In collaborating, the intention is to solve the problem by clarifying differences rather than by accommodating various points of view. This approach seeks win-win solutions that incorporate the viewpoints of all those involved.

AVOIDING This conflict management style involves people who are both unassertive and uncooperative. When a manager chooses to withdraw from a discussion or a situation in which conflict is likely, his choice is based on a desire to avoid a fight as well as those with whom he may disagree.

ACCOMMODATING This style involves people who are unassertive but cooperative. A manager seeking to appease an opponent or an employee may be willing to place that other person's interests above her own, usually for the sake of maintaining a good working relationship. In spite of personal misgivings or doubts, accommodators are willing to "give in" and "get along," either to promote the goals of the other person or for the sake of group harmony. Consistent accommodation to the needs and interests of others is sometimes seen as another form of conflict avoidance.

COMPROMISING This approach involves people who are at the midpoint on both assertiveness and cooperativeness. Compromise occurs when each party to a conflict demonstrates a willingness to give up something in order to promote a solution. When sharing of this sort occurs, there are no clear winners or losers. Rather, there is "a willingness to ration the object of the conflict and accept a solution that provides incomplete satisfaction of both parties' concerns."[20]

SO, WHAT SHOULD YOU DO?

In approaching the challenge posed by conflict in your organization (or any organization, for that matter), it seems clear that a single approach simply won't work. To succeed—that is, to achieve many different goals and balance the tug among opposing values—you may have to demonstrate skill at each of the five styles of conflict management we've just discussed. In some situations, you may need to accommodate to keep a valued employee. In other circumstances, you wish to compromise on an issue that's not especially important to you in order to get what you want. On other occasions, you may be faced with situations that involve many competitors and few rewards; to stay in the game, your approach may be thoroughly competitive. On still other occasions, you may decide to pack up your armor and avoid a fight altogether.

As you gather information and assess the situation, however, negotiation and conflict experts have identified a number of additional important considerations and suggestions.

LISTEN, LISTEN, AND THEN LISTEN SOME MORE That helped Los Angeles attorney Alan Liker navigate the sensitive negotiations for the purchase of Budget Rent-a-Car from Ford Motor Company by a group of licensees he represented. In such deals, he says, you have to find out what people are sensitive about, and you can do that only by listening carefully. Then you can adjust negotiation terms "so that it's perceived as a win-win situation."

It takes a great deal of discipline to be a good listener, according to William P. Dunk, a management consultant in Chapel Hill, North Carolina. "You're tempted to start speaking and intervening," he says, unwisely taking ownership of the problem. "By talking too much, even if you're not posing a solution, you're not pushing the employee into self-awareness."[21]

SEPARATE THE PEOPLE FROM THE PROBLEM Having clarified the mutual benefits to be gained by successfully concluding a negotiation, it may be useful to focus attention on the real issue at hand—solving the problem. Negotiations are more likely to conclude satisfactorily if the parties involved depersonalize the discussions. You're much more likely to get what you want if "one-upmanship" or revenge isn't part of your agenda. How can you do that? Begin to see the other party as an advocate for a point of view rather than an adversary or a rival. It's far better to say, "I can't support that solution," than it is to say, "I can't support you."[22]

FOCUS ON INTERESTS, NOT POSITIONS A demand that a negotiator makes is also known as a position. Interests are the real reasons behind the demands. Experience shows that it is easier to establish agreement on interests, given that they tend to be broader and multifaceted. You should also recognize that a negotiating position may be driven more by emotion than logic. It may be useful to inquire about that: "Can you tell me why you feel that way?" Or perhaps a simple declarative statement will prompt the response you're looking for: "Help me understand why you are advocating that position."[23]

RECOGNIZE AND ACCEPT THE FEELINGS OF THE INDIVIDUALS INVOLVED Irrational feelings are often generated in the midst of controversy, even though the participants don't always want to recognize this fact. Each wants to believe that she is examining the problem objectively. Recognizing and accepting feelings such as fear, jealousy, anger, or anxiety may make it possible for the participants to accept their own true feelings. Effective managers don't adopt a critical attitude, saying, "You have no right to feel angry." Rather, they accept those feelings for what they are and work to communicate empathy for those people involved.[24]

KEEP YOUR OWN EMOTIONS IN NEUTRAL When John Day headed the transition team that closed down pharmaceutical manufacturer Sterling Winthrop in New York after its parts were sold to four different companies, he was faced with the anger of employees who were losing their jobs. "You've got to keep your cool and keep busy and focus on the positive side," he says. "After they got their point across, I'd say, 'I'm in the same situation. Here's what I'm trying to do.' " All the parties involved in a conflict have to focus on what they're going to do next to begin solving the dilemma, says Mr. Day, who is now an executive with Ingersoll Rand. "That defuses the situation."[25]

TRACK THE CONFLICT TO ITS SOURCE Conflicts may arise from a manager's personality or style. Outside influences may also contribute. "Maybe an employee's got a sick parent in Georgia or a horrible two-hour commute," says William Dunk. "An effective executive at any level must realize both the drain on productivity and the incremental amount of conflict coming from forces outside the workplace." Then, he says, you can get the employee some help in dealing with them.[26]

COMMUNICATE CONTINUALLY AND FRANKLY In the Sterling Winthrop negotiations, the transition team communicated as much as possible. "We had constant meetings and newsletters, even if there wasn't much to tell them," says John Day. That communication made employees feel involved and helped lessen the tension of the company's difficult, final days. Day's team was also brutally honest, telling employees it was unlikely they would be hired by the acquirers. That sort of honesty brought them credibility when other conflicts arose. "On reflection," Mr. Day says, "that was a big thing."[27]

GET PEOPLE TOGETHER ON THE SMALL STUFF FIRST When disagreements crop up, get the parties together and decide on three or four small measures that everyone can agree on and work on those. If people can agree on at least a few things, experts say, the big issues won't be quite as difficult. Moreover, if you establish a harmonious negotiating environment, a little goodwill can help to carry difficult conversations on other, larger issues.[28]

DEVISE OPTIONS FOR MUTUAL GAIN This approach will involve some creativity on your part as a manager. By focusing your collective attention on brainstorming alternative mutually agreeable solutions, the conversational dynamic shifts from competitive to collaborative. This effort can demonstrate to others that you are a person of goodwill whose perspective does not necessarily require winners and losers. Additionally, the more options, alternatives, and combinations you have to explore, the greater the probability of reaching a solution that will please everyone involved.[29]

DEFINE SUCCESS IN TERMS OF GAINS RATHER THAN LOSSES If a manager seeking a 10 percent raise receives only 6 percent, that outcome can be seen as either a 6 percent improvement (over current income) or a 40 percent shortfall (over desired outcome). The first interpretation focuses on gains, while the second focuses on losses (in this case, unrealized expectations). The outcome is the same, but the manager's satisfaction with it varies substantially. It is important to recognize that our satisfaction with an outcome is affected by the standards we use to judge it. A sensible manager might ask, "Is this a meaningful improvement over current conditions?"[30]

FOLLOW UP TO ENSURE SUCCESS Review all of the issues, definitions, discussions, data, and details with everyone involved. Make sure that you're in agreement on the solution you plan to implement and the ways in which you plan to go about it. Establish some means of determining whether your solution is working. If possible, quantify outcomes. Agree to revisit the problem at a specific point in the future if the solution you have chosen doesn't seem to work.

KNOW WHEN TO CUT YOUR LOSSES Sometimes the conflict has simply gone too far and you have to decide where and when to start cutting. "All conflicts don't get resolved," says management consultant William Dunk, "and all people aren't worth saving."[31]

WHAT IF YOU'RE THE PROBLEM?

"The fact is, people get angry an average of 10 to 14 times a day," says Hendrie Weisinger, a clinical psychologist and anger-management specialist. "But anger is especially endemic to work. If you have a job, you're guaranteed to get angry."[32] The worst cases of workplace anger can explode into violence that makes banner headlines. But according to most professionals who deal with such issues, anger rarely rises to such extremes. Most people deal with life's disappointments in a calm, evenhanded way. "Keep in mind," writes business journalist Jane Brody, "that even if your anger is fully justified, blowing your top can still cost you; you may lose your job, your spouse, or your health."[33]

Anger has become widely accepted as a part of contemporary culture, according to Phil D'Agostino, a therapist based in Raleigh, North Carolina. He cites popular television shows displaying a hard, angry edge. "In an office," he recalls, "a man calls a female co-worker 'honey' and another woman tells her, 'You have a right to get angry.' No one has a right to be angry," he says, "and it's delusional to think that anger can be productive. If you're passed over for a promotion, you can do three things: accept it, leave it, or change it."[34] In the case of the coworker's offense, a generation gap may be more to blame than a lack of respect. "Often, when we feel hurt by someone else, we're mixing up impact and intent," explains Mark Gordon of the Boston-based Vantage Partners, a consulting firm specializing in negotiation and relationship management. "In other words, we are attributing to them the intent to hurt us because we feel hurt, when in reality, there can be a negative impact on us even though they had a perfectly benign, if not positive, intent."[35]

Dr. D'Agostino and other anger management experts, such as Mitchell Messer of Chicago's Anger Institute, and Albert Mehrabian, a psychologist at the University of California at Los Angeles, offer a number of guidelines to help in controlling your emotions. These suggestions appear frequently in the anger-management literature:

- *Acknowledge your anger.* Left unmanaged, anger festers. Don't ignore it in the hope that it will go away or pretend it isn't there because it seems unjustified.
- *Don't look for slights.* A colleague who seems to snub you as you meet in the hallway may simply be headed for the bathroom.
- *Know what's provoking you.* If you're upset with your spouse or a jammed photocopier, don't take it out on your colleagues.
- *Don't become infected by coworkers' gripes.* The fact that they're angry doesn't mean you should join them in their rage.
- *Check your own anger signals.* Anger often reveals itself through physical and emotional responses: a racing pulse, shortness of breath, pacing. Learn to read these signs before your anger gets out of hand.
- *Take a breather.* Find ways to cool off before your anger consumes you. Try deep breathing, a brisk walk, or even busy work.
- *Write a letter.* If someone has enraged you, write him or her a letter. Pour out your feelings; be candid and direct. Just don't mail it. You will still feel better.
- *Confide in a friend.* If it seems unwise to direct your anger toward its source, discuss the problem with someone you trust.[36]

Having read these suggestions, keep two important things in mind: First, many—if not most—conflicts resolve themselves before they become generalized workplace dilemmas. Most people of goodwill are willing to work with one another for the benefit of the organization, as long as they can see their own best interests linked in some way with those of the organization. And second, managers get paid to listen to their employees, gather useful information, resolve disputes, and make tough decisions. The more of it you do, the better you'll get.

If all else fails, consider the advice of Canadian Zen master Albert Low. "Zen teaches that fundamental conflicts exist in every being and that striving to reconcile them is the cause of all suffering, and all life," Low explains. "Conflict abounds in business, too—in the turf wars between departments and in the competing demands of shareholders, employees, customers, and community. The conventional approach to settling the strife with trades-offs actually kills the only sources of growth." The director of the Montreal Zen Centre and author of *Zen and Creative Management* says, "Managers are always choosing between two or more equally desirable resolutions, but all of them are in conflict. The real management charter," he says, "is to harness the energy of opposing forces. And that requires a really creative act. Responding is about trying to catch up. Acting takes you to the future."[37]

For Further Reading

Borisoff, D. and D. A. Victor. *Conflict Management: A Communication Skills Approach*, 2nd ed. Boston: Allyn & Bacon, 1997.

Collins, S. D. *Managing Conflict and Workplace Relationships*, 2nd ed. Mason, OH: Cengage South-Western, 2008.

De Dreu, C. K. W. "Productive Conflict: The Importance of Conflict Management and Conflict Issue," in De Dreu, C. K. W. and E. Van de Vliert, *Using Conflict in Organizations*. London: Sage Publications, 1997.

Drory, A. and I. Ritov. "Effects of Work Experience and Opponent's Power on Conflict Management Styles," *International Journal of Conflict Management* 8, no. 2 (April 1997), pp. 148–161.

Gordon, J. *The Pfeiffer Book of Successful Conflict Management Tools.* Hoboken, NJ: Pfeiffer Publishing, Inc., 2007.

Janssen, O. and E. Van de Vliert. "Concern for the Other's Goals: Key to (De)escalation of Conflict," *International Journal of Conflict Management* 7, no. 2 (April 1996), pp. 99–120.

Parker-Pope, T. "When the Bully Sits in the Next Cubicle," *New York Times*, March 25, 2008, p. D5.

Rahim, M. A. and R. T. Golembiewski (eds). Styles of Managing Organizational Conflict: A Critical Review and Synthesis of Theory and Research. Greenwich, CT: JAI Press, 1997.

Ritov, I. and A. Drory. "Ambiguity and Conflict Management Strategy," *International Journal of Conflict Management* 7, no. 2 (April 1996), pp. 139–155.

Withers, B. *The Conflict Management Skills Workshop: A Trainer's Guide.* New York: American Management Association, 2002.

"Workplace Anger Viewed Differently by Gender: Antagonistic Men Admired, While Women Seen 'Out of Control.'" Reuters/MSNBC.com. Updated: 11:53 A.M. ET, August 3, 2007. Available online at http://www.msnbc.mns.com/20108425.

Endnotes

1. Felton, B. "When Rage Is All the Rage: The Art of Anger Management," *New York Times*, March 15, 1998, p. 12. Copyright © 1998 by The New York Times Company. Reprinted with permission.

2. Lancaster, H. "Solving Conflicts in the Workplace Without Making Losers," *Wall Street Journal*, May 27, 1997, p. B1. Reprinted by permission of *The Wall Street Journal.* Copyright © 1997 Dow Jones & Company, Inc. All rights reserved worldwide.

3. Bernstein, A., P. Galuszka, and R. Barker. "What Price Peace? GM Lost a Lot to the UAW, and Labor Relations Are Still Bad," *BusinessWeek*, August 10, 1998, pp. 24–25.

4. Krueger, A. B. and A. Max. *Strikes, Scabs, and Tread Separations: Labor Strife and the Production of Defective Bridgestone/ Firestone Tires.* A working paper of the Industrial Relations Section, Firestone Library, Princeton University, Princeton, NJ. Online at: www.irs.princeton.edu/wpframe.html. Retrieved November 22, 2002. See also Wessel, D. "The Hidden Cost of Labor Strife," *Wall Street Journal*, January 10, 2002, p. A1.

5. Warshaw, M. "The Good Guy's (and Gal's) Guide to Office Politics," *Fast Company*, April 1998, p. 156.

6. Stenson, J. "Desk Rage: Workers Gone Wild," MSNBC.com. Updated: 6:54 A.M. ET, November 27, 2006. Available online at http:// www.manbc. msn.com.

7. Wulfhorst, E. "Get Out of the Way, Road Rage. Here Comes Desk Rage," Reuters, Thursday, July 10, 2008. Retrieved from http://www.reuters.com/article/idUSN0947145320080710 on January 6, 2011 at 2:38 p.m.

8. Gulbranson, J. E. "The Ground Rules of Conflict Resolution," *Industrial Management* 30, no. 3 (May–June 1998), p. 4.

9. Lancaster. "Solving Conflicts."

10. Chao, L. "Not-So-Nice Costs: As Work Street Mounts, Rise in Office Rudeness Weighs on Productivity, Retention," *Wall Street Journal*, January 17, 2006, p. B4.

11. See, for instance, Fink, C. F. "Some Conceptual Difficulties in the Theory of Social Conflict," *Journal of Conflict Resolution*, December 1968, pp. 412–460.

12. Robbins, S. P. *Organizational Behavior: Concepts, Controversies, and Applications*, 11th ed. Upper Saddle River, NJ: Prentice Hall, 2004, p. 445.

13. Thomas, K. W. "Conflict and Negotiation Processes in Organizations," in Dunnette, M. D. and L. M. Hough (eds), *Handbook of Industrial and Organizational Psychology*, 2nd ed., Vol. 3. Palo Alto, CA: Consulting Psychologists Press, 1994.

14. Robbins. *Organizational Behavior: Concepts, Controversies, and Applications*, p. 445.
15. Ibid., pp. 446–447.
16. Warshaw. "The Good Guy's (and Gal's) Guide to Office Politics," p. 156.
17. Jehn, Karen A. "Enhancing Effectiveness: An Investigation of Advantages and Disadvantages of Value-Based Intragroup Conflict," *International Journal of Conflict Management* 5, no. 3 (July 1994), pp. 223–238.
18. Ibid., p. 4.
19. Thomas. *Handbook of Industrial and Organizational Psychology.*
20. Robbins. *Organizational Behavior: Concepts, Controversies, and Applications,* pp. 451–453.
21. Lancaster. "Solving Conflicts," p. B1.
22. Whetten, D. A. and K. S. Cameron. *Developing Management Skills: Managing Conflict.* New York: HarperCollins, 1993, p. 35.
23. Ibid.
24. Schmidt, W. H. and R. Tannenbaum. "Management of Differences," in *Harvard Business Review on Negotiation and Conflict Resolution.* Boston: Harvard Business School Press, 2000, pp. 18–19. Copyright © 2000 by the Harvard Business School Publishing Corporation; all rights reserved.
25. Lancaster, "Solving Conflicts," p. B1. See also, Brody, J. E. "Why Angry People Can't Control the Short Fuse," *New York Times*, May 28, 2002, p. D7. Copyright © 2002 by The New York Times Company. Reprinted with permission.
26. Ibid.
27. Ibid.
28. Ibid.
29. Whetten and Cameron. *Developing Management Skills*, p. 35.
30. Ibid., p. 36.
31. Lancaster. "Solving Conflicts," p. B1.
32. Felton. "When Rage Is All the Rage," p. 12.
33. Brody. "Why Angry People Can't Control the Short Fuse."
34. Felton. "When Rage Is All the Rage," p. 12.
35. Gordon, M. Telephone interview, Vantage Partners/Boston, November 25, 2002.
36. Felton. "When Rage Is All the Rage," p. 12.
37. Green, W. "Zen and the Art of Managerial Maintenance," *Fast Company*, June 1996, p. 50.

CASE STUDY 11-1

Hayward Healthcare Systems, Inc.

Bob Jackson is the new operations manager of the distribution center for Hayward Healthcare Systems, Inc., a midsize, nonunion company located in California. The distribution center is an $80-million-a-year operation that has 50 employees, including 15 minorities and 18 females in the workforce.

Jackson was transferred from another operations position in the company to fill this position because of some serious performance problems in the distribution center that had resisted all attempts at improvement. The center had experienced a very high level of defects (140 per month) and an unacceptable rate of errors in the orders taken from client hospitals. Jackson accepted the assignment knowing that top management would expect him to improve the performance of the distribution center in a relatively short period of time.

Jackson's first few weeks on the job were revealing, to say the least. He discovered that the five supervisors that his predecessor had selected to lead the center's workforce had little credibility with the employees. They had each been selected on the basis of their job seniority or their friendship with the previous manager.

The workforce was organized into three categories. Pickers identify supplies by code numbers in the storage area, remove packaged items from the shelves, and sort them into baskets. Drivers operate forklifts and electric trucks, moving baskets and boxes of supplies to different locations within the distribution center. Loaders transfer supplies onto and off of the forklifts and delivery trucks.

The Situation Mr. Jackson Encountered

Jackson found that his employees were either demoralized or had tough, belligerent attitudes toward management and other employees. Part of the problem, he soon learned, was a lax approach to background checks and prior job references. Seven employees were convicted felons who had been imprisoned for violent assaults on their victims. The previous manager had made all of the hiring decisions by himself without bothering to check on the applicants' references or backgrounds.

Jackson soon discovered that it was not unusual for employees to settle their differences with their fists or to use verbally abusive language to berate people who had offended them. His predecessor had unintentionally encouraged these disruptive activities by staying in his office and not being available to the other workers. He had relied largely on his discredited supervisors to handle their own disciplinary problems. Before long, the employees at the center felt they could handle their own affairs in any way they wanted, without any interference from management.

The Loading Dock Incident

While sitting in his office, planning to make several policy changes to improve the efficiency of the distribution center, one of Jackson's supervisors entered and reported that two of the loaders had just gotten into a heated dispute, and the situation on the loading dock was tense.

The dispute was between Ed Williams, an African-American male employee, and Buddy Jones, a white male employee, and focused on which radio station to play on the loading dock sound system. Williams is the only black employee who works on the loading dock. The company's policy permits employees to listen to music while they work and, in recent years, workers have considered listening to music to be a benefit that improves their working conditions. Williams insisted that he couldn't stand to listen to the country music that Jones preferred to play. For his part, Jones claimed that Williams's choice of rap and hip-hop music was offensive to him and made working conditions difficult. An emotional and angry argument developed between the two men over their choices in music, and each yelled racial slurs at the other. Neither the company nor the division [has] a policy governing the choice of music permitted in the workplace. Apparently, whoever gets to work first chooses the music for the day.

Both Jones and Williams were known as tough employees who had previous disciplinary problems at Hayward Hospital Supply. Jones had been incarcerated for 18 months prior to being hired by the company. Jackson knew that he should take immediate action to resolve this problem and to avoid a potentially volatile escalation of the conflict. His supervisors told Jackson that, in the past, the previous manager would simply have hollered at the two antagonists in the conflict and then departed with no further action.

Jackson's objectives in resolving the conflict included the establishment of his own control in the workplace. He knew that he would have to change "business as usual" in the distribution center so that employees would respect his authority and would refrain from any further unprofessional conduct.

Resolving the Problem

In determining the most appropriate solution to the dispute between Jackson's employees, you should consider the following questions:

1. What seems to be the cause of the conflict?
2. What style of conflict management are the distribution center's employees using in this case?
3. What style of conflict management have Hayward Healthcare System managers used in the past?
4. What should Mr. Jackson do to settle the conflict? Should either or both of the employees be punished for their behavior?
5. What can Mr. Jackson do over the long term to ensure that incidents such as the one described in this case are less likely to occur?
6. What can Mr. Jackson do to develop a group of supervisors who can provide the support he requires and who can properly direct the work of the employees in the distribution center?
7. How important is communication in this case? What should Mr. Jackson do to improve the quality of communication in the distribution center?

WRITING ASSIGNMENT

Please respond in writing to the issues presented in this case by preparing two documents: a communication strategy memo and a professional business letter.

In preparing these documents, you may assume one of two roles: you may identify yourself as a Hayward Healthcare Systems manager who has been asked to provide advice to Bob Jackson regarding the issues he and the company are facing. Or, you may identify yourself as an external management consultant who has been asked by the company to provide advice to Mr. Jackson.

Either way, you must prepare a strategy memo addressed to Bob Jackson that summarizes the details of the case, rank orders critical issues, discusses their implications (what they mean and why they matter), offers specific recommendations for action (assigning ownership and suspense dates for each), and shows how to communicate the solution to all who are affected by the recommendations.

You must also prepare a professional business letter for Mr. Jackson's signature. That document must be addressed to the employees of the distribution center. If you have questions about either of these documents, please consult your instructor.

This case was prepared by Kay Wigton with the assistance of James S. O'Rourke, Concurrent Professor of Management, as the basis for class discussion rather than to illustrate either effective or ineffective handling of an administrative situation. Personal and corporate identities have been disguised.

CASE STUDY 11-2

Dixie Industries, Inc.

Middle managers are frequently called upon to draft documents, including letters, memoranda, position papers, background reports, and briefing documents for senior people in their organizations. Sometimes, senior managers will ask subordinates not only to prepare a document for signature, but to gather the relevant supporting information, as well.

Often, the preparation of such documents requires no more than a quick referral to a balance sheet, database, or filing system to gather the information needed. Sometimes, though, a management response requires that the company—often in the person of the chief executive or president—take a position on an issue. It is in such circumstances that middle managers can reveal who among them is most perceptive, thoughtful, and insightful.

Some management problems are easily resolved. The issues are clear, the resources are available, and implementation is not difficult. Other problems are more difficult. Resources may be limited, intentions and agenda may not be clear, and more than one audience may be paying attention to the response.

The issue at hand deals with corporate policy, corporate actions in regard to that policy, and with the public perceptions of both. This case requires two documents: a brief (two- or three-page) communication strategy memorandum and a letter to an employee. The strategy memo should be directed to the president of Dixie Industries, Inc., and should describe in detail how you plan to handle the case and why. The letter will help to implement the strategy.

Assume that you are the vice president for human resources and report directly to the president of the firm. Dixie Industries, Inc., is a midsize, nonunion textile company located in the American South. The author of the study referred to by your president is a loom operator with ten years' experience and six years of job tenure with the firm. Your memorandum to the president and letter to Ms. Feldman should be in finished form and ready to transmit.

DIXIE INDUSTRIES, INC.
3128 Northeast Industrial Park Road Meridian, Mississippi 39201

DATE: [Today's Date]
TO: Vice President, Human Resources
FROM: Keith Harkins
            President, Dixie Industries, Inc.
SUBJECT: Dixie Industries Women's Group Study of Company Promotion Practices

Background

As you know, Dixie Industries, Inc., recently has been accused by an ad hoc committee of employees of "a continuing and pervasive bias in promotions in favor of men." You may recall that Ms. Linda Feldman, founder and chairperson of the Dixie Industries Women's Group, has produced a so-called study of this problem and has demanded that we respond. The DI Executive Committee has read her study (such as it is) and asked for my response. I have attached a copy of her letter.

As far as I can determine, we now have four women in positions above that of assistant department head. None of the senior executive positions, other than your own, has ever been filled by a female, but we're certainly open to hiring some as positions come open.

Now you know, of course, that more than 40 percent of our 1,800 employees are female—all of them industrious and hardworking. Many of them are quite loyal to the company, but many others (Ms. Feldman included) come and go with some frequency. We have experienced 23 maternity leave requests in the past 12 months. Others have poor attendance records (sick children, school problems, etc.).

Our Official Position

My position, and the position of Dixie Industries, Inc., is this: We will promote the most deserving individual who is available to fill a particular vacancy. We will certainly consider any qualified woman (or any qualified man, for that matter) when a job in the executive ranks comes open. Our long-standing policy of promoting from within remains firm. We go outside the company only when no fully qualified applicants are available in-house.

Ms. Feldman's complaint ignores a number of important points, including the fact that few, if any, of our loom operators and plant floor personnel have the education and background to become managers. Also, a number of the figures she cites in the study are simply wrong. She does have a point, however, in that we have very few women in management or executive positions.

The other issue she ignores is the fact that we haven't had much turnover in management or executive positions in the past five years. In 25 positions, we've had one retirement and one resignation. The retirement resulted in an internal promotion (to VP, finance from comptroller), and the resignation resulted in an external hire. We have such low turnover, in my view, because of employee loyalty. And, as you know, we are well ahead of the industry in this regard.

(Continued)

Issues To Be Resolved

I am concerned about several issues here.

- **Unionization.** If Ms. Feldman manages to get enough of our hourly wage employees excited about this issue, we could be looking at a petition for establishment of a collective bargaining unit— probably with the ILGWU. That's a distraction that would be costly and counterproductive.

Dixie Industries Women's Group Study of Promotional Practices
[Today's Date]
Page 2 of 3

- **Publicity.** This is just the sort of thing that could hurt our image in the local community and, ultimately, drive our stock price down even further. We just cannot afford to have employees airing their grievances in the newspapers. We could use a little positive publicity for a change.
- **Job Action.** We have had a difficult time over the past 18 months in recruiting and retaining dependable loom operators. I'm concerned that Ms. Feldman and her group may instigate a slow down, a walkout, or some other job action that will impair this company's ability to respond to customer orders and remain competitive. As you know, margins in this industry are shrinking every year because of foreign competition.
- **Productivity.** We are consistently below industry standards in productivity and have been for more than a year. We simply cannot afford to spend more time worrying about issues like this. Instead, we must work on absenteeism, turnover, and unit productivity.
- **The Right Thing to Do.** I am also concerned about more than simple appearance here. I want this company to do the right thing, whatever that may be. The problem, of course, is that I'm not at all certain what the right thing might be. We can't promote high-school educated loom operators to management positions simply because we don't have many women in management.

Give me your best thoughts on this. What should we do? Shall we confront Ms. Feldman and her group? Or, should we try to work with her to resolve the issues we face?

I'm ready to move on this issue. Please prepare a plan for me that will respond to Ms. Feldman and address her concerns, and do what you can to help us calm this situation. Please let me know whether or not you think we should meet with this women's group. Involve whichever members of the staff you think are appropriate and copy them on your memo. Make it confidential but don't leave our key players in the dark.

Additionally, I would like you to prepare a letter for my signature to Ms. Feldman. I don't want any publicity about this matter, and I certainly don't want any lawsuits. Let me see your draft within 48 hours.

-KJH

[Dated One Week Ago]
310 Azalea Lane
Meridian, MS 39203

Mr. Keith Harkins
Dixie Industries
3128 Northeast Industrial Park Road
Meridian, MS 39201

Dear Mr. Harkins:

The Dixie Industries Women's Group has asked me to write to you on behalf of the women of our company. We have some questions and concerns that we would like to share with you.

Mr. Keith Harkins
[Dated One Week Ago]
Page 2

The first concerns promotion opportunities for women at Dixie Industries. According to Mr. Darryl Robbins of the DI Human Resources Department, this company employs approximately 1,798 employees in various jobs. Mr. Robbins also says that about 720 of them are women. That seems to be about 40 percent of the Dixie Industries workers who are female.

At the same time, Mr. Robbins told me that the company has about two dozen upper management positions here, but only four are staffed by women. That's not much better than 16 percent. This company has, according to its own HR Department, 54 managers and 25 senior managers. Of those, just seven women are managers and only two are senior managers. In addition to that, one of just two female executives, Mrs. Dorothy Wyatt, left the company last year. Some of her close friends say she left because of the general working environment here and the lack of opportunity for women.

An informal survey of other firms in the textile industry (see table below) shows that Dixie Industries is below average in promotion opportunities for women employees. West Point Pepperell in Georgia has told a member of our group that 35 percent of their senior managers are women. That's twice the average of Dixie Industries. Berkshire Mills of Alabama told us more or less the same thing. On top of that, both of those firms offer college tuition and specialized training to their employees, which Dixie does not.

The fact of the matter, Mr. Harkins, remains that Dixie Industries has not promoted a woman to a management position in over two years. Dixie does nothing to encourage and retain good women in management. And Dixie has done nothing to show current women employees that they have any future with this company. The only conclusion our group can draw is that the company is demonstrating a continuing and pervasive bias in promotions in favor of men.

(Continued)

Women Managers in Regional Textile Mills, 2011–2012: Mississippi, Alabama, Georgia					
Mill Name	Location	Employees	Managers	Sr. Mgrs.	Women Mgrs.
Pepperell	West Point, GA	2,650	78	33	36 (32%)
Berkshire	Prattville, AL	2,245	72	30	19 (19%)
Hoover	Anniston, AL	1,277	36	21	16 (28%)
Cannon	Columbus, GA	2,130	65	29	28 (30%)
Dixie	Meridian, MS	1,798	54	25	11 (14%)

The second significant issue that I have been asked to bring to your attention concerns training opportunities. Most of the promotions to supervisory positions on the plant floor have gone to people with advanced training in textile production and automated loom operations. Those people, with very few exceptions, have been men. We would like to know when the company plans to establish a fair and equitable means for selecting employees for training, especially training that is likely to lead to better employment opportunities.

Mr. Keith Harkins
[Dated One Week Ago]
Page 3

Mr. Harkins, I have personally been employed here over six years and am certified as a master loom technician. My reason for writing to you is to explain that a number of women employees of Dixie Industries are upset about these facts and concerned that no opportunity for a better future exists for them here. On their behalf, I respectfully ask that you explain what the company plans to do.

Sincerely,

Mrs. Linda S. Feldman

This case was prepared by James S. O'Rourke, Teaching Professor of Management, as the basis for class discussion rather than to illustrate either effective or ineffective handling of an administrative situation. Personal and corporate identities have been disguised.

CASE STUDY 11-3

It's Time to Kiss and Make Up

Hershey Foods Chief Executive Richard Lenny was reviewing the deal's final details in an office in Philadelphia as his advisers drafted a press release to announce the sale of Hershey Foods. It was just then that he got the phone call from Robert Vowler. The Hershey Trust Company board of directors had decided to reject all bids and informed Lenny that the company was no longer up for sale. Lenny was livid, "We had a deal. You told me if I brought you a deal that was acceptable, we would all go ahead."[1]

Hershey Foods: The Company

The Hershey Foods Company was founded by Milton S. Hershey in 1905 and went public in 1927. It currently trades on the New York Stock Exchange under the symbol HSY. Last year it had $4.6 billion in sales, representing 43 percent of the domestic chocolate market. The company is headquartered in Hershey, Pennsylvania, and employs 6,200 of the town's 13,000 residents.[2]

Hershey Foods is divided into three product groups: the chocolate and confectionary group, restaurant operations, and other food products and service group. The chocolate and confectionary group is the most widely known to consumers, as it produces and markets popular brands such as Hershey's Kisses, Reese's peanut butter cups, Twizzlers licorice, Mounds, Super Bubble gum, and Kit Kat.

Milton Hershey was born in 1857 on a farm in central Pennsylvania. Throughout his youth Hershey lived in Denver, New Orleans, and New York City, but returned to Pennsylvania in 1886, where he founded the Lancaster Caramel Company. He started producing chocolate in 1893, and formed Hershey Chocolate Company (a subsidiary of Lancaster Caramel) in 1894. In 1900, Mr. Hershey sold the Lancaster Caramel Company for $1 million. With the proceeds from the sale he returned to his native Derry Church, Pennsylvania, and began to build his chocolate manufacturing plant.[3]

With the factory opening in 1905, Milton Hershey embarked on his two most ambitious endeavors: being a pioneer in the mass-production of chocolate and creating a utopian community. He was an ambitious businessman, but he wanted the money he made to be used for a purpose of enduring good. A sign on his office wall read, "Business is a matter of human service."[4]

Hershey not only produced chocolate, but also built houses and public buildings, ran the utilities and trolleys, and created the Hershey Trust Company to serve as the community's bank. During the Great Depression, Milton Hershey managed to not lay off any of his workers, although sales dropped by 50 percent. He employed them for alternate projects, such as the building of the Hotel Hershey.

Milton Hershey, in the view of many of his supporters, had built the "sweetest place on Earth,"

and a key element of this community was the Milton Hershey School for disadvantaged children that he and his wife established in 1909. His mission is summarized by this statement from about the same year:

I want all of my money for the benefit of my employees and the people of Hershey, for the education of the children in Derry Township and the children of my employees—all my money.[5]

Milton Hershey died in 1945, at the age of 81, but his legacy is still very much alive in Hershey, Pennsylvania. The town's residents celebrate his birthday each September 13 in Chocolatetown square and pictures of him are ubiquitous throughout the town.

Richard Lenny: Hershey Foods CEO

Hershey residents hold a strong sense of their legacy, but the current CEO of Hershey Foods, Richard Lenny, had a different view of how a company should operate. Lenny became CEO in early 2001, and was the first outsider to ever run the company. Before joining Hershey Foods, he had been a group vice president at Kraft Foods. Hershey was a profitable company, ranked 28th best performing stock of the past 30 years with annualized returns of 17.4 percent, but it had seen its margins decline in recent years relative to the industry.[6]

Lenny increased profits in 2002 by 10 percent from January to March over the same period for the previous year. However, this increase in profits did not make him especially popular in the town, as the profit increase was due in large part to savings from plant closures, and cocoa production outsourcing.

These cost-cutting efforts created opposition within the company, and resulted in a six-week strike in April of 2002 over a proposed health care change. The 44-day strike was the longest in the company's history. Richard Lenny was unwilling to negotiate with the workers, and focused on his mission, "I'm here to do what the shareholders want me to do, which is to increase shareholder value."[7]

Worker discontent with the CEO grew beyond the initial reticence, and Bruce Hummel, head of Hershey's union branch summarized Lenny's attitude, "The whole air about him is the fact that he is just corporate greed."[8]

Hershey Trust Company

The same year that his chocolate factory started operations, Milton Hershey established the Hershey Trust Company to assist in the creation of the model industrial community he envisioned. The trust began operations in June 1905 serving as the community's first bank. A few years later, the trust was appointed trustee for the newly established Hershey Industrial School (now Milton Hershey School). The trust company's responsibilities as trustee for the school increased significantly in 1918 when Milton Hershey gifted the school his entire stake in the Hershey Chocolate company, valued at $60 million. In 1935, in response to his growing concerns for the future of Derry [Township's] youth, Milton Hershey established the M. S. Hershey Foundation and again appointed the Hershey Trust Company as trustee. The foundation's chartered purpose was to provide educational and cultural opportunities to the citizens of Derry Township.

Today a 17-member board headed by president and chief executive officer, Robert Vowler, manages the Milton S. Hershey School Trust, valued at $5.4 billion. Approximately 58 percent of the trust's assets are invested in Hershey Foods Corporation stock. The trust's stake represents 31 percent of the outstanding shares of Hershey Foods and 77 percent of the voting stock.[9] The preferred class B voting stocks that provide the trust with controlling interest resulted from a series of stock repurchases executed between 1986 and 1993 by Hershey Foods Corporation totaling $1.3 billion. The stock buybacks were designed to reduce the trust's holdings in Hershey Foods stock and diversify its portfolio. The trust's return over the past five years has been solid: Its compound average annual return was 4.3 percent, compared with 0.44 percent for the Standard & Poor's 500 stock index.[10]

Milton S. Hershey School

On November 15, 1909, Milton and Catherine Hershey, eager to put their growing fortune to good use, founded the Hershey Industrial School for orphaned boys. The deed of trust that chartered the school stipulated the school's purpose as the education and "training of young men to useful trades and occupations, so that they can earn their own livelihood."[11] Hershey's

donation of stock after the death of his wife assured the financial future of the school and made the trust company majority owner in the Hershey Chocolate Company. The "home boys" as the students came to be known, often had their lives changed by attending Hershey Industrial School and as a result developed a fierce loyalty to Milton Hershey and the school. Many went on to become employees, managers, and even CEOs of Hershey Foods and Hershey Entertainment & Resorts Company (Herco).

The school was later renamed the Milton S. Hershey School and admission policies were modified to remove the orphan restriction and to include girls, minorities, and under-privileged youths from broken homes. The school, located on a picturesque 10,000-acre campus, provides not only education, but also room, board, medical and dental care, clothing, social work support, laptop computers, and college fund assistance for 1,200 disadvantaged children. Proceeds from the trust provided approximately $111 million to operate the Milton S. Hershey School during the 2001–2002 school year, or roughly $96,500 for each of its students.[12] Plans to increase the school's enrollment to 1,500 students are currently underway.

The Beginning of the Divide

Hershey Chocolate Company, the Hershey Trust Company, the Milton Hershey School, and the community of Derry Township all enjoyed a cozy, albeit fragile union while Milton Hershey was alive and occupied the chairman's seat on each board. After his death in 1945, fissures began to develop. Townspeople objected to the trust's gift of $50 million to Pennsylvania State University to construct a medical school and teaching hospital in 1963. Over the next several decades, the Hershey Junior College (est. 1938) that residents and employees could attend free of charge was closed, the community swimming pool was filled in, Hershey-run municipal services and utilities were sold, and the amusement park began charging an admission fee.

In the early 1970s, Hershey stock and dividends experienced a steep decline as the result of price-wage controls. The school trustees had to sell real estate holdings to satisfy their obligations and enrollment was negatively affected for several years. The Hershey Chocolate Company lost its market share leader position to Mars and encountered financial difficulties. Pursuing an aggressive strategy of diversification, Hershey Chocolate Company executed a number of non-chocolate acquisitions and changed its name to Hershey Foods. Restructuring and operations changes proved successful and Hershey regained market share lead in 1988.[13] Hershey Chocolate Company leaders' necessary focus on the bottom line began to erode the paternalistic, protective culture that was Milton Hershey's legacy.

In 1993, an outsider (not an alumnus), former Iowa educator William Lepley, was hired to run the Milton Hershey School[14] and appointed to the school trust board. The school's alumni association was at odds with Lepley and the school's trust over changes at the school. An ongoing feud ensued amidst allegations of mismanagement and misconduct. As a consequence of board diversification and disputes over control, chief executives of Hershey Foods and Hershey Entertainment and Resort Company no longer hold positions on the Hershey Trust Company board of directors.

A Turbulent Time in Chocolate Town

In December of 2001, following an 18-month investigation in response to alumni claims of mismanagement at the school, state of Pennsylvania deputy attorney general Mark Pacella presented his findings to the Hershey Trust Company board. Among the findings was a recommendation that the trust diversify its holdings and better position itself to fulfill its fiduciary responsibility to the school and other dependent organizations. At its quarterly board meeting in the spring of 2002, the trust voted 15–2 to diversify its portfolio by seeking a buyer for Hershey Foods Corporation.

A delegation of board members met with CEO Richard Lenny to inform him of the trust's intent. Lenny opposed the trust's plan, refusing to sell the company, and requested time to come up with an alternative plan to achieve the trust's diversification goal. With his attention diverted by a union strike over health care cost reductions, it was early May before Lenny approached the trust with his plan. Lenny presented a stock repurchase plan to the trust company's investment committee since he was prevented from addressing the entire board. The plan would have Hershey Foods purchase 50 percent of the

trust company's stock at a 10 percent premium and help the trust liquidate its remaining shares on the open market over the next three to five years. The proposal was rebuffed on May 14, 2002, in a letter from Hershey Trust Company CEO, Robert Vowler. Members of the trust board threatened to fire Lenny and replace members of the Hershey board if the company did not solicit bids, and a member was quoted as saying "We're going to sell this with or without you."[15] Reluctantly, Lenny agreed to the sale, if he and his advisers would be allowed to lead the sale process.

On July 25, 2002, the Hershey Trust Company publicly announced that in recognition of its fiduciary responsibility to the Milton S. Hershey School, it had decided to put Hershey Foods Corporation up for sale. Lenny addressed the sale in a memo to Hershey employees:

> I'm terribly disappointed that we may not be able to see it through as an independent company. I came here to build our brands and build our people, not to manage a potential sale and subsequent integration process. Having been your CEO for only one year, I had hoped to work with you for a long time to come.[16]

Market and public reaction was immediate. Investor speculation increased Hershey Foods share price by more than 20 percent to close at $79.49. Within days of the announcement, multiple shareholder suits had been filed seeking assurance that the trust would receive maximum value for its controlling shares. John M. McMillin, an analyst at Prudential Securities said, "Milton Hershey must be rolling over in his grave. He believed very strongly in the community of Hershey, in protecting it. I'm all for food industry consolidation, but this one surprised me."[17]

Grass-Roots Opposition

By the middle of the week following the announcement, the opposition had begun to organize. Community leaders, school alumni, employees, and government officials voiced their disapproval of the trust board's decision. Pennsylvania State Attorney General Mike Fisher, whose office has jurisdiction over charitable trusts, added his voice to the opposition and vowed his office's support to counter the sale. Bruce McKinney, a graduate of the Milton Hershey School, former Herco CEO, and trust company trustee, denounced the sale and indicated the idea was summarily rejected earlier in his tenure. McKinney would become a prominent resistance leader. Former Hershey Foods CEO, Ken Wolfe angrily disputed the trust's claim that a sale was necessary to protect the long-term health of the Milton Hershey School Trust. He predicted that a sale would result in layoff of local workers saying, "I can't believe they are going to destroy this company and put this pain on all the people."[18] Monty Stover, a 102-year-old former executive who knew Milton Hershey personally, was representative of the community's disdain for the planned sale, "Mr. Hershey would never have considered this proposition. He would have said: 'Gentlemen, you are wasting your time and mine. Goodbye.'"[19] Ric Foaud, president of the school's alumni association summarized the community's response, "We're not here to mourn; we're here to organize."[20]

At 11:30 A.M. on August 2, 2002, more than 500 ordinary citizens, school alumni, employees, and politicians braved the sweltering August heat to gather in Chocolatetown Square. The community park in downtown Hershey, at the corner of Chocolate and Cocoa Ave., was the site of an hour-long rally protesting the sale of Hershey Foods. The spirited protest concluded with a march up a rise overlooking the Hershey factory to the Hershey Trust Company offices located in Milton Hershey's former residence, High Point.

The grass-roots community opposition would grow to include an online petition to oust the trust board members hosted on the www.friendsofhershey.org Web site, a "derail the sale" yard sign campaign, and a union-organized protest to the nearby state capital of Harrisburg. Citizens who wanted to participate in the lawn sign campaign could stop by John Dunn's house at 712 Linden Road and find preprinted signs and yard stakes in the open garage. A can was located nearby for contributions to help defray the costs. Automobile placards could be downloaded from the Friends of Hershey Web site. The fall fashion sensation in Hershey was a t-shirt bearing Milton Hershey's picture and the words "Save the Dream."[21]

Government Officials Respond

During the first week of August, in direct response to citizen outcry, Pennsylvania lawmakers considered legislation that would require consideration of community impact before the sale of a corporation could be executed. The following day, Attorney General and Republican candidate for governor, Mike Fisher declared his intent to pursue legal avenues to block the sale of Hershey Foods. On August 12, 2002, Fisher filed a petition with the Dauphin County Orphan's Court asking that the sale be subject to the approval of the court since it maintains jurisdiction over charitable trusts. A hearing was scheduled for later that month.

On September 3, 2002, First Deputy Attorney General Jerry Pappert argued on Fisher's behalf before Orphan's Court Senior Judge Warren Morgan. Former Hershey Foods CEO Richard Zimmerman, testifying as a witness for the attorney general's office, said that a buyer would likely slash jobs in Hershey to help make up for the cost of buying the company. The attorney general's office was requesting a temporary injunction to prevent the sale of Hershey Foods citing the potential irreparable harm to the local community as cause.

On September 4, 2002, Judge Morgan granted the injunction and issued a stinging rebuke to the trust company in his ruling. Morgan said the "sale appears to be excessive and unnecessary," and claims by the trust company that a sale is the only option are an "affront to the intelligence."[22] The trust appealed the ruling the same day stating that the Orphan's Court did not have jurisdiction since Hershey was incorporated in the state of Delaware.

Bidding Begins

Prospective suitors began touring the Derry Township factories on August 17, 2002. By the September 14, 2002, deadline, Hershey had two options to consider: A $10.5 billion Cadbury Schweppes. The newly formed Nestle/Cadbury consortium was for bidding purposes only and the two companies were discussing how to divvy up Hershey's brands once the acquisition was complete. The Wm. Wrigley Jr. Company topped the Nestle/ Cadbury offer and agreed to important concessions. The $12.5 billion bid from Wrigley was a combination of cash and stock in the new company to be called Wrigley Hershey.

Sale Ends

After intense negotiations between Hershey Foods and Wrigley, a deal was reached in which the Wrigley Company committed to retain the factories and maintain the workforce in Hershey, Pennsylvania. Wrigley promised to make Hershey, Pennsylvania "the chocolate capital of the world."[23] But on September 17, 2002, after an emotional ten-hour meeting, the Hershey Trust Company board had a change of heart and rejected all the bids. In a brief public statement, the trust explained that neither offer met its objectives. The Nestle/Cadbury offer was considered to be too low and the Wrigley offer would have left the trust with 36 percent of it holdings still in Hershey Foods stock. Trust president and CEO Robert Vowler addressed community concerns the following day stating that intense public opposition prompted the board to abandon it sale plans.

What Now?

Markets reacted badly to the news that the sale of Hershey Foods was being scrapped, pushing share prices down near 15-year lows. Thousands of workers and citizens of Hershey celebrated the derailing of the sale but were uncertain if it was the end of the issue.

There has been significant disruption to our company, employees and the communities in which we live and work over the past few months. However, Hershey Foods remains a competitively advantaged market leader in an attractive category. We also have a truly outstanding workforce, one that consistently has maintained focus and shown courage in the face of significant uncertainty about our future as an independent company. Our mission, as always, is to bring our energy and attention to the task of building our brand and capitalizing on the immense strengths that were so clearly evident to potential acquirers.[24]

RICHARD LENNY

DISCUSSION QUESTIONS

1. Would the long-term financial health of Hershey Foods and the Hershey School have been improved by the execution of the sale? Does the trust's decision to forgo selling the company enhance Hershey's stability?

2. What are the critical issues facing Richard Lenny as he positions Hershey Foods for the future? Who are the constituents that he must address? How should he address them?

3. How does Lenny approach the strained relations with investors? What should his message be?

4. Is it possible for the community of Hershey to exist in the twenty-first century as the industrial garden city Milton Hershey envisioned? What responsibility does Hershey Foods have to the community?

5. Could the outcome of the sale process have been different if the Hershey Trust Company had anticipated public reaction? If so, what message and approach should they have employed?

WRITING ASSIGNMENT

Please respond in writing to the issues presented in this case by preparing two documents: a communication strategy memo and a professional business letter.

In preparing these documents, you may assume one of two roles: you may identify yourself as Hershey Foods senior manager who has been asked to provide advice to Richard Lenny regarding the issues he and the company are facing. Or, you may identify yourself as an external management consultant who has been asked by the company to provide advice to Mr. Lenny.

Either way, you must prepare a strategy memo addressed to Mr. Lenny that summarizes the details of the case, rank orders critical issues, discusses their implications (what they mean and why they matter), offers specific recommendations for action (assigning ownership and suspense dates for each), and shows how to communicate the solution to all who are affected by the recommendations.

You must also prepare a professional business letter for the CEO's signature. That document may be addressed to the Hershey Trust Company or to all Hershey shareholders. If you have questions about either of these documents, please consult your instructor.

References

1. Frank, Robert and Sarah Ellison. "Controlling Trust Calls Off Sale of Hershey to Wrigley," *Wall Street Journal*, September 19, 2002.
2. Gadsden, Christopher H. "The Hershey Power Play,"*Charitable Giving,* November 11, 2002.
3. www.hersheys.com/discover/milton/milton/asp.
4. Helyar, John. "Sweet Surrender," *Fortune*, October 14, 2002.
5. Hostetter, Dr. Herman H. *The Body, Mind and Soul of Milton Snavely Hershey.*
6. money.cnn.com/pf/features/superstocks/.
7. Associated Press. "Bitterness Coats Sweet Hershey," *Seattle Times*, May 30, 2002.
8. news.bbc.co.uk/2/hi/business/1973405.stm.
9. "Hershey Trust Decides Not to Sell Candy-maker," CNN.com, September 18, 2002. Online at: www.cnn.com/2002/US/Northeast/09/18/hershey.no.sale/.
10. Barrett, Amy. "Graduate with a Cause," *BusinessWeek*, September 2, 2002.
11. www.hersheyarchives.org/part1/milton/milton.html.
12. Strauss, Gary and Thor Valdmanis. "City of Hershey Tastes Fear," *USA Today*, September 3, 2002.
13. Heylar, John. "Sweet Surrender," *Fortune*, October 14, 2002.
14. Ibid.
15. Frank, Robert and Sarah Ellison. "Meltdown in Chocolatetown," *Wall Street Journal*, September 19, 2002, pp. B1, B5.
16. Sulon, Bill. "Hershey Foods Chief Spells Out Sale Discussion," *The Patriot-News*, July 31, 2002.
17. Winter, Greg. "Chocolate Maker's Dream Melts Away," July 27, 2002. Online at: www.theage.com.au/articles/2002/07/26/1027497411375.html.
18. Marcy, Brett and Peter Decoursey. "Hershey Sale Off," *The Patriot-News*, September 18, 2002.
19. www.pennlive.com/news/hershey/.
20. Heylar. "Sweet Surrender."
21. Ibid.
22. Marcy and Decoursey. "Hershey Sale Off."
23. Frank and Sarah. "Meltdown in Chocolatetown."
24. PR Newswire. "Hershey Foods Reaffirms Its Strength," September 18, 2002.

Appendix A

Timeline

Spring 2001: Former Kraft Foods executive, Richard Lenny takes over as CEO of Hershey Foods. Lenny is the first outsider to run the company.

October 2001: Under CEO Richard Lenny's direction, Hershey Foods begins a $275 million restructuring. The restructuring efforts are intended to cut costs and include the closing of three manufacturing plants and a distribution center, the sale of non-chocolate food products, outsourcing of cocoa production, and the offering of a voluntary separation package to a large portion of Hershey's management.

December 2001: Following an 18-month investigation prompted by alumni charges of mismanagement by the trust board, deputy attorney general Mark Pacella advises Hershey Trust Company to diversify its holdings. Diversification would assure the financial future of Milton Hershey School and other dependent organizations.

March 2002: The trust board votes 15–2 to seek a buyer for Hershey Foods. A trust board delegation meets with Hershey Foods CEO Richard Lenny and tells him to put the company up for sale. Lenny opposes the sale and requests time to develop an alternative plan.

April 26, 2002: Chocolate Workers Local 464 union members reject a proposed contract that would double employee contributions for health insurance premiums and begin a 44-day strike.

May 2002: Richard Lenny presents a stock buyback plan to the trust as an alternative to the sale of Hershey Foods. Hershey Foods Corporation would [buy back] 50 percent of shares held by the trust and would help the trust liquidate its remaining shares in the open market over the next three to five years.

May 14, 2002: Hershey Trust Company CEO, Robert Vowler, sends a letter to Lenny rejecting the buyback plan. Members of the trust threaten to fire Lenny if he does not solicit bids. Trust indicates that they will sell the company with or without his assistance.

July 2002: Richard Lenny reluctantly agrees to the sale of the company if the Hershey Foods management team is allowed to lead the sale process.

July 25, 2002: Hershey Trust Co. publicly announces that it is seeking a buyer for Hershey Foods. The trust states the reason for the sale as a need to diversify its more than $5 billion portfolio and guarantee the fiscal future of the Milton Hershey School.

July 29, 2002: Multiple shareholder suits are filed seeking assurance that the trust would receive maximum value for its controlling shares.

July 30, 2002: Community leaders, school alumni, and government leaders voice opposition to the sale.

July 31, 2002: Pennsylvania Attorney General, Mike Fisher, expresses his disapproval of the trust's plan to sell Hershey Foods. The attorney general's office has jurisdiction over charitable trusts.

August 1, 2002: Former trust company trustees denounce the sale indicating the idea was rejected during their tenure.

August 2, 2002: Community protest rally draws 500 participants to picket offices of Hershey Trust Company. Community opposition expands to include friendsofhershey.org Web site, online petition to oust trust board members, "derail the sale" lawn sign campaign, and a protest rally at the state [capitol].

August 7, 2002: Amidst the firestorm of protest, the trust board meets and reaffirms its decision to sell the company.

August 8, 2002: Pennsylvania lawmakers consider legislation requiring consideration of community impact before the sale of a corporation can be executed.

August 9, 2002: Attorney General and Republican candidate for governor, Mike Fisher, vows to take legal action to prevent sale.

August 12, 2002: Fisher files a petition with the Dauphin County Orphan's Court asking that the sale be subject to approval of the court.

August 15, 2002: Dick Zimmerman and Ken Wolfe, former Hershey Foods chief executives, add their voices to the opposition.

August 17, 2002: Potential bidders begin to tour Hershey factories in Derry Township. Final bids are due September 14.

August 20, 2002: Trust board member Bill Alexander issues a letter suggesting growing uncertainty in the board's commitment to sell the company.

September 3, 2002: Attorney General Mike Fisher appears in Dauphin County Orphan's Court seeking an injunction to block the sale of Hershey Foods based on the detrimental financial impact the sale would have on the community of Hershey.

September 4, 2002: Judge Warren G. Morgan grants an injunction prohibiting the sale of Hershey Foods. News of the injunction caused a $3 decline in the price of Hershey Foods stock.

September 17, 2002: Wrigley makes presentation of its $12.5 billion proposal that includes concession to uphold the company's commitment to the community. Trust board scheduled to meet Wednesday, September 18, 2002, to accept Wrigley's offer.

Late evening, September 17, 2002: Trust board rejects all bids and requests Hershey Foods discontinues the process of finding a buyer.

Appendix B

Impact on Hershey Stock

HERSHEY FOODS CP
as of 25-Nov-2002   Splits: ▼

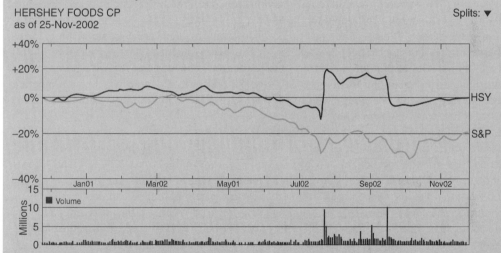

FIGURE 11-2 Impact on Hershey Stock

This case was prepared by Research Assistants Michaelyn M. McCoy and Laura A. Castrillo under the direction of James S. O'Rourke, Concurrent Professor of Management, as the basis for class discussion rather than to illustrate either effective or ineffective handling of an administrative situation.

Chapter *12*

Business Meetings That Work

Say the word in a small group of your colleagues. Go ahead, say it. *Meeting.* Suggest that your group schedule a meeting; tell them that you think they can resolve the issue they're discussing by setting up a meeting. Now watch the nonverbal reactions: eyes roll, noses scrunch up, people begin hyperventilating. Eyes that don't roll begin to glaze over.

You know the reason: No one likes meetings. "Too many of them are a waste of time," says Marge Boberschmidt. "Too many people walk out of too many meetings feeling that they didn't accomplish anything." Boberschmidt is a former public relations executive at AT&T who now runs her own consulting firm—planning meetings. "My greatest fear is that people will leave a meeting I've planned—having spent time, money, energy, and all sorts of lost opportunity—and come to the conclusion that it just wasn't worthwhile."[1]

Boberschmidt's reactions are common among managers who know that people and productivity are at the top of their list of current concerns. "People are my most important asset," says Bill Mountford, founder of a chain of Midwestern restaurants called *Studebagels*. "And I know that, even though I have information to share with them and they have information to share with me, I'm almost certain that having a meeting is among the least productive things I can do."[2]

Meetings are the most universal—and universally despised—part of business life. But bad meetings do more than ruin an otherwise pleasant day. William R. Daniels, senior consultant at American Consulting & Training in Mill Valley, California, is adamant about the real stakes: Bad meetings make bad companies. "Meetings matter because that's where an organization's culture perpetuates itself," he says. "Meetings are how an organization says, 'You are a member.' So if every day we go to boring meetings full of boring people, then we can't help but think that this is a boring company. Bad meetings are a source of negative messages about our company and ourselves."[3]

Bad meetings waste time and money, but they may also harm employee health. Professors in the United States and Britain recently surveyed 676 employees, who said they spend an average of 5.6 hours a week in meetings. The more time they spent in meetings they considered ineffective, says Steven Rogelberg, a principal researcher, the more gloomy and anxious they became about their jobs.[4]

It's not supposed to be this way. In a business world that is faster, tougher, leaner, and more downsized than ever, you might expect the sheer demands of competition (not to mention the impact of e-mail, texting, and groupware) to curb our appetite for meetings. In reality, according to author Eric Matson, the *opposite* may be true. As more work becomes teamwork and fewer people remain to do the work that exists, the number of meetings is likely to increase rather than decrease.[5]

Roger Mosvick, a communications professor at Macalester College in St. Paul, Minnesota, says meetings are on the upswing. The average number of meetings jumped from seven to about ten a week, based on surveys of business professionals done over a 15-year period. Many participants, says Mosvick, reported that they don't even know why they're attending some meetings. "It's an alarming statistic," he says. "Many meetings are mind-numbing in their mundaneness."[6]

Teresa Taylor, chief operating officer of Quest, begins each of her meetings by saying, "Do we all know why we're here?" When asked if she really does that, she replied "Yes, because so many people say, 'No, I don't know. I was invited.' It's usually the bigger meetings—not so much my direct report team." Her motivation is to get everyone on the same page. "I get invited to a lot of meetings where someone wants to brief me, or bring me up to speed on something. So I open with 'Do we all know why we're here? Are you going to ask me for something at the end?' I try to get that out right away. It's amazing, there will be eight people in the room and they all have a different answer of what's going on there."[7]

Meetings are also a time drain. Business professionals spend about half of their time in meetings, according to the 3M Meeting Network, an online resource covering meeting issues. As much as 50 percent of that time is unproductive, and up to 25 percent of meeting time covers irrelevant issues, according to professionals surveyed by 3M. "People just have a tendency to ramble," says J. Doug Batchelor, owner of Dalcom Systems, a software firm in Fort Worth, Texas. "There's entirely too much time spent on meetings." And meetings can trigger stress. Workers asked to rank emotionally charged situations on the job listed people taking up more time than necessary with meetings as a top problem, according to a survey by the American Management Association. "So often people get into a meeting and talk around an issue," says Beryl Loeb, a consultant and executive training specialist in Needham, Massachusetts. "Then they have to meet again."[8]

A recent survey of 613 workers by Office Team, a temporary-staffing agency in Menlo Park, California, indicated what most workers think about the subject. On a list of workplace time-wasters, "meetings that last too long" came in first, chosen by 27 percent of the respondents. According to Patti Hathaway, an author and change management consultant, "Nobody can afford to waste time anymore, sitting in a meeting that isn't productive. And the reality is, most corporate meetings are a colossal waste of time."[9]

WHAT'S THE MOTIVATION FOR MEETING?

So why do people have meetings? Most management experts tell us that there are really three reasons: First, because they're scheduled and attendance is not optional; second, because participants have ulterior or nonmeeting-related motives for attending (those meetings are usually in nice hotels located far from the company headquarters); and third, because they have no other options for achieving their goals.

There is one other reason for meeting, and that's the potential for human contact. "The drive for social connection is a very strong one," says Nicholas Epley, a professor of behavioral science at the University of Chicago's Booth School of Business. "Sitting in a cubicle is stupefying and isolating," he says, "only intensifying a social need."[10]

In some industries where product development and marketing programs rely heavily on teamwork across departments, meetings are simply unavoidable. Survey results published by the Annenberg School of Communications at the University of Southern California and the University of Minnesota's Training and Development Research Center confirm what the people at 3M found: Executives, on average, spend 40–50 percent of their working hours in meetings. Further evidence of the pervasiveness of meetings comes from facility consultant Jon Ryburg, who says he advises corporate clients to provide twice as much meeting space as they did 20 years ago.[11]

According to a recent survey by a large telecommunication company, managers now attend an average of 60 meetings a month, more than a third of which they say are difficult or unproductive.[12] In some professions, that percentage is much higher. "I must spend three-quarters of my working day in meetings," says Nancy Hobor. "I meet with our CFO regularly. I meet with my staff, with investment analysts, with mutual fund managers, with dozens of different people during the day." Hobor is the vice president for corporate communications and investor relations at W. W. Grainger and Company in Lake Forest, Illinois. "Time to myself is a luxury, so I have to use it wisely. I also have to use my meeting time wisely, as well as the time I take from other people."[13]

SO, WHY MEET?

An unspoken but widely accepted rule of business meetings is this: You should never, ever call a meeting—especially one that involves the time, energy, and budget of a considerable number of people—unless you have no other choice. A formal meeting is a communication alternative available when you cannot accomplish your goals or objectives in any other way. It is, in other words, the communication tool of last resort, after you have considered and discarded other forms of information exchange.

Professional meeting consultants see six legitimate reasons for taking people's time, spending their company's money, and devoting both energy and effort into a meeting.

- *To motivate.* A sales force, for instance, may get the jump start it needs to begin a highly competitive new season by meeting with people who can provide both motivation and methods for successful selling.
- *To educate.* An investor relations manager may meet with analysts or fund managers to brief them on new earnings growth projections, an update to the company's strategic plans, or a proposed product line.
- *To recreate.* Team building exercises often take place off-site in a hotel or conference center setting or, perhaps, in a wooded, outdoors setting designed to build confidence and unity.
- *To initiate.* Gathering employees together prior to a new product launch or brand line extension might help to explain product features and the market position management is hoping to sell to customers.
- *To network.* Members of professional societies and trade associations often gather to meet and speak with each other as much as they do to hear scheduled speakers or participate in carefully planned panel discussions or breakout sessions.
- *To reward.* Management can show employees that they genuinely care about them by offering a trip—often with family members accompanying them—to a company meeting in a desirable location (think warm in the winter, cool in the summer). A resort hotel or theme park can combine the professional and social goals of meeting, as long as costs are kept within reason and recreational goals are specified as an important part of the meeting agenda.[14]

WHAT IS A BUSINESS MEETING?

A business meeting is a gathering in which a purposeful exchange or transaction occurs among two or more people with a common interest, purpose, or problem. Many meetings, of course, turn out to be neither purposeful nor productive, but the best of them can help to solve problems, build consensus, provide training, gather opinion, and move an organization forward. Many, in fact, are not only productive but actually fun.

WHEN SHOULD I CALL A MEETING?

As we've already noted, people meet for a variety of reasons. Generally, they gather together to move group actions forward, often referred to as a *task focus*. To meet this goal, participants usually do two things in meetings: They present information to others and they collaborate. That is, they review, evaluate, discuss, solve problems, and decide what to do next. When any of these actions is essential to your business, consider a meeting.

As we've also noted, people want to meet for social reasons. Numerous studies show that people gather in meetings because they feel a need to belong, a need to achieve or make a difference of some sort, or because of a desire to communicate, to build and share a common reality.[15]

Why else should you consider meeting? Here are 10 more reasons why a meeting may be your best communication option:

Talk about goals.	Build morale.
Listen to reports.	Reach a consensus.
Train people.	Discover or solve problems.
Explain plans and programs.	Gather opinions.
Tell people what they're supposed to do and how they're to do it.	Keep things moving.

WHEN SHOULD I *NOT* CALL A MEETING?

You should consider some other communication alternative when a phone call, a memo, or an e-mail message would do just as well. Frequently, managers think they must meet with people—usually their employees and coworkers—in order to simply pass along information. If the flow of information is entirely one-way, you certainly should consider alternative routes for it. Unless the information is highly sensitive or personal—the death of a colleague or the sale of the company—a face-to-face meeting is usually not necessary.

You should also not plan a meeting when:

- **A key person is not available**. Often, a substitute can fill in for a colleague, but in some instances, it simply makes no sense to meet without a particular person in the room.
- **Participants don't have time to prepare**. If the group needs certain data or information to guide its discussion, make sure you have time to gather and distribute it. If preliminary reading or small group discussions must take place first, don't short-circuit your intentions by scheduling a meeting before all of that can happen.
- **Personality conflicts or the plans of higher management might make the meeting a waste of time**. If the issue you plan to discuss has become highly polarized in your organization, gathering people on opposite sides of the issue may provoke conflict rather than discussion. Preliminary, one-on-one meetings may be necessary to smooth the way for larger discussions to follow. Of course, if you know (or think you know) that organizational executives have other plans, a meeting to discuss the issue *may* be unproductive. Planning a rebuttal or

response might be a good reason for meeting, but if the issue has already been resolved higher up in the organization, save your time and energy. Cancel the meeting.

WHAT SHOULD I CONSIDER AS I PLAN FOR A MEETING?

Three issues—the objective, the agenda, and the participants—are essential to the success of any meeting, regardless of size, length, or purpose.

THE OBJECTIVE Your foremost consideration should be your purpose in getting together. What is the meeting's objective? Why is this important? If participants aren't clear on your purpose for meeting, they'll make up one of their own. When that happens, it's easy to lose control and watch your participants wander off in a dozen different directions.

How can you build clarity into your purpose for meeting? Christopher Avery, a communications consultant who owns Partnerwerks in Austin, Texas, thinks the following steps may help.

First, consider why you want people to meet. Ask yourself what you will accomplish face-to-face (or via conference call) that you wouldn't accomplish otherwise. Are you meeting to share information, build relationships, make decisions, design something, or solve a problem? After you know the objective of the meeting, think about the outcomes you're hoping for and write down at least two of them: What is the *perfect* outcome for this meeting? What is your *minimum acceptable* outcome?

Next, validate the objective and outcomes to the best of your ability. Can you reasonably expect this group to produce your outcome in the time allotted? What can they achieve? What sort of preparation will they need? Include others whom you trust in this process if it will help you achieve clarity. Finally, start the meeting by clearly stating the objective and outcomes. Make sure all of the participants understand the objective and are willing to work toward it.[16]

THE AGENDA Create a solid agenda. It's nothing more than an outline of things to be discussed at the meeting, along with a time budget for each item. To create an effective agenda, ask yourself three questions: To achieve our objectives, what do we need to do in this meeting? What conversations will be important to the people who attend? What information will we need to begin?

Two important considerations: First, prioritize your agenda items. Make sure you don't spend most of your time on more immediate but less important issues. Leaving the most crucial or urgent items until last runs the risk of running out of time and not considering them at all. Second, assign realistic amounts of time to each agenda item. When you have exhausted the time allocated for discussion of a particular item, the meeting chair must gently nudge the group: "Any other thoughts on this? It's time to move on."

What's the most effective use of your agenda? Conventional wisdom says that agendas should be created and distributed in advance. For formal meetings and meetings requiring preparation, that approach makes considerable sense. For informal meetings or for those called in the midst of change, however, you can easily build an agenda as you begin. Simply poll the participants on topics they think should be covered, establish a set of priorities, and budget the meeting time.[17]

The most important thing you can do with your agenda, once it's written, is to stick to it. In too many meetings, too many participants wander off topic, spending too much time discussing issues irrelevant to the reason they are in the room. Michael Schrage, a consultant on collaborative technologies, acknowledges that most meetings in most companies are decidedly agenda-free. "In the real world," he says, "agendas are about as rare as the white rhino. If they do exist, they're about as useful. Who hasn't been in meetings where someone tries to prove that the agenda isn't appropriate?"[18]

Agendas are worth taking seriously, however. Intel Corporation, the Silicon Valley semiconductor manufacturer, is fanatical about them. They've developed an agenda template that everyone in the company uses. A typical Intel agenda, which circulates several days before a meeting to let participants react to and modify it, lists the meeting's key topics, who will lead which parts of the discussion, how long each segment will take, and what the expected outcomes will be.

Of course, even the best of agendas can't ensure the success of a meeting. The challenge, according to Kimberly Thomas, a former director of small business services for a telecommunication firm in Chicago, is to keep meetings focused without stifling creativity or insulting participants who stray. "When comments come up that aren't related to the issue at hand," she says, "we record them on a flip chart labeled 'The Parking Lot.' We always track the issue and the person responsible for it," she adds. "We use this technique throughout the company."[19]

THE PARTICIPANTS The people on your participant list should be only those people who are directly related to the goals for the meeting. Failing to invite key decision makers or influencers invites frustration and failure. Including people either because they're interesting or simply to fill up chairs in the room is a waste of your time and theirs. So who should you include? Think carefully about inviting people who:

- Will have to carry out or implement what's been decided
- Have valuable information or good ideas
- Can approve the results
- Can act as an advocate on behalf of the group's ideas at a higher level
- Represent divergent views or traditionally excluded viewpoints
- Are indispensable to the success of the decision

Once you know whose input is needed, as well as those whose buy-in will be necessary to move forward, you're ready to secure the facilities and issue invitations.

HOW DO I PREPARE FOR A SUCCESSFUL MEETING?

We mentioned three essential considerations as you plan for a meeting—the objectives, the agenda, and the participants—but there's more. Here are some additional steps you should think about carefully.

ARRANGE FOR A MEETING TIME, DATE, AND PLACE Think carefully about what times and dates would be most convenient for everyone concerned. In the absence of convenience, when can people be there? Although it may not be possible to accommodate literally *everyone's* schedule as you plan for a meeting, be as flexible as possible in trying to arrange a time that the largest number of participants will find workable. Mealtimes are often used as an opportunity to get an otherwise difficult-to-assemble group together. Most people have at least something to eat at breakfast and lunch each day, and if you offer to buy, they may be willing to join you.

Keep in mind that it's generally a bad idea to convene a meeting outside of normal business hours. Sometimes you must, but the editors of the *Harvard Management Communication Letter* say such occasions should be reserved for real emergencies. "People who schedule meetings for evenings and weekends are merely advertising the embarrassing fact that they have no life—and they're expecting others to give up theirs. That kind of person should not be allowed to run anything, much less part of a modern corporation, because they lack the basic humanity to do a good job."[20]

Selecting a location for your meeting can be just as important as drafting your objectives and drawing up a participant list. "If people are meeting for recreational reasons or are being rewarded in some way by the company, think very carefully about where you want to meet," says meeting consultant Marge Boberschmidt. "A world-class hotel or even a nice corporate conference center can often compensate for an otherwise uninspired panel of speakers or weak agenda."[21]

COORDINATE DETAILS AT THE MEETING SITE "The small stuff will always come back to bite you," says Boberschmidt. "Pay attention to the size of the room, the quality and comfort levels of the seating, the conference table, projection equipment, lighting, temperature controls, refreshments, and anything else that will influence a participant's frame of mind."[22] Everything from parking to pencils and pads will affect how people feel about the experience of being in a meeting room, she says, and all of it is worth considering.

Consider, as well, all of those issues related to travel requirements, location, and cost. Make absolutely certain that every participant knows how to find the meeting location. Anticipate commonly asked questions, then provide a telephone number for last-minute questions or unanticipated problems. Having a real human being to talk with can be comforting as a busy manager tries to pull his act together at the last minute before an important business meeting.

If you're responsible for planning the meeting, talk to or meet with those responsible for supporting or carrying out your plans, including audiovisual technicians, caterers, front-desk managers, and banquet and meeting managers. Make certain they know how to find you—no matter what the hour—and be explicit about what you want. Be pleasant to them, though. Keep in mind that they are probably overworked and underpaid, and the success of your meeting is in their hands. A generous tip at the right moment wouldn't hurt, either.

ANNOUNCE THE AGENDA Unless secrecy is essential, your meeting is more likely to succeed with a published agenda that everyone has had an opportunity to examine and think about in advance. State your objectives and explain the outcomes you're hoping for. Be sure to include all relevant detail in the announcement, including themes, topics, speakers, times, dates, places, directions, and the specific responsibilities of the participants. If you e-mail the agenda, ask for a return receipt to make sure everyone received and displayed the document. If you are at all nervous about getting everyone on the same page, follow up with paper copies and, perhaps, a phone call to confirm that the event is a high priority.

ASSIGN ROLES An important part of the planning process involves the assignment of roles. Any well-run meeting will involve at least four important roles.

- Facilitator
- Recorder
- Leader
- Participant

Some meeting planners like to add a fifth role, the timekeeper, so that each agenda item gets its fair share of attention and the discussion stays on track. Different people can play each of these roles, or one person can play them all, but they all have to be accounted for if the meeting is to flow well and produce results. Determining role assignments at the beginning engages everybody in the process and, if done properly, validates each participant's expectations and contributions.[23]

A Weekly Meeting at Wal-Mart Becomes a Competitive Advantage

The idea of it is very simple. Nothing very constructive happens in the office. Everybody else had gone to regional offices—Sears, Kmart, everybody—but we decided to send everybody from Bentonville out to the stores Monday through Thursday and bring them back Thursday night.

On Friday morning, we'd have our merchandise meetings. But on Saturday morning we'd have the sales for the week. And we'd have all the other information from people who'd been out in the field. They're telling us what the competitors are doing, and we get reports from people in the regions who had been traveling through the week. So we decide then what corrective action we want to take. And before noon on Saturday, the regional manager was required to be hooked up by phone with all his district managers, giving them direction as to what we were going to do or change.

By noon on Saturday we had all our corrections in place. Our competitors, for the most part, got their sales results on Monday for the week prior. Now they're ten days behind, and we've already made the corrections.

David Glass
CEO, Wal-Mart Stores, Inc.
1988–2000

Source: Gilman, H. "The Most Underrated CEO Ever," *Fortune*, April 5, 2004, pp. 244–246.

WHAT FORM OR MEETING STYLE WILL WORK BEST?

Each organization has its own style that is based in part on the personalities of both the leadership and participants, as well as the organizational culture. The style you select has to fit the preferences of those who will participate as well as the business needs of the organization. Here are three styles or meeting forms that are well suited to smaller business-oriented meetings.

THE STAFF CONFERENCE This military-style meeting often works well if you clearly outrank everyone else in the room. In this format, each team member reports to you on how his or her project is going, answers your questions, and makes recommendations. The two of you then discuss strategy, usually with little input from other team members.

This style keeps everyone informed of what each team member is doing, forces all team members to be ready with reports and to be accountable in front of their peers, and lets you control the flow of the meeting. Disadvantages include a limited exchange of ideas, an autocratic management style, and the potential for conflict if participants' responsibilities overlap.

THE "CONGRESSIONAL" SYSTEM If you're chairing an association meeting, where officers are elected and all members are of equal standing, your role in the chair will be that of a presiding officer rather than an executive. In this case, a parliamentary format is almost always the right choice. In this style of meeting, people don't just talk when they please: It's hands up, like in school, and when everyone's had their say, they vote.

This system is useful if you have particularly argumentative members or if the issues to be discussed are especially contentious. As chair of a parliamentary meeting, you must be careful not to take sides publicly. If you want something specific to happen, you'll have to ensure that other members bring the matter up and get it passed with very little help from you. You can't let participants think that you're forcing your own agenda through.

This meeting style allows input from whoever wants to give it; it encourages people to think before speaking; and agreed-upon rules of order make it easier to maintain decorum. To prevent interruptions or side-tracking, the chair simply says, "Hold that thought, Jeff. Carolyn has the floor." An obvious disadvantage is that the chair has severely limited power, and it does encourage a certain amount of intrigue and power-brokering in advance of the meeting.

THE "HOUSE OF COMMONS" SYSTEM In the British House of Commons, the prime minister is the head of government, but that person sits on the floor of the House like any other member; the prime minister does not preside. If you're clearly the ranking person present but want to make the meeting as democratic as possible, appoint (or elect) another member to chair the meeting. Remind the presiding officer beforehand that you are subject to the same rules as every other member and to treat you accordingly.

One obvious advantage to this approach is that you will spend less time planning the meeting. It also provides leadership experience to other members and encourages subordinates to speak frankly. If the newly elected (or appointed) meeting leader isn't careful, however, this approach can create the impression that no one is in charge.[24]

HOW DO I KEEP A MEETING ON TRACK?

Meetings don't actually go off-topic, people do. It usually takes at least two people adrift to take the meeting off course. Sometimes, a participant with ulterior motives can try to hijack a meeting and use it for his or her own purposes, but that's a less common threat than these three.

TOPIC DRIFT Almost any meeting can attract comments or observations from participants who will take the discussion in an unintended direction. Sometimes a brief discussion of non-agenda items can lighten the mood in the room and may, in fact, be helpful in getting certain people to speak, but you can tolerate such diversions for just so long. When this drifting off course happens, the meeting chair has a couple of choices: Call the group back on topic, "OK, let's see if we can focus on the problem we need to solve . . . ." Or, the chair can ask if the group would like to consider the new topic separately: "This discussion seems to be outside the scope of the agenda. Can we table it for now or do we need to add it as a separate discussion item?"[25]

BREAKING TIME AGREEMENTS A meeting that doesn't start or end at the times advertised in the agenda or doesn't honor the time budgeted for a given agenda item breaks the meeting time agreement. This issue can become a serious problem that prevents the group from reaching its goals. Dealing with the agenda time budget is generally easier; the chair can either continue the discussion and reschedule other agenda items or limit the discussion and move on to the next item.

What happens if people don't show up on time, leave early, or fail to show up at all? Improving the "crispness" of meetings means getting participants to take them seriously. How often have you heard someone declare at the end of a gathering, "Well, meeting's over. Let's get back to work." The mind-set at Intel Corporation is that meetings *are* work. They're an important part of the job and each participant has to take them seriously. Other companies punish latecomers with a penalty fee or reprimand them in the minutes of the meeting for being late or absent.

SUBGROUP FOCUS Sometimes agenda items will spawn dialogue among members of a small group who have important views and ideas to share with each other. When other participants have no interest in that conversation, however, they become bystanders at their own meeting. How should the meeting chair handle such conversations? The chair has two choices: First, ask subgroup participants to rejoin the main discussion, or if that approach is unsuccessful, ask those involved in the spontaneous breakout session if the topic they're exploring is something that would interest the entire group. Either way, the leader must reassert control or risk losing the direction and commitment of the larger group.[26]

WHAT SHOULD I LISTEN FOR?

Some people have such a deep-seated need to be right that they simply can't stand evidence to the contrary. They are the ones who work overtime to prove others are wrong and disparage anyone who offers a different point of view. These folks make meetings difficult because, for them, meetings become a win/lose occasion, an opportunity to show other people just how wrong they really are. If they can't argue the evidence, they'll debate the procedure. If that doesn't work, they'll attack or threaten others in the room. They'll bluff, bluster, pull rank, and—if all else fails—they'll get up and leave.

How do you get people to listen? Well, that's not an easy question to answer. The key is showing them how cooperating with others is in their own best interest. At a minimum, you can lead by example, trying to improve your own listening behavior in meetings.

- Consider all of your knowledge, ideas, and opinions as functions of your unique perspective. Consider each other person's knowledge, ideas, and opinions as functions of their perspective. Each person is entitled to his or her own point of view, though they are not entitled to their own set of facts.
- Pay attention to your own point of view, especially as it relates to others. Such deliberate reflection will help you discern your own beliefs and values and be more comfortable with them.
- Remember that considering an issue from many different viewpoints is what makes a team smart. Value the opportunity to meet with people who see things differently than you do.
- Practice what collaboration consultant Christopher Avery calls "playback listening." Pay careful attention to what others say so that you can play back their words to them exactly. This powerful practice will help you develop the capacity to acknowledge others' points of view and help them to be heard.
- Hear others with the intention of integrating your point of view with as many others as you can. This goal means you must be willing to hear and validate all other points of view consistently over time, not just when you agree with them.
- Try not to think in terms of *right* and *wrong*, but rather in terms of what works and doesn't work. Think about outcomes for the group and achieving the group's goals, not merely your own goals of contributing to the process.[27]

WHAT SHOULD I LOOK FOR?

Have you ever been to a meeting where, even though the leader said she wanted high participation, she stood at the end of the table and "talked at" the participants, each of whom was seated silently down both sides? It's not all that uncommon. Leaders who don't plan for participation in a meeting won't get it, no matter what they say they want. Standing at the end of a long table sends a strong nonverbal message: Don't talk, just listen. It's a great setup for discouraging participation.

As you saw in Chapter 9, actions not only speak louder than words but often speak in ways that words simply cannot. Think about what that means as you look around your meeting room and where people will sit. In his book *Silent Messages*, Albert Mehrabian tells us the words we say account for just 7 percent of total message communication. Our tone of voice accounts for another 38 percent. More than half (55%) of received message communication in an interpersonal setting comes from body language, including such issues as eye contact, posture, gestures, hand movement, and position in the room.[28]

Deliberately conveying nonverbal messages is not all that difficult. When you are the leader and you need to maintain control of a meeting, run the meeting yourself to signal that you have both authority and control. Stand while others are sitting to signal that you have the floor. And, of course, sit at the head of the table to show that you are in charge.

On the other hand, if you want a more participative or collaborative meeting, ask a team member or facilitator to run the meeting to signal shared control. Sit while others are sitting to signal that your views are equally important. And consider taking a seat along the side of the conference table to demonstrate that you're one of them, rather than in charge of them.[29]

You can even defuse confrontation by changing the furniture in the room. A living room atmosphere with sofas, upholstered chairs, and low-rise coffee tables is likely to encourage people to speak up in a more participative way. Conference tables clearly denote authority and who outranks whom.

To minimize participation and interruptions:

- Set up a long, narrow table for a smaller meeting, placing the leader at the end.
- Choose a seating arrangement that minimizes eye contact between participants (classroom-style seating), where one presenter faces the audience.
- Create an expectation that speech only comes from the front of the room.

To maximize participation and collaboration:

- Choose a round or square table, with the leader seated as a member of the group.
- For longer meetings, set up chairs in a U-shape, instead of using classroom-style row seating, so that participants face each other.
- For large groups, arrange banquet-style seating to accommodate five to eight people, using as many round tables as necessary.[30]

WHAT SHOULD I WRITE DOWN?

In every meeting, someone should be designated to take notes. At the very least, the names and titles of those present, the agenda items discussed, the participant comments, and the ideas generated should find their way onto paper. If the group leader is to follow up on decisions, new ideas, or opportunities discussed during the meeting, a simplified, streamlined method of recording and sharing the minutes of each meeting must be a priority.

Increasingly, technology has begun to play a role in note-taking during meetings. 3M Corporation has developed a digital whiteboard that's as simple to write on and erase as a traditional whiteboard. The difference? The board captures a complete record of the evolution of ideas during a meeting. Every board full of information can be saved as a page on your iPad or PC, ready to edit, print, e-mail, and cut and paste into other applications.

In too many organizations, discussions are held and ideas are written onto flip charts, chalk boards, and white boards, but somehow, nothing happens. Decisions don't get turned into actions. According to Michael Schrage, a consultant on collaborative technologies, the best way to avoid that is to convert from *meeting* to *doing*—where the doing focuses on the creation of shared documents that lead to action. At most computer-enabled meetings, the most powerful role for technology is also the simplest: recording comments, outlining ideas, generating written proposals, projecting them for the entire group to see, and printing them so people leave with real-time minutes.

"You're not just having a meeting," says Schrage, "you're creating a document. I can't emphasize enough the importance of that distinction. It is the fundamental difference between ordinary meetings and computer-augmented collaborations. Comments, questions, criticisms, insights should enhance the quality of the document. That should be the group's mission."[31]

HOW CAN I MAKE MY MEETINGS MORE PRODUCTIVE?

Technology may be one answer. Gordon Mangione, a product-unit manager at Microsoft Exchange Group, uses video technology to improve the experience for his team in Redmond, Washington. "Daily meetings are a valuable tool for keeping projects on track," he says. "But as the number of participants grows—our team includes about 60 key managers—we face a dilemma: How do we ensure real-time interaction, keep everyone informed, and maintain cohesiveness—without tying up the whole team?"

Team meetings are critical at Microsoft. "Teams come together, review daily builds, and identify any developments from the past 24 hours. We haven't found an 'enabling technology' that works better than face-to-face conversation," he observes. "But when meetings turn into standing-room only affairs, the disadvantages are overwhelming."

Mangione's answer is a hybrid meeting, part physical and part virtual. "We still hold the daily meeting in our conference room, but now just 20 people sit in the room. The other 40 'attend' from their offices." Three technicians make the meetings work. Video cameras and microphones in the conference room and on everyone's computer screen allow "virtual" and "physical" participants to see and hear one another. A large-screen TV captures presentations that are broadcast to the desktops, and people pass notes to one another via instant messaging technology.[32] Microsoft isn't alone in embracing new technology to improve meetings. WebEx of San Jose, California, now offers software that plugs into your browser, permitting people in different physical locations to look at the same document and discuss changes as they are being made.

They can talk on the phone, even though the calls are being sent via the Web.[33] Technology, of course, can do more than just bring people in different locations together. It can also increase productivity—that is, help generate more ideas and decisions per minute. One of the main benefits of "meetingware" is that it allows participants to violate the first rule of good behavior in most other circumstances: *Wait your turn to speak.* With Ventana Corporation's *GroupSystems V*, a powerful meeting software program, participants enter their comments and ideas into workstations which, in turn, organize the comments and project them onto a monitor for the whole group to see. Nearly everyone who has studied or participated in computer-enabled meetings agrees that this capacity for simultaneity produces dramatic gains in the number of ideas and the speed with which they are generated.[34]

Other companies have tried different methods for making meetings more productive and more interesting. Kaufman and Broad Home Corporation, one of the top home builders in the United States, recognized that the grind of workday pressures made group meetings especially difficult. Their solution? The "After Five" meeting. Jeff Charney, a senior vice president of marketing and communications, began gathering his team for freewheeling brainstorming sessions after 5:00 P.M., when the workday normally concludes. "Without all the day-to-day pressures," says Charney, "it's much easier to engage our imaginations and let them run wild."

Keep in mind that we explicitly warned you a few pages back against holding meetings after 5:00 P.M. Kaufman and Broad, however, think the culture of their organization is appropriate for such late-afternoon gatherings. During one of their After Five sessions not long ago, the team devised a major promotional campaign that used a full-scale replica of the home of Marge and Homer Simpson—a marketing gambit that got worldwide media attention. "Nine-to-five," says Charney, "we're in a taking-care-of-business mode. By holding the meeting at the day's end, we can switch gears and leave behind phones and pagers. Those things just kill creativity."[35]

Still others have tried an updated version of an old military stand-by: the "7:30 A.M. Stand-Up." Researchers at the University of Missouri wanted to test the notion that one way to make better, certainly shorter, meetings was to take away the chairs. And sure enough, after comparing outcomes for 111 meetings, they found that those conducted while the participants were seated lasted an average of 34 percent longer than meetings in which the participants remained standing. More importantly, they discovered the quality of decision making was the same for both formats. Dr. Mary Waller, a professor who specializes in organizational behavior at the University of Illinois, and who was not involved with the study, added: "I think it's a pretty important finding. If I were consulting with an organization, I would probably suggest that they combine sit-down and standing-up meetings."[36]

The Ritz-Carlton hotel chain—the only hotel company ever to receive a Malcolm Baldrige National Quality Award—uses the same idea with considerable success. Every day at precisely 9:00 A.M., about 80 of the company's top executives gather for a 10-minute stand-up meeting in the hallway outside the office of President and COO Horst Schulze. Just as important, within 24 hours, every hotel from Boston to Bali, along with the rest of the company's 16,000 employees, gets the same concentrated dose of the Ritz credo at their daily shift meetings. "We prepare a monthly calendar of lineup topics," says Leonardo Inghilleri, a senior vice president for human resources, "ranging from the opening of a new hotel in Dubai to meeting-planner programs—and e-mail them weekly to each hotel. For one critical moment each day," he says, "the entire organization is aligned behind the same issue."[37]

CAN BUSINESS MEETINGS EVER IMPROVE?

Bernard DeKoven, founder of the Institute for Better Meetings in Palo Alto, California, remains hopeful about the improvement of meetings. "People don't have good meetings because they don't know what good meetings are like. Good meetings aren't just about work. They're about fun— keeping people charged up. It's more than collaboration. It's 'coliberation'—people freeing each other up to think more creatively."[38]

For Further Reading

Crockett, R. "The 21st Century Meeting: The Latest Gear May Finally Deliver on the Promise of Videoconferencing," *BusinessWeek*, February 26, 2007, pp. 72–79.

Dvorak, P. "Corporate Meetings Go Through a Makeover," *Wall Street Journal*, March 6, 2006, p. B3.

Farivar, C. "How to Run an Effective Meeting," Bnet.com. Retrieved from http://www.bnet.com on April 10, 2007 at 11:28 A.M.

Fricks, H. "The Five W's: Tips for Planning Your Company Meeting," *Indiana Business Magazine*, July 1998, pp. 34–37.

Goldberg, M. "The Meeting I Never Miss," *Fast Company*, February 1997, pp. 28–30.

Kopytoff, V. G. "The Necessary Art of the Impromptu Meeting," *New York Times*, August 24, 1997, p. A11.

Korkki, P. "Another Meeting? Say It Isn't So," *New York Times*, July 20, 2008, p. BU-8.

Lohr, S. "Face Time That Relies on Screens," *New York Times*, July 22, 2008, pp. C1, C8.

McAdams, S. "Engage Employees in Nine Minutes? Yes, It's Possible," Ragan.com. Retrieved from http://www.ragan.com on February 4, 2008, at 1:44 P.M.

McGarvey, R. "Making Meetings Work: The Benchmark Hospitality Formula for Successful Conferences," *Harvard Business Review*, March 2003, pp. 51–58.

Mosvick, R. K. and Nelson, R. B. *We've Got to Start Meeting Like This: A Guide to Successful Meeting Management.* Indianapolis, IN: Jist Works, 1996.

Yeaney, J. "The Top Ten Meeting Personalities," *Fast Company*, November 18, 2009. Retrieved from http://www.fastcompany.com/node/1460895.

Zimmerman, E. "Staying Professional in Virtual Meetings," *New York Times*, September 29, 2010. Retrieved from http://www.nytimes.com/2010/09/26/jobs/26career.html

Endnotes

1. Boberschmidt, M. Personal communication, July 25–26, 2005.
2. Mountford, W. Personal communication, September 19, 1999.
3. Matson, E. "The Seven Sins of Deadly Meetings," *Fast Company*, April 1996, pp. 122–128.
4. Dvorak, P. "Corporate Meetings Go Through a Makeover: Better Productivity Is Goal as Methods Differ to Boost Effectiveness of Employees," *Wall Street Journal*, March 6, 2006, p. B3.
5. Ibid.
6. Armour, S. "Business' Black Hole: Spiraling Number of Meetings Consume Time and Productivity," *USA Today*, December 8, 1997, pp. Al, A2.
7. Bryant, A. "Everything on One Calendar, Please." *New York Times*, Sunday, December 27, 2009, p. D7.
8. Ibid.
9. Ligos, M. "Cutting Meetings Down to Size," *New York Times*, January 11, 2004, p. 10. Copyright © 2004 by The New York Times Company. Reprinted with permission.
10. Sandberg, J. "Another Meeting? Good. Another Chance to Hear Myself Talk," *Wall Street Journal*, March 11, 2008, p. B1.
11. "Making Meetings Work," *The 3M Meeting Guides.* Online at: www.3M.com/meetings/. Accessed August 2, 2005.
12. "Men and Women Fall Back into Kids' Roles at Corporate Meetings," *Wall Street Journal*, December 15, 1998, p. B1. Reprinted by permission of *The Wall Street Journal.* Copyright © 1998 Dow Jones & Company, Inc. All rights reserved worldwide.
13. Hobor, N. Personal communication, January 7, 2000.
14. Boberschmidt. Personal communication.
15. "Anatomy of Great Meetings," *The 3M Meeting Guides.* Online at: www.3M.com/meetings/. Accessed August 2, 2005.
16. Avery, C. M. "Clear Objectives Make Powerful Meetings," *The 3M Meeting Guides.* Online at: www.3M.com/meetings/. Accessed August 2, 2005.
17. "Building Great Agendas," *The 3M Meeting Guides.* Online at: www.3M.com/meetings/. Accessed August 2, 2005.
18. Matson. "The Seven Sins of Deadly Meetings."
19. Ibid.
20. *Harvard Management Communication Letter*, 2, no. 11 (November 1999), pp. 1–3.
21. Boberschmidt. Personal communication.
22. Ibid.
23. "Anatomy of Great Meetings," *The 3M Meeting Guides.*
24. "Chairing a Meeting: To Keep Order, Be True to Form," *New York Times*, September 22, 1999, p. C25. Copyright © 1999 by The New York Times Company. Reprinted with permission.
25. Mann, Merlin. "9 Tips for Running More Productive Meetings," Retrieved from

http://www.43folders.com/2006/02/21/
meetings on July 21, 2008 at 11:41 A.M.

26. "Keeping a Meeting on Track," *The 3M Meeting Guides.* Online at: www.3M.com/meetings/. Accessed August 2, 2005.

27. Avery, C. M. "Listening to Others in Meetings," *The 3M Meeting Guides.* Online at: www.3M.com/meetings/. Accessed August 2, 2005.

28. Mehrabian, A. *Silent Messages: Implicit Communication of Emotions and Attitudes.* Belmont, CA: Wadsworth Publishing, 1981.

29. "Nonverbal Messages in Meetings," *The 3M Meeting Guides.* Online at: www.3M.com/meetings/. Accessed August 2, 2005.

30. Ibid.

31. Matson. "The Seven Sins of Deadly Meetings."

32. Olofson, C. "So Many Meetings, So Little Time," *Fast Company*, January–February 2000, p. 48.

33. Mardesich, J. "Putting the Drag in WebEx's Ad Campaign," *Fortune*, January 10, 2000, p. 174.

34. Matson. "The Seven Sins of Deadly Meetings."

35. Olofson, C. "Open Minds After Closing Time: Meetings I Never Miss," *Fast Company*, June 1999, p. 72.

36. Berger, A. "The All-Rise Method for Faster Meetings," *New York Times*, June 22, 1999, p. D7. See also, Germer, E. "Meeting I Never Miss: Huddle Up!" *Fast Company*, December 2000, p. 86.

37. Olofson, C. "The Ritz Puts on Stand-Up Meetings." *Fast Company*, September 1998, p. 62. See also: Farivar, C. "Shake It Up: Alternative Meeting Strategies," Retrieved from http://www.bnet.com on April 10, 2007, at 11:29 A.M. See also: Farivar, C. "Shake It Up: Alternative Meeting Strategies," BNET, April 9, 2007. Retrieved from: http://www.bnet.com/article/shake-it-up-alternative-meeting-strategies/61204 on January 7, 2011 at 1:00 P.M.

38. Matson. "The Seven Sins of Deadly Meetings."

CASE STUDY 12-1

Spartan Industries, Inc.

Background

Managers are often called on to recognize the achievements and accomplishments of their employees and others within their organizations. Public acknowledgment of exceptional work, career milestones, and special events in people's lives is important, not only to those being recognized, but to others who carefully observe how the organization treats its people.

Those who have worked in and for large, complex organizations will often acknowledge that it's difficult to monitor and properly appreciate individual achievements. Many financial, sales, production, and profit goals are predicated on group activities; individuals often are made to bask in the reflected glory of group membership.

Promotions are one means of rewarding employees who have performed especially well, but promotions are given for just two reasons: A vacancy exists in a position that must be filled, and the company has identified an individual with demonstrated potential to serve in that position. Promotion announcements are generally carefully guarded secrets within a business until the moment they are made public. This is usually the case because a promotion for one employee often means that others were considered but not selected.

Promotion letters must convey several pieces of information: the fact of the promotion, the new position or title, and the effective date. Additionally, such letters often convey congratulations to the recipient of the promotion, along with appropriate expressions of appreciation for past accomplishments.

Spartan Industries, Inc., is a midsized manufacturer of specialty metal products, most of which are used in the automotive industry. They produce lathed and stamped metal products to contract specifications for both domestic and overseas manufacturers of automobiles and automotive equipment. Spartan Industries, Inc., is a nonunion firm.

You may assume that you are an assistant manager in the metal specialties stamping division of the Jackson, Michigan, plant. The company retains a firm in Detroit, Michigan, specializing in manufacturing and labor law to handle all legal matters.

Spartan Industries, Inc., conducts no internal corporate communication activity other than a monthly desktop newsletter produced by the human resources division. You may entertain any reasonable structural or procedural assumptions in this case.

WRITING ASSIGNMENT

This case requires three documents:

- A communication strategy memo (one-and-a-half to two pages in length). The memo should be directed to the company's general manager, with appropriate copies to other officers/agencies, and should respond to the questions posed in the case.

- A letter to the employee selected for promotion.
- A sample letter addressable to those employees who were considered but not selected for promotion. All three documents should be in final form and ready to dispatch.

SPARTAN INDUSTRIES, INC.
2200 Spring Arbor Road
Jackson, Michigan 48138 USA

DATE:	[Today's Date]
TO:	Assistant Manager
	Metal Specialties Stamping Division
FROM:	William A. Bissell
	General Manager, Jackson Plant
SUBJECT:	Employee Promotion Announcements

I am pleased to inform you that we're going to promote several people in the Jackson plant, and one of the employees to be promoted is a member of your division.

Robert S. Johnson currently serves as lead operator in the punch-press section of the stamping division and, effective the first of next month, will assume the responsibilities of punch-press foreman.

Bob has been with us seven years and has performed superbly in his duties. You may recall that he served on our safety committee following a series of accidents last year. He's been indispensable to the company, and I want to make sure we not only retain our best people, but put our very best people in positions of responsibility. It seems to me, based on your recommendations and his work record, that Johnson is the right employee for the foreman's job.

Now, as you know, we interviewed and considered several other current employees for that position. I want them to know how much we appreciate their work, but there is only one opening at the moment, and the job goes to Johnson. I'd like your help with a couple of matters related to this promotion:

- First, draft a letter to Johnson telling him of the promotion. Congratulate him on my behalf and explain how valuable he is to us. Say whatever else you think may be necessary or important.

- Second, give me your thoughts regarding notification of the employees. What should we say to those whom we considered but did not select? And, how should we go about it? Prepare a sample letter for them; I want to know what you think we should say.

- Third, when should we let Johnson know about this—before or after we tell the others? Give me some sense of timing and your best judgment on how we should handle a general announcement to the entire plant.

- Finally, I am interested in garnering some positive publicity for the Jackson plant. I would think a promotion of this type would be of some interest to the local news media. Please give me your specific suggestions regarding this. How should we go about placing this story in the local press? I think we should move quickly on this. There is no real point in delaying the notifications. I would like to see your [thoughts] no later than tomorrow morning. As always, your help is indispensable [to] me. Please accept my thanks for your good work.

This case was prepared from public sources and personal interviews by James S. O'Rourke, Concurrent Professor of Management, as the basis for class discussion rather than to illustrate either effective or ineffective handling of an administrative situation.

CASE STUDY 12-2

American Rubber Products Company (A)

Thursday, March 4, 1993

As the clock in his study struck 10:00 P.M., Jeff Bernel stood up, stretched, and walked over to the window. The lake effect snow blowing in from Lake Michigan had picked up intensity and was beginning to accumulate on the lawn. Wet, slippery snow on the streets and roadways wouldn't be far behind. "It's nice to be home tonight," he thought, "even if I still have another ninety minutes of finance ahead of me."

Jeff Bernel, Chairman, President, and Chief Executive Officer at American Rubber Products Company, headquartered in LaPorte, Indiana, was also an Executive MBA student at the University of Notre Dame, 40 miles to the east. Late nights, team study meetings, telephone conferences, and group projects were a fact of life for a second-semester MBA.

As he settled back into his finance text, the phone rang. It was Mark Dilley, his Executive Vice President and Chief Operating Officer. "Jeff," he said, "there appears to have been an accident at work. Some kind of explosion. We have to get there." A brief pause followed and Bernel responded: "See you there." Bernel bounded down the steps, grabbed a coat and left a note for his wife, Liz. As he backed out of the driveway, he knew in an instant the usual two-mile drive would take more than a few minutes.

The Company Jeff Bernel Leads

American Rubber Products Company is a midsize manufacturing firm with annual revenues in excess of $35 million. The firm employs 600 people at four locations in Indiana, Michigan, Kentucky, and New York. The company was founded in 1933 and is a supplier of seals and gaskets to the North American Original Equipment Manufacturers and 1st tier automotive markets.

The Scene at the LaPorte Plant

When he arrived at the LaPorte, Indiana, headquarters of American Rubber Products, he was certainly unprepared for what he saw: fire trucks, ambulances, rescue vehicles, police cars, chaos, and considerable confusion. The main gate was blocked with a pumper unit, so he pulled around to the side entrance on Tipton Street. As he did, a familiar face greeted him.

Sheriff's deputy Greg Bell, a friend from church, knocked on the car window. "You've had a boiler explosion, Mr. Bernel. You have two fatalities." The news was stunning. In 20 years of business experience and 6 years of submarine duty in the Navy, Jeff had never experienced anything like this.

He pulled his car into the parking lot, grabbed a flashlight from the glove box and went through the center door to Press Room C. There, he ran into Ida Allen, Press Room supervisor. "Give me an update," he said. Mrs. Allen, a loyal employee of more than [a] dozen years, gave Bernel an accounting of all those at work. "We were just at the end of the second shift, Jeff. We had about forty people in the building."

"It could have been a lot worse," he thought to himself. "If this had been the first shift, we'd have had 60 or 70 people in here, plus another 40 in an adjoining area."

Mrs. Allen, obviously shaken and upset, continued with her update for Bernel. She detailed where each employee had been, where the injured were, and how she had rung 9-1-1 and then cared for the most seriously injured until help arrived. Though visibly shocked, she used full names for the five injured and described in detail what had happened. Among those hurt, two were critical, two were in serious condition, the other was listed by paramedics as "fair."

The two deceased employees had been in the press room adjacent to the boiler room when the accident occurred. "They were press operators," Bernel later recalled, "who took raw pre-formed rubber stock and placed it in a mold attached to a steam press. The press would close hydraulically for whatever length of time it would take to shape and cure the rubber into auto gaskets."

The presses at American Rubber Products were timed to open after each cure cycle. Press operators would remove cured gaskets and put them on a conveyor to a post-treatment trim area. Operators would then clean the mold with a brush and an air-gun. That process would be repeated three-to-five times each hour. One person is charged with responsibility for six to ten presses, producing from 100 to 300 gaskets per hour, depending on the size and weight of the product.

"These are semi-skilled laborers," Bernel said later. "They receive on-the-job training from senior mold/press operators responsible for new employees. We also supply problem-solving training and statistical process control training for each." On the evening of Thursday, March 4, 1993, Press Room C was staffed by about a half-dozen employees. It was 10:30 P.M. and now two of them were dead: a 32-year-old mother of two and an 18-year-old woman hired earlier in the week as a temporary employee.

The Boiler Room Equipment

The boiler room adjacent to Press Room C is essentially a barrel on its side, measuring 10-to-12 feet in diameter and 30 feet long. According to industry experts, it's known as a "marine boiler," which uses natural gas fed through tubing at one end. An electrically controlled gas burner fires the combustion gasses down a 20-inch pipe called a "Morrison Tube."

As they move horizontally through the boiler, the combustion gasses are blown down the Morrison Tube, then diverted 180 degrees through hundreds of small tubes, each one-and-a-half inches in diameter, directing the gasses back toward the burner. These tubes are surrounded by cool, fresh water. Gasses in the stainless steel tubes heat more than 20,000 pounds of that water to create steam. Gasses are then diverted 180 degrees again at the burner end and passed through another set of tubes before being vented out an exhaust stack more than 100 feet high.

The boiler, manufactured by the York Shipley Company of St. Louis, Missouri, features two large compartments: one containing low pressure, the other containing high pressure. In the low-pressure compartment, atmospheric pressure aided by blower fans totals approximately 10 pounds per square inch (ppsi). The high-pressure compartment is where water is heated to 125 ppsi. The higher the water pressure, the hotter the steam.

The Boiler's History

A marine boiler, properly maintained is considered to have a useful lifetime of approximately 30 years in continuous service. Because of the risk posed to human life in their operation, marine boilers are licensed by Occupational Safety and Health Administration authorities in all 50 states. And, because of the number of moving parts, high steam pressure, and extremely high temperatures involved a boiler's operation, state-licensed inspections are mandated at regular intervals. The frequency of those inspections varies according to state regulation, boiler type, and variety of operational uses.

The boiler at American Rubber Products Company was slightly more than 15 years old on the day of the accident. Five years prior to the accident, Power Plant Services of Fort Wayne, Indiana, had installed a new, more efficient gas burner. Annual and semiannual safety inspections were performed each summer by Hartford Steam Boiler Insurance Company under a license issued by the State of Indiana. During those inspections, the boiler was completely disassembled, both ends were opened and all internal parts were examined. A state-specified series of inspection parameters was then tested for by Power Plant Services, who also performed any repairs deemed necessary.

As far as Jeff Bernel knew, the boiler was in good condition, conformed to the operational specifications of the State of Indiana, and—until a few minutes ago—posed no threat or hazard to his employees. Although he was an engineer who understood the inner-workings of the boiler, Bernel left the inspection and certification of the equipment in his plant to the state-certified experts from Power Plant Services and Hartford Steam Boiler Insurance.

Every Executive's Nightmare

"As I exited the building by the South entrance," Bernel recalled, "people were everywhere." LaPorte Hospital, by sheer coincidence, had just completed a disaster preparedness exercise and the trauma team was already on site. "An emergency technician confirmed that ambulance response was just nine minutes to the scene. Within 20 minutes, all injured were in the hospital, receiving treatment." After his brief tour of the darkened, powerless building, he gathered one, final situation report from employees, fire and police officials. Competent professionals were there doing their jobs, but could Bernel do his?

As he walked back to his car, Bernel noticed that reporters and cameras crews from South Bend and Chicago were already on scene. The parking lot was filling up with gawkers and media-types and he had to do something, fast. As he slipped into the driver's seat and slammed the door, one thought came to him: "I've got to get help."

At that point, he got out his cell phone and called David Haist, lead attorney with Barnes & Thornburg. As the phone rang at Haist's home, it was 11:30 P.M.

WRITING ASSIGNMENT

Please respond in writing to the issues presented in this case by preparing two documents: a communication strategy memo and a professional business letter.

Haist was quick with a reply: "I can't help you, Jeff, but Doug Dieterly can. He's our best product liability lawyer and you should talk with him tonight." After an exchange of telephone numbers, Bernel dialed Dieterly and explained as much as he could. By this point, the car was growing cold.

"Do you think it's your fault?" Dieterly asked.

"No," Bernel replied, "I really don't. We've done everything we were supposed to do. We've followed the State safety guidelines scrupulously. That boiler is torn down and inspected semiannually and certified as safe by State of Indiana boiler inspectors."

"If you're not at fault," Dieterly counseled, "appoint someone to speak, open the doors and tell them everything you know." After a pause, he added: "If you are at fault, or think you may be, lock the doors, gather all management employees and direct them not to speak to anyone." Dieterly's final words were clear: "Don't practice conjecture."

Bernel rubbed his glove against the car window to clear the condensation, and realized that meeting the media was just the first of many problems he would face. The tools in his LaPorte plant were the property of his customers—the Big Three domestic automakers and a handful of important overseas customers. If he couldn't produce steam to cure rubber in ten days, his customers would simply reclaim the molds and American Rubber Products would be out of business.

More than talking to the press, Bernel was faced with two basic issues, one dealing with people and the other dealing with his business. The people issue was more pressing, more urgent. "How do I keep this group together?" he thought. "How do I care for the injured and the families of the deceased? And how in the world do I convince them it's safe to return to work?"

The other issue was his business. If he couldn't restore manufacturing capacity soon, he wouldn't have a business. It was too late to draft a crisis response plan now. As he glanced at his watch, he could see that it was 12:05 A.M. Tomorrow had already come.

In preparing these documents, you may assume one of two roles: you may identify yourself as an American Rubber Products manager who has been asked to provide advice to Mr. Jeffrey Bernel regarding the issues he and the company are facing. Or, you may identify yourself as an external management consultant who has been asked by the company to provide advice to Mr. Bernel.

Either way, you must prepare a strategy memo addressed to Jeff Bernel, Chairman and Chief Executive Officer of the company, that summarizes the details of the case, rank orders critical issues, discusses their implications (what they mean and why they matter), offers specific recommendations for action (assigning ownership and suspense dates for each), and shows how to communicate the solution to all who are affected by the recommendations.

You must also prepare a professional business letter for Mr. Bernel's signature. That document may be addressed to ARPC suppliers or to the employees of American Rubber Products Company. If you have questions about either of these documents, please consult your instructor.

This case was prepared from personal interviews and public sources by James S. O'Rourke, Concurrent Professor of Management, as the basis for class discussion rather than to illustrate either effective or ineffective handling of an administrative situation.

Chapter *13*

Dealing with the News Media

Some people are simply better than others at saying what they mean and sounding sincere in the process. When a federal grand jury accused Chrysler Corporation of odometer tampering some years ago, it was clear to Chairman Lee Iacocca that there was only one way to stem public concern: confront it head on and nip it in the bud. So he called a news conference, apologized for "breaking the law of common sense," and pledged to fix the mistakes.

Iacocca told reporters that Chrysler had done nothing illegal. But in his familiar, blunt style, he also pointed a finger at his own company for "dumb" and "stupid" practices. "Did we screw up? You bet we did," he admitted. He outlined how Chrysler would make it right with their customers, and he promised it wouldn't happen again.

Apparently it worked. Four days after the charges were announced, 55 percent of adult Americans polled in a public opinion survey thought Chrysler faced a serious problem. In a follow-up survey four days after the press conference, 67 percent of those contacted felt Chrysler had adequately dealt with the issue. Chrysler officials added that there had been no ill effect on vehicle sales or stock prices.[1]

On the other side of the coin, during the massive oil spill in the Gulf of Mexico, BP chief executive Tony Hayward famously said, "I think the environmental impact of this disaster is likely to be very, very modest." That same day, when asked about whether he was able to sleep at night in light of the oil spill's effects, he replied, "Of course I can." Just two weeks later, in a televised interview in Louisiana, he addressed the people of the Gulf region, saying, "We're sorry for the massive disruption it's caused to their lives. There's no one who wants this thing over more than I do. I'd like my life back." Those words, played over and over again on evening newscasts came to haunt Mr. Hayward until he was relieved of his duties weeks later by BP's chairman.[2]

INTRODUCTION

Maintaining a positive, honest, accessible relationship with the news media who report on your industry and your company will never be easy, but it will be essential. Few managers and virtually no executives will make it through a career successfully without responding to the media—in good times and in bad.

More than 30 years ago, management consultant and former president of CBS News, Chester Burger said:

A corporate president is not chosen for his outstanding ability to articulate corporate problems. He is selected by his board of directors because of his management know-how, or his financial expertise, or his legal proficiency, or whatever particular combination of these talents may be required by the immediate problems facing the company. In utilizing his own skills, he is usually very good indeed.

But the skills of management are not the same as those required to deal with the news media. Reporters, whether they are employed by television (where most people still get most of their news these days), newspapers, magazines, radio, or an Internet blog, are trained in their ability to talk with someone and unearth a newsworthy story, one that will stimulate their viewers or readers. This ability is why they were selected; it is their surpassing talent; and it is precisely what unnerves corporate managers who choose to face their questions.[3] Most media relations and corporate communication experts will acknowledge that reporters are not only well-trained in their profession, but most are also quite good at the process of asking good questions in pursuit of a newsworthy story. What few outsiders understand, however, is that managers and executives have faced others—many of them better informed and better prepared to ask tough questions—whom they respect but do not fear.

"There's little in this world tougher than a bond road show," says Jordan Industries President and COO Tom Quinn. "The people in that audience have money to invest and plenty of tough questions about what you're planning to do with it." In many respects, investors in the debt market are sharper than equities investors. "People who manage mutual funds, retirement plans, or insurance companies know dozens of tough questions to ask and they take their measure of you as you sit there on a stool or stand in front of them with nothing but your wits and charm to defend yourself."[4]

The fact is that managers get paid to answer difficult questions every day from people who know the facts, understand the business, and are familiar with the products and services involved. Everyone from worried or irate shareholders to curious government regulators have posed questions that managers must answer—many of them on the spot, without reference to files, databases, or conversations with others in the organization.

The relationship between the media and business is essentially adversarial, which is simply part of doing business in a democratic society. NBC reporter and later ABC News commentator David Brinkley once said, "When a reporter asks questions, he is not working for the person being questioned, whether businessman, politician, or bureaucrat, but he is working for the readers and listeners."[5] He also once said, "News is what you don't want to tell me. Everything else is public relations."

Can you do it? Are you equal to the challenge of facing a reporter and straightforwardly answering questions about your business? Sure you are. It won't be easy, but you certainly have the talent and the motivation to do the job. What you need is the preparation.

This chapter looks at why it will be in your best interest to cooperate with reporters and editors who wish to interview you and suggests a number of ways to prepare yourself. Specifically, we examine six issues that confront any manager who faces the prospect of a press interview, whether for good news or bad.

- Why interviews are important
- Should I or shouldn't I?
- A look at the media

- Getting ready
- Making it happen
- Follow-up

WHY INTERVIEWS ARE IMPORTANT

THEY ARE A CHANCE TO REACH A LARGE AUDIENCE An interview with a reporter is an unparalleled opportunity to reach a large audience. You simply cannot attend enough Kiwanis Club breakfasts or Rotary Club luncheons to tell your story directly. Those events, by the way, are wonderful opportunities, and you should take advantage of every invitation you receive to speak before such groups. They represent a chance to network, to meet community leaders, and to put your message forward in a direct and unfiltered fashion. The disadvantage is that they offer a limited audience for your message.

If you must reach thousands or millions of people with your message in a short period of time, you have very few choices. One choice is to take out newspaper and magazine advertisements (television advertisements are usually too expensive and inappropriate for most corporate information campaigns). People usually look at such ad campaigns as one-sided and biased and pay little attention to the content of the message.

If you need to speak to a metropolitan, statewide, or national audience, the mass media are— or should be—your first choice. Arranging for dinner or luncheon speeches will be helpful, as will the information you plan to post on your company's Web site or share with selected bloggers. But there is simply no substitute for speaking directly to a newspaper or television reporter. Their reach is global; their speed is near-instantaneous; and their reputation for objectivity is your guarantee that "informed attenders" in the public (those who read newspapers and watch national television newscasts) will see, hear, or read your message. It may not be pleasant, but you have few other choices.

THEY REPRESENT AN OPPORTUNITY TO TELL YOUR STORY For better or worse, most people in your target audience really don't know much about you. If your company is typical, many people will recognize the company's name; some will know of your products and services; a few will understand issues related to ownership, organization, or the industry in which you compete; and no one will seem to understand much about the issues that worry you the most. Like it or not, most people are basically ignorant about your people, your mission, and your goals as an organization.

Is this all bad? Not necessarily. Anonymity can have its rewards. The owner of a small bookshop near campus once remarked, "Whenever some stink about book publishing, censorship, or objectionable publications hits the news, reporters in this town always go over to interview the manager at Barnes & Noble. Good," she said. "I don't want to answer those kinds of questions." Being anonymous, however, often means you must fight to be noticed when it's important for the public to know who you are.

THEY ARE AN OPPORTUNITY TO INFORM Talking to a reporter is a chance for you, as a manager, to establish yourself as an expert on certain subjects, or at least as a specialist who knows something about the market, the product category, or the industry. Being friendly with those who are in search of information to support a newsworthy story can buy some goodwill for you when times are more difficult and the story is about you rather than someone else.

If you make it a regular practice to offer information to the news media about your company and your industry, chances are much greater that the readers and viewers of those news outlets will associate your name, your company's name, and your product or service line with such important attributes as quality, currency, value, and desirability. You can't afford to be shy when the media come looking for a comment on a story related to your business, even if it doesn't involve you directly.

THEY OFFER AN OPPORTUNITY TO ADDRESS PUBLIC CONCERNS The public at large are worried about any number of things, including the environment, the economy, job opportunity, working conditions, security, and product safety. Where does your company fit into those concerns? Do you know what concerns are most important to people across the nation or in your own community? If not, you should because those issues are most likely to become the motivating factors that frame a reporter's questions.

You should be ready with little or no notice to address questions that concern how your company treats the environment. Do you produce hazardous waste or non-biodegradable by-products? How do you dispose of that waste? How does your company treat its workers? What are the wages, conditions of employment, or benefits for those who make your products or deliver your services? If a company across town or somewhere else in the country makes an unsafe product and you happen to compete in the same industry, are you ready to answer detailed, direct questions in an honest and believable manner?

When people watch television news interviews—particularly in a crisis or during a breaking news story—they tend to ask one question of themselves as they observe a businessperson responding to a reporter: "Is anyone smart in charge here?" If so, they go on about their own business and don't think much about yours. They're confident in the knowledge that some smart young man or woman is taking care of that messy business they saw on television. If the answer is "no," then the viewers tend to think less of the company involved, and may decide that company shouldn't be permitted to do business in their community any longer.

Keep in mind that just because you may have a license to do business—to assemble things, to transform raw materials into finished goods, or to store or process various materials—doesn't mean you'll be in business forever. Your real license to continue what you're doing depends directly on the goodwill and permission of the people who live in your community, who work in your facilities, and who buy your products and services. If they lose confidence in you, you're done. It's up to you to convince them that someone smart is in charge. AT&T vice president Arthur W. Page may have said it best when he wrote: "All business in a democratic country begins with public permission and exists by public approval. Real success," he said, "both for big business and the public, lies in large enterprise conducting itself in the public interest and in such a way that the public will give it sufficient freedom to serve effectively."[6]

THEY GIVE YOU AN OPPORTUNITY TO SET THE RECORD STRAIGHT Although many people know little (and some want to know even less) about your company and its business practices, much of what some people know just isn't true. American humorist Will Rogers once said, "It ain't what he don't know that bothers me. It's what he knows for sure that just ain't so that I'm worried about."

You'd be surprised, indeed, if you were to speak directly with many people about your business or your industry. Misconceptions, stereotypes, distortions, and often some disinformation will form the bulk of what they "know for sure." A news media interview is an opportunity to set the facts straight, to offer your own perspective, to refute allegations or stories that are simply untrue.

THEY OFFER AN OPPORTUNITY TO APOLOGIZE Investors have lost trillions in recent business scandals; popular anger with corporate executives is at its highest level since the Great Depression; and foreign allies are questioning the vitality of American capitalism. So how do the executives responsible for these improprieties, illegalities, and bad judgment respond? Jeffrey K. Skilling says he is "immensely proud" of what he accomplished at Enron. Marc Shapiro, vice-chairman of J. P. Morgan Chase, insists his bank's transactions with the Houston energy company were "entirely appropriate." Duke Energy's round-trip power trades were "well within the market rules," says CEO James Donnell, while Martha Stewart called insider-trading allegations "ridiculous."

The first reaction of many executives is to hunker down; deny everything; hire tough, expensive lawyers; and try to wait out the mess, hoping the headlines, animosity, and bad feelings will eventually pass. A more productive approach to such problems might involve a sincere, unrestrained, and heartfelt apology. New academic research indicates that goodwill generated by such *mea culpa* could more than make up for the legal costs involved. State legislatures, meanwhile, are quietly passing laws that encourage contrition by making apologies inadmissible as evidence against those making them.[7]

Professor Lamar Reinsch of Georgetown University's McDonough School of Management has studied the effects of public apologies and their effect on liability. After reviewing hundreds of recent cases, he concludes:

> The risk of litigation is one that corporations balance against public backlash and loss of consumer base. In the end, judges and juries have demonstrated an understanding that expression of remorse and apology are not necessarily admissions of responsibility or liability, as evidenced by protections enacted by federal and state bodies. When a plaintiff goes to court armed with naught but an apology, courts are likely to find that the apology is useless in fulfilling the legal elements necessary to impose liability.
>
> Liability is not admitted when a corporation publicly pronounces regret that its customers have been injured, and that the corporation is willing to use its power to cure problems faced by its customers. . .Well-timed apologies and promises to investigate the root of the injury can often diffuse a potential crisis, or at least lessen its intensity.
>
> In sum, corporations must carefully weigh the factors of their particular situation when contemplating a public apology and decide whether the risk of potential liability is worth the possible alleviation of public censure and legally mitigating effects of public contrition on rulings of judge and jury. In other words, executives are advised to seek advice both from public relations professionals and from attorneys who are familiar with the details of the specific circumstances.[8]

According to business journalist Mike France, companies may be overestimating the costs of apologies and underestimating their benefits. "For one thing," he writes, "juries weigh the fact that a company has faced up to its problems when assessing punitive damages. More important, apologies can defuse victims' anger." Some evidence suggests that people may be just as interested in apologies as they are in money. In one recent study of British medical malpractice patients, 37 percent said they wouldn't have brought suit if the doctor had provided them with an explanation and an apology.[9]

The details differ, but the laws generally prevent expressions of sympathy from being used as evidence of fault after an accident. They do not, however, apply to expressions of guilt. So the statement "I'm sorry your son died in the crash" would not be admissible as evidence of guilt, whereas "I'm sorry your son died because of the faulty brakes in the automobile we made," probably would be.

Apologies can have surprising power when they are delivered well. Not long ago, for instance, Joette Schmidt, a vice president for customer service at America West Airlines Inc., appeared on NBC television's *Today* show to ask the forgiveness of Sheryl Cole, a passenger who had been thrown off a flight for joking about the company's recent drunken-pilot episode. Ignoring interviewer Matt Lauer's invitation to defend the airlines' conduct, Schmidt declared: "I'm here primarily to apologize to Ms. Cole. We overreacted." The victim, who had spent the first minute of the segment tearing into America West, was caught off guard. "I appreciate the apology," Cole responded. "I'm sympathetic to America West right now. I know they're going through a tough time."[10]

THEY ARE AN OPPORTUNITY TO REINFORCE CREDIBILITY When the public stops believing in you, you're finished. An important part of your task as a manager is to reinforce public belief in what you do, what you make or provide, and in who you are as an organization. How do you do that? One easy way for a manager to find credibility for his or her statements to the press is to cite the speeches, public pronouncements, or public statements of the company's executive team. Where will you find such statements? In your company's advertising brochures, on your corporate Web site, in the annual report, or in the company's 10-K and 10-Q filings with the Securities and Exchange Commission. You needn't spend a great deal of time inventing clever things to say about your organization; people have already done that for you, including public relations and advertising firms, the corporate communication staff, and the company's senior team. Read those documents; look for ideas, phrases, and concepts that you can easily include in a conversation with a reporter. Remember, the more often you say it, the more likely it is a reporter will eventually use it in a story.

SHOULD YOU OR SHOULDN'T YOU?

In deciding whether to respond to a reporter's request for an interview or whether to call a press conference to attract attention to your message, here are a few basic considerations.

FOLLOW THE FEW BLANKET RULES THAT APPLY One of the most important rules is "Never talk to strangers." If your mother passed along that bit of wisdom to you as a child, consider yourself well-raised. Your mother was wise, indeed. Dealing with strangers is a high-risk proposition, especially in the news media.

If you are approached by a reporter and asked to respond to a series of questions about your company, your products or services, or the industry, do what you can to gather some basic information first: Who is the reporter? Which organization does he or she work for? What sort of deadline is the reporter working against? Then ask for some time to gather information, consult with others, and formulate a decision about participating.

Public relations expert Vic Gold once said, "There are no blanket rules in this business, except one: If Mike Wallace calls, hang up."[11] Did the venerable CBS journalist do something to anger or upset Mr. Gold? Probably not, but the advice is useful, anyway. His point is simple: *60 Minutes*, the program for which Mr. Wallace was a reporter for so many years, is not a news program. It's owned and operated by the News Division of the CBS Television Network. The program employs journalists and former reporters—Anderson Cooper, Lara Logan, Scott Pelley, Steve Kroft, and others—to report the stories you see on air. Executive producer Jeff Fager and his staff are long-experienced in the business of television news. So why isn't *60 Minutes* a news program? What makes it different?

60 Minutes is merely the longest-running and most successful of a television genre that includes such programs as NBC's *Dateline*, ABC's *20/20*, *PrimeTime Live*, and a host of equally profitable but less reputable programs such as *Hard Copy, Inside Edition, American Journal, E!, Access Hollywood*, and many others. These programs are clearly not news programs. They are entertainment programs. Often, they are dressed up to look like news: Well-known news reporters are hired to speak into the camera; news editing techniques are employed to create movement and tension in their stories; and studio sets as well as field reporting techniques create the impression of a news program. Nothing could be further from the truth.

The objective standards and search for the truth that characterize legitimate news operations are frequently strangers to these programs and those who produce them. Stories on such programs are usually chosen more for their emotional value or audience appeal than their news value. Producers have been known to accept an assignment or begin reporting on a story because of preconceived views or an ideologically driven perspective.

The truth about such programs as *60 Minutes* and others is that they are wonderfully entertaining. But as you smile or nod when Scott Pelley disassembles some poor soul on camera, think to yourself: "That could be me." Few people have the skills or abilities to present themselves and their argument in a fashion that a producer could not edit to suit his or her own taste. Even experienced politicians, long skilled in the arts of dealing with the press, have been eaten alive by the interviewers and producers of these "magazine format" shows. Former Alaska Governor Sarah Palin fumbled for an answer when Katie Couric asked her what newspapers and magazines she regularly reads.

Some businesspeople have agreed to *60 Minutes* interviews and have lived to tell of it. Others have emerged successfully: They've told their stories to a large audience; they were treated fairly; the facts were presented in an evenhanded and professional manner. Joseph and William Coors of Coors Brewing Company made the deliberate decision to be interviewed by CBS's *60 Minutes* in the midst of an ongoing labor dispute and emerged looking like conscientious, caring, responsible businesspeople. Keep in mind, they are an exception to the rule.

The same general considerations we've discussed here also apply to print publications that pass themselves off as newspapers. They include *The National Enquirer, The Globe, Midnight, Weekly World News*, and other supermarket tabloids. Even their most loyal readers admit that they don't buy those publications for serious news; they see them for what they are: entertainment. Some focus on celebrities, others on the bizarre, and still others on the near-believable. It would be difficult, indeed, to see how you and your company could benefit from being quoted or featured in an edition of one of these papers.

ASK YOUR PUBLIC AFFAIRS OR CORPORATE COMMUNICATION OFFICE FOR HELP Unless you work in a small company, chances are good that the firm employs people with public relations skills. Your organization, no doubt, will have people who are experienced professionals, able to advise you in making your decision to participate in an interview.

"Why doesn't the public affairs person do the interview?" you ask. The reason is simple enough: No self-respecting reporter wants to talk to a public affairs specialist. They know full well that the public affairs office or corporate communication media specialists have an agenda to discuss. Reporters understand that experienced public affairs and public relations people will say only what they want a reporter to hear and report.

Should that make you cautious? It should, primarily because a reporter will feel more comfortable with you, hoping for more candid and revealing statements. In a reporter's eyes, you will have more credibility because you're closer to the action in the organization; you are on the front lines where business decisions are made and the essence of the business happens each day. Your public affairs or corporate communication office can still be of great help to you, though, as you search for information, bring yourself up-to-date on the story, and gather details that will be useful in determining whether to participate in the interview. Ask them for assistance—they won't say "no."

GET SOME BACKGROUND BEFORE COMMITTING Among the many things you'll want to know before agreeing to a press interview is whether this story is primarily about you and your business or whether it's simply an industry trend story that you're being asked to comment on.

It will be especially useful for you to know the background of the story before saying yes to an interview. Simply ask the reporter, "What's the backdrop here? How did this story develop?" You should also consider asking who else is participating in this interview. What sources has the reporter consulted? If you know a competitor is talking to him or her, your awareness may influence your decision to participate. If you know that a well-recognized industry critic or media gadfly is being quoted, that knowledge may influence your decision, as well.

PAY ATTENTION TO GUT FEELINGS If the story is sufficiently negative, or if you think the news organization you are dealing with won't give you an opportunity to tell your story accurately, fairly, and completely, you may well decide not to participate. If a reporter has deceived you about his or her identity, affiliation, or intentions, you might not want to cooperate. If the news organization that this reporter works for has an unsavory reputation, that may influence your feelings.

You have to trust your instincts. They have taken you a long way in life and have served you well. They have helped you get through college, find a job, and get into business school. They usually won't fail you if you simply let them work on your behalf. Don't agree to participate if:

- You don't trust the reporter.
- You aren't clear on the direction or intent of the story.
- A reporter tries to high-pressure or blackmail you into cooperation.
- A reporter says, "I'm on deadline and need an answer now."
- The nature of the story is so strongly negative that you do not want your name or your company's name associated with the report.

Remember, if you don't participate, you won't have an opportunity to tell your side of the story, from your perspective, or to set the record straight on issues that are most important to your firm. On the other hand, if you honestly think you won't get a fair shake from the reporter or the news organization, you're perfectly within your rights as a citizen and an employee to back off and think about it. The advantage is that your remarks won't be misquoted or taken out of context, and you won't be a part of a story you consider unseemly. The disadvantage may be that others set the tone and direction of the story, and you may be running to catch up.

A LOOK AT THE NEWS MEDIA

In order to know what you're getting into, we should examine a few basics about the news media.

IT'S A BUSINESS First and foremost, news is a business; it is not a philanthropic enterprise. Newspapers, magazines, television stations and networks, and radio broadcasters make money not by selling news but by selling airtime and space to commercial advertisers. It's a straightforward exchange of audience for money. The greater the audience for commercial advertisements, the more the publisher or broadcaster can charge for the time or space.

One interesting aspect of this arrangement is that many businesspeople sign contracts with broadcasters without knowing exactly how much the ads they run will cost them. They know what the rate per thousand households will be, but they won't know until the rating estimates have come in just how much they will pay for the privilege of airing their commercial announcement. Again, the greater the audience, the larger the invoice.

If broadcasters want greater revenues for the airtime they sell, the easiest way to obtain it is to increase the size of the audience that watches their programming. In the case of news broadcasts, that may mean anything from a new hairdo for the news anchor to new graphics or a dramatic new set design. It may also mean more controversial news stories—stories designed to pique the interest of the audience and draw in more viewers. Newspapers and news Web sites do it with dramatic headlines ("Mom Locks Tot in Trunk at JFK"), more stories about celebrities ("Lindsay Lohan Checks into Rehab . . . Again!"), sports figures (O. J. Simpson, Barry Bonds, Marv Albert), and other people (Britney Spears, Paris Hilton) who—in the greater scheme of things—really don't matter.

Journalist and newspaper editor Pete Hamill recently wrote:

> True accomplishment is marginal to the recognition factor. There is seldom any attention paid to scientists, poets, educators, or archaeologists. Citizens who work, love their spouses and children, pay taxes, give to charities, and break no laws are never in a newspaper unless they die in some grisly murder. Even solid politicians, those who do the work of the people without ambitions for immense power, and do so without scandal, are ignored. The focus of most media attention, almost to the exclusion of all other subjects, is those big names.[12]

Does this mean you can't get into the news unless you're famous? No, although it certainly helps to be famous if you want attention. Chrysler Corporation's Jim Tolley said: "[Lee] Iacocca's prominence and personality put us in an unusual and enviable situation. Other professionals spend their careers trying to get publicity for their company or client; at Chrysler, we get paid to cope with it."[13]

News organizations are also eager to boost ratings by searching for bad guys, wrongdoers, and companies whose products bring people to grief. Of course, that's good. You would expect that the media would perform a public watchdog function, looking out for our best interests. But what if they get the story wrong? What if someone feeds a reporter some details about your company or your products that are simply not true? To keep from becoming a ratings booster for a news program or a local paper out to do good for the community and its readers, you should consider taking the initiative, demonstrating both good citizenship and good sense by helping a reporter see your company's perspective.

MARKETS AND SOPHISTICATION Most market areas are served by broadcasters and newspaper publishers who are loathe to mistreat businesspeople, and for good reason. Those same businesspeople are the lifeblood of their advertising program. If word gets around that the local paper has misquoted, misrepresented, or mishandled a business or its management, the publisher will hear about it. And, in turn, so will the editors and reporters.

News gathering and advertising are supposed to be separate but rarely ever are, which doesn't mean that reporters will spike a legitimate investigation or important news story just because an advertiser is involved. Nor does it mean that a businessperson can buy his or her way off the front page with a healthy advertising account. It does mean that in a small to medium-sized market of 50,000–750,000 people, you can generally expect courteous, fair, and professional treatment most of the time. In large markets of 1 million or more people, life is a bit different. For one thing, it's tougher to get your story into the news when you want exposure for your company or your products. Announcing good news is difficult in a large market because it's usually a much bigger deal to those who generate it than it is to those who report it. And in a large market there's simply a lot more news, good and bad.

Reporters in large markets are also much less sensitive to the relationship between advertising and profits. When they smell a good story, they'll go after it with little regard for the names involved. Big cities also produce a certain amount of "hit-and-run" journalism in which reporters will do just about anything to get the details or the pictures of a story, including climbing the fence to your property, bribing the gate guards, or hassling your employees until they've found one who's disgruntled enough to talk. Once the story is done, they don't need you any more, and you have little leverage with them. If you're located in a metropolitan area and become involved in an important breaking news event, you should seek professional help from your corporate communication office or a professional public relations firm at once. Even a few hours' delay can be disastrous.

Another aspect of market size and sophistication is that media outlets in smaller markets can rarely afford to develop reporters who are genuine specialists. In New York, financial and economics reporters often know more about the market and the issues than the people they are interviewing. In Detroit, dozens of reporters focus exclusively on the automotive industry and have a professional lifetime's experience in writing about cars and auto-making. In San Francisco, literally hundreds of journalists specialize in the information technology industry; many of them have advanced degrees and are highly sophisticated in their approach to the issues they write about.

You get the picture. If you live and work in a big city, you can and should expect the journalists you deal with to know a great deal about your business. Be careful: They know the issues in your industry; they understand the vocabulary; and they know the questions to ask. The real danger here is not that you will be misquoted. The danger is that you'll say something dumb and they will get it right. Worse yet, a broadcast journalist will save the video.

In a smaller market—say Syracuse, New York; Montgomery, Alabama; or South Bend, Indiana—the danger is just as great for a manager, but it's danger of a different type. The risk in small to medium-sized markets is that a general assignment reporter will know little or nothing of your business or industry. So if she gets it wrong in the story that appears on tonight's six o'clock news or in tomorrow's newspaper, it's probably your fault.

In such cases, you're dealing with a bright, curious, capable journalist but one who is probably overworked and underpaid, and ends up covering a car wreck and a cat show later that same day. Your story is just one stop along the way. It's up to you to explain the story in simple, everyday terms the audience will understand. It's your job to make complex issues simple, to make difficult terms clear, and to turn a confusing story into one that's easy to understand. You can do so by offering your company's perspective early and often in the interview and by flagging the interview with easy-to-follow cues: "The key issue here, Maureen, is . . ." or "If there's one thing I think is more important for your viewers to understand than any other, Mark, it's this . . ."

THEY DO MAKE MISTAKES Daily newspapers contain literally thousands of facts and dozens of opinions. Occasionally, a reporter will simply get it wrong by copying down the wrong fact, transposing numbers, or worse, speaking with someone who doesn't know anything.

This sort of thing happens from time to time, even in large markets with sophisticated and highly regarded news operations. The reporters who make such mistakes rarely ever do so because of malice or bad feelings about the source. Mistakes most often occur because of naiveté or pressure to get a story done before deadline. Occasionally, reporters feel a kind of internal pressure to sensationalize a story when neither hype nor hyperbole are called for.[14]

If it happens to you, if you are misquoted or your words are taken from context, if the facts in the story about your company are distorted or just plain wrong, you should respond, but do so carefully.

Deal first with the reporter. On the telephone or in person, ask if he misunderstood you or if you weren't clear in your response to his questions. Try to begin such conversations with this phrase: "I know you don't want your readers to be misinformed, so . . ." Complete the thought with words such as these: "I thought you should know that some of what appears in your story on page 3 this morning is inaccurate."

DEMANDING A RETRACTION You should never, ever, under any circumstances, demand a retraction or threaten a reporter. For one thing, it won't work. For another, it puts you in a position of obligation to a reporter who's just misquoted you. In exchange for retracting the incorrect story, you now "owe her one." In addition, reporters are threatened all the time; they have grown accustomed to hearing threats from news sources. Your best bet is to appeal to a reporter's sense of integrity and credibility. Without credibility, a reporter has nothing. Stories about journalists making up details of a story or inventing sources for feature reports invariably end with the notation that the reporter has been fired by the paper or the television station. Once you have a reporter's full attention, give him the details or the perspective you hope to reach the public with and conclude the conversation with the phrase, "Thanks. I know you'll do the right thing."

If dealing directly with the reporter who wrote or broadcast your story doesn't work, your next step is the news director (in broadcasting) or the managing editor (in newspapers). The approach should be exactly the same: "I know you don't want your viewers to be misinformed, so . . . ." Editors and news directors are seasoned professionals who know their business and who want to make sure that the sources and subjects of their news stories are treated fairly.

Your last resort is the publisher or station manager, but it's unlikely they will be of much help. Such executives are reluctant to back a version of the truth other than the one presented to them by their news managers. Only in rare circumstances of willful misconduct will publishers or general managers back down, apologize, or retract a story. If all else fails, you can threaten to sue, but that's a lengthy and expensive process that often ends in disappointment. Only in the most egregious cases do publishers or broadcasters end up losing in court.

FACTS VERSUS OPINIONS If the mistake is an error in fact, editors and news directors will be quick to correct it and will usually do so with a sincere and direct apology to the person or organization who was misrepresented. If the mistake, however, is a matter of opinion, perspective, or viewpoint, it will be much more difficult—if not downright impossible—to get a correction or response from the paper or broadcaster. Editors and news directors feel strongly that they are entitled to report opinion, even if it's a minority viewpoint, and as long as it's labeled as such, they owe an irate reader or viewer little in the way of an apology. Bill Moyers of CBS News once said, "Our business is truth as much as news."[15] Even though facts can be easy to produce and easy to correct, truth can be highly subjective. One man's "ecological calamity" can be another man's "routine clean-up."

FEW REPORTERS ARE DECISION MAKERS Although you want to deal directly with and try to make friends of the reporters who cover your business and your industry, it's important to note that few reporters are influential enough to make key decisions about the stories they cover. Brian Williams can decide whether a story is big enough for him to be there personally, but Anne Thompson cannot. Reporters, even big-name anchors, are responsive to the decisions made by their managing editors and news directors. Some stories become big enough, fast enough for general assignment reporters to be bumped aside in favor of a bigger name on the byline. On other occasions, reporters know they are in the doghouse with their bosses because of the insignificance or remoteness of the stories they have been assigned to cover.

Business executives find it useful to cultivate the friendship and favor of certain reporters. In fact, unless they involve breaking news or a crisis of some sort, most news stories rarely get any attention when they're first suggested to a media outlet. Corporate communication professionals will tell you it may take six months to a year to convince someone at *Fortune*, *Barron's*, or *Bloomberg BusinessWeek* to cover a soft feature. But you should know that reporters rarely make the decisions that lead to extensive reporting, the investment of photography or research talent, or the assignment of airtime or print space to a story. Those decisions are made by news management professionals, and regardless of what you do for a living, you should make it your job to get to know them.

GET TO KNOW LOCAL MANAGEMENT If you work in a metropolitan market, the professionals in your corporate communication department will help you and others in the organization tell your story through the media. Follow their lead. If you work in a smaller market, you may need to take the initiative to meet and speak with news professionals on your own.

You should systematically set about, with the assistance of your corporate communication people, meeting radio and television news directors, newspaper managing editors, and—if your community has a business newsweekly—the editors of that publication. Meeting with them may take no more than 20 minutes, and you may do little more than offer them your business card, a brief overview of your business and its products and services, and an offer to help if a story should ever develop on a subject related to your business. Conclude the conversation by asking for an opportunity to comment on any story, whether it deals directly with your company or not. "Call me," you should say. "Give me a chance to help you tell the story accurately, fairly, and completely."

If you maintain a regular, steady dialogue and keep open lines of communication with local editors and news directors, you're unlikely to be surprised by bad news. You're also unlikely to have serious disagreements with them about how a story should be covered. Do your part and respond each time you are asked for a comment. Be there ahead of their deadline and respect their rules; you won't get to edit your own comments, nor will you get to look over a story before it goes to press. But you certainly can get a news organization into the habit of calling you back to check a quote or ask for additional details if you treat them as intelligent professionals and respect the work they do.

GETTING READY

Preparing to meet with a reporter or to be interviewed by a journalist will involve some homework on your part, beginning with your strategy. If you don't have a strategy, it means that you don't know what your objectives are; if you have no specific objectives, you shouldn't agree to the interview.

DEVELOP A STRATEGY Both your supervisor and your public affairs office should know of your interest in meeting with and working with local news managers, and you should go about cultivating a good working relationship with a strategy in mind. That strategy should specify the following in clear terms:

- The goals you hope to achieve by working with local news professionals
- The general content of your message
- The intended audience for your message
- The visuals or photo opportunities you intend to offer
- The timing and sequence of events involved in your story
- What makes this story different from others
- What makes your story newsworthy
- The media you plan to work with to tell your story

Your strategy should be committed to paper as soon as you have a story to tell. Keep in mind that a strategy on paper is not a commitment to one course of action; it should be a living, changing document as you discover new ways to tell the story, new ideas for promoting your message, and new opportunities to use the news media to your advantage. Review it and revise it as often as you need to.

RESEARCH THE REPORTER Make a point of getting to know the reporter you've agreed to interview with. Find out as much as you can: writing and reporting style, story types, experience, general reputation in the community. The best place to start is with the media relations staff of your corporate communications office. They'll know something about nearly every reporter who takes an interest in your company and can help prepare you.

If you have the time, look at some of this reporter's previous stories. Read some clips from the company archives and get a sense of the reporter's style. Does she frequently use direct quotes? Is the style friendly, professional, or aggressive? Should you prepare background information on your company and its products or services to take with you to an interview? Would this reporter welcome a tour of your facilities?

The same is true of television reporters. If time permits, look for online video clips of your reporter's work. If you've been invited to a regularly scheduled local program for an interview, make certain you watch at least one episode of the program in advance to get some idea of the style the interviewer uses with his or her guests.

REFINE AND PRACTICE YOUR MESSAGE Even the most experienced of professionals can benefit from practice occasionally. CEOs, board chairmen, and senior managers will often draft a message they want to convey during a press interview, edit it carefully, review it, and rehearse it. Most important, they will work on sound bites, those 10- to 12-second memorable phrases that they hope will appear again and again on television and in the newspaper.

Do you know the *central theme* of your message—the one nugget of truth that you really want a reporter to record or write down? Begin with your central theme and work from there to develop *examples*, *illustrations*, and *anecdotes* to support that message. Make sure all of the evidence you plan to use is *accurate*, *current*, and *easy to understand*.

Speak in terms of the public's interest, not the company's. Don't talk about what the company wants or needs, but speak instead of how the company will benefit the community, the consumer, your customers, and others, including your employees. Speak in personal terms, showing how you and your coworkers are involved in making better products, providing better services, building a better community.

Rehearse the words you actually plan to use during a press interview. Don't assume that you'll be able to ad lib the content of your interview when the pressure is on. You won't. You'll rely on what you know, what you have rehearsed, and what you feel most comfortable with. Practice your message until you know it so thoroughly you would feel comfortable conducting the interview in the middle of the night.

And when all else fails: Go to the mission statement. Make sure you know your company's mission statement, because when you really can't think of another thing to say, you can always offer the mission statement and then show how the subject at hand is related to the company's basic goals. It'll give you time to think and an opportunity to link the basic vision, values, and beliefs of your firm to the subject of the interview.

CONFIRM THE DETAILS AND GROUND RULES Double-check the time, day, date, and location of the interview. If it's a studio interview and you've never been to that location, you might consider driving by that location *before* you actually need to be there. Can you find the studio or offices you've agreed to meet in? Do you know where you can park? Do you know how long it will take you to get there? Will traffic patterns be different at the time of day you've agreed to meet?

If you've arranged for a telephone interview, make sure you tell the reporter up front how much time you can devote to the conversation. Make certain you know whether the interview is being recorded. In a face-to-face interview, it's not a bad idea for you to bring along a digital recorder so that you'll have your own copy of what you were asked and what you said in response. The presence of the recorder will keep a reporter honest. A reporter who knows you have a copy of the conversation will feel little temptation to get inventive with a direct quote, a fact or figure, or some important element of the story. If you're using a telephone and plan to record the interview, both parties must know of and agree to the recording. Otherwise, you may be in violation of one or more wiretap laws. As you double-check the rules, ask if you can stop or correct quotes as you speak. Almost all reporters will allow such corrections. Also inquire about what the reporter's interests are one more time. What in particular would he like to talk about?

REVIEW THE NEWS OF THE DAY Even if your interview is scheduled early in the day, make sure you check the morning paper, watch the headlines on CNN, and briefly tune into the local news. If you have the time and network access, you may want to check the Internet to see whether any stories regarding your company or your industry are on the Net. You never want to be surprised.

If a reporter offers a story or a headline to you that you haven't seen or heard before, you aren't obligated to respond. You can never be certain that the report is accurate, or that you've been told the whole story. Journalists sometimes ask you to respond to a quote from someone else. If you haven't seen or heard that quote before, say so. "I'm sorry, Erin, I haven't seen that story yet. I'd rather read the full story before I respond." Don't be goaded into responding to a quote or a story you haven't read and haven't had an opportunity to think about.

REMEMBER, YOU ARE THE EXPERT Often lost in all of the anxiety and rush to prepare for an interview is the idea that you know more about the subject than the reporter does. Granted, some financial and business press journalists know a great deal about the subject, but it's rare that they would know your company, your projects, your products, your services, your strategy, and your plans for the future as well as you. Rely on the confidence and detailed preparation that got you this far to take you one step further.

MAKING IT HAPPEN

When the moment of the interview arrives, here's a final checklist to consider.

A PREPARED POCKET CARD MAY HELP Many executives carry a small 3" × 5" (or slightly larger) index card to record and review important details. A manufacturing facility manager in Michigan carries a card in his jacket pocket that contains the number of acres inside the perimeter fence, the square footage on the plant floor, the number of employees per shift, the hourly output in each division, production goals for the week, and other important, quantifiable information.

What's most important about your work? Can you jot down a few things that are unlikely to change in the next few days and keep them on hand? What about those issues related directly to the reason you're being interviewed? Write down one or two main points you hope to impress the reporter with. Include supporting details, numbers, and examples, if you can. Think about jotting down several key points you could talk about if the interview runs long. What *good news subjects* would you like to talk about if time permits?

ARRIVE EARLY, CHECK OUT THE SETTING Again, if you're being interviewed at a studio, the offices of a newspaper or magazine, or at some neutral location, plan to arrive early. Even if your schedule is busy that day, squeeze out a few extra minutes so that when the interviewer arrives or it's your turn to go on, you're calm, relaxed, and familiar with the surroundings.

APPEARANCE AND MAKEUP ARE IMPORTANT Television is a visual medium and it's one that favors close-up shots. If a production assistant offers you an opportunity to apply makeup, take it. Men: Swallow your pride and let the makeup artist improve your looks. A little light powder will help to reduce glare produced by perspiration under the studio lights and, most importantly, it will help to prevent dark shadows from forming under and around your eyes. Women: If you routinely wear makeup, don't do anything differently for a television appearance. If you don't routinely wear makeup, follow the same rules offered for men.

One reminder: Make sure you stop in the rest room on your way out and remove the makeup. If you show up at work wearing makeup, the staff may not understand.

GET YOUR POINTS IN EARLY Most interviews, especially in broadcasting, will move quickly. Lead with your main point. Rephrase it in the next sentence. Then, mention your key issues or principal concerns again before a minute has elapsed. Don't assume that a reporter will get around to asking you what you want to say. He may never get around to asking you about those subjects you would most like to talk about. Raise your principal concerns early and often.

TAKE THE MOTHER-IN-LAW TEST This simple test asks whether your mother-in-law would understand the explanation you've just given. Does your response to a question or does your prepared statement for the press contain acronyms, technical terms, and industry lingo? Is it filled with insider jargon?

Remember that those people watching your interview or reading the report of your conversation with a journalist are generally pretty smart, but they probably don't know much about your business. Use everyday terminology, simple explanations, and direct, declarative sentences. Draw pictures for them, tell stories, use anecdotes. Do what you can to make the subject both real and interesting for them. And if you don't have a mother-in-law, borrow mine. She's a lovely woman named Edna who'd be more than happy to tell you if she understands what you have just said.

BE YOURSELF Unless you're the Boston strangler or someone with a personality no one would want to meet, you're much better off simply being yourself. Don't pretend, don't posture, and don't try to be someone you're not. A great reservoir of goodwill exists in this country for ordinary people who look and act like they're honest. The audience will give you the benefit of the doubt, as long as you act like yourself and play it straight.

STAYING IN CONTROL OF AN INTERVIEW

Among the worst things that could happen is for you to lose control of an interview. It's no different from managing a project or a business event. If you lose control, you cannot determine the outcome; other people will do that for you.

THE IMPORTANCE OF STAYING IN CONTROL Simply focus on your goals for the interview and offer responses that are directed toward those goals. Keep your objective in mind, get your key points in early, and repeat them as often as you can. Don't let a reporter take the interview in a direction that is negative, counterproductive, or off-topic.

Say what you want to say. If they don't use it, you're only out the time and effort you spent preparing. If you say something in response to a question that you hadn't planned on or didn't intend to say, you're asking for trouble. If a reporter asks you a question you don't want to answer, answer a question you wish he had asked. If a journalist asks you a question you can't answer, say why it is you can't offer an answer ("That information is confidential," "We don't yet know what caused the accident," or "Those details are protected by the Privacy Act").

Avoid responding with simple yes or no responses, even if the questions are posed in that way. Use the opportunity to seize control of the interview and get your key points across. It's free airtime or print space that's at stake here. Use it to your best advantage.

YOU DON'T HAVE TO ACCEPT A REPORTER'S PREMISE If a reporter begins a question with the phrase, "Isn't it true . . .," watch out. What usually follows is often not true and is usually designed to put you on the spot. Don't accept what a reporter says as gospel truth, even if the reporter seems especially well informed. Stick to what you know and repeat your most important contentions. If a reporter uses words you wouldn't use or phrases you wouldn't say, don't repeat them, even to deny the accusation.

TELL THE TRUTH Being completely truthful is a novel idea for some managers, but it's one that usually works. If you've done what you are accused of doing—unless your attorney advises otherwise—admit it, but explain in the next breath what you are doing to correct the problem or improve the issue. Don't invent, embellish, stretch, or puff up the facts. Reporters are exceedingly good at finding the truth in most stories; they're trained professionals in research and investigation. If they smell a liar, they'll come after you like a pack of dogs. You needn't reveal everything, of course, but what you do say should be honest, accurate, and truthful.

AVOID ARGUMENTS Don't pick a fight. Journalists are trained in the techniques of combative interviews, and you are unlikely to win. If you get angry and lash out at a reporter, he or she will likely remain quiet and let you look foolish. Stay calm, under control, and professional. You'll win the respect of the reporter and the audience in the process.

YOU ARE ALWAYS ON THE RECORD People who watch television shows about reporters often think they can go *off the record* to tell an interviewer something confidential, hoping that it won't make it into the story. People who tell reporters something off the record usually have an ulterior motive: "You can use this information any way you want, just don't attach my name to it." Reporters are suspicious of sources who pass along information that is off the record.

Bob Franken, who was assistant managing editor of the *Arizona Republic* for many years, once said, "If you don't want it to appear in the paper, don't ever say it to a reporter."[16] He meant simply that saying something to a reporter will somehow, someday eventually work its way to the surface and appear in print, on the air, or in public. If you're concerned about keeping something secret, don't say it. You can't fault a reporter for using something you've said, even though you tried to preface (or backpedal) with the words, "off the record." Every successful manager's career steers clear of off-the-record comments to a reporter.

USE EXAMPLES, ILLUSTRATIONS, BRIEF ANECDOTES People respond to stories, especially those with circumstances they can easily envision or identify with. Illustrate your response or press statement with tales that will capture the hearts and imagination of those listening or reading. Rather than talk about how many metric tons of snow were removed from your company's property during last week's blizzard, relate a story that involves one of your employees; talk about how long he worked and what the experience was like. Examples and stories will work much better than dry facts, figures, and statistics.

IF YOU CAN'T SPEAK TO THE QUESTIONS, SPEAK TO THE ISSUE Individual questions may be phrased in a way that makes them tough to answer. More important, your response to this particular question may be of little help in assisting the audience to understand the larger issue. You may need to deflect the question slightly: "That would be interesting to know, Jay, but the more important issue at the moment is . . ." Or you may simply need to refocus the question: "The number of units involved in this recall is much less important than the overall issue of product safety . . ."

A number of experts cite New York City mayor Rudolph W. Giuliani and his remarkable performance before the cameras during the autumn of 2001. His daily press conferences dealing with the city's exposure to anthrax provide a model for how to handle a crisis effectively. Most observers said the mayor had consistently done the right thing by appealing to people's most rational selves. While literally millions of people were afraid they might be exposed to a terrifying and unpredictable microbe that could attack without warning, Giuliani offered perspective on the issue and reminded them that just one person had died. Dr. Arieh Shalev of Hadassah University Hospital in Jerusalem cautions senior officials to be sensible in their approach, especially to bad news. "Information," he says, "always has to be seen as accurate and reliable and not contaminated by efforts to encourage people."[17]

ABOVE ALL ELSE, STAY LIKEABLE If the audience doesn't like you, you're dead meat. A great reservoir of goodwill and understanding is available out there for people who work hard, play by the rules, and respond honestly to a question. If the audience decides that they like the reporter better than they like you, it will be all but impossible to win any friends for your company or your cause. Use humor, be self-effacing, stay humble. You've got a lot to lose if you don't.

FOLLOW-UP

After it's over, you shouldn't simply put the experience behind you. Each press interview should be an opportunity to learn, grow, and improve your abilities. Another event, another product rollout, another small crisis may be just around the corner.

REVIEW THE ARTICLE OR TAPE Read what's been written about you, watch the videotape, and look carefully at the way the story came together. Did the reporter get it right? Are the key facts there? If most of it's right and if your company is cast in a generally favorable light, be glad. That's the most you can ask. Few reporters will get every detail exactly right; even fewer will say things the way you'd have said them if you had written the story yourself.

INFORM THE CHAIN OF COMMAND No surprises. Keep your boss informed about every interview you do. Tell the people in corporate communication how it went; they may wish to pass along information to others in the company who may be contacted for an interview. No one expects perfection from each encounter with the media, but no one in higher management wants to be blindsided by employee quotes or statements in the press.

PROVIDE FEEDBACK It's not a bad idea to pick up the phone and call the reporter who interviewed you. He or she will likely enjoy hearing from you, especially if the experience was a good one. If it didn't work out the way you had planned or hoped, talk with the reporter and see what went wrong. If it did work, consider a follow-up opportunity. Perhaps there's another story in your organization that would be of interest to that reporter or another opportunity to show what your company can do.

LEAVE A RECORD FOR YOUR SUCCESSOR Don't walk away from an encounter with the Fourth Estate and simply press on with business as usual. Take a few minutes to draft a memo for the record, explaining how the request for an interview developed, what the key issues were, who was involved, where the interview took place, and what your impressions were. Include a copy of the newspaper or magazine clipping or a copy of the videotape. The more information your successor has to work with, the greater the chances for success if the same reporter or news outlet should call again.

For Further Reading

Bland, M., Theaker, A., and D. Wragg. *Effective Media Relations: How to Get Results.* Sterling, VA: Kogan Page, 2005.

Cutlip, S. M., Center, A. H., and Broom, G. M. *Effective Public Relations*, 9th ed. Upper Saddle River, NJ: Prentice Hall, 2005.

Evans, F. J. *Managing the Media: Proactive Strategies for Better Business-Press Relations.* Westport, CT: Quorum Books, 1997.

Harmon, J. F. *Feeding Frenzy: Crisis Management in the Spotlight.* New York: AEG Publishing Group, 2009.

Henderson, D. *Making News: A Straight-Shooting Guide to Media Relations.* Lincoln, NE: iUniverse, 2006.

Howard, C. M. and Matthews, W. K. *On Deadline: Managing Media Relations*, 3rd ed. Prospect Heights, IL: Waveland Press, 2000.

Hoover, J. D. *Corporate Advocacy: Rhetoric in the Information Age.* Westport, CT: Greenwood Publishing Group, 1997.

Johnson, J. *Media Relations: Issues and Strategies.* Crows Nest NSW, Australia: Allen & Unwin, 2007.

Matthews, W. *How to Create a Media Relations Program.* International Association of Business Communicators, 1997.

Mathis, M. E. *Feeding the Media Beast: An Easy Recipe for Great Publicity.* West Lafayette, IN: Purdue University Press, 2002.

Mayhew, L. H. *The New Public: Professional Communication and the Means of Social Influence.* Cambridge, UK: Cambridge University Press, 1997.

Moore, S. *An Invitation to Public Relations.* London, UK. Cassell, 1996.

Overholt, A. "Are You Ready for Your Close-Up?" *Fast Company*, November 2002, p. 53.

Stewart, S. *Media Training 101: A Guide to Meeting the Press.* New York: Wiley & Sons, 2003.

Wilcox, D. L., Ault, P. H., Cameron, G. T., and Agee, W. K. *Public Relations: Strategies and Tactics*, 7th ed. Boston, MA: Allyn & Bacon, 2002.

Yale, D. R. *Publicity and Media Relations Checklists.* New York: NTC Business Books, 1995.

Endnotes

1. Tolley, J. L. "Iacocca Still Charms the Media," *ABC Communication World*, September 1987, p. 22.

2. : Durando, J. "BP's Tony Hayward: 'I'd Like My Life Back.'" *USA Today*, June 1, 2010. Retrieved from http://content.usatoday.com/communities/greenhouse/post/2010/06/bp-tony-hayward-apology/1

3. Reprinted by permission of *Harvard Business Review* from Burger, C. "How to Meet the Press," *Harvard Business Review*, July–August 1975, p. 63. Copyright © 1975 by the Harvard Business School Publishing Corporation; all rights reserved.

4. Quinn, T. President and Chief Operating Officer, Jordan Industries, Inc., Chicago, Illinois, in a personal interview, November 20, 1997, Notre Dame, Indiana.

5. Burger. "How to Meet the Press," p. 62.

6. The Arthur W. Page Society: Background and History, The Page Philosophy. Retrieved from http://www.awpagesociety.com/site/about/page_philosophy/ on July 21, 2008 at 3:00 P.M.

7. France, M. "The Mea Culpa Defense," *BusinessWeek Online*, p. 2. Online at: www.businessweek.com/magazine/content/02_34/b3796604.htm. Retrieved November 21, 2002.

8. Patel, A., and Reinsch, L. "Companies Can Apologize: Corporate Apologies and Legal Liability," *Business Communication Quarterly*, 66, no. 1 (2003), pp. 9–25. See also Cooper, D. A. "CEO Must Weigh Legal and Public Relations Approaches," *Public Relations Journal*, January 1992, pp. 39–40; and Fitzpatrick, K. R. and M. S. Rubin. "Public Relations vs. Legal Strategies in Organizational Crisis Decisions," *Public Relations Review*, 21 (1995), pp. 21–33.

9. France. "The Mea Culpa Defense," pp. 2–3.

10. Ibid., p. 3.

11. Gold, V. "If Mike Wallace Calls, Hang Up: Ten Rules for Dealing with Today's Journalists," *The Washingtonian*, September 1984, pp. 87–89.

12. Hamill, P. *News Is a Verb: Journalism at the End of the Twentieth Century.* New York: The Ballantine Publishing Group, 1998, p. 80.

13. Tolley. "Iacocca," p. 21.

14. Hamill. *News Is a Verb*, pp. 79–94.

15. Lichter, S. R., S. Rothman, and L. S. Lichter. *The Media Elite: America's New Powerbrokers.* Bethesda, MD: Adler & Adler, 1986, p. 132.

16. Franken, R. Personal interview, May 19, 2005. Notre Dame, Indiana.

17. Goode, E. "Anthrax Offers Lessons in How to Handle Bad News," *New York Times*, October 23, 2001, pp. D1, D6. Copyright © 2001 by The New York Times Company. Reprinted with permission.

CASE STUDY 13-1

L'Oreal USA.

Do Looks Really Matter in the Cosmetic Industry?

The cosmetic and fragrance floor of the Macy's in San Jose was bustling with shoppers as Elysa Yanowitz, regional sales manager for L'Oreal, and John (Jack) Wiswall, general manager of L'Oreal's designer fragrance division, to whom Yanowitz reported, walked together through the store on a routine visit in the fall of 1997. As the two walked past the Polo Ralph Lauren counter, which is licensed to L'Oreal, Wiswall noticed a woman of Middle Eastern descent selling fragrances behind the counter. He instructed Yanowitz to "get [him] someone hot" and fire the Middle Eastern employee. Passing by a young good-looking blonde, Wiswall pulled Yanowitz aside and said, "Get me one that looks like that."

A few weeks later Wiswall visited the store again and was upset to discover that Yanowitz had not dismissed the saleswoman as instructed. Visibly frustrated with her refusal to follow his order, he asked Yanowitz upon leaving the store, "Didn't I tell you to get rid of her?"[1] Despite repeated inquires from Wiswall, Yanowitz refused to fire the sales associate, claiming later that she could not dismiss the woman without adequate justification. Additionally, the employee was one of the top-selling sales associates in the region.

Wiswall became frustrated and with the help of Richard Roderick, vice president of designer fragrances and Yanowitz's immediate supervisor, he began to solicit complaints from Yanowitz's subordinates. In their quest for negative feedback on Yanowitz, they claimed that she maintained a dictatorial style of leadership and was disliked by her subordinates. Wiswall and Roderick also performed audits on Yanowitz's expense reports and prepared memos about problems with her performance. They told her she had become a liability and was making too many mistakes. Ironically, only one year prior, she had been awarded "L'Oreal's Regional Sales Manager of the Year."[2]

Yanowitz, typically a first-rate manager, became distressed and preoccupied to the extent that it affected her job performance. As a result, her sales numbers began to slip and in July 1998 she was forced to take a medical leave of absence. She cited job-related stress as the cause of her departure.[3] After three months, L'Oreal replaced her.

Elysa Yanowitz

Elysa Yanowitz started as a sales representative with L'Oreal in 1981 when the company name was licensed by Cosmair, Inc. Yanowitz rose through the ranks to become a sales manager in 1986. She was responsible for managing L'Oreal's sales force and dealing with the department and specialty stores that sold L'Oreal's fragrances. Yanowitz's performance was consistently rated as "Above Expectations" or just short of "Outstanding." During her career she received multiple awards for her sales performance.[4] In 1997, L'Oreal restructured to merge its European Designer Fragrances Division (where Yanowitz worked), with its Polo Ralph Lauren fragrances division. At this time, Yanowitz received the additional responsibilities of marketing Polo Ralph Lauren fragrances in her region.

L'Oreal

L'Oreal S.A. Paris is the world's number one cosmetic company specializing in the development and manufacturing process of hair care, hair color, skincare, color cosmetics, and fragrances for the consumer and professional markets.

The history of L'Oreal began in 1907 when Eugene Schueller, a young French chemist, developed an innovative hair color formula and sold it to Parisian hairdressers. Mr. Schueller started a small company that would later be L'Oreal and put in place the guiding principles of the company: research and innovation in the interest of beauty. By 1912, Schueller was exporting his hair color products to Holland, Austria, and Italy. A few years later, he was selling products to the United States, Russia, South America, and the Far East. While L'Oreal got its start in the hair color business, it soon expanded its operations to include other cleansing and beauty products. Today, L'Oreal is the world's largest cosmetic company marketing 500 brands and more than 2,000 products in all areas of the beauty business. In 2002, L'Oreal recorded over 14 billion (euros) in consolidated sales.[5]

L'Oreal USA, a wholly owned subsidiary of L'Oreal S.A. Paris, was founded in 1953 (by exclusive licensee Cosmair, Inc.). Since its foundation, the company has acquired a host of big-name consumer product brands, including Maybelline, Garnier, and Softsheen Carson. The company also owns several salon product lines including Redken, Matrix, Kérastase, and Mizani, as well as fragrance brands Ralph Lauren and Giorgio Armani. L'Oreal USA's upscale Lancôme, Shu Uemura and Biotherm cosmetic and skincare lines are also sold in department stores nationwide. With a broad distribution network of salons, mass-market, specialty, and department stores, L'Oreal USA is the most comprehensive beauty company in the United States.

The Polo Ralph Lauren Brand

In 1967, Ralph Lauren began the Polo Ralph Lauren company with 26 boxes of ties. Interested in promoting a lifestyle with his ties, Ralph Lauren named his line after Polo, a sport of discreet elegance and classic style. Today, 35 years later, the company is a $10 billion global business of menswear, womenswear, childrenswear, home collections, accessories, and fragrances.

Polo Ralph Lauren's brand and distinctive image have been consistently developed across an expanding number of products, brands, and international markets. Defined by its all-American style and combination of classic taste, quality, and integrity, Polo Ralph Lauren is a leader in the fashion industry. The company's products are distributed through upscale department stores such as Macy's, Nordstrom's, and Neiman Marcus.[6]

Polo Ralph Lauren's brand names, which include *Polo*, *Polo by Ralph Lauren*, *Ralph Lauren Purple Label*, *Polo Sport*, *Ralph Lauren*, *RALPH*, *Lauren*, *Polo Jeans Co.*, *RL*, *Chaps*, and *Club Monaco* among others, constitute one of the world's most recognized families of consumer brands. Through an exclusive partnership with Polo Ralph Lauren, L'Oreal USA markets and manages the Polo Ralph Lauren fragrance line. However, not all of the company's [brand] products are licensed through L'Oreal, just the fragrance line. In 1997, L'Oreal's European Designer Fragrance Division merged with its Polo Ralph Lauren Fragrance Division.

The Cosmetic Industry

Cosmetic products are generally grouped into five main categories: perfumes and fragrances, decorative cosmetics, skincare, hair care, and toiletries. The marketing of these products represents an important part of building cosmetic brands. The cosmetic industry typically markets its products using creative packaging and superior formulations. Employees in the cosmetic industry must have the ability to monitor and interpret fashion and consumer trends both locally and internationally in order to offer the latest in product innovation and packaging technology. They also must work closely with clients while creating products and developing marketing strategies to maximize the sales potential within specific market segments.[7]

The cosmetic industry is fortunate to operate in markets that are less sensitive to economic cycles than others.[8] When the economy is difficult, customers who delay purchase of a consumer durable will continue to buy cosmetics products because they provide a sense of well-being at a reasonable price. However, Lindsey Owen-Jones, Chairman and CEO of L'Oreal, recently warned investors that the current cosmetic market is "one of the worst we've seen for years."[9]

The target consumers for the cosmetic market are primarily working, college-educated women over the age of 20 who have an active lifestyle. However, there is an emergence of teenagers as a market segment as they wish to assert their identity and personality. Another consumer trend is the spread of skincare products and cosmetics for men. Although the market for men is in its infancy, it constitutes another promising opportunity for the cosmetics industry.

Appearance-Based Discrimination: Human Resources/Legal Implications

Appearance in the fashion and cosmetic industries is very important because beauty products are tied directly to the brand's image. Companies in these industries depend on their sales associates to be "brand ambassadors" and project the qualities of the brand to the customer. In today's competitive environment and particularly in the fashion and beauty industries, it is critical that beauty-based companies create an experience that is appealing to the target customer. For example, at some Abercrombie stores, applicants are required to submit a professional head shot with their application to ensure that they are a good match with the "Abercrombie style."[10] This trend of hiring attractive employees is occurring in other industries as well. Hotels, bars, and other businesses also are beginning to recruit only the best-looking employees to attract customers and charge premium prices.

Hiring someone who is attractive isn't illegal, per se. In recent years, however, several cases have emerged disputing whether employers can base employment decisions solely on physical appearance. In a 1981 case, *Wilson v. Southwest Airlines Co.*,[11] Southwest defended its then-existing policy that only attractive women could be hired as flight attendants and ticket agents. Southwest argued that female sex appeal was a bona fide occupational qualification (BFOQ) under Title VII because the airline wanted to project "a sexy image and fulfill its public promise to take passengers skyward with love."[12] However, since Southwest is not in the business of providing "vicarious sex entertainment," the district court rejected its defense.

What is and is not discrimination? Employers may fire their best employee; they may also fire a woman, a person who practices a certain faith, a pregnant woman, a disabled person, a gay or lesbian, or a foreigner. However, they cannot terminate them *because* they are a woman, of a certain religion, pregnant, disabled, gay or lesbian, or from a foreign country. The motive for the termination is the single governing factor in a lawsuit for discrimination when an employee falls within a protected category.[13]

Employees are protected under Title VII of the Civil Rights Act from discrimination based on sex, race, religion, color or national origin, but height, weight, and physical appearance discrimination are not included.[14] Part of the problem is the fact that attractiveness is subjective; people have different opinions on what is appealing. To protect themselves, some companies have created policies that state that

employees must be "well-groomed and attractive," but these companies run into difficulty when the policy is not consistently enforced across sexes and races.[15]

The Court of [Appeals] ruled that the L'Oreal case was one of sex discrimination: A male executive cannot insist that a female subordinate be terminated because she is not sexually appealing to him, when no similar orders are issued with respect to male employees. Just as an employer may not enforce rules that regulate men and women differently based on their appearance or sexual desirability, an employer may also not discriminate against employees on these bases.

The L'Oreal case also raises the question of wrongful termination. The state of California operates under an "at will" employment model. This means that employees work at the will of their employer—subject to two exceptions, discrimination and contract—and an employer may terminate without reason or notice. Employers cannot discriminate against employees on the basis of age, race, sex, national origin, and several other criteria. Employers also cannot fire contracted employees who are hired to work for the company for a specified time period or purpose but are not directly employed by the company.

Working at L'Oreal

L'Oreal's sales team includes employees with different educational backgrounds and work experiences. For some positions, the company requires sales associates to have a cosmetology license, previous experience, and specific knowledge. L'Oreal is particularly interested in employees who are enthusiastic about fashion and beauty, possess customer service abilities, are analytical, have excellent negotiation skills, are willing to travel and relocate, and are computer literate.[16]

L'Oreal describes itself as a fast-paced, energetic company that employs smart, focused individuals who enjoy their work. The company boasts that it is not a "cookie-cutter corporation." In fact, L'Oreal claims that its workforce diversity "will amaze and inspire you." Since the company strives for diversity, would it seem reasonable to terminate a sales associate on the basis of her appearance and background?

Yanowitz vs. L'Oreal

In 1999, Elysa Yanowitz filed a sexual discrimination suit against L'Oreal. During a four-year court battle, Yanowitz insisted that Wiswall had violated California's fair employment law barring sexual discrimination when he sought to fire the saleswoman. She further argued that it was illegal for L'Oreal to retaliate against her for not carrying out an order she believed violated the law. L'Oreal's legal representatives argued that Wiswall and other company officials did nothing wrong and took action to reprimand Yanowitz for her errors and oversights.[17]

On March 7, 2003, a three-judge panel of the Court of Appeals for the First Appellate District in San Francisco reinstated her claim of retaliation, which was dismissed previously by the trial court. The panel wrote: "An explicit order to fire a female employee for failing to meet a male executive's personal standards for sexual desirability is sex discrimination." The panel also said, "A lower-level manager's refusal to carry out that order is protected activity, and an employer may not retaliate against her for that refusal." On June 11, 2003, the California Supreme Court voted 6 to 1 to review the appellate court's ruling.[18]

Rebecca Caruso

On August 4, 2003, L'Oreal USA named Rebecca Caruso as its Executive Vice President of Corporate Communications. She replaced John Wendt, Executive Vice President, Corporate and Public Affairs, who [would] retire in December after 23 years with L'Oreal USA. Prior to joining L'Oreal USA, Caruso worked in communications and public relations for Toys "R" Us, Inc., McDonald's Corporation, and Chrysler Corporation of America.

Caruso must decide the best way for her department to handle L'Oreal's communication response concerning Yanowitz's lawsuit. Because she joined the L'Oreal team in August 2003, she faces an interesting challenge of dealing with this case after all the major events have occurred. In her new capacity, Caruso is responsible for the management of all internal and external communications and diversity initiatives for L'Oreal USA. She must work closely with Mr. Jean-Paul Agon, President and CEO of L'Oreal USA, to deal with this lawsuit and prevent it from developing into a public relations disaster. With the upcoming trial date and the media heavily covering the case, she must determine how to retain L'Oreal's strong brand identity and reputation.

DISCUSSION QUESTIONS

1. How should L'Oreal handle the negative press surrounding this lawsuit?
2. Would an outside consulting firm be useful? How?
3. Who should handle the communication with the public, stakeholders, and the media?
4. What should the message be and how should it be delivered?
5. What actions should L'Oreal take to protect itself in the future?
6. What are the critical issues and who are the major stakeholders in this case?
7. What options does L'Oreal have regarding the lawsuit, and is battling the case with Yanowitz in court the best decision?

WRITING ASSIGNMENT

Please respond in writing to the issues presented in this case by preparing two documents: a communication strategy memo and a professional business letter.

In preparing these documents, you may assume one of two roles: you may identify yourself as a L'Oreal manager who has been asked to provide advice to Ms. Rebecca Caruso, Executive Vice President for Corporate Communications and External Affairs, regarding the issues she and the company are facing. Or, you may identify yourself as an external management consultant who has been asked by the company to provide advice to Ms. Caruso.

Either way, you must prepare a strategy memo addressed to Ms. Caruso that summarizes the details of the case, rank-orders critical issues, discusses their implications (what they mean and why they matter), offers specific recommendations for action (assigning ownership and suspense dates for each), and shows how to communicate the solution to all who are affected by the recommendations.

You must also prepare a professional business letter for the signature of Mr. Frederic Roze, President and Chief Executive Officer, L'Oreal USA. That document may be addressed to any of L'Oreal's key stakeholders, including customers, retailers, investors, or others. If you have questions about either of these documents, please consult your instructor.

References

1. "Refusal to Fire Unattractive saleswomen Led to Dismissal, Suit Contends." *The New York Times*, April 11, 2003, p. A10.
2. Ibid.
3. Leff, Lisa. "Women Who Wouldn't Fire Cosmetics Clerk Over Looks Can Sue," *Associated Press*, April 12, 2003.
4. Ofgang, Kenneth. "Firing Woman for Lack of Attractiveness Violates Anti-Bias Law," *Metropolitan New-Enterprise*, March 10, 2003.
5. L'Oreal at www.loreal.com.
6. Ralph Lauren at www.polo.com.
7. Cosmetic, Toiletry, and Perfumery Association at www.ctpa.org.uk.
8. Ibid.
9. L'Oreal Finance at www.loreal-finance.com.
10. Houston, David. "Abercrombie & Fitch Ads Offend Critics, Who Say Company Shuns Minority Workers," *Daily Journal*, June 23, 2003.
11. *Wilson v. Southwest Airlines Co.* N.D. Texas (1981) 517 F.Supp. 292 (Wilson).
12. Ibid.
13. www.discriminationattorney.com.
14. Kranke, Bell, Iyer & Hoffman, University of Northern Colorado. "Appearance Discrimination and Small Business." Online at: www.eeoc.gov/laws/vii.html. Retrieved December 16, 2003.
15. Ibid.
16. L'Oreal at www.loreal.com.
17. Associated Press. "US Judge Lets L'Oreal Sex Discrimination Suit Proceed," *Morning Star*, April 11, 2003.
18. *Yanowitz v. L'Oreal USA, Inc.* Legal Brief, California Court of Appeal, March 7, 2003.

This case was prepared by Research Assistants Allison A. Petty, Cynthia G. Reimer, and Ross R. Swanes under the direction of James S. O'Rourke, Concurrent Professor of Management, as the basis for class discussion rather than to illustrate either effective or ineffective handling of an administrative situation.

CASE STUDY 13-2

Taco Bell: How Do We Know It's Safe to Eat?

I was vomiting, had diarrhea; I was in so much pain. I thought I was going to die.[1]

These were the words of Stephen Minnis, a 27-year-old from Limerick, Pennsylvania. On November 25, 2006, only a few weeks after he was discharged from the U.S. Air Force, Minnis dined at a Taco Bell in nearby Gilbertsville. Little did he know that the chicken chalupa he devoured for lunch that day would nearly kill him.

On November 30, Taco Bell officials learned that several customers had become sick with a virulent strain of *E. coli* after eating at one of the chain's restaurants in New Jersey. Day by day, new cases of *E. coli* bacteria relating to Taco Bell were popping up throughout the Northeast in New Jersey, New York, Pennsylvania, and Delaware. Several of the victims were vegetarians, leading authorities to focus on produce rather than ground beef. Although green onions were initially suspected to be the culprit, extensive testing of Taco Bell ingredients had yet to determine the source of the outbreak. As word of the outbreak quickly reached the media, and more cases continued to arise, 1-800-TACO-BELL was flooded with telephone calls. Was Taco Bell food safe to eat? What was the source of the *E. coli*? What was Taco Bell doing to eliminate the problem?

Upon hearing the news, Laurie Gannon, Public Relations Director at Taco Bell Corporation, probably asked herself how many times lightning was going to strike her company. In November of 1999, ground beef from a San Francisco Bay-area Taco Bell restaurant was implicated in an *E. coli* scare that sickened ten. In September of 2000, Taco Bell's genetically modified taco shells sold in grocery stores were determined to contain a corn ingredient unapproved for human consumption. In December of the same year, green onions from Taco Bell restaurants were implicated in a hepatitis A outbreak in Florida, Kentucky, and Nevada. Now, as several Taco Bell customers became infected with *E. coli*, Laurie found herself in a difficult, yet all-too-familiar position.

The Outbreak

The first reported case of potentially deadly *E. coli* O157:H7 was in Middlesex County, New Jersey on November 17, six days before Thanksgiving. In the last two weeks of November, more cases were reported in the same county, leading county health officials to review the data and look for connections. Infected patients were asked whether they had recently eaten out, and if so, where. Officials determined that signals pointed to a single Taco Bell restaurant in South Plainfield, New Jersey, where nine out of eleven reported victims had eaten. On November 30, the owners of the franchise agreed to shut down, dispose of all its existing supplies, and have the restaurant professionally cleaned. Officials in the restaurant found no contaminated food, leading them to believe a Taco Bell worker was to blame. However, when four Taco Bells nearby were also found to be involved, county health authorities realized they might be dealing with a much bigger issue.[2]

On December 4, Taco Bell decided to voluntarily close eight of its other restaurants in Suffolk and Nassau counties in New York. As a precaution, the restaurants threw out all existing food and brought in new food. They also completely cleaned and re-sanitized all of their utensils and cooking equipment.[3]

Cases of the *E. coli* infection relating to Taco Bell food continued to pop up throughout the Northeast, specifically New Jersey, New York, Pennsylvania, and Delaware. One case in South Carolina involved a patient who ate at a Pennsylvania Taco Bell. As the extent of the outbreak grew, the Food and Drug Administration (FDA) and the Centers for Disease Control (CDC) became involved in an extensive investigation and began the testing of Taco Bell facilities and ingredients.

Taco Bell responded by hiring Certified Laboratories of Plainview, New York, an independent scientific laboratory to conduct tests on 300 samples of all ingredients. In Suffolk County, New York, a Taco Bell food safety team was flown in to collect samples of just about every type of tortilla, tomato, and Mexican seasoning from a Deer Park restaurant. Similar samples were collected by Taco Bell representatives from restaurants in multiple states and sent to Certified Laboratories for testing. Quick tests determined that three samples of green onions, also known as scallions, were contaminated with the *E. coli* bacteria. Although follow-up Federal testing of those samples were negative for *E. coli*, on December 6, the company announced that it had removed green onions from all of its restaurants nationwide.[4] Taco Bell President, Greg Creed, said, "In an abundance of caution, we've decided to pull all green onions from our restaurants until we know conclusively whether they are the cause of the *E. coli* outbreak."[5]

On December 9, 2006, Taco Bell Corporation affirmed that its restaurants were safe and that after more extensive testing by Certified Laboratories, all ingredients had tested negative for *E. coli* O157:H7, with the possible exception of green onions. However, on December 11, Taco Bell announced that the samples of green onions that tested positive for *E. coli* were confirmed negative by the company and the FDA. The results came from an open bin of white onions that tested positive for *E. coli*, but it was a different strain of the bacteria and no illnesses were linked to this strain.[6]

It was not until December 13, 2006, that Taco Bell determined lettuce from one of its California suppliers was the most probable source of the *E. coli* outbreak. The FDA and the CDC confirmed this through additional statistical analysis of the company's food ingredients. Lettuce is served in approximately 70 percent of all Taco Bell menu items which, according to the CDC, increases the probability that it would be the source.

Finally, on December 14, 2006, Taco Bell was informed by the CDC that the *E. coli* outbreak was over. The CDC also indicated that "contamination of lettuce likely occurred before reaching the restaurants."[7] By this time, all 90 Taco Bell restaurants that had been voluntarily close were up and running again. However, there were more than 400 confirmed or suspected cases of *E. coli* poisoning linked to Taco Bell restaurants.[8]

Taco Bell Corporation

Taco Bell is the nation's leading Mexican-style quick service restaurant. The company was founded in Downey, California, by Glen Bell on March 21, 1962. The company went public in 1969, and in 1978, Glen Bell sold all 868 restaurants to PepsiCo, Inc., and became a major shareholder in PepsiCo. In October of 1997, PepsiCo spun off KFC, Pizza Hut, and Taco Bell to form Tricon Global Restaurants, which became the world's largest restaurant company with annual revenues in excess of $22 billion.[9]

In May of 2002, Tricon changed its name to Yum! Brands, Inc., after acquiring Long John Silver's and A&W All-American Food. The company is headquartered in Louisville, Kentucky, and is the largest restaurant company in the world (in terms of "system units") with more than 34,000 restaurants in over 100 countries.[10] Yum! Brands generated over $9 billion in total revenues in 2005. The company is also a leader in multi-branding, putting two restaurants under one roof, with KFC and Taco Bell being the most productive combination.[11]

Taco Bell began franchising in 1964. Of its 5,800 restaurants nationwide, almost 75 percent of its restaurants are owned and operated by independent franchisees, while the rest are company-operated.[12] In 2005, Taco Bell itself exceeded $6 billion worldwide, with $4.4 billion in sales from franchises and $1.8 billion in company-operated sales.[13]

Taco Bell serves more than two billion consumers a year, or more than 35 million per week. According to company President, Greg Creed, nearly half of the entire U.S. adult population eats at a Taco Bell at least once a month.[14] The company has more than 5,800 restaurants in the U.S., and over 278 restaurants operating outside the U.S. Taco Bell's "left-of-center" thinking and commitment to marketing helps the company to target the 18–24 year-old demographic.[15]

The company is also committed to forward-thinking and updating its marketing campaign as needed. The first most nationally acclaimed marketing campaign was for the 1997 "Yo Quiero Taco Bell!" Chihuahua dog, which won the company an American Marketing Association advertising award. Taco Bell has used other very creative marketing tools, one of which was free tacos for every American if the falling Russian space station MIR landed on a Taco Bell target in the Pacific Ocean in March of 2001. The company has also established multiple partnerships with MTV, X Games, Viacom, Microsoft, and Fox for various projects displaying the brand name. Currently Taco Bell maintains its originality in marketing with its current tagline "Think Outside the Bun."

Related Health Concerns and Issues

Taco Bell has survived several previous health issues. In November of 1999, ten customers were sickened with an *E. coli* infection after eating at Taco Bell restaurant in San Francisco. Although testing of ingredients came back negative, ground beef was suspected to be the source of the *E. coli*.[16] In September of 2000, the company was accused of selling genetically modified Kraft taco shells in grocery stores. The shells contained a protein molecule (Cry9c) that was unapproved for human consumption.[17] In December of the same year, Taco Bell restaurants were implicated in a hepatitis A outbreak in multiple counties in Florida, Kentucky, and Nevada. Analysis revealed that the green onions were likely the source, but that the ingredients were contaminated prior to arrival at the Taco Bell restaurants.[18] The company has also endured criticism for the general quality of its food and ingredients, especially the beef it uses. However, Taco Bell is not alone in these health concerns.

In late 2006, around the same time as Taco Bell's *E. coli* outbreak, nearly three dozen people fell ill with symptoms consistent with an *E. coli* infection after eating at a Taco John's restaurant in Cedar Falls, Iowa. Several people also became ill after eating at a Taco John's in Albert Lea, Minnesota. The first illness was reported to the Black Hawk County Health Department on November 28, 2006.[19] Kevin Teale of the Iowa Department of Health said approximately 40 people had reported symptoms consistent with *E. coli* and 14 had been hospitalized.[20] Although the outbreak had no connection to that of Taco Bell, lettuce from a California farm was determined to be the likely source.[21]

E. coli

E. coli is an abbreviation for *Escherichia coli* bacteria, commonly found in the intestinal tracts of humans and other animals. Most *E. coli* infections are associated with undercooked meat that has come in contact with animal feces, but the bacteria can also manifest itself in leafy vegetables, such as spinach and lettuce. Generally, *E. coli* is harmless, but certain strands, especially *E. coli* O157:H7, can cause abdominal cramps, fever, kidney failure, blindness, paralysis, and even death.

Where is it Found?

E. coli is generally found in a cow's large intestine, and it is ever-present in cattle lots. Because of this, the bacterium is most likely to be found in ground beef or vegetables that are grown near animals or irrigated with water contaminated by the cow manure in fertilizer.[22] *E. coli* can also be found in drinking water, lakes, or swimming pools that have sewage in them; milk that is not pasteurized; and produce that is grown or washed in contaminated water.

Effects

Many times, *E. coli* goes unnoticed because it is difficult to detect and nearly impossible to treat or eradicate. There are an estimated 73,000 cases and 60 related deaths reported annually in the United States, and fortunately this number has decreased over the past decade due to guidelines implemented by the FDA, CDC, and USDA.[23] Of these 73,000 cases, an estimated 2,100 result in hospitalization in the United States. Because the symptoms are not necessarily specific to *E. coli*, illnesses are often misdiagnosed, and hospitals spend considerable resources on treatment.[24]

There are thousands of strands of *E. coli*, mostly harmless, but it only takes one strand to cause an outbreak. The *Escherichia coli* O157:H7 strand was traced to the Taco Bell outbreak, and it is also the same strand that was linked to the California spinach outbreak in September and October of 2006. This particular strand of *E. coli* makes a potent toxin that latches onto intestinal cells. Just ten cells of *E. coli* O157:H7 are enough to infect a person, compared to the hundreds of thousands of cells needed to infect a person with Salmonella or cholera.[25]

Symptoms

The *E. coli* bacteria can cause many symptoms, including mild fever, diarrhea, bloody diarrhea, or dehydration. These symptoms usually occur within two to three days of exposure, but they can arise within one day or up to a week later. Fortunately, most healthy adults recover completely within one week. Another possible result of contact with the bacteria is hemolytic uremic syndrome (HUS), which can cause decreased urine production, kidney failure, anemia, edema, hypertension, blood-clotting, seizures, or death. HUS can be diagnosed through stool sample testing, but it does result in an estimated 61 fatalities each year.[26]

Taco Bell's Suppliers

According to Taco Bell's president Greg Creed, extensive testing determined that the current outbreak was an "ingredient issue" and said it "was not about the hygiene of our restaurants."[27] As a result, the *E. coli* outbreak put the spotlight on Taco Bell's produce suppliers.

After being harvested, most produce is moved to processing plants where it is washed, sorted, and cooled for transport to supermarkets or distribution centers around the country. There are resting guidelines in place at various steps along the distribution chain that major food distributors follow. Bryan Silbermann, President of the Produce Marketing Association, a trade group that represents restaurants, farmers, and other companies in the produce supply chain, confirms that for the past decade, all the major restaurant and supermarket chains have insisted that outside auditors monitor suppliers.[28]

Taco Bell's produce suppliers typically purchase lettuce and onions from multiple farms, many of which are in California. As for the lettuce, suppliers clean, rinse, shred, and pack the produce into sealed containers for shipment to Taco Bell's distributors, which in turn send them to the company's stores.[29]

The onions undergo an even more extensive process: they are washed with a chlorine solution to kill contaminants, rinsed with water, trimmed, sanitized again, rinsed with water, dried, and put into 8-ounce bags that are not air-tight. No human skin contact is allowed during this process and the produce bags are coded and traceable. These bags are then packed and shipped to Taco Bell restaurants by way of McLane distribution in New York. Inventory turnover of the onions is dozens of times every two to three weeks.[30]

Despite these procedures, there is still the possibility that shipments can be contaminated. Michael Hansen, a senior scientist at Consumers Union, a consumer advocacy group, said "Because we have more industrialized systems now where things are concentrated, we need more tracking of produce. You'll continue to see these types of outbreaks until people start looking at the whole food chain to find out where this is happening."[31]

Franchisees

With 5,800 restaurants nationwide and millions spent on television ads and marketing campaigns, Taco Bell is an enormous operation with a largely corporate image. However, at the companies core is a collection of businesses, franchises owned by individuals. While most of the focus after an *E. coli* outbreak is on the corporate parent, the hardship can be worse for those franchise owners. According to Paul Argenti, a professor of corporate communications at the Tuck School of Business at Dartmouth College, "[Franchisees] stand to lose the most. It's unfortunate. They are suffering because of the problems that developed at the corporate level."[32]

While restaurants in the area of the outbreak stand to lose much in sales, franchises around the country can also take a large hit. Some estimates indicate that same store sales may fall by as much as 20 percent.[33] In 1993, when people in the Northwest fell ill after eating tainted hamburgers from Jack in the Box, one franchise in El Paso, Texas, far from the outbreak

saw a $10,000 per week drop in sales. The manager of the franchise said it took several years for the store to fully recover.[34]

Of the 90 stores that closed temporarily, all but four were franchises. After such a crisis, being a franchise owner is both a blessing and a curse. While the franchisees have the marketing and financial strength of Taco Bell Corporation to back them up, they are also largely dependent on their parent company's public relations and advertising to lure customers back.[35]

Another disadvantage for some franchisees is that they, rather than their parent company, may be held liable for serving contaminated food. In response to the *E. coli* outbreak, some Taco Bell franchisees were named in lawsuits filed on behalf of customers who were sickened. The law holds the server of the food liable for such illnesses, but the franchise owners often try to pass the liability on to the parent company, the suppliers, distributors, or farmers. Franchise owners do not think they should be held liable for following company protocol and using the food suppliers dictated by the corporate parent.[36]

Government's Role and Response

Following the *E. coli* outbreak in the Northeast, lawmakers in New York called on the United States Food and Drug Administration (FDA), the Centers for Disease Control and Prevention (CDC), and the United States Department of Agriculture (USDA) to create a joint task force to examine the *E. coli* outbreak and recommend changes in laws and regulations to prevent contamination of food.[37] In April of 2007, the USDA published new guidelines for the produce industry to prevent contamination throughout the food supply chain, from before planting to the dinner table. Fortunately, food-borne illness has generally declined over the past decade. In an effort to maintain this trend, the industry is pushing for voluntary changes and not more government regulation.[38] The CDC, FDA, and USDA are all working together with state and local health departments to rapidly detect infections, identify sources, and provide information on treatment and prevention of *E. coli* O157:H7. According to Ken August from State Health Services, "The USDA is looking at [Taco Bell] distribution centers and trying to trace back products; the FDA is looking at [produce] products, and the CDC is continuing to look at the individual cases of illness."[39]

Center for Disease Control and Prevention (CDC)

The CDC is the leading federal agency for conducting disease surveillance and outbreak investigations in the United States.[40] It was founded in 1946 to help control malaria and now monitors the extent of outbreaks, either ongoing or concluded.

The CDC uses a case-control study with a standard epidemiological method to investigate an outbreak that involves comparing foods consumed by ill and well persons to show statistical links to particular food ingredients. This method focuses on ingredients consumed more often by ill rather than well persons. The PulseNet system matches illness in people to those in an outbreak and allows for rapid comparison of "DNA fingerprints" of E. coli O157.

The top priority of the CDC is to communicate health messages to the general population. It is one of thirteen major operating components of the Department of Health and Human Services (DHHS) and its primary goal is "protecting the health and safety of all Americans and providing essential human services, especially for those people who are least able to help themselves."[41]

Food and Drug Administration (FDA)

The FDA is responsible for regulating everything Americans eat, except meat, poultry, and processed egg products, which are regulated by the USDA. The FDA's role has grown more important in recent years as consumption of produce, and particularly "ready-to-eat" products, has greatly increased.

The FDA launched the Lettuce Safety Initiative in August 2006 due to spinach contamination in the Salinas Valley in California. The objectives of this initiative were to assess current industry approaches, alert customers early and respond rapidly once outbreaks occur, obtain information for use in developing guidance in hopes to minimize outbreaks in the future, and to consider regulatory action, if necessary.[42]

United States Department of Agriculture (USDA)

The USDA develops and executes policy on farming, agriculture, and food. It aims to meet the needs of farmers and ranchers, promote agricultural trade and production, and works to assure food safety. The USDA also concerns itself with assisting farmers with the sale of crops on both a domestic and world market. The USDA currently inspects the manufacturing plants where Taco Bell's ground beef is cooked and then shipped to restaurants.[43]

Financial Effects

As a result of the E. coli outbreak, Taco Bell sales at all U.S. restaurants nationwide decreased by 2 percent in the fourth quarter while operating profits fell $20 million. About half of the $20 million was due to lost sales, while the other half related to marketing, consumer research, legal and other expenses.[44] During the lowest point in the middle of December, sales were down as much as five percent. Since then, sales have begun to recover, but Taco Bell has still not completely won back its customer base. David Novak, Yum Chairman and Chief Executive, said, "loyalty among core customers remains strong, but the challenge is to get occasional diners back in Taco Bell restaurants."[45]

Despite the negative impact of the E. coli outbreak in the northeast U.S., Yum Brands fourth-quarter profits grew 3 percent thanks to strong international sales. Same store sales for Taco Bell fell 5 percent for the three months ended December 30, compared to a seven percent gain the previous year.[46]

Current and Impending Litigation

By March of 2007, 11 lawsuits had been filed against Yum Brands, Inc., and its Taco Bell Corp. subsidiary in response to the 2006 E. coli outbreak. At least five of the lawsuits named franchises that were not company owned, and Yum stated in its 2006 annual report that it was not liable for any losses at these restaurants. However, Yum said it had provided these franchises the estimated litigation costs.[47]

One of the first lawsuits was filed by Jared Keller when he fell ill with E. coli and was hospitalized for two days after eating food from a Taco Bell restaurant in Utica, New York, on November 25. The lawsuit accused the restaurant chain and a California farm of negligence and breach of warranty for serving tainted food. Keller's lawyer said the companies failed in their obligation to "prepare, serve and sell food that was fit for human consumption" and violated federal, state, and local food safety regulations.[48] The lawsuit names Yum Brands as a defendant, as well as Boskovich Farms, Inc., of Oxford, California, and Ready Pac Produce, Inc., of Irwindale, California. Keller is seeking unspecified damages but has already accumulated thousands of dollars in medial expenses.[49]

Taco Bell has made no comment on the lawsuits so far, but a spokesman for the restaurant chain, Rob Poetsch, stated, "All our efforts are focused on helping authorities get to the bottom of this. But I can say we are very concerned about all the people who have gotten ill."[50]

What Have Other Restaurant Chains Done?

In response to the recent *E. coli* outbreak, Taco John's made substantial efforts to win back its customers' loyalty and appetites. Company executives flew to Minnesota and Iowa, where the outbreak had occurred, and vowed to pay customers' medical bills. The company also advertised how it was changing its food-safety practices to make sure another outbreak did not occur. To increase positive publicity, Paul Fisherkeller, CEO of Taco John's, ate several chicken and beef tacos at the restaurants that had served the tainted food. The chain has also been very open with franchise owners, constantly updating them with new information and keeping "their confidence and energy strong."[51] Taco John's even provided financial assistance to three franchises and gave additional marketing and customer support.

What's Next For Taco Bell?

After the *E. coli* outbreak had ended, many Taco Bell customers responded to the issue:

> I eat there because it is cheap for how much food you get. Statistically, I thought I would be fine.
>
> —*Myles* Jeffrey, *16-year old high school senior*[52]

> Think about it, just because it happened, they are going to be cleaner.
>
> —*Hiral Patel, 20-year-old*[53]

> It didn't really bother me, I figure it's all safe, and they've taken care of it. Do you notice there's no one else here but me?
>
> —*Randy McLain, Data Processing Consultant*[54]

Sentiments like these may have offered Taco Bell a slight glimmer of hope, but Laurie Gannon knew the beleaguered food chain had a monumental task on it hands in convincing customers that its food was once again safe to eat. How should Taco Bell respond to the *E. coli* outbreak? How will the company rebuild customer confidence? Who should Taco Bell communicate with to alleviate the problem? What steps should the company take to improve the quality of its food and prevent future health concerns? How long would it be before lightning strikes Taco Bell again?

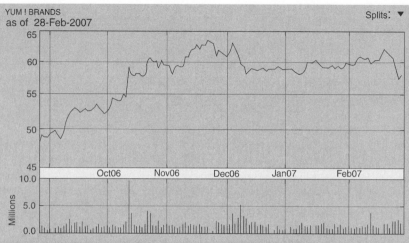

FIGURE 13-1 Yum! Brands Six-Month Stock Chart, September 2006–February 2007.

DISCUSSION QUESTIONS

1. What is Laurie Gannon's primary concern? What should be her first course of action? Which actions should follow from those?
2. Who are the key stakeholders in the case? Who has the most to gain or lose? What's at stake for each of them?
3. What should Taco Bell do to rebuild its customers' confidence and loyalty? What message should the company communicate to its customers? How should the message be communicated?
4. Whose responsibility is it to ensure the safety of the food served at Taco Bell? Who is to blame for the current *E. coli* outbreak?
5. What steps should Taco Bell take to prevent future contamination and to ensure that the entire supply chain is held to a high standard?
6. Should the FDA, CDC, and USDA impose more regulations on the food industry and suppliers, or should these industries be self-regulated?
7. How should Taco Bell respond to the current litigation? Should it accept liability or leave it in the hands of the franchisees? Should either Taco Bell Corp. or Yum Brands, Inc., provide litigation assistance to the affected franchises?
8. Will Taco Bell be able to maintain its customer base and sales levels in lieu of all the food quality and safety issues the company continues to face? What is unique about Taco Bell has allowed the company to survive similar health concerns in the past?

WRITING ASSIGNMENT

Please respond in writing to the issues presented in this case by preparing two documents: a communication strategy memo and a professional business letter.

In preparing these documents, you may assume one of two roles: you may identify yourself as a Taco Bell corporate manager who has been asked to provide advice to Ms. Laurie Gannon, Director of Public Relations, regarding the issues she and the company are facing. Or, you may identify yourself as an external management consultant who has been asked by the company to provide advice to Ms. Gannon.

Either way, you must prepare a strategy memo addressed to Ms. Gannon that summarizes the details of

the case, rank-orders critical issues, discusses their implications (what they mean and why they matter), offers specific recommendations for action (assigning ownership and suspense dates for each), and shows how to communicate the solution to all who are affected by the recommendations.

You must also prepare a professional business letter for the signature of Mr. David C. Novak, Chairman, CEO and President, Yum! Brands, Inc. That document may be addressed to any of Yum! Brands' key stakeholders, including customers, franchisees, investors, or others. If you have questions about either of these documents, please consult your instructor.

References

1. Martin, Andrew. "Left Holding the Bag in the Land of Fast Food," *The New York Times.* February 20, 2007.
2. DePalma, Anthony and Lambert, Bruce. "Gumshoe Work and Luck Helped in E. coli Case," *The New York Times.* December 10, 2006.
3. Tacobell.com. Our Company—Latest News.
4. Ibid.
5. Ibid.
6. Ibid.
7. Ibid.
8. Martin. "Left Holding the Bag in the Land of Fast Food."
9. Tacobell.com. Our Company—Interesting Facts.
10. Yum.com
11. Yumfranchises.com
12. Tacobell.com. Our Company—Interesting Facts.
13. Ibid.
14. The Associated Press. "Onions May Not Be E. coli Source After All," Msnbc.com. December 12, 2006.
15. Tacobell.com. "Taco Bell Tunes in to the New TNN with Multimillion-Dollar Viacom Marketing Deal."
16. Brazil, Eric. "Officials probe Bay Area E. coli cases," *The San Francisco Chronicle.* December 10, 1999.
17. Carver, Tom. " 'GM Tacos' Recalled," *BBC News.* September 25, 2000.
18. Marler, Bill. "Not to pile on Taco Bell, but how many times does lightning need to strike?" http://www.marlerblog.com, December 6, 2006.
19. Ibid.
20. Miller, Dan. "64 Sickened by Taco Bell E. coli; More Onions Test Positive." Cnn.com. December 12, 2006.
21. The Associated Press. "Taco John's Drops Supplier Amid E. coli Scare," Msnbc.com. December 12, 2006.
22. Pearson
23. Cdc.gov
24. Ibid.
25. Pearson
26. Cdc.gov
27. Jerry Hirsch and Rong-Gong Lin. "Lettuce is Suspect in Taco Bell E. coli Case," LATimes.com. December 14, 2006.
28. The Associated Press. "Onions may not be E. coli source after all."
29. Ibid.
30. Ken Belson and Ronald Smothers. "Reports on Illness Spread as Searchers Zero In on E. coli Source."
31. Ibid.
32. Martin. "Left Holding the Bag in the Land of Fast Food."
33. Hirsch and Lin. "Lettuce is Suspect in Taco Bell E. coli Case."
34. Martin. "Left Holding the Bag in the Land of Fast Food."
35. Ibid.
36. Ibid.
37. The Associated Press. "Onions May Not Be E. coli Source After All."
38. "E. Coli Spurs New Industry Guidelines." *The Wall Street Journal*, January 2, 2007. p. D.6.
39. Liddle, Alan. "Feds, Calif. Officials Probe E. coli Link to Taco Bell Units," *Nation's Restaurant News.* December 20, 1999.
40. Cdc.gov
41. Ibid.
42. FDA.gov
43. Liddle. "Feds, Calif. Officials Probe E. coli Link to Taco Bell Units."
44. Strott, Elizabeth. "Taco Bell and KFC: Not so YUM-my?" MSNMoney.com. February 23, 2007.
45. Msnbc.com. "E. coli Takes Bite out of Taco Bell Earnings."
46. Ibid.
47. "Eleven Suits Filed Over Taco Bell E. coli Outbreak." Bizjournals.com, February 28, 2007.
48. Kates, William, "NY Lawsuit Claims Taco Bell Served Food Unfit for Consumption," http://www.health.state.ny.us/diseases/communicable/e_coli/outbreak/, December 11, 2006.
49. Ibid.
50. Ibid.
51. Martin. "Left Holding the Bag in the Land of Fast Food."
52. Hirsch, Jerry. "E. coli Incident Takes a Bit Out of Taco Bell," *The Los Angeles Times.* February, 13, 2007.

53. Martin. "Left Holding the Bag in the Land of Fast Food."

54. Martin, Andrew. "With Onions No Longer the Top Suspect, the Search for E. coli Resumes." *The New York Times*. December 13, 2006.

This case was prepared by Research Assistants Andree Johnson, Daniel VanDerWerff, Steven Howenstein, and Kathryn Fromm, under the direction of James S. O'Rourke, Concurrent Professor of Management, as the basis for class discussion rather than to illustrate either effective or ineffective handling of an administrative situation. Information was gathered from corporate as well as public sources.

EXERCISE 13-1

Buon Giorno Italian Foods, Inc.

Please read and familiarize yourself with the information contained in this case. You have been designated to serve as an official representative of your firm and can expect to be interviewed by broadcast or print reporters on the incident described here. You may keep this fact sheet at hand during an interview and, if necessary, refer to it. Be aware that your credibility depends, to a degree, on your familiarity with the facts. Be aware, also, that a reporter may ask related questions not addressed by the information provided by this sheet. Do your best.

Background

You are a senior production manager with Buon Giorno Italian Foods, Inc., of Mishawaka, Indiana. Your supervisor, Mr. Anthony Delgado, is vice president for production for the firm. Your company has just one plant but grosses nearly $30 million per year, producing specialty Italian food items for wholesale distribution through food brokers to restaurants. Your company has recently launched a highly successful line of similar food items under the Buon Giorno label that are designed for retail sale through supermarkets and specialty food shops.

Your new line of specialty Italian soups has proven particularly successful throughout the Midwestern United States. The Mishawaka plant now produces more than 2,000 cases a month of the soups, including pasta e'fagiole, minestrone, and rigatoni aribiata. Your retail sales of these soups have tripled in the past six months and now account for 15 percent of

sales. The national and North American markets appear virtually unlimited.

Your firm purchases ingredients for your specialty food line from a number of different importers, most of them in New York and New Jersey. Your largest supplier of pasta is Dellafina Imports of Secaucus, New Jersey. Many of the fresh food stocks, including beans, onions, and other vegetables come from local and regional green grocers. Specialty items, such as anchovies, pimentos, dill, and other ingredients come from literally dozens of small food brokers in the Midwest and along the East Coast. Such items are price sensitive and you shop for the best bargains wherever they may be found.

The Facts of the Case

Your supervisor called you this morning and told you that the company president, Mr. Carmine Matuso, was notified by the Michigan Public Health Commissioner that your company's food products have been implicated in a series of mysterious deaths in the Midwest. The Michigan Public Health Service and several Michigan county coroners have quickly begun gathering data and reviewing autopsies dating back several months.

The link, according to Michigan Public Health Commissioner, Dr. Viola Nelson, was established tentatively over the weekend in Detroit when three people became seriously ill after eating what they claim were cans of your company's soup. Dr. Nelson [. . .] notified the FDA and regional public health officials, and contacted your CEO, Mr. Matuso, three days ago. Since that time, one additional death has been recorded under similarly suspicious circumstances in the

Birmingham, Michigan, area. Your boss has delayed telling you about this until today.

Health officials now suspect the culprit may be a deadly botulism bacterium in one or more batches of your Minestrone Milano. A quick series of telephone calls to production supervisors in the Mishawaka plant reveals that your people had heard rumors over the weekend and, in fact, several phone calls from Detroit area hospitals had been received.

The Executive Committee Decision

Following an executive committee meeting this morning at Buon Giorno Foods, the company has decided to begin an immediate recall of all Minestrone Milano. Some 6,000 cans of the soup are thought to be on supermarket shelves and in consumer cupboards throughout a seven-state area. The Minestrone Milano in question bears the lot number G-7114-AB9. That number is stamped on the bottom of the cans.

The committee has decided not to recall any other soup lines or any of the company's other products. Supermarkets are being asked to pull their shelf stocks and return them to the broker who supplied them. Consumers are asked to return the soups to the stores where they bought them. Above all, the committee feels, no one should panic over this matter. After all, no definitive link has yet been established between your products and the illnesses and deaths in Michigan.

The company has retained the service of Blank, Hobbes, Harter and Freeman, a Chicago law firm specializing in product liability. Your firm has also contracted the services of an epidemiologist and a pathologist from St. Joseph Hospital, South Bend, Indiana. They're planning to examine your production and processing equipment and packaging facilities, perhaps as early as tomorrow. Your task is to explain this to the press and the public.

This case was prepared from public sources by James S. O'Rourke, Concurrent Professor of Management, as the basis for class discussion rather than to illustrate either effective or ineffective handling of an administrative situation. Personal identities have been disguised.

EXERCISE 13-2

O'Brien Paint Company

Please read and familiarize yourself with the information contained in this case. You have been designated to serve as an official representative of your firm and can expect to be interviewed by broadcast or print reporters on the incident described here. You may keep this fact sheet at hand during an interview and, if necessary, refer to it. Be aware that your credibility depends, to a degree, on your familiarity with the facts. Be aware, also, that a reporter may ask related questions not addressed by the information provided by this sheet. Do your best.

The Facts of the Case

A fire broke out early this morning in the Western Avenue plant of the O'Brien Paint Company. A night security officer smelled smoke in one of the bulk storage facilities and called local fire officials on the 9-1-1 emergency line. When the officer returned from the telephone to the scene of the fire, he saw flames and immediately recognized the danger to various paints and chemicals stored in the area. He removed a handheld fire extinguisher from the wall unit in the storage facility and attempted to extinguish the flames himself; he was largely unsuccessful.

A pumper unit, a hook-and-ladder unit, one rescue unit, and a command vehicle responded to the fire call from the Fire Department's #7 Station, located at 1616 Portage Avenue. Those units were under the command of Fire Captain Cazimir Pelazinski and arrived on the scene 4 minutes and 30 seconds after the emergency call was received, at approximately 3:25 A.M.

By the time the fire units arrived, flames had spread from the bulk storage area to a production unit, a packaging room, and a box and dry-storage facility. Because of the spreading flames, Captain Pelazinski upgraded the fire designation from one alarm to three and called for two backup pumper units from Fire Station #6 at 4302 Western Avenue; those units were on scene by 3:41 A.M. Fire officials briefly considered evacuating the surrounding neighborhood, mostly low-income, single-family dwellings and a few low-rise apartment buildings, because of the toxic nature of smoke and fumes from the fire. A significant danger of explosion from paint, chemicals, varnish, turpentine, and other products also existed at the time.

For a variety of reasons, fire officials elected not to evacuate the neighborhood. The fire was eventually brought under control by approximately 7:20 A.M. but has not yet been declared fully extinguished.

The security officer, Rupert J. Watson, 37, of 819 Christiana Street, was unhurt in the incident. He has been employed by O'Brien Paints, Inc., since October 14, 2007, as a security specialist. Mr. Watson is a native of the local area and a veteran of the U.S. Army; he served as a combat infantryman in [the] Persian Gulf during Operation Iraqi Freedom in 2005–2006.

Your supervisor, Mr. Fredrick J. McQuethy, who is assistant vice president for production, spoke with you by telephone this morning for several minutes. At this point, apparently, no cause for the fire can be specified, though both you and Mr. McQuethy are aware that several small fires have broken out in the Western Avenue Plant in recent months, none of them causing extensive damage. Mr. McQuethy is personally convinced that militant trade unionists in the plant set the fire. The collective bargaining agreement with members of International Brotherhood of Oil, Atomic and Chemical Workers, local 326, is set to expire in less than 30 days. The union is adamant about renegotiating elements of the contract dealing with compensation, job security, and working conditions in the Western Avenue plant.

The building was last inspected 11 months ago by a local fire marshal and was due for inspection in about 30 days. Several minor fire safety discrepancies were noted in the previous inspection but were corrected in a matter of weeks. The production area was equipped with a fire suppression system that functioned satisfactorily. The storage units, however, were equipped a bit differently. They were protected by a sprinkler system that apparently failed, permitting a substantial amount of damage to occur. All areas were in compliance with state and local fire ordinances.

One last item: The police have been called in by the fire department within the past hour to investigate the charred remains of an individual found in the fire rubble. As far as you know, that individual is not an employee of the firm. The security officer, Mr. Watson, claims no knowledge of anyone on the plant grounds last evening and has told investigators he has no idea how someone could have gotten in the building without his knowledge or permission. Police, thus far, are silent on this matter.

Damage to portions of the plant is extensive, but production could probably resume within a week to ten days, depending on the findings of the fire investigators. Most short-term orders could be filled by the O'Brien Paint plants in Alameda, California, and Linden, New Jersey, until that time.

Your task is to explain all of this to the press and the public. Keep in mind that the news media may have interests that are different from those of the immediate neighborhood, the community at large, O'Brien Paint employees, and O'Brien shareholders.

APPENDIX A
ANALYZING A CASE STUDY

Among the many tools available to business educators, the case study has become increasingly popular. Professors use it to teach the complexities of many different, modern business problems. That's not a surprising development. Beyond the fundamentals, memorization and description will take you just so far. The real test of whether you are ready to manage a business will come when you are asked to assume the role of a manager, step into an authentic business situation, make sense of the circumstances you see, draft a plan, and take action.

WHY STUDY CASES?

Schools of law have studied cases for many years as a means of exploring legal concepts and understanding the practices of the courts. Harvard Business School began inviting executives and managers into their classrooms after the First World War, hoping to provide students with some insight into the thinking of successful businesspeople. Not long afterward, professors of business began writing down the narratives of these business managers in an effort to capture the ambiguities and complexities involved in the day-to-day practice of commerce and administration.

The idea spread to other schools of business and migrated from graduate to undergraduate programs. Today, many business educators use case studies because their narratives are so valuable in developing analytic and critical thinking abilities, as well as organizational and communication skills. You can memorize lists, procedures, and attributes. You can occasionally guess successfully at the answer to a multiple-choice question. But you cannot memorize the answer to a problem you have never encountered, nor can you guess at the options available to a manager who must resolve a complex, difficult, often ambiguous situation.

TYPES OF CASES

Although each case is different, you are likely to encounter three basic types of case studies, depending on the subject you are studying: field cases, library cases (sometimes referred to as *public record cases*), and armchair cases.

Field Cases

Field cases are written by professors and students of business with the cooperation of managers and executives who experienced the events and problems described in the case. They involve extensive interviews with people who are often identified by name as the narrative unfolds. Information contained in these cases is known best—and sometimes only—to insiders in a business. Newspaper accounts and descriptions of events contained in the business press may play a role in establishing key facts, but the sequence of events—what was said to whom, what each manager knew at the time, and which managerial options were open to the principals of the case—are often a mystery to the public-at-large.

Extensive interviews with employees, managers, and executives will often reveal more. Careful examination of business records and databases can provide background and context for the events. And, frequently, the active cooperation of a company is the only way a case author will ever know exactly what happened with any measure of certainty.

Field cases are often more extensive and thorough than other case types but present a dilemma for the case writer: What does the company have to gain by granting access to its premises, its records, and its employees? Is this merely an attempt to make executives look good after the fact? Are such cases an attempt at public relations when things go wrong in a business? Often, to gain access to a business, a case writer must have some special relationship with those who own or manage it and must have a reputation for reporting on events in an accurate and fair manner. One disadvantage of such cases is that, once they are published, they are difficult to modify and may quickly become dated.

Library Cases

Unlike a field case, library or public record cases do not involve special access to the businesses being studied. They do not involve interview material or direct quotes that are unavailable elsewhere. And they most often do not include figures, data, or information that are not somehow a part of the public record, available to anyone with a library card, Internet access, and basic research skills.

Companies that have failed somehow—blown a great opportunity, overlooked the obvious, chosen the wrong path, or failed to act when they should have—are understandably reluctant to permit case writers to speak with their employees or look at the evidence. If they've done something terribly wrong—committed a crime or imperiled the public welfare—a company may do all it can to withhold, obscure, or cover up what has happened. That is precisely the challenge facing most business reporters as they gather information for publication each day.

Writers who produce library cases, however, have a wealth of information available to them. In addition to stories produced for broadcast, print, and online news organizations, business case writers can look to numerous government documents and other sources, particularly for publicly held firms. Annual filings with the Securities and Exchange Commission, such as forms 10-Q, 10-K, and 8-K can be very helpful, as well.

When one company declares its intention to acquire another or is sued in federal court, numerous documents relevant to the issues at hand may become a part of the public record. When a company prepares to launch an IPO or float a bond offering, numerous public disclosures are required. Case writers have a high degree of confidence in the accuracy of such records, because the penalty for falsifying them may involve heavy fines or jail time.

Armchair Cases

Armchair cases are fictional documents about companies that don't really exist and events that have never really occurred. Although they bear some resemblance to authentic cases, they are often lacking in the richness of detail and complexity that accompany real events. They may be useful, however, in introducing basic concepts to students or in provoking a discussion about key issues confronting businesses.

Business educators produce armchair cases when they are denied access to the people and data of real businesses or when they wish to reduce complex events to a series of simple decision opportunities. Armchair cases are often useful to begin a discussion about change management, the introduction of technology, or a rapidly unfolding set of events in other cultures. A principal advantage of these cases is that they can be modified and updated at will without securing the permission of the fictional companies and managers they describe.

PRODUCING A CASE SOLUTION

Producing a case solution that demonstrates you are ready for management-level responsibility will involve the following steps:

Read the Case

The first step to a successful case solution is to read the case, carefully and with an eye for detail, more than once. Personality theorists tell us that some people are eager to get to the end of a story quickly. "Don't bother me with details," they say. "Just tell me what happened." Such people, often dependent on *Cliff's Notes* and executive summaries, will bypass the details of a case in order to reach a conclusion about what happened in the story. They are often reluctant to read the case attachments and will frequently avoid tables of numbers altogether. Many arrive at conclusions quickly and begin formulating responses before they have all the facts. The less clever in this crowd see the details of a case as a nuisance; reading the facts will only interfere with their preparation of a response.

After you have read and thought about the issues in a case, if you are uncertain about what to do, read it again. As you mature in the experiences of business school, you will get better at this, but at first, your best defense against being surprised or frustrated by a case is to read it thoroughly.

Take Notes

College students typically want to either underline or highlight much of what is contained in a book chapter, reprint, or essay. Case studies, however, are constructed a bit differently. Textbook chapters are typically organized in a hierarchical fashion, with key points and sub-points listed in order of importance, carefully illustrated and summarized. Not so with case studies, which are often simply arranged in chronological order. Textbooks usually proceed in logical fashion, with one concept building on others that came before it. Case studies, on the other hand, are seemingly chaotic: Many events happen at once, order and discipline are sometimes missing, and key issues are not always self-evident.

Case studies may also contain substantial amounts of information in tabular form: annual revenues, product shipment rates, tons of raw materials processed, or cost data organized by business units. To know what such data mean, you will have to read the tables and apply what you have learned about reading a balance sheet, or about activity-based costing. You may find crucial information contained in a sequence of events or a direct quote from a unit manager. Sometimes you will discover that the most important issues are never mentioned by the principals in the case—they are simply ideas or tools that they weren't clever enough to think of, or didn't think were important at the time.

Your notes should focus on the details you will need to identify the business problems involved in the case, the issues critical to solving those problems, as well as the resources available to the managers in the case. Those notes will be helpful in producing a case solution.

Identify the Business Problem

In each case, at least one fundamental business problem is present. It may be a small, tactical issue, such as how this company will collect money from a delinquent customer. But the issue may be broader in nature: "How can they reduce accounts receivable ageing to 30 days or less?" Larger, more strategic problems might involve the company's chronic, critical cash-flow difficulties. "If this company were no longer cash-starved, what longer-term opportunities might open up?"

You may identify more than one problem in a case. Complex cases often involve several such problems simultaneously. They may be technical in nature and involve accounting or cost control systems. They may involve the use of technology. You might see supply-chain problems in the business you are studying. You may identify marketing deficiencies. Or, you might see human problems that involve supervision, communication, motivation, or training.

Specify an Objective for the Managers Involved

Once you have identified one or more business problems present in the case, think about the outcome(s) you would most hope to see for the company and people you have read about. If you were asked to consult on this company's problems—and that is the role most business students are playing as they read a case study—what results would you hope for? Don't limit your thinking to what the company should *do*, but what the most *successful outcome* would look like. Be specific about how the company will know whether it has succeeded. Quantify the desired results whenever you can.

Identify and Rank Order the Critical Issues

These issues are at the heart of the case. If you miss a critical issue, you may not be able to solve the case to the satisfaction of your professor.

- *Some issues are interdependent.* That is, a solution to one issue might necessarily precede or depend on another. In a product-contamination case, for example, a media relations team can't draft a press release until the production or packaging team knows what's wrong with the product. The team responsible for a new product launch can't make final advertising and promotion decisions until issues related to packaging, transportation, and distribution have been solved.
- *Some issues are more important than others.* A company may have a great opportunity to launch a product line extension but not have sufficient market research data to support the idea. More to the point, they may not have the talent on staff to understand and properly use such data. Thus, hiring a market research chief might be more important than simply contracting with an outside firm to find the data.
- *Each issue has a time dimension.* Even though two problems may be equally important to the success of a company, one may be near term in nature while the other is long term. Upgrading a corporate Web site may be important, but it won't solve the longer-term issue of marketing strategy: Should we sell directly over the Web or use retail partners to market our products? Specify which problems must be addressed first, but think, as well, about the duration of the solutions—how long will it take to fix this?
- *Some issues are merely symptoms of larger or deeper problems.* Two managers in open warfare with each other about budget or resource issues may be symptomatic of more serious, long-term budget problems, inadequate communication among the management team, or perhaps a corporate culture that encourages confrontation over minor issues. When Sears Roebuck & Co. discovered that auto service managers in California were charging customers to replace parts that were not yet worn out, the problem was deeper than a few overzealous managers. After analyzing the complaints brought by the California Attorney General, Sears realized that their compensation system rewarded managers for selling more parts, and not for simply servicing customers' vehicles.

Consider Relevant Information and Underlying Assumptions

Accept the fact that much of the information contained in the case will not be useful to your analysis. You should also accept the fact that you will never know all that you would like in order to produce a solution. Life is like that. So are case studies. Identify the relevant facts contained in the case and think carefully about them. Identify additional information you might like to have—that might be part of your solution—but don't dwell on it.

Separate facts from assumptions. Recognize that there are some things you will know for sure and others that you will not. Recognize further that you may be required to subjectively interpret some evidence and to assume other evidence not directly stated in the case. The more suppositions you make, however, the weaker your analysis becomes.

List Possible Solutions to the Problem

Just about every problem lends itself to more than one solution. Keep looking for good ideas, even when you have already thought of one that will solve the problem. Listing possible solutions is a form of brainstorming that will later permit you to assign values or weights to those ideas: Is one solution less expensive than another? Will one be more effective than another? Will one idea work more quickly? Will one of these ideas have a more enduring effect?

Select a Solution

After assigning weights and values to the various solutions you have thought about, select the one you like best and prepare to defend it. Show why the ideas you have thought about are superior and how they will work. If you have rejected other, more obvious ideas, you may want to explain why.

Decide How to Implement the Best Solution

Having good ideas is insufficient. You must be able to put them to work. Graduate students of business are often praised by executives for being theoretically well-grounded but criticized for lacking practical application. "A team of young MBAs told me that we needed to sell this division of my company," said an executive in the chemical industry. "But they couldn't tell me what to do or how to go about it. All they knew was that we should try to find a buyer. Interesting," he concluded, "but not very helpful."

Explain How to Communicate the Solution

In a management communication case study, you will be asked to identify key audiences for your message. That means identifying which groups you want to communicate with and the means you will use to reach them. Think carefully about the broad range of *stakeholders* in the case: employees, customers, shareholders, business partners, suppliers, regulators, and the marketplace at large. Identify exactly how you would plan to transmit your message, assure that it has been received and understood, and think about how you would analyze feedback from those audiences. You should think, as well, about timing and sequencing of messages. Who should you speak with first? Who should send the message? How should this particular audience hear about this particular message?

Write It Up

Different professors will have different expectations about what they want from you in a written case solution. They will probably not provide you with specific, detailed instructions regarding their expectations, but they will certainly tell you if you've missed the boat or have produced a solid response. Some will ask for wide-ranging responses that cover many issues, while others will expect a more focused response. Just provide your professor with your best thinking and be as detailed as you think you can within the page limits you've been given.

WHAT YOU SHOULD EXPECT

If you have read the case thoroughly, identified the business problems, rank ordered the critical issues, proposed various solutions, and then identified how you will implement and communicate them, you can expect to be relatively well prepared for classroom case discussion. Here's what else you should expect:

- *An occasional cold call.* Be prepared for your professor to ask you to provide key details from the case, sometimes referred to as a "shred." Simply explain what happened in the case, identifying the business and its principals, and give your best thinking on critical issues in two minutes or less. Don't worry about providing a solution just yet. Your professor is likely to want a more thorough discussion of the issues first. If you are feeling especially confident, you may wish to volunteer.
- *A logical, step-by-step approach.* If classmates offer information that is useful but not relevant or in line with the question the professor asks, wait for the discussion to return to the issues the professor thinks are most important before you move on.
- *Different approaches from different professors.* No two professors are exactly the same in their approach or preferences. Virtually all of them, however, appreciate a bold, "do something" approach over hedging, caution, and a reluctance to act.

WHAT YOU SHOULD NOT EXPECT

- *More information.* From time to time, your professor will present you with a "B" case that offers new or subsequent information. Such cases represent an extension of the facts in the "A" case and usually provide another managerial decision opportunity. For the most part, though, the information given in the "A" case is all you will have and you must make do with that.
- *A "right answer."* Because case studies are most often based on real events, no one can say for certain what would have happened if your ideas or other, "better" ideas had been implemented. Some solutions are clearly better than others, but many ideas will work. Some of the very best ideas may not yet have been thought of or spoken aloud.
- *An explanation of what "actually happened."* Many professors either don't know what happened to the managers and the businesses described in your case studies or they don't think that your having that information will be useful or productive in the learning process. Your own thinking may be limited or skewed if you focus on actual outcomes.
- *A single discipline focus to each case.* Although some cases are principally about accounting, they may contain issues related to finance, operations management, human resources, or communication. Authentic business problems are rarely, if ever, unidimensional. The more you are willing to think about other dimensions of business and their interdependency, the more you will learn about how real businesses work.
- *That your response will solve all of the problems in the case.* Focus on the most important, most urgent, and most relevant problems first. You may wish to identify issues for further thought or investigation by the management team described in the case, but you cannot and should not try to solve all the problems in the case.

In summary, your task is to read, identify, and understand the business problems in the case. By identifying, rank ordering, and exploring the critical issues it contains, you should be able to propose a workable solution, identifying how to implement and communicate it. From that point forward, you must explain your choices in writing and be ready to defend them in the classroom.

For Further Reading

Barnes, L. B., Christensen, C. R., and A. J. Hansen. *Teaching and the Case Method*, 3rd ed. Boston, MA: Harvard Business School Press, 1994.

Bouton, C. and Garth R. (ed.). *Learning in Groups.* San Francisco, CA: Jossey-Bass, 1983.

Corey, R. "The Use of Cases in Management Education," Harvard Business School Case No. 376–240.

Erskine, J., Leenders, M. R., and Mauffette-Leenders, L. A. *Teaching with Cases.* London, Ontario: School of Business, University of Western Ontario, 1981.

Gragg, C. J. "Because Wisdom Can't Be Told," *The Case Method at the Harvard Business School.* New York: McGraw-Hill, 1954, p. 6.

McNair, M. P. "The Genesis of the Case Method in Business Administration," *The Case Method at the Harvard Business School.* New York: McGraw-Hill, 1954, pp. 25–33.

Penrose, J. M., Raspberry, R. W., and R. J. Myers. "Analyzing and Writing a Case Report," *Advanced Business Communication*, 3rd ed. Cincinnati, OH: South-Western College Publishing, 1997.

Wasserman, S. *Put Some Thinking in Your Classroom.* Chicago, IL: Benefic Press, 1978.

This teaching note was prepared from personal interviews and public sources by James S. O'Rourke, Teaching Professor of Management, as the basis for class discussion.

APPENDIX B
WRITING A CASE STUDY

For the better part of a century now, business schools worldwide have used the case study as a principal learning tool in business education. Schools in North America, such as Harvard, Wharton, Darden, Mendoza, Ivey, Tuck, and others, have made the case study method a central part of the way they prepare managers to step into authentic business situations, analyze the circumstances they have encountered, and take action.

WHAT IS A BUSINESS CASE STUDY?

A business case study is, essentially, a story. It's a narrative tale about a problem, challenge, or opportunity faced by a manager or executive that students are asked to read, think about, and respond to. The contents of a case study—including narrative details, direct quotations from those involved in the events of the case, and attachments—will form the basis for an analytic discussion. Those discussions are often conducted aloud in a classroom, while others are conducted on paper between professor and student.[1]

THE CHARACTERISTICS OF A CASE STUDY

The stories offered up in a business case usually do not include either direct answers or disclosure of the resolution to the business problem. The point of such documents is to gather as much information as possible to explain what happened to the business as accurately, fairly, and completely as possible, incorporating as many viewpoints as the author can reasonably accommodate. Such cases are never written for the purpose of identifying heroes and villains, but for the purpose of beginning a discussion about business problems.

Case studies are different from case histories in several important respects. First, as noted, a case study does not provide answers, outcomes, alternatives, or resolution to the problems encountered by the managers depicted in the story. Instead, they provide enough detail for readers to understand the nature and scope of the problem, and they serve as a springboard for discussion and learning.

A case history, on the other hand, often summarizes events, describing not only what happened to create the problem, conditions, or opportunity facing the manager, but frequently revealing the manager's response in detail. Case histories are usually more focused on managerial responses and solutions than they are on the events leading to a decision point. And, by revealing what the company actually did in response to the crisis or events, such brief, historical summaries often limit student thinking and suppress the wide-ranging, open forms of imagination that case studies are designed to stimulate.

A business case study, then, is really a learning tool. It's an instrument that provides a discussion leader with an opportunity to explore issues that do not lend themselves to deduction or memorization. It is designed to promote analytic problem solving and teach critical thinking.

Case studies are not particularly well suited to training in which learners will be asked to memorize approved responses to carefully defined stimuli. They're really much better at promoting learning in situations that involve ambiguity, uncertainty, and multiple outcomes. If an instructor aims at having all students arrive at a single, correct solution, a case study might not be the best tool to facilitate learning.

On the other hand, if an instructor has learning objectives in mind that focus on the process of identifying and analyzing business problems, followed by a discussion in which various possible responses might be implemented, a case study may be a suitable tool.

WHY STUDY BUSINESS CASES?

The principal difference between training and education, according to educational philosopher John Dewey, is that—however necessary it may be—training merely modifies external habits of action. Learners are presented with a menu of stimuli and taught to respond with an approved behavior. It's fairly easy to test for learning proficiency when a trainer can offer a stimulus or situation to a learner who can, in turn, exhibit the approved response.

Education, on the other hand, is designed to provide learners with the intellectual and analytic skills they will need to solve problems they've never seen, and to respond to stimuli they could not have imagined as students. Without a comprehensive menu of stimuli and responses, students must rely on the values acquired during their education. Knowing what they value, what the hierarchy of those values is, and why they have arranged them in that fashion will be enormously useful to a student later in life. Training and education are both essential to our success, of course, but only education can prepare us for circumstances we have yet to encounter.[2]

TYPES OF CASES

Although each case is different, you are likely to encounter three basic types of case studies, depending on the subject you are studying: field cases, library cases (sometimes referred to as *public record cases*), and armchair cases. For a detailed description of each, please refer to Appendix A, "Analyzing a Case Study."

SELECTING A SUBJECT

If you're interested in writing a business case study, you should begin by selecting a topic that is interesting both to you and to your prospective audience. If you have some passion for the subject, you'll be more likely to know what the issues are, who the key players may be, and which sources would be most useful to consult. The subject must also be of interest to a significant number of people in your prospective audience. A case study—no matter how well researched, organized, and expressed—that interests only a few people is unlikely to reach a wide audience and achieve the goals you've set for the project.

In choosing a topic to write about, you must understand the audience for whom you are writing. Will they have the intellectual and professional skills to understand the issues and events in the case? Will they have a working knowledge of the processes, structures, and organizations you plan to describe? Will they understand the vocabulary of the industry or profession you're writing about? The more general knowledge your audience has about the subject, the better. If necessary, you may need to define terms, explain concepts, and provide examples that will help your audience better understand the issues in the case.

It also helps if the events you plan to write about are not seriously out-of-date. If most events described in your case are more than five years old, you might consider switching to a more current topic. Finally, you must have access to accurate, reliable, and current information about the events that you hope to describe. It's one thing to select an interesting subject. It's quite another to get informed sources to talk with you about it.

BEGINNING YOUR RESEARCH

Once you've selected your subject, you must begin preliminary research to make certain you have a viable topic. This would include a review of newspaper files and online databases such as Factiva or NYTimes.com; broadcast Web sites, such as CNN.com or MSNBC.com; or, other news-gathering sources such as Associated Press and Reuters. You may even wish to pick up the telephone and ask to speak with relatively low-ranking people who may know something about the topic you've chosen.

If you are not yet confident that you have access to enough information to write the case, you should set a firm "go/no-go" decision date, backed up by at least one or two alternative topic ideas. Knowing whether you have enough information is often very subjective but you'll quickly develop a sense of confidence about whether your principal problem is too much information and not enough perspective, or too little information and not enough cooperation.

Make Some Choices

When you are confident that you have a viable topic, you must then select:

- **The perspective** from which the story is to be told. Who is the decision maker in this case? From whose perspective will the reader see the details of the case?
- **The start-and-stop dates** for the story. Each story begins at a moment in time and concludes with a decision point for the manager. You may choose to start at the beginning of the story, or you may select a relatively recent but crucial moment in the sequence of events, and then move back to the beginning to lay out other details. Either way, this decision is important for you as a writer.
- **The kind and level of detail** that you plan to include in the story. Some issues can be included as a passing reference in the dependent clause of just one sentence. Others will require their own boldface heading and several paragraphs (or pages) to describe in detail. Don't overwhelm your readers with detail that is unnecessary to understand the story and issues involved, but—on the other hand—don't assume that they already understand the finer points, or know who each of the principal characters is.

Make Some Lists

The next step in your research will involve several issues that you may wish to include in your Teaching Notes.

- **Construct a timeline** with key events in chronological order. This timeline may run to several pages, but it will help you (and, perhaps, your readers) to keep people, issues, and events straight. It's easy to forget what happened when, and in what sequence; a detailed timeline will be helpful.
- **Identify key players** in the story, by name and by role. Explain to the readers who they are, what their background is, and why they're important to the case. Again, if more than just a few people are involved, an alphabetical list may be helpful to you as you begin writing.
- **Identify the critical issues** in the case, rank ordering them by importance to the executive decision maker. You would not wish to directly reveal these issues to your readers, but you will want to include them in your Teaching Notes. This list would include, from most important to least important, those issues the executive or manager will need to think about and address, along with a brief explanation of why they are important. Remember, what seems crucial to one observer may not be important at all to another. This list will be the basis for an interesting and animated discussion.

Consider a Spreadsheet

Although it's not essential, a two-axis matrix or text-based spreadsheet (Excel, Lotus, QuatroPro, and others) may be useful in tracking the details of your case. Along the x-axis (horizontal), list the key events or issues as reported in the public record or documented in your interviews. Along the y-axis (vertical), list the source for each of those. Check off each item so that you'll know where you found it and how many sources have reported the same information.

You will, of course, have greater confidence in those facts that are reported by just about every source. You may wish to pay special attention to those items that are "one of a kind," or available to you from just one source. Ask yourself why that may be so. Is that one source particularly knowledgeable or well informed? Are you sure it's accurate? If you are unable to confirm (or corroborate) that information, you must decide whether you believe it. If you don't believe it, cross it off and do not include it in the case. If you do believe it, you are obligated to explain in your narrative that the information comes from just one source and, if possible, identify that source in the text.

The Division of Labor

Once you're sure you have a viable case and enough information to begin, it may be useful to assign responsibility for various actions:

- Gathering financial data information about the firm
- Doing historical research on the companies and people involved
- Saving photos and screen-grabs for your PowerPoint presentation
- Saving videotape of the evening news, if your case involves ongoing events or breaking news
- Looking for streaming video of press conferences, interviews, commercials, or other products that may be useful in framing a discussion of the case
- Scheduling personal or telephone interviews with key figures in the case

TIME TO BEGIN WRITING

Once you're sure of your topic, your sources, and your approach to the issues—and you have established the key decision maker's perspective, your timeline, and the start–stop dates—and all team members are clear on their obligations, it's probably time to begin writing.

Your case need not be written in sequence, beginning with the opening paragraph, and it need not be written entirely by one person. But your writing style must be consistent throughout and must flow easily and effortlessly for the reader. You can certainly delegate different research and writing tasks to different members of the team, but one person—preferably the best writer—must be responsible for reading, integrating, editing, and revising the final product.

As you begin, make absolutely certain that you have at least one reliable source (preferably more) for everything you plan to say or include in the case. Insert the footnotes or endnotes as you write, not later on. Don't create additional work for yourself by saying, "I'll come back later and figure out which sources each of these facts and quotes came from." The opportunity for error grows with each draft of the paper. You must be scrupulous about accurately documenting everything.

To make life easier as you write, make photocopies and keep detailed notes. Copy down dates, times, page numbers, volume and edition numbers, and anything else that will help to reveal to your readers where this information came from. Avoid any confusion about who said something or about the source of a fact important to your case.

PREPARE A FIRST DRAFT

As you begin writing, it is important to grab the reader's attention directly with an anecdote, a quote, an event, or a revealing fact of some sort. If you cannot convince your reader in the first few paragraphs that the case is worth reading, many of them may give up or simply skim through to pick up highlights. No matter how you begin, you must make the sequence of events clear from the first paragraph. Don't give your readers an opportunity to get lost or become confused.

Move next to an explanation of the company or organization's history, the industry in which it operates, the products or services it produces, and the annual revenues it generates. You should give some attention, as well, to the size of the company's employee base and market share.

Having established a big-picture overview of the company and industry, you should next introduce key characters in the case, along with various role players and decision makers. As readers move from paragraph to paragraph, they should develop a clear notion of who will be responsible for the decisions you will ask them to think about in the final few sentences.

Here are a few suggestions to keep in mind as you get your first draft down on disk and, later, on paper:

- Explain in plain English what happened, when, and how.
- Identify all relevant assumptions.
- Reveal your sources in text, where necessary.
- Don't look for conclusions, causal factors, or solutions just yet.
- Be specific. Quantify where possible.
- Use direct quotes, identifying and qualifying those whom you quote.
- Identify those issues you don't understand and those questions you cannot answer. Save them for the executive or managerial interviews you hope to schedule later.

CONSULT MULTIPLE SOURCES

A one-source case is dangerous. Your principal or sole source could, quite simply, be mistaken about things. He or she could have a political point of view or an axe to grind that would skew or color the information you receive. The result could be a case study that is simply embarrassing as other important details emerge. Protect yourself and your teammates by consulting as many sources and viewpoints as you possibly can.

Consider frontline supervisors, hourly workers, as well as senior executives for telephone, e-mail, or face-to-face interviews. Remember, though, that each has a point of view and a motive for talking with you. Your goal is accuracy, completeness, and fairness in your presentation of the facts.

Read broadly. Consider out-of-town publications, even foreign publications for differing viewpoints. If you can't make sense of all the facts, consider calling a reporter who has written on or covered this story. Ask if he or she will speak with you. Many of them are more than happy to share what they know with sincere, well-mannered students.

Talk to various stakeholders, including customers, suppliers, shareholders, community and civic officials, regulatory agency officials, employees, or competitors. You might even think about speaking with people who live in the neighborhood around the company or others who may have been affected by the events of the case.

If people won't talk with you, be polite and offer to show them the preliminary draft of your work. Offer to let them mark it up or suggest changes. Make them a partner in the process. Your work is, in some ways, like that of a journalist, but the rules of the game are different. A reporter would never let a source see the story before it's published. You have nothing to lose by showing your work to a source. If the reasons they offer for suggesting changes make sense to you, the case will be better for your having asked.

PREPARE A SECOND DRAFT

Assemble what you've written. Read it for storyline flow as well as grammar and syntax. Your goal is to make it lively, tightly written, cogent, and correct. It must be interesting to read, but it must—above all else—be right.

Consider including tables, figures, stock charts, diagrams, maps, or other visual devices in the text to help explain the story to your reader. If you devise these yourself, you won't need the permission of a publisher or Internet site to use them. If you download a stock chart from Yahoo! Finance or CNN.com, you'll have to e-mail them and ask if you can use the graphic. Most news-gathering organizations will gladly let you use their work for free, as long as you acknowledge the source and indicate that it was used by permission. Some sources, particularly print magazines, will ask that you pay a royalty for the privilege of reprinting large portions of their work. You'll have to decide for yourself whether you are willing or able to do that.

Don't even think about publishing your second draft. Show it to a trusted colleague, an associate, your professor, or someone whose professional opinions you value. Make certain it's as good as you can possibly make it, and as grammatically correct as you are able. Then, read it again, just to be sure.

PREPARE YOUR TEACHING NOTE

Every good case study includes a Teaching Note. That's simply a document that explains what the case is about, what the issues and options may be, and how an instructor might go about leading a discussion of the case. Most Teaching Notes are just a few pages in length but will contain valuable information about how to probe for student thinking, how to time the discussion, and what to expect as students offer various viewpoints. At the least, a comprehensive Teaching Note should include:

- The purpose of the case study.
- A clear statement of the *business problem.* Not the communication or public relations problem, but the central business problem in the case.
- A forecast of the most desirable outcome. If you could write a "Hollywood ending" for this case, what would it be? What do the various stakeholders most want or hope for?
- A statement and rank-ordering of the critical issues in the case. You might also briefly explain why each issue is important.
- A list of stakeholders and what's at stake for each of them.
- A list of definitions for specialized or unusual terms. You might also think about issues, concepts, or ideas that students might have trouble with. What sort of things need additional explanation as the discussion moves along?
- A list of possible solutions to the problem.
- A plan for implementing and communicating the optimal solution.
- A plan for teaching the case, including what you believe the instructor should do prior to the discussion to prepare the class, and suggestions on how to spend class time during the first 5–10 minutes, the next 30 minutes, and so on. Suggest ways to summarize and wrap up the discussion, as well.
- A timeline of events and a series of five or six discussion questions would also be helpful.

You need not suggest a specific course of action in your Teaching Notes, if you'd rather not, but you should acknowledge various approaches that students may mention in discussion. You may also wish to reveal what actually happened in the case (if you know), but you would certainly not want to include any of those details in the case itself.

Complex cases may include not only a printed timeline, but also a glossary of specialized terms, and financial data, such as balance sheets, profit-and-loss statements, or cash statements. You must have permission, of course, to use those documents unless they are made public as part of an annual report or SEC filing.

PREPARE YOUR POWERPOINT

Think visually as you prepare your ideas for the big screen. Look for ways to show people what happened. Include visual images that will help carry your message:

- Photos of key characters or company officials
- Company logotypes, symbols, or trademarks
- Products, people, events, or other images that will generate visual interest

Keep background templates clean, crisp, simple, and uncluttered. The less visual distraction, the better. Keep animation to a minimum and avoid sound effects, except under the most unusual of circumstances. Be consistent and straightforward as you prepare those images. Think, as well, about hyperlinks, streaming video, and VHS news clips from commercial television and cable networks. You're entitled to capture newscasts on videotape and use them in the classroom as long as the use is brief, and not for profit.

PULLING IT ALL TOGETHER

Meet regularly as a team. Talk with one another about progress, deadlines, and next steps. Much of your work can be done by telephone and e-mail, but occasional face-to-face sessions will prove helpful. As the process moves along, respect each other and offer to help whenever you can. Your teammates will appreciate that and, in return, give you their best effort.

Finally, as you prepare your publication draft of the case, admit that you may need to update or correct it, and then rehearse your presentation. Your task is to make it all look as sincere and professional as possible. If you've done it right, you'll be rewarded with the attention and approval of a number of important audiences.

Endnotes

1. Barnes, Louis B., C. Roland Christensen, and Abby J. Hansen. *Teaching and the Case Method*, 3rd ed. Boston, MA: Harvard Business School Press, 1994.

2. Dewey, John. *Democracy and Education: An Introduction to the Philosophy of Education.* New York: Simon and Schuster, 1997. Originally published 1916.

This teaching note was prepared by James S. O'Rourke, Teaching Professor of Management, as the basis for class discussion.

APPENDIX C
SAMPLE BUSINESS LETTER

BIG DOG SOFTWARE

Innovative Applications • Enterprise Software • Business Control Systems

October 25, 2012
Mr. Ryan P. McCarthy
786 Elliott Street
Seattle, WA 91277-3022

Dear Mr. McCarthy:

This is an example of the Full Block Letter style, one of the most popular styles in business use today. The primary reason the Full Block style is so popular is its clean, efficient look. Typists favor this style, too, because it's easy to prepare and simple to compose.

Each element in this letter style begins at the left-hand margin. That includes the date, the inside address, the salutation, each body paragraph, the complimentary close, and the signature block. There is no need to use additional keystrokes to center the date or to move the complimentary close and signature block to the other side of the page.

Please note that this letter style uses full punctuation, including the colon following the salutation and the comma following the complimentary close. The open, or ragged, right-hand margin gives the letter a slightly informal appearance, yet requires no additional work on the typist's part.

This is the most common variation of business letter format in use today. Some writers prefer other styles, especially if the letter extends beyond one page, because it's easy to tell where a paragraph begins if it's indented. In the Full Block Letter style, none of the paragraphs are indented. The letter is composed with a single space between lines within each paragraph and two spaces between paragraphs.

The vast majority of business correspondence in North America features the one-page letter. There are two reasons for this: First, most business letters are focused on just one subject and most writers can say what they must in three or four paragraphs. Second, the Full Block Letter style doesn't use indented paragraphs.

P.O. Box 1743 • LaJolla, California 92037 • 858-555-4321
www.bigdogsoftware.com

Mr. Ryan P. McCarthy
October 25, 2012
Page 2

There is another reason for the popularity of the one-page letter and it's cultural. Most North American business writers come directly to the point in the first—or at the very least—second paragraph. European, Asian, and Latin American business writers will spend more time developing personal relationships, inquiring about the health and well-being of the readers, but most U.S. and Canadian writers prefer to put their main point up front and say what they mean, using fewer words.

If you choose to write a multipage later, the Full Block Letter style can easily accommodate that. You must simply be sure to enter a page heading in the upper left-hand corner of each succeeding page. That page heading should contain the name of the letter recipient, the page number, and the date of the letter.

Remember, if you write a two-page letter, the second page must contain at least two lines of text. Most writers prefer to include at least a full paragraph. The final paragraph of the letter is followed by a complimentary close, a signature block, and—if circumstances require—a copy line or an enclosure line, indicating that either others have received a copy of the letter or that the envelope contains other documents.

Sincerely,

Paul Magers
General Manager

Enclosures

cc: Doug Hemphill

APPENDIX D
SAMPLE STRATEGY MEMO

The Eugene D. Fanning Center
University of Notre Dame • Mendoza College of Business

DATE:	October 25, 2012
TO:	Management Writing Students
COPY:	Interested People with a Need to Know But No Responsibility for Action
FROM:	J. S. O'Rourke (234 Mendoza College of Business; Phone 555-8397) Fanning Center for Business Communication
SUBJECT:	**STRATEGY MEMO: FORMAT AND CONTENTS**

This memo format recommends a communication plan in response to a specific event or circumstance facing a company or organization. It will briefly summarize the details of the event/circumstance; discuss their implications, importance, or probable outcome; and will provide a specific list of actions taken and actions recommended.

Background

In this portion of the memo, the writer briefly but completely reviews the *facts* of the case. This paragraph will contain historical data, information that is a matter of public record, and facts that are relevant to the recommended communication strategy.

- Crisp, tightly expressed sentences set apart from the main paragraph by bullet points are often useful in highlighting factual information.
- This paragraph *does not* include assumptions, suppositions, or speculative information. Nor does it include gratuitous references in the first person singular, such as "I think . . .," "In my opinion . . .," or "I feel. . . ."
- If a specific source is available for each piece of information in this paragraph, the writer should consider embedding it directly in a sentence, that is, "2000 Census figures reveal that. . . ." Another approach is to list a source in parentheses following the information you provide, that is, "Mead Corporation's Stevenson, Alabama, mill has an annual production capacity of 400,000 tons of corrugated containerboard (Source: *Mead Financial Fact Book*, Mead Corp., 2003, p. 5)."

Discussion

In this portion of the memo, the writer expands on the implications of the facts cited in the Background. This is where the writer explains to the reader what those facts mean and why they matter. The discussion paragraph often becomes the basis for the recommendations that follow. If the discussion is extended or complex, writers often use separate paragraphs, subheadings, and bullet points to highlight various issues.

This section of the memo is frequently much longer than either the Background or Recommendation sections. It often contains a robust, detailed discussion of the issues and events present in the Background, followed by some sense of what they mean and why they matter.

Recommendations

In this paragraph, the writer lays out each recommendation in specific terms. Where possible, recommendations lead with a verb, are separated from one another with white space, are underlined or printed in boldface type for emphasis, and are either numbered (if the writer recommends more than three actions) or bullet-pointed. For example:

1. **Sign the attached letter of apology to the customer.** The letter not only apologizes for the flaw discovered in our shipment of July 1, but also offers a 2 percent discount on the shipment and a full replacement of all defective parts. (Action: President)
2. **Forward the defective parts to Quality Control for examination.** When the QC report is complete, copies of their findings should be shared with Sales & Marketing, Customer Service, and members of the Senior Management Team. (Action: Customer Service)
3. **Contact the retailer who sold the equipment to review return/refund procedures.** We must make certain that each retailer handling our products fully understands his/her obligation to accept customer returns and to provide full refunds, if appropriate. (Action: Sales Manager)
4. **Follow up with the customer to make sure he is satisfied with our actions on his behalf.** This is a particularly large account and, while each customer is important to this company, some customers are more important than others. Direct, personal contact to assure customer satisfaction, followed by an after-action report for company files, is essential. (Action: Customer Service)

Other Issues

On occasion, the Recommendations paragraph will be labeled "Actions Recommended" and would be preceded by a paragraph labeled "Actions Taken." The difference is a matter of authority in the organization. The memo writer clearly has authority to take certain actions on his or her own and to *backbrief* the supervisor or manager by means of this memo. That same writer might propose actions for his superiors or for other divisions/agencies in the company that the reader is asked to agree to. It's always useful for the reader to know what tasks have already been done and what tasks he or she is being asked to approve.

Most memoranda *do not* include a signature block, nor do they feature salutation lines ("Dear . . .") or complimentary closing lines ("Sincerely yours,"). Rather than a full signature, most memos will include the initials of the writer next to the "FROM:" line.

Strategy Memo: Format and Contents
October 28, 2009
Page 3 of 3

Please note that this two-page memo requires a "second page header" that includes the subject line (exactly as written on page one), a date line, and a page number.

To conclude, most memos will feature some distinctive typographical mark just beneath the last line of type. Some authors will use their initials; others simply use the pound sign or other mark of their choice.

###

APPENDIX E
DOCUMENTATION
ACKNOWLEDGING THE SOURCES OF YOUR RESEARCH

BACKGROUND

The idea is simple: When you borrow the words or ideas of others, your readers or listeners must know where they came from and who wrote them. In practice, it's not so easy. Who among us has had a *truly original* idea today? A few, perhaps, but not many. Most of what we know is derived from what we have read and heard from others. The more innovative among us might modify or adapt ideas that others have thought and put them to work in a new context, but few of us take the time to properly credit our sources.

Your Management Communication instructors look at this a bit differently. If you use the words, ideas, or intellectual property of another, your instructors will insist that you scrupulously document all of it. If it's not common knowledge or your own original work, they'll expect to see a source note. If you use the words of another directly, they'll look for quotation marks.

It's a matter of fairness, honesty, and candor. Showing your readers where you found a statistic or a quotation is simply being fair—with them and with the source of your information. In addition, it's a matter of credibility. If you insist that we believe you (and only you) as we examine the evidence in your argument, then you place yourself in a difficult position, indeed. It's much easier to let the evidence and the experts speak for themselves. Your own credibility is probably not as great as the source you've consulted, so why not explain who wrote those words? Why not use their title, position, and accomplishments to help carry your argument?

Some folks think this just isn't that big a deal. Two notable (and once well-respected) historians might disagree. According to Martin Arnold of the *New York Times*, "Recently Stephen E. Ambrose and Doris Kearns Goodwin, both best-selling authors of some admirable books, have been caught lifting material from other people's books, kidnapping the words of others. So far, they have gotten off easy, as nearly as can be determined. There has been some criticism. . . ."[1]

More to the point, there's been trouble. Goodwin recently resigned from the prestigious Pulitzer Prize committee at Colombia University, and Ambrose promised to correct the problems in subsequent editions of his work. Mr. Arnold and others who follow these issues have stepped up their expressions of concern:

> For Mr. Ambrose, with so much to do, naturally a careless slip occurs. People shrug. But they shouldn't: a writer of Mr. Ambrose's reputation should read every sentence before he ships a manuscript to this publisher and he certainly should be able to recognize his own sentences when sees them.[2]

"Those are professional historians," you say. "They're held to a higher standard than students." Perhaps, but not everyone thinks carelessness or intellectual theft should be quickly or easily forgiven in college and high school students. A tenth-grade botany project in Piper, Kansas, resulted in multiple teacher resignations—in protest over the local school board's refusal to back a teacher who uncovered plagiarism in her students' work.[3]

Christine Pelton concluded that 28 of her 118 students had plagiarized portions of a major project and gave them grades of zero for it. When the school board superintendent reversed her decision and gave passing grades to the students who had cheated, an uproar ensued that is still the subject of controversy to this day. Ms. Pelton resigned, as did her principal, Michael Adams. When Nick A. Tomasik, the Wyandotte County, Kansas, district attorney began looking into the case, he said, "So much is unknown. A large concern for teachers is that if this happens to one of us, one of our own, what's going to keep it from happening to me?"[4]

WHAT IS PLAGIARISM?

As a college student, you will encounter the work of other people every day: you'll see their paintings, hear their music, read their words, and work with their inventions. That's part of the magic of college: Learning directly from people who are considered to be gifted or insightful. To help measure your understanding and, from time to time, your achievement of learning objectives, your instructors will ask that you write or speak in class. They won't expect that everything you say or write will be your own ideas. They will, however, expect that you will tell your readers and listeners when and from where you found the ideas and words you're using.

"Plagiarism," in the view of Indiana University's writing center, "is using others' ideas and words without clearly acknowledging the source of that information."[5]

This appendix will examine your responsibilities as a writer and as a student. We'll show you the distinction between *informal documentation* and *formal documentation*. We'll also look at the difference between *paraphrasing* and *direct quotes*. We'll show you the value of an *attribution line* in the text of your work, as well. We will also look at *framing* both quotations and paraphrased material, and we'll show you how to properly set up a footnote or endnote so that your reader knows exactly where to find the source of the information in your paper.

WHAT IS COPYRIGHT?

First though, a quick distinction between *plagiarism* and *copyright infringement*. A plagiarist is one who would have you believe the words and ideas in a paper are his own when, in reality, he's simply lifted them from someone else (usually a better writer who is both more famous and not around to object). Such papers are often submitted for credit in colleges and universities.

A copyright infringer, on the other hand, is trying to borrow the works of others for profit. It does not matter that she has properly credited the source of her material; she doesn't have the *right to copy* and sell it. That's what copyright means. If you copy someone else's poetry and include it in a book you plan to sell, you must first get permission from the copyright holder (usually the author or a publisher) and then you may be asked to pay for the right.

Brief passages or small portions of a copyrighted work may be used in a student paper, a newspaper review, or even a textbook sold for profit. According to Richard Posner of the *Atlantic Monthly*, "The doctrine of 'fair use' permits brief passages from a book to be quoted in a book review or critical essay; and the parodist of a copyrighted work is permitted to copy as much of that work as is necessary to enable readers to recognize the new work as a parody."[6]

How much of a work is considered suitable for "fair use"? According to Stanford University Professor and former U.S. Secretary of State, Condoleeza Rice, "The concept of fair use is necessarily somewhat vague when discussed in the abstract. Its application depends critically on the particular facts of the individual situation. Neither the case law nor the statutory law provides bright lines concerning which uses are fair and which are not."[7] Like insider trading, the law is deliberately vague, but will permit educational institutions to copy small portions of a protected document for one-time use. It's also important to note that the courts take a dim view of copying work that is available for purchase in the campus bookstore.

Works that are no longer protected by copyright law are said to be "in the public domain" and may be used without obtaining permission or paying a fee. Even so, they may not be cited in a college paper without proper documentation (to do so would be plagiarism).

WHEN SHOULD I DOCUMENT SOMETHING?

When it's clear that the words or ideas aren't your own. Documentation comes in two forms: informal and formal.

- *Informal documentation* includes an acknowledgment of the source as the information is revealed. For example, "Michelin has become a world leader in tire production and sales. Chairman Edouard Michelin recently revealed the creation of a joint-stock company with the number one tire manufacturer in China, Shanghai Tire and Rubber Company." It's clear from this reference that the ideas came from Mr. Michelin and not from the student who wrote the paper.
- *Formal documentation* includes footnotes, endnotes, or parenthetical documentation that clearly establishes exactly where the information, statistics, ideas, or direct quotes came from. They follow one of several conventions and will permit the reader to find the same information for herself. For example, "Michelin demonstrated that they could remain profitable under difficult market conditions, achieving a 6.6% operating margin in 2001" (*Michelin 2001 Annual Report*, p. 3).

Formal documentation means that you will use a style that is consistent, widely accepted, and useful to your reader. Three sources for documentation are commonly used by business writers:

- *The author-date method* (*Publication Manual of the American Psychological Association*).[8] The source is identified by the last name of the author(s) and the date of publication. Example:

Professor Carolyn Boulger (2003, p. 2) says the transformation to integrated communications will begin when "businesses and large organizations train their people to recognize appropriate channels for communication within and among various audience groups."

At the end of the paper, you would include a section entitled "Works Cited" or "References" and you would include the following entry: Boulger, C. *e-Technology and the Fourth Economy*. Cincinnati, OH: Thomson South-Western College Publishing, 2003.

The APA manual encourages writers to be as specific as possible in directing readers to the original source material. So, if you're citing a specific passage as we've just done in the paragraph above, you should include the page number. If you're referring broadly to information contained in just one chapter of that book, you should cite the chapter number (Boulger, 2003, ch. 1).

If you're simply referring to the author's findings in general but aren't focused on a particular page or chapter, you should cite just the author's name and the year of publication (Boulger, 2003). Be as helpful to your readers as you can. If you want them to pay attention to a particular passage or quote in your sources, tell them where to find it.

- *The author-page method* (*MLA Handbook for Writers of Research Papers*).[9] The source is identified by the last name of the author(s) and the page number in the source where the information can be found. Example:

Work groups are an indisputable Twenty-First Century necessity for most of us, one likely to continue to dominate organizational life as industries, businesses, organizations, institutions, and communities adapt to a dramatically evolving global marketplace (Yarbrough 1).

At the end of the paper, you would include a section entitled "Works Cited" or "References" and you would include the following entry: Yarbrough, B. *Leading Groups and Teams.* Cincinnati, OH: Thomson South-Western College Publishing, 2008.

- *The numerical method* (*The Chicago Manual of Style*).[10] The source is identified by a raised (superscript) numeral in the text, with a corresponding numbered footnote or endnote that provides complete documentation for the source. Example:

After more than a year of animosity, suspicion and distrust between Ford Motor Company and the Firestone division of Bridgestone, Inc., the gloves finally came off. Not only were the world-famous automaker and the global tire manufacturer no longer cooperating, but they had chosen to end their century-long relationship by blaming each other for a disastrous series of tire failures and auto wrecks that had injured thousands and taken more than 100 lives around the world.[11]

At the end of the paper, you would include a section entitled "Works Cited" or "References" and you would include the following entry: 11. O'Rourke, J. "Bridgestone/Firestone, Inc. and Ford Motor Company: How a Product Safety Crisis Ended a Hundred-Year Relationship," *Corporate Reputation Review*, 4, no. 3 (Autumn 2001), pp. 255–264.

If you plan to be a college student for the next few years, you might consider having a copy of one of these reference books handy. Please consult your instructors to see what advice they might have or which system of documentation they prefer.

PARAPHRASING

A paraphrase is the simple rephrasing of someone else's words. This approach is often helpful when you want to explain complex ideas simply and in your own words. Some years ago, investment executive Warren Buffet saw a mutual fund prospectus that read:

Maturity and duration management decisions are made in the context of an intermediate maturity orientation. The maturity structure of the portfolio is adjusted in the anticipation of cyclical interest rate changes. Such adjustments are not made in an effort to capture short-term, day-to-day movements in the market, but instead are implemented in anticipation of longer term, secular shifts in the levels of interest rates (i.e., shifts transcending and/or not inherent to the business cycle).

Adjustments made to shorten portfolio maturity and duration are made to limit capital losses during periods when interest rates are expected to rise. Conversely, adjustments made to lengthen maturity for the protfolio's maturity and duration strategy lies in analysis of the U.S. and global economies, focusing on levels of real interest rates, monetary and fiscal policy actions, and cyclical indicators.

He paraphrased that prospectus, putting the ideas into his own words:

We will try to profit by correctly predicting future interest rates. When we have no strong opinion, we will generally hold intermediate-term bonds. But when we expect a major and sustained increase in rates, we will concentrate on short-term issues. And, conversely, if we expect a major shift to lower rates, we will buy long bonds. We will focus on the big picture and won't make moves based on short-term considerations.[12]

ATTRIBUTION LINES

Another form of paraphrasing is the *attribution line*, in which you explain in the text of your paper or talk where the ideas came from:

According to authors Majken Schultz and Jo Hatch, organizational identity refers to how people inside a company see and understand who they are and what they stand for.[13]

Professor Cees B.M. van Riel of The Netherlands thinks of a "sustainable corporate story" as a means of maintaining key relationships with customers and investors. While that's certainly true, a consistent, interesting corporate story is more than that. It's also a way to signal the marketplace about who you are and who you hope to become.[14]

In each paraphrase above, the writer has taken the ideas of others and put them into his own words. At the same time, he's been careful to explain whose ideas they were and where they came from. (You wouldn't use *italics* to identify an attribution line or a paraphrase, but I've used them here to help you recognize them.)

QUOTATIONS

If you use words written by someone else—and don't paraphrase them by putting the ideas into your own words—you must surround the words with *quotation marks*.

"If you go to a good hotel and ask for something, you get it," says John Collins, the HR director. "If you go to a great hotel, you don't even have to ask."[15]

If you directly quote someone who is, in turn, quoting someone else, you have what's known as a quote within a quote, or an *indirect quote.* To identify an indirect quote, use *single quote marks.*

"Today, the subject is Basic 14, which admonishes employees to use the right sort of language with guests and one another. For example, we are to say, 'Please accept my apologies,' rather than 'I'm sorry'; 'Certainly, my pleasure,' instead of 'Okay.'"[16]

Note that the period goes *inside* the quote mark and that single and double quote marks may be used to end a sentence.

BRACKETS

Square brackets are used to indicate that the words are *yours* and not those of the author being quoted. For example:

At the midpoint of the twentieth century, management philosopher Peter Drucker wrote, "Managers have to learn to know language, to understand what words are and what they mean. Perhaps most important, they have to acquire respect for language as [our] most precious gift and heritage."[17]

ELLIPSES

Use ellipses (plural) or ellipsis periods to show that you've left words out of a quotation. Please note that a space follows the word preceding the ellipses and the next word of the quote. You must also insert a space between each of the periods. For example:

> No matter how much money your clothes cost, an omission or error in grooming can sabotage the entire effect. If you have trouble paying attention to small details, post a grooming checklist in your home . . . run down the list and check yourself, point by point, so that when people see you, they will see nothing out of place.[18]

USING THE INTERNET FOR RESEARCH

The *Internet* has become the go-to research tool, both for businesspeople and for students studying to become one of them. Hundreds of millions of computers, linked together worldwide, have instantaneous (well, perhaps immediate) access to information by, from, and about businesses across the globe.

The Internet, however, is not without its problems. For one thing, the information it contains is not organized. Stephen Hayes, a university business services librarian, has described the Internet as "a library with all the books on the floor."[19] It's no ordinary library, either. Literally anyone can set up a home page, buy an address, and begin doing business on the Internet. The U.S. Supreme Court ruled in 1997 that government censorship of Internet content is unconstitutional. So, a student in search of information can—and often does—find inaccurate information alongside something of value on the Internet. "There's little we can do to verify the accuracy of the information contained in most sites on the World Wide Web," said Mr. Hayes. "Thus, each of us should approach what we find with appropriate caution and skepticism—just as we would a print source."[20]

The *World Wide Web* is organized broadly into four categories of sites: government, educational, commercial, and not-for-profit. Internet addresses, known as URLs, reflect these categories in the letters they contain. Corporate home pages (usually ending in ".com") will tell you things about a company that they want you to know, such as where to buy their products, how their stock price is doing, and how to apply for employment. In many ways, it's simply another form of advertising.

Government-sponsored Web sites (ending in ".gov") provide large categories of information, including census data, international trade and banking data, and regulatory information. These sites usually have a legal mandate to maintain the authority of the data. Educational institutions, such as colleges and universities, sponsor Web sites (ending in ".edu") that permit students, alumni, and others to find out more about everything from academic curricula to how the varsity lacrosse team is doing.

Finally, Web sites sponsored by not-for-profit organizations (usually ending in ".org"), such as the American Red Cross, Goodwill Industries, and National Public Radio, offer everything from program schedule and broadcast transcripts to detailed descriptions of current activities in their organizations.

Search engines and directories are among the most useful tools to someone looking for information on the Internet. Simply speaking, search engines and directories are programs that will search for information that you ask about. If you visit www.yahoo.com, you will find one of the most popular and widely used directories. Simply type in the keywords that best describe the product, service, company, or industry that you want information about and the Yahoo! directory will produce numerous references with links to Web sites that may prove useful. *Directories* will search only the higher levels of a Web site, such as the title and author, while *search engines* will explore deeply for the data requested.

The more precisely or narrowly you define what you're looking for, the greater the chance that one of the more widely used search engines will find what you're seeking. Among the more popular search engines are www.google.com, www.dogpile.com, www.bing.com, and www.altavista.com.

CITING INTERNET SOURCES

Search engines have made it so easy to find information on the Web that it takes little more than a phrase or question in the Google search to generate hundreds of sources for academic research papers, business proposals, reports, and business correspondence. In addition to heeding Stephen Hayes's comment about not believing everything you see on the Internet, two other issues become important. We've already talked about the first, that is, not plagiarizing the work of others. You must scrupulously document absolutely everything you borrow or quote from another source. And, of course, if you use a lot of it, you may have to obtain permission and pay a royalty fee.

For the vast majority of your work in college, however, your real challenge is twofold: First, figuring out whether the information you've found is accurate, current, and reliable. Second, you must figure out how to cite the source of that information so that others will know where it came from. Complicating your task is the simple fact that home pages and Web sites on the Internet are constantly undergoing change each day. What was there last night won't necessarily be there tomorrow morning. And what's available today may be "down" or unavailable in a week.

Here are some examples that may prove helpful:

How to cite a book in a bibliography:

Dickens, C. *A Tale of Two Cities.* New York: Vintage Classics, 1990.

How to cite an e-book in a bibliography:

Dickens, C. *A Tale of Two Cities* [Internet]. Charlottesville, VA: University of Virginia Library, Electronic Text Center; 1994; © 1999 [updated 1996 May; cited 2002 June 24]. Available from etext.lib.virginia.edu/toc/modeng/public/DicTale.html.

How to cite a newspaper article:

Stanley, A. and C. Hayes. "Martha Stewart's New Project Is Reconstructing Her Image," *New York Times*, June 23, 2002, pp. A1, A24.

How to cite the same article taken from a Web site:

Stanley, A. and C. Hayes. "Martha Stewart's To Do List May Include Image Polishing," *New York Times* [Internet]. 2002 June 23 (cited 2002 June 23): Available from http://www.nytimes.com/2002/06/23/business/23MART.html?todaysheadlines.

How to cite a Web site:

The Eugene D. Fanning Center for Business Communication [Internet]. Notre Dame, IN: Mendoza College of Business, University of Notre Dame; [updated 2002 May 14; cited 2002 Jun 23]. Available from www.nd.edu/~fanning.

How to cite an e-mail:

Rodgers, Priscilla (University of Michigan.psr@umich.edu). Materials for ORA Nomination [Internet]. Message to: James S. O'Rourke, IV (jorourke@nd.edu). 2002 Jun 18, 13:22:28 (cited 2002 Jun 23).

According to Kathleen Sheedy of the American Psychological Association, the purpose of a bibliography is to identify an author's sources so a reader can look them up. The APA wants the bibliographies used in its journals to "get the user as close to the source as possible. You want to point him to the specific page."[21]

The problem with Web sites, of course, is they don't have page numbers or chapters. In addition, you may find that the article posted online is shorter or a bit different from the article printed in the paper version of the magazine or newspaper you're hoping to cite. If you've compared the two *New York Times* stories above, you'll note that they're the same story but with different headlines. And, according to June Kronholz of the *Wall Street Journal*, there is no single authority on bibliography style. Social scientists follow the style set by the APA. Historians follow *The Chicago Manual of Style*, and anyone writing about the humanities follows the Modern Language Association, or MLA style.[22]

Will any of those manuals help you in citing information taken from an Internet Web site? Well, the APA updated its manual last year, devoting 19 pages to the intricacies of citing electronic publications. And, according to Ms. Kronholz, the MLA has already updated its style manual twice to accommodate the Internet and is now working on another edition. So is the *Chicago Manual*. But, says Ms. Kronholz, "styles still differ: some manuals dictate square brackets around Web addresses. Some decree angle brackets instead. Punctuation and abbreviation are still thorny matters."[23]

If this is all a matter of heated debate among professional bibliographers—people who do this sort of thing for a living—then what should you do? The answer is relatively simple: Do your very best to show your reader where and when you found the work and, if you know, who wrote the work. With some luck, perhaps they'll be able to find it, as well.

Here's some additional advice from Ms. Kronholz and her sources at the *Wall Street Journal*:

What should you do if you can't find a page number on a Web site?
Answer: Use [about page 5] or [about screen 6].

What should you do if you can't find the title of an article on a Web site?
Answer: Make one up, using the first words on the screen.

What should you do if you can't find an author's name on a Web site?
Answer: Look. Look hard, make sure you really can't find it, then forget about it.[24]

Do everything you can to be fair, honest, and candid with your readers and the sources you've taken your information from. Double-check things, proofread your work carefully, then sleep well, knowing you've done your best.

Endnotes

1. Arnold, M. "Historians Who Resort to Cutting and Pasting," *New York Times*, February 28, 2002, p. B1.

2. Ibid.

3. Trotter, A. "Plagiarism Controversy Engulfs Kansas School," *Education Week*, April 2, 2002, 21, no. 9, p. 5.

4. Ibid.

5. "Plagiarism: What It Is and How to Recognize and Avoid It," Writing Tutorial Services, Indiana University, Bloomington, IN. Available online at: www.indiana.edu/~wts/wts/plagiarism.html. Retrieved June 22, 2002.

6. Posner, R. A. "On Plagiarism," *Atlantic Monthly*, April 2002. Available online at: www.the atlantic. com/issues/2002/04/posner.htm. Retrieved June 22, 2002.

7. Rice, C. "Copyright Reminder," A memo to members of the faculty, Hoover Institution fellows, academic staff, and library directors, Stanford University, October 30, 1998. Retrieved June 22, 2002, from firuse.stanford.edu/rice.html.

8.   *Publication Manual of the American Psychological Association*, 4th ed. Washington, DC: American Psychological Association, 1994.

9.   Gibaldi, J. and H. Lindenberger. *MLA Style Manual and Guide to Scholarly Publishing*, 2nd ed. New York: Modern Language Association of America, 1998.

10. *The Chicago Manual of Style: The Essential Guide for Writers, Editors, and Publishers*, 14th ed. Chicago, IL: University of Chicago Press, 1993.

11. O'Rourke, J. "Bridgestone/Firestone, Inc. and Ford Motor Company: How a Product Safety Crisis Ended a Hundred-Year Relationship." *Corporate Reputation Review*, 4, no. 3 (Autumn 2001), pp. 255–264.

12. *USA Today*, October 14, 1994, p. C1.

13. Schultz, M. and J. Hatch. "Scaling the Tower of Babel: Relational Differences Between Identity, Image, and Culture in Organizations," in *The Expressive Organization: Linking Identity, Reputation, and the Corporate Brand.* Oxford, UK: Oxford University Press, 2000, p. 15.

14. Van Riel, C. "Corporate Communication Orchestrated by a Sustainable Corporate Story," in *The Expressive Organization: Linking Identity, Reputation, and the Corporate Brand.* Oxford, UK: Oxford University Press, 2000, pp. 157–181.

15. Hemp, P. "My Week as a Room-Service Waiter at the Ritz," *Harvard Business Review*, 80, no. 6 (June 2002), p. 54.

16. Ibid.

17. Drucker, P. F. *The Practice of Management.* New York: Harper & Row, 1954.

18. Baldrige, L. *Letitia Baldrige's New Complete Guide to Executive Manners.* New York: Rawson Associates, 1993, p. 225.

19. Hayes, S. Mahaffey Center for Business Information, Mendoza College of Business, University of Notre Dame. Personal communication, April 2001.

20. Ibid.

21. Kronholz, J. "Bibliography Mess: The Internet Wreaks Havoc with the Form," *Wall Street Journal*, May 2, 2002, p. A1.

22. Ibid.

23. Ibid.

24. Ibid.

APPENDIX F
MEDIA RELATIONS FOR BUSINESS PROFESSIONALS
HOW TO PREPARE FOR A BROADCAST OR PRESS INTERVIEW

INTRODUCTION

During the course of your career in business, it will be virtually impossible for you to avoid meeting and dealing with the news media. Inevitably, the media will want access to you as a functional expert when you are least prepared and willing to deal with them—often during a crisis of some sort.

Even they are not a surrogate for dealing with the public directly and their influence on public opinion formation is indirect and somewhat limited, the news media can provide a useful service and valuable opportunity to reach large numbers of people with a carefully prepared message. Those people who have been most successful in dealing with the news media have discovered that such encounters require careful preparation and some understanding of how media representatives operate.

DISCUSSION

Have you ever done a media interview before? How did it go? What was your impression of the reporter? Did you have an opportunity to see the broadcast or read the interview after it was completed? Did the reporter treat you fairly in the interview and in the story to which it contributed?

A separate series of questions concerns the news media in general. What's your impression of the media? Of reporters in general? Do you think it's a good idea to cooperate when reporters or editors ask for your reaction to something?

Regardless of your initial experience, are you ready to do it again?

In general, most businesses and profit-making organizations take a positive stance regarding press interviews and public appearances by company officials, particularly those in positions of senior responsibility. Most not-for-profit institutions follow a policy that requires that you work with and through your public relations office to arrange and prepare for such interviews, but contact with reporters is not limited, by any means, simply to the public relations office. In fact, most news organizations would rather speak with a "newsmaker" or responsible official than an "official spokesperson."

If you are asked to do an interview, look on it as a positive experience, an opportunity to tell your company's story, a chance to get your point of view across to the public. It is, at the very least, an inexpensive means of communicating your message to a very large audience. It's an opportunity to show the flag and to talk about your agenda—regardless of what the interview was called for—with the public at large.

If you agree to an interview, though, remember that it's not without risk. You can fail—it's not common, but it can happen if you're unprepared for the occasion. Preparing yourself is not difficult if you keep a few basic suggestions in mind.

ONE WEEK BEFORE THE INTERVIEW

Several things you may wish to consider at least a week before you're to be interviewed:

- Consult with your public relations director on his or her plan for the interview. When and where will it take place? What's the subject? Will we plan to limit the questions to a particular subject or will the reporter want to talk about many subjects? Remember, it's best to focus or limit the interview and prepare yourself well to answer a narrow range of questions than it is to let a reporter "go fishing." If your business does not have a public relations officer, prepare yourself by speaking with a knowledgeable, senior colleague whom you trust. Think about the questions you're most likely to be asked, and think about those you would most like to answer. Think, as well, about those you really hope you don't have to answer. After a thorough review session with a trusted colleague, if you still aren't confident, consider asking a professional media relations consultant for help. The time and money spent on such help will pay huge dividends down the road in protecting your company's reputation, share price, market share, and public image.
- Read some of the reporter's work, or watch a video copy of the show you're to appear on. Get some idea of how the interviewer or reporter works, what his style may be, how she works.
- Begin to assemble information for and to define your "agenda." What's on your mind? What's your message? What three or four key issues do you want to talk about? Get the most current facts and figures together and focus your mind on how best to package that information. Practice expressing your point of view in 15- to 20-second segments that could stand alone if they were edited out of a longer interview. Say your message aloud until you are thoroughly familiar with the words, numbers, and phrases you will use. Practice until you are confident, self-assured, and professional in your approach to the subject.
- Prepare a pocket or purse card. Be sure to include the time, place of the interview, name of the interviewer, and his or her media outlet. Include other key details, as well, such as how you will get there, who will accompany you, phone numbers, and names. On the other side, write down your three or four key points, along with supporting detail, numbers or facts you want to talk about.

ONE DAY BEFORE THE INTERVIEW

The day before you do the interview, check on a few final details.

- Have your corporate communication director confirm the time and place of the interview with the reporter or host. Who will you follow on the show? Who else is being interviewed? Who will ask the questions? You don't need any surprises at this point.
- Check your card to make sure it's complete and accurate and fully reflects your position on the issues to be discussed. Make sure that position also reflects institutional policy and current administration views. Remember, you represent not only your business, but its employees, shareholders, and other stakeholders, as well.
- Check on transportation, parking, and other elements in your schedule for tomorrow. How will you get there? Where will you park? How long will it take to get there? Will traffic or weather be a problem?
- Make sure your clothing is among the best you own. Dress conservatively so that your attire doesn't detract from your message. Consider getting a haircut.

THE DAY OF THE INTERVIEW

On the day you're to be interviewed, you'll have a few, final details to attend to.

- Watch the news that morning; read the papers; search your favorite news-gathering sites on the Internet. Check the local news and have a look at the morning's latest stories. Is there anything late-breaking that could serve as a springboard for a reporter's question? Even though the issues in the morning's news may be well beyond your expertise or influence, they could still become part of a reporter's question. Prepare yourself to respond.
- If the interview is scheduled for late afternoon or later in the day, men may want to shave again, particularly if you have a heavier beard. Check your shirt, suit coat, and shoes. You want to make the best impression possible.
- Plan to arrive early. Give yourself a few minutes to calm down, examine your surroundings, and review your notes before you go on the air.
- Unbutton your suit jacket if it's a sit-down interview. To remove wrinkles and "collar creep," pull the jacket down from the rear. Button your jacket if it's a stand-up interview.
- Men: Wear over-the-calf socks. Choose complementary colors and plain patterns.
- Women: Wear plain, unpatterned hosiery. Keep jewelry simple. Those diamonds may look terrific at a dinner party, but on television, they will catch the light and distract the audience.
- Wear your glasses if you need them to see. They will make you more comfortable and, often, people will develop facial marks if they wear glasses all the time. You don't want those to show.
- Don't wear sunglasses, either indoors or outdoors if at all possible, or tinted photochromatic lenses while you're on camera. Studio lights will turn those lenses very dark and you don't want to hide your eyes from the audience.
- Men: Don't wear vests, wide stripes, or checks. Solid colors, pinstripes, or narrow chalkstripes are best.
- Women: Don't wear extremely light or exceptionally dark dresses. Extremely short skirts can be difficult during a sit-down interview, as well.

BEFORE YOU GO ON CAMERA

As you arrive at the studio, there are a few things to think about.

- Look at the studio and set. Observe the cameras, mikes, lighting equipment, and positions of the crew members. Talk with crew members if you have the opportunity—it will make you seem more human to them and it will dispel any nervousness you may be experiencing.
- Men: If they offer makeup, swallow your pride and take it. You will look better on-camera and it's easy to remove once you're done.
- Women: Don't do anything different or unusual about your makeup. If it's suitable for a business meeting, it's suitable for television.
- Check out the position of the studio floor monitor, then ignore it while you're on the air. Focus only on your host.
- Introduce yourself to people. The act of reaching out to someone, psychologically, will help you to feel friendly, generous, and relaxed.
- Tell the program staff if you have a genuine physical reason for preferring one profile or side (e.g., a hearing disability).
- Sit on the front of the chair, turning your body 45 degrees to the camera lens, facing the interviewer. Hands on your knees or in your lap; don't slouch, sit up straight.

- Gestures are constructive communication. Hold your hands lightly, loosely on your legs so they're free to gesture when you need to. Gestures will also help dispel nervous energy.
- Plan to look at the person conducting the interview about 90 percent of the time. Look away infrequently, only to focus your thoughts as necessary. Try as best you can to maintain eye contact to heighten sincerity.
- About 7 percent of the meaning in our statements comes through in our words; some 38 percent is delivered in our voice and vocal quality, while about 55 percent of our total meaning is communicated in other, purely nonverbal ways, including muscle tone, facial expression, body posture, body movement, and hand gestures. Some of this happens at the conscious level, but much of it goes on with little or no awareness on our part. Your goal is to project a relaxed, confident, professional image. People will listen to what you say, but they will take their measure of you by watching how you behave.
- Try to remember that your audience will remember less of what you say than they will of the way in which you've said it. How your message is packaged and delivered is important. That's unfortunate, but it's true—they'll come away with few facts from a television interview, but many impressions and images.
- Use the audio-level check, or "mike check" to identify yourself and make a positive point about your organization or your cause.
- Don't ever say anything into or near a microphone that you wouldn't want broadcast to the rest of the world. Assume that all cameras are "on" and all microphones are "live." Remember, you're always on the record and if you say or do something dumb, they will save the tape.

GETTING YOUR CONVICTIONS ACROSS

- Your presentation must contain not only your thoughts, but also your feelings. Your emotions, energy, and enthusiasm will account for much of your success in this interview—stress the affective more than the cognitive.
- You need to get your points across through your voice, your gestures, proxemics, and body motion, as well as your words. Those words won't stand alone; they're accompanied by facial expressions, vocal tone, and a host of other nonverbal mannerisms.

THE KINDS OF QUESTIONS YOU ARE LIKELY TO FACE

In most interviews, you will find a number of different question types. Your success in handling those questions depends, in part, on your being able to identify what sort of question is being asked.

- *Focus Questions.* Those that give you an opportunity to expand on a point by going into further detail, or by giving an illustration.
- *Avoidance Questions.* Those that you would just as soon not have to answer, probably because they put you or your business in a bad light. Acknowledge the question by repeating the key part in a positive way and then bridge to the point you want to make.
- *Control Questions.* Those that seem relatively simple, but which you would like to pass back to the interviewer. You should respond to these questions by making a positive point about the thrust of the question, not by dealing with the question itself. You may even consider restating the question in a way you'd like to have it asked.

- *Factual Questions.* Those that seem very direct or straightforward. They ask for factual data. Don't stop with the facts or the numbers, though. Show how they're related to a positive point you want to make.
- *Hypothetical Questions.* Those that require you to speculate about the future or provide a response to a set of assumptions that may never prove to be true. Don't be drawn into speculation, assumptions, or guessing. Deflect a hypothetical question by answering one you wish the interviewer had asked.
- *Forced Choice Questions.* Those that require you to adopt either of two unacceptable viewpoints put forward by the interviewer. Don't be drawn into accepting a reporter's terminology, choices, analysis, or alternatives. Use your own words and avoid the trap of selecting one or another of the extremes presented in a question. Most issues are rarely black-and-white, this choice or that; most issues are sufficiently complex to have several points of view.
- *False Facts or False Assumption Questions.* Those that begin with an error in fact by the reporter or host, leading to a mistaken impression in the audience. Set the record straight directly and politely, but don't ever let a mistaken or erroneous statement of any significance go unchallenged in the course of answering a question.
- *Leading or Loaded Questions.* Those that are clearly headed in the direction of a predetermined conclusion on the part of the questioner. Don't be led down the garden path by a reporter who is looking for evidence to support a conclusion he or she has already reached; take control of the interview by raising the "more important issue" or by refocusing the discussion on the one point you think the audience most needs to understand.

MAINTAINING CONTROL OF THE INTERVIEW

A few simple techniques will help you to control the interview, rather than the reporter or host. If you're in control, you get to focus on your agenda, say what you want and put your point of view forward. If you don't maintain control, the reporter or host takes the interview in whatever direction he or she wants and it's a lost opportunity for you, your company, and your people.

- *Gaining Time to Think.* You can create a few moments of thinking or organizing time for yourself by asking the reporter to repeat the question or by asking for the question to be restated in another way. Don't overuse this technique, but once or twice in a long interview, it may buy you some time.
- *Set the Pace Yourself.* Don't let a reporter rush or badger you by picking up the pace of the interview. Just because a questioner jumps in at the end of a response with another question or interrupts you is no reason to change your pacing, timing, or frame of mind. Stay cool, slow down, and stay in charge.
- *Bridging.* If you're faced with a tough question that you simply can't duck, go ahead and acknowledge it. After acknowledging the factual aspect of what's been asked, bridge to a point you want to make.
- *Flagging.* In a long interview that may be subject to editing, you can help yourself, the interviewer, and the editor by identifying the key points, the one thing to remember, the principal issue at hand.
- *Hooking.* You can draw the interviewer into asking a question that might not otherwise have occurred to him or her by addressing an issue at the end of a response to another question that leaves the area open for questioning.

- *Stay Positive.* Don't repeat negative words or phrases. Don't let the reporter put words in your mouth; don't use any emotionally loaded words or phrases just because that's the way the interviewer chose to describe things.
- *Don't Say More than You Intend.* Once you have answered a reporter or talk-show host's question fully and accurately, once you've said all you need to say on a given subject, it's perfectly all right to remain silent. After all, it is not your responsibility to "feed the microphone," it is the host or reporter's responsibility. If the adrenalin[e] rush produced by standing or sitting before the camera and microphone leads you to talk more than you usually might, protect yourself by preparing and offering responses that are complete, accurate, and thoughtful, but that don't lead you to continuous, nonstop talking. Don't ramble on and say things you might later wish you hadn't.

OTHER THINGS TO KEEP IN MIND

- *Know Your Interviewer and Your Audience.* Who are you talking to? Who is watching, listening, or tuning in?
- *Tell the Truth.* Answer honestly. If you don't know the answer, say so, but don't ever say "no comment." That simply sounds like you're guilty and are afraid to talk about it.
- *Avoid an Argument.* You can't win when you grow antagonistic with a professional journalist or talk-show host. They've been doing this sort of thing much longer than you have.
- *Protect the Record.* You are *never* off the record.
- *Use Your Experience, Ethos, Authority, and Expertise.* You, after all, are the one they want to see, hear, and talk to.

IN CONCLUSION

An interview with a reporter or talk-show host can be a win-win situation for you both: He or she gets an interview, fills air-time or column inches, and you get an opportunity to get your agenda or point of view across. You must prepare yourself, though, stay confident, and maintain control. If you do, your company, your coworkers, shareholders, and customers will be better for it.

This teaching note was prepared by James S. O'Rourke, Teaching Professor of Management, as the basis for class discussion.

INDEX